THE
unofficial GUIDE®
TO New York City

7TH EDITION

THE
unofficial GUIDE®
TO New York City

7TH EDITION

EVE ZIBART *with* LEA LANE
and AARON STARMER

WILEY

Please note that prices fluctuate in the course of time and that travel information changes under the impact of many factors that influence the travel industry. We therefore suggest that you write or call ahead for confirmation when making your travel plans. Every effort has been made to ensure the accuracy of information throughout this book, and the contents of this publication are believed to be correct at the time of printing. Nevertheless, the publishers cannot accept responsibility for errors or omissions, for changes in details given in this guide, or for the consequences of any reliance on the information provided by the same. Assessments of attractions and so forth are based upon the authors' own experiences; therefore, descriptions given in this guide necessarily contain an element of subjective opinion, which may not reflect the publisher's opinion or dictate a reader's own experience on another occasion. Readers are invited to write the publisher with ideas, comments, and suggestions for future editions.

Published by:
John Wiley & Sons, Inc.
111 River Street
Hoboken, NJ 07030

Produced by Menasha Ridge Press

Cover design by Michael J. Freeland

Interior design by Vertigo Design

For information on our other products and services or to obtain technical support, please contact our Customer Care Department from within the United States at 877-762-2974, from outside the United States at 317-572-3993, or by fax at 317-572-4002.

John Wiley & Sons, Inc., also publishes its books in a variety of electronic formats. Some content that appears in print may not be available in electronic formats.

ISBN 978-0-470-53327-7

Manufactured in the United States of America

5 4 3 2 1

CONTENTS

LIST *of* MAPS

ACKNOWLEDGMENTS

MANY THANKS TO Lea Lane and Aaron Starmer for their time and taste.

As always, thanks to the folks at Menasha Ridge Press, particularly Molly Merkle, Ritchey Halphen, Amber Henderson, Annie Long, and Steve Jones. Many thanks as well to Steve Millburg, Gabriela Oates, and Ann Cassar—who read about our vacations but hardly ever get the chance to take one.

Special thanks and a farewell toast to Johnny, who made the Oak Bar my favorite Manhattan sanctuary; and to Walter Weintz, who must have been a Zibart separated at birth.

Finally, this book is for my brother Michael, the best companion.

—*Eve Zibart*

ABOUT *the* AUTHOR *and* CONTRIBUTORS

EVE ZIBART has written more about dining, entertainment, travel, and lifestyles than most people experience in a lifetime. In her early years as the pop-music-and-culture reporter for the (Nashville) *Tennessean* and then the *Washington Post*, Eve quickly exhibited a flair for scene and sensory detail. She rapidly moved through the ranks of the *Post* as a feature writer and spent her last ten years there as restaurant critic. She now freelances for *BookPage* and *Washingtonian* and has written for *Cosmopolitan, Four Seasons, Town & Country,* and *Playboy*. Given an amazing ability to turn 24 hours into 30, Eve has found time to author several books, including *The Ethnic Food Lover's Companion; The Eclectic Gourmet Guide to Washington, D.C.; The Unofficial Guide to New Orleans; The Unofficial Guide to Walt Disney World for Grown-Ups;* and *Inside Disney: The Incredible Story of Walt Disney World and the Man Behind the Mouse.*

LEA LANE is a hotel maven, having visited and researched thousands of rooms around the world—including in the Big Apple—for many guidebooks and trade publications, such as Birnbaum's *United States* and *STAR Service,* the premier travel-agent reference. Lea has also been a columnist for Gannett Suburban Newspapers, a television travel and lifestyle reporter, and managing editor of the newsletter *Travel Smart*. She is a major contributor to guidebooks about Greece, Naples, the Amalfi Coast, and Belgium. Her book *Solo Traveler: Tales and Tips for Great Trips,* and her Web site, **www.sololady.com,** make her an expert on solo travel.

AARON STARMER is a writer and editor who has worked, dined, and played in New York City for more than ten years. Along with his wife, Catharine Wells, and his brother, Tim Starmer, he is coauthor of the guidebook *The Best in Tent Camping: New York State* (Menasha Ridge Press). His first novel, DWEEB, was published in 2009. A humorous adventure for the young and nerdy, it is set across the Hudson River from Manhattan, in the land of New Jersey.

INTRODUCTION

"NEW YORK, NEW YORK, IT'S *a* HELLUVA TOWN . . ."

IF YOU'RE EVER A PASSENGER IN A TAXICAB IN NEW YORK, look at the city map affixed to the back of the driver's seat. Chances are, it will show only the tourist territories, cutting Manhattan off partway up Central Park, only hinting at Brooklyn, and likely dispensing with the Bronx, Long Island, and Staten Island altogether. Most guidebooks about New York do the same. They get you from the Staten Island Ferry (the landing point, at least) on the Battery to the Metropolitan Museum of Art at 82nd Street. A few mention Harlem and the River Café across the Hudson. But for the most part, it's "East Side, West Side" rather than "all around the town."

Worse, tour guides rarely draw connections, convey waves of progress, or point up ironies of development. In a city literally embraced by the spirits of multiculturalism—with the Statue of Liberty, that monumental icon of hope for immigrants, at one end, and the shrine of Mother Cabrini, their patron saint, at the other—most visitors peer through the most homogeneous of filters, the endless barrage of Big Apple boosterism and crime or inflation news trotted out every day. Watch enough TV and you'd think the whole city was painted with red ink, white ticker tape, pinstripes, and blue uniforms.

What a waste. New York City is one of the most original, elaborate, eccentric, and irresistible creatures—it clearly has a life of its own—you will ever encounter. And we want you to experience it all, in not just three but four dimensions: underground, above the cloud line, and most definitely at street level, and through time; its past, present, and future. And for that we need your cooperation. We need you to be open to the city's charm. And we need you to turn off that damn TV.

We often speak of visiting a new place as "seeing" it. "See Rock City," read those famous barns. "Join the Navy and see the world."

But the strange thing about sightseeing is that people get too absorbed in the "sights" and forget about the "seeing." It may sound odd for an author to say, but having your nose buried in a book, even this book, is not the way to travel.

Many guidebooks will tell you that New York is not for the faint-hearted; we would say that it is not for the unimaginative. Part of its fascination is its complexity: all the accents, the rhythms, the smells. In this most famous melting pot, New York has yet to produce a truly creole society; minorities here are not so much assimilated as incorporated. That means food, gifts, clothes, and "roots" of a hundred cultures. It's a permanent World's Fair, free for the strolling. Diversity isn't just a souvenir of Ellis Island or dim sum in Chinatown; it's daily life, the greatest attraction of them all.

unofficial **TIP**
Don't miss the "outdoors" of New York. Every borough has a large public park—and no, Central Park is not the largest—and four have botanical gardens. There are five zoos and an aquarium, a wildlife refuge, and beaches and marinas.

New York is also the great silent witness to American culture. There is not a single block in the city, whether residential, renovated, commercial, or even crumbling, that does not speak of its restless and often reckless history: expansionist, extravagant, fickle, fashionable. All you have to do is look. Broadway or off-Broadway, here, all the world truly is a stage.

And a stage set: if there had not been such a thing as a skyline, New York would have had to invent it. Skyscrapers are the cathedrals of Manhattan's private religion—commerce—just as the scores of exquisite churches and temples salute the spiritual. You can almost relive the evolution of the city by glancing around at the architecture, from the 18th-century purity of St. Paul's Chapel to the 19th-century neoclassicism of Federal Hall, the French Renaissance of the Jewish Museum, and the Gothic Revival of St. Patrick's; from the Beaux Arts Grand Central Terminal (with staircases copied from the Paris Opéra) and the Art Deco Chrysler Building to the Wright-stuff Guggenheim and the Bauhaus Seagram Building.

Even "ordinary" office buildings can have extraordinary features: friezes, carvings, gilding, capitals, cornice pieces, decorative sills—all of the showy elements of European palaces, only bigger and brasher and designed to make aristocrats out of merchants. For these are the great palaces of trade, tributes to the variety and vitality of American industry. New York was one of the first cities to abandon class distinction, at least as far as the purveyors were concerned, between the carriage trade and the merchant class, between the custom-tailored and the store-fitted. It was the natural preserve of the department store, with its abundance of luxuries (which gradually became, by long acquaintance and by the nature of human ambition, necessities). And, after all, it was those capitalist princes of old New York—the Rockefellers, Guggenheims, Fricks, and Morgans—whose often-competitive collecting and philanthropy produced the great art collections that are now public treasures.

This book is about seeing New York. Not just Midtown Manhattan, but the whole city. It's about shopping and art-gazing and theatergoing, of course, but mostly it's about looking past the sales pitches to the piers, beyond the boutiques to the brownstones. It's about the green spaces as well as the grand hotels, about going off-Broadway as far as Brooklyn and seeing the Battery as the birthplace of America. If you want a top-ten list of tourist attractions, you can find one on any corner and at any souvenir stand; but if you want to know ten lovely things to do for yourself, ten splendors to share with your children, or ten places where beauty really is truth, read on.

ABOUT *this* GUIDE

"INSIDE" NEW YORK FOR OUTSIDERS

IT'S A FUNNY THING ABOUT NEW YORK TRAVEL GUIDES: most of them tell you too much, and a few tell you too little. This is because New York is such a complex city, so ornate and enveloping and layered with history that it's hard to stop acquiring good stories and passing them on. And the more time you spend there, the more you realize you don't know.

But statistics show that the majority of visitors to New York stay only three or four days—and even that average span likely includes time spent in business meetings or conventions. How much can you squeeze into a long weekend? How much do you want to see? This city's attractions are among the most frequently photographed in the world, yet package tours often haul you around as if you didn't already know what the Empire State Building looks like. Some tour books either skimp on shopping or endorse every dealer in town; some overlook any museum too small for blockbuster exhibits. Some short-change any theater outside Lincoln Center or Broadway, and any restaurant outside Manhattan. Some are too uncritical, some too "insider." Some have all the right stuff but are poorly organized; some are easy to read but oversimplified.

Not only that, but most guidebook writers also seem so attached to the modern stereotype of the city—the New York of loudmouthed cabbies, TV cop shows, the "if I can make it there" rat race, and the Wall Street shark pool—that they don't express the great romance of this rich, inimitable, and electrifying metropolis. It's an asphalt wonder, sure, but there are cobblestones still to be seen; a world-famous skyline, yes, but an architectural creation, not just a higher-rent district. It's a magnet for immigration, but that also means it's a tapestry of ethnic revival. And in an era when the Statue of Liberty is animated for a deodorant commercial, it's too easy to forget what an icon it really is and has been to millions of Americans and would-be Americans.

So as hard and heartbreaking as it is to limit a book like this, we've done so by doubling up whenever possible. The profiles in Part Five, New York's Neighborhoods, are partly geographical descriptions and partly historical romances: they're designed to help you get your bearings, but they include enough sights and stories to serve as do-it-yourself walking tours. In Part Six, Sightseeing, Tours, and Attractions in Depth, we've listed some attractions by type—family-style, theatrical, genealogical, and so on—to help you customize your visit. Major museums and sites in each neighborhood are explored in more detail and rated for interest by age group. In Part Eight, Shopping, we've combined best bets with do-it-yourself walking tours so you can see the sights and fill out your wish list at the same time. The maps are designed to help you with the logistics of arranging accommodations, dining, and sightseeing.

As for the hundreds of tourist attractions, we've tried to pick out the first-rate and special-interest best and skip the hype jobs. Truth is, even if you visit New York a dozen times, you won't be able to see as much as we've described for you, and by then you'll have discovered your own favorite places But we don't want you to waste any of your time, either. If it isn't fun, if it isn't informative, if it isn't accurate, we don't want you to go. If there's a better alternative, we want you to know. We hope to keep the quality of your visit high and the irritation quotient low. (And if we'd known that would turn into a poem, we'd have let you know.)

We've covered these attractions in these various ways, often overlapping, because we want to make sure you can pick out the ones you'd most enjoy. And for those who don't wish to do it themselves at all, we have listed a number of commercial and customized tours tailored to almost any interest, also in Part Six.

unofficial **TIP**
Remember that prices and hours change constantly. We have listed the most up-to-date information we can get, but you should double-check times in particular (if prices of attractions change, it is generally not by much). And remember, this is one of the busiest tourist towns in the world, drawing more than 30 million visitors a year, so make your reservations early and reconfirm at least once.

Even granting that your time will be tight, we've included a list of opportunities for exercise or play. That's partly because we at the *Unofficial Guides* try to keep up with our workouts when we're on the road, and also because you may be visiting old friends or old teammates. Even if you don't think you'll want to make time for a run or ride, experience has taught us that sightseeing and shopping can be exhausting, make you stiff, make you long for a little outdoors—or at least a little calorie countering.

WHY "UNOFFICIAL"?

MOST GUIDES TO NEW YORK TOUT the well-known sights, promote the local restaurants and hotels indiscriminately, and leave out a lot of good stuff. This one is different. We're reader-friendly. We sent in a team of evaluators—opinionated and often irreverent—to tour the museums, eat in the restaurants, perform critical evaluations of the hotels, and sample the wide variety of nightclubs. If a museum is boring, or standing in line for two hours to view a famous attraction is a waste of time, we say so—and, in the process, hopefully we will make your visit more fun, efficient, and economical. In fact, we got into the guidebook business in the first place because we were unhappy with the way travel guides make the reader work to get any usable information.

Most guidebooks are compilations of lists. This is true regardless of whether the information is presented in a list form or artfully distributed through pages of prose. There is insufficient detail in a list, and prose can present tedious helpings of nonessential or marginally useful information. Not enough wheat, so to speak, for nourishment in one instance, and too much chaff in the other.

And while many guides are readable and well researched, but they tend to be difficult to use. To select a hotel, for example, a reader must study several pages of text, and because each description essentially deals with the same variables, it's hard to recall what was said concerning a particular hotel. Readers generally must work through all the write-ups before beginning to narrow their choices. Restaurants, nightclubs, and attractions are treated the same way. Using such a guide means doing nearly as much research and comparison as starting from scratch, whereas we hope to simplify the task by narrowing travelers' choices to a thoughtfully considered, well-distilled, and manageable few.

HOW *UNOFFICIAL GUIDES* ARE DIFFERENT

READERS CARE ABOUT THE AUTHORS' OPINIONS. The authors, after all, are supposed to know what they are talking about. This, coupled with the fact that the traveler wants quick answers (as opposed to endless alternatives), dictates that authors should be explicit, prescriptive, and, above all, direct. The authors of the *Unofficial Guides* try to be just that. They spell out alternatives and recommend specific courses of action. They simplify complicated destinations and attractions and allow the traveler to feel in control in the most unfamiliar environments. The objective of the *Unofficial Guide* authors is not to give the most information or all of the information, but to offer the most accessible, useful information.

An *Unofficial Guide* is a critical reference work. Our authors and research team are completely independent of the attractions, restaurants, and hotels described. *The Unofficial Guide to New York* is designed for individuals and families traveling for the fun of it, as well as for business travelers and conventioneers, especially those visiting the Big Apple for the first time.

Special Features

The *Unofficial Guide* offers the following special features:

- Friendly introductions to New York's most fascinating neighborhoods
- "Best of" listings giving our well-qualified opinions on things ranging from raw oysters to blackened snapper and five-star hotels to multistory views
- Listings that are keyed to your interests, so you can pick and choose
- Advice to sightseers on how to avoid the worst of the crowds; advice to business travelers on how to avoid traffic and excessive costs
- Recommendations for lesser-known sights that are away from Times Square but are no less worthwhile
- Maps to make it easy to find places you want to go to and avoid places you don't
- Expert advice on avoiding New York's notorious street crime
- A hotel chart that helps you narrow down your choices fast
- Shorter listings that include only those restaurants, clubs, and hotels we think are worth considering
- Insider advice on best times of day (or night) to go places

HOW THIS GUIDE WAS RESEARCHED AND WRITTEN

ALTHOUGH MANY GUIDEBOOKS HAVE BEEN WRITTEN about New York City, very few of them have been evaluative. Some guides come close to regurgitating the hotels' and tourist offices' own promotional material. In preparing this work, team members not only visited each hotel, restaurant, shop, and attraction, evaluating them according to formal criteria, they interviewed tourists of all ages to determine what they enjoyed most and least during their New York visits. And while our observers are independent and impartial, they visited New York not as critics or VIPs but as tourists or business travelers, just as readers would.

In compiling this guide, we recognize that a tourist's age, background, and interests will strongly influence his or her taste in New York's wide array of attractions and will account for a preference for one sight or museum over another. Our sole objective is to provide the reader with sufficient description, critical evaluation, and pertinent data to make knowledgeable decisions according to individual tastes.

LETTERS, COMMENTS, AND QUESTIONS FROM READERS

WE EXPECT TO LEARN FROM OUR MISTAKES, as well as from the input of our readers, and to improve with each new book and edition. Many of those who use the *Unofficial Guides* write to us asking questions, making comments, or sharing their own discoveries or lessons learned in New York. We seriously appreciate all such input, both positive and critical, and we encourage our readers to continue writing.

How to Write the Authors

Eve, Lea, and Aaron
The Unofficial Guide to New York City
P.O. Box 43673
Birmingham, AL 35243
unofficialguides@menasharidge.com

When you write, be sure to put your return address on your letter as well as on the envelope—sometimes envelopes and letters get separated. And remember, our work takes us out of the office for long periods of time, so forgive us if our response is delayed.

Reader Survey

At the back of the guide you will find a short questionnaire that you can use to express opinions about your New York visit. Clip out the survey along the dotted line and mail it to the previous address.

HOW INFORMATION IS ORGANIZED

IN ORDER TO GIVE YOU FAST ACCESS TO INFORMATION about the best of New York, we've organized material in several formats.

HOTELS Since most people visiting New York stay in one hotel for the duration of their trip, we have concentrated on the specific variables that differentiate one hotel from another—location, size, room quality, services, amenities, and cost—and summarized our ratings in charts and maps that will help you streamline your decision-making.

RESTAURANTS We provide plenty of detail when it comes to restaurants. Since you will probably eat a dozen or more restaurant meals during your stay, and since not even you can predict what you might be in the mood for on Saturday night, we provide detailed profiles of the best restaurants in and around New York.

ENTERTAINMENT AND NIGHTLIFE Visitors frequently try several different clubs or nightspots during their stay. Since clubs and nightspots, like restaurants, are usually selected once travelers are actually in the city, we provide tips on getting tickets to big-name shows and in-depth profiles of the best nightspots and lounges in Part Ten, Entertainment and Nightlife.

SPECIAL TIPS In addition to singling out not-to-be-missed sites in the city and attractions ideally suited to younger tourists, we've marked some insider tips, shortcuts, and "only in New York" features throughout the book.

New York Metropolitan Area

GREAT NECK
LONG ISLAND

Throgs Neck Bridge

Clearview Expwy.

Cross Island Pkwy.

John F. Kennedy Int'l. Airport

495

295

678

Bronx-Whitestone Bridge

THE BRONX

278

278

Yankee Stadium

87

Citi Field

Flushing Meadows Corona Park

Grand Central Pkwy.

Van Wyck Expwy.

678

Forest Park

Cross Bay Blvd.

Jamaica Bay Wildlife Refuge

Shore Pkwy.

Pennsylvania Ave.

Rikers Island

LaGuardia Airport

RFK Bridge (formerly Triborough Bridge)

QUEENS

Northern Blvd.

278

Central Pkwy.

Grand

Woodhaven

Jackie Robinson Pkwy.

Linden Blvd.

Queensboro Bridge

Queens Blvd.

Long Island Expwy.

278

BQE (Brooklyn-Queens Expwy.)

Broadway

BROOKLYN

Flatbush Ave.

Queens-Midtown Tunnel

Williamsburg Bridge

Manhattan Bridge

George Washington Bridge

9A

125th St.

Central Park

Fifth Ave.

FDR Drive

East River

MANHATTAN

Henry Hudson Pkwy.

Hudson River

Broadway

42nd St.

23rd St.

West Side Hwy.

Delancey

Canal St.

N.Y.U.

Brooklyn Bridge

478

278

Brooklyn-Battery Tunnel

Lincoln Tunnel

95

HOBOKEN

Holland Tunnel

9

1

Ellis Island

Governors Island

Statue of Liberty

Upper New York Bay

NEW JERSEY

95

3

95

JERSEY CITY

78

STATEN ISLAND

N

3 mi

3 km

0

0

Passaic River

280

Newark Bay

NEWARK

1

95

9

Newark Int'l. Airport

78

95

Bayonne Bridge

PART ONE

UNDERSTANDING
the CITY

A VERY SHORT HISTORY *of* *an* EXTREMELY COMPLEX CITY

COLONIALISM AND CAPITALISM

IF IT WEREN'T FOR A DETERMINED JAG of geography (or, rather, political arm-twisting), New York City might not even connect with the rest of the state. It's like the little tail on a stylized comma or the pointed throat of some vulturous bird cutting down the Hudson River toward the Atlantic.

Before the arrival of the Europeans, the region was inhabited by two groups of related native tribes: the Algonquins along the Hudson and on Long Island, and the Iroquois Confederacy, among it the Mohawks and Seneca, who roamed to the west and upstate. Some historians theorize that the colony reportedly established in the year 1010 by Greenlander Thorfinn Karlsefni was in fact on the island of Manhattan, but if so, his village's existence left no trace.

As was common in the 16th and 17th centuries, the explorers who sailed for one European empire were often citizens of another, so fascinated by the prospect of travel that they accepted commissions from rival powers. So John Cabot of Genoa became a citizen of Venice, then moved to Bristol and sailed for England; he landed in Newfoundland in 1497 and disappeared while attempting to return to the region in 1498. His son Sebastian, who may have reached the Hudson Bay a decade later, sailed for the Spanish. Venetian Giovanni da Verrazano, who sailed into New York Bay in 1524, was in the pay of the French. Esteban Gomez, who sighted Manhattan a year later, was a Portuguese Moor flying the Spanish flag. Henry Hudson, who was English, was working for the Dutch. At least Samuel de Champlain, who was also carrying the French flag when he mapped eastern Canada, was working in his own language.

With its fine natural port, access to areas near Canada via the Hudson River, and the agricultural wealth of the surrounding territory—not to mention European dreams of a vast paradise of gold in the land beyond and a marine shortcut to the Asian trade—New York was destined to be the target of political and colonial struggles. Champlain and Hudson worked their way into almost the same area at the same time, in 1609, and left their names behind as a handy reminder: the Frenchman sailed south from Canada along what is now known as Lake Champlain to its tip, while the Englishman sailed north along the waterway ever after called the Hudson River, nearly as far as modern Albany.

The French, who had earlier allied themselves with the Huron in Canada, immediately became embroiled in trade and territorial struggles with the tribes of the Iroquois, a strategy that would haunt them for more than a century. The Dutch, on the other hand, went right for the open water: in 1624, representatives of the newly created Dutch West Indies Company famously acquired the land at the south end of the island of Manhattan from the easygoing Manates tribe for trinkets worth less than $25, naming the settlement New (or Nieuw) Amsterdam. They were sometimes referred to as the Manhattan Indians, as they called the area *Man-a-hatt-ta*. However, that may have been a bad omen: one other possible interpretation of the term is "island of drunkenness," because Hudson's landing apparently turned into quite a party. Under a series of practical-minded Dutch administrators, the port prospered and expanded, and they almost certainly got their money's worth in the next 40 years. Workers, whether voluntary or involuntary, were highly desirable: the first African slaves were imported in 1625, and the first Jewish settlers arrived in 1626. By the 1660s, there were about 300 permanent homes listed in the records.

But during the Second Dutch War, England re-declared its right to the region, basing its claim on the voyages of John Cabot; in 1664, when the English fleet sailed into New York Harbor, then-Governor Peter Stuyvesant struck his colors and quietly surrendered. (Actually, his constituents surrendered for him; a puritanical tyrant with a wooden leg, Stuyvesant ordered every tavern in the city to close by 9 p.m., which clearly proves he was in the wrong place.) He left behind the names of **Wall Street** (so called because a protective wall was raised there); **Broadway** (originally Breede Wegh, a cobbled route that ran the entire length of the island); the **Bowery** (from Stuyvesant's own country home, or *bouwerie*) in the farmland a mile uptown; **Harlem,** after Haarlem, the capital of North Holland; **Bloomingdale** (Bloemendaal), or "vale of flowers," which, though now pretty much known only as the name of the department store, once referred to much of the West Side (from 23rd Street to above Central Park, by some accounts); and, of course, **Stuyvesant Square.** With one very brief resurgence of the Dutch in 1673, New York—now renamed in honor of King Charles's brother, the Duke of York (later James II)—was firmly in the hands of the British.

Back in Europe, the imperial and often internecine struggles between Britain and France only intermittently gave way to peace. So the colonial governor, Thomas Donegan, increasingly wary of French expansionism from the Canadian border, assiduously cultivated friendly relationships with the Iroquois. It was a good strategy, and the tribes were an invaluable ally during the decades of the French and Indian Wars, which stretched from the late 17th century into the mid-18th. The Battery got its name early in that struggle, when nearly a hundred cannons were lined up along the waterfront to prevent an attack on the harbor. The Treaty of Paris in 1763 confirmed the British domination of the North American territories, and the long and bitter campaigns gave way to a burst of settlement and expansion.

There was a brief period of self-satisfied prosperity. The area was covered in wheat fields and farms, such as the one in the Bronx on which the **Van Cortlandt House,** now a museum, was built in 1748. King's College (now **Columbia University**) was founded in 1754; **St. Paul's Chapel** was dedicated in 1766.

Then, in one of those ironies history is made of, the British crown tried to pay off its war debts by levying huge taxes on the very American colonies it had fought so hard to retain. With the passage of the Stamp Act in 1765, the resentment of many formerly loyal colonists reached a crisis. Shippers and "bolters" (millers) turned to smuggling and tariff-dodging. Fledgling Sons of Liberty took on the British authorities in the Battle of Golden Hill as early as 1770, and in 1774 they threw a "tea party" of their own in New York Harbor. Tensions increased to the point that many older landowners returned to England. William Tryon, the popular colonial governor of North Carolina, was transferred to New York in an attempt to contain the troubles, but he was forced out in 1775. Rebellion-minded New Yorkers—notably including English-born but radical-hearted Thomas Paine and 19-year-old Alexander Hamilton, whose eloquence would later be turned to persuading the colonies to ratify the Constitution—published scathing denunciations of the Crown's policies toward the colonies. With the capture of Fort Ticonderoga later that year, war was all but declared.

This was the crucial region of the American Revolution. Fully a third of all battles were fought in the state, including the tide-turning Battle of Saratoga. New York produced both America's first martyr, Nathan Hale, who was hanged in the city, and its most infamous hero-turned-traitor, Benedict Arnold.

Unhappily, New York City's active role in the Revolution was very short and not too sweet. General Washington suffered a series of defeats in the late summer and fall of 1776, including the battles of Long Island, Harlem Heights, and White Plains, and though the Americans held on to most of the upper and western part of the state, they eventually had to abandon the city to the British forces, who sailed into the harbor in a fleet of 500 ships and occupied it for the full seven years until the end of the war.

During the British occupation, unfortunately, the city was swept by two massive and somewhat suspicious fires: a 1776 conflagration that destroyed 1,000 homes and **Trinity Church,** and the second in 1778. Consequently, there are few buildings from the Colonial period visible outside **Historic Richmond Town** and the **Alice Austen House,** both on Staten Island; even the **Fraunces Tavern,** site of Washington's famous farewell to the troops in 1783, is a partial re-creation of the original.

THE EMPIRE STATE

ALMOST FROM THE MOMENT PEACE WAS PRONOUNCED, New York boomed—and bickered. From 1785 until 1790, New York served as the nation's capital; it was here that Washington was sworn in as the first president; and it was from here that Hamilton, John Jay, and Virginian James Madison published the so-called Federalist Papers, which eventually persuaded the states to ratify the Constitution. Hamilton served as Washington's secretary of the treasury and founded both the Bank of New York and the *New York Post*. But he and John Adams opposed the French Revolution, which widened the gap between the Federalists and the Jeffersonians, among whom were Hamilton's former collaborator Madison and the brilliant young senator Aaron Burr. Burr might have been President, but a close House of Representatives vote made him Jefferson's vice president instead; Burr blamed Hamilton, and when Hamilton later blocked his election as governor, Burr challenged him to a duel. The 1804 shootout left both Hamilton and Burr's political career fatally wounded.

About the time that political power shifted, first to Philadelphia and then to the new capital at Washington, the **New York Stock Exchange** opened, and New York's indefinite term as a financial capital began. The agricultural order gradually began to yield to an industrial and shipping society. Staten Island ferry boy Cornelius Vanderbilt gradually bought up the local freight lines and built his shipping force into an empire, becoming a millionaire while still in his teens. German-born John Jacob Astor, whose China trading, land sales, and fur-trade companies enjoyed comfortable monopolies in the nation, was the first in New York's long line of millionaire tycoons (and first to establish the city's philanthropic tradition by leaving money for what became the **New York Public Library**). Confident of its own importance as early as 1804, the city established the **New York Historical Society** collection.

Already it was the largest city in the country, with more than 33,000 residents; ten years later the population had nearly doubled. A series of virulent epidemics—yellow fever, cholera, typhoid, smallpox—gradually drove residents from the old downtown area into what is now Greenwich Village. Another huge fire in 1835 and yet another in 1845 again destroyed most of Lower Manhattan and cleared the way for ever more ambitious construction. They also inspired the creation of **Croton Reservoir** in 1842, in the heart of Midtown where the New York Public Library is now; this project marked the beginning of fresh public water and a citywide sewer system.

The **Erie Canal** was completed in 1825, drawing even more trade, and immigrants as well, through New York's already booming port. The great potato famine forced a huge influx of Irish immigrants—at least 200,000—in the 1840s and 1850s. A wave of German immigrants followed in the 1860s; the Chinese began arriving in the 1870s; and in the 1880s, an estimated 1.5 million Eastern European Jews flooded the Lower East Side. They were accompanied by thousands of Italians, Irish, and displaced Southern blacks, and by 1900 the city held an astonishing 3.4 million people. That would double again, to 7 million, in just 30 years. And an estimated 17 million more transient immigrants passed through the city between 1880 and 1910.

The widespread poverty and incredibly unsanitary living conditions of the underclass produced not only disease but also rampant and almost institutional crime—that is, street gangs at one level and political machines at the other. The Five Points neighborhood, re-created by Martin Scorsese in his 2002 epic *Gangs of New York,* was only blocks from Cherry Street, where William "Boss" Tweed held court. Tweed and his Tammany Hall organization looted the city of more than $160 million over the years, though they did do the immigrants the favor of registering them as Democrats by way of maintaining control.

New York took on the role of intellectual capital as well. The rest of the state might be known to have a sort of wild and bucolic beauty, thanks to the efforts of such writers as Washington Irving, James Fenimore Cooper, and William Cullen Bryant, and the Hudson River School artists, including Thomas Cole and Frederic Church, but New York City was determined that everything be modern and smart.

Horace Greeley's *New York Tribune,* the most influential newspaper before and during the Civil War, was founded in 1841; the *New York Times* followed in 1851. The **University of the City of New York** was chartered in 1831; the **Philharmonic Society of New York** gave its first concert in 1842. The **Crystal Palace,** modeled on the pavilion erected for London's Great Exposition of 1851, hosted the World's Fair in 1853 (and later burned to the ground, just as the London palace had). Numerous progressive and reformist movements made New York their headquarters, including that of the suffragettes (the first women's rights convention was held in Seneca Falls in 1848); Greeley's *Tribune* editorialized in favor of organized labor, profit sharing (both of which he instituted at his paper), abolition, and women's suffrage. The California gold rush electrified Wall Street in 1849; a scheme by Jay Gould to corner the gold market 20 years later would nearly bankrupt it.

And in 1858, one of New York's most beloved landmarks, **Central Park,** opened its gates, ensuring that even the poorest sweatshop worker in the city would always have a place to walk like a prince.

CIVIL WAR AND THE "SECOND EMPIRE"

NEW YORK WAS NO STRANGER TO SLAVERY. The first slaves had been imported by the Dutch in 1625, and in fact it was slave labor that built the original fortress, including the "wall" that was Wall Street. With painful irony, Wall Street also featured the first slave market, a mercenary operation that predated the Stock Exchange by nearly a century. But New York was also in the vanguard of the abolitionist movement, outlawing slavery in the city as early as 1799 (phasing it out over 30 years) and increasingly agitating for nationwide abolition. Frederick Douglass's influential *North Star* newspaper was headquartered in Rochester; Greeley's *Tribune* was the country's most vociferous antislavery mainstream paper (though originally a passivist one). It was the growing split between the outspoken antislavery and laissez-faire elements within the long-dominant Democratic Party that helped swing New York to the Republicans and Abraham Lincoln in 1860.

Nevertheless, while the intellectual element in New York favored abolition, not even all of the abolitionists—and even fewer members of the laboring class and immigrant communities, who could not hope to raise the $300 "replacement fee" that was the rich man's alternative to active service—supported a war to free the Southern slaves. With the passage of the Conscription Act, draft riots broke out all over the country; those in New York City, which lasted four days in July 1863 and resulted in the deaths of 120 men, nearly all black, and the displacement of close to a thousand more, were the most serious.

In general, however, New York vigorously supported the war effort, especially as the need for continual military supplies and transportation fueled the city's industries. The city provided battleships (including the ironclad *Monitor*) and freighters, textiles for uniforms and supplies, provisions, and, most important, the railroads that carried them. And for all the occasional Wall Street panics, the momentum never really slackened: the end of the war was for New York the beginning of what Mark Twain christened the "Gilded Age."

Luxury hotels such as **The Waldorf-Astoria** and **The Plaza** (original versions) opened their doors; so did the **Metropolitan Museum of Art** and the **Metropolitan Opera House** (then on Broadway near Times Square). Fifth Avenue became known as "Mansion Row."

Henry Villard, publisher of the *New York Evening Post* and president of the Northern Pacific Railway, began his gilded palace (now part of the **New York Palace Hotel**) at Madison Avenue and 50th Street in 1882; W. K. Vanderbilt built an Italianate mansion at 52nd and Fifth, just one of a long line—or avenue—of Vanderbilt family extravagances leading up to his cousin Cornelius II's fantastic French Renaissance chateau at the foot of Central Park (the house seen in the painting in The Plaza Hotel's Oak Bar).

Elevated railroads, or "Els," running above Second, Third, Sixth, and Ninth avenues suddenly made it easier to get uptown, and newly electrified streetlights made it safer. Telephone and telegraph wires crisscrossed the city, at least until the blizzard of 1888 ripped them down and launched the city on a buried-cable program. The first great luxury apartment building, the **Dakota,** staked out a new frontier on Central Park West at 72nd Street. Andrew Carnegie built his mansion, complete with Otis elevator and central heating, on the east side of the park in the "wilds" of 91st Street. The **Statue of Liberty, St. Patrick's Cathedral,** the **Brooklyn Bridge, Carnegie Hall**—all these monuments to the New York spirit were in place a quarter century after war's end.

And the city was stretching in other directions, too, especially to the southeast. The **Brooklyn Academy of Music** had been founded in 1861; Brooklyn's **Prospect Park,** designed by Central Park architects Frederick Law Olmsted and Calvert Vaux (and considered by many to be superior to the Manhattan park), was opened in 1867; the **Brooklyn Museum of Art** opened in 1897. In fact, Brooklyn was the third-largest city in the country in 1898, when the five boroughs officially consolidated.

No economy benefited more than New York's during the postwar period. Shipping, trade, industry, government contracts, and, inevitably, corruption in the awarding of them, made millionaires out of manufacturers, mob bosses, political-influence peddlers, and sweatshop operators alike. Samuel Tilden became an early example of New York's periodic hero, the crusading reformer, when he prosecuted Boss Tweed of the Tammany Hall ring, but he made little real dent in the power of Tammany itself. (A few years later, city Police Commissioner Theodore Roosevelt would build a more successful political career on his reformist reputation.) The Republicans were not much cleaner, and the semiunderground power struggle led to a more overt political distance between the city's Democrats and the Republicans upstate.

The hundreds of thousands of immigrants who arrived near the end of the 19th century were herded into warehouses, mills, and industrial sweatshops, while labor leaders fought to establish minimal hour and wage (and age) standards. The tenement, the flophouse, the drug den, and the gang took up permanent positions in the city structure. Despite periodic catastrophes—most famously the Triangle Shirtwaist Factory fire of 1911, which killed 140—and the increase of institutionalized poverty, most New Yorkers were intoxicated by the flow of commercial goods and boastfully smug about the prosperity of the city.

To a great extent, both this vast prosperity and the narrowness of its beneficiaries are exemplified by the spread of the railroads and the great fortunes their owners made from them. And one way or another, most of the rail barons had New York connections. The gold rush of 1849 may have lured Collis Huntington from Oneonta, New York, to California, but he quickly realized that the real money was to be made in railroads stretching from coast to coast. The fortunes of Andrew Carnegie and his partner-turned-rival Henry Frick were forged in steel and railroading. "Commodore" Cornelius Vanderbilt expanded into railroads as well and became lord of the New York–Chicago routes. Jay Gould was forced out of the Erie Railroad and other state rails, but he merely headed west and wound up with four more.

Stockbroker E. H. Harriman took over the Union Pacific, Southern Pacific, and Central Pacific railroads. J. Pierpont Morgan, already extremely wealthy thanks to his financier father, J. S. Morgan, took a lesson from all of these preceding examples, wresting away control of Gould's eastern railway holdings, founding U.S. Steel with Frick, and lending gold to the federal government at usurious rates during the Panic of 1895. These families, along with the Astors and Vanderbilts and their financial rivals, built lavish mansions on the East Side, establishing Midtown and Central Park as the social center of Manhattan and defining what came to be known as "The Four Hundred," the city's social elite. (It may be worth remembering that the life of luxury wasn't necessarily a safe one: John Jacob Astor IV went down on the *Titanic,* and a Vanderbilt who had to postpone journey on the same ship died on the *Lusitania.*)

John D. Rockefeller's fortune, grounded in the oil-refining business, was almost incalculable, well into the hundreds of millions by the turn of the century. And he was not alone. By 1900, 70% of the nation's corporations were headquartered in Manhattan, and 65% of all import trade passed through the harbor.

THE EARLY 20TH CENTURY

IN CHARACTERISTIC FASHION, New York was too impatient to wait for the calendar to announce a new era. The age of American imperialism, such as it was, was hastened by New York newspaper tycoons William Randolph Hearst and Joseph Pulitzer, whose respective (if not entirely respectable) dailies, the *Journal* and *World,* so twisted coverage of Cuban-Spanish tensions that the United States was eventually lured into the Spanish-American War, from which it gained the Philippines, Guam, and Puerto Rico, not to mention the toothy New York–born hero Teddy Roosevelt.

Even so, 1900 was a landmark year. Ground for the first subway was broken in 1900; when it was completed, it was suddenly possible to cross the nine miles from City Hall to 145th Street in a little more than 20 minutes. (A steam-driven version, a single car that rocketed about 300 feet along Broadway between Warren and Murray streets and then was sucked backward, was constructed in 1870, but it made little impression.)

The city of the future had already been forged from the five boroughs in 1898. New Yorkers were so confident of their home's position as First City that the Vanderbilts launched a railroad line between Manhattan and Chicago, the "Second City"; its flagship express train was described as the overland version of a luxury liner, and it was grandly titled *The Twentieth Century Limited*. The "new" **Grand Central Terminal,** the Beaux Arts beauty now restored to its original glory, was begun in 1903; **Pennsylvania Station** (the original, not the existing building) would follow only a few years later. The city took over operation of the **Staten Island Ferry** in 1905; the first metered taxi challenged the old omnibus system in 1907.

The scramble for the skyline began with the construction of the almost-300-foot **Flatiron Building** at Broadway, Fifth Avenue, and 23rd Street in 1902; skeptics confidently predicted its collapse, though it stands proudly today as the symbol of its own "district." At 60 stories, the 1913, Gothic-style **Woolworth Building** at Broadway and Park Place reigned for 17 years, until the construction of the 77-story **Chrysler Building** in 1930, and that topped the city for only a few months, until the 102-story **Empire State Building** opened in 1931. (The Empire State Building held the world height title until 1972 with the opening of the **World Trade Center,** but it was overshadowed a year later by the Sears Tower, now the Willis Tower, in Chicago.)

The early years of the 20th century were a golden age for songwriters, playwrights, musicians, and vaudeville performers. Publishing firms crowded into a dilapidated 28th Street neighborhood, which became known as **Tin Pan Alley.**

The **Apollo Theater** in Harlem opened in 1913. Blacks and Hispanics settled on the West Side, in an area of the 60s then called San Juan Hill (which got its nickname shortly after Roosevelt's famous Rough Riders victory in Cuba), and on the north side of Manhattan in Harlem. That had been a prosperous Jewish neighborhood, but it gradually became a center for black art, literature, and music during a period called the Harlem Renaissance. In the 1920s alone, Harlem's population increased from 83,000 to more than 200,000.

World War I only boosted the city's economy, which went into overdrive to supply the troops; stocks continued to rise throughout the 1920s, which roared in New York as nowhere else. Prohibition became the law in 1920, but just as war boosted profits, so did the relatively genteel, or at least socially tolerated, crime of bootlegging. Smart, brittle, and literary characters went hand in hand with the

Ziegfeld Follies. American women were not only emancipated, in the phrase of the time, but were also finally enfranchised. (They got to vote.) The *New Yorker* magazine debuted in 1925, with its quintessential Gilded Age fop of a symbol, Eustace Tilley, on the cover. Charles Lindbergh flew across the Atlantic Ocean in the *Spirit of St. Louis* while New Yorkers drove under the Hudson River through the brand-new **Holland Tunnel.** Big bands and Broadway filled the airways; so did baseball player Babe Ruth, who in 1927 hit 60 home runs for the Yankees. The **Museum of Modern Art** was founded in 1929, and a year later Samuel Guggenheim began collecting the art that would eventually form the heart of the **Guggenheim Museum.**

Everything glittered until 1929, when New York once again led the nation, this time into disaster. The crash of the stock market in October turned Central Park into a shantytown and the city's greatest artists into federal employees, thanks to the Works Progress Administration (WPA). At the same time, growing political tensions in Europe, particularly in Germany, inspired a whole new generation of writers and artists to emigrate to America. During the slow reconstruction of the 1930s, Mayor Fiorello La Guardia, the "Little Flower," was able to institute a series of municipal reforms so that the poorer classes could also share in the recovery. He also persuaded President (and former New York Governor) Franklin Roosevelt to provide New Deal funds to build the **Triborough** and **Hudson bridges,** the **Brooklyn Battery Tunnel,** and dozens of other public projects. In 1939, multimillionaire philanthropist John D. Rockefeller Jr. personally drove the final rivet into the beautiful Art Deco complex at **Rockefeller Plaza.** Flush with visions of a bright new future, the New York World's Fair of 1939–40 drew a staggering 45 million visitors to Queens.

THE MODERN ERA

ONCE AGAIN, WAR FUELED THE ECONOMY. The outbreak of World War II kicked the stock market back into high gear, and it was not to slow for nearly 30 years. With the ending of the war, America the melting pot took its place at the head of international power as well; the **United Nations** headquarters was established in New York in 1946. Large numbers of Puerto Ricans and other Hispanic immigrants arrived, and many of them moved to the Upper East Side, to what became known as **El Barrio** or **Spanish Harlem;** the Chinese arrived in even greater numbers throughout the 1940s and 1950s. By 1950, New York was the largest city in the world.

The 1960s were famously feverish in New York, in the arts world, in the cultural sphere, and in politics. Queens's **Flushing Meadows Corona Park** hosted another World's Fair in 1964, and its symbolic Unisphere still holds up the one-world promise. The Beatles set foot on American soil for the first time at **Kennedy Airport** in 1965, and they played to 55,600 fans at **Shea Stadium.** Builder and power broker Robert Moses remade the face of the West Side, culturally and physically, by sweeping away the crumbling buildings in the San Juan district and designing a huge arts complex, now **Lincoln Center for the Performing Arts,** in its place.

Columbia University students staged famous sit-ins. *Hair* opened in 1967, and Mikhail Baryshnikov and Rudolf Nureyev led the list of Soviet writers, dancers, and artists who fled to the United States. A new sense of irony, expressed in various ways—the Beat generation of writers and so-called bohemians, and later Pop Art and the stereotypically neurotic New Yorker made famous by Woody Allen, among others—made New York City seem both exotic and depraved to many conservative Americans.

New York's black intelligentsia, from Langston Hughes and Zora Neale Hurston to James Baldwin, Richard Wright, and Ralph Ellison, had been exposing racism in scathing essays, novels, and plays throughout the 1950s; now their writings and *The Autobiography of Malcolm X* became required reading. The flamboyant lifestyle of Harlem congressman Adam Clayton Powell and the charges of corruption and political favoritism that surrounded him were reminiscent of the Prohibition-era reign of Mayor Jimmy Walker. Greenwich Village became first the symbol and center of the gay-rights movement, and then the equally vivid shorthand for the burgeoning AIDS epidemic. Militant civil-rights groups, antigovernment radical political parties, anti–Vietnam War demonstrators, and women's groups seemed to have transformed New York society top to bottom.

And perhaps they did—but in New York, money always seems to have more pull than politics. By the early 1970s, President Nixon was beginning to withdraw the troops from Southeast Asia, the hippies were on the way out, and the yuppies had arrived. A burst of luxury hotels and apartment buildings and huge, showy corporate structures jacked the skyline ever higher (and led, though too late for Stanford White's Penn Station, to a greater appreciation of historic restoration and preservation). Moreover, the expansion of New York, specifically the exodus of Manhattanites into the suburbs, began to drain the city of vital income. And as the upper middle class moved out, the city became a playground for the superrich and a prison for the poor.

The pride of the 1970s nearly led to a great fall. Just as the World Trade Center was completed in 1973, the city began to spiral toward bankruptcy, a fate just barely averted with the fraternal assistance of Wall Street. The Great White Way and the entire rest of the city went dark in the Blackout of 1977. Stocks ballooned again, only to crash again in 1987. The first terrorist attack on the World Trade Center, in 1993, killed six people; eight years later, the death toll would be nearly 3,000. But markets never stay slow in a city that never sleeps, and downtown construction, repair and improvement of mass transit, and the restaurant and entertainment industries are stronger than ever.

Heading into the millennium, and having celebrated its own official first century as a unified city, New York seemed to be turning over its own chronometers, spiritual and literal. **Ellis Island,** which reopened as the **Immigration Museum** in 1990, is one of the most visited sites in New York, even as another great wave of immigration is bringing greater ethnic variety to the city. Crime, the city's long-standing shadow empire, is succumbing to the police department's continual investigations into corruption both external and internal. During the administration of Mayor Rudolph Giuliani, a former federal prosecutor, crime rates began to plummet. They are now at the lowest level in a half-century. (The murder rate in 2007 was the lowest in statistical history.) **Times Square,** once a byword of prostitution, gambling, and purse-snatching, began an astonishing revitalization campaign that has not only reshaped the entire area but also attracted a new generation of theatrical producers and media conglomerates. Pollution levels have been substantially lowered, thanks in part to the city's growing fleet of natural-gas and diesel-hybrid buses and to the fact that so many New Yorkers use public transportation. The air has also improved on a person-to-person level, thanks to the citywide smoking ban that went into effect in 2003.

There can be no question, however, that the two great blows—September 11, 2001, and the Wall Street crash of 2008—have forever changed this great city, sobering its financial, cultural, and architectural hubris. Yet even those events have shown the city's character at its best—heroic, united, stubborn, determined. They have also demonstrated the inherent power of the American Dream: the **Statue of Liberty,** whose lamp remains the most recognizable symbol of hope in the world, reopened in its entirety, base to crown, on Independence Day 2009. Despite many delays and design changes for rebuilding on the World Trade Center site, the neighborhood now known as **Ground Zero** has obviously become fixed in the minds of Americans as a crucial bit of history. In fact, with the reopening of the **Port Authority Trans-Hudson (PATH) terminal** near the World Trade Center site in Lower Manhattan, the construction of high-end condos in that same 9/11-blasted neighborhood, along with a network of public parks and green spaces around the border of the island's southern tip promised to make it more of landmark than ever. New York may wind up with an even greater sense of its original skyline than it had before 9/11.

PART TWO

PLANNING YOUR VISIT

WHEN *to* GO

NEW YORK MAY SOUND NORTHERN to a lot of folks, and in winter it can certainly scrape up some low temperatures and shine up the sidewalks; but in the heart of summer, especially August, it can be as thick and muggy as any Southern city, with the temperature nudging up toward the three-figure mark and sudden, sweeping rains leaving the asphalt steaming. Why do you think the Hamptons were invented? Of course, if you're inured to the humidity, or if business or school vacations require you to travel in July or August, you will still find a lot of free programs, indoors and out, all over town (and you can count on all the restaurants and museums cranking up the air-conditioning).

Actually, there's something to be said for almost any time of year in the Big Apple. If you go for the sidewalk show, spring and fall are absolutely gorgeous in New York; average temperatures are in the 60s and 70s, making for perfect walking weather, and there are flower shows, the ballet and opera spring seasons, and circus rings.

Summer is freebie heaven: opera, classical music, and Shakespeare in **Central Park;** Tuesday-night chamber concerts in **Washington Square Park,** weekend concerts at **South Street Seaport,** and jazz in the **Museum of Modern Art**'s sculpture garden; swing dance

unofficial **TIP**
January is a good time to visit with all those sales (including discounts on coats), **Ice Capades** at **Madison Square Garden,** several major antiques shows, perhaps an early **Chinese New Year** (of course there's a parade), and quiet time in the museums that are otherwise usually full of kids.

unofficial **TIP**
If you do wish to go during a major holiday or around a special event, such as Christmas, be sure to make your reservations well in advance and confirm at least once. Manhattan is a madhouse at prime time, although the excitement may be worth it. If you need your space, however, pick another time.

on **Lincoln Center Plaza;** at least one street fair every week; Fourth of July fireworks; and sunbathing in **Strawberry Fields.**

Fall is one party after another, starting with **Halloween**—the parade in Greenwich Village is the largest in the country, and elaborate **haunted houses** materialize uptown and down—and running through Thanksgiving; the **Big Apple Circus** sets up in the Lincoln Center Plaza through the holidays; and Central Park is absolutely brilliant. For all its chill—the really brutal winds don't usually hit until after the New Year—New York is a city that really knows how to dress for the holidays, with musical programs, lighting displays, elaborate window settings, and parades. (In fact, a parade is practically guaranteed for your visit: there are so many excuses for parading in this town, you'd have to look for a month to miss one.) Many parks, including the **Bronx Zoo,** light up and stay open late around the holidays; the **New York Botanical Garden** presents a huge model train display; the music of the Central Park and **Rockefeller Center** ice rinks fills the air. The South Street Seaport is a winter fantasy of lights, and the carolers—assembled in a "singing tree"—are a family favorite. Department-store windows are almost worth the visit by themselves, particularly at the tradition-minded **Macy's** and **Saks,** the hipper-than-thou **Barney's** (in 2009, it featured the Coneheads), and the extravagantly unpredictable and meticulously fantastic **Bergdorf Goodman,** Eve's perennial favorites. This really is the town that never sleeps. See the final section of this chapter for a calendar of special events.

WHAT*to* PACK

PERHAPS A LITTLE SADLY, this once most elegant of societies has become extremely informal; you'll be unlikely to see a tie or even a tuxedo outside of a wedding party unless you are fortunate enough to be invited to a serious social event. Even the old, established restaurants rarely require a tie for lunch; most only "recommend" a jacket, although it's a good idea to have a tie on hand at night. (See the dress code advisories in our restaurant profiles.) However, the great majority of Manhattanites are dressed either for success or to impress, in classic style or not, so if you like to blend in with the shopping or art crowd, go for the reasonably neat look.

If you're simply sightseeing, you can pretty much do as you please; street wear is every-wear, especially during the day. Shorts, T-shirts, or polo shirts (athletic-logo sportswear for kids) are common well into autumn, and a casual dress or reasonably neat pair of khakis will make you look downright respectable. The one "touristy" craze we do not recommend is the fanny pack. Not only does it mark you as an outsider, but it also can be more easily cut off and stolen than wallets or even purses.

As for outerwear, try to get something with dual use. A rainproof top of some sort, a lightweight jacket you can layer, or a sweater is probably the most you'll need in the summer, just in case a breeze comes up at night. However, remember that you will probably be going in and out of air-conditioning. If you're planning to jump in and out of buses or stores or even theaters, a light jacket you can easily unbutton or remove and carry without difficulty will keep you from alternately sweating and freezing. (A medium-weight or heavy shawl, which can be both decorative and warming, is a great alternative and easy to pack.) Those small, fold-up umbrellas are preferable to the traditional sort, not only because you can stash them in your bag but also because a crowd of people wielding pointed implements or hanging them on chair backs and such can be dangerous. (They're available on the street if you lose or forget one.) However, coming down through those "tunnels" of skyscrapers, wind gusts down city streets can pick up surprising force, and the trash-can graveyards of inside-out umbrellas are numerous, so a jacket or slicker with a hood might be a better bet.

Something along the lines of a trench coat with zip-in lining or a wool walking coat with a sweater will usually do in winter, though it's smart to have the anti-wind accessories—gloves, earmuffs, hats, and scarves—tucked in your bag. And if you have pull-on, thin, plastic galoshes or waterproof boots of some sort, it wouldn't hurt to bring them; snowstorms can move in pretty quickly. Fur coats are no longer much of an issue in the moral sense in New York, but unless you're planning to go to the nicer hotels and restaurants, you may find your fur more trouble to worry about than it's worth. Lugging a fuzzy through the **Metropolitan Museum of Art** gets to be extremely sweaty. Of course, if you're sticking to the **Metropolitan Opera,** fur away.

Just don't overload yourself. Frankly, years of travel (and packing) have convinced us that most people carry more clothes than they really need. (And these days, with stricter limits on carry-ons and baggage weights, and ever-increasing charges for checked luggage, it's even sillier to overindulge.) As obvious as those easy-packing tips you see in travel magazines may be (pick a basic color and a few bright accessories or a change of ties, things that don't wrinkle, lots of light layers, and so on), most visitors fill up their suitcases with whole new outfits for every day and evening event. Whom are you trying to impress? Plan your packing the way you'd plan everyday life at home. Unless you have a really formal event to go to, high heels are tiring and take up a lot of room. Similarly, men can easily wear one nice jacket and carry assorted slacks, or a suit and different shirts, perhaps a vest. A dark suit is next to formality, anyway. Besides, it is difficult to resist buying something new and fashionable when you're visiting, and then you have even more clothes to carry.

unofficial **TIP**
A pair of shock-absorbent sole inserts can dramatically reduce foot and back pain.

Two really important things to consider when packing are comfortable shoes—this is a culture of the streets, and what isn't asphalt is concrete—and expandable or forgiving waistlines. Even if you don't think you're going to eat much, the scent of food is constantly in the air; every bar lays out those mixed nuts or something similar; and somehow even the most careful dieters seem to join the clean-plate club when they visit one of the world's most famous restaurant centers. Seasoned travelers know that a change in schedule can often cause bloating as well as, paradoxically, dehydration. Make sure you have a change of shoes, too; this is not the place to save space, because wearing the same shoes through and after hours of walking or even standing around sightseeing is a good way to have sore feet, if not worse. The new antiblister patches and sprays may be helpful as well. If you don't want to pack "fat day" clothes, you had better be packing your running shoes. Or let them double as your walking shoes.

The other traveling "musts" are over-the-counter medications and ointments. People tend to drink more coffee and more cocktails on vacation, or even when taking important clients out, so be sure to pack headache medicines, Alka-Seltzer, and the like. If you are on prescription medicine, carry a little more of it than you actually need: you might drop some while sightseeing or find yourself staying a day or so longer than you expected for business or pleasure or even because of bad traveling weather. (It wouldn't hurt to photocopy the prescription or label, either, particularly if the medication contains any controlled substances.) If you are allergic to bites or stings, remember the antihistamines. For scratches and small annoyances, a small tube of Neosporin or other antiseptic ointment is helpful. You can get these things at a drugstore or the hotel shop, of course, but those little "travel sizes" are wildly overpriced; you'd be better off putting a small amount of each in your own containers (but remember the Transportation Security Administration restrictions at airports). Be absolutely sure to pack bandage strips and muscle-pain antidotes as well; blisters can ruin an otherwise wonderful trip. Similarly, you might want to bring an extra pair of eyeglasses or contact lenses.

Most better hotels have small sewing kits in the rooms for quick fixes, although bigger emergencies will be better served by valets or a dry cleaner around the corner. But if you're staying in a basic hotel, a needle and thread may come in handy. So may a multitool pocketknife, though you must pack it with your checked baggage (any such implements in carry-on luggage, including corkscrews, might still be confiscated). If you find that

unofficial **TIP**
A good way to keep medications fresh is to use those small zip-top plastic bags sold for jewelry (or even the sandwich-sized bags).

you forgot to take your grandfather's pocketknife out of your kit bag, find the nearest express office and send it home.

We have found four other tiny items to be extremely useful: a handkerchief, mini–magnifying or reading glasses, disposable stain-remover pads, and one of those tiny flashlights. We mean an old-fashioned man's handkerchief, not a pretty little showpiece. In the event of bad weather, allergies, air-conditioning, damp subway seats, and similar eventualities, a good 12-inch square is a lifesaver. Restaurant menus keep getting more ornate, the lighting dimmer, and—it seems—the type smaller. If you plan to spend time on the subways or the sidewalks, you will be in near-contact with a lot of coffee cups, snacks, and so on; if you find yourself having an even closer encounter thanks to a jerking subway ride, one of those towelette-sized spot treatments can save you a lot of heartache. And as more and more museums have to lower or narrowly focus their lighting to protect fragile canvases and textiles, we increasingly find ourselves squinting at the plaques and captions. A penlight comes in handy (but be sure to train it only on the information, not the art).

GATHERING INFORMATION

BROCHURES, HISTORICAL BACKGROUND, and up-to-date schedules are available from **NYC & Company,** which updates its material frequently. It's best to call in advance and get the information package mailed to you (☎ 800-NYC-VISIT or **www.nycgo.com**), but NYC & Company also has offices around Manhattan if you don't get to it beforehand (call ☎ 212-484-1222). There you can pick up lots of maps, free tickets or discounts, shopping guides, and so on.

The **main visitor center,** which boasts a wall-sized computer map, interactive-screen trip planners, and other high-tech attractions, is in **Midtown Manhattan** on Seventh Avenue between 52nd and 53rd streets and is open weekdays 8:30 a.m. to 6 p.m., weekends 9 a.m. to 5 p.m., and holidays 9 a.m. to 3 p.m. Not far away, a visitor center at the historic **Embassy Theater** in **Times Square** (Broadway between 46th and 47th streets) has information from both NYC & Company and the Times Square Alliance; it's open daily 8 a.m. to 8 p.m. (except Christmas and New Year's Day) and has multilingual tourist advisers and brochures.

There are others in Harlem (at the **Studio Museum** on 125th Street between Adam Clayton Powell Jr. Boulevard and Malcolm X Boulevard; open 9 a.m. to 6 p.m., weekends 10 a.m. to 6 p.m., closed holidays) and the Financial District (in **Federal Hall National Memorial,** 26 Wall Street; weekdays 9 a.m. to 5 p.m. except federal holidays), plus kiosks downtown at the southern tip of **City Hall Park** (on the

Broadway sidewalk at Park Row; open weekdays 9 a.m. to 6 p.m., weekends and holidays 10 a.m. to 5 p.m.) and in **Chinatown** (the triangle where Canal, Walker, and Baxter streets meet; open 10 a.m. to 6 p.m. daily). Be sure to pick up the free subway map.

New York has a large gay and lesbian population and many services and attractions for the homosexual traveler. Among local publications reporting gay events are the *Village Voice* and *New York Press,* both free in the city (and both with online versions), and the more specialized *Next* and *Blade,* free weeklies available at many bars and restaurants; both also have Web sites. Gay bookstores (see the relevant section in Part Eight, Shopping) can also serve as bulletin boards for community information.

When it comes to Internet sites, no city outdoes New York. Among them are the online versions of the weekly *City Guide,* provided to hotels (**www.cityguideny.com**); *Citysearch* (**www.citysearch.com**); the downtown monthly *Paper* (**www.papermag.com**); and *Time Out New York* (**newyork.timeout.com**).

New York magazine, which in its print form is among the most influential publications in the city, also puts cultural events and restaurant and entertainment listings up at **www.nymag.com.** Even booming Times Square has a Web site with info on local attractions (**timessquare.nyctourist.com**).

For those who are into the blogging game, there is only one site: **www.gothamist.com.** For lists of coffeehouses, independent bookstores, and even art cinemas by zip code, try **www.delocator.net.** And while the gossip-heavy **www.gawker.com** has moved beyond blogging, the site is still reporting—as it formerly mentioned on the front page—from the center of the universe; occasionally there's some information of use to outsiders.

Once in New York, look for free publications in your hotel room (most often the *New York Visitors Guide* and weekly editions of the *City Guide*), and the monthly *Where New York* and *In New York* magazines. Check current issues of *New York* and the *New Yorker* magazines and the daily *New York Times* for special events and performances. The Spanish-language daily *El Diario* is available at most newsstands. There are also several entertainment and cultural hotlines to call for daily opportunities: see Part Ten, Entertainment and Nightlife.

SPECIAL CONSIDERATIONS

TRAVELING WITH CHILDREN

NEW YORK IS MOST FAMOUS as a sort of adults' playground, but if you're considering a family vacation here, don't worry: for all the bars and "the-ah-tuh," New York is absolutely packed with family-style attractions and hands-on, state-of-the-art children's museums, both in and outside of Manhattan, not to mention the special events (such as the Macy's Thanksgiving Day Parade), the area zoos (five of them!) and botanical gardens, ice skating in Rockefeller Center, harbor tours, high views, antique carousels, and so on.

And sightseeing with small children can be a bargain if you use public transportation: kids less than 44 inches tall ride free on the buses and subways (there are handy-dandy lines by the bus driver's seat and toll gates for measuring). Remember that warnings about dehydration go double for small children, even in winter. For specific recommendations, see the "Best Children's Fare" list in Part Six, Sightseeing, Tours, and Attractions in Depth. And for kid-friendly hotels and restaurants and the best museums to visit with young ones, check out **www.newyorkkids.net.**

If you do bring the kids but would like to have a little adults-only time, contact the **Baby Sitters' Guild** (☎ 212-682-0227; **www.baby sittersguild.com**) or **American ChildCare Service** (☎ 212-244-0200; **www .americanchildcare.com**), which have bonded members who will stay in or carry out, so to speak, to Central Park or some other play spot. Also check with your hotel; most have a list of reliable sitters.

In the case of illness or medical emergency, first call the front desk of your hotel; many have arrangements with physicians for house calls. Otherwise, contact **Dial-a-Doctor** (☎ 212-971-9692).

Not surprisingly, the town that never sleeps is rife with 24-hour pharmacies, especially in the nightlife neighborhoods. (The Times Square–Broadway stretch is lit up with them.) Depending on your "extra points" accounts, you can call into the homegrown **Duane Reade** stores (including those at Broadway and 94th Street, ☎ 212-663-1580; Broadway and 57th Street, ☎ 212-541-9708; and Third Avenue at East 74th Street, ☎ 212-744-2668); the **CVS** stores at Third Avenue and East 91st Street (☎ 212-876-7016), 59th Street at Columbus Avenue (☎ 212-245-0617), Lexington Avenue and 53rd Street (☎ 917-369-8688), and Second Avenue at 72nd Street (☎ 212-249-5699); and the **Walgreens** at Second Avenue and 70th Street (☎ 212-734-6076).

TRAVELING WITH PETS

IF IT'S FIDO OR FLUFFY you simply cannot leave at home, there are some pet-friendly hotels in Manhattan, among them the **W hotels** (**whotels.starwoodhotels.com**); the **Affinia** hotels (**www.affinia .com**); **Marriott** and its sibling **Renaissance** hotels (**www.marriott.com**);

the **Loews Regency,** on Park at 61st Street (**www.loewshotels.com**); the **Soho Grand,** on West Broadway (**www.sohogrand.com**); **Le Parker Meridien,** south of Central Park (**www.parkermeridien.com**); the **Ritz-Carlton, Battery Park** (**www.ritzcarlton.com**); the **Hotel Indigo Chelsea** (**www .indigochelsea.com**) and the **Doubletree Chelsea** (**doubletree1.hilton .com**; and the **Sheraton** hotels (**www.sheraton.com**). Fees and damage-deposit policies vary; call the individual hotels for details. If your hotel doesn't accept pets, the concierge can probably give you the name of a kennel or pet-sitting service.

TIPS FOR INTERNATIONAL TRAVELERS

VISITORS FROM THE UNITED KINGDOM, western Europe, Australia, New Zealand, Japan, and a few other countries need only a valid, machine-readable passport to enter the United States, not a visa. Canadian citizens need a passport if arriving by air, but most do not need a visa. If arriving by land or sea, Canadian citizens can get by with an Enhanced Driver's License or Enhanced Identification Card (government-issued documents available only in certain provinces), or a Trusted Traveler Program card. Citizens of other countries must have a passport, good for at least six months beyond the projected end of the visit, and a tourist visa as well, available from any U.S. consulate. Some airlines and travel agents may also have forms available. For full requirements, see **travel.state.gov.**

If you are taking prescription drugs that contain narcotics or require injection by syringe, be sure to get a doctor's signed prescription and instructions. Also check with the local consulate to see whether travelers from your country are required to have any inoculations; there are no set requirements for entering the United States, but if there has been any sort of epidemic in your homeland, there may be temporary restrictions.

If you arrive by air, be prepared to spend two hours or more entering the United States and getting through U.S. Customs. Every adult traveler may bring in, duty-free, up to one liter of wine or hard liquor, 200 cigarettes or 100 non-Cuban cigars or three pounds of loose tobacco, and $100 worth of gifts, as well as up to $10,000 in U.S. currency or its equivalent in foreign currency. Most food or plants may not be brought in.

The dollar is the basic unit of monetary exchange, and the entire system is decimal. The smaller sums are represented by coins. One hundred cents (or pennies, as the one-cent coins are known) equal one dollar; five cents equal a nickel (20 nickels to a dollar);

unofficial **TIP**
If you have an emergency or need special assistance, contact the **Traveler's Aid Society,** which has booths at **Kennedy airport** (☎ 718-656-4870) and **Newark airport** (☎ 973-623-5052).

the ten-cent coin is called a dime (ten dimes to a dollar); and the 25-cent coin is called a quarter (four to a dollar). Beginning at the $1 level, money is in currency bills (although there are some $1 coins around as well). Bills come in denominations of $1, $2 (rare), $5, $10, $20, $50, $100, $500, and so on, although you are unlikely to want to carry $1,000 or more.

Banks in the United States are closed on federal holidays, which are New Year's Day (January 1), Martin Luther King Jr. Day (third Monday in January), Presidents' Day (third Monday in February), Memorial Day (last Monday in May), Independence Day (July 4), Labor Day (first Monday in September); Columbus Day (second Monday in October), Veterans Day (November 11), Thanksgiving (fourth Thursday in November), and Christmas (December 25).

The credit card is by far the most common form of payment in New York, especially American Express, Visa (also known as Barclaycard in Britain), and MasterCard (Barclaycard in Britain, Eurocard elsewhere in western Europe). Other popular cards include Diners Club, Discover, and Carte Blanche.

Traveler's checks will be accepted at most hotels and restaurants if they are in American dollars; checks in other currencies should be changed into dollar denominations. There are currency-exchange booths in such major traffic areas as **Kennedy** and **LaGuardia** airports, **Grand Central Terminal, Times Square,** and even **Macy's** and **Bloomingdale's** department stores.

unofficial **TIP**
Stick to $20 bills for taxicabs; drivers rarely make change for anything larger.

Public telephones require 35 cents; although area codes must be dialed for all calls inside or between boroughs, there is no additional charge for such local calls. Throughout the United States, if you have a medical, police, or fire emergency, dial ☎ **911,** even on a pay telephone without inserting coins, and an ambulance, police cruiser, or fire truck will be dispatched to help you.

The main area code for Manhattan is ☎ **212,** though recent years have seen the addition of ☎ **646** and ☎ **917** (mostly for cell phones). Outer-borough area codes include ☎ **718** and ☎ **347.**

Incidentally, New York has one of the most stringent antismoking programs in the country, something international visitors might need to consider in advance. Smoking is prohibited on buses, on subways, and in taxicabs; in public buildings or the lobbies of office buildings; in all but designated areas in theaters; in most shops and all museums; and in all restaurants and bars.

TIPS FOR THOSE WITH DISABILITIES

NEW YORK IS FAR MORE RECEPTIVE to the tourist with disabilities than its tough reputation might lead you to believe. All **city buses** are

unofficial **TIP**
An online brochure covering the transit authority's policies for all riders with disabilities, which can be downloaded, is available at **www.mta.info/mta/ada/ada.pdf.**

equipped with wheelchair lifts and "kneeling" steps (though admittedly they don't always work); disabled riders with a reduced-fare **MetroCard** pay half fare ($1) and can sometimes ride free. **Gray Line Tours** has an entire fleet of wheelchair-accessible double-decker touring buses. An increasing number of subway stops—currently more than 30—are wheelchair-accessible as well; for a list of services for the disabled, go to **mta .nyc.ny.us,** or contact the **Metropolitan Transit Authority's Customer Service Division** (370 J Street, Suite 702, Brooklyn, NY 11201; ☎ 718-330-3322), or see **www.mta.info/mta/ada/stations.htm.**

Travelers with visual impairments can get a Braille subway map and other materials free by calling the MTA's **accessibility office** at ☎ 646-252-5031. The traveler with hearing impairment can get similar help from the **New York Society for the Deaf** (817 Broadway, Seventh Floor, New York, NY 10003; TDD ☎ 212-777-3900).

A list of wheelchair-accessible museums, hotels, and restaurants is available from the **Society for Accessible Travel and Hospitality** (347 Fifth Avenue, New York, NY 10016; ☎ 212-447-7284 or **www.sath.org**). A similar guidebook, "Audiences for All: A Guide for People with Disabilities to New York City Cultural Institutions," is available from **Hospital Audiences** for $5 (548 Broadway, Third Floor, New York, NY 10012; ☎ 212-284-4100 or 212-575-7676). Or see the information on the organization's Web site at **www.hospaud.org/database/intro.htm.** And many members of the volunteer **Big Apple Greeter,** warmly recommended in Part Six, will partner visitors with disabilities around town, but you should call at least several days in advance (☎ 212-669-3602; **www.big applegreeter.org**).

Visitors who use walking aids should be warned that some older museums, especially smaller art collections housed in what were once private homes with stairs, may not be entirely wheelchair-accessible. Even shops or restaurants at sidewalk level may not have wide aisles or specially equipped bathrooms. Also, New York's roads and sidewalks are among the most used and hence most battered surfaces in the country, so beware.

The restaurants that we profile later in the book all have a disabled-access rating, as do most of the major attractions, but you need to call any other eatery or any store in advance. (In fact, you might check with some restaurants that were listed as not accessible at press time, as it's quite possible they've renovated their facilities since.) Similarly, you should call any stores you're particularly interested in; increased accessibility has been public policy for quite some time now.

CALENDAR*of*
SPECIAL EVENTS

HERE ARE THE MAJOR CELEBRATIONS and a sampling of the less well-known but unique events around New York and their approximate dates (specific ones where possible). Remember, if the event requires tickets, it's best to try to arrange them before leaving home; otherwise you may find yourself paying extra or being locked out entirely. Tickets for the **U.S. Open tennis championships** in August and September, for instance, go on sale in May, and the scalpers' prices are astonishingly high by the opening rounds.

Please note that many festivals, especially in the summer, move around from year to year, and that some close down or are replaced by others; so if you are interested, contact organizers as soon as possible. For many of the municipal functions, you may call NYC & Company at ☎ 212-484-1222, or check the Web at **www.nycgo.com.** Parade routes and times will usually be listed in the *New York Times* on the appropriate days. The local newspapers will also mention numerous street fairs, art shows, and concerts, particularly in summer.

In addition to the contacts listed in the following section, **Ticketmaster** (☎ 212-307-7171 or 866-448-7849; **www.ticketmaster.com**) may be able to supply tickets to particular events, although there will be an additional handling charge. Another ticket source is **StubHub!** (**www.stubhub.com**), which buys and resells tickets to concerts, sporting events, and other special events.

January

WINTER ANTIQUES SHOW   Third week in January. One of the largest and most prestigious (read: expensive) antiques gatherings in the city, this is held in the historic Park Avenue Armory on Park Avenue at 67th Street. For information, call ☎ 718-292-7392 or see **www.winterantiques show.com.** Over the first weekend of the big collection, **Antiques at the Armory,** a sort of counter-show featuring less-established or edgier collectors, is held at the 26th Street Armory at Lexington Avenue, and shuttle buses run between the two. For information, call ☎ 212-255-0020 or see **www.stellashows.com.**

WINTER RESTAURANT WEEK   Usually the third week in January into early February. A sit-down "taste of the town" event, when some of the biggest-name restaurants offer special cut-price meals. As soon as you see the ads in the *New York Times* or elsewhere listing the participating establishments, get on the phone to the restaurant of your choice, or you'll be out of luck. Call ☎ 212-397-8222 or see **www.nycvisit.com.**

CHINESE NEW YEAR PARADE At the new moon in late January or early February. A fortnight of fireworks, street fairs, and food festivals leads toward the big dragon parade through Chinatown. Call ☎ 212-484-1222 for information. A theatrical spectacular of Chinese dance, music, and arts is held at Radio City Music Hall in conjunction with the New Year; call ☎ 212-736-8535 or see **www.nyshow.net** for information.

February

EMPIRE STATE BUILDING RUN-UP Early February. Hundreds of athletes race not horizontally but vertically: 1,576 steps from the lobby to the 86th-floor observation deck. The best make it in less than 11 minutes. Contact the New York Road Runners at ☎ 212-860-4455 or visit **www.nyrr.org.**

WESTMINSTER KENNEL CLUB DOG SHOW Midmonth. This most prestigious of canine parades brings thousands of familiar, unusual, and rare dogs, all blow-dried and maybe even ribboned for judging, to Madison Square Garden. Call ☎ 800-455-3647 or 212-465-6741 or visit **www .westminsterkennelclub.org.**

March

ARTEXPO Early or mid-March. This huge affair at the Javits Convention Center specializes in what dealers call popular art, and that means anything from nice lithographs to the stuff you get on the sidewalk or see in chain motels. Call ☎ 216-328-8926 or visit **www.artexpos.com.**

ST. PATRICK'S DAY PARADE On March 17, everyone is Irish, so pack something green or get out of the way. The parade, at more than 200 years old, is one of the oldest anywhere, includes an estimated 150,000 marchers, and kicks off at 11 a.m.; the route is along Fifth Avenue (of course) from 44th to 86th streets, with the thickest crowd around St. Patrick's Cathedral (of course). See **www.saintpatricksday parade.com.** There's also a South Street Seaport Irish Stroll along Pier 17, with food and beverage vendors and buskers. Call ☎ 301-652-7712 for information.

THE PIER ANTIQUES SHOW Mid-March. Vast antiques exhibit and sale brings together 500 dealers on Pier 94 (along the Hudson River). There's also a companion show later in the year; see November listings. Call ☎ 212-255-0020 or visit **www.stellashows.com.**

RINGLING BROS. AND BARNUM & BAILEY CIRCUS PARADE Late March. Another great traditional procession, this one is now (thanks to animal protests) a semi-secret wee-hours train of elephants and lions and tigers making their way from Long Island City through the Queens-Midtown Tunnel to Madison Square Garden. For information, call ☎ 212-465-6741 or visit **www.ringling.com.**

CIRQUE DU SOLEIL Late March. Beginning in 2010, the strange and fantastic Canadian one-tent circus will present three shows annually: one in the warmer months at the Beacon Theater, a summer show at Randall's Island, and a winter holiday show at Madison Square Garden's WaMu Theater. Cirque's blend of astonishing acrobats and contortionists with eerie music is famous. Call ☎ 800-678-5440 or visit **www.cirquedusoleil.com.**

EASTER PARADE Late March to late April. A parade so famous they made a Fred Astaire–Judy Garland movie about it. Don that bonnet—the bigger the better—and promenade along (what else?) Fifth Avenue from 49th to 57th. Macy's Flower Show at the famous department store at Herald Square (on Broadway between 34th and 35th) starts the week leading up to Easter Sunday; for information, call ☎ 212-695-4400 or visit **www.macys.com.**

EASTER EGG ROLL Saturday before Easter (late March through April). In the East Meadow of Central Park; call ☎ 212-360-3456 or 888-NYPARKS.

NEW DIRECTORS/NEW FILMS FESTIVAL Late March to early April. A cutting-edge cinematic collaboration between the Museum of Modern Art, which hosts the screenings, and the Film Society of Lincoln Center. Call ☎ 212-721-6500 or see **www.filmlinc.com.**

INTERNATIONAL ASIAN ART FAIR March or early April. Increasingly the premier Asian-antiques showcase on the East Coast; 583 Park Avenue at 63rd Street. Call ☎ 212-642-8572 or visit **www.haughton.com/asian.**

BASEBALL SEASON OPENING DAY End of March to early April. If you're a pinstriper, or just an American Leaguer at heart, you can try for tickets by contacting the box office for the new Yankee Stadium at ☎ 718-293-6000 or **www.yankees.com.** For fans of the senior league, those heartbreaking Mets are enjoying their own new ballpark, Citi Field; call ☎ 718-507-8499 or visit **www.mets.com.**

April

ANTIQUARIAN BOOK FAIR April. First editions, rare titles, and autographed copies fill the Park Avenue Armory on Park at 67th Street. Call ☎ 212-944-8291 or visit **www.sanfordsmith.com.**

HANAMI: CELEBRATING THE CHERRY-VIEWING SEASON April to early May. A celebration of the Japanese, or flowering Kwanzan, cherry trees of the Brooklyn Botanic Garden; call ☎ 718-623-7200 or visit **www.bbg.org.**

May

FIVE BORO BIKE TOUR Early May. This 42-mile for-fun bike race—it draws 30,000 wheelers and dealers—links all five boroughs, with the kickoff downtown and the finish line in Staten Island. Picnic at the end of pedaling. Call ☎ 212-932-2453 or check **www.bikenew york.org.**

MARTIN LUTHER KING JR. DAY PARADE Third Sunday in May. A salute to the civil-rights leader starts on Fifth Avenue at 44th and streams up to 86th. Contact NYC & Company at ☎ 212-397-8222.

AIDS WALK NEW YORK Mid-May. The world's largest AIDS fund-raising walk—it usually draws a field 45,000—marches 6.2 miles along the Upper West Side; **www.aidswalk.net.**

WASHINGTON SQUARE OUTDOOR ART EXHIBIT Memorial Day weekend plus the following weekend and the first two weekends of September. This huge outdoor art show is a giant block party, with easels (and food carts) in the streets all around the park. Call ☎ 212-982-6255 or visit **www.washingtonsquareoutdoorartexhibit.org.**

LOWER EAST SIDE FESTIVAL OF THE ARTS Memorial Day weekend. An arts festival and street party held in and around Theater for the New City on First Avenue between Ninth and Tenth streets. Call ☎ 212-254-1109 or visit **www.theaterforthenewcity.net/les.htm.**

June

SHAKESPEARE IN THE PARK From June into September, this now-famous, free, and star-studded series (call ☎ 212-539-8750 or visit **www.public theater.org**) takes over the Delacorte Theater stage in Central Park. There are fewer than 2,000 seats, and the box office opens at 1 p.m. every day, but the line forms much earlier. (See "Ticket Tips" in Part Ten.)

CONCERTS IN THE PARK June through August. Some concerts in Central Park, Prospect Park, and other city greens are put on by the New York Philharmonic (call ☎ 212-875-5709 or visit **www.nyphil.org**) and the great Metropolitan Opera (call ☎ 212-362-6000 or visit **www .metopera.org**).

SUMMERSTAGE Similarly, there are free or nominally priced pop, rock, country, folk, reggae, and jazz concerts **throughout the summer** in Central Park. Remember Simon and Garfunkel? Garth Brooks? It's big, but it's fun. Call ☎ 212-360-2777 or look up **www.summerstage.com.**

BELMONT STAKES The second (occasionally the first) Saturday in June. The final leg of thoroughbred 3-year-old horse racing's Triple Crown, and a full schedule of other races, go off at Belmont Park on Long Island; call ☎ 516-488-6000 or visit **www.nyra.com/belmont.**

PUERTO RICAN DAY PARADE Second Sunday in June. A lively musical march along Fifth Avenue from 44th to 86th streets. Call ☎ 718-401-0404 or visit **www.nationalpuertoricandayparade.org.**

SUMMER RESTAURANT WEEK Usually the third week in June. A sit-down "taste of the town" event, when some of the biggest-name restaurants offer special cut-price meals. As soon as you see the ads in the *New York Times* or elsewhere listing the participating establishments, get on the phone to the restaurant of your choice, or you'll be out of luck. Call ☎ 212-397-8222 or see **www.nycvisit.com.**

GAY AND LESBIAN PRIDE DAY PARADE Late June. A weeklong series of public and private events culminates in the parade, commemorating the Stonewall Riot of June 28, 1969. It struts down (rather than up) Fifth Avenue from 52nd Street to the West Village. Call ☎ 212-807-7433 or visit **www.nycpride.org.**

MERMAID PARADE Late June. A sort of pre-Halloween bash along the Coney Island–Brighton Beach Boardwalk. A few years ago, the grand merman, uh, marshall, was former Talking Head David Byrne. Call ☎ 718-372-5159 or see **www.coneyisland.com/mermaid.shtml.**

July

FOURTH OF JULY FESTIVAL July 4. Independence Day celebrations include street fairs, concerts, and, after dark, the famous Macy's fireworks over the East River. Call ☎ 212-484-1222 or see **www.nycvisit .com.** All-day festivities downtown around Battery Park climax with fireworks over the harbor. And the Brooklyn Independence Day Parade, which claims to be the oldest in the city, kicks off at 10 a.m. from Bay Ridge and winds its way to John Paul Jones Park. Call ☎ 718-415-3945 or see **www.visitbrooklyn.org.**

LINCOLN CENTER FESTIVAL July. An array of dance, drama, children's shows, and multimedia and performance art that involves both the repertory companies and special guests and that moves through the indoor venues and sometimes outdoors as well, through July and August. Call ☎ 212-875-5928 or visit **www.lincolncenter.org.**

TAP CITY, THE NEW YORK TAP FESTIVAL Early July. Hundreds of kids and adults—students, beginners, masters—as well as celebrity dancers and tap legends gather for classes and rehearsals leading up to performances around town. Call ☎ 646-230-9564 or see **www.atdf.org.**

August

LINCOLN CENTER OUT OF DOORS Throughout the month. Some of the outdoor series taper off in August, but the music and other performances on the plaza (information at ☎ 212-546-2656 or **www .lincolncenter.org**) keep the joint jumpin'.

HONG KONG DRAGON BOAT FESTIVAL First weekend in August. Some 50 teams of 22 rowers, plus drummer and helmsman, race Chinese-style 40-foot teak boats on the lake at Flushing Meadows Corona Park in Queens. Call ☎ 718-767-1776 or visit **www.hkdbf-ny.org.**

HARLEM WEEK Mid-August. Films, art exhibits, concerts, exhibition games, and street fairs celebrating the neighborhood's rich cultural history build up to Uptown Saturday Nite, a combination block party and black-arts expo along 135th Street between Lenox (also called Malcolm X Boulevard) and St. Nicholas avenues. Call ☎ 212-862-7200 or see **www.harlemweek.com.**

MOSTLY MOZART FESTIVAL Most of the month. A famous phrase, and one brought to life with a wide variety of concerts at Lincoln Center. Call ☎ 212-875-5000 or see **www.lincolncenter.org.**

U.S. OPEN TENNIS TOURNAMENT Late August to early September. In its expanded digs at Flushing Meadows, this Grand Slam event is one of the sport's hottest tickets—literally. Don't forget the drinking water and the sunblock, if you can get in. Call ☎ 888-673-6849 or visit **www.usopen.org.**

NEW YORK INTERNATIONAL FRINGE FESTIVAL Mid-August. Multimedia, dance, theater, street, and musical performances, many of them free, at venues around the Lower East Side and East Village. Call ☎ 212-279-4488 or visit **www.fringenyc.org.**

September

WEST INDIAN AMERICAN DAY CARNIVAL AND PARADE Labor Day weekend. It's big, it's loud, it's delicious, and it's relatively underpublicized, perhaps because it's in Brooklyn, but fans of world or Caribbean music, food, and dance won't mind the short trip to Crown Heights. Call 718-467-1797 or see **www.wiadca.org.**

THE GREAT NORTH RIVER TUGBOAT RACE Labor Day weekend. Part parade, part true tug competition at Pier 84 (44th Street and Twelfth Avenue); **www.workingharbor.org.**

WASHINGTON SQUARE OUTDOOR ART EXHIBIT First two weekends of September. The late-summer edition of an old and revered Greenwich Village gathering that also takes place in May. This huge outdoor art show is a giant block party, with easels (and food carts) in the streets all around the park. Call ☎ 212-982-6255 or visit **www.washington squareoutdoorartexhibit.org.**

BROADWAY ON BROADWAY Early to mid-September. For one enchanted day and evening in Times Square—where else?—the casts of the big Broadway shows sing and step out in public for free. Call ☎ 888-BROADWAY or see **www.broadwayonbroadway.com.**

CLOISTERS MEDIEVAL FESTIVAL Mid- to late September. Falconry, food, tomfoolery, jousting, and feasting, all with a Middle Ages flavor. Call ☎ 212-795-1600 or see **www.whidc.org.**

AFRICAN AMERICAN DAY PARADE Mid-September. Close to a million spectators line Adam Clayton Powell Jr. Boulevard (Seventh Avenue) from 111th to 142nd Street. Call ☎ 212-348-3080 or go to **www.african americanparade.org.**

FEAST OF SAN GENNARO Mid-September. This Little Italy street fest is pretty famous, probably because it lasts a long (two-weekend) week, although its rumored "family" connections have gotten a lot of publicity; along Mulberry Street. Call ☎ 212-768-9320 or see **www .sangennaro.org.**

THE NEW YORK MUSICAL THEATRE FESTIVAL Mid-September into October. New shows premiere and are evaluated, which means public concerts and stagings. Call ☎ 212-352-3101 or go to **www.nymf.org.**

BROADWAY CARES/EQUITY FIGHTS AIDS ANNUAL FLEA MARKET AND GRAND AUCTION Late September. The theatrical garage sale, memento scuffle, and costume clearinghouse of the year. Shubert Alley and West 44th Street. Call ☎ 212-840-0770 or see **www.broadwaycares.org.**

NEW YORK FILM FESTIVAL Late September to mid-October. Not so avant-garde as the New Films series, this prestigious series at Lincoln Center lasts two weeks and usually has a big-name premiere or two on the schedule; call ☎ 212-875-5050 or visit **www.filmlinc.com.**

GREENWICH AVENUE FESTIVAL Late September. Vendors, food, and entertainment along Greenwich Avenue between Sixth and Seventh avenues. This festival occurs several times spring through fall; the weather can be particularly lovely this time of year. Call ☎ 646-230-0489 or see **www.clearviewfestival.com.**

NEW YORK UNDERGROUND COMEDY FESTIVAL Late September to early October. More than 350 emerging and established comedians perform over a week at venues all over the city, including Tompkins Square Park. Go to **www.nycundergroundcomedy.com,** which includes phone numbers for each venue.

CHILE PEPPER FIESTA Late September or early October. The Brooklyn Botanic Garden puts its mouth where its money is, so to speak, hosting a festival that showcases the hundreds of types of the American spice that conquered the world's cuisines. Guacamole, Jamaican jerk chicken, chili, wraps—it's hot, hot, hot. Call ☎ 718-623-7200 or visit **www.bbg.org.**

October

BIG APPLE CIRCUS October through January. You might have forgotten how this cheery little one-ring operation got its name, but watch the little big top go up in the park outside Lincoln Center and then try to resist. Call ☎ 212-268-2500 or see **www.big applecircus.org.**

NEW YORK CITY OKTOBERFEST Early October. More than 500 ethnic food (and beer), art, craft, and clothing exhibits turn Lexington Avenue from 42nd to 57th streets into a street fair. Call ☎ 212-809-4900 or see **www.nycstreetfairs.com.**

OPEN HOUSE NEW YORK First weekend in October. More than 200 homes, museums, churches, historical sites, and other buildings are open for tours during this free annual event. Call ☎ 212-991-6470 or go to **www.ohny.org.**

FEAST OF ST. FRANCIS OF ASSISI First Sunday in October. The Francis-like blessing of the animals at the Cathedral Church of Saint John the Divine used to be a fairly sedate affair, but nowadays it's a sort of well-bred circus, with snakes, rabbits, ferrets, exotic birds, and, yes, even elephants being offered for prayer. Call ☎ 212-316-7490 or see **www.stjohndivine.org.**

GRAMERCY PARK ANTIQUES SHOW Mid-October. Art glass, 17th-, 18th-, and 19th-century porcelain, furniture, and fine art at the 69th Regiment Armory at Lexington Avenue and 26th Street; call ☎ 212-255-0020 or see **www.stellashows.com.**

PULASKI DAY PARADE Sunday nearest October 5. Polish American festival, sometimes called Polish Day, marches Fifth Avenue from 26th to 53rd streets. Call ☎ 877-4-PULASKI or see **www.pulaskiparade.com.**

COLUMBUS DAY PARADE Second Monday in October. A combination founder's day, display of Italian pride, and star-spangled celebration up Fifth Avenue from 44th to 79th streets. Call ☎ 212-249-9932 or see **www.columbuscitizensfd.org.**

INTERNATIONAL FINE ART AND ANTIQUE DEALERS SHOW Mid- to late October. The last (actually, the first, as dealers consider the season) of New York's major shows comes just in time for holiday shopping, if you can afford it. At least you can look. At the Park Avenue Armory on Park Avenue at 67th Street; call ☎ 212-642-8572 or visit **www .haughton.com.**

THE NEW YORKER FESTIVAL Early October. This three-day gathering of journalists, authors, performers, artists, and other cultural icons has become a huge draw; schedules are printed in the magazine's mid-September issues. See **festival.newyorker.com.**

THE NEW YORK CABARET CONVENTION Late October or early November. For a week, more than 100 classic crooners work their way through the American popular songbook at the Rose Theater in the Time Warner Center. Call ☎ 212-721-6500 or see **www.mabelmercer.org.**

NEW YORK'S VILLAGE HALLOWEEN PARADE October 31. Yet another over-the-top and inimitable dress function, this annual party-on-legs (and some wheels) circles Greenwich Village; check local papers for the exact route. Walk-ups welcome; gather at Sixth Avenue between Canal and Spring streets at dusk. Call ☎ 845-758-5519 or visit **www .halloween-nyc.com.**

HULAWEEN October 31. Bette Midler and various of her superstar friends (Elton John, Sting, and so on) dress up, get down, and raise money at The Waldorf-Astoria for the New York Restoration Project (which restores parks, community gardens, and other open spaces). Call ☎ 212-333-2552 or visit **www.nyrp.org.**

NEXT WAVE FESTIVAL October through mid-December. The Brooklyn Academy of Music showcases avant-garde, experimental, and new music, dance, and performance; call ☎ 718-636-4100 or visit **www .bam.org.**

CMJ MUSIC MARATHON AND FILM FESTIVAL Late October. More than 1,000 bands attend workshops by day and perform—at 50 or so venues all around town—sometimes three or four times a night, all in hopes of catching the ear of a music industry exec or booking agent. Not all of the venues are clubs in the real sense, but anyone interested in new and upcoming rock, alternative, roots rock, or rock 'n' roll acts should flip through the local listings. Call ☎ 917-606-1908 or visit **www.cmj.com.**

NEW YORK CITY MARATHON Last Sunday in October or first Sunday in November. One of the big races—not counting the 2.5 million cheering onlookers and volunteers—and with one of the most scenic courses, which includes the Verrazano-Narrows Bridge, stretches of Fifth Avenue, and a finish line in Central Park. Call ☎ 212-423-2249 or visit **www.nycmarathon.org.**

November

CHRISTMAS SPECTACULAR AT RADIO CITY MUSIC HALL Early November through late December or early January. Traditional family favorite featuring the Rockettes in their toy-soldier kick line, music, costumes, and so on. Call ☎ 212-307-1000 or visit **www.radiocity.com.**

CHOCOLATE SHOW/CHOCOLATE WEEK Mid-November. Cooking demonstrations, tastings, cooking classes, even chocolate couture are on display for a whole week, plus area restaurants and sweet shops offer special chocolate menus and treats. At the Metropolitan Pavilion & Altman Building, 125 West 18th Street. Call ☎ 212-889-5112 or go to **www.chocolateshow.com.**

THE PIER ANTIQUES SHOW Mid-November. This shopping-season version of the spring Pier Antiques Show (see March listings) features 500 antiques dealers and a special section of vintage fashions, all on Pier 94 on the Hudson River. An art show takes place simultaneously on adjacent Pier 92. Call ☎ 212-255-0020 or visit **www.stellashows.com.**

MACY'S THANKSGIVING DAY PARADE Late November. How else would Santa Claus—not to mention Snoopy and Woodstock and Garfield and Bullwinkle and half of Broadway—make it to Herald Square on time? The parade begins at Central Park West and 77th and works down Broadway to the store at 34th Street. Santa takes up his station in Macy's the next day. *Hints:* The evening before, you can watch the balloons being inflated while storytellers entertain the kids; head up to the American Museum of Natural History between 77th and 81st and Central Park West and Columbus Avenue between 3 and 10 p.m. Bands form up in Herald Square starting at 2 a.m. Thursday; the clowns collect near 77th Street and Central Park West, and the baton regiments around 70th, both usually by 6 a.m. Call ☎ 212-494-4495 or see **www.macys.com.**

December

LIGHTING OF THE CHRISTMAS TREE AT ROCKEFELLER CENTER The first Monday evening in December, the mayor pulls the switch, and people sing, ice skate, make wishes, you name it; the tree will be lit throughout the month. Call ☎ 212-332-7654 or see **www.rockefellercenter.com.**

ANTIQUES & ART AT THE ARMORY Around the second weekend in December. Another blockbuster sale drawing 70 dealers in serious 17th-, 18th-, and 19th-century American, European, and Asian furniture and art at the Park Avenue Armory, 67th Street and Park. Call ☎ 914-437-5983 or see **www.antiquesandartatthearmory.com.**

THE NUTCRACKER BALLET Throughout December. The Sugar Plum Fairy is absolutely everywhere. The American Ballet Theater version, for sentimentalists (it features George Balanchine's original choreography), is in the New York State Theater in Lincoln Center (call ☎ 212-870-5570 or see **www.nycballet.com**), but the local papers will list many others.

MESSIAH SING-IN AT LINCOLN CENTER Mid-December. Huge public performance of Handel's popular oratorio in Avery Fisher Hall, with rehearsals and coaching beforehand; call ☎ 212-875-5030 or see **www .nationalchorale.org.** Dozens of other sing-alongs, carolings, and family performances will be listed in the local papers.

KWANZAA CELEBRATIONS Mid- through late December. Watch for listings of African American ethnic festivities around town.

THE BALL December 24. Billed as the world's largest Jewish singles party, this bash requires five clubs for its 4,500-plus guests (a "Jewniversal pass" gets you into all). Go to **www.letmypeoplego.com** for information.

NEW YEAR'S EVE December 31. Times Square must be one of the most famous addresses in New Year's folklore. It's a heck of a street party, complete with countdown and lighted ball. For those who have made their resolutions a day early, there's a midnight run through Central Park; call ☎ 212-860-4455 or visit **www.nyrr.org.**

PART THREE

ACCOMMODATIONS

TOUGH TIMES, LOWER RATES, MORE ROOMS

NYC REMAINS A MUST-VISIT FOR TRAVELERS everywhere, every year. That said, prices came down 30% in 2009 from the year before and now average about $350 a night for a midlevel hotel. If you've avoided the Big Apple in years past because of steep room rates, you can now find lower prices, some new budget-oriented hotels, and a better chance for an upgrade or discount.

The economic downturn has not stopped hotel growth: in 2009, more than 5,000 new rooms became available, including the reopening of such classics as **The Pierre** and **The Mark.** Entering the century's second decade, New York has almost 90,000 hotel rooms—20,000 of them new or refurbished, with the emerging outer boroughs getting (and needing) about half of these fresh rooms.

And more than 10,000 additional rooms are scheduled to open throughout the five boroughs in the next two years.

New properties tend to be small or midsized, midpriced, reconverted, or niche-oriented. But chains catering to business travelers are expanding throughout the greater New York City area. Add on the newish luxury apartment hotels and luxury hotels with kitchenette amenities, and you have excellent options in all price ranges. Despite tight financial times, the hotel scene continues to be tough but appealing—a melting pot worthy of New York, New York.

ALL THINGS CONSIDERED

NEW YORK HOTELS FLAUNT BREATHTAKING VIEWS and grand lobbies, business services and concierges, superb restaurants and

Uptown Accommodations

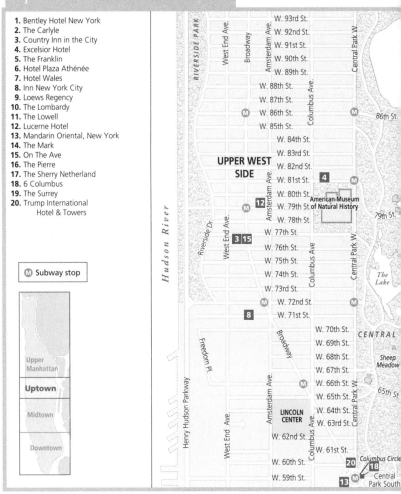

1. Bentley Hotel New York
2. The Carlyle
3. Country Inn in the City
4. Excelsior Hotel
5. The Franklin
6. Hotel Plaza Athénée
7. Hotel Wales
8. Inn New York City
9. Loews Regency
10. The Lombardy
11. The Lowell
12. Lucerne Hotel
13. Mandarin Oriental, New York
14. The Mark
15. On The Ave
16. The Pierre
17. The Sherry Netherland
18. 6 Columbus
19. The Surrey
20. Trump International
    Hotel & Towers

Ⓜ Subway stop

Upper Manhattan

Uptown

Midtown

Downtown

trendy bars. But even in luxury establishments, guest rooms are often minuscule, and recreational facilities will not match those in most major cities. Why? Cost per square foot to build in Manhattan is outrageous, so to turn a profit, hotels opt for creating more guest rooms and appealing watering holes where payback is high. Thus, rather than provide pools and tennis courts, many otherwise great hotels offer only small fitness centers or passes to nearby health clubs.

The hotel scene here is different in other ways as well, since New York is as much a world city as an American one. Because about a quarter

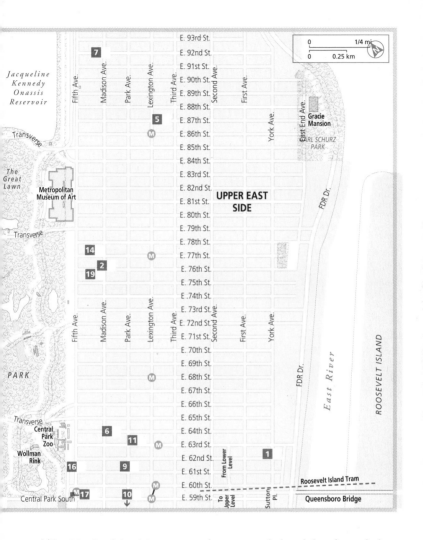

of the Big Apple's visitors come from around the globe, front-desk people speak many languages, translation services are easy to obtain, concierges abound even at small hotels, shops sell international goods familiar to overseas customers, and many bathrooms offer bidets.

Luxury—at least the illusion of it—is important, so uniformed doormen (these greeters are almost exclusively men), standard personnel at upscale city apartments, are also a tradition at top hotels, even if there is a revolving door. These people exist as much for show and small services as for security: giving a friendly greeting, hailing

Midtown Accommodations

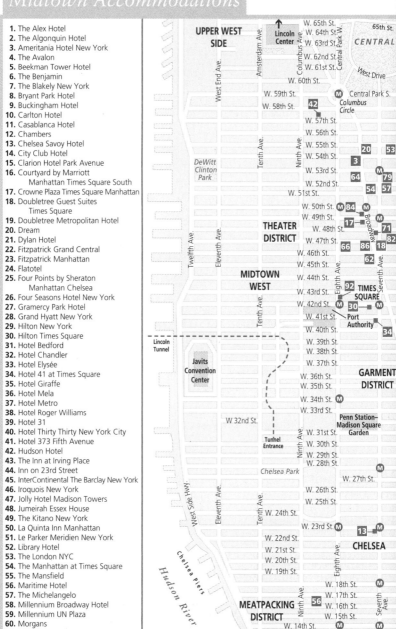

1. The Alex Hotel
2. The Algonquin Hotel
3. Ameritania Hotel New York
4. The Avalon
5. Beekman Tower Hotel
6. The Benjamin
7. The Blakely New York
8. Bryant Park Hotel
9. Buckingham Hotel
10. Carlton Hotel
11. Casablanca Hotel
12. Chambers
13. Chelsea Savoy Hotel
14. City Club Hotel
15. Clarion Hotel Park Avenue
16. Courtyard by Marriott
        Manhattan Times Square South
17. Crowne Plaza Times Square Manhattan
18. Doubletree Guest Suites
        Times Square
19. Doubletree Metropolitan Hotel
20. Dream
21. Dylan Hotel
22. Fitzpatrick Grand Central
23. Fitzpatrick Manhattan
24. Flatotel
25. Four Points by Sheraton
        Manhattan Chelsea
26. Four Seasons Hotel New York
27. Gramercy Park Hotel
28. Grand Hyatt New York
29. Hilton New York
30. Hilton Times Square
31. Hotel Bedford
32. Hotel Chandler
33. Hotel Elysée
34. Hotel 41 at Times Square
35. Hotel Giraffe
36. Hotel Mela
37. Hotel Metro
38. Hotel Roger Williams
39. Hotel 31
40. Hotel Thirty Thirty New York City
41. Hotel 373 Fifth Avenue
42. Hudson Hotel
43. The Inn at Irving Place
44. Inn on 23rd Street
45. InterContinental The Barclay New York
46. Iroquois New York
47. Jolly Hotel Madison Towers
48. Jumeirah Essex House
49. The Kitano New York
50. La Quinta Inn Manhattan
51. Le Parker Meridien New York
52. Library Hotel
53. The London NYC
54. The Manhattan at Times Square
55. The Mansfield
56. Maritime Hotel
57. The Michelangelo
58. Millennium Broadway Hotel
59. Millennium UN Plaza
60. Morgans

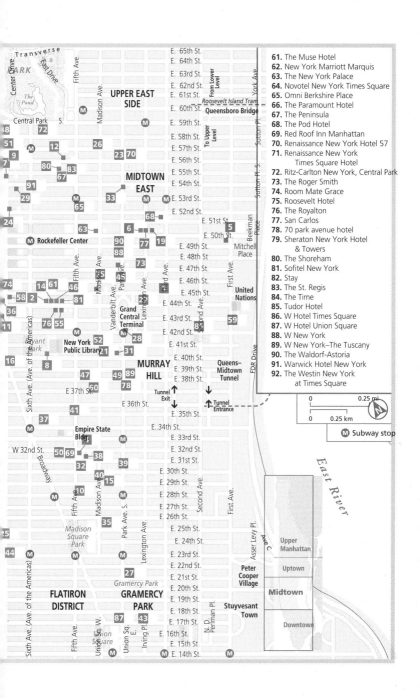

61. The Muse Hotel
62. New York Marriott Marquis
63. The New York Palace
64. Novotel New York Times Square
65. Omni Berkshire Place
66. The Paramount Hotel
67. The Peninsula
68. The Pod Hotel
69. Red Roof Inn Manhattan
70. Renaissance New York Hotel 57
71. Renaissance New York
    Times Square Hotel
72. Ritz-Carlton New York, Central Park
73. The Roger Smith
74. Room Mate Grace
75. Roosevelt Hotel
76. The Royalton
77. San Carlos
78. 70 park avenue hotel
79. Sheraton New York Hotel
    & Towers
80. The Shoreham
81. Sofitel New York
82. Stay
83. The St. Regis
84. The Time
85. Tudor Hotel
86. W Hotel Times Square
87. W Hotel Union Square
88. W New York
89. W New York–The Tuscany
90. The Waldorf-Astoria
91. Warwick Hotel New York
92. The Westin New York
    at Times Square

Downtown Accommodations

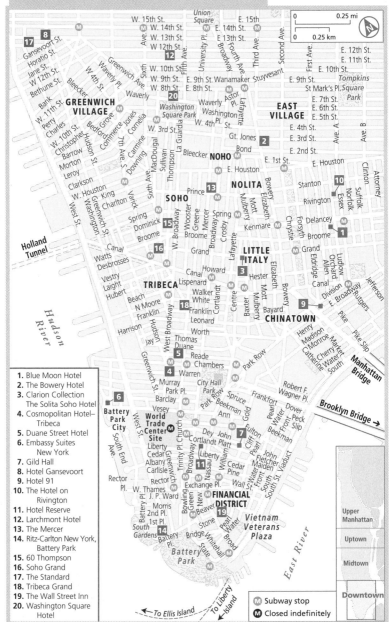

1. Blue Moon Hotel
2. The Bowery Hotel
3. Clarion Collection The Solita Soho Hotel
4. Cosmopolitan Hotel–Tribeca
5. Duane Street Hotel
6. Embassy Suites New York
7. Gild Hall
8. Hotel Gansevoort
9. Hotel 91
10. The Hotel on Rivington
11. Hotel Reserve
12. Larchmont Hotel
13. The Mercer
14. Ritz-Carlton New York, Battery Park
15. 60 Thompson
16. Soho Grand
17. The Standard
18. Tribeca Grand
19. The Wall Street Inn
20. Washington Square Hotel

Ⓜ Subway stop
Ⓜ Closed indefinitely

cabs, holding umbrellas, and bringing luggage into the lobby.

Crime rates may be down, but the threat of
terrorism remains a factor in these uncertain
times, and since many guests are wealthy and/
or famous, high-profile security is the norm.
New York hotels usually provide key cards
rather than old-fashioned keys and maintain

unofficial **TIP**
If you use a travel agent,
explain carefully what
matters most to you in
selecting a hotel, and have
the agent write those
requests down.

regular floor checks by in-house guards. Most upscale hotels have
in-room safes, and all comply with strict city fire codes. The safest
element of city hotels is that even in the wee hours of the morning,
staff will be at the front desk, and usually you will find other guests
in the lobby—New York does, after all, go on around the clock.

So which hotel should you stay in? Consider the following factors
when choosing, and check availability before booking. Our hotel
chart at the end of the chapter will help in your selection, or you
could call, peruse brochures, or access computer information.

PURPOSE OF STAY If you know why you're traveling, you'll know which
hotel services and amenities are vital and what location is best.

- **On business?** You might need special services, meeting space, banquet rooms, translation services, and extensive room facilities. Most
  big hotels are well equipped in these areas. But if you're a leisure traveler, why pay for them? Major chains such as **Marriott, Hilton, Hyatt,**
  and **Sheraton** will have the business facilities, of course, but nowadays
  upscale independents often have state-of-the-art room facilities—such
  as cell phone rentals—even if they lack meeting space. Hotels with
  excellent, updated meeting space include the **Mandarin Oriental
  New York; The Ritz-Carlton New York, Central Park; Flatotel;** the
  Grand Hyatt New York; and the **Jolly Hotel Madison Towers.** Also,
  lower-priced hotel groups such as **Apple Core** (**www.applecorehotels
  .com**) offer clean, budget accommodations. For experiencing the city
  over the long term, extended-stay lodgings such as **Club Quarters**
  (**www.clubquarters.com**) and the **Affinia** properties (formerly **Manhattan East,** ☎ 866-246-2203; **www.affinia.com**), with kitchens and
  maid and shopping services, are convenient and cost-effective.
- **Out to impress?** Then concentrate on location, location, location. But
  different parts of Manhattan impress in different ways. The **Upper East
  Side** is the luxury address, but the **Meatpacking District** and **Downtown** are cutting-edge and creative. Public space and decor may be
  especially important if you're entertaining or on business, so you should
  scan brochures and Internet sites carefully. The **St. Regis, Four Seasons,
  Carlyle, Gramercy Park, The Waldorf-Astoria, Jumeirah Essex House,
  Pierre, Lowell, Elysée, Soho Grand, The Mercer,** and **W New York** are
  among the most impressive hotels for New York style of differing kinds.

- **Spending lots of time in your room?** Then size, view, and amenities will matter more than if you're on the town 24-7. But everyone appreciates Wi-Fi; a flat-screen, high-def TV; a DVD player; a CD player; big windows; and good lighting. Again, check out our chapter or chart, or hotel brochures, and have your travel agent ask about these features.
- **Want to weave a romantic spell?** Smaller, specialized hotels can add to the mood, and around-the-clock room service, king-size beds, whirlpool tubs, and soft lighting will help. The **Elysée, The Inn at Irving Place,** and the **Casablanca Hotel** are oases of romance in this tough and hectic city.

unofficial **TIP**
Check the Hotel Information Chart to see which hotels are closest to public-transportation lines—safe, affordable, and efficient ways to get around. You can save big money if you don't have to spend it on long cab rides or parking fees.

CONVENIENCE Time is perhaps your most precious commodity when traveling, especially in a city where crossing against the light to save a minute is a code of conduct. So think in terms of what you will be doing and where you will be doing it, then choose a hotel from our maps, in close proximity to your needs.

For ultimate convenience, if you'll be spending a weekend seeing **Broadway shows,** stay at a nearby hotel such as **The Time, The Westin New York at Times Square,** or **New York Marriott Marquis.** Like to jog and enjoy the country? Stay as close to country as Manhattan gets—across from **Central Park** at **6 Columbus, Trump International,** or **Jumeirah Essex House.** If you plan on lining up to get tickets for *The Late Show with David Letterman,* the **Ameritania Hotel New York** is around the corner. The **Excelsior Hotel** is near the **Museum of Natural History.** If you're strolling in **SoHo,** check out **The Mercer.** When visiting your cousin in Westchester, you'll appreciate the **Grand Hyatt,** connected to **Grand Central Terminal,** and if your cousin is on Long Island, **Hotel Metro** is near **Penn Station.** The time and money saved by being able to walk or take public transportation to your destination will make your stay more special.

VIEW What New York lacks in horizontal space it makes up for in height, and a stunning by-product is the view. Whether your favorite is a landmark, river, or park, a hotel somewhere in this city is sure to overlook it.

For example, if you like to watch the tugboats, water traffic, and bridges of the **East River,** hotels along First Avenue, such as the **Beekman Tower** and **Millennium UN Plaza,** overlook that watery scene (and the bonus of the **United Nations** complex). Want to overlook the **Hudson?** Try **The Standard.** Hotels that rim the Park on Fifth Avenue, Central Park South, and Central Park West offer bucolic views in this hyperurban environment. **Midtown East** hotels in the 30s and 40s, such as **373 Fifth Avenue,** are most likely to include views of such landmarks as the **Chrysler Building** or **Empire State Building.** Hotels closest to the southern tip of Manhattan have rooms overlooking **New York Harbor** and the **Statue of Liberty.** Hotels near Broadway, such as **Novotel New York Times Square,** the **New York Marriott Marquis,** the **Renaissance New York Times Square Hotel,** and the **Crowne Plaza Times Square Manhattan,** have blazingly colorful neon vistas. And the tallest hotels throughout the city provide panoramas that include huge sections of dramatic skyscrapers, rivers, and parks. When reservations are made, request a high floor and the best view possible, or, even more specifically, ask for a view of whatever it is that you want to see.

NOISE The city may never sleep, but you probably want to. In general, **Downtown** (especially the **Financial District** at night) and **Uptown** are quieter than **Midtown,** which according to traffic experts has more vehicles per square mile than any other place in the country—around 700,000 motorists daily.

If noise is a primary concern to you, stay away from hotels near hospitals, police stations, firehouses, or nightclubs. Major hospitals are at First Avenue and 16th Street, First Avenue and 32nd Street, York Avenue and 68th Street, East End Avenue and 88th Street, Park Avenue and 77th Street, Seventh Avenue and West 11th Street, and Tenth Avenue and West 59th Street. Ask for a room away from street noise (or elevator noise, if that matters). High up is better but, surprisingly, not all that much, as sound seems to echo against the skyscrapers. Older hotels built before World War II usually have the thickest walls, but most luxury hotels are exceptionally well insulated. Check our survey to make sure your hotel's windows are at least double-glazed; triple-glazing is even better and keeps most street noise out. Hotels on heavily trafficked routes, such as **The Kitano New York** on Park Avenue, are well soundproofed because of this. And some hotels, such as the Casablanca, even have quadruple-glazed windows!

unofficial **TIP**
Streets are generally less noisy than avenues—and avenues closer to the rivers than to Midtown are often quietest, although West Side Highway along the Hudson and FDR Drive along the East River are heavily trafficked and often have emergency vehicles.

AMENITIES New York City is the quintessential urban environment—culture, all-night action, superb restaurants, clubs, bars—and as a result many hotels offer only basic amenities. If you have special needs, mention them when booking. Physically challenged guests should clarify whether rooms designated for disabled guests just have handrails in bathrooms or have made-to-order furnishings and complete wheelchair access. If you have a car, a garage is a major convenience, and free parking a big bonus. If you are with your family or are planning a longer stay, a suite situation or a kitchenette can be a wonderful addition. Most New York hotels offer Wi-Fi, data ports, fax and copying services, and e-mail retrieval, and big hotels have conference rooms of all sizes, with state-of-the-art facilities. Some have kitchenettes.

The **Millennium UN Plaza** offers both an indoor pool and tennis courts—rarities in the city. But there are more-unusual amenities as well. The **Four Seasons** provides toys for kids and food for pets. **The New York Palace** sets out personalized stationery and business cards in its Towers section. **The Benjamin** has 13 types of pillows. **Trump International** provides magnifying glasses and telescopes (presumably to look at Central Park vistas, not into other windows). **The Premier** offers Champagne ice pops, and the **Algonquin** presents dinner and a cabaret show for guests. We have investigated to find other hotels with amenities that might appeal, so check out our hotel information chart at the end of the chapter.

FOOD AND DRINK If you enjoy the convenience of dining en suite or a mere elevator ride from your room, check our charts at the end of the chapter for hotels that include restaurants. Most hotels in the city have at least a coffee shop or an adjacent restaurant, and you can otherwise count on minibars and coffeemakers to tide you over. If there's a restaurant, room service is also often available, especially at larger establishments. A pleasant trend, especially at smaller hotels, is inclusion of a Continental breakfast in the price. Among hotels offering this are the **Avalon, Bentley Hotel New York, Franklin, Iroquois New York, Mansfield, Roger Smith, Roger Williams, Shoreham,** and **Millennium Broadway Hotel.** Hotel dining establishments have become among the best in the city, with star chefs, luxury decor, and multicourse tasting menus. Count on a three-course dinner at a top hotel restaurant costing at least $60 per person with a glass of wine, tax, and tip. Lunches are a better deal, and pre-theater dinners or prix-fixe special meals are also good values.

unofficial **TIP**
When you book your hotel, ask for restaurant reservations at the same time; although hotel guests have priority, some of these restaurants are booked months in advance.

As for watering holes where you can drink, nibble, and schmooze day and night, New York hotels have superb examples—and they may include light meals, sophisticated entertainment, or at least live piano music. The decor is often dramatic, as are the patrons—many of them power brokers or stylish singles. You can people-watch in style.

SERVICE The level of service in hotels here varies from world-class polished and refined to straightforward, no-nonsense Noo Yawk style, which can border on rude. The city is used to assertive people, and to hold your own in this competitive atmosphere, hang tough, as New Yorkers do. Good manners are essential anywhere, but here you can ask a little louder or longer if there's something you'd like, or like changed. (Around here, that's called "chutzpah.") Although the service may vary from one front desk person to the next, good management ensures an atmosphere where "the guest is always right"—or at least starts out that way.

Smaller hotels that cater to independent travelers are more likely to give better service, as they can't compete in terms of physical plant and amenities and focus instead on making guests feel special. So if you like to be pampered, luxury hotels and small independents will be your best bets. Word of mouth based on the actual experience of travel agents, friends, or coworkers is a great indicator. Otherwise, note:

- Is there a service desk or service representative, such as a concierge?
- How are you greeted? Is there a doorman? Are you taken to your room by a hotel representative? Are you provided with clear information and asked if you need anything?
- Are requests fulfilled promptly and courteously?
- What services are offered as standard—secretarial, translation, goods procurement, babysitting, concierge, luggage handling, valet parking?
- Is your bed turned down at night, and are towels replaced?
- Is there 24-hour room service?

Most luxury hotels pride themselves on service, which translates into luxury and in the final analysis is what often makes a hotel great. For example, **The Michelangelo** offers a kit with everything from dental floss to condoms, and the **St. Regis** provides 24-hour butler service. Other hotels with reps for great service include the **Carlyle, Four Seasons, Lowell,** and **Peninsula.**

SIZE Most New York hotels, even the finest, have smaller rooms than hotels in other major cities. But in a few cases, hotels, such as **Flatotel,** that have been converted from apartment houses (*flat* equals "apartment," get it?) offer huge units.

kids Fictional Eloise and that *Home Alone* boy may be the most famous ones, but kids regularly stay and play in New York hotels. Suites, especially with kitchenettes, are a real cost-saver and a good idea. And many hotels offer free lodging to kids staying in their parents' room. Some of New York's best hotels are surprisingly kid-friendly, with many family amenities, playrooms, increasingly lavish kids' programs, and, in some cases, big discounts.

For instance, **Le Parker Meridien** has a family-friendly "Smart Aleck" service, which includes cartoons in the elevator to the rooftop pool. The **Westin New York at Times Square** hosts a Kids Club; members receive a sports bottle, toys, coloring books, and a bedtime story. Toddlers get an amenity box including a step stool and potty seat. **Doubletree Guest Suites Times Square** dedicates a playroom. **Inter-Continental The Barclay New York** offers a backpack filled with goodies, including night-lights, a baseball cap, and a guidebook of kid events. **Novotel New York Times Square** provides a Kid's Corner. And **The Ritz-Carlton New York, Battery Park** includes a toy menu from **FAO Schwarz,** a telescope for viewing the Statue of Liberty, and bikes for touring Battery Park. Ritz Kids also have their own butler to prepare bubble baths and leave a teddy bear on their pillows.

unofficial **TIP**
When staying in a large hotel, insist on a floor where no tour group is booked.

Other kid innovations? **The Waldorf-Astoria** hosts a children's tea, featuring etiquette tips. **Loews** hotels offer several packages specifically for grandparents and grandkids.

TOUR AND CONVENTION GROUPS Some New York hotels specialize in hosting convention or tour groups. For individual travelers, trying to compete with large groups can be time-consuming and frustrating. Even more maddening is to find yourself on the same floor with a tour group of 100 high-school seniors running up and down the corridor in the middle of the night, partying, and slamming doors. (We've been there.)

BE HOTEL WISE

NEW YORKERS LEARN TO USE WHAT'S AVAILABLE and make do with what isn't. Here are some general tips to help:

- Check out rooms ahead of time if possible, by Internet or brochure. Try **www.hoteldiscount.com** or **www.quikbook.com.**
- Request a renovated room (even if you aren't sure there are any). New York hotels are constantly improving, often floor by floor, and newest is usually best, often at the same price. Even if the hotel has not recently renovated, asking shows that you want the best available room for the price.
- If in doubt, visit the room before committing your luggage to it, and if you are not satisfied, ask for a better one. This is a common action in Europe, and New York hoteliers are not surprised by it. If you have a specific and legitimate gripe, such as small size, poor housekeeping, lack of view, or excessive noise, chances are you will get results and a better room.
- Make the most of the concierge. The best NYC hotels have extensively trained professionals who can book anything and advise about everything in the city. You can often acquire hard-to-get tickets this way, even at the last minute—if you're willing to pay the top fee for them; a good concierge has the savvy and connections needed. Book restaurants through concierges to get better tables, better service, and more response to complaints. If the meal was memorable and the reservation hard to get, factor that into your tip for the concierge.
- If you reserve in the hotel restaurant, be sure to mention if you are staying at the hotel. You'll probably get better attention.
- Be assertive. Don't accept the first "no" for major requests if you really want something.
- When you're on business, select a room with at least a portion of a sitting area. If you meet there, you'll save time, money, and hassle, and it will be more appropriate than sitting on a bed.
- Check in early and out late. Often you can extend your stay by several hours. If you arrive around noon for a 3 p.m. check-in, your room may

already be made up. At worst, you can leave your bags in a locked room and return later. If you ask politely for a late checkout on your last day, you can often get it. But 2 p.m. checkout is usually the latest hotels are willing to give.

• If you have a great view, open the curtains all the way! The greater your sense of place here in New York, the more you get for your money.

HOTEL NEIGHBORHOODS

UNLESS BUSINESS OR FRIENDS AND FAMILY take you to one of the outer boroughs, the place to stay is Manhattan. Within the narrow island are hundreds of choices—from the finest in the world to faded but acceptable. Most are clustered in the Midtown area, from 42nd Street to 59th. However, fine new and refurbished hotels are turning up from the 90s down to the Battery, from SoHo and the Meatpacking District and Chelsea to Chinatown, the Village, and the West Side. Generally, Downtown is trendy, Uptown is tony, and Midtown is bustling.

DOWNTOWN AND LOWER MANHATTAN (BELOW CANAL STREET, INCLUDING TRIBECA)

PETER MINUIT MAY HAVE BOUGHT Manhattan for $25, but that hardly covers a minibar snack today. Among the concrete canyons of the megamillionaire hedge-funders and traders of Wall Street and the sightseers at a rising (noisy) **Ground Zero** are several modern hotels, geared to the business and leisure traveler. Because many visitors are on work assignments, most hotels in this area are large and pricey and offer complete business services. But visitors also flock to the walking paths of Battery Park, the Statue of Liberty and **Ellis Island,** the **Jewish Heritage Museum, South Street Seaport, Chinatown,** and **Little Italy.** Many developers are converting existing buildings into hotels in the next five years to add to the room inventory. Downtown remains quiet at night, with fewer nightspots than the rest of the island. Although subways are convenient, bus service is erratic, and cab fares to Midtown are expensive. New hotels such as **Gild Hall, Hotel on Rivington,** and the **Blue Moon** (a kosher hotel built from an old tenement) reflect the area's historic character. The **Tribeca Grand** has become a hip landmark downtown, and **The Smyth** has just opened in TriBeCa.

SOHO, GREENWICH VILLAGE, MEATPACKING DISTRICT

THIS IS THE HOTTEST, HIPPEST AREA IN THE CITY. Restaurants, galleries, shops, boutiques, and small theaters abound on winding streets. Students and creative types and a convenient subway system make the **East** and **West Village** magnets for both tourists and the bridge-and-tunnel crowd. But surprisingly, relatively few hotels rise here, and aside from bed-and-breakfasts and conversions of small properties, the hotel scene has lagged behind the street scene. Hotels include the **The Bowery Hotel, Washington Square Hotel, The Mercer,** and the **Soho Grand. Clarion Collection The Solita Soho Hotel** and **60 Thompson** are stylish favorites. In the Meatpacking area, trendy hotels include **The Maritime,** the **Gansevoort,** and the **Standard,** which straddles the beginning of the **High Line elevated park.**

14TH TO 30TH STREETS: CHELSEA, THE HIGH LINE, GRAMERCY

CHELSEA IS ARTSY. Galleries, boutiques, and restaurants abound. The 30-acre **Chelsea Piers sports complex** on the Hudson River offers everything from bowling to volleyball to indoor golf. Artists are converting old buildings into studios and galleries, and with the High Line park along the former elevated rail line, hundreds more will be following. Right now, though, good hotels are few and far between. Visitors to **Chelsea Market** and the **Joyce,** the city's modern-dance theater, will like the **Chelsea Savoy Hotel** on the West Side. The East Side seems more residential—the **Inn at Irving Place** is a tiny, choice place near leafy and quiet **Gramercy Park.** The rediscovered star is the **Gramercy Park Hotel,** a faded beauty now again draped in luxury by hotel icon Ian Schrager.

31ST TO 41ST STREETS, MURRAY HILL

ON THE WEST SIDE, this bustling area of offices, sports complexes, the **Jacob Javits Convention Center,** and transportation terminals is no-nonsense, and large. Midrange hotels reflect the group clientele and convention needs. Visitors to **Madison Square Garden,** by a possibly-to-be-redeveloped Penn Station, can stay at the small **Hotel Metro.** On the East Side, with still-limited subway service, quiet **Murray Hill,** with many historic town houses, is home to the expanded **Morgan Library and Museum** and nearby small hotels, such as the still-stylish **Morgans, The Avalon,** the spiffy **Roger Williams,** and the Japanese-influenced **Kitano.** The new **Hotel 373 Fifth Avenue** is across from the Empire State Building.

42ND TO 59TH STREETS: THE EAST SIDE

MIDTOWN DRAWS COMMUTERS, delegates and visitors to the United Nations, Fifth Avenue shoppers, sidewalk TV-studio gawkers, **Rockefeller Center** ice skaters, business travelers at corporate headquarters, and diners at pricey restaurants. This is the center of the city's energy and power (though things quiet down around 9 p.m.). Some of the best hotels in the world offer great views of the East River and landmark buildings. Grand Central Terminal provides easy access by rail to the northern suburbs and Connecticut. Among the dozens of fine skyscraper hotels clustered here are the classic Art Deco **Waldorf-Astoria** and the **Fitzpatrick Grand Central.**

42ND TO 59TH STREETS: THE WEST SIDE

Times Square, Broadway, Carnegie Hall, theme restaurants, TV studios, and the office buildings along **Columbus Circle** and **Avenue of the Americas** all draw throngs. Lodgings from moderately priced chains, such as **Holiday Inn, Marriott, Howard Johnson,** and **Days Inn,** and older hotels abound, catering to tour groups and individual tourists. But the great hotels rimming the southern end of sprawling Central Park, including the **Jumeirah Essex House,** are among the best in the city. Noteworthy: The **London NYC hotel** (formerly the **RIGHA Royal**) was designed by David Collins and features a restaurant by star chef Gordon Ramsay. The midpriced **Portland Hotel at Times Square** on West 47th Street is being transformed into the more luxurious **Sanctuary Hotel New York.**

60TH STREET AND ABOVE

UPTOWN—REFINED, FASHIONABLE, EXCLUSIVE, cultured, quiet. **Central Park** is the oasis of this area, but Uptown also offers world-famous museums along **Museum Mile** and top hospitals. Two-storied **Madison Avenue** is one of the most fascinating shopping areas of the world, and **Lincoln Center** is a renowned cultural focal point on the West Side Great views abound. Not surprisingly, some of the fanciest older hotels stand here, including **The Carlyle** and the newly refurbished **Pierre.**

WAY UPTOWN AND OTHER BOROUGHS

A NEW HARLEM RENAISSANCE IS UNDER WAY, with clubs, dining, and new residential areas. In Harlem, check out **Harlem Landmark Guest House,** a restored town house.

If you don't mind not being in "the city" (and don't mind saving some big bucks), commute into Manhattan by subway, bus, or ferry, or splurge on a taxi, and check out the wonders of the outer boroughs and the following hotels: in Brooklyn, the **Best Western Gregory** and **New York Marriott at the Brooklyn Bridge;** in Queens, **Comfort Inn Long Island City** and **Holiday Inn Express Queens Midtown;** in Staten Island, **Hilton Garden Inn New York/Staten Island** and **Harbor House Bed & Breakfast.**

New or coming soon in the boroughs are **Hotel Le Jolie, aloft Brooklyn/Downtown, The Smith Hotel,** and **Sheraton Brooklyn** in Brooklyn, and **Hampton Inn & Suites Staten Island** in Staten Island.

CAN YOU EVEN GET IN?

EVEN WITH INCREASING NUMBERS OF HOTEL ROOMS in New York City, with apologies to songwriters Kander and Ebb, if you can make a reservation (t)here, you can make one anywhere. It's up to you—and your resourcefulness—to get a room in New York, New York

- Try **NYC & Company**'s online reservation system (**www.nycvisit.com**) to check out almost 200 New York hotels. It's powered by Orbitz.

- Check out the **Peak Season Hotel Hotline.** It provides access to rooms at more than 80 hotels in all price categories from September 1 to December 31. As a last resort, on nights when travel agents and consumers believe the city is "sold out," the hotline can find rooms. Call ☎ 800-846-7666. And note the other reservations services listed later in the chapter.

- Book as far in advance as possible. Holidays and special events such as **Fashion Week** are always busy, but even when occupancy is down in many parts of the country, hotels often are fully booked here, as huge conferences reserve blocks of rooms years in advance, frequently at odd times. Traditionally, the easiest time to get a room is during January and February. Sunday is the slowest day of the week.

- Call just after 6 p.m. on the day you want to stay. That is when most properties cancel reservations not guaranteed with a credit card on the day of arrival. (In the industry, these nonguaranteed reservations are called "timers.")

- Try the Web. Sites are always expanding and new ones popping up, so use a search engine such as Yahoo! or Google to find a selection.

- Use travel and tour agencies that do lots of NYC convention business. They often have the clout to find a room, even when you're on your own. Usually the major agencies will do the most convention business; otherwise, ask those who have traveled on business to New York, or ask around locally. As for tour operators, some who frequently handle New York City are **ATI (American Tours International), AlliedTPro,** and **City Tours.** Your travel agent will help you reserve through tour operators.

- Be flexible. The more rigid your requests, the harder it may be to fill them. Ask what's available. Management may not have many standard rooms but can sometimes offer luxury suites or relatively unappealing rooms—poor view, low floor, not yet refurbished. If you're willing, you can often negotiate a deal for these white elephants.

- Think small. Hotels with few rooms are least likely to host huge groups, and, surprisingly, you can often find a room at small places even at busy times.

- Think independent. When rooms are scarce, nonchain hotels often have availability, as they are less well known and have smaller advertising and marketing budgets than chains.

Queens, Brooklyn, Staten Island, and the Bronx have some chain hotels, and around **Kennedy, LaGuardia,** and **Newark airports** you will find many midlevel choices (see our hotel listings). But nearby Westchester County, southern Connecticut, and Long Island have a varied selection of luxury hotels, inns, resorts, and bed-and-breakfasts, with more recreational space at generally lower cost than comparable accommodations in the city. You may miss out on urban excitement, but you're more likely to get a room.

The following notable accommodations are in the suburbs within an hour or so of the city. All are near subway or train lines (taxis usually meet trains), are in safe neighborhoods, and offer free parking, outstanding settings and decor, and excellent on-site or nearby restaurants.

Westchester County, New York

CASTLE ON THE HUDSON 400 Benedict Avenue, Tarrytown; ☎ 800-616-4487, 914-631-1980; fax ☎ 914-631-4612; **www.castleonthe hudsonhotel.com**

CRABTREE'S KITTLE HOUSE 11 Kittle Road, Chappaqua; ☎ 914-666-8044; fax ☎ 914-666-2684; **www.kittlehouse.com**

DORAL ARROWWOOD 975 Anderson Hill Road, Rye Brook; ☎ 866-428-9739, 914-939-5500; fax ☎ 914-323-5500; **www.doralarrowwood.com**

Long Island, New York

GARDEN CITY HOTEL 45 Seventh Street, Garden City; ☎ 877-549-0400, 516-747-3000; fax ☎ 516-747-1414; **www.gardencityhotel.com**

INN AT GREAT NECK 30 Cutter Mill Road, Great Neck; ☎ 516-773-2000; fax ☎ 516-773-2020; **www.innatgreatneck.com**

Southern Connecticut

HOMESTEAD INN 420 Field Point Road, Greenwich; ☎ 203-869-7500; fax ☎ 203-869-7502; **www.homesteadinn.com**

HYATT REGENCY GREENWICH 1800 East Putnam, Old Greenwich; ☎ 203-637-1234; fax ☎ 203-637-2940; **greenwich.hyatt.com**

THE INN AT NATIONAL HALL 2 Post Road West, Westport; ☎ 800-628-4255, 203-221-1351; fax ☎ 203-221-0276; **www.innatnationalhall.com**

SLICE *the* PRICE *of* ROOMS *in the* APPLE

THE BAD NEWS: Tourists from around the world, it seems, will pay any price to visit New York and stay "in the city."

The good news: compared to many other great international cities, New York is a relative bargain. Remember that as you plunk down your plastic, signing off on what seems like the GNP of Honduras. Here are some helpful ideas for lowering costs:

- **Check out the Internet.** Last-minute bargains are now available online at sites such as **www.hotels.com, www.priceline.com, www .expedia.com, www.orbitz.com,** and **www.travelocity.com.** You can judge comparative value for money by seeing a listing of hotels—what they offer, where they are located, and what they charge.

- **Choose a less-than-fashionable neighborhood.** New York is made up of many distinct enclaves, and this emphasis on address influences pricing. Unless you need to be there for convenience, it may not be worth it to stay on the Upper East Side when the same-quality room on the **Lower West Side** may be half the cost. The East Side is priciest; Midtown and up to 96th Street is the fanciest area. The good deals are on the **Upper West Side.** You will occasionally find a budget hotel in pricey areas, such as **The Pod,** in the 50s on the East Side.

- **Leave your car at home.** Garaging a car overnight in New York can cost as much as a motel room off the highway (with doughnuts and coffee).

- **For longer stays, try an apartment hotel.** These typically offer daily maid service and kitchen and laundry facilities. **Club Quarters** is one example. Several upscale hotels offer an apartment option, including **The Waldorf-Astoria.** These hybrids combine hotel services with a kitchen and a residential feel and are wonderful for entertaining, or as an alternative to getting an apartment.

- **Seek a suite, which offers the potential of whole families in one room.** And if there's a kitchenette, even better. Several hotels, such as **Trump International Hotel & Tower,** offer kitchenettes even in standard rooms.

- **Stay at the least expensive room at a good hotel rather than the most expensive at a lesser one.** The cost differential can be considerable, although the rest of the hotel services, amenities, and public rooms remain available for your pleasure. You're getting the biggest bang for your buck when you ask for the low-priced, smallest room with the worst view on the lowest floor at an otherwise-good hotel.

- **Avoid room service and minibars.** Bring food up from delis, take-out groceries (which usually have salad bars), or sidewalk vendors, which purvey fresh fruits as well as hot dogs, falafel, and other ethnic delights. Or, if possible, make like a resident and have a restaurant deliver (frowned on by some hotels—check first). Neighborhood restaurants, especially the old-fashioned coffee shops and "ethnics," are good and surprisingly reasonable.

- **Accept shared baths.** Some hotels, such as **The Pod,** are set up with some shared facilities, at around $100 a night. If price means more than privacy, you'll enjoy the savings.

- **Go really basic. YMCAs** and youth hostels are available in the city. Bare-bones, but cheap. There are Ys on the East Side (☎ 212-912-2500), on the West Side (☎ 212-875-4100), and in Harlem (☎ 212-281-4100, ext. 210); see **www.ymcanyc.org. Hostelling International** offers a hostel on the Upper West Side (☎ 800-909-4776 or 212-932-2300; **www.hinewyork.org**). For dormitory accommodations, check with universities in the city, including New York University. Judith Glynn's **Manhattan Getaways** (☎ 212-956-2010; **www.manhattangetaways.com**) is a great source for home-style getaways, such as reconverted apartments and guesthouses.

- **Find a discounted rate.** Check out deals through ads, agents, special events, and openings. These include weekend and convention deals, frequent-mileage clubs, automobile or other travel clubs, senior rates (some specify ages as young as 50), military or government discounts, corporate or shareholder rates, packages, long-stay rates (usually at least five nights), and travel-industry rates. Some hotels might even give lower rates if you are visiting because of bereavement or medical care.

Special Weekend Rates

Most hotels that cater to business, government, and convention travelers offer special weekend discount rates ranging 15% to 40% below normal weekday rates. Find out about weekend specials by calling individual hotels or by consulting your travel agent.

Corporate Rates

Many hotels offer discounted corporate rates (5% to 20% off rack rate). Usually you don't need to work for a large company or have a special relationship with the hotel—simply ask for this discount. But some others may make the rate conditional on your providing some sort of bona fides—for instance, a fax on your company's letterhead requesting the rate or a company credit card or business card on check-in. Generally, the screening is not rigorous.

Half-price Programs

Larger discounts on rooms (35% to 60%), in New York or anywhere else, are available through half-price hotel programs, often called travel clubs. Program operators contract with an individual hotel to provide rooms at deep discounts, usually 50% off rack rate, on a "space available" basis. You can usually reserve a discounted room whenever the hotel expects less than 80% occupancy. A little calendar sleuthing to avoid citywide conventions and special events increases your chance of finding this kind of discount.

Most half-price programs will charge an annual membership fee or directory-subscription charge of $25 to $125. You'll get a membership card and a directory that lists participating hotels. But note the restrictions and exceptions. Some hotels "black out" certain dates or times of year. Others may offer the discount only certain days of the week or require you to stay a certain number of nights. Still others may offer a much smaller discount than 50% off rack rate.

Programs specialize in domestic travel, international travel, or both. More-established operators offer members thousands of hotels to choose from in the United States. All of the following programs have a heavy concentration of hotels in California and Florida, and most have a limited selection in New York City.

Encore ☎ 800-444-9800 **www.virtual-encore.com**

Entertainment Publications ☎ 888-231-7283 **www.entertainment.com**

ITC50 ☎ 800-513-7000 **www.itc50online.com**

Quest ☎ 800-742-3543 **www.questprograms.com**

unofficial **TIP**
As a rule, if you travel several times a year, your room-rate savings will easily compensate for membership fees in half-price programs.

One caveat: If something seems too good to be true, it usually is, and some hotels figure the discount on an exaggerated rack rate. A few may deduct the discount from a supposed "superior" or "upgraded" room rate, even though the room you get is standard.

But the majority of participating properties base discounts on the published rate in the Hotel and Travel Index (a reference work used by travel agents) and work within the spirit of their agreement with the program operator.

Deeply discounted rooms through half-price programs are not commissionable to travel agents, so you'll probably have to make your own calls and reservations. But if you travel frequently, your agent will probably do your legwork anyway.

Preferred Rates

This discount helps travel agents stimulate booking activity or attract a certain class of traveler. Most preferred rates are promoted through travel-industry publications, and they are often accessible only through an agent. Sound out your travel

unofficial **TIP**
Hotel reps respond positively to travel agents because agents represent a source of additional business. There are certain specials that hotel reps will disclose only to travel agents.

agent about possible deals, but note that the rates shown on travel agents' computerized reservations systems are not always the lowest rates obtainable. Zero in on a couple of hotels that fill your needs in terms of location and quality of accommodations, then have your agent call the hotels for the latest rates and specials. A personal appeal from your agent to the hotel's director of sales and marketing will often get you a room.

Consolidators, Wholesalers, and Reservation Services

The discount available (if any) from a reservation service depends on whether the service functions as a consolidator or as a wholesaler. Consolidators are strictly sales agents who do not own or control the room inventory they are trying to sell. Discounts offered by consolidators are determined by the hotels with rooms to fill. Consolidator discounts vary enormously depending on how desperate the hotel is to unload the rooms. When you deal with a room-reservation service that operates as a consolidator, you pay for your room as usual when you check out of the hotel.

Wholesalers have long-standing contracts with hotels to buy rooms at an established deep discount. Some wholesalers hold purchase options on blocks of rooms, whereas others actually pay for rooms and own the inventory, so they can offer whatever discount is consistent with current demand. Most discounts fall in the 10%-to-40% range, and you'll usually pay for your entire stay in advance with your credit card. The service then sends you a written confirmation and usually a voucher (indicating prepayment) to present at the hotel.

Reservation services are probably more useful when availability is scarce than when generally trying to obtain deep discounts. Calling the hotels ourselves, we were often able to beat the reservation services' rates (when rooms were available). When the city was booked, however, the reservation services were able to find rooms at a fair price.

Ask for a rate quote for a particular hotel, or for the best available deal, in your preferred area. If you say you're on a budget, the service might even shave a bit off its profit.

Services that frequently offer substantial discounts include

Accommodations Express ☎ 800-444-7666

Hotel Reservations Network ☎ 800-964-6835 **www.180096hotel.com**

Quikbook ☎ 800-789-9887 **www.quikbook.com**

HOW TO EVALUATE A TRAVEL PACKAGE

PACKAGE VACATIONS CAN BE WIN–WIN. The buyer has only to make one phone call and deal with a single salesperson to set up the whole vacation: transportation, lodging, meals, guided tours, and Broadway shows. The seller eliminates separate sales, confirmations, and billing. Some packagers also buy hotel rooms and airfares in bulk on contract, like a broker playing the commodities market, which can mean a significant saving from posted fares.

Choose a package with features you are sure to use; you will be paying for them. If cost is more important than convenience, make a few calls to price individual components (airfare, lodging, shows, etc.). If the costs are about the same, the package is probably worth buying just for the convenience. If your package includes a choice of rental car or transfers to and from the airport, take the transfers. Driving in the city is difficult, and parking in a garage is expensive, often up to $50 for a 24-hour period.

Buyer beware. You're dealing with a lot of money and trust here, and, alas, a packager could cash in on discounts without passing them on or load packages with extras that cost the packager next to nothing but inflate the retail price higher than the Empire State Building. So if something seems "off," check with a supervisor or a major travel agency, and be sure you're with a reputable company.

IS YOUR TRAVEL AGENT NYC SAVVY?

THE CITY HOTEL SCENE IS COMPLEX and constantly changing. Has your travel agent recently been to New York? And does the agency keep up-to-the-minute info?

Some travel agents unfamiliar with the Apple may try to plug you into a tour operator's or wholesaler's preset package, allowing the agent to set up your whole trip with a single phone call—and still collect an 8%-to-10% commission. And many agents will place almost all their New York business with only one or two wholesalers or tour operators, which doesn't provide much choice for you.

Agents will often use wholesalers who run packages in conjunction with airlines, such as Delta Vacations or American Airlines Vacations, and because of the wholesaler's exclusive relationship with the carrier, these trips are easy to book. However, they can be more expensive than a package offered by a high-volume wholesaler who works with airlines in a primary New York City market.

To help your travel agent get you the best possible hotel deal, follow these five steps:

1. Determine which area is best for you, and, if possible, choose a specific hotel. Review the hotel information provided in this guide and contact hotels that interest you, if necessary.

2. Check out the hotel deals and package vacations advertised on the Internet and in the Sunday travel sections of major newspapers, such as the *New York Times, New York Daily News, Philadelphia Inquirer,* or *Boston Globe.* They often advertise deals that undercut anything offered in your local paper. See if you can find specials that fit your plans and include a hotel you like.

3. Call the hotels, wholesalers, or tour operators whose ads you have collected. Ask any questions you have concerning their packages, but do not book your trip with them directly.

4. Ask if your travel agent can get you something better. The deals in the paper will serve as a benchmark.

5. Choose from the options, then have your travel agent book the best one. Even if you go with one of the packages in the newspaper, it will probably be commissionable (at no additional cost to you) and will provide the agent some return on the time invested on your behalf. Also, as a travel professional, your agent should be able to verify the quality and integrity of the deal.

IF YOU MAKE YOUR OWN RESERVATION

CHECK OUT THE INTERNET. A great tool in the hotel-hunting arsenal is **www.travelaxe.com.** Travelaxe offers free software you can download to your PC (it won't run on Macs) that will scan an assortment of hotel-discount sites and find the cheapest rate for each of more than 200 New York hotels. The site offers filters such as price, quality rating, and proximity to a specific location (Midtown, convention center, airport, and so on) to allow you to narrow your search. The same software also scans for the best rates in cities throughout the United States and the world. Also, call the specific hotel (as opposed to the hotel chain's national toll-free number, where operators are usually unaware of local specials). Always ask about specials before inquiring about corporate rates—and don't be afraid to bargain. If you're buying a hotel's weekend package, for example, and want to extend your stay into the following week, you can often obtain at least the corporate rate for the extra days. However, do your bargaining before you check in, preferably when you make your reservations.

ARE YOU COMING TO NYC ON BUSINESS?

IDENTIFY THE NEIGHBORHOOD(S) where your business will take you, then use the hotel chart to cross-reference the hotels located in that area. Once you have developed a short list of possible hotels that fit your budget and offer the standards you require, you (or your travel agent) can apply the cost-saving suggestions discussed earlier to obtain the lowest rate.

Convention Rates: How They Work and How to Do Better

If you're attending a major convention or trade show, your group has probably negotiated convention rates, and hotels have booked rooms at an agreed-on price, sometimes citywide.

Because the convention sponsor brings big business to New York and reserves many rooms, often annually, it usually can negotiate volume discounts substantially below rack rate. You may get a housing list that includes the special rates, and you can compare them with the rates obtainable using the strategies covered in the previous section.

If the negotiated convention rate doesn't sound like a good deal, try to reserve a room using an Internet bargain, a half-price club, a consolidator, or a tour operator. Remember, however, that deep discounts are usually available only when the hotel expects to be at less than 80% occupancy, a rarity when a big convention is in town.

Strategies for Beating Convention Rates: Easy as 1-2-3

1. Reserve early. Most big conventions and trade shows announce meeting sites one to three years in advance. If you book well ahead of the time the convention sponsor sends out the housing list, chances are good that the hotel will accept your reservation.

2. Compare your convention's housing list with the list of hotels presented in this guide. You may be able to find a suitable hotel not on the housing list.

3. Use a local reservations agency or consolidator. This is also a good strategy if you need to make reservations at the last minute. Local reservations agencies and consolidators almost always control some rooms, even during a huge convention or trade show.

HOTELS RATED *and* RANKED

WHAT'S IN A ROOM?

UNFORTUNATELY, IN NEW YORK, some beautifully appointed rooms are cramped and poorly designed. *Unofficial Guide* researchers

unofficial **TIP**
Rooms at the **Four Seasons,** at 600 square feet, are among the largest in the city—as large as many New York one-bedroom apartments.

are aware of this and spend many weeks inspecting hotel rooms. Here are a few of the things we check.

ROOM SIZE Spacious rooms are preferable, but New York's hotel rooms are generally smaller than those in other major cities (as small as 100 square feet!), and the trend is high-style and cramped. Note the other luxuries, and if size will be a problem, ask about it when booking. (Smaller rooms can be cozy, but not if you bump your shins in the middle of the night trying to maneuver between the walls and the bed.) If a room is well designed, with big windows, mirrored walls, nooks, and alcoves, that can compensate for lack of space.

TEMPERATURE CONTROL, VENTILATION, AND ODOR Hotel rooms should be odor-free and smoke-free and not feel stuffy or damp. The most quiet and responsive system is central heating and air-conditioning, controlled by the room's own thermostat. Next best is a room module heater and air conditioner, controlled preferably by an automatic thermostat, but usually by manually operated button controls. Central heating and air without any sort of room thermostat can leave you sweltering or shivering in the changeable New York climate, without much control.

Most hotel rooms have windows or balcony doors that have been permanently sealed. Though there are legitimate safety and liability issues involved, we prefer windows and balcony doors that can be opened. A room with a view is preferable, and a balcony or terrace is especially exciting (and rare) in New York City.

ROOM SECURITY We'll start with front-desk staffers, who need to be discreet about calling out your room number. Better rooms have locks that require a plastic card instead of the traditional lock and key; card-and-slot systems allow the hotel to change the combination or entry code of the lock with each new guest. Though larger hotels and hotel chains with lock-and-key systems usually rotate their locks once each year, they remain vulnerable to hotel thieves much of the time, and many smaller or independent properties rarely rotate their locks.

In addition to the entry-lock system, the door should have a dead bolt and perhaps a chain that can be locked from the inside, but a chain by itself is not sufficient. Peepholes allow you to check out visitors. Any windows and balcony doors should have secure locks. Room safes are becoming standard, and the bigger the better, so that technical devices, cameras, and other large items can be stored.

SAFETY New York codes are tough. Fire or smoke alarms, clear fire instructions, and sprinkler systems are musts for rooms. Bathtubs should have a nonskid surface, and shower stall doors are safest if they either open outward or slide side-to-side. Bathroom electrical outlets high on the wall and not too close to the sink are best. Balconies should have sturdy, high rails.

NOISE If traffic and street noises are around-the-clock problems, make sure windows are double- or triple-glazed. In better hotels, wall and ceiling construction effectively screens routine noise, carpets and drapes absorb and muffle sounds, and mattresses mounted on stable platforms or sturdy bed frames don't squeak much, even when challenged by the most acrobatic lovers. Televisions enclosed in cabinets, and with volume governors, rarely disturb guests in adjacent rooms.

unofficial **TIP**
If you are easily disturbed by noise, ask for a room on a higher floor, off main thoroughfares, and away from elevators and ice and vending machines.

Optimally, the air-conditioning and heating system operates without noise or vibration. Likewise, plumbing is quiet and positioned away from the sleeping area. Doors to the hall and to adjoining rooms are thick and well fitted to block out noise.

DARKNESS CONTROL Ever wake up at sunrise in a hotel room where the curtains would not quite meet in the middle? Thick, lined curtains that close completely in the center and extend beyond the edges of the window or door frame are ideal. In a well-planned room, the curtains, shades, or blinds should almost totally block light at any time of day.

LIGHTING Poor lighting is a problem in American hotel rooms, and New York rooms, sorry to say, are no exception. Lighting may be dramatic, and adequate for dressing, relaxing, or watching television, but not for reading or working. Light needs to be bright over tables and desks and beside couches or easy chairs. Because many people read in bed, best is a separate light for each person, high enough to shed light on books, but illuminating a small area so that a sleeper will not be bothered by a roommate's light. A bedside console that controls most lights and electronics is especially desirable. The worst situation is a single bedside lamp, sometimes compounded by weak light bulbs.

Closet areas should be well lit, with a switch near the door that turns on room lights when you enter. Bathroom lighting should be adequate for grooming purposes—and a heat lamp is a nice bonus.

FURNISHINGS Minimum sleep requirements are top-grade mattresses, pillows with nonallergenic fillers, warm blankets, and high-thread-count bed linens changed daily. Better hotels usually provide extra blankets and pillows in the room or on request, and they sometimes use a second top sheet between blanket and spread. Duvets over down comforters are the New York standard of cleanliness and comfort.

Dressers should be large enough to hold clothes for two people during a long stay, and a luggage rack and full-length mirror are useful. As for electronics, televisions today are expected to be large as well as cable-connected—and, preferably, flat-screen and high-def. A local TV program guide helps. In-room movies are nice options. CD/DVD players, iPod chargers, and top-grade digital clock radios are pluses.

Telephones should be capable of international direct dialing and conveniently situated, with easy-to-understand dialing instructions and a rate card. Local white and yellow pages should be provided. Better hotels install phones in the bathroom and furnish portable phones or equip room phones with long cords. Two lines, data ports for faxing and laptop computers, and mobile phones are offered at luxury and business-oriented hotels.

A table with chairs, or a desk, and a sitting area—perhaps with screens or French doors to block off work and sleep areas—are important elements. Well-designed hotel rooms usually have armchairs and sometimes a sleeper sofa for lounging and reading. Nice extras in any hotel room include small refrigerators or minibars, irons and ironing boards, coffeemakers, and trouser presses.

BATHROOM Marble, granite, and tile look best and are easy to keep clean. Two sinks are better than one, and you cannot have too much counter space. A sink outside the bath is a great convenience when one person bathes as another dresses. A separate toilet area is nice for privacy, and bidets are important options, especially for international travelers. Better bathrooms have both a tub and a separate shower with a nonslip bottom. The bath needs to be well lit and should have an exhaust fan and a guest-controlled bathroom heater. Towels and washcloths should be large, thick, and generously supplied. An electrical outlet for each sink, conveniently and safely placed, is a big convenience when you're shaving or drying hair.

Magnifying mirrors, scales, bathrobes and slippers, phones, hair driers, TVs or extra speakers, and amenities such as fine soaps, shampoos, and lotions all add to the luxury of the bathroom.

VENDING If there is no minibar, a complimentary ice machine and a drink machine should be conveniently located, or nibbles and drinks should be easily available from room service. Welcome additions at midrange properties include access to snacks and sundries (combs, toothpaste, etc.) in restaurants and shops. Luxury hotels will provide sundries in the room or on request.

MAINTENANCE Your eyes, nose, and fingers will tell you how your room is maintained. Even if a room is large and luxurious, if it isn't clean, it isn't habitable. On the other hand, a basic but clean room may be just fine. Check whether the hotel offers daily maid service. Luxury hotels offer turndown service (and that nice chocolate—or more—on the pillow).

"YOU'RE THE GREATEST": OUR FAVORITE NEW YORK HOTELS

WITH APOLOGIES TO NEW YORK'S OWN Ralph Kramden (of the classic TV series *The Honeymooners*), here's our totally subjective listing of superlative New York hotels. (Some of these listed here don't appear in our ratings, but because they have special reputations for particular attractions, we include them here.)

HOTEL RATINGS

★★★★★	Superior	*Tasteful and luxurious by any standard*
★★★★	Extremely nice	*What you would expect at a Hyatt Regency or Marriott*
★★★	Nice	*Holiday Inn or comparable quality*
★★	Adequate	*Clean, comfortable, and functional without frills—like a Motel 6*
★	Budget	*Spartan, not aesthetically pleasing, but clean*

OVERALL QUALITY To distinguish properties according to relative quality, tastefulness, state of repair, cleanliness, and size of standard rooms, we have grouped the hotels and motels into classifications denoted by stars. Star ratings in this guide apply to New York–area properties only and do not necessarily correspond to stars awarded by Mobil, AAA, or other travel critics. Because stars carry little weight when awarded in the absence of common standards of comparison, we have linked our ratings to expected levels of quality established by specific American hotel corporations.

Star ratings describe the property's standard accommodations. For most hotels, a "standard accommodation" is a room with either one king bed or two queen beds. In an all-suite property, the standard accommodation is either a one- or a two-room suite. In addition to standard accommodations, many hotels offer luxury rooms and special suites not rated here. Star ratings are assigned without regard to whether a property has restaurants, recreational facilities, entertainment, or other extras.

ROOM QUALITY In addition to stars (which delineate broad categories), we also employ a numerical rating system. Our rating scale is 0 to 100, with 100 as the best possible rating and zero (0) as the worst. Numerical ratings are presented to show the difference we perceive between one property and another. Rooms at the Sheraton New York, The Maritime, and The Avalon are all rated as four-star (★★★★). In the supplemental numerical ratings, the Sheraton is rated an 89, The Maritime an 88, and The Avalon an 84. This means that within the four-star category, the Sheraton and The Maritime are comparable, and both have slightly nicer rooms than The Avalon.

COST Price estimates are based on the hotel's published rack rates for standard rooms. Each "$" represents $80. Thus, a cost symbol of "$$$" means a room (or suite) at that hotel will cost about $240 a night.

HOW THE HOTELS COMPARE

THE NICEST ROOMS IN TOWN are featured in the charts on pages 70–73. We've focused strictly on room quality and excluded any consideration of location, services, recreation, or amenities. In some instances, a one- or two-room suite can be had for the same price as or less than a hotel room.

If you've used previous editions of this guide, you will notice that many of the ratings and rankings have changed. In addition to the inclusion of new properties, these changes also consider guest-room renovations or improved maintenance and housekeeping. A failure to properly maintain guest rooms or a lapse in housekeeping standards can negatively affect the ratings.

Finally, before you begin to shop for a hotel, take a hard look at this letter we received from a couple in Hot Springs, Arkansas:

We canceled our room reservations to follow the advice in your book and reserved a hotel room highly ranked by the Unofficial Guide. *We wanted inexpensive but clean and cheerful. We got inexpensive, but also dirty, grim, and depressing. I really felt disappointed in your advice and the room. It was the pits. That was the one real piece of information I needed from your book! The room spoiled the holiday for me aside from our touring.*

Needless to say, this letter was as unsettling to us as the bad room was to our reader. Our integrity as travel journalists, after all, is based on the quality of the information we provide our readers. Even with the best of intentions and the most conscientious research, however, we cannot inspect every room in every hotel. What we do, in statistical terms, is take a sample: we check out several rooms selected at random in each hotel and base our ratings and rankings on those rooms. The inspections are conducted anonymously and without the knowledge of management.

Although it would be unusual, it is certainly possible that the rooms we randomly inspect are not representative of the majority of rooms at a particular hotel. Another possibility is that the rooms we inspect in a given hotel are representative but that by bad luck a reader is assigned a room that is inferior. When we rechecked the hotel our reader disliked, we discovered that our rating was correctly representative but that he and his wife had unfortunately been assigned to one of a small number of threadbare rooms scheduled for renovation.

The key to avoiding disappointment is to snoop around in advance. We recommend that you search the Web and ask for a photo of a hotel's standard guest room before you book, or at least get a copy of the hotel's promotional brochure. Alas, some hotel chains use the same guest-room photo in their promotional literature for all their properties; a specific guest room may not resemble the brochure photo. Find out how old the property is and when your guest room was last renovated. If you arrive and are assigned an inferior room, demand to be moved.

TOP 30 BEST DEALS IN NEW YORK

LET'S REORDER THE LIST TO RANK THE BEST COMBINATIONS of quality and value in a room. As before, the rankings are made without consideration of location or the availability of restaurants, recreational facilities, entertainment, or amenities. Remember that a ★★★ room at $120 may rank closely with a ★★★★ room at $240, but that does not mean the rooms will be of comparable quality. Regardless of whether it's a good deal or not, a ★★★ room is still a ★★★ room. These are the best room buys for the money, regardless of location or star classification, based on averaged rack rates (see chart on pages 76 and 77.)

How the Hotels Compare

HOTEL	STAR RATING	ROOM QUALITY	COST ($ = $80)
Mandarin Oriental, New York	★★★★★	98	$$$$$$$$$$$$+
The St. Regis	★★★★★	98	$$$$$$$$$$$$–
Four Seasons Hotel New York	★★★★★	97	$$$$$$$$$$$$–
The Pierre	★★★★★	97	$$$$$$+
Ritz-Carlton New York, Battery Park	★★★★★	97	$$$$$$+
Trump International Hotel & Towers	★★★★★	97	$$$$$$$$$–
The Carlyle	★★★★★	96	$$$$$$$$$–
Jumeirah Essex House	★★★★½	95	$$$$$$$
The Lowell	★★★★½	95	$$$$$$$$–
The Mark	★★★★½	95	$$$$$$$$+
Renaissance NY Times Square Hotel	★★★★½	95	$$$$$$–
W Hotel Times Square	★★★★½	95	$$$$+
The Waldorf-Astoria	★★★★½	95	$$$+
Inn at Irving Place	★★★★½	94	$$$$$$$–
Inn New York City	★★★★½	94	$$$$$$$+
The Kitano New York	★★★★½	94	$$$$
Le Parker Meridien New York	★★★★½	94	$$$$$
New York Palace	★★★★½	94	$$$$$$+
Ritz-Carlton New York, Central Park	★★★★½	94	$$$$$$$$$$$$–
The Alex Hotel	★★★★½	93	$$$$+
City Club Hotel	★★★★½	93	$$$$–
Flatotel	★★★★½	93	$$$$+
Loews Regency	★★★★½	93	$$$$$$
The Lombardy	★★★★½	93	$$$$+
The London NYC	★★★★½	93	$$$$$$$+
The Muse Hotel	★★★★½	93	$$$$$+
The Peninsula	★★★★½	93	$$$$$$$$+
Soho Grand	★★★★½	93	$$$
Bryant Park Hotel	★★★★½	92	$$$$
Duane Street Hotel	★★★★½	92	$$$+
Hotel Gansevoort	★★★★½	92	$$$$$$–
The Hotel on Rivington	★★★★½	92	$$$$$$
The Manhattan at Times Square	★★★★½	92	$$$$+
The Michelangelo	★★★★½	92	$$$$$$$$–
Millennium Broadway Hotel	★★★★½	92	$$$+

HOTEL	STAR RATING	ROOM QUALITY	COST ($ = $80)
Omni Berkshire Place	★★★★½	92	$$$$$
Sherry Netherland	★★★★½	92	$$$$$+
The Surrey	★★★★½	92	$$$$$$
Embassy Suites New York	★★★★½	91	$$$
The Mercer	★★★★½	91	$$$$$$$+
6 Columbus	★★★★½	91	$$$
The Standard	★★★★½	91	$$+
W New York	★★★★½	91	$$$+
The Benjamin	★★★★½	90	$$$+
The Blakely New York	★★★★½	90	$$$$−
The Bowery Hotel	★★★★½	90	$$$$$−
Gramercy Park Hotel	★★★★½	90	$$$$$$$−
Hotel Chandler	★★★★½	90	$$$
Hotel Plaza Athénée	★★★★½	90	$$$$$$$$$−
InterContinental The Barclay New York	★★★★½	90	$$$$+
La Quinta Inn Manhattan	★★★★½	90	$$$$+
Millennium U.N. Plaza	★★★★½	90	$$$$+
Morgans	★★★★½	90	$$$$$+
San Carlos	★★★★½	90	$$$$$−
70 park avenue hotel	★★★★½	90	$$$$$−
Tribeca Grand	★★★★½	90	$$$
The Westin New York at Times Square	★★★★½	90	$$$$−
Chambers	★★★★	89	$$$$$+
Dream	★★★★	89	$$$$−
Fitzpatrick Manhattan	★★★★	89	$$$−
Hotel 373 Fifth Avenue	★★★★	89	$$+
Hotel Elysée	★★★★	89	$$$
Hilton New York	★★★★	89	$$$$
Sheraton New York Hotel & Towers	★★★★	89	$$$$$−
60 Thompson	★★★★	89	$$$$$$−
Sofitel New York	★★★★	89	$$$+
Clarion Collection The Solita Soho Hotel	★★★★	89	$$$
Algonquin Hotel	★★★★	88	$$$$$
Bed-and-Breakfast on the Park	★★★★	88	$$$$
Beekman Tower Hotel	★★★★	88	$$+

How the Hotels Compare (continued)

HOTEL	STAR RATING	ROOM QUALITY	COST ($ = $80)
Bentley Hotel New York	★★★★	88	$$–
Carlton Hotel	★★★★	88	$$$
Courtyard by Marriott Manhattan Times Square South	★★★★	88	$$$
Hilton Times Square	★★★★	88	$$$+
Hotel Giraffe	★★★★	88	$$$+
Novotel New York Times Square	★★★★	88	$$$+
The Paramount Hotel	★★★★	88	$$$$+
The Shoreham	★★★★	88	$$$$–
Time	★★★★	88	$$$
Warwick New York Hotel	★★★★	88	$$$+
Buckingham Hotel	★★★★	87	$$$$–
The Mansfield	★★★★	87	$$$$+
Maritime Hotel	★★★★	87	$$$$$–
Stay	★★★★	87	$$
Tudor Hotel	★★★★	87	$$$+
W New York–The Tuscany	★★★★	87	$$$+
Casablanca Hotel	★★★★	86	$$$$$
Crowne Plaza Times Square Manhattan	★★★★	86	$$$$+
Grand Hyatt New York	★★★★	86	$$$+
Hotel Roger Williams	★★★★	86	$$$+
Iroquois New York	★★★★	86	$$$$$$
Library Hotel	★★★★	86	$$$$$
Room Mate Grace	★★★★	86	$$$$–
The Royalton	★★★★	86	$$$$$
W Hotel Union Square	★★★★	86	$$$$$–
The Wall Street Inn	★★★★	86	$$+
Fitzpatrick Grand Central	★★★★	85	$$+
Hotel Wales	★★★★	85	$$$+
Hudson Hotel	★★★★	85	$$$$+
The Avalon	★★★★	84	$$$$+
Blue Moon Hotel	★★★★	84	$$$$$$$+
Doubletree Metropolitan Hotel	★★★★	84	$$–
Dylan Hotel	★★★★	84	$$$

HOTEL	STAR RATING	ROOM QUALITY	COST ($ = $80)
Hotel Bedford	★★★★	84	$$
Hotel Mela	★★★★	84	$$$$
New York Marriott Marquis	★★★★	84	$$$$$$+
Excelsior Hotel	★★★½	83	$$+
Four Points by Sheraton Manhattan Chelsea	★★★½	83	$$$$–
Hotel 41 at Times Square	★★★½	83	$$+
Red Roof Inn Manhattan	★★★½	83	$$$$+
Clarion Hotel Park Avenue	★★★½	82	$$$–
The Franklin	★★★½	82	$$$+
Hotel Metro	★★★½	81	$$$$
The Roger Smith	★★★½	81	$$$$$
Washington Square Hotel	★★★½	81	$$$–
Ameritania Hotel New York	★★★½	80	$+
Country Inn in the City	★★★½	80	$$$$
Doubletree Guest Suites Times Square	★★★½	80	$$$$$+
Hotel Reserve	★★★½	80	$$+
Jolly Hotel Madison Towers	★★★½	80	$$$$$–
Le Refuge Inn	★★★½	80	$$–
On the Ave	★★★½	80	$$$$+
Roosevelt Hotel	★★★½	80	$$$$$$–
Gild Hall	★★★½	78	$$$
Hotel 91	★★★½	78	$$$+
Hotel Thirty Thirty New York City	★★★½	78	$$$–
Chelsea Savoy Hotel	★★★½	77	$$–
Inn on 23rd Street	★★★½	76	$$$$$–
Hotel 31	★★★½	75	$+
Renaissance New York Hotel 57	★★★½	75	$$$$–
Cosmopolitan Hotel–Tribeca	★★★	74	$$–
Lucerne Hotel	★★★	74	$$$$
The Pod Hotel	★★★	72	$$$$–
Akwaaba Mansion	★★★	70	$$+
Larchmont Hotel	★★★	70	$+
Harbor House	★★★	68	$$

New York Hotels by Neighborhood

DOWNTOWN

Blue Moon Hotel
The Bowery Hotel
Cosmopolitan Hotel–Tribeca
Duane Street Hotel
Embassy Suites New York
Gild Hall
Hotel Gansevoort
Hotel 91
The Hotel on Rivington
Hotel Reserve
Larchmont Hotel
The Mercer
Ritz-Carlton New York, Battery Park
60 Thompson
Soho Grand
Clarion Collection Solita Soho Hotel
Tribeca Grand
The Wall Street Inn
Washington Square Hotel

CHELSEA, GRAMERCY PARK, AND MIDTOWN

The Alex Hotel
Algonquin Hotel
Ameritania Hotel New York
The Avalon
Beekman Tower Hotel
The Benjamin
The Blakely New York
Bryant Park Hotel
Buckingham Hotel
Carlton Hotel
Casablanca Hotel
Chambers
Chelsea Savoy Hotel
City Club Hotel
Clarion Hotel Park Avenue

Courtyard by Marriott Manhattan
    Times Square South
Crowne Plaza Times Square Manhattan
Doubletree Guest Suites
    Times Square
Doubletree Metropolitan Hotel
Dream
Dylan Hotel
Fitzpatrick Grand Central
Fitzpatrick Manhattan
Flatotel
Four Points by Sheraton Manhattan
    Chelsea
Four Seasons Hotel New York
Gramercy Park Hotel
Grand Hyatt New York
Hilton New York
Hilton Times Square
Hotel Bedford
Hotel Chandler
Hotel Elysée
Hotel 41 at Times Square
Hotel Giraffe
Hotel Mela
Hotel Metro
Hotel Roger Williams
Hotel Thirty Thirty New York City
Hotel 31
Hotel 373 Fifth Avenue
Hudson Hotel
Inn at Irving Place
Inn on 23rd Street
InterContinental The Barclay New York
Iroquois New York
Jolly Hotel Madison Towers
Jumeirah Essex House
The Kitano New York
La Quinta Inn Manhattan

Le Parker Meridien New York

Library Hotel

The Lombardy

The London NYC

The Manhattan at Times Square

The Mansfield

Maritime Hotel

The Michelangelo

Millennium Broadway Hotel

Millennium UN Plaza Hotel
New York

Morgans

The Muse Hotel

New York Marriott Marquis

New York Palace

Novotel New York Times Square

Omni Berkshire Place

The Paramount Hotel

The Peninsula

The Pod Hotel

Red Roof Inn Manhattan

Renaissance New York Times Square
Hotel

Renaissance New York Hotel 57

Ritz-Carlton New York, Central Park

The Roger Smith

Room Mate Grace

Roosevelt Hotel

The Royalton

San Carlos

70 park avenue hotel

Sheraton New York Hotel & Towers

The Shoreham

Sofitel New York

The Standard

Stay

The St. Regis

The Time

Tudor Hotel

W Hotel Times Square

W Hotel Union Square

W New York

W New York–The Tuscany

The Waldorf-Astoria

Warwick New York Hotel

The Westin New York at Times Square

UPTOWN

Bentley Hotel New York

The Carlyle

Country Inn in the City

Excelsior Hotel

The Franklin

Hotel Plaza Athénée

Hotel Wales

Inn New York City

Loews Regency

The Lowell

Lucerne Hotel

Mandarin Oriental, New York

The Mark

On the Ave

The Pierre

6 Columbus

The Sherry-Netherland

The Surrey

Trump International Hotel &
Towers

BROOKLYN

Akwaaba Mansion

Bed-and-Breakfast on the Park

BRONX

Le Refuge Inn

STATEN ISLAND

Harbor House

The Top 30 Best Deals in New York City

HOTEL	STAR RATING	ROOM QUALITY	COST ($ = $80)
1. Mandarin Oriental, New York	★★★★★	98	$$$$$$$$$$$$+
2. Four Seasons Hotel New York	★★★★★	97	$$$$$$$$$$$$−
3. The St. Regis	★★★★★	98	$$$$$$$$$$$$−
4. Ritz-Carlton New York Central Park	★★★★½	94	$$$$$$$$$$$$−
5. The Carlyle	★★★★★	96	$$$$$$$$$−
6. Trump International Hotel & Towers	★★★★★	97	$$$$$$$$$−
7. Hotel Plaza Athénée	★★★★½	90	$$$$$$$$$−
8. The Peninsula	★★★★½	93	$$$$$$$$+
9. The Mark	★★★★½	95	$$$$$$$$+
10. The Michelangelo	★★★★½	92	$$$$$$$$−
11. The Lowell	★★★★½	95	$$$$$$$$−
12. The Mercer	★★★★½	91	$$$$$$$+
13. Inn New York City	★★★★½	94	$$$$$$$+
14. The London NYC	★★★★½	93	$$$$$$$+
15. Blue Moon Hotel	★★★★	84	$$$$$$$+

HOTEL	STAR RATING	ROOM QUALITY	COST ($ = $80)
16. Gramercy Park Hotel	★★★★½	90	$$$$$$$–
17. Jumeirah Essex House	★★★★½	95	$$$$$$$
18. The Pierre	★★★★★	97	$$$$$$+
19. Ritz-Carlton New York, Battery Park	★★★★★	97	$$$$$$+
20. Inn at Irving Place	★★★★½	94	$$$$$$$–
21. New York Marriott Marquis	★★★★	84	$$$$$$+
22. The Surrey	★★★★½	92	$$$$$$
23. New York Palace	★★★★½	94	$$$$$$+
24. Loews Regency	★★★★½	93	$$$$$$
25. The Hotel on Rivington	★★★★½	92	$$$$$$
26. San Carlos	★★★★½	90	$$$$$$–
27. Hotel Gansevoort	★★★★½	92	$$$$$$–
28. Iroquois New York	★★★★	86	$$$$$$
29. Renaissance NY Times Square Hotel	★★★★½	95	$$$$$$–
30. Morgans	★★★★½	90	$$$$$+

Hotel Information Chart

Akwaaba Mansion ★★★
347 MacDonough Street
New York, NY 11233
☎ 718-455-5958
TOLL-FREE 888-INN-DULJ
www.akwaaba.com

ROOM QUALITY	70
COST ($ = $80)	$$+
LOCATION	Brooklyn
DISCOUNTS	–
NO. OF ROOMS	4
ROOM SQUARE FEET	185
MEETING FACILITIES	–
POOL/SAUNA	–
EXERCISE FACILITIES	–
WINDOW GLAZE	Single
PARKING PER DAY	Free
NEAREST SUBWAY	20 minutes
BAR	
ON-SITE DINING	African/Caribbean/ Mediterranean
EXTRA AMENITIES	Free breakfast, terry-cloth robes
BUSINESS AMENITIES	–

The Alex Hotel ★★★★½
205 East 45th Street
New York, NY 10017
☎ 212-867-5100
TOLL-FREE 888-765-2370
www.thealexhotel.com

ROOM QUALITY	93
COST ($ = $80)	$$$$+
LOCATION	Chelsea, Gramercy Park, and Midtown
DISCOUNTS	Gov't
NO. OF ROOMS	203
ROOM SQUARE FEET	320
MEETING FACILITIES	•
POOL/SAUNA	–
EXERCISE FACILITIES	•
WINDOW GLAZE	Single
PARKING PER DAY	$32–$52
NEAREST SUBWAY	1½ blocks
BAR	•
ON-SITE DINING	Japanese American
EXTRA AMENITIES	Concierge
BUSINESS AMENITIES	Data port, 2 phone lines, fax access

Algonquin Hotel ★★★★
59 West 44th Street
New York, NY 10036
☎ 212-840-6800
TOLL-FREE 888-304-2047
www.algonquinhotel.com

ROOM QUALITY	88
COST ($ = $80)	$$$$$
LOCATION	Chelsea, Gramercy Park, and Midtown
DISCOUNTS	AAA, gov't
NO. OF ROOMS	174
ROOM SQUARE FEET	170
MEETING FACILITIES	•
POOL/SAUNA	–
EXERCISE FACILITIES	•
WINDOW GLAZE	Double
PARKING PER DAY	Public lot $30
NEAREST SUBWAY	1 block
BAR	•
ON-SITE DINING	Dinner show, pub fare, Continental
EXTRA AMENITIES	–
BUSINESS AMENITIES	Data port

Beekman Tower Hotel ★★★★
3 Mitchell Place
New York, NY 10017
☎ 212-355-7300
TOLL-FREE 800-637-8483
www.thebeekmanhotel.com

ROOM QUALITY	88
COST ($ = $80)	$$+
LOCATION	Chelsea, Gramercy Park, and Midtown
DISCOUNTS	–
NO. OF ROOMS	170
ROOM SQUARE FEET	250
MEETING FACILITIES	•
POOL/SAUNA	Whirlpool, sauna
EXERCISE FACILITIES	•
WINDOW GLAZE	Triple/double
PARKING PER DAY	$50–$60
NEAREST SUBWAY	5 blocks
BAR	•
ON-SITE DINING	American
EXTRA AMENITIES	All-suite property
BUSINESS AMENITIES	Data port

The Benjamin ★★★★½
125 East 50th Street
New York, NY 10022
☎ 212-753-2700
TOLL-FREE 1-800-278-7757
www.nyc-hotels.net

ROOM QUALITY	90
COST ($ = $80)	$$$+
LOCATION	Chelsea, Gramercy Park, and Midtown
DISCOUNTS	AAA, gov't
NO. OF ROOMS	209
ROOM SQUARE FEET	–
MEETING FACILITIES	•
POOL/SAUNA	Spa
EXERCISE FACILITIES	•
WINDOW GLAZE	Triple
PARKING PER DAY	$35
NEAREST SUBWAY	1 block
BAR	•
ON-SITE DINING	American
EXTRA AMENITIES	Concierge
BUSINESS AMENITIES	Data port, 2 phone lines, fax, DSL

Bentley Hotel New York ★★★★
500 East 62nd Street
New York, NY 10085
☎ 212-644-6000
TOLL-FREE 1-800-278-7757
www.nyc-hotels.net

ROOM QUALITY	88
COST ($ = $80)	$$–
LOCATION	Uptown
DISCOUNTS	–
NO. OF ROOMS	197
ROOM SQUARE FEET	235
MEETING FACILITIES	–
POOL/SAUNA	–
EXERCISE FACILITIES	Discount access
WINDOW GLAZE	Double
PARKING PER DAY	$20
NEAREST SUBWAY	5 blocks
BAR	•
ON-SITE DINING	American
EXTRA AMENITIES	Continental breakfast, valet, capPucCino Bar
BUSINESS AMENITIES	Data port, 2 phone lines

Ameritania Hotel
New York ★★★½
230 West 54th Street
New York, NY 10019
☎ 212-247-5000
TOLL-FREE 1-800-278-7757
www.nyc-hotels.net

ROOM QUALITY	80
COST ($ = $80)	$+
LOCATION	Chelsea, Gramercy Park, and Midtown
DISCOUNTS	Gov't
NO. OF ROOMS	210
ROOM SQUARE FEET	210
MEETING FACILITIES	—
POOL/SAUNA	—
EXERCISE FACILITIES	$20 access
WINDOW GLAZE	Double
PARKING PER DAY	$30
NEAREST SUBWAY	3 blocks
BAR	•
ON-SITE DINING	Italian
EXTRA AMENITIES	Free Continental breakfast
BUSINESS AMENITIES	Data port

The Avalon ★★★★
16 East 32nd Street
New York, NY 10016
☎ 212-299-7000
www.avalonhotelnyc.com

ROOM QUALITY	84
COST ($ = $80)	$$$$+
LOCATION	Chelsea, Gramercy Park, and Midtown
DISCOUNTS	AAA, gov't
NO. OF ROOMS	99
ROOM SQUARE FEET	200
MEETING FACILITIES	•
POOL/SAUNA	—
EXERCISE FACILITIES	access
WINDOW GLAZE	Double
PARKING PER DAY	$29–$39
NEAREST SUBWAY	1 block
BAR	—
ON-SITE DINING	American
EXTRA AMENITIES	Continental breakfast, concierge
BUSINESS AMENITIES	Data port, 2 phone lines

Bed-and-Breakfast
on the Park ★★★★
113 Prospect Park West
New York, NY 11215
☎ 718-499-6115
www.bbnyc.com

ROOM QUALITY	88
COST ($ = $80)	$$$$
LOCATION	Brooklyn
DISCOUNTS	AAA
NO. OF ROOMS	7
ROOM SQUARE FEET	140
MEETING FACILITIES	—
POOL/SAUNA	—
EXERCISE FACILITIES	—
WINDOW GLAZE	Single
PARKING PER DAY	Free
NEAREST SUBWAY	3 blocks
BAR	—
ON-SITE DINING	American
EXTRA AMENITIES	Roof garden, free breakfast
BUSINESS AMENITIES	—

The Blakely
New York ★★★★½
136 West 55th Street
New York, NY 10019
☎ 212-245-1800
TOLL-FREE 800-735-0710
www.blakelynewyork.com

ROOM QUALITY	90
COST ($ = $80)	$$$$–
LOCATION	Uptown
DISCOUNTS	AAA
NO. OF ROOMS	117
ROOM SQUARE FEET	310
MEETING FACILITIES	•
POOL/SAUNA	—
EXERCISE FACILITIES	•
WINDOW GLAZE	Double
PARKING PER DAY	$33
NEAREST SUBWAY	100 feet
BAR	•
ON-SITE DINING	Italian
EXTRA AMENITIES	—
BUSINESS AMENITIES	Wireless network, 2 phone lines, fax access

Blue Moon Hotel ★★★★
100 Orchard Street
New York, NY 10002
☎ 212-533-9080
www.bluemoon-nyc.com

ROOM QUALITY	84
COST ($ = $80)	$$$$$$$+
LOCATION	Downtown
DISCOUNTS	—
NO. OF ROOMS	22
ROOM SQUARE FEET	—
MEETING FACILITIES	—
POOL/SAUNA	—
EXERCISE FACILITIES	—
WINDOW GLAZE	Double
PARKING PER DAY	—
NEAREST SUBWAY	2 blocks
BAR	—
ON-SITE DINING	—
EXTRA AMENITIES	—
BUSINESS AMENITIES	Wireless network, 1 phone line

The Bowery Hotel ★★★★½
335 Bowery
New York, NY 10003
☎ 212-505-9100
www.theboweryhotel.com

ROOM QUALITY	90
COST ($ = $80)	$$$$$–
LOCATION	Downtown
DISCOUNTS	—
NO. OF ROOMS	135
ROOM SQUARE FEET	220–1,275
MEETING FACILITIES	•
POOL/SAUNA	—
EXERCISE FACILITIES	—
WINDOW GLAZE	Single
PARKING PER DAY	$45–$55
NEAREST SUBWAY	2 blocks
BAR	•
ON-SITE DINING	Italian
EXTRA AMENITIES	Concierge, free DVD library, marble baths
BUSINESS AMENITIES	Free Wi-Fi

Hotel Information Chart (continued)

Bryant Park Hotel ★★★★½	**Buckingham Hotel** ★★★★	**Carlton Hotel** ★★★★
40 West 40th Street	101 West 57th Street	88 Madison Avenue
New York, NY 10018	New York, NY 10019	New York, NY 10016
☎ 212-869-0100	☎ 212-246-1500	☎ 212-532-4100
TOLL-FREE 877-640-9300	TOLL-FREE 888-511-1900	TOLL-FREE 800-601-8500
www.bryantparkhotel.com	www.buckinghamhotel.com	www.hotelcarltonnewyork.com

	Bryant Park	Buckingham	Carlton
ROOM QUALITY	92	87	88
COST ($ = $80)	$$$$	$$$$–	$$$
LOCATION	Chelsea, Gramercy Park, and Midtown	Chelsea, Gramercy Park, and Midtown	Chelsea, Gramercy Park, and Midtown
DISCOUNTS	–	–	AAA, gov't
NO. OF ROOMS	129	–	317
ROOM SQUARE FEET	330	405	250
MEETING FACILITIES	•	•	•
POOL/SAUNA			–
EXERCISE FACILITIES	•	•	Privileges
WINDOW GLAZE	Double		–
PARKING PER DAY	$45	$39	$35
NEAREST SUBWAY	½ block	4 blocks	1 block
BAR	•	–	•
ON-SITE DINING	Seasonal/European		American
EXTRA AMENITIES	Concierge	–	Concierge
BUSINESS AMENITIES	Data port, 2 phone lines		Data port, 2 phone lines, DSL, fax access

Chelsea Savoy Hotel ★★★½	**City Club Hotel** ★★★★½	**Clarion Collection The Solita Soho Hotel** ★★★★
204 West 23rd Street	55 West 44th Street	159 Grand Street
New York, NY 10011	New York, NY 10036	New York, NY 10013
☎ 212-929-9353	☎ 212-921-5500	☎ 212-925-3600
TOLL-FREE 866-929-9353	TOLL-FREE 888-256-4100	TOLL-FREE 888-SOLITA-8
www.chelseasavoynyc.com	www.cityclubhotel.com	www.clarionhotel.com

	Chelsea Savoy	City Club	Clarion Collection
ROOM QUALITY	77	93	89
COST ($ = $80)	$$–	$$$$–	$$$
LOCATION	Chelsea, Gramercy Park, and Midtown	Chelsea, Gramercy Park, and Midtown	Downtown
DISCOUNTS	–	–	AAA, gov't
NO. OF ROOMS	90	65	42
ROOM SQUARE FEET	–	300	–
MEETING FACILITIES	–	–	–
POOL/SAUNA	–	–	–
EXERCISE FACILITIES	–	–	$15 access
WINDOW GLAZE	Double	Double	–
PARKING PER DAY	$25	$41	$35
NEAREST SUBWAY	1 block	½ block	2 blocks
BAR	•	•	•
ON-SITE DINING	Cafe	Bistro	
EXTRA AMENITIES	–	Safe deposit box in room	Plasma TV, dual shower heads
BUSINESS AMENITIES	–	Internet, 2 phone lines, bath phone	Data port, 2 phone lines, fax access

The Carlyle ★★★★★
35 East 76th Street
New York, NY 10021
☎ 212-744-1600
TOLL-FREE 800-227-5737
www.rosewoodhotels.com

ROOM QUALITY	96
COST ($ = $80)	$$$$$$$$$$–
LOCATION	Uptown
DISCOUNTS	–
NO. OF ROOMS	188
ROOM SQUARE FEET	180
MEETING FACILITIES	•
POOL/SAUNA	Sauna, steam room
EXERCISE FACILITIES	•
WINDOW GLAZE	Double
PARKING PER DAY	$50
NEAREST SUBWAY	2 blocks
BAR	•
ON-SITE DINING	Dinner club, American/French, tea room
EXTRA AMENITIES	Continental cafe with live music
BUSINESS AMENITIES	Data port, 2 phone lines, fax

Casablanca Hotel ★★★★
147 West 43rd Street
New York, NY 10036
☎ 212-869-1212
TOLL-FREE 888-922-7225
www.casablancahotel.com

ROOM QUALITY	86
COST ($ = $80)	$$$$$
LOCATION	Chelsea, Gramercy Park, and Midtown
DISCOUNTS	–
NO. OF ROOMS	48
ROOM SQUARE FEET	270
MEETING FACILITIES	Small conf. room
POOL/SAUNA	Privileges, free
EXERCISE FACILITIES	Privileges
WINDOW GLAZE	Quadruple
PARKING PER DAY	$25
NEAREST SUBWAY	½ block
BAR	–
ON-SITE DINING	–
EXTRA AMENITIES	Free Continental breakfast, wine, hors d'oeuvres
BUSINESS AMENITIES	Data port, 2 phone lines

Chambers ★★★★½
15 West 56th Street
New York, NY 10019
☎ 212-974-5656
TOLL-FREE 866-204-5656
www.chambershotel.com

ROOM QUALITY	89
COST ($ = $80)	$$$$$+
LOCATION	Chelsea, Gramercy Park, and Midtown
DISCOUNTS	–
NO. OF ROOMS	77
ROOM SQUARE FEET	300
MEETING FACILITIES	•
POOL/SAUNA	–
EXERCISE FACILITIES	Privileges
WINDOW GLAZE	Double
PARKING PER DAY	$35
NEAREST SUBWAY	1 block
BAR	•
ON-SITE DINING	American
EXTRA AMENITIES	Concierge, CD, DVD, library
BUSINESS AMENITIES	Fax

Clarion Hotel Park Avenue ★★★½
492 Park Avenue South
New York, NY 10016
☎ 212-545-9727
TOLL-FREE 800-258-4290
www.clarionhotelny.com

ROOM QUALITY	82
COST ($ = $80)	$$$–
LOCATION	Chelsea, Gramercy Park, and Midtown
DISCOUNTS	AAA, AARP
NO. OF ROOMS	60
ROOM SQUARE FEET	260
MEETING FACILITIES	–
POOL/SAUNA	Sauna
EXERCISE FACILITIES	Privileges, $15
WINDOW GLAZE	Double
PARKING PER DAY	$24
NEAREST SUBWAY	2 blocks
BAR	–
ON-SITE DINING	Lunch and dinner
EXTRA AMENITIES	Free breakfast
BUSINESS AMENITIES	Data port, business center

Cosmopolitan Hotel– Tribeca ★★★
95 West Broadway
New York, NY 10007
☎ 212-566-1900
TOLL-FREE 888-895-9400
www.cosmohotel.com

ROOM QUALITY	74
COST ($ = $80)	$$–
LOCATION	Downtown
DISCOUNTS	–
NO. OF ROOMS	150
ROOM SQUARE FEET	160
MEETING FACILITIES	•
POOL/SAUNA	–
EXERCISE FACILITIES	–
WINDOW GLAZE	Single
PARKING PER DAY	$35
NEAREST SUBWAY	1 block
BAR	–
ON-SITE DINING	–
EXTRA AMENITIES	–
BUSINESS AMENITIES	Data port, fax, study desk

Country Inn in the City ★★★½
270 West 77th Street
New York, NY 10024
☎ 212-580-4183
www.countryinnthecity.com

ROOM QUALITY	80
COST ($ = $80)	$$$$
LOCATION	Uptown
DISCOUNTS	–
NO. OF ROOMS	4
ROOM SQUARE FEET	550
MEETING FACILITIES	–
POOL/SAUNA	–
EXERCISE FACILITIES	–
WINDOW GLAZE	Single
PARKING PER DAY	–
NEAREST SUBWAY	2 blocks
BAR	–
ON-SITE DINING	–
EXTRA AMENITIES	Kitchenette, welcome basket
BUSINESS AMENITIES	–

Hotel Information Chart (continued)

Courtyard by Marriott Manhattan Times Square South ★★★★
114 West 40th Street
New York, NY 10018
☎ 212-391-0088
TOLL-FREE 800-321-2211
www.marriott.com

ROOM QUALITY	88
COST ($ = $80)	$$$
LOCATION	Chelsea, Gramercy Park, and Midtown
DISCOUNTS	AAA, gov't
NO. OF ROOMS	244
ROOM SQUARE FEET	187
MEETING FACILITIES	•
POOL/SAUNA	–
EXERCISE FACILITIES	•
WINDOW GLAZE	Single
PARKING PER DAY	$52
NEAREST SUBWAY	1 block
BAR	–
ON-SITE DINING	Continental/European
EXTRA AMENITIES	Concierge, valet, dry cleaning
BUSINESS AMENITIES	2 phone lines, Internet

Crowne Plaza Times Square Manhattan ★★★★
1605 Broadway
New York, NY 10019
☎ 212-977-4000
TOLL-FREE 800-243-6969
www.crowneplaza.com

ROOM QUALITY	86
COST ($ = $80)	$$$$+
LOCATION	Chelsea, Gramercy Park, and Midtown
DISCOUNTS	Gov't
NO. OF ROOMS	770
ROOM SQUARE FEET	–
MEETING FACILITIES	•
POOL/SAUNA	Pool, sauna
EXERCISE FACILITIES	•
WINDOW GLAZE	Single
PARKING PER DAY	$39–$49
NEAREST SUBWAY	2 blocks
BAR	•
ON-SITE DINING	American
EXTRA AMENITIES	Concierge
BUSINESS AMENITIES	Business center, Internet

Doubletree Guest Suites Times Square ★★★½
1568 Broadway
New York, NY 10036
☎ 212-719-1600
TOLL-FREE 800-222-TREE
www.doubletree.com

ROOM QUALITY	80
COST ($ = $80)	$$$$$+
LOCATION	Chelsea, Gramercy Park, and Midtown
DISCOUNTS	AAA, AARP, gov't, military
NO. OF ROOMS	460
ROOM SQUARE FEET	442
MEETING FACILITIES	•
POOL/SAUNA	–
EXERCISE FACILITIES	•
WINDOW GLAZE	Single/double
PARKING PER DAY	$35
NEAREST SUBWAY	½ block
BAR	•
ON-SITE DINING	American
EXTRA AMENITIES	Kitchenette, tour desk, robes
BUSINESS AMENITIES	3 phone lines, Internet

Dylan Hotel ★★★★
52 East 41st Street
New York, NY 10017
☎ 212-338-0500
TOLL-FREE 800-553-9526
www.dylanhotel.com

ROOM QUALITY	84
COST ($ = $80)	$$$
LOCATION	Chelsea, Gramercy Park, and Midtown
DISCOUNTS	–
NO. OF ROOMS	107
ROOM SQUARE FEET	210
MEETING FACILITIES	•
POOL/SAUNA	–
EXERCISE FACILITIES	•
WINDOW GLAZE	Triple
PARKING PER DAY	$45
NEAREST SUBWAY	2 blocks
BAR	•
ON-SITE DINING	Continental breakfast
EXTRA AMENITIES	Concierge, safe, valet
BUSINESS AMENITIES	Data port, voice mail, 2 phone lines

Embassy Suites New York ★★★★½
102 North End Avenue
New York, NY 10282
☎ 212-945-0100
TOLL-FREE 800-HILTONS
www.embassysuites.com

ROOM QUALITY	91
COST ($ = $80)	$$$
LOCATION	Downtown
DISCOUNTS	AAA
NO. OF ROOMS	463
ROOM SQUARE FEET	450
MEETING FACILITIES	•
POOL/SAUNA	–
EXERCISE FACILITIES	•
WINDOW GLAZE	Single
PARKING PER DAY	$60
NEAREST SUBWAY	5 blocks
BAR	•
ON-SITE DINING	Steakhouse, American
EXTRA AMENITIES	Cocktails, breakfast
BUSINESS AMENITIES	Fax, Internet, 2 phone lines

Excelsior Hotel ★★★½
45 West 81st Street
New York, NY 10024
☎ 212-362-9200
TOLL-FREE 800-368-4575
www.excelsiorhotelny.com

ROOM QUALITY	83
COST ($ = $80)	$$+
LOCATION	Uptown
DISCOUNTS	–
NO. OF ROOMS	200
ROOM SQUARE FEET	250
MEETING FACILITIES	•
POOL/SAUNA	–
EXERCISE FACILITIES	–
WINDOW GLAZE	Double
PARKING PER DAY	$25–$35
NEAREST SUBWAY	½ block
BAR	–
ON-SITE DINING	Charge for breakfast room
EXTRA AMENITIES	Library
BUSINESS AMENITIES	Data port, fax, 2 phone lines

Doubletree Metropolitan Hotel
★★★★
569 Lexington Avenue
New York, NY 10022
☎ 212-752-7000
TOLL-FREE 800-695-8284
www.hilton.com

ROOM QUALITY	84
COST ($ = $80)	$$–
LOCATION	Chelsea, Gramercy Park, and Midtown
DISCOUNTS	AAA, AARP
NO. OF ROOMS	760
ROOM SQUARE FEET	215
MEETING FACILITIES	•
POOL/SAUNA	–
EXERCISE FACILITIES	•
WINDOW GLAZE	Double
PARKING PER DAY	$30
NEAREST SUBWAY	2 blocks
BAR	•
ON-SITE DINING	American
EXTRA AMENITIES	Barber/beauty shop
BUSINESS AMENITIES	Data port

Dream   ★★★★
210 West 55th Street
New York, NY 10019
☎ 212-247-2000
TOLL-FREE 866-IDREAMNY
www.dreamny.com

ROOM QUALITY	89
COST ($ = $80)	$$$$–
LOCATION	Chelsea, Gramercy Park, and Midtown
DISCOUNTS	–
NO. OF ROOMS	228
ROOM SQUARE FEET	155
MEETING FACILITIES	–
POOL/SAUNA	Sauna
EXERCISE FACILITIES	•
WINDOW GLAZE	–
PARKING PER DAY	$40
NEAREST SUBWAY	2 blocks
BAR	•
ON-SITE DINING	Italian
EXTRA AMENITIES	Concierge, 24-hour room service, Deepak Chopra Spa
BUSINESS AMENITIES	Data port, 2 phone lines, DSL, fax access

Duane Street Hotel   ★★★★½
130 Duane Street
New York, NY 10013
☎ 212-964-4600
www.duanestreethotel.com

ROOM QUALITY	92
COST ($ = $80)	$$$+
LOCATION	Downtown
DISCOUNTS	AAA, AARP, Corp.
NO. OF ROOMS	45
ROOM SQUARE FEET	200
MEETING FACILITIES	–
POOL/SAUNA	–
EXERCISE FACILITIES	Privileges
WINDOW GLAZE	Double
PARKING PER DAY	–
NEAREST SUBWAY	3 blocks
BAR	•
ON-SITE DINING	New American/ Mediterranean
EXTRA AMENITIES	Oversize loft windows, slate baths, laptop safe, 24-hr. business concierge
BUSINESS AMENITIES	High-speed and Wi-Fi Internet

Fitzpatrick Grand Central
★★★★
141 East 44th Street
New York, NY 10017
☎ 212-351-6800
TOLL-FREE 800-367-7701
www.fitzpatrickhotels.com

ROOM QUALITY	85
COST ($ = $80)	$$+
LOCATION	Chelsea, Gramercy Park, and Midtown
DISCOUNTS	AAA
NO. OF ROOMS	155
ROOM SQUARE FEET	500
MEETING FACILITIES	–
POOL/SAUNA	–
EXERCISE FACILITIES	Privileges
WINDOW GLAZE	Double
PARKING PER DAY	$49–$54
NEAREST SUBWAY	Across street
BAR	•
ON-SITE DINING	Irish/American
EXTRA AMENITIES	Valet
BUSINESS AMENITIES	Data port, 2 phone lines

Fitzpatrick Manhattan
★★★★
687 Lexington Avenue
New York, NY 10022
☎ 212-355-0100
TOLL-FREE 800-367-7701
www.fitzpatrickhotels.com

ROOM QUALITY	89
COST ($ = $80)	$$$–
LOCATION	Chelsea, Gramercy Park, and Midtown
DISCOUNTS	AAA, AARP
NO. OF ROOMS	91
ROOM SQUARE FEET	300
MEETING FACILITIES	•
POOL/SAUNA	Pool, privileges
EXERCISE FACILITIES	Privileges
WINDOW GLAZE	Double
PARKING PER DAY	$59–$64
NEAREST SUBWAY	2 blocks
BAR	•
ON-SITE DINING	Continental
EXTRA AMENITIES	Irish theme
BUSINESS AMENITIES	Data port, fax

Flatotel
★★★★½
135 West 52nd Street
New York, NY 10019
☎ 212-887-9400
TOLL-FREE 800-FLATOTEL
www.flatotel.com

ROOM QUALITY	93
COST ($ = $80)	$$$$+
LOCATION	Chelsea, Gramercy Park, and Midtown
DISCOUNTS	–
NO. OF ROOMS	272
ROOM SQUARE FEET	–
MEETING FACILITIES	Suites
POOL/SAUNA	Sauna, pool privileges
EXERCISE FACILITIES	•
WINDOW GLAZE	Double
PARKING PER DAY	$30–$47
NEAREST SUBWAY	2 blocks
BAR	–
ON-SITE DINING	Breakfast only
EXTRA AMENITIES	Kitchenettes, free breakfast 24 hours
BUSINESS AMENITIES	Data port, 2 phone lines, business center

Hotel Information Chart (continued)

Four Points by Sheraton Manhattan Chelsea ★★★½
160 West 25th Street
New York, NY 10011
☎ 212-627-1888
TOLL-FREE 800-403-4176
www.starwoodhotels.com

ROOM QUALITY	83
COST ($ = $80)	$$$$–
LOCATION	Chelsea, Gramercy Park, and Midtown
DISCOUNTS	AAA, gov't
NO. OF ROOMS	158
ROOM SQUARE FEET	200
MEETING FACILITIES	•
POOL/SAUNA	
EXERCISE FACILITIES	•
WINDOW GLAZE	–
PARKING PER DAY	$25–$35
NEAREST SUBWAY	2 blocks
BAR	•
ON-SITE DINING	Asian Fusion
EXTRA AMENITIES	–
BUSINESS AMENITIES	Data port, 2 phone lines, fax access

Four Seasons Hotel New York ★★★★★
57 East 57th Street
New York, NY 10022
☎ 212-758-5700
TOLL-FREE 800-819-5053
www.fourseasons.com

ROOM QUALITY	97
COST ($ = $80)	$$$$$$$$$$$–
LOCATION	Chelsea, Gramercy Park, and Midtown
DISCOUNTS	–
NO. OF ROOMS	368
ROOM SQUARE FEET	600
MEETING FACILITIES	•
POOL/SAUNA	Whirlpool
EXERCISE FACILITIES	•
WINDOW GLAZE	Triple
PARKING PER DAY	$42
NEAREST SUBWAY	4 blocks
BAR	•
ON-SITE DINING	Contemporary American
EXTRA AMENITIES	Spa suite packages
BUSINESS AMENITIES	2 phone lines

The Franklin ★★★½
164 East 87th Street
New York, NY 10128
☎ 212-369-1000
TOLL-FREE 877-847-4444
www.franklinhotel.com

ROOM QUALITY	82
COST ($ = $80)	$$$+
LOCATION	Uptown
DISCOUNTS	–
NO. OF ROOMS	50+
ROOM SQUARE FEET	150
MEETING FACILITIES	–
POOL/SAUNA	–
EXERCISE FACILITIES	Privileges, charges vary
WINDOW GLAZE	Double
PARKING PER DAY	$25–$35
NEAREST SUBWAY	1 block
BAR	–
ON-SITE DINING	–
EXTRA AMENITIES	Free breakfast
BUSINESS AMENITIES	(Some rooms) 2 phone lines, data port; request ahead

Harbor House ★★★
One Hylan Boulevard
Staten Island, NY 10305
☎ 718-876-0056
www.nyharborhouse.com

ROOM QUALITY	68
COST ($ = $80)	$$
LOCATION	Staten Island
DISCOUNTS	Multiroom
NO. OF ROOMS	11
ROOM SQUARE FEET	260–285
MEETING FACILITIES	–
POOL/SAUNA	–
EXERCISE FACILITIES	–
WINDOW GLAZE	Single
PARKING PER DAY	Free
NEAREST SUBWAY	25 minutes
BAR	–
ON-SITE DINING	–
EXTRA AMENITIES	Free Continental breakfast
BUSINESS AMENITIES	–

Hilton New York ★★★★
1335 Avenue of the Americas
New York, NY 10019
☎ 212-586-7000
TOLL-FREE 800-HILTONS
www.hilton.com

ROOM QUALITY	89
COST ($ = $80)	$$$$
LOCATION	Chelsea, Gramercy Park, and Midtown
DISCOUNTS	AAA, AARP, gov't
NO. OF ROOMS	1,980
ROOM SQUARE FEET	320
MEETING FACILITIES	•
POOL/SAUNA	Sauna
EXERCISE FACILITIES	•
WINDOW GLAZE	Double
PARKING PER DAY	$46
NEAREST SUBWAY	3 blocks
BAR	•
ON-SITE DINING	American, International, Italian
EXTRA AMENITIES	Spa services
BUSINESS AMENITIES	Data port, 2 phone lines

Hilton Times Square ★★★★
234 West 42nd Street
New York, NY 10036
☎ 212-840-8222
TOLL-FREE 800-HILTONS
www.hilton.com

ROOM QUALITY	88
COST ($ = $80)	$$$+
LOCATION	Chelsea, Gramercy Park, and Midtown
DISCOUNTS	AAA, gov't
NO. OF ROOMS	460
ROOM SQUARE FEET	300
MEETING FACILITIES	•
POOL/SAUNA	Sauna
EXERCISE FACILITIES	•
WINDOW GLAZE	Single
PARKING PER DAY	$52
NEAREST SUBWAY	2½ blocks
BAR	•
ON-SITE DINING	American
EXTRA AMENITIES	Valet, safe
BUSINESS AMENITIES	Data port, laptop, 2 phone lines, business center

Gild Hall ★★★½
15 Gold Street
New York, NY 10038
☎ 212-232-7700
TOLL-FREE 800-268-0700
www.thompsonhotels.com

ROOM QUALITY	78
COST ($ = $80)	$$$
LOCATION	Downtown
DISCOUNTS	–
NO. OF ROOMS	126
ROOM SQUARE FEET	200
MEETING FACILITIES	–
POOL/SAUNA	–
EXERCISE FACILITIES	•
WINDOW GLAZE	–
PARKING PER DAY	$45–$55
NEAREST SUBWAY	1 block
BAR	•
ON-SITE DINING	–
EXTRA AMENITIES	–
BUSINESS AMENITIES	–

Gramercy Park Hotel ★★★★½
2 Lexington Avenue
New York, NY 10010
☎ 212-920-3300
TOLL-FREE 866-784-1300
www.gramercyparkhotel.com

ROOM QUALITY	90
COST ($ = $80)	$$$$$$$–
LOCATION	Chelsea, Gramercy Park, and Midtown
DISCOUNTS	–
NO. OF ROOMS	185
ROOM SQUARE FEET	275
MEETING FACILITIES	•
POOL/SAUNA	•
EXERCISE FACILITIES	•
WINDOW GLAZE	Single
PARKING PER DAY	$47 self, $55 valet
NEAREST SUBWAY	1 block
BAR	•
ON-SITE DINING	Chinese/Dim Sum
EXTRA AMENITIES	Access to private park, private roof club
BUSINESS AMENITIES	Data port, 2-line phone; high-speed Internet, laptop, mobile phone, fax on request

Grand Hyatt New York ★★★★
109 East 42nd Street at
Grand Central
New York, NY 10017
☎ 212-883-1234
TOLL-FREE 800-633-7313
grandnewyork.hyatt.com

ROOM QUALITY	86
COST ($ = $80)	$$$+
LOCATION	Chelsea, Gramercy Park, and Midtown
DISCOUNTS	AAA, seniors
NO. OF ROOMS	1,311
ROOM SQUARE FEET	210
MEETING FACILITIES	•
POOL/SAUNA	–
EXERCISE FACILITIES	•
WINDOW GLAZE	Single/double
PARKING PER DAY	$44–$65
NEAREST SUBWAY	½ block
BAR	•
ON-SITE DINING	American
EXTRA AMENITIES	Theater desk, fax
BUSINESS AMENITIES	Business center

Hotel Bedford ★★★★
118 East 40th Street
New York, NY 10016
☎ 212-697-4800
TOLL-FREE 800-221-6881
www.bedfordhotel.com

ROOM QUALITY	84
COST ($ = $80)	$$
LOCATION	Chelsea, Gramercy Park, and Midtown
DISCOUNTS	AAA
NO. OF ROOMS	135
ROOM SQUARE FEET	300
MEETING FACILITIES	–
POOL/SAUNA	–
EXERCISE FACILITIES	–
WINDOW GLAZE	Single/double
PARKING PER DAY	$22
NEAREST SUBWAY	1 block
BAR	•
ON-SITE DINING	American/Italian
EXTRA AMENITIES	Kitchenettes, free breakfast
BUSINESS AMENITIES	Data port

Hotel Chandler ★★★★½
12 East 31st Street
New York, NY 10016
☎ 212-889-6363
TOLL-FREE 866-MARQUIS
www.hotelchandler.com

ROOM QUALITY	90
COST ($ = $80)	$$$
LOCATION	Chelsea, Gramercy Park, and Midtown
DISCOUNTS	AAA, AARP
NO. OF ROOMS	124
ROOM SQUARE FEET	200
MEETING FACILITIES	•
POOL/SAUNA	Sauna
EXERCISE FACILITIES	•
WINDOW GLAZE	Double
PARKING PER DAY	$40–$45
NEAREST SUBWAY	½ block
BAR	–
ON-SITE DINING	–
EXTRA AMENITIES	–
BUSINESS AMENITIES	Data port, 2 phone lines, Internet

Hotel Elysée ★★★★
60 East 54th Street
New York, NY 10022
☎ 212-753-1066
TOLL-FREE 800-535-9733
www.elyseehotel.com

ROOM QUALITY	89
COST ($ = $80)	$$$
LOCATION	Chelsea, Gramercy Park, and Midtown
DISCOUNTS	–
NO. OF ROOMS	101
ROOM SQUARE FEET	300
MEETING FACILITIES	Small
POOL/SAUNA	–
EXERCISE FACILITIES	Privileges
WINDOW GLAZE	Double
PARKING PER DAY	$30–$35
NEAREST SUBWAY	1 block
BAR	•
ON-SITE DINING	Continental
EXTRA AMENITIES	Wine, snacks, free Continental breakfast
BUSINESS AMENITIES	Data port, 2 phone lines

Hotel Information Chart (continued)

	Hotel 41 at Times Square ★★★½ 206 West 41st Street New York, NY 10036 ☎ 212-703-8600 TOLL-FREE 877-847-4444 www.hotel41nyc.com
ROOM QUALITY	83
COST ($ = $80)	$$+
LOCATION	Chelsea, Gramercy Park, and Midtown
DISCOUNTS	—
NO. OF ROOMS	47
ROOM SQUARE FEET	100
MEETING FACILITIES	—
POOL/SAUNA	—
EXERCISE FACILITIES	Privileges, $10
WINDOW GLAZE	Double
PARKING PER DAY	$30
NEAREST SUBWAY	½ block
BAR	•
ON-SITE DINING	Bar food
EXTRA AMENITIES	Pet-friendly
BUSINESS AMENITIES	Internet

	Hotel Gansevoort ★★★★½ 18 Ninth Avenue New York, NY 10014 ☎ 212-206-6700 TOLL-FREE 877-726-7386 www.hotelgansevoort.com
ROOM QUALITY	92
COST ($ = $80)	$$$$$$–
LOCATION	Downtown
DISCOUNTS	—
NO. OF ROOMS	210
ROOM SQUARE FEET	300
MEETING FACILITIES	•
POOL/SAUNA	•
EXERCISE FACILITIES	•
WINDOW GLAZE	Double/Triple
PARKING PER DAY	—
NEAREST SUBWAY	1 block
BAR	•
ON-SITE DINING	Japanese
EXTRA AMENITIES	Roof garden, feather beds
BUSINESS AMENITIES	Internet, 2 phone lines

	Hotel Giraffe ★★★★ 365 Park Avenue South New York, NY 10010 ☎ 212-685-7700 TOLL-FREE 877-296-0009 www.hotelgiraffe.com
ROOM QUALITY	88
COST ($ = $80)	$$$+
LOCATION	Chelsea, Gramercy, and Midtown
DISCOUNTS	—
NO. OF ROOMS	72
ROOM SQUARE FEET	325
MEETING FACILITIES	•
POOL/SAUNA	—
EXERCISE FACILITIES	•
WINDOW GLAZE	Triple
PARKING PER DAY	$34
NEAREST SUBWAY	1 block
BAR	•
ON-SITE DINING	—
EXTRA AMENITIES	Wine/cheese, free breakfast, refreshments
BUSINESS AMENITIES	Internet, 2 phone lines

	The Hotel on Rivington ★★★★½ 107 Rivington Street New York, NY 10002 ☎ 212-475-2600 TOLL-FREE 800-915-1537 www.hotelonrivington.com
ROOM QUALITY	92
COST ($ = $80)	$$$$$
LOCATION	Downtown
DISCOUNTS	—
NO. OF ROOMS	111
ROOM SQUARE FEET	Average 380
MEETING FACILITIES	•
POOL/SAUNA	•
EXERCISE FACILITIES	•
WINDOW GLAZE	Single
PARKING PER DAY	$60
NEAREST SUBWAY	1 block
BAR	•
ON-SITE DINING	French cuisine
EXTRA AMENITIES	—
BUSINESS AMENITIES	Data port, 3 phone lines, fax

	Hotel Plaza Athénée ★★★★½ 37 East 64th Street New York, NY 10021 ☎ 212-734-9100 TOLL-FREE 800-447-8800 www.plaza-athenee.com
ROOM QUALITY	90
COST ($ = $80)	$$$$$$$$–
LOCATION	Uptown
DISCOUNTS	—
NO. OF ROOMS	149
ROOM SQUARE FEET	300
MEETING FACILITIES	•
POOL/SAUNA	—
EXERCISE FACILITIES	•
WINDOW GLAZE	Double
PARKING PER DAY	$54
NEAREST SUBWAY	7 blocks
BAR	•
ON-SITE DINING	Modern American
EXTRA AMENITIES	—
BUSINESS AMENITIES	Data port, 2 phone lines

	Hotel Reserve ★★★½ 51 Nassau Street New York, NY 10038 ☎ 212-227-3007 TOLL-FREE 888-693-5353 www.hotelreservenyc.com
ROOM QUALITY	80
COST ($ = $80)	$$+
LOCATION	Downtown
DISCOUNTS	—
NO. OF ROOMS	113
ROOM SQUARE FEET	200
MEETING FACILITIES	—
POOL/SAUNA	—
EXERCISE FACILITIES	•
WINDOW GLAZE	—
PARKING PER DAY	$35
NEAREST SUBWAY	2 blocks
BAR	•
ON-SITE DINING	American
EXTRA AMENITIES	Room service
BUSINESS AMENITIES	—

Hotel Mela ★★★★
120 44th Street
New York, NY 10036
☎ 212-710-7000
TOLL-FREE 877-452-MELA
www.hotelmela.com

ROOM QUALITY	84
COST ($ = $80)	$$$$
LOCATION	Chelsea, Gramercy Park, and Midtown
DISCOUNTS	AAA, gov't
NO. OF ROOMS	228
ROOM SQUARE FEET	220
MEETING FACILITIES	•
POOL/SAUNA	—
EXERCISE FACILITIES	•
WINDOW GLAZE	Double
PARKING PER DAY	$50
NEAREST SUBWAY	1 block
BAR	—
ON-SITE DINING	Eclectic, French bistro
EXTRA AMENITIES	Concierge, fitness studio
BUSINESS AMENITIES	2-line phone, Wi-Fi

Hotel Metro ★★★½
45 West 35th Street
New York, NY 10001
☎ 212-947-2500
TOLL-FREE 800-356-3870
www.hotelmetronyc.com

ROOM QUALITY	81
COST ($ = $80)	$$$$
LOCATION	Chelsea, Gramercy Park, and Midtown
DISCOUNTS	—
NO. OF ROOMS	179
ROOM SQUARE FEET	150
MEETING FACILITIES	•
POOL/SAUNA	—
EXERCISE FACILITIES	•
WINDOW GLAZE	Double
PARKING PER DAY	$27
NEAREST SUBWAY	1 block
BAR	•
ON-SITE DINING	American
EXTRA AMENITIES	Free Continental breakfast, beauty salon
BUSINESS AMENITIES	Data port

Hotel 91 ★★★½
91 East Broadway
New York, NY 10002
☎ 643-438-6600
www.thehotel91.com

ROOM QUALITY	78
COST ($ = $80)	$$$+
LOCATION	Downtown
DISCOUNTS	—
NO. OF ROOMS	70
ROOM SQUARE FEET	200
MEETING FACILITIES	—
POOL/SAUNA	—
EXERCISE FACILITIES	—
WINDOW GLAZE	—
PARKING PER DAY	$55–$65
NEAREST SUBWAY	3 blocks
BAR	—
ON-SITE DINING	—
EXTRA AMENITIES	—
BUSINESS AMENITIES	—

Hotel Thirty Thirty New York City
★★★½
30 East 30th Street
New York, NY 10016
☎ 212-689-1900
TOLL-FREE 800-804-4480
www.thirtythirty-nyc.com

ROOM QUALITY	78
COST ($ = $80)	$$$–
LOCATION	Chelsea, Gramercy Park, and Midtown
DISCOUNTS	AAA, gov't
NO. OF ROOMS	253
ROOM SQUARE FEET	200
MEETING FACILITIES	—
POOL/SAUNA	—
EXERCISE FACILITIES	—
WINDOW GLAZE	Single
PARKING PER DAY	$25
NEAREST SUBWAY	2 blocks
BAR	—
ON-SITE DINING	—
EXTRA AMENITIES	—
BUSINESS AMENITIES	2 phone lines

Hotel Roger Williams ★★★★
131 Madison Avenue
New York, NY 10016
☎ 212-448-7000
TOLL-FREE 888-448-7788
www.hotelrogerwilliams.com

ROOM QUALITY	86
COST ($ = $80)	$$$+
LOCATION	Chelsea, Gramercy Park, and Midtown
DISCOUNTS	AAA
NO. OF ROOMS	193
ROOM SQUARE FEET	300
MEETING FACILITIES	—
POOL/SAUNA	—
EXERCISE FACILITIES	—
WINDOW GLAZE	Single
PARKING PER DAY	$42
NEAREST SUBWAY	2 blocks
BAR	—
ON-SITE DINING	—
EXTRA AMENITIES	Free Continental breakfast, free dessert buffet
BUSINESS AMENITIES	Data port; some rooms have 2 phone lines

Hotel 31 ★★★½
120 East 31st Street
New York, NY 10016
☎ 212-685-3060
www.hotel31.com

ROOM QUALITY	75
COST ($ = $80)	$+
LOCATION	Chelsea, Gramercy Park, and Midtown
DISCOUNTS	Gov't
NO. OF ROOMS	60
ROOM SQUARE FEET	Very small
MEETING FACILITIES	—
POOL/SAUNA	—
EXERCISE FACILITIES	—
WINDOW GLAZE	—
PARKING PER DAY	$25
NEAREST SUBWAY	1½ blocks
BAR	—
ON-SITE DINING	—
EXTRA AMENITIES	Concierge
BUSINESS AMENITIES	Data port, DSL

Hotel Information Chart (continued)

Hotel 373 Fifth Avenue ★★★★

373 Fifth Avenue
New York, NY 10016
☎ 212-213-3388
TOLL-FREE 888-382-7111
www.hotel373.com

ROOM QUALITY	89
COST ($ = $80)	$$+
LOCATION	Chelsea, Gramercy Park, and Midtown
DISCOUNTS	AAA
NO. OF ROOMS	70
ROOM SQUARE FEET	220
MEETING FACILITIES	–
POOL/SAUNA	–
EXERCISE FACILITIES	–
WINDOW GLAZE	Double
PARKING PER DAY	$33–$43
NEAREST SUBWAY	1 block
BAR	–
ON-SITE DINING	On-site Starbucks
EXTRA AMENITIES	Concierge, marble bath, bathrobes, iPod docks
BUSINESS AMENITIES	Wi-Fi, high-speed Internet

Hotel Wales ★★★★

1295 Madison Avenue
New York, NY 10128
☎ 212-876-6000
TOLL-FREE 877-847-4444
www.waleshotel.com

ROOM QUALITY	85
COST ($ = $80)	$$$+
LOCATION	Uptown
DISCOUNTS	–
NO. OF ROOMS	88
ROOM SQUARE FEET	150
MEETING FACILITIES	–
POOL/SAUNA	Privileges
EXERCISE FACILITIES	Privileges + small on-site
WINDOW GLAZE	Double
PARKING PER DAY	$49, $10 per in/out fee
NEAREST SUBWAY	5 blocks
BAR	–
ON-SITE DINING	American, Italian
EXTRA AMENITIES	Harp music in lobby, spa, videos, CD, free breakfast
BUSINESS AMENITIES	–

Hudson Hotel ★★★★

356 West 58th Street
New York, NY 10019
☎ 212-554-6000
TOLL-FREE 800-444-4786
www.hudsonhotel.com

ROOM QUALITY	85
COST ($ = $80)	$$$$+
LOCATION	Chelsea, Gramercy, and Midtown
DISCOUNTS	–
NO. OF ROOMS	1,000
ROOM SQUARE FEET	150
MEETING FACILITIES	•
POOL/SAUNA	•
EXERCISE FACILITIES	•
WINDOW GLAZE	Single
PARKING PER DAY	$55
NEAREST SUBWAY	1 block
BAR	•
ON-SITE DINING	International comfort food
EXTRA AMENITIES	Valet, music
BUSINESS AMENITIES	Internet, 2 phone lines

InterContinental The Barclay New York ★★★★½

111 East 48th Street
New York, NY 10017
☎ 212-755-5900
TOLL-FREE 877-660-8550
www.ichotelsgroup.com

ROOM QUALITY	90
COST ($ = $80)	$$$$+
LOCATION	Chelsea, Gramercy Park, and Midtown
DISCOUNTS	–
NO. OF ROOMS	686
ROOM SQUARE FEET	210
MEETING FACILITIES	•
POOL/SAUNA	–
EXERCISE FACILITIES	•
WINDOW GLAZE	Single/double
PARKING PER DAY	$60
NEAREST SUBWAY	½ block
BAR	•
ON-SITE DINING	American
EXTRA AMENITIES	–
BUSINESS AMENITIES	Courier, Internet, business center

Iroquois New York ★★★★

49 West 44th Street
New York, NY 10036
☎ 212-840-3080
TOLL-FREE 800-332-7220
www.iroquoisny.com

ROOM QUALITY	86
COST ($ = $80)	$$$$$$
LOCATION	Chelsea, Gramercy Park, and Midtown
DISCOUNTS	–
NO. OF ROOMS	114
ROOM SQUARE FEET	275
MEETING FACILITIES	•
POOL/SAUNA	Sauna
EXERCISE FACILITIES	•
WINDOW GLAZE	Single
PARKING PER DAY	$30
NEAREST SUBWAY	2 blocks
BAR	•
ON-SITE DINING	French
EXTRA AMENITIES	Concierge, safe, CD
BUSINESS AMENITIES	Data port, 2 phone lines

Jolly Hotel Madison Towers ★★★½

22 East 38th Street
New York, NY 10016
☎ 212-802-0600
TOLL-FREE 800-221-2626
www.jollymadison.com

ROOM QUALITY	80
COST ($ = $80)	$$$$$–
LOCATION	Chelsea, Gramercy Park, and Midtown
DISCOUNTS	–
NO. OF ROOMS	215
ROOM SQUARE FEET	80
MEETING FACILITIES	•
POOL/SAUNA	•
EXERCISE FACILITIES	•
WINDOW GLAZE	Single
PARKING PER DAY	$42
NEAREST SUBWAY	½ block
BAR	•
ON-SITE DINING	American, Italian
EXTRA AMENITIES	–
BUSINESS AMENITIES	Data port, 2 phone lines, Internet

Inn at Irving Place ★★★★½
56 Irving Place
New York, NY 10003
☎ 212-533-4600
TOLL-FREE 800-685-1447
www.innatirving.com

ROOM QUALITY	94
COST ($ = $80)	$$$$$$–
LOCATION	Chelsea, Gramercy Park, and Midtown
DISCOUNTS	–
NO. OF ROOMS	12
ROOM SQUARE FEET	360
MEETING FACILITIES	•
POOL/SAUNA	–
EXERCISE FACILITIES	Privileges $20
WINDOW GLAZE	None
PARKING PER DAY	$33
NEAREST SUBWAY	3 blocks
BAR	•
ON-SITE DINING	Tea room, pub fare, cafe
EXTRA AMENITIES	Library, Continental breakfast
BUSINESS AMENITIES	Data port, 2 phone lines

Inn New York City ★★★★½
266 West 71st Street
New York, NY 10023
☎ 212-580-1900
www.innnewyorkcity.com

ROOM QUALITY	94
COST ($ = $80)	$$$$$$$+
LOCATION	Uptown
DISCOUNTS	–
NO. OF ROOMS	4
ROOM SQUARE FEET	800
MEETING FACILITIES	–
POOL/SAUNA	–
EXERCISE FACILITIES	–
WINDOW GLAZE	Single
PARKING PER DAY	Free
NEAREST SUBWAY	3 blocks
BAR	–
ON-SITE DINING	–
EXTRA AMENITIES	Kitchenette, fruit basket, wine, flowers
BUSINESS AMENITIES	–

Inn on 23rd Street ★★★½
131 West 23rd Street
New York, NY 10011
☎ 212-463-0330
TOLL-FREE 877-387-2323
www.innon23rd.com

ROOM QUALITY	76
COST ($ = $80)	$$$$$–
LOCATION	Chelsea, Gramercy Park, and Midtown
DISCOUNTS	–
NO. OF ROOMS	12
ROOM SQUARE FEET	215
MEETING FACILITIES	–
POOL/SAUNA	–
EXERCISE FACILITIES	–
WINDOW GLAZE	Double
PARKING PER DAY	$42
NEAREST SUBWAY	2 blocks
BAR	–
ON-SITE DINING	American Creative
EXTRA AMENITIES	Free breakfast
BUSINESS AMENITIES	Data port, 2 phone lines

Jumeirah Essex House ★★★★½
160 Central Park South
New York, NY 10019
☎ 212-247-0300
www.westin.com

ROOM QUALITY	95
COST ($ = $80)	$$$$$$$
LOCATION	Chelsea, Gramercy Park, and Midtown
DISCOUNTS	AAA, gov't
NO. OF ROOMS	515
ROOM SQUARE FEET	170
MEETING FACILITIES	•
POOL/SAUNA	Sauna, steam room
EXERCISE FACILITIES	•
WINDOW GLAZE	Double
PARKING PER DAY	$52
NEAREST SUBWAY	1 block
BAR	•
ON-SITE DINING	French, Nouveau, American
EXTRA AMENITIES	Spa
BUSINESS AMENITIES	Data port, 2 phone lines, fax

The Kitano New York ★★★★½
66 Park Avenue
New York, NY 10016
☎ 212-885-7100
TOLL-FREE 800-KITANO-NY
www.kitano.com

ROOM QUALITY	94
COST ($ = $80)	$$$$
LOCATION	Chelsea, Gramercy Park, and Midtown
DISCOUNTS	Gov't
NO. OF ROOMS	167
ROOM SQUARE FEET	460
MEETING FACILITIES	•
POOL/SAUNA	Privileges
EXERCISE FACILITIES	Privileges
WINDOW GLAZE	Double
PARKING PER DAY	$42
NEAREST SUBWAY	4 blocks
BAR	•
ON-SITE DINING	American, Japanese
EXTRA AMENITIES	Safe
BUSINESS AMENITIES	Data port, 2 phone lines, fax

La Quinta Inn Manhattan ★★★★½
17 West 32nd Street
New York, NY 10001
☎ 212-736-1600
TOLL-FREE 866-725-1661
www.lq.com

ROOM QUALITY	90
COST ($ = $80)	$$$$+
LOCATION	Chelsea, Gramercy Park, and Midtown
DISCOUNTS	AAA, AARP, gov't
NO. OF ROOMS	182
ROOM SQUARE FEET	160
MEETING FACILITIES	•
POOL/SAUNA	–
EXERCISE FACILITIES	–
WINDOW GLAZE	Single
PARKING PER DAY	Self $30
NEAREST SUBWAY	½ block
BAR	•
ON-SITE DINING	American, Chinese
EXTRA AMENITIES	Continental breakfast
BUSINESS AMENITIES	Data port

Hotel Information Chart (continued)

Larchmont Hotel ★★★
27 West 11th Street
New York, NY 10011
☎ 212-989-9333
www.larchmonthotel.com

ROOM QUALITY	70
COST ($ = $80)	$+
LOCATION	Downtown
DISCOUNTS	—
NO. OF ROOMS	65
ROOM SQUARE FEET	"small"
MEETING FACILITIES	—
POOL/SAUNA	—
EXERCISE FACILITIES	—
WINDOW GLAZE	Single
PARKING PER DAY	$40 public
NEAREST SUBWAY	4 blocks
BAR	—
ON-SITE DINING	Free Continental breakfast
EXTRA AMENITIES	Shared baths, robes, slippers, ceiling fans
BUSINESS AMENITIES	—

Le Parker Meridien New York ★★★★½
119 West 57th Street
New York, NY 10019
☎ 212-245-5000
TOLL-FREE 800-543-4300
www.parkermeridien.com

ROOM QUALITY	94
COST ($ = $80)	$$$$$
LOCATION	Chelsea, Gramercy Park, and Midtown
DISCOUNTS	AAA, gov't, seniors
NO. OF ROOMS	698
ROOM SQUARE FEET	312
MEETING FACILITIES	•
POOL/SAUNA	Pool
EXERCISE FACILITIES	•
WINDOW GLAZE	Double
PARKING PER DAY	$50, no in/out privileges
NEAREST SUBWAY	½ block
BAR	•
ON-SITE DINING	American/Continental, pub fare
EXTRA AMENITIES	Track, health club
BUSINESS AMENITIES	Data port, 2 phone lines, fax on request

Le Refuge Inn ★★★½
586 City Island Avenue
New York, NY 10464
☎ 718-885-2478
www.lerefugeinn.com

ROOM QUALITY	80
COST ($ = $80)	$$–
LOCATION	Bronx
DISCOUNTS	—
NO. OF ROOMS	7
ROOM SQUARE FEET	—
MEETING FACILITIES	—
POOL/SAUNA	—
EXERCISE FACILITIES	—
WINDOW GLAZE	Double
PARKING PER DAY	Free
NEAREST SUBWAY	—
BAR	—
ON-SITE DINING	Country French
EXTRA AMENITIES	Continental breakfast
BUSINESS AMENITIES	—

The London NYC ★★★★½
151 West 54th Street
New York, NY 10019
☎ 212-468-8856
TOLL-FREE 866-690-2029
www.thelondonnyc.com

ROOM QUALITY	93
COST ($ = $80)	$$$$$$+
LOCATION	Chelsea, Gramercy Park, and Midtown
DISCOUNTS	—
NO. OF ROOMS	561
ROOM SQUARE FEET	500
MEETING FACILITIES	•
POOL/SAUNA	—
EXERCISE FACILITIES	•
WINDOW GLAZE	Double
PARKING PER DAY	$55–$65
NEAREST SUBWAY	3 blocks
BAR	•
ON-SITE DINING	French/French-Asian
EXTRA AMENITIES	Concierge, bath environments
BUSINESS AMENITIES	High-speed Internet, iPod docking stations, and LG flat-screen LCD TVs

The Lowell ★★★★½
28 East 63rd Street
New York, NY 10021
☎ 212-838-1400
TOLL-FREE 800-221-4444
www.lowellhotel.com

ROOM QUALITY	95
COST ($ = $80)	$$$$$$$–
LOCATION	Uptown
DISCOUNTS	AAA
NO. OF ROOMS	70
ROOM SQUARE FEET	350
MEETING FACILITIES	Small
POOL/SAUNA	—
EXERCISE FACILITIES	•
WINDOW GLAZE	Double
PARKING PER DAY	$50–$65
NEAREST SUBWAY	2 blocks
BAR	•
ON-SITE DINING	Tea room, New American
EXTRA AMENITIES	—
BUSINESS AMENITIES	Data port, 2 phone lines, fax

Lucerne Hotel ★★★
201 West 79th Street
New York, NY 10024
☎ 212-875-1000
TOLL-FREE 800-492-8122
www.thelucernehotel.com

ROOM QUALITY	74
COST ($ = $80)	$$$$
LOCATION	Uptown
DISCOUNTS	AAA, AARP, gov't blacked out
NO. OF ROOMS	184
ROOM SQUARE FEET	204
MEETING FACILITIES	•
POOL/SAUNA	—
EXERCISE FACILITIES	Privileges
WINDOW GLAZE	Double
PARKING PER DAY	$30
NEAREST SUBWAY	1 block
BAR	•
ON-SITE DINING	Bar and grill, French, Mediterranean
EXTRA AMENITIES	Continental breakfast
BUSINESS AMENITIES	Data port, 2 phone lines, fax in suites

Library Hotel ★★★★
299 Madison Avenue
New York, NY 10017
☎ 212-983-4500
TOLL-FREE 877-793-READ
www.libraryhotel.com

ROOM QUALITY	87
COST ($ = $80)	$$$$$
LOCATION	Chelsea, Gramercy Park, and Midtown
DISCOUNTS	Gov't
NO. OF ROOMS	60
ROOM SQUARE FEET	200
MEETING FACILITIES	•
POOL/SAUNA	–
EXERCISE FACILITIES	Privileges
WINDOW GLAZE	Single
PARKING PER DAY	$30
NEAREST SUBWAY	1 block
BAR	–
ON-SITE DINING	American Bistro
EXTRA AMENITIES	Continental breakfast, wine, CD
BUSINESS AMENITIES	Data port, business center, 2 phone lines

Loews Regency ★★★★½
540 Park Avenue
New York, NY 10021
☎ 212-759-4100
TOLL-FREE 800-233-2356
www.loewshotels.com

ROOM QUALITY	93
COST ($ = $80)	$$$$$$
LOCATION	Uptown
DISCOUNTS	AAA, AARP, gov't
NO. OF ROOMS	362
ROOM SQUARE FEET	220
MEETING FACILITIES	•
POOL/SAUNA	Sauna, whirlpool
EXERCISE FACILITIES	•
WINDOW GLAZE	Double
PARKING PER DAY	$60 no in/out privileges
NEAREST SUBWAY	2 blocks
BAR	•
ON-SITE DINING	Lounge, French-American
EXTRA AMENITIES	Hair salon, concierge, massage
BUSINESS AMENITIES	Data port, 2 phone lines, fax

The Lombardy ★★★★½
111 East 56th Street
New York, NY 10022
☎ 212-753-8600
TOLL-FREE 800-223-5254
www.lombardyhotel.com

ROOM QUALITY	93
COST ($ = $80)	$$$$+
LOCATION	Chelsea, Gramercy Park, and Midtown
DISCOUNTS	–
NO. OF ROOMS	115
ROOM SQUARE FEET	470
MEETING FACILITIES	In restaurant
POOL/SAUNA	–
EXERCISE FACILITIES	•
WINDOW GLAZE	Double
PARKING PER DAY	$40
NEAREST SUBWAY	3 blocks
BAR	•
ON-SITE DINING	French
EXTRA AMENITIES	Kitchens, laundry, breakfast
BUSINESS AMENITIES	Data port

Mandarin Oriental, New York ★★★★★
80 Columbus Circle
New York, NY 10023
☎ 212-805-8800
TOLL-FREE 800-526-6566
www.mandarinoriental.com

ROOM QUALITY	98
COST ($ = $80)	$$$$$$$$$$$+
LOCATION	Uptown
DISCOUNTS	–
NO. OF ROOMS	248
ROOM SQUARE FEET	400
MEETING FACILITIES	•
POOL/SAUNA	Pool, sauna
EXERCISE FACILITIES	•
WINDOW GLAZE	Double
PARKING PER DAY	$65 no in/out privileges
NEAREST SUBWAY	½ block
BAR	•
ON-SITE DINING	Contemporary with Asian Influence
EXTRA AMENITIES	Bathrobes
BUSINESS AMENITIES	Computer, Internet, cell phone rentals

The Manhattan at Times Square ★★★★½
790 Seventh Avenue
New York, NY 10019
☎ 212-581-3300

ROOM QUALITY	92
COST ($ = $80)	$$$$+
LOCATION	Chelsea, Gramercy Park, and Midtown
DISCOUNTS	AAA, AARP, gov't
NO. OF ROOMS	665
ROOM SQUARE FEET	180
MEETING FACILITIES	•
POOL/SAUNA	Pool
EXERCISE FACILITIES	•
WINDOW GLAZE	Double
PARKING PER DAY	$42
NEAREST SUBWAY	2 blocks
BAR	•
ON-SITE DINING	Bistro
EXTRA AMENITIES	Convention center
BUSINESS AMENITIES	Data port, 2 phone lines, fax in some rooms

The Mansfield ★★★★
12 West 44th Street
New York, NY 10036
☎ 212-277-8700
TOLL-FREE 877-847-4444
www.mansfieldhotel.com

ROOM QUALITY	87
COST ($ = $80)	$$$$+
LOCATION	Chelsea, Gramercy Park, and Midtown
DISCOUNTS	–
NO. OF ROOMS	126
ROOM SQUARE FEET	150
MEETING FACILITIES	Small
POOL/SAUNA	–
EXERCISE FACILITIES	•
WINDOW GLAZE	Double
PARKING PER DAY	$30–$50
NEAREST SUBWAY	2 blocks
BAR	–
ON-SITE DINING	–
EXTRA AMENITIES	–
BUSINESS AMENITIES	Data port, access to copier and fax

Hotel Information Chart (continued)

Maritime Hotel ★★★★	
363 West 16th Street	
New York, NY 10011	
☎ 212-242-4300	
TOLL-FREE 866-601-9330	
www.themaritimehotel.com	
ROOM QUALITY	87
COST ($ = $80)	$$$$$–
LOCATION	Chelsea, Gramercy Park, and Midtown
DISCOUNTS	–
NO. OF ROOMS	125
ROOM SQUARE FEET	300
MEETING FACILITIES	•
POOL/SAUNA	•
EXERCISE FACILITIES	•
WINDOW GLAZE	Double
PARKING PER DAY	$25–$50
NEAREST SUBWAY	1 block
BAR	•
ON-SITE DINING	Italian, Japanese
EXTRA AMENITIES	Banquet room
BUSINESS AMENITIES	Data port, 2 phone lines, Internet

The Mark ★★★★½	
Madison Avenue at 77th Street	
New York, NY 10075	
☎ 212-744-4300	
TOLL-FREE 866-744-4300	
www.themarkhotel.com	
ROOM QUALITY	95
COST ($ = $80)	$$$$$$$$+
LOCATION	Uptown
DISCOUNTS	–
NO. OF ROOMS	–
ROOM SQUARE FEET	400
MEETING FACILITIES	–
POOL/SAUNA	–
EXERCISE FACILITIES	–
WINDOW GLAZE	–
PARKING PER DAY	$55
NEAREST SUBWAY	2 blocks
BAR	•
ON-SITE DINING	–
EXTRA AMENITIES	–
BUSINESS AMENITIES	–

The Mercer ★★★★½	
147 Mercer Street	
New York, NY 10012	
☎ 212-966-6060	
TOLL-FREE 888-918-6060	
www.mercerhotel.com	
ROOM QUALITY	93
COST ($ = $80)	$$$$$$$+
LOCATION	Downtown
DISCOUNTS	–
NO. OF ROOMS	75
ROOM SQUARE FEET	320
MEETING FACILITIES	–
POOL/SAUNA	–
EXERCISE FACILITIES	Privileges
WINDOW GLAZE	Single
PARKING PER DAY	$50
NEAREST SUBWAY	1 block
BAR	•
ON-SITE DINING	American, Provençal
EXTRA AMENITIES	Valet, CD, safe
BUSINESS AMENITIES	Data port, 2 phone lines, fax, computer

Morgans ★★★★½	
237 Madison Avenue	
New York, NY 10016	
☎ 212-686-0300	
TOLL-FREE 800-334-3408	
www.morganshotelgroup.com	
ROOM QUALITY	90
COST ($ = $80)	$$$$$+
LOCATION	Chelsea, Gramercy Park, and Midtown
DISCOUNTS	Gov't
NO. OF ROOMS	113
ROOM SQUARE FEET	220 standard
MEETING FACILITIES	•
POOL/SAUNA	–
EXERCISE FACILITIES	Privileges, free
WINDOW GLAZE	Double
PARKING PER DAY	$50, no in/out privileges
NEAREST SUBWAY	4 blocks
BAR	•
ON-SITE DINING	Asian-Cuban
EXTRA AMENITIES	Free breakfast
BUSINESS AMENITIES	Data port, 2 phone lines

The Muse Hotel ★★★★½	
130 West 46th Street	
New York, NY 10036	
☎ 212-485-2400	
TOLL-FREE 877-692-6873	
www.themusehotel.com	
ROOM QUALITY	92
COST ($ = $80)	$$$$$+
LOCATION	Chelsea, Gramercy Park, and Midtown
DISCOUNTS	AAA
NO. OF ROOMS	200
ROOM SQUARE FEET	350
MEETING FACILITIES	•
POOL/SAUNA	–
EXERCISE FACILITIES	•
WINDOW GLAZE	Single
PARKING PER DAY	$50
NEAREST SUBWAY	2 blocks
BAR	•
ON-SITE DINING	American
EXTRA AMENITIES	Valet, safe, refreshments
BUSINESS AMENITIES	Internet, 2 phone lines

New York Marriott Marquis ★★★★	
1535 Broadway	
New York, NY 10036	
☎ 212-398-1900	
TOLL-FREE 800-228-9290	
www.marriott.com	
ROOM QUALITY	84
COST ($ = $80)	$$$$$$+
LOCATION	Chelsea, Gramercy Park, and Midtown
DISCOUNTS	Gov't, military
NO. OF ROOMS	1,949
ROOM SQUARE FEET	570
MEETING FACILITIES	•
POOL/SAUNA	Sauna, whirlpool
EXERCISE FACILITIES	•
WINDOW GLAZE	Double
PARKING PER DAY	$55
NEAREST SUBWAY	3 blocks
BAR	•
ON-SITE DINING	Continental, steak house, American, deli
EXTRA AMENITIES	Hair salon, Barber
BUSINESS AMENITIES	–

The Michelangelo ★★★★½
152 West 51st Street
New York, NY 10019
☎ 212-765-1900
TOLL-FREE 800-237-0990
www.michelangelohotel.com

ROOM QUALITY	92
COST ($ = $80)	$$$$$$$–
LOCATION	Chelsea, Gramercy Park, and Midtown
DISCOUNTS	–
NO. OF ROOMS	179
ROOM SQUARE FEET	Average 475 (350–1,200)
MEETING FACILITIES	•
POOL/SAUNA	–
EXERCISE FACILITIES	•
WINDOW GLAZE	Double
PARKING PER DAY	$42
NEAREST SUBWAY	2 blocks
BAR	•
ON-SITE DINING	Italian
EXTRA AMENITIES	Free breakfast
BUSINESS AMENITIES	Data port, 2 phone lines, fax, copy, print

Millennium Broadway Hotel ★★★★½
145 West 44th Street
New York, NY 10036
☎ 212-768-4400
TOLL-FREE 800-622-5569
www.millennium-hotels.com

ROOM QUALITY	92
COST ($ = $80)	$$$+
LOCATION	Chelsea, Gramercy Park, and Midtown
DISCOUNTS	AAA, gov't blacked out
NO. OF ROOMS	625
ROOM SQUARE FEET	150
MEETING FACILITIES	•
POOL/SAUNA	Steam room
EXERCISE FACILITIES	•
WINDOW GLAZE	Double
PARKING PER DAY	$50
NEAREST SUBWAY	2 blocks
BAR	•
ON-SITE DINING	New American
EXTRA AMENITIES	–
BUSINESS AMENITIES	Data port, 2 phone lines

Millennium UN Plaza Hotel New York ★★★★½
1 United Nations Plaza
New York, NY 10017
☎ 212-758-1234
TOLL-FREE 866-866-8086
www.millenniumhotels.com

ROOM QUALITY	90
COST ($ = $80)	$$$$+
LOCATION	Chelsea, Gramercy Park, and Midtown
DISCOUNTS	AAA blacked out
NO. OF ROOMS	427
ROOM SQUARE FEET	240
MEETING FACILITIES	•
POOL/SAUNA	Pool, sauna, whirlpool
EXERCISE FACILITIES	•
WINDOW GLAZE	Double
PARKING PER DAY	$28–$35
NEAREST SUBWAY	4 blocks
BAR	•
ON-SITE DINING	New American
EXTRA AMENITIES	Harpist in lobby
BUSINESS AMENITIES	Data port, 2 phone lines, fax

New York Palace ★★★★½
455 Madison Avenue
New York, NY 10022
☎ 212-888-7000
TOLL-FREE 800-NYPALACE
www.newyorkpalace.com

ROOM QUALITY	94
COST ($ = $80)	$$$$$$+
LOCATION	Chelsea, Gramercy Park, and Midtown
DISCOUNTS	AAA, gov't blacked out
NO. OF ROOMS	892
ROOM SQUARE FEET	320
MEETING FACILITIES	•
POOL/SAUNA	Steam room
EXERCISE FACILITIES	•
WINDOW GLAZE	Double
PARKING PER DAY	$60
NEAREST SUBWAY	2 blocks
BAR	•
ON-SITE DINING	Modern American, bistro-style
EXTRA AMENITIES	Spa services
BUSINESS AMENITIES	Data port, 2 phone lines, fax

Novotel New York Times Square ★★★★
226 West 52nd Street
New York, NY 10019
☎ 212-315-0100
TOLL-FREE 800-221-3185
www.novotel.com

ROOM QUALITY	88
COST ($ = $80)	$$$+
LOCATION	Chelsea, Gramercy Park, and Midtown
DISCOUNTS	AAA, gov't
NO. OF ROOMS	480
ROOM SQUARE FEET	276
MEETING FACILITIES	•
POOL/SAUNA	–
EXERCISE FACILITIES	•
WINDOW GLAZE	Double
PARKING PER DAY	$30
NEAREST SUBWAY	1 block
BAR	•
ON-SITE DINING	French
EXTRA AMENITIES	Live music in lounge weeknights
BUSINESS AMENITIES	Data port, 24-hour business center

Omni Berkshire Place ★★★★½
21 East 52nd Street
New York, NY 10022
☎ 212-753-5800
TOLL-FREE 800-843-6664
www.omnihotels.com

ROOM QUALITY	92
COST ($ = $80)	$$$$$
LOCATION	Chelsea, Gramercy Park, and Midtown
DISCOUNTS	AAA, gov't
NO. OF ROOMS	396
ROOM SQUARE FEET	300
MEETING FACILITIES	•
POOL/SAUNA	–
EXERCISE FACILITIES	•
WINDOW GLAZE	Triple
PARKING PER DAY	$35–$45
NEAREST SUBWAY	1 block
BAR	•
ON-SITE DINING	Asian-Mediterranean
EXTRA AMENITIES	Sundeck, electronic controls suite
BUSINESS AMENITIES	Data port, 2 phone lines, fax

Hotel Information Chart (continued)

On the Ave ★★★½
2178 West 77th Street
New York, NY 10023
☎ 212-362-1100
TOLL-FREE 800-509-7598
www.ontheave-nyc.com

ROOM QUALITY	80
COST ($ = $80)	$$$$+
LOCATION	Uptown
DISCOUNTS	AAA
NO. OF ROOMS	196
ROOM SQUARE FEET	375
MEETING FACILITIES	•
POOL/SAUNA	Sauna privileges
EXERCISE FACILITIES	Privileges, $20, passes available
WINDOW GLAZE	Double
PARKING PER DAY	$50
NEAREST SUBWAY	2 blocks
BAR	•
ON-SITE DINING	French comfort, Malaysian
EXTRA AMENITIES	Hair dryers, irons
BUSINESS AMENITIES	Data port, 2 phone lines, fax

The Paramount Hotel ★★★★
235 West 46th Street
New York, NY 10036
☎ 212-764-5500
TOLL-FREE 800-225-7474
www.nycparamount.com

ROOM QUALITY	88
COST ($ = $80)	$$$$+
LOCATION	Chelsea, Gramercy Park, and Midtown
DISCOUNTS	AAA, gov't
NO. OF ROOMS	601
ROOM SQUARE FEET	150
MEETING FACILITIES	•
POOL/SAUNA	–
EXERCISE FACILITIES	•
WINDOW GLAZE	Double
PARKING PER DAY	$50
NEAREST SUBWAY	2 blocks
BAR	•
ON-SITE DINING	Continental
EXTRA AMENITIES	
BUSINESS AMENITIES	Data ports, 2 phone lines, 24-hour business center

The Peninsula ★★★★½
700 Fifth Avenue
New York, NY 10019
☎ 212-956-2888
TOLL-FREE 800-262-9467
www.peninsula.com

ROOM QUALITY	93
COST ($ = $80)	$$$$$$$$+
LOCATION	Chelsea, Gramercy, and Midtown
DISCOUNTS	–
NO. OF ROOMS	239
ROOM SQUARE FEET	350
MEETING FACILITIES	•
POOL/SAUNA	•
EXERCISE FACILITIES	•
WINDOW GLAZE	Triple
PARKING PER DAY	$60
NEAREST SUBWAY	3 blocks
BAR	•
ON-SITE DINING	American, Chinese
EXTRA AMENITIES	Marble baths, robes, minibar, spa
BUSINESS AMENITIES	Data port, 2 phone lines, in-room fax

Renaissance New York Times Square Hotel ★★★★½
714 Seventh Avenue
New York, NY 10036
☎ 212-765-7676
TOLL-FREE 800-236-2427
www.marriott.com

ROOM QUALITY	95
COST ($ = $80)	$$$$$$–
LOCATION	Chelsea, Gramercy Park, and Midtown
DISCOUNTS	AAA, AARP blacked out, senior
NO. OF ROOMS	310
ROOM SQUARE FEET	340
MEETING FACILITIES	•
POOL/SAUNA	–
EXERCISE FACILITIES	•
WINDOW GLAZE	Double
PARKING PER DAY	$54
NEAREST SUBWAY	Beneath hotel
BAR	•
ON-SITE DINING	American
EXTRA AMENITIES	–
BUSINESS AMENITIES	Data port, 2 phone lines

Renaissance New York Hotel 57 ★★★½
130 East 57th Street
New York, NY 10022
☎ 212-753-8841
TOLL-FREE 1-866-240-8604
www.hotel57.com or
www.marriott.com

ROOM QUALITY	75
COST ($ = $80)	$$$$–
LOCATION	Chelsea, Gramercy Park, and Midtown
DISCOUNTS	–
NO. OF ROOMS	200
ROOM SQUARE FEET	100
MEETING FACILITIES	–
POOL/SAUNA	–
EXERCISE FACILITIES	–
WINDOW GLAZE	–
PARKING PER DAY	$55–$65
NEAREST SUBWAY	2 blocks
BAR	Open for dinner
ON-SITE DINING	Continental breakfast
EXTRA AMENITIES	–
BUSINESS AMENITIES	Data port, 2 phone lines

Ritz-Carlton New York, Battery Park ★★★★★
2 West Street
New York, NY 10004
☎ 212-344-0800
TOLL-FREE 800-241-3333
www.ritzcarlton.com

ROOM QUALITY	97
COST ($ = $80)	$$$$$$+
LOCATION	Downtown
DISCOUNTS	AAA
NO. OF ROOMS	298
ROOM SQUARE FEET	425
MEETING FACILITIES	•
POOL/SAUNA	Spa
EXERCISE FACILITIES	•
WINDOW GLAZE	Single/double
PARKING PER DAY	$60
NEAREST SUBWAY	½ block
BAR	•
ON-SITE DINING	Modern American
EXTRA AMENITIES	Telescope
BUSINESS AMENITIES	Data port, 2 phone lines

The Pierre ★★★★★
2 East 61st Street
New York, NY 10065
☎ 212-838-8000
www.tajhotels.com

ROOM QUALITY	97
COST ($ = $80)	$$$$$$+
LOCATION	Uptown
DISCOUNTS	–
NO. OF ROOMS	189
ROOM SQUARE FEET	200
MEETING FACILITIES	•
POOL/SAUNA	
EXERCISE FACILITIES	•
WINDOW GLAZE	–
PARKING PER DAY	–
NEAREST SUBWAY	1 block
BAR	•
ON-SITE DINING	–
EXTRA AMENITIES	–
BUSINESS AMENITIES	–

The Pod Hotel   ★★★
230 East 51st Street
New York, NY 10022
☎ 212-355-0300
TOLL-FREE 800-742-5945
www.thepodhotel.com

ROOM QUALITY	72
COST ($ = $80)	$$$$–
LOCATION	Chelsea, Gramercy Park, and Midtown
DISCOUNTS	–
NO. OF ROOMS	350
ROOM SQUARE FEET	100
MEETING FACILITIES	–
POOL/SAUNA	–
EXERCISE FACILITIES	–
WINDOW GLAZE	Double
PARKING PER DAY	$35–$45
NEAREST SUBWAY	2 blocks
BAR	•
ON-SITE DINING	Modern, French bistro
EXTRA AMENITIES	Concierge, lobby lounge, rooftop garden bar
BUSINESS AMENITIES	Business center at front desk, data ports

Red Roof Inn Manhattan
★★★½
6 West 32nd Street
New York, NY 10001
☎ 212-643-7100
TOLL-FREE 800-REDROOF
www.redroof.com

ROOM QUALITY	83
COST ($ = $80)	$$$$+
LOCATION	Chelsea, Gramercy Park, and Midtown
DISCOUNTS	AAA
NO. OF ROOMS	171
ROOM SQUARE FEET	–
MEETING FACILITIES	•
POOL/SAUNA	–
EXERCISE FACILITIES	•
WINDOW GLAZE	Double
PARKING PER DAY	$26–$42
NEAREST SUBWAY	1 block
BAR	•
ON-SITE DINING	
EXTRA AMENITIES	Concierge, free breakfast, paper
BUSINESS AMENITIES	2 phone lines

Ritz-Carlton New York, Central Park   ★★★★½
50 Central Park South
New York, NY 10017
☎ 212-308-9100
TOLL-FREE 800-241-3333
www.ritzcarlton.com

ROOM QUALITY	94
COST ($ = $80)	$$$$$$$$$$–
LOCATION	Chelsea, Gramercy Park, and Midtown
DISCOUNTS	AAA, AARP
NO. OF ROOMS	259
ROOM SQUARE FEET	425
MEETING FACILITIES	•
POOL/SAUNA	Spa
EXERCISE FACILITIES	–
WINDOW GLAZE	Double
PARKING PER DAY	$60
NEAREST SUBWAY	½ block
BAR	•
ON-SITE DINING	French/American
EXTRA AMENITIES	Telescope, robes, library
BUSINESS AMENITIES	Internet, 2 phone lines

The Roger Smith   ★★★½
501 Lexington Avenue
New York, NY 10017
☎ 212-755-1400
TOLL-FREE 800-445-0277
www.rogersmith.com

ROOM QUALITY	81
COST ($ = $80)	$$$$$
LOCATION	Chelsea, Gramercy Park, and Midtown
DISCOUNTS	Gov't, AAA
NO. OF ROOMS	136
ROOM SQUARE FEET	204
MEETING FACILITIES	•
POOL/SAUNA	Sauna privileges
EXERCISE FACILITIES	Privileges, $25
WINDOW GLAZE	Double
PARKING PER DAY	$40
NEAREST SUBWAY	2 blocks
BAR	•
ON-SITE DINING	New American
EXTRA AMENITIES	Free Continental breakfast, gallery, videos
BUSINESS AMENITIES	Data port, computer available

Room Mate Grace   ★★★★
125 West 45th Street
New York, NY 10036
☎ 212-354-2323
www.room-matehotels.com

ROOM QUALITY	86
COST ($ = $80)	$$$$–
LOCATION	Chelsea, Gramercy Park, and Midtown
DISCOUNTS	Gov't
NO. OF ROOMS	139
ROOM SQUARE FEET	200
MEETING FACILITIES	–
POOL/SAUNA	•
EXERCISE FACILITIES	•
WINDOW GLAZE	–
PARKING PER DAY	$27
NEAREST SUBWAY	1 block
BAR	•
ON-SITE DINING	American
EXTRA AMENITIES	Continental breakfast
BUSINESS AMENITIES	Data port, 2 phone lines

Hotel Information Chart (continued)

Roosevelt Hotel ★★★½	
45 East 45th Street	
New York, NY 10017	
☎ 212-661-9600	
TOLL-FREE 888-TEDDY-NY	
www.theroosevelthotel.com	
ROOM QUALITY	80
COST ($ = $80)	$$$$$$–
LOCATION	Chelsea, Gramercy Park, and Midtown
DISCOUNTS	AAA, gov't
NO. OF ROOMS	1,015
ROOM SQUARE FEET	200
MEETING FACILITIES	•
POOL/SAUNA	–
EXERCISE FACILITIES	–
WINDOW GLAZE	Single/double
PARKING PER DAY	$50
NEAREST SUBWAY	1 block
BAR	•
ON-SITE DINING	American
EXTRA AMENITIES	Concierge
BUSINESS AMENITIES	2 phone lines, fax, modem

The Royalton ★★★★½	
44 West 44th Street	
New York, NY 10036	
☎ 212-869-4400	
TOLL-FREE 800-635-9013	
www.royaltonhotel.com	
ROOM QUALITY	86
COST ($ = $80)	$$$$$
LOCATION	Chelsea, Gramercy Park, and Midtown
DISCOUNTS	Gov't
NO. OF ROOMS	168
ROOM SQUARE FEET	250
MEETING FACILITIES	–
POOL/SAUNA	–
EXERCISE FACILITIES	•
WINDOW GLAZE	Double
PARKING PER DAY	$60
NEAREST SUBWAY	4 blocks
BAR	•.
ON-SITE DINING	American
EXTRA AMENITIES	Concierge
BUSINESS AMENITIES	Data port, 2 phone lines

San Carlos ★★★★½	
150 East 50th Street	
New York, NY 10022	
☎ 212-755-1800	
TOLL-FREE 800-722-2012	
www.sancarloshotel.com	
ROOM QUALITY	90
COST ($ = $80)	$$$$$$–
LOCATION	Chelsea, Gramercy Park, and Midtown
DISCOUNTS	–
NO. OF ROOMS	147
ROOM SQUARE FEET	350
MEETING FACILITIES	•
POOL/SAUNA	–
EXERCISE FACILITIES	•
WINDOW GLAZE	Double
PARKING PER DAY	$40
NEAREST SUBWAY	1 block
BAR	•
ON-SITE DINING	Indian American
EXTRA AMENITIES	Concierge, Continental breakfast, laundry service
BUSINESS AMENITIES	Data port, 2 phone lines, DSL, fax access

The Shoreham ★★★★	
33 West 55th Street	
New York, NY 10019	
☎ 212-247-6700	
TOLL-FREE 877-847-4444	
www.boutiquehg.com	
ROOM QUALITY	88
COST ($ = $80)	$$$$–
LOCATION	Chelsea, Gramercy Park, and Midtown
DISCOUNTS	–
NO. OF ROOMS	177
ROOM SQUARE FEET	250
MEETING FACILITIES	–
POOL/SAUNA	Privileges
EXERCISE FACILITIES	Privileges, free
WINDOW GLAZE	Single
PARKING PER DAY	$45–$55
NEAREST SUBWAY	1 block
BAR	•
ON-SITE DINING	French
EXTRA AMENITIES	–
BUSINESS AMENITIES	Data port, 2 phone lines

6 Columbus ★★★★½	
6 Columbus Circle	
New York, NY 10019	
☎ 212-204-3000	
www.sixcolumbus.com	
ROOM QUALITY	91
COST ($ = $80)	$$$
LOCATION	Uptown
DISCOUNTS	–
NO. OF ROOMS	88
ROOM SQUARE FEET	175
MEETING FACILITIES	–
POOL/SAUNA	–
EXERCISE FACILITIES	–
WINDOW GLAZE	Single
PARKING PER DAY	$45
NEAREST SUBWAY	1 block
BAR	•
ON-SITE DINING	Japanese/Sushi
EXTRA AMENITIES	Concierge, rooftop members lounge
BUSINESS AMENITIES	Flat-screen TV and iPod docking station

60 Thompson ★★★★	
60 Thompson Street	
New York, NY 10012	
☎ 212-431-0400	
TOLL-FREE 800-325-3535	
www.thompsonhotels.com	
ROOM QUALITY	89
COST ($ = $80)	$$$$$$–
LOCATION	Downtown
DISCOUNTS	AAA, AARP, gov't
NO. OF ROOMS	100
ROOM SQUARE FEET	180
MEETING FACILITIES	Small
POOL/SAUNA	–
EXERCISE FACILITIES	Privileges
WINDOW GLAZE	Single
PARKING PER DAY	$55
NEAREST SUBWAY	3 blocks
BAR	•
ON-SITE DINING	American
EXTRA AMENITIES	Concierge, breakfast
BUSINESS AMENITIES	Internet, fax

70 park avenue hotel
★★★★½
70 Park Avenue
New York, NY 10016
☎ 212-973-2400
TOLL-FREE 877-707-2752
www.70parkave.com

ROOM QUALITY	90
COST ($ = $80)	$$$$$–
LOCATION	Chelsea, Gramercy Park, and Midtown
DISCOUNTS	AAA, AARP, gov't
NO. OF ROOMS	188
ROOM SQUARE FEET	270
MEETING FACILITIES	•
POOL/SAUNA	Whirlpool
EXERCISE FACILITIES	Privileges
WINDOW GLAZE	Double
PARKING PER DAY	$52
NEAREST SUBWAY	3 blocks
BAR	•
ON-SITE DINING	New American
EXTRA AMENITIES	–
BUSINESS AMENITIES	Data port

Sheraton New York Hotel & Towers ★★★★
811 Seventh Avenue
New York, NY 10019
☎ 212-581-1000
TOLL-FREE 800-325-3535
www.sheraton.com

ROOM QUALITY	89
COST ($ = $80)	$$$$$–
LOCATION	Chelsea, Gramercy Park, and Midtown
DISCOUNTS	AAA, AARP, gov't
NO. OF ROOMS	1,750
ROOM SQUARE FEET	180
MEETING FACILITIES	•
POOL/SAUNA	–
EXERCISE FACILITIES	•
WINDOW GLAZE	Single
PARKING PER DAY	$42
NEAREST SUBWAY	Beneath hotel
BAR	•
ON-SITE DINING	Cafe, American
EXTRA AMENITIES	Convention center
BUSINESS AMENITIES	Data port, 2 phone lines, fax

The Sherry-Netherland
★★★★½
781 Fifth Avenue
New York, NY 10022
☎ 212-355-2800
TOLL-FREE 800-247-4377
www.sherrynetherland.com

ROOM QUALITY	92
COST ($ = $80)	$$$$$+
LOCATION	Uptown
DISCOUNTS	–
NO. OF ROOMS	50
ROOM SQUARE FEET	400
MEETING FACILITIES	Small
POOL/SAUNA	–
EXERCISE FACILITIES	•
WINDOW GLAZE	Single
PARKING PER DAY	$45
NEAREST SUBWAY	½ block
BAR	•
ON-SITE DINING	Italian
EXTRA AMENITIES	Concierge, breakfast
BUSINESS AMENITIES	Data port, 2 phone lines, fax in some rooms

Sofitel New York ★★★★
45 West 44th Street
New York, NY 10036
☎ 212-354-8844
TOLL-FREE 800-SOFITEL
www.sofitel.com

ROOM QUALITY	89
COST ($ = $80)	$$$+
LOCATION	Chelsea, Gramercy Park, and Midtown
DISCOUNTS	–
NO. OF ROOMS	356
ROOM SQUARE FEET	–
MEETING FACILITIES	•
POOL/SAUNA	–
EXERCISE FACILITIES	•
WINDOW GLAZE	Triple
PARKING PER DAY	$45
NEAREST SUBWAY	2 blocks
BAR	•
ON-SITE DINING	French
EXTRA AMENITIES	Concierge
BUSINESS AMENITIES	Data port, DSL, computer

Soho Grand ★★★★½
310 West Broadway
New York, NY 10013
☎ 212-965-3000
TOLL-FREE 800-965-3000
www.sohogrand.com

ROOM QUALITY	93
COST ($ = $80)	$$$
LOCATION	Downtown
DISCOUNTS	–
NO. OF ROOMS	363
ROOM SQUARE FEET	275
MEETING FACILITIES	•
POOL/SAUNA	–
EXERCISE FACILITIES	•
WINDOW GLAZE	Triple
PARKING PER DAY	$55–$65
NEAREST SUBWAY	1 block
BAR	•
ON-SITE DINING	New England
EXTRA AMENITIES	Goldfish in room by request
BUSINESS AMENITIES	Data port, 2 phone lines

The St. Regis ★★★★★
2 East 55th Street
New York, NY 10022
☎ 212-753-4500
TOLL-FREE 800-759-7550
www.stregis.com

ROOM QUALITY	98
COST ($ = $80)	$$$$$$$$$$–
LOCATION	Chelsea, Gramercy Park, and Midtown
DISCOUNTS	–
NO. OF ROOMS	229
ROOM SQUARE FEET	425
MEETING FACILITIES	•
POOL/SAUNA	Sauna, steam room
EXERCISE FACILITIES	•
WINDOW GLAZE	Double
PARKING PER DAY	$45
NEAREST SUBWAY	2 blocks
BAR	•
ON-SITE DINING	American, French
EXTRA AMENITIES	Live piano and harp in salon
BUSINESS AMENITIES	Data port, 2 phone lines

Hotel Information Chart (continued)

The Standard ★★★★½
848 Washington Street
New York, NY 10014
☎ 212-645-4646
TOLL-FREE 877-550-4446
www.standardhotels.com

ROOM QUALITY	91
COST ($ = $80)	$$+
LOCATION	Downtown
DISCOUNTS	–
NO. OF ROOMS	337
ROOM SQUARE FEET	250
MEETING FACILITIES	•
POOL/SAUNA	–
EXERCISE FACILITIES	–
WINDOW GLAZE	
PARKING PER DAY	$55–$65
NEAREST SUBWAY	2 blocks
BAR	•
ON-SITE DINING	–
EXTRA AMENITIES	–
BUSINESS AMENITIES	–

Stay ★★★★
157 West 47th Street
New York, NY 10036
☎ 212-768-3700
www.stayhotelny.com

ROOM QUALITY	87
COST ($ = $80)	$$
LOCATION	Chelsea, Gramercy Park, and Midtown
DISCOUNTS	–
NO. OF ROOMS	210
ROOM SQUARE FEET	200
MEETING FACILITIES	•
POOL/SAUNA	–
EXERCISE FACILITIES	•
WINDOW GLAZE	
PARKING PER DAY	$45–$55
NEAREST SUBWAY	2 blocks
BAR	•
ON-SITE DINING	–
EXTRA AMENITIES	Robes
BUSINESS AMENITIES	–

The Surrey ★★★★½
20 East 76th Street
New York, NY 10021
☎ 212-288-3700
www.thesurrey.com

ROOM QUALITY	92
COST ($ = $80)	$$$$$$
LOCATION	Uptown
DISCOUNTS	–
NO. OF ROOMS	190
ROOM SQUARE FEET	330–570
MEETING FACILITIES	–
POOL/SAUNA	–
EXERCISE FACILITIES	•
WINDOW GLAZE	
PARKING PER DAY	$55
NEAREST SUBWAY	3 blocks
BAR	–
ON-SITE DINING	–
EXTRA AMENITIES	–
BUSINESS AMENITIES	–

Tudor Hotel ★★★★
304 East 42nd Street
New York, NY 10017
☎ 212-986-8800
TOLL-FREE 800-879-8836
www.tudorhotelny.com

ROOM QUALITY	87
COST ($ = $80)	$$$+
LOCATION	Chelsea, Gramercy Park, and Midtown
DISCOUNTS	AAA, AARP
NO. OF ROOMS	300
ROOM SQUARE FEET	248
MEETING FACILITIES	•
POOL/SAUNA	Whirlpool
EXERCISE FACILITIES	•
WINDOW GLAZE	Single/Triple
PARKING PER DAY	$40
NEAREST SUBWAY	2 blocks
BAR	•
ON-SITE DINING	Bistro
EXTRA AMENITIES	–
BUSINESS AMENITIES	Data port, 2 phone lines

W Hotel Times Square ★★★★½
1567 Broadway
New York, NY 10036
☎ 212-930-7400
TOLL-FREE 877-946-8357
www.whotels.com

ROOM QUALITY	95
COST ($ = $80)	$$$$+
LOCATION	Chelsea, Gramercy Park, and Midtown
DISCOUNTS	AAA, gov't, military
NO. OF ROOMS	550
ROOM SQUARE FEET	210
MEETING FACILITIES	•
POOL/SAUNA	–
EXERCISE FACILITIES	•
WINDOW GLAZE	Single
PARKING PER DAY	$45
NEAREST SUBWAY	½ block
BAR	•
ON-SITE DINING	Seafood, sushi
EXTRA AMENITIES	Spa, bathrobes, library
BUSINESS AMENITIES	Internet, 2 phone lines, data port

W Hotel Union Square ★★★★
201 Park Avenue South
New York, NY 10003
☎ 212-253-9119
TOLL-FREE 877-946-8357
www.whotels.com

ROOM QUALITY	86
COST ($ = $80)	$$$$–
LOCATION	Chelsea, Gramercy Park, and Midtown
DISCOUNTS	AAA, gov't
NO. OF ROOMS	270
ROOM SQUARE FEET	390
MEETING FACILITIES	•
POOL/SAUNA	–
EXERCISE FACILITIES	•
WINDOW GLAZE	Triple
PARKING PER DAY	$45
NEAREST SUBWAY	½ block
BAR	•
ON-SITE DINING	Italian
EXTRA AMENITIES	Concierge, CD, DVD, library
BUSINESS AMENITIES	Data port, 2 phone lines

The Time ★★★★
224 West 49th Street
New York, NY 10019
☎ 212-246-5252
TOLL-FREE 877-846-3692
www.thetimeny.com

ROOM QUALITY	88
COST ($ = $80)	$$$
LOCATION	Chelsea, Gramercy Park, and Midtown
DISCOUNTS	–
NO. OF ROOMS	194
ROOM SQUARE FEET	235
MEETING FACILITIES	•
POOL/SAUNA	–
EXERCISE FACILITIES	–
WINDOW GLAZE	Double
PARKING PER DAY	$25
NEAREST SUBWAY	1 block
BAR	•
ON-SITE DINING	American
EXTRA AMENITIES	–
BUSINESS AMENITIES	Data port, 2 phone lines, fax, WebTV

Tribeca Grand ★★★★½
2 Avenue of the Americas
New York, NY 10013
☎ 212-519-6600
TOLL-FREE 877-519-6600
www.tribecagrand.com

ROOM QUALITY	90
COST ($ = $80)	$$$
LOCATION	Downtown
DISCOUNTS	Gov't
NO. OF ROOMS	203
ROOM SQUARE FEET	–
MEETING FACILITIES	•
POOL/SAUNA	Pool
EXERCISE FACILITIES	•
WINDOW GLAZE	Single
PARKING PER DAY	$55–$65
NEAREST SUBWAY	2 blocks
BAR	•
ON-SITE DINING	American
EXTRA AMENITIES	Champagne, breakfast
BUSINESS AMENITIES	2 phone lines, business center

Trump International Hotel & Towers ★★★★★
1 Central Park West
New York, NY 10023
☎ 212-299-1000
TOLL-FREE 888-448-7867
www.trumpintl.com

ROOM QUALITY	97
COST ($ = $80)	$$$$$$$$$–
LOCATION	Uptown
DISCOUNTS	–
NO. OF ROOMS	167
ROOM SQUARE FEET	–
MEETING FACILITIES	•
POOL/SAUNA	Pool
EXERCISE FACILITIES	•
WINDOW GLAZE	Single
PARKING PER DAY	$49–$59
NEAREST SUBWAY	1 block
BAR	•
ON-SITE DINING	American, French
EXTRA AMENITIES	Concierge, CD, safe
BUSINESS AMENITIES	Data port, 2 phone lines, fax

W New York ★★★★½
541 Lexington Avenue
New York, NY 10022
☎ 212-755-1200
TOLL-FREE 877-946-8357
www.whotels.com

ROOM QUALITY	91
COST ($ = $80)	$$$+
LOCATION	Chelsea, Gramercy Park, and Midtown
DISCOUNTS	Gov't, military
NO. OF ROOMS	688
ROOM SQUARE FEET	200
MEETING FACILITIES	•
POOL/SAUNA	Sauna, whirlpool
EXERCISE FACILITIES	•
WINDOW GLAZE	Double
PARKING PER DAY	$45
NEAREST SUBWAY	1 block
BAR	•
ON-SITE DINING	–
EXTRA AMENITIES	–
BUSINESS AMENITIES	Data port

W New York– The Tuscany ★★★★
120 East 39th Street
New York, NY 10016
☎ 212-686-1600
TOLL-FREE 877-946-8357
www.whotels.com

ROOM QUALITY	87
COST ($ = $80)	$$$+
LOCATION	Chelsea, Gramercy Park, and Midtown
DISCOUNTS	Gov't, military
NO. OF ROOMS	113
ROOM SQUARE FEET	400
MEETING FACILITIES	•
POOL/SAUNA	–
EXERCISE FACILITIES	•
WINDOW GLAZE	Double
PARKING PER DAY	$50
NEAREST SUBWAY	2 blocks
BAR	•
ON-SITE DINING	Tuscan
EXTRA AMENITIES	Packages
BUSINESS AMENITIES	Data port, 2 phone lines

The Waldorf-Astoria ★★★★½
301 Park Avenue
New York, NY 10022
☎ 212-355-3000
TOLL-FREE 800-WALDORF
www.waldorfastoria.com

ROOM QUALITY	95
COST ($ = $80)	$$$+
LOCATION	Chelsea, Gramercy Park, and Midtown
DISCOUNTS	AAA, gov't
NO. OF ROOMS	1,245
ROOM SQUARE FEET	–
MEETING FACILITIES	•
POOL/SAUNA	Whirlpool
EXERCISE FACILITIES	•
WINDOW GLAZE	Double
PARKING PER DAY	$45
NEAREST SUBWAY	1 block
BAR	•
ON-SITE DINING	French, American, Japanese
EXTRA AMENITIES	Cocktail terrace with pianist, salon, spa
BUSINESS AMENITIES	Data port, 2 phone lines, fax

Hotel Information Chart (continued)

The Wall Street Inn ★★★★
9 South William Street
New York, NY 10004
☎ 212-747-1500
TOLL-FREE 877-747-1500
www.thewallstreetinn.com

ROOM QUALITY	86
COST ($ = $80)	$$+
LOCATION	Downtown
DISCOUNTS	Gov't
NO. OF ROOMS	46
ROOM SQUARE FEET	250
MEETING FACILITIES	•
POOL/SAUNA	Sauna, steam room
EXERCISE FACILITIES	Small
WINDOW GLAZE	Double
PARKING PER DAY	–
NEAREST SUBWAY	3 blocks
BAR	–
ON-SITE DINING	–
EXTRA AMENITIES	Free Continental breakfast, hair dryers
BUSINESS AMENITIES	Data port, 2 phone lines

Warwick New York Hotel ★★★★
65 West 54th Street
New York, NY 10019
☎ 212-247-2700
TOLL-FREE 800-223-4099
www.warwickhotels.com

ROOM QUALITY	88
COST ($ = $80)	$$$+
LOCATION	Chelsea, Gramercy Park, and Midtown
DISCOUNTS	AAA, gov't
NO. OF ROOMS	422
ROOM SQUARE FEET	240
MEETING FACILITIES	•
POOL/SAUNA	–
EXERCISE FACILITIES	•
WINDOW GLAZE	Double
PARKING PER DAY	$45
NEAREST SUBWAY	2 blocks
BAR	•
ON-SITE DINING	Italian cafe
EXTRA AMENITIES	–
BUSINESS AMENITIES	Data port, 2 phone lines

Washington Square Hotel ★★★½
103 Waverly Place
New York, NY 10011
☎ 212-777-9515
TOLL-FREE 800-222-0418
www.washingtonsquarehotel.com

ROOM QUALITY	81
COST ($ = $80)	$$$–
LOCATION	Downtown
DISCOUNTS	–
NO. OF ROOMS	150
ROOM SQUARE FEET	120
MEETING FACILITIES	Small
POOL/SAUNA	–
EXERCISE FACILITIES	•
WINDOW GLAZE	Single
PARKING PER DAY	n/a
NEAREST SUBWAY	1 block
BAR	•
ON-SITE DINING	American
EXTRA AMENITIES	Free Continental breakfast
BUSINESS AMENITIES	Data port

The Westin New York at Times Square ★★★★½
270 West 43rd Street
New York, NY 10036
☎ 212-201-2700
TOLL-FREE 866-837-4183
www.westinny.com

ROOM QUALITY	90
COST ($ = $80)	$$$$–
LOCATION	Chelsea, Gramercy Park, and Midtown
DISCOUNTS	AAA, gov't
NO. OF ROOMS	863
ROOM SQUARE FEET	310
MEETING FACILITIES	•
POOL/SAUNA	Spa
EXERCISE FACILITIES	•
WINDOW GLAZE	Double
PARKING PER DAY	$27–$48
NEAREST SUBWAY	½ block
BAR	•
ON-SITE DINING	Steak house, American
EXTRA AMENITIES	Theater-ticket desk
BUSINESS AMENITIES	Data port, 2 phone lines

PART FOUR

GETTING *in* *and* GETTING AROUND

IF YOU ARE AN AMERICAN, there's a good chance that at least some of your forebears entered the United States through New York, steaming west out of the Atlantic Ocean into Lower New York Bay, through the Narrows between **Staten Island** and **Brooklyn,** north into Upper New York Bay, and finally past the **Statue of Liberty** to docks near the southern tip of **Manhattan Island,** or to ports north, or south to the terminals of nearby New Jersey. Today, it's possible to arrive in New York by just about any means imaginable, making it one of the most accessible cities in the world.

However—and this should be part of your travel planning not only in this case but wherever you go from now on—no matter which form of transportation you choose, getting into and out of the New York area, and Manhattan in particular, changed forever in the aftermath of 9/11. If you intend to drive, especially if you're considering bringing a truck or van into the city, be forewarned that some bridges and tunnels may be closed to commercial vehicles. At all bridges and tunnels, all vehicles are subject to being searched at the discretion of the authorities. (And remember, Manhattan, Staten Island, Brooklyn, and **Queens** are all on islands, which means you're just about doomed to use a bridge or tunnel.) While a vehicle search itself is a minor inconvenience, the traffic backups attending such searches are not so minor.

And, once you do arrive, there's still a huge amount of surface traffic congestion to be navigated, most obviously in **Lower Manhattan,** at the heavily disrupted construction area surrounding **Ground Zero,** and in the **Midtown** areas on both sides—that is, those areas served by intraborough bridges and tunnels.

It may be even more of a pain to have a car *in* Manhattan. Traffic is never less than

unofficial **TIP**
We cannot be too emphatic about this: leave your vehicle outside the city, and train, bus, cab, subway, bike, hike, or even kayak in.

boggling, generally intimidating, and frequently terrifying. This is truly a city where you should leave the driving to the experts—even though, as you will discover, "expertise" in New York cab driving translates to a sort of inspired insanity. (And multilingual at that. If you happen to be an aficionado of foreign-language cursing, as Eve is, riding in cabs can be very educational, if nerve-wracking.)

And then you have to pay for parking (which, even if your hotel has its own lot, will cost you $25 to $50 a day) and gas (much of which you'll eat up idling in traffic or circling the one-way streets to your destination—not to mention avoiding aggressive pedestrians).

Despite recurrent complains about service cuts, ticket-price hikes, and proliferating fees, air travel is still the primary option for visitors coming from several hundred miles away, or from another country. At the four New York–area airports, you can expect the lengthy security screenings that are now routine at U.S. facilities, so be sure to arrive two or more hours prior to departure time.

Train travel has been less affected by new security procedures than has air or automobile travel, though spot security checks are increasingly frequent, especially at holiday times. If you previously considered flying up from Washington or down from Boston on one of the air shuttles, you'll probably save time by switching from the plane to the train—or to one of the new upscale bus services that are even more competitively priced, if you're in the right city to book one. And for many European or Canadian visitors, and even some U.S. residents along the East Coast, there are more affordable cruise-ship options than ever before—one upside to the rough financial seas.

ARRIVAL STRATEGIES

BY CAR

IF YOU ARE DETERMINED TO DRIVE INTO MANHATTAN, there are several major accesses. (If you're willing to stay in one of the outer boroughs and stop before you actually cross onto the island, the directions are generally the same, but abbreviated, of course. You've got a GPS app on your smart phone, right?)

For those Luddite drivers who use maps the old-fashioned way: from southeast of New York, you can take Interstate 95 (the New Jersey Turnpike) north directly into Manhattan via the **George Washington Bridge,** which is more convenient if you are headed uptown. (Be aware that the bridge, which is a double-decker with a total of 14 lanes, can be pretty scary, especially at rush hour.) If you're going into **Midtown,** you can transfer to NJ 495 and go in through the **Lincoln Tunnel.** If you're headed into **Lower Manhattan,** you can get off I-95 onto I-78 near Jersey City and go into the city via the **Holland Tunnel.** If you're staying in the southern suburbs, you could also turn off I-95 onto I-278 near Elizabeth, New Jersey (a stretch sometimes called the Union Freeway), cross the **Goethals Bridge** through Staten Island, and continue across the **Verrazano-Narrows Bridge** into Brooklyn.

From areas northwest of the city, you could take Interstate 80 to I-95 to the George Washington Bridge. From Connecticut and other sites northeast of town, the main choices are taking I-95 south (again using the George Washington Bridge) or connecting to I-87, which begins at the Canadian border, becomes the Major Deegan Expressway in the **Bronx,** and enters the city through the **Robert F. Kennedy Bridge** (known until 2008 as the **Triborough Bridge** and still generally referred to that way).

Incidentally, don't get so focused on "visiting the city" that you forget other suburban options. Many visitors save money by staying in Jersey City, New Jersey—which has an increasingly impressive skyline of its own and great views of Manhattan—and taking the subway into town. Or you might consider driving to the Metropark train station in New Jersey, leaving the car there ($9 a day instead of $20), and taking New Jersey Transit ($13.75 round-trip or $16 at rush hour) into the city. (Amtrak also stops at Metropark but is more expensive.) To reach Metropark, take the New Jersey Turnpike to the Garden State Parkway, then go about two miles and take Exit 131 to Metropark.

BY AIR

THE NEW YORK AREA IS SERVED BY THREE MAJOR AIRPORTS— LaGuardia, Kennedy, and Newark—and the smaller but useful Islip on Long Island.

LaGuardia Airport, in Queens, is the closest to Manhattan, about eight miles east. **John F. Kennedy International Airport** (JFK), south of Queens on Jamaica Bay, and **Newark Liberty International Airport** in New Jersey are both approximately 15 miles from the city. Islip, formally **Long Island MacArthur Airport,** is 50 miles east on Long Island.

LaGuardia primarily serves domestic flights and carriers. Islip serves only Southwest and US Airways. JFK and Newark handle both international and domestic air traffic.

In general, LaGuardia is closer and more convenient than JFK or Newark, though the difference is not all that great—about 20 or so additional minutes and about $10 in cab fare to most Manhattan destinations. However, there are free shuttles from JFK to the Howard Beach subway station, so you could make it into Manhattan for only $2. There is also bus service via **New York Airport Service Express Bus** (☎ 212-875-8200; **www.nyairportservice.com**) from JFK ($15 one-way or $27 round-trip) and LaGuardia ($12 or $21).

unofficial **TIP**
All the bridges and tunnels into Manhattan require tolls, and the interstates and expressways do as well. It's well worth getting an E-ZPass, a windshield-mounted "debit card" that allows you to use express toll lanes, before you head out; go to **www.e-zpass ny.com** for information.

unofficial **TIP**
If you're booking your ticket online, here are the official abbreviations for the airports: LaGuardia is **LGA**; John F. Kennedy is (not surprisingly) **JFK**; Newark is **EWR** (yep, no *N*), and Islip is **ISP**.

If you're visiting over the winter, we recommend flying into either Newark or JFK. These airports have longer runways and electronic instrumentation allowing them to operate in weather that might shut LaGuardia down. And because they are larger than LaGuardia, Newark and JFK can de-ice airplanes near the active runways. At LaGuardia, planes are usually detoured to a remote staging area for de-icing.

There's actually a fifth option: fly into **Baltimore/Washington International Thurgood Marshall** (BWI), and then take an Amtrak train directly to **New York Penn Station.** There are more than 20 trains a day, and there is a free shuttle to the Amtrak station.

TRANSPORTATION CHART

NAME	SERVICE	PHONE
Airlink	Bus service	☎ 212-812-9000
Air-Ride	Airport transfer info	☎ 800-247-7433
Amtrak	Train service	☎ 800-872-7245
JFK International Airport	Airport	☎ 718-244-4444
LaGuardia Airport	Airport	☎ 718-533-3400
Long Island Rail Road	Commuter railroad	☎ 718-217-LIRR
Metro-North Railroad	Commuter railroad	☎ 212-532-4900
New Jersey Transit	Buses and trains to NYC	☎ 800-772-2222
NYC Bridges & Tunnels	Bridge and tunnel info	☎ 800-221-9903
NYC DOT	Parking, etc.	☎ 212-639-9675
NYC Taxi & Limo Commission	New York City taxis	☎ 212-692-8294
NYC Transit Authority	Subways and buses	☎ 718-330-1234
New York Airport Service	NYC–airports bus service	☎ 718-875-8200
New York Waterway	Commuter ferry service	☎ 800-533-3779
Newark Liberty International Airport	Airport	☎ 973-961-6000
Olympia Newark Liberty Airport Express Buses	Newark airport bus service	☎ 877-863-9275
PATH Train	New Jersey–NYC train	☎ 800-234-7284
Port Authority Bus Terminal	Bus and subway station	☎ 212-564-8484
Road Conditions	Road condition information	☎ 800-847-8929, 212-639-9675
Super Shuttle	Airports–NYC shuttle	☎ 800-258-5826

Conventional trains take about three hours and a quarter, and at press time cost between $65 and $95 for a standard seat. The **Acela Express** makes the trip in two and a half hours and costs between $110 and $190 depending on the day of the week and time of day. Also, if you can fly directly from your home airport to BWI, the plane–train combo can sometimes get you to New York faster than an air itinerary that requires a change of planes.

Plus it can be a bargain. *Unofficial Guide* patriarch Bob Sehlinger has found that taking the BWI-Amtrak route from Birmingham saved him about 40% over even an economy fare to LaGuardia, JFK, or Newark. (Eve's brother uses a similar strategy flying from Nashville to Islip: see next page.) And because Amtrak deposits you in the heart of Manhattan, you also save taxi or bus fares (and tolls) from the airport.

LaGuardia Airport

LaGuardia, the smallest of the four airports, is just off Grand Central Parkway in Queens. LaGuardia has four terminals. All airlines use the Central Terminal except Delta and US Airways. Delta also uses the Marine Air Terminal for Delta Shuttle flights. Because the Delta Shuttle operates at the opposite end of the airport from Delta's other flights, make sure you know from which terminal your flight departs.

Flying to LaGuardia *usually* gets you to Manhattan the quickest. During nonrush periods, it takes about 20 to 25 minutes by cab or limo and 35 to 45 minutes by bus from LaGuardia to Midtown. During busy periods it may take up to an hour; however, going to the airport in afternoon rush-hour traffic is more problematic. If you're booked on a flight that departs between 4:30 and 8 p.m. on weekdays, it'd be smart to leave three hours in advance by cab, more by shuttle bus.

John F. Kennedy International Airport (JFK)

JFK is a sprawling, confusing eight-terminal facility that most savvy travelers avoid. Almost 100 airlines, including most foreign ones, use JFK. International travelers make domestic connections here, as do Americans bound for international destinations. Upside: you can go between JFK and Manhattan by cab, limo, bus, or subway.

Newark International Airport

Newark Liberty International Airport has three terminals serving about 50 domestic and foreign airlines. All of the terminals and long-term parking lots are connected by monorail. Newark is better organized and less intimidating than JFK and generally more efficient than LaGuardia. If your Manhattan destination is on the **West Side,** you should consider flying into Newark. Bus service, especially to **Downtown** and to the **Port Authority Terminal** in Midtown, is excellent, with buses departing every 20 to 30 minutes, 24 hours a day. Amtrak runs between the airport and **New York Penn Station.**

PUBLIC-TRANSPORTATION ROUTES FROM LAGUARDIA AIRPORT			
SERVICE	TO	DEPARTS	TRAVEL TIME
Super Shuttle Fare: $20	Drop-off any-where between Battery Park and 227th Street; also stops at certain hotels	24 hours	55–110 minutes depending on destination
Cab Fare: $21–$30 plus tolls and tip	Any stop in Manhattan	At your convenience	20–35 minutes depending on destination (nonrush)
Limo Fare: $35–$130 depending on vehicle type	Any stop in Manhattan	At your convenience	20–35 minutes (nonrush)
New York Airport Service (bus) Fare: $12–$15 one-way; $21–$33 round-trip	Grand Central Terminal & Port Authority Terminal	Every 30 minutes, 6:45 a.m.– midnight	35–45 minutes (nonrush)

Long Island MacArthur Airport (Islip)

Islip services only about 2 million travelers a year, so if either Southwest or US Airways is your preferred carrier, flying there may not only less expensive but also less exasperating than using one of the other three. (Ireland's Ryanair has proposed adding service to Dublin, which would mean constructing an immigration-customs area.)

Islip has only one terminal, with about eight gates and a food court (and free Wi-Fi). Eve's brother, Michael, to whom this book is dedicated, finds that when flying Southwest from Nashville, even taking a town-car service the 50 miles or so into Manhattan saves him money. Depending on the company and the size of the car, it's roughly $75 to $175, which in some cases includes the tolls and tip. The companies servicing Islip, their contact numbers, and their prices are listed on the airport's Web site, **www.macarthurairport.com**.

*un*official **TIP**
The great advantage of booking a limo is that you can go directly to your destination, whereas with public transportation you will still have to get from Midtown to your hotel.

If you want to go the bargain way, the **Long Island Rail Road** (LIRR) Ronkonkoma train station is very near the airport. A shuttle from Islip to the train station departs every 30 minutes from 5:30 a.m. to 10:30 p.m., picking up just outside the baggage-claim area; one-way fare is $5 (cash or credit card). There is also bus service every hour, the Suffolk Country

PUBLIC-TRANSPORTATION ROUTES FROM JFK AIRPORT			
SERVICE	TO	DEPARTS	TRAVEL TIME
Super Shuttle Fare: $17–$19	Drop-off anywhere between Battery Park and 227th Street; also stops at certain hotels	24 hours; reservations required for return service	Varies with destination
New York Airport Service (bus) Fare: $15	Grand Central Terminal & Port Authority Terminal	Every 30 minutes, 6 a.m.–midnight	45–65 minutes (nonrush)
Subway, "A" Line	Manhattan—all stops from Fulton Street to 207th Street, Howard Beach Station to Midtown, plus stops in Queens and Brooklyn	24 hours	60–75 minutes
Cab Fare: $45 flat rate plus tolls and tip	Any stop in Manhattan	At your convenience	40–60 minutes
Limo Fare: $45–$150 depending on vehicle type	Any stop in Manhattan	At your convenience	40–60 minutes

S-57 route; it costs only $1.50 but is unavailable Sundays or major holidays.

The LIRR runs into New York Penn Station, where you can hop the subway or hail a cab. Fare is $10.75 off-peak, $15 at rush hour, with discounts for seniors and disabled passengers. The ticket office is open most of the time. If you have a large party, you might want to book a van; **SuperShuttle** will cost about $175 and is good for up to 11 people; call ☎ 800 BLUE-VAN or go to **www.supershuttle.com.**

Getting into Manhattan from the Airports

Here, we opt for simplicity, even if it costs a dollar or two more. The fewer times you must heft your luggage, the better, and the fewer stops or transfers necessary, the less complicated the trip.

From LaGuardia, we always take a cab or limo. The JFK A-train subway looks good on paper and is definitely the least expensive way to get into town, but it takes a long time because of the intermediate

PUBLIC-TRANSPORTATION ROUTES FROM NEWARK INTERNATIONAL			
SERVICE	TO	DEPARTS	TRAVEL TIME
Olympia Newark Liberty Airport Express Bus Fare: $12.50–$14	Port Author-ity Terminal at 42nd and Eighth Avenue	Every 20–30 minutes; no service 1:45–4:45 a.m.	40–50 minutes
Olympia Newark Liberty Airport Express Bus Fare: $13	Grand Central Terminal or Penn Station	Every 20–30 minutes; no service 1:45–4:45 a.m.	50–70 minutes
Airlink Bus Fare: $16–$20 one-way; $31–$36 round-trip	Anywhere between Battery Park and 125th Street	On demand, 24 hours	75 minutes
Cab Fare: $50–$75 plus tolls and tip	Any stop in Manhattan	At your convenience	40–60 minutes
Limo Fare: $45–$150 depending on vehicle type	Any stop in Manhattan	At your convenience	40–60 minutes
Train New Jersey Transit Fare: $7.75–$14	New York Penn Station	Every 20–30 minutes; no service 2–5 a.m.	30–45 minutes
Train Amtrak Regional Fare: $30–$40	New York Penn Station	Every 25–60 minutes, 6 a.m.–9 p.m.	20 minutes

stops. From Newark, we usually take the Olympia Newark Liberty Express Bus to the Port Authority Bus Terminal on Manhattan's West Side. Because of preferential treatment at the Lincoln Tunnel and a direct "buses only" throughway, the bus can often make it to Manhattan faster than a cab (once the bus leaves the airport). If you plan to return to the airport the same way, locate the Airport Transportation Lobby on the first floor of the northern (42nd Street) side of the terminal. From the Port Authority Terminal, you can catch a cab or the subway to your destination—there's a taxi stand just outside the 42nd Street entrance.

First-time visitors may find all this intimidating: Port Authority's a maze, and the underground connection to the Times Square–42nd Street subway station is a traffic jam in itself. On the other hand, if you are brave, sturdy, not overburdened with luggage, and reasonably

PUBLIC-TRANSPORTATION ROUTES FROM ISLIP AIRPORT			
SERVICE	TO	DEPARTS	TRAVEL TIME
Limo-van Fare: $75–$175	Any stop in Manhattan	At your convenience	40–60 minutes
Train Long Island Rail Road Fare: $10.75–$15	New York Penn Station	Every 15–60 minutes	85 minutes

subway savvy, it offers you the most options for continuing to your hotel.

Though New York has made great progress in reducing crime in public places, the Port Authority Terminal is not a great spot to hang around. Unless, as we Southerners say, "you're fixin' to explode," wait until you reach your hotel to use the restroom.

If you want to take Amtrak into the city, catch an **AirTrain** monorail to the airport train station. The monorail is free if you have a pre-purchased Amtrak or NJ Transit ticket, or $5.50 if you don't (free for children under age 5). Trains from the airport station depart every 25 to 60 minutes, depending on time of day, and they stop at Newark Penn Station en route. The commute via Amtrak takes only about 20 minutes, making it the fastest way into the city. It is also, however, the most expensive option short of a private cab, costing about $30 to $40 one-way, depending on the time of day, not including any monorail charges.

unofficial **TIP**
New Jersey Transit trains run almost the same route from Newark as their faster Amtrak counterparts, and they are much cheaper. At the entrance to the AirTrain monorail, vending machines sell NJ Transit tickets. Buy a ticket for New York Penn Station (about $15), and use this ticket to get through the AirTrain turnstiles; the monorail will take you to the train station.

From LaGuardia and JFK, if there are two or more in your party, a cab is not much more expensive than the bus, plus it takes you right to your hotel. The New York Airport Service Express Bus from LaGuardia to **Grand Central Terminal,** for example, is $12 for the first passenger and $7 for the second (and $6 for the third). A couple using the bus would spend $19 to get to Grand Central, Penn Station, or Port Authority, and then would probably need a cab to reach their hotel. By the time you add it all up, the cost is very comparable to the price of a cab straight from the airport, including tolls and tip.

Each terminal at all the airports has a monitored taxi queue, so it usually takes only a couple of minutes in line to get a cab.

Michael Zibart isn't the only savvy traveler to have discovered limo services. Limos encompass a diverse assortment of vehicles in addition to stretch Cadillacs and can be reserved by the trip or by the hour. For

unofficial TIP
Do not accept a ride from any person who approaches you in the terminal or on the side-walk. Official, licensed cabs load only at des-ignated taxi stands, supervised by a dispatcher.

sometimes even less than a cab, a limo and driver will meet your flight and transport you into Manhattan. Rates range from about $35 for a trip from LaGuardia to Manhattan in a modest sedan to more than $150 for a ride from Newark International in something fancy. Although you can occasionally beat the price of a cab, the big advantage to reserving a limo is having somebody there waiting for you—that is, no taxi queue. (The operators listed on the next page are just a sampling; you can also comparison-shop online.) Have your flight information handy, including airline, flight number, and arrival time. The service will also ask for your Manhattan destination. Although you can request that your driver meet you in the terminal, it's customary (and sometimes cheaper) to meet him or her curbside. Most limo services will accept prepayment by credit card, or you can pay the driver. Tolls, parking fees, and gratuities are extra.

AIRPORT LIMO SERVICES

Classic Limousine
☎ 800-666-4949, 631-567-5100;
www.classictrans.com

Dial Car www.dialcar.com
☎ 800-DIAL-743, 718-743-8200;

Super Saver by Carmel
☎ 800-922-7635, 212-666-6666;
www.carmellimo.com

Tel Aviv Car & Limo Service
☎ 800-222-9888, 212-777-7777;
www.telavivlimo.com

Westchester Express
☎ 800-910-5466, 201-997-7368;
www.republictransportation.com

Getting to the Airports from Manhattan

Essentially, you have the same options available when it's time to go to the airport for your return flight. For LaGuardia and JFK, your best bet is a cab. For Newark, take a cab to the Port Authority Terminal, and then board a Newark Airport Express bus for the airport. You can take the LIRR back to Islip, although, as we said, it might be worth the limo ride.

There is one additional option for commuting to the airports: shared-ride services. These services offer reserved-space door-to-door transportation to the airports.

To Islip, LaGuardia or JFK
Classic Airport Share-Ride ☎ 800-666-4949, 631-567-5100;
www.classictrans.com

To Islip or Newark International
SuperShuttle ☎ 800-258-3826, 212-315-3006; www.supershuttle.com

With shared-ride services, you call the service and advise it of your flight time. It integrates you into the pickup schedule and tells you what time to be ready to go. If you are the first person collected, you have a bit of riding to look forward to. On the other hand, if you are the last person in the van, straight to the airport you go. The service to Newark is a bargain, starting at $19, and eliminates carting all your stuff through the Port Authority Terminal or paying big bucks for a cab. Ride-share service to JFK for one person will save you about $5 to $10 over the cost of a cab. Going to LaGuardia, you're better off in terms of convenience and cost to take a taxi. The same companies also provide shared-ride service from the airports to Manhattan.

BY TRAIN

NEW YORK HAS EXCELLENT TRAIN CONNECTIONS south to Baltimore and Washington, D.C.; north to upstate New York, Boston, and New England; and west to New Jersey and eastern Pennsylvania. From these areas you can commute directly to Midtown Manhattan in a time span that rivals or betters that of traveling by air. From Baltimore, for example, we departed our hotel for the 10-minute ride to the Amtrak station, waited less than 20 minutes for the train to arrive, and then buzzed up to New York's Penn Station in about two and a half hours—a total of slightly less than three hours for the whole trip. (Using the high-speed **Acela Express** trains, you can make it even faster.) By contrast, our colleagues commuted 20 minutes to the airport, then consumed two hours and ten minutes checking in, walking to the departure gate, waiting, and boarding. The flight to LaGuardia took another hour from gate to gate. They had no checked luggage, but it took 15 minutes to disembark and make it to the taxi queue, where the wait for a cab was a modest five minutes. Cabbing from LaGuardia to Midtown consumed a little more than 20 minutes—for a total of four hours and ten minutes.

Acela high-speed service from Washington, D.C., to New York, and from Boston to New York, is **Amtrak**'s version of European bullet trains. Reaching speeds of 150 miles an hour, Acela Express trains provide first- and business-class service, while Regional trains (which make more stops) offer both business and coach accommodations. Seat-side computer plugs, club cars with conference tables, and "quiet cars" are standard on all trains, as is complimentary full meal and beverage service for first-class passengers. With departures throughout the day, and business and first-class fares comparable to airfares, it's hard to figure why anyone in the Boston–New York–DC corridor would opt to fly. For

unofficial **TIP**
It's worth spending the extra money to get a ticket on a reserved-seating train, especially if you're traveling during a holiday or heavy convention time.

additional information, check out **www.amtrak.com** or call ☎ 800-USA-RAIL.

If you are traveling from farther afield, the train may require more time than you want to invest. Sometimes, however, the longer haul has an unexpected upside. Bill, traveling from Atlanta to New York, caught the **Amtrak *Crescent*** at 7:30 p.m. His first-class ticket included a sleeping compartment, and his meals were covered as well. He arrived in New York at 2:10 the following afternoon. Because he could work on the train, Bill arrived relaxed and prepared for his afternoon meeting. His partner, Jane, by contrast, spent a busy morning hustling to the airport, flying to LaGuardia, cabbing into the city, and then trying to catch a bite to eat on the run. Other cities with fairly attractive Amtrak schedules and fares include Richmond, Norfolk, Raleigh-Durham, Charlotte, Charleston (SC), Birmingham, Savannah, Jacksonville, Orlando, Cleveland, Pittsburgh, Chicago, and Montreal.

In addition to Amtrak, several commuter lines serve the greater New York area. **New Jersey Transit** (☎ 800-772-2222, 973-762-5100; **www.njtransit.com**) uses New York Penn Station along with Amtrak and the Long Island Rail Road (☎ 718-217-LIRR; **www.mta.info/lirr**). The **Metro-North Railroad** (☎ 800-638-7646, 212-532-4900; **www.mta .info/mnr**), serving towns north along the Hudson River, arrives and departs from Grand Central Terminal.

BY BUS

IF YOU'RE LOOKING FOR A BARGAIN, leave the driving to somebody else. **Greyhound** may have invented the slogan (more or less), but in recent years, it's been the upstart upscale motorcoach companies that have been setting the pace (and driving Greyhound into upscaling its own coaches). Nowadays, Wi-Fi and computer plugs are almost standard; individual video screens and bottled water are common.

unofficial **TIP**
To get the best fares from the bus companies, book online and in advance. **Bolt Bus** fares start at $1 for early bookers, and Bolt has a "buy eight rides, get the ninth free" members-incentive program.

Most of these new companies serve only limited markets, while Greyhound serves New York from almost all major cities (☎ 800-231-2222 or TDD-TTY 300-345-3109; **www.grey hound.com**). However, considering the cost of a ticket—starting at $20 from Washington—trying to make a connection to a bus-friendly city could be a bargain. And, unlike Greyhound, which goes straight to at Port Authority, the new-style coaches may offer three or even more pickup and drop-off points.

The easiest way to track the options is to go to **Bus Junction** (**www .busjunction.com**), which monitors 14 companies, including **DC2NY, Megabus, Bolt, Vamoose,** and even Greyhound.

BY SHIP

IN THE OLD DAYS, if you arrived in New York on a cruise ship, you probably tied up at the **Manhattan Cruise Terminal,** on the far west side of the city between West 47th and West 53rd streets. However, since cruise ships are ever larger and ever heavier, some of the piers and the industrial-style passenger terminal are undergoing major renovation. Some companies, including **Royal Caribbean** and **Celebrity Cruises,** sail out of the **Cape Liberty Pier,** which is directly across from Lower Manhattan on the New Jersey side of the Statue of Liberty. **Cunard,** which operates the *Queen Mary 2,* and **Princess Cruise Lines** dock at the new **Brooklyn Cruise Terminal** in Red Hook. As yet, the bus and cab service options are minimal, but they are being improved; contact your cruise company for details.

GETTING *around* TOWN

BY TAXI

WHEN IT COMES TO TAXICABS, Manhattan is the land of plenty, a revelation for tourists from towns where you have to reserve one in advance. The main thoroughfares sometimes look like rivers of yellow, with four and five lanes of cabs whipping along. The New York City Taxi and Limousine Commission licenses and regulates the yellow "medallioned" taxis (the "medallion" is the illuminated light on top of the cab), and there are currently more than 12,000 Yellow Cabs alone. These taxis must be hailed on the street—in other words, you cannot call them on the phone to pick you up. (And don't think the cabbies don't take this really seriously: a couple of years ago, when a longtime driver retired, he sold his medallion for a staggering $600,000.)

There is little trick to hailing one. First, make sure you're not on a one-way street trying to wave somebody down on the wrong side. (This happens more often than you'd think.) Then stand at the edge of the curb— try not to walk out into traffic unless you're blocked by parked vehicles, and even then be very careful—and raise your arm high. You don't need to wave it about frantically unless you're in an emergency: cabbies have a sort of radar.

unofficial **TIP**
If you feel a little awkward at first, pay a visit to the corner of Park Avenue and 49th Street; there you will find a J. Seward Johnson bronze of a very harried salaryman semaphoring for a cab in a sort of urban despair. Only in New York . . .

It's rude to cut off someone who's already signaling by getting upstream; however, you may approach a cab that's letting someone else out and wait by the open door.

To avoid unnecessary frustration, realize that in New York, unlike some other cities, passengers are guaranteed a private ride. That is,

unofficial **TIP**
If you are not encumbered by luggage and the like, you can save time and money by walking to the closest one-way street heading in your direction and hailing a cab there. Similarly, if you find yourself gridlocked in a cab within a block or two of your destination, pay your fare and hoof it.

the cabbie cannot just veer over and see if you happen to be going in the same direction as the first passenger, and then pop you into the front seat. So don't swear at cabs with shadowy figures in the back. (At press time, New York was experimenting with a very few number of shared-ride routes, all headed from uptown to Grand Central Station.) Of course, if there are several in your party who get in together, you can drop off some riders before others. Also note that the cab is not on duty unless the little light in the middle of the rooftop sign—the "medallion" that proves the cab is legit—is lit: if the yellow ones on the sides that read OFF DUTY are lit, the cabbie is headed home.

If you're staying at one of the nicer hotels, a doorman is likely to be available to whistle up a cab for you. This also allows for a bit of cheating if you are a little timid or loaded down. You can walk into the hotel lobby from one entrance, pass through to the other side, and, looking as though you have just left your room, ask the doorman there to hail you one. (Please tip him $1 or $2 if it's really busy or raining and he has to go way out into traffic to haul someone in.)

Some New York cabbies speak limited English. You can expect them to be familiar with major hotels, train and bus terminals, and major attractions. For more obscure destinations or addresses, you will do yourself (and the cabbie) a favor by writing down the exact address where you want to go.

Once inside the cab, you should make sure the driver's license with photograph and name are clearly displayed on the passenger-side visor. This is required for your protection in case of disagreement (for complaints, contact the **Taxi and Limousine Commission** simply by dialing ☎ 311). It doesn't hurt to notice the number, either, in case you leave something behind; perhaps then you can get the dispatcher to send the cab to your hotel.

In our experience, New York cabbies usually take the most direct route—or the quickest which may depend on traffic patterns and time of day. (They live here, remember.) Sometimes there is a little fudging, as when a driver circles an entire block to deliver you to a corner address on a one-way street, but in the main you can count on cabbies to keep it short and simple. (Or you could ask to be dropped on the corner.) If you prefer, you can specify the route you want your driver to take, and sometimes on longer fares the cabbie will actually ask if you have a preference. Still, many New York first-timers are a bit paranoid about cabbies taking them for a ride. In particular, LaGuardia Airport to Midtown via the Kennedy (Triborough) Bridge arouses suspicions, though it is a perfectly acceptable route.

In addition to the medallion on the roof, a legitimate cab will have an automatic receipt machine mounted on the dashboard so that you can get an immediate record. (Fares begin at $2.50, and the meter ticks over 40¢ for each fifth of a mile of driving or 60 seconds of standing time; there's a dark-hours surcharge of 50¢ between 8 p.m. and 6 a.m. plus a $1 rush-hour surcharge from 4 to 8 p.m., and passengers are responsible for tolls.)

All licensed taxis now have credit-/debit-card machines mounted in the back seat, so you don't have to pay cash if you're running low. You don't have to sign the receipt, either, unless it's more than $25. The machines take Visa, American Express, MasterCard, and Discover; some accept JCB. However, there are as yet no keypads, so only signature-based cards will work, not those that require a PIN.

If you are making two stops—as when you are picking someone else up at one location and proceeding somewhere else—you need to tell the cabbie this. After you get in the cab, simply say, "Two stops," and provide your destinations in order. This lets the cabbie know not to turn off the meter when you reach the first destination.

unofficial **TIP**

Licensed drivers are not allowed to use cell phones while driving, even phones with hands-free devices. Of course, if you take a gypsy cab, you're on your own.

Don't be surprised if your cabbie drives fast and aggressively. More often than not, you will feel like an extra in a movie chase scene as you careen through the concrete canyons, weaving in and out of traffic. The good news is that these guys are excellent drivers. The other good news is that cabs now have seat belts in the back, and celebrity-voice recordings to remind you to buckle up.

Although cabs range throughout Manhattan and the boroughs, they are most plentiful in Midtown. If you find yourself below Canal Street after business hours or on a weekend, for example, finding an empty yellow medallioned taxi cruising down the street may be a challenge. Your alternative is to phone one of the many companies listed under "Taxicab Service" in the yellow pages. Although these companies are also licensed by the Taxi and Limousine Commission, their cars will probably not be yellow or have a medallion. Some companies dispatch cars on demand 24 hours a day, seven days a week, but others require advance arrangements. Fares, as you would expect, are generally higher than those of metered and medallioned yellow cabs. Late at night, in bad weather, or in isolated areas, however, phoning for a taxi is a safer and less stressful option than trusting to luck on the street. Ask your concierge, hotel desk clerk, or restaurant maître d' for a recommendation; often one of the services is on speed-dial or standby. If you call, tell the dispatcher where you want the car to pick you up and where you are going, and ask to be quoted a fare. Almost all of the car-on-demand companies accept credit cards. As always, tips and tolls are extra.

Now, as to illicit taxis: New York has a lot of limousines and luxury cars because of all its executives and celebrities. Consequently, it also has a lot of chauffeurs with time on their hands. So frequently, when you are standing on the street trying to hail a cab—and this is particularly true if you are a woman or if it is clearly theater-rush or dinner time and you look a little harried—a nice-looking sedan or town car may pull over and the driver may offer to take you to your destination. These are sometimes referred to as gypsy cabs; although few of them pose a threat in the sense that they are unlikely to kidnap you, they will almost certainly want to charge you a very hefty fee. If it's raining or snowing or you're really late, or you really want to make an entrance, you might want to take the driver up on it. Just be prepared to pay the fee—and realize that you won't have any legal recourse if you're ripped off.

The **SUBWAY**

ONE OF THE FIRST THINGS THAT YOU NOTICE about New York is the snarled traffic. But the key to the city is just beneath the sidewalk, and it will set you free. Underground, far removed from the cursing, horn blowing, and bumper-to-bumper slog of the mean streets, is one of the world's largest subway systems, a fast, efficient network that carries more than 5 million passengers over 850 miles 24 hours every weekday (and nearly 3 million on Saturdays). Close to 470 stations connect the boroughs of Manhattan, the Bronx, Brooklyn, and Queens, with others under construction; so you are likely to find one near where you want to go.

unofficial **TIP**
The subways do not run particularly close to the far east or the far west sides of the island. Thus, subway travel to such destinations as the Javits Center, the Passenger Ship Terminal, or the United Nations is not recommended.

The nexus of the system is the complex of stations and routes below **Central Park,** extending to the southern tip of Manhattan Island. Though service to other areas of Manhattan and the outlying boroughs is more than adequate, this Midtown and Downtown ganglion of routes, connections, and stops provides the most frequent and flexible level of service in America. Learn a little about how it operates, and you will be able to get around New York quickly and affordably. For an online introduction, visit **www.nycsubway.org** or **mta.nyc.ny.us.**

However, you should be aware that only a few stations have restrooms. Grand Central, Penn Station, and the 34th Street–Port Authority stations have facilities, as do the stations at Lexington–59th Street, Fifth Avenue at 57th Street, and 125th and Chambers streets, and a few in the outer boroughs as well. But in general, don't plan on making a stop at the stop. On the other hand, if you're visiting between Thanksgiving and New Year's Eve, you'll find the fully staffed, 20-room **Charmin rest stop** on Broadway between West 45th and 46th streets.

The Subway versus Cabs

We recommend cabs whenever you are encumbered by luggage, multiple shopping bags, or the like; in the evening after rush-hour traffic has abated; after 11 p.m. or so for safety reasons; or if you need door-to-door service (say, in bad weather). If there are two or more in your party and you are heading to different destinations, sharing a cab makes more sense than taking the subway.

But between about 6:30 a.m. and 8 p.m., especially on weekdays, New York streets are insanely congested. This is when the subway really shines. While cabs are stuck for three changes of the same traffic signal, the subways are zipping along. Of course, if you have to walk several blocks to the closest station, wait for the train, ride to your destination, and then walk to wherever you're going, you may or may not save time over a short cab ride. On weekends, when the streets are somewhat less congested and when trains run less frequently, the cab may also be faster. But if you are traveling a relatively long distance, say, 35 blocks or more, the subway will beat the cab about 60% of the time, especially during business hours on a weekday. Plus, the subway is much less expensive. With fare and tip, the shortest cab ride will likely cost you about $5, compared with $2.25 on the subway.

unofficial **TIP** Any time of day, if you are carrying packages, a briefcase, or luggage, sit as far from the doors as possible. A favorite ploy of thieves is to grab the purse or package of a person sitting near a door and escape onto the platform just as the doors are closing.

Note: Although you'll find some subway stations equipped with elevators or escalators, stairs are the norm. If you're hauling stuff, especially through one of the deeper stations, it will require some stamina. See the tips for disabled travelers in Part Two, Planning Your Visit.

Safety

Once the butt of talk-show jokes, the New York subway system is now clean, scoured of (most) graffiti, and well policed. Muggings and violent crime are extremely rare these days, though riders on SRO trains and in crowded stations should continue to be alert for pickpockets.

In recent years, many subway stations have been renovated to include various kinds of artwork—murals, paintings, even mosaics—reflecting neighborhood attractions. The station at 81st Street near the **Museum of Natural History** has mosaics of reptiles, birds, butterflies, sharks, scorpions, and the like.

unofficial **TIP** The NYNEX Manhattan Yellow Pages book includes complete color maps of both the subway system and Manhattan bus routes; you'll find them at the beginning of the book.

In the **Times Square** station are murals by Jacob Lawrence and Jack Beal. Houston Street station shows a man sitting on a bench reading a newspaper while a whale kibitzes over his shoulder. Alice—she of the "Adventures Underground"—and her mad company are in evidence at 50th Street. Coffee cups and poetry come together beneath **Bloomingdale's,** and 100 eyes, like Argus's, peer out at Chambers Street travelers.

From 6 a.m. until 11 p.m. or so, you can ride the subway with no more concern for your personal safety than you feel on the streets during business hours. After 11 p.m., it's wise to use the special "Off-Hours Waiting Areas" that are monitored by subway security. When the train arrives, we suggest that you ride in the same car as the train's conductor (usually one of the middle cars).

Finding the Subway

Everybody should have a copy of the **New York City Transit Subway Map,** which shows all routes and stations and offers information about fares and frequency of service, among other things. Once you know the address of your New York hotel, you can use the subway map to plan your travel around town. You can begin to familiarize yourself with the routes by logging on to **mta.nyc.ny.us.** You can also have a map mailed to you at home by calling Subway Travel Information at ☎ 718-330-1234 (open 24 hours), or you can easily pick one up at the airports, Penn Station, Grand Central Terminal, or the Port Authority Terminal. Many hotel front desks and concierges also stock a supply of maps.

If you step out without a subway map, look for the lighted globes (about the size of bowling balls) that mark most subway entrances. A green globe means the subway entrance is open and staffed 24 hours a day. A red (or red and white) globe indicates that the entrance is open only during hours posted above the station. (Some of the larger subway entrances are accessed through buildings; although most have

Subway Map Symbols

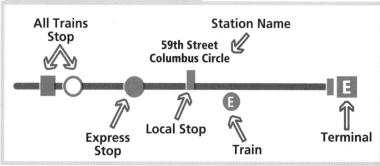

good street signage, a few do not. Don't be one of those folks who won't ask for directions.)

In Midtown and Downtown where various lines converge, there may be several stations close together. The subway map will help you sort out the stations. If you don't have a map, descend into the closest station and check the system map displayed on the wall.

The Subway Map: Reading Along and Between the Lines

Each line is shown in a different color. Though some lines diverge into separate routes above Central Park in Manhattan and in the boroughs, they all bear the color of the trunk (main) line. Each diverging route is designated by a letter or number in a circle or diamond of the same color (see graphic on facing page). End-of-line terminals are indicated by squares; on some online maps, the ends of rush-hours-only routes are marked as diamonds.

Each station's name is shown in bold type. Station names are usually streets or avenues—the **Houston Street Station** on the Red Line is shown on the map as **Houston St.** Some stations, however, have place names, such as **Penn Station** or **Times Sq** (Times Square). Underneath the station name, the map shows which routes stop at that particular station (see illustration). If the station is wheelchair-accessible, the visual wheelchair graphic will be printed alongside the station name.

The Lexington Avenue line, for example, which runs all the way from the Bronx through Manhattan and into Brooklyn, is represented on the subway map in green. The map shows three primary routes— the 4-Circle, 5-Circle, and 6-Circle—as well as a 6-Diamond and a second No. 5 branch marked on some maps and timetables with a dotted line and on some with a black-and-white diamond.

Diamonds indicate part-time service: the 6-Diamond is express service to the **Pelham Bay Park** subway at rush hour, which means that it skips some stations in the Bronx (between **Third Avenue– 138th Street** and **Hunts Point Avenue,** and between **Hunts Point** and **Parkchester**) at rush hour. The regular 6-Circle always stops at all stations. (The 5-Half-diamond, so to speak, branches off from the 180th Street station and makes several stops before ending at **Nereid Avenue,** but it runs only one way, into town during morning rush and back out in the evening, and has very few trains.)

As they head south from the Bronx, the routes converge at the **125th Street** station in Manhattan, but though they all follow Lexington Avenue south through the island, they have different itineraries, meeting again only four times, at the **86th Street** station, the **59th Street** station, the **Grand Central–42nd Street** station, and the **Brooklyn Bridge–City Hall** station. The 6-Circle becomes the "local," making every stop, until it terminates at Brooklyn Bridge–City Hall, so the symbol there is a 6 in a green square. Both the 4 and 5 are considered express trains, but they have different routes. The 4 train ends at **Crown Heights–Utica Avenue** in Brooklyn, which is where you see the number

4 in a green square. The No. 5 goes along with the 4 to **Franklin Avenue,** then branches south to end at **Flatbush Avenue–Brooklyn College.**

So the 86th Street Station on the green Lexington Avenue line looks like this on the map:

86 St 4-5-6

This means that all three routes stop at this station, and no others. However, there are few twists: some lines skip certain stations during rush hour and late at night (11 p.m. to 5:30 a.m. weekdays and 10:15 p.m. to 6 a.m. on weekends); others make all stops at rush hour but not at night. The No. 4 ends at Crown Heights except after hours, when it follows the No. 3 route as far as **New Lots Avenue;** it also turns from an express into a local. The No. 5 makes seven stops in Manhattan between 125th Street and **Bowling Green** throughout the day, but after 8:45 p.m., southbound trains end at Bowling Green, and during those late hours, the train makes only a few stops in the Bronx.

This means you will also see stations where some of the routes are not depicted in bold, such as:

Franklin Av 2-3-4-5

This means that the 4 train offers regular service to Franklin Avenue but that the 5-Circle train provides only part-time service. It also means that the Red Line 2 and 3 routes also stop at this station. The Red Line parallels the Green Line in Brooklyn, but in Manhattan it has a different route along the west side of the island; that means you could take the Red Line train as well as the Green No. 4 after the 5 has stopped service.

Don't think you're stuck on any one train. For instance, if you are staying in a hotel on the Upper East Side and heading down to the Battery to see the Statue of Liberty, you can take an express 4 or 5 train from 86th or 59th Street all the way to Bowling Green at the foot of Manhattan, which means you stop only a few times; or you can take the No. 6 local as far as Brooklyn Bridge–City Hall and transfer at that station to a 4 or 5. (Similarly, if you're staying near one of the other Lexington Avenue or Park Avenue stops, you could start on the 6 and transfer.) The express will save you time, but because expresses are commuter-oriented routes, they are much more crowded and hectic, especially at rush hour (although they seem pretty busy at all times). You might have better luck getting a seat on the 6, if that matters.

To find out where you can transfer between lines without exiting the system, look for the symbol shown at right.

unofficial **TIP**
There are enough variables that, if you're going to be out late, it's best to ask the station manager as you go in which lines will be running when you return.

This means there is a pedestrian pathway or tunnel between two or more neighboring stations where you can transfer without going above ground. However, some of these can be quite lengthy, and you will have to wait for the other train as well, so if you are planning to transfer along the way, allow extra time.

unofficial **TIP**
When you buy a card or pay to increase your balance, always run your card through the reader before you leave the fare window to make sure your purchase was properly recorded.

Fares

It costs $2.25 to ride the subway, no matter how long the trip or at what hour. (There is no charge for children under 44 inches in height.) Tokens are no longer accepted; you must buy a **MetroCard.** Available at subway stations and at more than 2,000 neighborhood stores, the credit-card-sized MetroCard can be purchased in any amount from $2.25 (a single ride) to $80. Each time you ride the subway, you swipe your card—back to front, with the stripe facing you—through an electronic reader on the right side of the turnstile. The electronic reader reads the amount of credit you have on the card and deducts $2.25 for every ride. When you use your card, your balance is displayed on the turnstile. All the accounting is maintained electronically, so there's no way to tell the fare credit remaining by looking at the card. If you want to check your balance, there are "reader" machines at most stations that will show the card's current balance without deducting anything. You don't have to get a new card when your balance gets low: just take the card to a fare booth or to one of the automated machines inside the station and pay to have your balance increased. MetroCards expire after one year, but any amount remaining on the card can be transferred to a new card. For additional information on the MetroCard, call ☎ 212-METROCARD or see **www.mta.info/metrocard.**

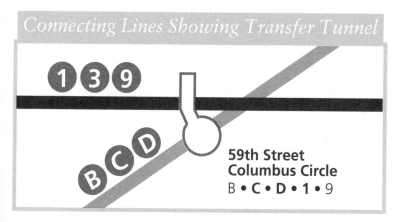

Connecting Lines Showing Transfer Tunnel

59th Street
Columbus Circle
B • C • D • 1 • 9

It's most economical to get at least $8 on your MetroCard at a time, which earns you a 15% bonus. An even better bargain is the one-day unlimited-ride MetroCard, which costs $8.25 (so after only four rides in a day you're already ahead) and which is good until 3 a.m. the morning after it's activated, so you can really see the town. Seven-day unlimited-ride MetroCards cost $27, and if you're in town for the long haul, 14-day cards cost $51.50, and 30-day cards cost $89.

unofficial **TIP**
Unlimited-ride MetroCards are bargains, as they can be used for the buses all day as well as the subway.

In addition to being available anywhere regular MetroCards are sold, these prepackaged cards can be purchased at **Hudson News** and many drugstores.

We are not great fans of New York City buses—not because of the vehicles themselves but because of traffic time—but you should know that with MetroCard you can transfer free from subway to bus, bus to subway, or bus to bus. You must use your MetroCard to start your trip and must make your transfer within two hours. Transfers from subway to subway are also free, with or without the MetroCard, as long as you do not exit the system.

Riding the Subway: A Primer

Using the subway map (or at one of the poster-sized subway maps on display in the stations), try to locate the stations closest to your starting point and to your destination. If the nearest station offers no service in the general direction you'll be going, check to see whether there are any other stations reasonably close by that do. Try to find a subway route that requires no transfers. It is generally faster to get within a few blocks of your destination on the subway and then cover the remaining distance on foot than it is to make a transfer (though bad weather may affect that). As a rule of thumb, it takes less than two minutes to walk the short blocks between streets. Walking crosstown, you can cover the long blocks between avenues in four to five minutes each.

Check to see which trains stop at stations you have identified. In general, the more options, the better. But remember "locals" versus "express" trains, and make sure that the train you're hopping also stops at your destination.

unofficial **TIP**
Repeat this mantra: "The station manager is my friend." If you're not sure of something, ask.

Except for the crosstown 7-Circle Flushing Local, the 7-Diamond Flushing Express, and the L-Circle 14th Street Canarsie Local, most trains travel more or less north–south, or, in subway-speak, uptown (north) and downtown (south). If you want to go crosstown (east or west), you may need to check the map to see where the train terminates. If, for instance, you're taking the E-Circle train from Penn Station to a hotel or restaurant south of Central Park or are headed to Long Island City, the signs for this train will not say EAST or CROSSTOWN, but UPTOWN–JAMAICA/QUEENS. If, on the other hand, you were headed toward Greenwich Village, you'd look for DOWNTOWN–WORLD TRADE CENTER, indicating the train's final destination to the south. More confusingly, if you were headed from Lexington Avenue back toward the Port Authority stop so you could walk through the passage to Times Squares, you would also be headed (by subway logic) "downtown," not "west."

When you approach the station, there may be one or multiple entrances. If there is only one entrance, proceed inside and follow the signs directing you to the Uptown or Downtown train platforms, whichever applies. If you are standing at a street intersection and there are subway entrances on all four corners, or on both sides of an avenue, the entrance(s) on the west side of the avenue will lead to downtown platforms, and the entrance(s) on the east side of the avenue will lead to uptown platforms. Normally there is good signage at the entrances identifying the line, trains (routes), and direction that the particular entrance serves. Usually, because you do not have to swipe your MetroCard until you are within spitting distance of the platform, you can verify that you have chosen the correct entrance by checking the signage on the platform. If you want to travel uptown and you descend to a platform that reads DOWNTOWN, do not pass through the turnstiles. Instead, return to the street, cross the avenue, and descend to the uptown platform.

Though most stations are served by only one line, a number of stations, particularly in Midtown and Downtown, are served by several lines. What you have here, essentially, is a sort of double- or even triple-decker station. With these stations, it's a little more complicated than understanding uptown versus downtown. At these multiline stations, you may have a choice of lines going uptown and downtown as well as, possibly, some crosstown lines.

Be aware that in the larger stations you may have to pay and go through the turnstiles before you get anywhere near the train platforms. Don't worry. The inside signage is good, and there are interior passages that will allow you to correct your mistake if you end up on the wrong platform.

Once on the platform, double-check the signs, and if necessary recheck the system map. The platform sign will show the trains that stop at that platform, indicate their direction (usually uptown or downtown), and specify the terminal (end of the line) for each route.

Sometimes a single waiting platform will serve two tracks. Trains arriving on one side of the platform will go in one direction,

unofficial **TIP**
On overhead signs, an arrow pointing up doesn't mean "up," even if there are stairs nearby; it means "forward." An arrow leading you out will either angle upward or turn 90 degrees to the side.

unofficial **TIP**
If you are going a long way, you may want to hold out for an express train.

and trains on the other side will go in the opposite direction. If you descended a long way or had to navigate a spiraling stairwell, you may arrive on the platform somewhat disoriented. Check the signage to determine the correct direction for your travel. If the signs don't help, simply ask another waiting passenger.

If there are several trains that stop at both your departure and destination stations, you can take your choice. If you are going a relatively short distance (30 blocks or less), go ahead and hop on the first train that comes along. If it's a "local," it will make a lot of stops, but you will still probably arrive sooner than if you had waited for an express.

When the train comes into the station, it will be well marked. The A-Circle train on the Eighth Avenue Blue Line, for example, will sport big blue circles with the letter A inside. The conductor usually rides in the middle of the train and will usually stick his head out the window when the train stops. If you are really confused, ask him if the train goes to your destination station. If you have mistakenly boarded the right train in the wrong direction, wait until the train stops at one of the larger stations, where internal passages allow you to cross over to the opposite platform without leaving the station and having to pay to reenter.

You've probably seen film footage of people crowding onto and battling off subways. Although this does sometimes occur at the height of rush hour in the larger stations, usually things are much more civil. When the train stops, approach the door and wait for it to open. Allow passengers getting off to disembark, then step into the car. The conductor observes the loading process, so unless you're trying to leap on or off at the last second (not recommended), you shouldn't have to worry about getting caught in a closing door.

If you are still a little confused about which direction you're headed, look for the system map on the wall of the car. Check the next scheduled stop for the direction you wish to travel. When the train pulls in, verify by the signs on the platform that you are traveling in the right direction, and if necessary get off and cross over. Newer trains have electronic signs inside the car, telling you which station is next.

BUSES

IN ADDITION TO BEING SUBJECT TO ALL THE PROBLEMS that afflict Manhattan surface traffic, buses are slow, make innumerable stops, and have difficulty maneuvering. Even so, there are several good reasons to use public bus service. After 11 p.m., buses are safer than walking if you don't want to spring for a cab. Though subways excel in north–south, uptown–downtown service, there is less crosstown (east–west) subway service than one would hope (especially because no subways cross beneath Central Park). Buses fill this public transportation gap, running a good number of crosstown routes. You can get a vague idea of the bus's destination by making a note of the letter or letters that precede the route number: *M* for Manhattan, *Q* for Queens, *B* for Brooklyn, and *Bx* for the Bronx. That's "up," remember? Finally, of course, buses are inexpensive to ride, especially with the MetroCard, which allows bus-to-bus, bus-to-subway, and subway-to-bus transfers. Maps of Manhattan bus routes can be found in the front of the NYNEX Manhattan Yellow Pages book. MTA buses cost $2.25 and require either exact change or a MetroCard (and express buses take MetroCard only). For more information, check out **mta.nyc.ny.us.**

unofficial **TIP**
Some buses, like the 1, 5, 6, 10, and 15, run very interesting routes and are a dirt-cheap, if slow, option for sightseeing. Ride on weekends, when traffic is lighter. Check them out at **www.mta .info/nyct/maps.**

WALKING

NEW YORK IS A GREAT TOWN FOR WALKING. Like most cities, it has neighborhoods that are not ideally suited for an evening stroll, but these are easily avoided. If you observe a few precautions and exercise some common sense, you will find the sidewalks of New York not only interesting and exhilarating but also quite hospitable.

The blocks between the (usually numbered) east–west streets are quite short. Thus, walking south (toward Downtown) on Seventh Avenue, most folks will be able to cover the blocks from 59th Street to 49th Street in about 12 minutes, even assuming a wait for traffic at several intersections. Crossing town from east to west (or vice versa), the blocks are much longer. A walk from First Avenue to Tenth Avenue along 42nd Street is a real hike, requiring more than 30 minutes for most people. If you want to try a restaurant eight blocks away, and the address is north or south of where you are, you won't even need a cab. If the restaurant is eight blocks away across town (east–west), take the subway or hail a taxi.

If you become disoriented during a walk, proceed to the nearest street corner and see what the street is (as opposed to an avenue). Then walk one additional short block in either direction. If the next cross street is higher in number, you are heading north (uptown). East will be to your right, and west to your left. If the next cross street is lower in number, then you are walking south. East will be to your left, and west to your right.

Or you can go by the traffic: Fifth and Lexington avenues are one-way streets going south; Madison and Third go north; Park Avenue is two-way. Seventh and Broadway go south; Eighth goes north until it becomes Central Park West, when it is two-way (but, of course, you can see the park from there anyway), and so on.

Because there is no better or more direct way to experience New York than to explore it on foot, we recommend that you do as much hoofing as your time and stamina permit. To help you organize your walking, we include several walking tours (guided and self-guided) in Part Six, Sightseeing, Tours, and Attractions in Depth.

THINGS *the* LOCKS
Already KNOW

TIPPING

NEW YORK'S UNFRIENDLY REPUTATION is highly exaggerated, but the city requires a little "friendliness" on your part too. This is a society accustomed to—one might almost say built on—the tipping system, and you should be prepared right from the start. Cabbies generally expect 15% to 20% of the fare as a tip, and you should certainly be generous if traffic is as bad as it generally is. If your hotel doorman gets you the cab, it's customary, though still optional, to slip him a dollar bill (besides, you don't want to have to wait next time, do you?). However, if you pick up the cab from one of the managed taxi stands at the train stations or airports, do not tip the traffic conductor.

unofficial **TIP**
If you are staying several days in the same hotel room, leave cash for the day and evening maids separately, as the night shift is usually shorted when it comes to tips.

Once at the hotel, expect to slip the bellhop a dollar per suitcase ($2 if it's really heavy or clumsy); when you check out, leave behind at least $2 a day for the maids, $3 if the room has a second visit for turndown service or extra care. Tipping the concierge is a question of letting the reward fit the service: if she merely makes dinner reservations, a warm thank you may suffice, but if she finagles them in the hottest restaurant in town, or gets opening-night tickets to a Broadway blockbuster, go for the 20% rule.

Bartenders typically get a dollar a drink for a simple cocktail, but the elaborate ones now common—and especially the "signature" creations at the trendier bars, which may involve infusions, muddlings, or fancy garnish—get $2 or $3. (Look around: if you notice the regulars leaving larger tips, follow suit, and service or portions are likely to be improved.) Waiters generally get 15% to 20%, although you should look to see whether an automatic gratuity has been built into the total. If you check your coats, tip the attendant $1 per wrap when you pick them up, and perhaps another dollar for large umbrellas or briefcases. Legends to the contrary, it is rare that slipping the maître d' a bribe will do you much good, and it makes you look like a rube unless some actual rearrangement has been necessary. If you have summoned the sommelier to consult on the wine choice, you should leave him something in the range of 10% of the cost of the bottle. (Remember to check the bill; give the sommelier his tip, and then figure the waiter's on the remaining cost.)

Any personal services you arrange, such as a massage, hairstyling, a manicure, or the like, also require a tip of about 20%. And if you get a shoeshine—an underestimated pleasure, incidentally—you should surely throw in a similar bonus.

JAYWALKING

YES, IT'S ILLEGAL, and no, we're not actually encouraging it, but the fact is, New Yorkers are rarely in the mood to wait for the traffic signals to change. Even the police officers assigned to guard traffic intersections are accustomed to the problem, usually whistling or yelling only to those who are truly oblivious to their danger.

If you wish to do as the locals do, here is some advice. The biggest rule, if it can be called that, is not to interfere with the flow of traffic; if your stepping into the road will cause the oncoming taxi to have to brake or swerve, you are doubly in the wrong. (And remember, large commercial vehicles take longer to slow than cars.) If the way is clear, or if the light is already turning yellow—although only if the oncoming traffic is some ways away—you are acceptably transgressing. If traffic has become backed up in the intersection, which is not uncommon, you may walk between the vehicles, but keep at least one eye on the drivers, who may be frustrated and concentrating only on getting on.

Don't step off the curb just become someone else does. Talking on cell phones tends to distract pedestrians, and there is a certain hypnotic effect that walking many blocks seems to induce even in experienced commuters. Also, there are those who still think their time is more important than anyone else's and who will disrupt the rhythm of the traffic, but that's seriously not recommended.

And if you are crossing the street in the middle of a block, do look both ways, even if it seems to be a one-way street: Manhattan has a lot of active parking lots and enclosed but active driveways. In addition, double-parked delivery trucks, utility trucks, police cars, etc., might be pulling out or backing up, and not all have those nice, handy-dandy beep alerts.

RADIO AND TELEVISION STATIONS

NEW YORK HAS A THOUSAND RADIO STATIONS—well, maybe it just sounds that way, getting in and out of taxis and shopping malls—

but among the most useful for out-of-towners are National Public Radio's flagship **WNYC** (AM 820 and FM 93.9); sports **WFAN** (AM 660); and the all-news **WCBS** (AM 880). For those runners who haven't yet succumbed to the MP3 craze (or who would rather lose a cheap radio), the music choices include classical **WQXR** (FM 105.9), rock and adult contemporary **WXPK** (FM 107.1), adult-contemporary **WPLJ** (FM 95.5); classic-rock **WAXQ** (FM 104.3), and **WQHT** (FM 97.1), which claims to be the biggest hip-hop and R&B station in the country.

Most hotels have cable TV, and if you're lucky, the list of stations in your room will more or less correspond to what you actually get. The major networks are easy to find, however: **CBS** on **Channel 2, NBC** on **Channel 4, Fox** on **5, ABC** on **7,** and **PBS** on **13.**

PUBLIC ACCOMMODATIONS

THE *UNOFFICIAL GUIDES* ARE STARTING TO GET a reputation for worrying about restrooms or, rather, about your being able to find them. This is a, uh, tribute to the relatively short staying power of our founder, Bob Sehlinger, and someday we'll stop teasing him about it. But he has a good point; being uncomfortable doesn't help you enjoy a walking tour or a museum. And especially in summer, when New York can be so hot, it's tempting to drink a lot. (When on a vacation is it not tempting to drink a lot?) There are plenty of restrooms in the transportation terminals, such as Grand Central and Penn Station, which are much cleaner and safer than they used to be; the large theaters (though most lobbies will be inaccessible during the day) and museums have them, too, but the lines can be rather long.

In Central Park, look for the restrooms near the **Delacorte Theater** at 79th Street. There are also public facilities behind the **New York Public Library** in **Bryant Park** on Sixth Avenue and 42nd Street. In fact, the ones in Bryant Park were saluted by the Web site **RestroomRatings .com** as "the best truly public restroom anywhere." (The restrooms in **Washington Square Park** also get high ratings for cleanliness, although no points for privacy.) In **Herald Square,** where a brief flirtation with French automated self-cleaning kiosks was quietly abandoned, the renovated and now manually cleaned restrooms are now among the city's most, um, visited.

Castle Clinton in Battery Park is nice and not usually crowded. The nearby **Robert Wagner Park** facility is even better. Big tourist centers such as **Chelsea Piers,** department stores, and malls are good bets, though the quality varies with the age and general atmosphere (in the **Manhattan Mall,** check the seventh floor). The large hotel lobbies have restrooms, of course, although you should take advantage of them only in an emergency and when you are reasonably well dressed.

Finally, there are very few stretches in New York that don't have at least one bar or restaurant. If you are really in a pinch for a restroom, go to the bar and at least order a soda before you hit the john.

HOW *to* AVOID CRIME *and* KEEP SAFE *in* PUBLIC PLACES

OKAY, SO NEW YORK is not the sort of place to leave your door wide open. But you don't need a false bottom on your boot heel for your credit cards, either. All you need is a little common sense.

For many years, New York's "mean streets" were the national symbol of America's crime problem. Statistics were big; headlines were bigger. TV police shows and legal procedurals, series after series of precinct crime novels, and big-name movies played on that reputation. It wasn't organized crime that began to worry out-of-towners (although it did produce even more famous movie characters), or professional burglars, or con men; it was the independent and unpredictable punk, the street hood, the drug addict who might corner you on the subway or go "wilding" with his friends like the kids who gang-raped, beat, and left comatose a runner in Central Park.

But all of a sudden, in the past decade, the word *crime* has been back on New Yorkers' lips—and they're smiling. Although analysts and politicians argue over who gets the credit, it is clear that crime has been sharply reduced. Homicide is at its lowest rate in three decades. Subway crime has been curtailed to an amazing degree: robberies on the system, the threat of which formerly made late-night or solo travel worrisome, are down fully 80% since the beginning of the 1990s. (Intriguingly, transit police have demonstrated that one out of every six fare-evaders is either carrying a weapon or already has an outstanding warrant against him, so try to spot someone with a MetroCard and stick close.) And in one of those strange psychological victories, the renovation of many subway stations is improving users' attitudes toward the system; littering is down, onboard soliciting has nearly disappeared (except for the occasional itinerant musician or candy seller), and the level of civility has greatly increased.

One of the most obvious changes is around Times Square, once the byword for X-rated urban sleaze and now the site of a frenetic rebuilding and restoration movement. Crime is no longer much of an issue in the area, although the crowding and milling about does make some pocket-picking possible.

Similarly, many of the neighborhoods that were once a little questionable after dark, especially in the southern part of Manhattan around **TriBeCa** or **Chelsea,** are now busy with restaurants and young urban dwellers. Perhaps you still don't want to hang around the northern stretch of Central Park at night, and it never hurts to carry pepper spray (which

unofficial **TIP**
Do *not* carry your wallet in a fanny pack. Thieves can easily snip the belt and disappear before you realize what's happened. The safest place to carry valuables is under your arm in a holster-style shoulder pouch, or in a money belt or pouch inside your clothes.

you'll have to purchase locally if you arrive by air) and a strong whistle, but a reasonable amount of street smarts should keep you in good health.

Most of Manhattan is pretty safe during the day, but after dark you should stick to the more populated streets. If you need to use an ATM, either go into one of the enclosed bank lobbies or use one inside a convenience store, hotel lobby, or restaurant. Don't leave a lot of money or traveler's checks in your hotel room, even though the employees are probably dependable. And if you buy any valuables of the sort that can be easily pawned, such as silver, gems, or electronics, ask the hotel to lock them in the safe.

Remember: the upside of a lively street scene is almost all-hours shopping; the downside is that the sidewalks of New York can be a gold mine, literally, for rip-offs. Although pickpockets, scam artists, and tricksters work throughout Manhattan, they are particularly thick in the bus and train terminals, along Broadway and Seventh Avenue near Times Square, and along 42nd Street between Grand Central Terminal and the Port Authority Terminal. Although some of the scams are relatively harmless, others can be costly as well as dangerous.

PART FIVE

NEW YORK'S NEIGHBORHOODS

The SIDEWALKS of NEW YORK

OBVIOUSLY, NO ONE CAN SEE ALL OF NEW YORK in a single visit, and probably only a few people are interested in all of its neighborhoods, but each is fascinating in its own way. So here are a series of neighborhood "character studies" that could serve either as self-guided walking tours or simply armchair tours for future reference. Even if you don't have time to see more than a little of the city, you might enjoy reading about the rest to see how all the pieces fit together.

The profiles in this chapter are designed to convey a little of the geographical layout, history, tourist attractions, and a sense of the spirit of the areas. Many, particularly downtown **Manhattan,** are in a feverish state of change, which makes them both fascinating and a little frustrating; it's like a giant game of musical chairs. The generally accepted boundaries of various neighborhoods shape-shift, subdivide, upscale, downscale; if you pick up two visitors' maps, whole blocks of the city may be marked off differently. (And we should warn you that at any moment, construction or redevelopment may hamper your strolls or challenge your patience, as well as your eardrums.)

We have included some phone numbers and Web sites, and some of the most important historical buildings, museums, and landmarks in each neighborhood are described in detail in Part Six, Sightseeing, Tours, and Attractions in Depth. Most of the buildings mentioned here are public structures, notable for their history or exteriors. Some have particularly stunning interiors or lobbies, but sad to say, in the years since 9/11 many are closed to the public. Most of the city's churches continue to welcome visitors throughout the day, but a few smaller or older churches (or

unofficial **TIP**
For information on all New York City parks, dial ☎ 311 from inside the city; from outside, call ☎ 212-NEW-YORK.

Manhattan Neighborhoods

HARLEM↑

Central

↑EAST HARLEM

Riverside Park

West End Ave.

86th St.

FDR Drive

American Museum of Natural History

Park

Metropolitan Museum of Art

Broadway

79th St.

Columbus Ave.

UPPER EAST SIDE

72nd St.

QUEENS

West Side Hwy.

UPPER WEST SIDE

Lincoln Center

59th St.

Fifth Ave.

Lexington Ave.

First Ave.

Roosevelt Island

Eighth Ave.

Rockefeller Center

ⓘ

MIDTOWN EAST

Queensboro Bridge

MIDTOWN WEST

ⓘ

Grand Central Terminal

42nd St.

TIMES SQUARE

Lincoln Tunnel

Port Authority Terminal

Eleventh Ave.

34th St.

Seventh Ave.

Empire State Building

MURRAY HILL

East River

BROOKLYN

Penn Station

GRAMERCY PARK

Broadway

FDR Drive

23rd St.

CHELSEA

FLATIRON DISTRICT

Union Square

MEAT-PACKING DISTRICT

14th St.

Hudson River

Washington Square Park

GREENWICH VILLAGE

The Bowery

EAST VILLAGE

NOHO

Williamsburg Bridge

Houston St.

LOWER EAST SIDE

SOHO

NOLITA

Broadway

Hudson St.

Delancey St.

Grand St.

East Broadway

Holland Tunnel

Canal St.

West St.

LITTLE ITALY

TRIBECA

CHINATOWN

Manhattan Bridge

Chambers St.

Park Row

World Trade Center Site

Brooklyn Bridge

Battery Park City

FINANCIAL DISTRICT

South Street Seaport

BROOKLYN

ⓘ Information

Battery Park

0   0.5 mi

0   0.5 km

those with valuable antiques) may also have limited viewing hours. In any case, apply common sense and courtesy; be quiet for the sake of those using the premises for their original purposes, and try not to interrupt religious services.

Some museums or collections may charge admission or ask for donations. Most will be closed on major holidays and perhaps one weekday. All museums, parks, and zoos are smoke-free.

LOWER MANHATTAN, WALL STREET, THE BATTERY, AND THE WORLD TRADE CENTER

ALWAYS A MAJOR TOURIST AREA because of the **Statue of Liberty, Lower Manhattan** has become an even more emotionally powerful destination since the World Trade Center's Twin Towers were blasted off the skyline by the hijacked jetliners. New York's historical and spiritual footprint is here, at the tip of the island.

This area, which is generally agreed to extend up to Chambers Street and the **Brooklyn Bridge**, is actually sort of four neighborhoods in one: the historical center; the **Financial District**; **Battery Park,** which is also the gateway to the Statue of Liberty and **Ellis Island;** and the former World Trade Center section and the surrounding office-hotel cluster. (At press time, there was no public access to the construction site where the 9/11 memorial will be.)

From the Battery on the south tip of the island to **City Hall Park** and the courthouse complex at the "north pole" of the neighborhood; from the **South Street Seaport,** New York's original port, on the east to **Battery Park City**—created in part from rock and landfill materials cast aside during construction of the World Trade Center—on the west; and with the glorious **Trinity Church** eye-to-eye with Wall Street—God and Mammon in daily competition—it covers far and away the greatest range of New York history of any single region. From here, the soaring Brooklyn Bridge joins Manhattan to one sibling borough; the **Staten Island Ferry** loops it to a second; and Broadway, which runs all the way from **Bowling Green** to the **Bronx,** to a third.

The area below Chambers Street is the original New York—Nieuw Amsterdam, the port "bought" from the natives and the village occupied by the British for virtually the entire Revolutionary War. The colonial administrators lived in the mansion on **Governors Island** out in the harbor. The entire Battery was once just that, a fortification: **Castle Clinton** (☎ 212-344-7220; **www.nps.gov/cacl**), on the west side of the Battery, was still 300 feet offshore when the Battery pointed its 28 cannons against the threat of British invaders in 1811. Castle Clinton had a second life as

unofficial **TIP**
Take a break at **Battery Gardens** restaurant on State Street at the southernmost tip of the Battery (☎ 212-809-5508; **www .batterygardens.com**); it has outdoor seating and panoramic views of Ellis Island, the harbor, and the Statue of Liberty (as well as a nice bar).

an entertainment venue in the 19th century—P. T. Barnum brought "Swedish Nightingale" Jenny Lind here in 1850—then a third as the pre-Ellis Island immigration point; it's now a history museum, a National Park Service station, and the departure point for the Statue of Liberty tours.

As befits the original Manhattan, the Battery contains memorials ranging through events and people from New York's history. In fact, one might say that Battery Park is to New York as the Mall is to Washington—not so much the museum center, though there are several here, but a major cluster of statues and memorials. Many are reminders of the city's long history as a melting pot and refuge; others salute members of the armed forces; and one, of course, recalls the shattering events of September 11, 2001. At the north end of the park is the huge bronze **Sphere** by Fritz Koenig, which originally stood between the Twin Towers of the World Trade Center, and which sustained visible damage in the collapse. (Ironically, it originally represented global peace.) It was moved to the park, and an eternal flame was placed before it as a memorial to the victims of the attack. It will be returned to its original site when the National September 11 Memorial is completed.

unofficial **TIP**

Manhattan was first sighted by Europeans in 1524, an event celebrated by the **Giovanni da Verrazano Monument** in the southwest corner of Battery Park. And the **African Burial Ground** near City Hall dates back to the 17th century, a reminder that the labor of slaves, as well as so many others, built this city (**www.nps.gov/afbg**).

Many of the Battery's memorials salute the courage of servicemen (and, eventually, women). The **World War II** memorial is a gantlet of four huge tablets, inscribed with the names of members of the Navy, Army, Army Air Forces, and Coast Guard who lost their lives, which leads to a huge steel eagle facing straight toward the Statue of Liberty. **New York Korean War Veterans Memorial** is a "ghost"—the silhouette of an infantryman missing from his granite tomb: it is also known as the **Universal Solider.** Just to the east of the landing slip for the Statue of Liberty tours is the **American Merchant Marine Memorial,** which shows the rescue of a sailor seemingly right from the waters of the harbor. Among others are the three-figure **Coast Guard** tribute and a memorial to the **wireless operators** lost at sea. There's a marker saluting **Admiral George Dewey** and the Spanish-American War victory at Manila Bay. And though it is not a military tribute in the usual sense, there is a figure of engineer **John Ericsson** holding a model of his ironclad USS *Monitor*, the launching of which arguably heralded the end of the Civil War.

Though not in Battery Park itself, the **Vietnam Veterans Plaza**, a simple glass-block wall, is only two blocks east, on South Street at Water. And the **New York City Police Museum,** with its collection of badges and weapons dating to 1658 (including a gun used by Al Capone in a Manhattan murder) and displays on fingerprinting and forensics, has moved into the old First Precinct station on Old Slip Street (☎ 212-480-3100; **www.nycpolicemuseum.org**); its third floor has been turned into a permanent tribute to the heroics of 9/11 first responders.

However, the more moving memorials may be those that pay tribute to the many "outsiders" who became the Americans. The flagpole in **Peter Minuit Plaza,** a corner of Battery Park near the ferry building, salutes the courage of New York's first Jewish immigrants, who had been caught up in the Portuguese-Dutch wars and were harried back and forth between Europe and Brazil, attacked by pirates, and finally carried to Nieuw Amsterdam, where they were allowed to settle in 1626. Another plaque salutes the **32 Belgian Huguenots** who were turned away by the virulently anti-Catholic British in Virginia but allowed to land here by the Dutch East India Company in 1724. The bronze *Immigrants* near Castle Clinton, with its eager arms and hopeful postures, is a tribute to the spirit of the immigrants (an estimated 8 million between 1855 and 1890) who landed here.

A plaque in Battery Park salutes Emma Lazarus, whose poem about the Statue of Liberty, "The New Colossus," made "Give me your tired, your poor . . ." a motto of hope for all those millions. And it is from here, of course, that most visitors look to the Statue of Liberty and the **Ellis Island Immigration Museum,** perhaps the most lasting memorials to the American spirit to be found anywhere. Both are described in detail in Part Six.

Across State Street from the park green is the shrine to **Mother Elizabeth Ann Seton,** the first American-born saint of the Catholic Church (☎ 212-269-6865; **www.setonshrine.com**). The shrine itself adjoins the curve-fronted, circa-1800 **Watson House,** later a home for immigrant Irish women, sheltering as many as 170,000 after the Civil War.

Although it's not in Battery Park proper, the **Irish Hunger Memorial** is only a promenade away, above the North Cove. The little fieldstone cottage is a real one, brought over from Ireland and reconstructed on the site; and the garden includes more than 60 species of wildflowers and plants native to Ireland—along with, as a quiet reminder of the great famine, rows of potato vines.

Two full-sized museums adjoining Battery Park remind us to remember the "forgotten peoples": the **George Gustav Heye Center** of the **National Museum of the American Indian** within the fine Beaux Arts **U.S. Custom House**

unofficial **TIP**
Battery Park's mirror image, so to speak, is **Liberty State Park,** across the Hudson River in Jersey City, which houses a science center, an IMAX theater, a nature center, memorials, and a waterfront promenade that leads to the Central Railroad of New Jersey Terminal. The terminal was where immigrants arriving at Ellis Island began the land portion of their journey to their new American homes and is part of the freedom vista of the Museum of Jewish Heritage.

(☎ 212-514-3700; **nmai.si.edu**), at Broadway and Bowling Green; and the **Museum of Jewish Heritage—A Living Memorial to the Holocaust** in Battery Park City (☎ 646-437-4200; **www.mjhnyc.org**). Both are profiled in Part Six.

And for architecture fans, the **Skyscraper Museum,** at 39 Battery Place in Battery Park City (☎ 212-945-6324; **www.skyscraper.org**), offers a fascinating glimpse into the creation of New York and its famous "profile." It's a small, sleek, mirror-floored museum, easily viewed, and the models of the proposed Twin Towers memorials alone are worth a trip.

unofficial **TIP**
Check out the doors reading "First Class" and "Cabin Class" on the building at **1 Broadway**; it used to belong to International Mercantile Marine, which owned the White Star ship line, although not until after the *Titanic* sank.

The Battery is famously one terminus of the **Staten Island Ferry** (**www.siferry.com**)— still offering one of the greatest views of the Statue of Liberty, and absolutely free. The second-best thing about riding the ferry is that you can do it anytime, whenever your schedule is open for about an hour (or a little more, if you have to wait in line). Ferries leave every 30 minutes 24/7, and every 15 minutes at rush hour. (It is a commuter ferry, after all.) You can choose to see Manhattan by dawn or sunset or even moonlight. It's a very cooling trip in summer and picturesque in the snow. (The third-best thing about it? The concession stand sells beer.)

Another park in the harbor visible from the Battery is the 172-acre Governors Island, site of the 1988 Reagan–Gorbachev meetings. It has become a popular escape for bikers, hikers, concertgoers, etc., but it's open only from May through October, when it hosts arts fairs, dances, lectures, movie screenings, and occasional open-house tours. The ferry leaves from a fabulous building at Slip 7 just east of the Staten Island Ferry terminal; visit **www.govisland.com** for more information.

Statues and museums aside, Lower Manhattan is a treasure trove of American history.

The Declaration of Independence was read aloud on the **Bowling Green** on July 9, 1776; the crowd then pulled down the statue of King George III that stood there and melted it for ammunition. George Washington prayed here, in the simplicity of **St. Paul's Chapel** on Broadway (profiled in Part Six); he bade farewell to his officers here, on the site of the **Fraunces Tavern Museum,** at Pearl and Broad streets (☎ 212-425-1778; **www.frauncestavernmuseum.org**). Washington was sworn in as the first president here as well, on the site of what is now the Greek Revival **Federal Hall National Memorial** at 26 Wall Street (☎ 212-825-6888; **www.nps.gov/feha**), though not on the front steps, as the bronze statue there suggests; he stood on the balcony and swore on the Bible that is inside in one of the hall's exhibit rooms.

The most startling thing to consider as you stroll around this area is just how very small the original city was. Nearly a third of Lower Manhattan—including the entire Battery Park area and the eastern strip from Pearl Street to the East River up to the South Street Seaport area—was actually constructed from landfill after the War of 1812. **Wall Street,** literally a wooden wall built in 1653, was the northern border of Nieuw Amsterdam. Even in colonial times the town (population 20,000) was only ten blocks square, counting the Bowling Green—which in those days really was one. **Stone Street,** which along with Coenties Slip has become a pedestrian mall and open-air restaurant row, was the city's first paved throughway, dating to the 1650s (though the current cobbles are new).

> *unofficial* **TIP**
> The Fraunces Tavern wasn't only a military watering hole; it also housed some offices of the Continental Congress and various government agencies, including the War Department. It was also a hangout for the Sons of Liberty and the site of New York's own Boston-style "tea party" in 1765.

It wasn't until the early decades of the 19th century that the lawyers and stockbrokers had so taken hold of what is now known as the Financial District that residences began to be built farther north. In fact, when **City Hall** was constructed in 1811, a little more than half a mile up Broadway, it was considered so far out of town that the north face was covered in brownstone instead of marble because city officials never expected anyone to view it from that side.

Nowadays, Lower Manhattan is one of the most fascinating areas of the city, still the financial capital of the nation—with the **Federal Reserve Bank** on Liberty Street, the **New York Stock Exchange**—closed to visitors but instantly recognizable by its huge American flag—facing Federal Hall at Broad and Wall streets, the **American Stock Exchange** on Trinity Street, and the **Mercantile Exchange,** also now closed to the public, and, surprisingly for so relatively young a city, the financial capital of the world. The various bank buildings along Wall Street and around the exchanges are New York's version of the Forum in Rome, veritable temples of finance—the building at **14 Wall Street** was modeled on the Mausoleum of Halicarnassus, one of the Seven Wonders of the World, and J. P. Morgan's private apartment on the 31st floor had an emperor's view of the city—so be sure to look up at the elaborate friezes and colonnades. (Many of these elaborate old buildings, such as the old **National City Bank,** at 55 Wall Street, are being turned into luxury condominiums; most still have wrought-iron balconies or door handles with financial symbols.)

> *unofficial* **TIP**
> The Financial District was also where New York's fine-dining scene was born in 1837 with the opening of the original **Delmonico's** on Beaver Street at William (☎ 212-509-1144; www .delmonicosny.com), creator of not only the eponymous steak and potatoes but also Lobster Newburg, Eggs Benedict, and Baked Alaska.

If you're of a bearish temperament, you can visit the **Museum of American Finance** (48 Wall Street; ☎ 212-908-4110; **www.financial history.org**), in the former headquarters of the Bank of New York; its exhibits include various bits of Wall Street exotica, including the only remaining piece of ticker tape from the infamous "Black Tuesday" crash of 1929. If, on the other hand, you prefer your assets in a more tangible form, you can tour the vaults of gold and museum exhibits at the **Federal Reserve Bank,** (33 Liberty Street between William and Nassau; ☎ 212-720-6130; **www.newyorkfed.org**), though you'll have to go through screening, and, depending on the current threat level, the Fed may suspend the tours.

unofficial **TIP**
If you're more of a bull, be sure to visit the **Charging Bull** statue in Bowling Green Park at the bottom of Broadway and rub it for luck.

Lower Manhattan was also where New York's newspaper industry was born. In the 19th century, what was then Chatham Street, now **Park Row,** along the southeast edge of **City Hill Park,** was known as "Newspaper Row." At one time the offices of the *New York Times* (41 Park Row), Joseph Pulitzer's *New York World*, and the *New York Tribune* were all here—and the block known as "Printing House Square" is presided over by a statue of Benjamin Franklin holding a copy of the *Pennsylvania Gazette*. The Beaux Arts building at 15 Park Row was one of the first real skyscrapers, completed in 1899; for a decade, it was—at less than 400 feet high—the world's tallest building.

(Perhaps this cluster of would-be statesmen and media tycoons is one of the reasons that the original Brooks Brothers store, founded in 1818 as H. & D. H. Brooks & Co., was here at the intersection of Catherine and Cherry streets.)

Just across the tip of City Hill Park, at 233 Broadway between Park and Barclay, is the glorious Gothic **Woolworth Building,** which in its turn was, from 1913 to 1930, the world's tallest building, twice as tall as 15 Park Row; it is still one of New York's 20 tallest spires. Its 58th-floor observation deck was until World War II one of the country's greatest attractions; these days, the exterior, with its tiered crown and gargoyles, is more famous as the home of *Mode* magazine on the TV show *Ugly Betty*. It has one of the most famous lobbies in New York as well, with remarkable caricatures of F. W. Woolworth counting his pennies and architect Cass Gilbert holding a model of the building, among others; sadly, the lobby has been closed to the public since 9/11.

unofficial **TIP**
The **Potter Building,** at 38 Park Row, was widely admired as the city's first fireproof building and is still a visual stunner, with its ornate terra-cotta capitals, its vertical piers, and the 11-story embedding column around the back on the corner of Nassau Street and Beekman Place.

Even more depressingly, many of the elegant municipal buildings you can see from the park—including **Surrogate's Court,** inspired by the Paris Opéra and arrayed with a pageant of sculpture and a neo-Egyptian mosaic ceiling in the lobby that, like Grand Central's, reproduces the zodiac; and the **State Supreme Court,** with its restored 1930s murals—are no longer open to the public (without a subpoena). The exception at press time is City Hall itself, a French Renaissance beauty with elaborate lobby murals, double-hanging staircase, and cases of official gifts to the city, which can be toured free on weekdays. Stop by the kiosk on the Broadway side of the park for tickets, call ☎ 311 for information, or see **www.nyc .gov/html/artcom/html/tours/tours.shtml.**

Three blocks east, the 32-story Art Deco **Barclay-Vesey Building,** at 140 West Street (between Barclay and Vesey, of course), was built in 1926 for what was then the New York Telephone Company, later NYNEX, and is now the **Verizon Building.** Extensively damaged on 9/11, the building, including its vaulted lobby, with ceiling murals illustrating the history of human communications from the Aztec relay runners to the invention of the telephone, has been beautifully restored at a cost of nearly $1.5 billion.

> *unofficial* **TIP**
> Two Presidents, Lincoln and Grant, lay in state in the rotunda of City Hall.

SOHO AND TRIBECA

NOW THAT POPULAR-MUSIC TITLES and hip industry logos have made odd capitalizations common, the names "**SoHo**" and "**TriBeCa**" don't stand out the way they used to. Both are purely physical descriptions, only in shorthand: SoHo is **So**uth of **Ho**uston Street— it has nothing to do with the Soho of London—and TriBeCa is an acronym for the **Tri**angle **Be**low **Ca**nal, although these days it more closely resembles a slightly left-leaning rectangle extending down to Chambers Street.

In some ways, SoHo gave rise to TriBeCa, in that as the former evolved from rundown warehouse neighborhood to chic loft space to ultra-chic shopping central, the trendy but less-prosperous loft-dwellers, artists, and restaurateurs were pushed south.

> *unofficial* **TIP**
> Note that Houston is pronounced *"house*-ton," not like the Texas city.

Though it's now one of the most prosperous (and fashionable) retail neighborhoods in the city, great swaths of SoHo were largely rural until well after the turn of the 19th century. Remnants of the old Canarsie-Manate Indian tribe continued to live here throughout the Dutch and early British Colonial eras. Through the 18th century, it was largely farmland (like much of Manhattan) and country estates of the more prosperous residents. It was gradually consumed by town houses after the turn of the 19th century; there is a three-block area at the north-central corner, bordered by Sixth Avenue and West Houston, Varick, and Vandam streets, that is a historic district of its own; developed by John Jacob Astor in the late 1820s, it contains the city's largest concentration of Federal-style row houses.

But SoHo came into its own in the mid–19th century, when Manhattan's residential tide began to flow uptown. The architectural movement called American Industrial—huge spaces covered with pseudoclassical columns and cornices made of cast iron—swept in and transformed it into the light-industrial and retail center of the city. Tiffany & Co. was here, and Lord & Taylor. It is still home to the largest concentration of cast-iron ornamentation in the city, and many of those oversized buildings have been transformed into art galleries, furniture display rooms, and even museums.

As a commercial throughway, **Broadway** was, then as now, a barometer of the city's growth. Tiffany & Co. was originally on Broadway near **City Hall,** then moved up to **Washington Square,** then **Union Square** before shifting to Fifth Avenue, first at 37th and then at its current famous location at 57th Street. The great nine-foot Atlas clock that is Tiffany's "face" was originally mounted on the Union Square branch; it's been moving northward with the company ever since.

Here, and throughout downtown New York, the boundaries of neighborhoods are particularly fluid. At various times the eastern boundary of SoHo has been described as Broadway or Crosby Street; currently it seems to be Lafayette, in practice if not in theory. Similarly, while SoHo is said to end at West Broadway, many maps put the western edge at Sixth Avenue—and the phrase "West SoHo" is beginning to be used for the blocks west to the Hudson River. TriBeCa itself was formerly referred to as the Lower West Side.

The five cobblestone blocks of **Greene Street** from Canal to Houston are the centerpiece of the **Cast-Iron Historic District,** with more than 50 intact 19th-century buildings sporting facades in the neoclassical, Renaissance Revival, and Corinthian styles. The building (now a luxury condo) at 72–76 Greene, with a five-story Second Empire facade, is called the "**King of Greene Street.**" The "**Queen of Greene,**" built by the same developer, Isaac Duckworth, is the mansard-roofed building at 28–30 Greene. (For more on this area, see "Great Neighborhoods for Shopping" in Part Eight.)

There is one particularly family-friendly attraction in "West SoHo." The **New York City Fire Museum,** at 278 Spring Street (☎ 212-691-1303; **www.nycfiremuseum.org**), contains the largest collection of antique firefighting equipment, engines, pumps, bells, and hydrants in the country. Its displays feature a parade of fire engines, including a 1790 Farnam engine and one that was present at the opening of the Statue of Liberty; leather fire buckets and speaking trumpets; and its own 9/11 memorial. The guided tour includes a burning "apartment" with mock smoke and lasers.

TriBeCa is also increasingly "hot," although it affects a kind of gritty urban chic, and the shops are a little funkier still. It has been getting a reputation (with good reason) as a restaurant and nightlife haven, possibly because of the many old and family-owned food-import businesses around. And thanks to the well-advertised presence of actor Robert De Niro, part owner of such hot spots as **Tribeca Grill** and **Nobu,** as well as restaurants from chefs David Bouley and David Waltuck (whose groundbreaking Chanterelle has recently closed), TriBeCa is developing a certain celebrity population and upscale aspirations.

unofficial **TIP**
TriBeCa's in the midst of a real population boom. Forty years ago, only about 250 people lived in the area; now it has about 25,000 residents.

The **Clock Tower Building,** on Broadway at Leonard Street, designed in 1898 by McKim, Mead & White for the New York Life Insurance Company, is notable for two reasons. First, thanks to clockmaster Marvin Schneider, who climbs a (lovely) iron spiral staircase to wind it every Wednesday—it's powered by two 800-pound weights and rings with a 5,000-pound bell—the giant timepiece once again keeps perfect time. Second, the space just below the actual works was originally intended by Stanford White as his "entertaining" apartment. Unfortunately, his entertaining of actress Evelyn Nesbit, "the girl in the red velvet swing," led to his murder by Nesbit's husband, Harry Thaw.

Oh, and have you ever wondered about Duane Reade, the apparent founder of New York's busy pharmacy chain? It's not a who; it's a where. The original store was on Broadway in the middle of the block between, you guessed it, Duane Street and Reade Street.

CHINATOWN, LITTLE ITALY, AND THE LOWER EAST SIDE

TIME WAS WHEN THESE THREE ETHNIC NEIGHBORHOODS were not just distinct; they were rigorously segregated. In recent years, however, the outlines of the three have blurred and overlapped, and **Little Italy** in particular is being subsumed as Chinese businesses spill north of Canal Street, south to Cherry, west toward Lafayette, and up alongside the long strip of **Sara Delano Roosevelt Park.** The **Eldridge Street Synagogue,** one of the most important markers of the Jewish experience on the **Lower East Side,** has been surrounded. **Chinatown** has even encircled Little Italy's prize "marker," **Columbus Park;** the cheek-by-jowl (or cacciatore-by-pasta) restaurant strip along Mulberry Street is almost all that's left. One local historian estimates that fewer than 1,000 Italian Americans still live in the area.

In contrast, Chinese immigrants have been one of the fastest-growing communities in the city for several decades. An estimated 175,000—the older population mostly Cantonese, the newer immigrants heavily Fujianese—now live in Chinatown alone. In addition, Chinatown is now far more broadly Asian. The signs and sounds of Vietnamese, Thai, and Indonesian society are almost as common as Chinese. Hence, the entire hybridizing area is now frequently referred to simply as the Lower East Side. (The most visible reminder of the old days is the fact that each ethnic group has a history museum here.)

At the same time, the gradual eastward expansion of SoHo chic, and even the infiltration of some neo-1960s-style hippie culture from the **East Village** to the north, is turning the old Lower East Side bargain territory into the latest bohemian and art-warehouse hangout. Hence the latest "neighborhood" nicknames, **NoLita**—North of Little Italy, the section between Broome and Houston and Lafayette and the Bowery—and **NoHo,** for the cheese wedge of territory north of Houston and between the East Village and Washington Square.

The first Chinese residents arrived on Mott Street in the mid–19th century, and Chinatown's history is as dramatic as any Manhattan neighborhood's, dominated by family networks, community associations, and criminal gangs, but all operating in so closed a circle as to be nearly invisible to outsiders. Chinatown has little architectural style in comparison to, say, San Francisco's Grant Avenue area, but it is full of street vendors (most selling cheap knockoffs, but highly popular in themselves), produce and fish markets, restaurants, and import shops. More popular in recent years are herbal apothecaries—herbal pharmacies with remedies dating back thousands of years.

The **Museum of Chinese in America** (MOCA) has moved into an impressive new home designed by Maya Lin at 215 Centre Street, between Grand and Howard streets (☎ 212-619-4785; **www.mocanyc .org**), a space six times larger than the old truly huddled-masses space. Its collection of old photographs, business leases, and oral histories is first class; you might also be able to piggyback onto one of the walking tours the museum sometimes puts on, but you can also arrange a guided tour, either a general look at Chinatown or a foodie version.

The **Eastern States Buddhist Temple,** on Mott near Canal, houses more than 100 golden statues of the Enlightened One (☎ 212-966-6229), and a statue of Confucius stands in monumental contemplation in **Confucius Plaza,** on the Bowery near Pell Street. Ironically, the nearby block of Doyers Street, which takes a sharp turn between the Bowery and Pell, was known as Chinatown's **"Bloody Angle"** back when the opium dealers lured rivals into ambush. The Chinese Music Hall, which once stood at 12 Pell Street, was the first Asian theater on the East Coast; it became a saloon—a young waiter and hopeful entertainer named Irving Berlin reportedly complained to his manager about the dubious quality of the clientele and was promptly fired—that was simultaneously an opium den and the site of some famous assassinations.

Of course, Little Italy was no stranger to gang violence. **Columbus Park,** a small green oasis between Bayard and Worth streets, was once the heart of the Five Points slum, one of the city's largest gang havens and red-light districts. (If you've seen *Gangs of New York,* then you've seen The Points.) And if you loved those old *Untouchables* shows, then you'll want to know that the sidewalk in front of the original **Umberto's Clam House,** at Mulberry and Hester (two blocks south of the current Umberto's; ☎ 212-431-7545 or **www.umbertosclamhouse .com**), was the scene of "Crazy" Joey Gallo's last breath in 1972.

On the other hand, even criminals back then were often habitual churchgoers, and presumably regular contributors. **Old St. Patrick's Cathedral,** at Mott and Prince (☎ 212-226-8075; **www.oldsaintpatricks .com**), begun in 1809, is still the parish church, although the big St. Patrick's uptown is now the archdiocesan seat.

As indicated earlier, Little Italy is a shadow of its former self, except perhaps during the Feast of San Gennaro in the fall and when the old-timers gather to play bocce in Roosevelt Park. Its most famous thoroughfare is **Mulberry Street.** Its most infamous is probably the Bowery, thanks to that street's role in the "Bowery Boys" serials. The buildings at 185–189 Grand Street (at Mulberry), once an Italian bank, have been renovated as the home of the **Italian American Museum** (☎ 212-541-1021; **www.italianamericanmuseum.org**), which points out the more reputable roles Italian immigrants played in American history.

To give equal time to the "coppers," walk by the luxury apartment building at Grand and Centre streets, with its Baroque clock-tower dome, stone friezes, and guardian lions; it used to be the police head-quarters, and gazing up the front steps at the guard's desk, you can just imagine how impressive it must have been to be hauled up in front of the sergeant in the heyday of New York's Irish finest. The jagged Art Moderne **Criminal Courts Building,** on Centre near Lafayette, used to be the jail. At Lafayette and White streets is **Engine Co. No. 31,** an 1895 gem that looks more like a French country castle than a fire-house. (It's now a community TV and film center.)

The Lower East Side, generally on the south side of East Houston from the Bowery east, was not particularly desirable land in the early decades of New York development because it was largely wetlands. It had served as temporary quarters for a series of the poorest immigrants, first Irish victims of the potato famine and then German farmers whose own potato crops were gradually infected, followed by periodic influxes of Turkish and Greek families.

It held on to the name Kleindeutschland, or Little Germany, for decades; it was the site of literally hundreds of burials in 1904, when the burning and then sinking of the paddlewheel steamboat *General Slocum,* carrying a load mostly of German immigrant women and children on a picnic excursion up the East River, killed an estimated 1,021—the city's deadliest disaster prior to 9/11.

However, the most famous and lasting immigration began in the late 19th century, when as many as 1.6 million Eastern European Jews arrived, creating the neighborhood famous from photographs of tenement houses, sidewalk carts, and Orthodox scholars. It was both a slum and a cultural haven (not an unusual paradox for a people used to ghettos), filled with synagogues, debating clubs, and community banks as well as vendors and sweatshops. At its height, New York provided jobs for more than 5,000 kosher butchers and 1,000 ritual slaughterers. (For more on this area, see "Great Neighborhoods for Shopping" in Part Eight.)

In recent years, the Lower East Side has made a concerted effort to turn itself into a historical as well as retail tourist attraction. The irony is that many of the Jewish families have moved up-island to the wealthier areas on either side of the park and out to Brooklyn, and large numbers of Hispanic, black, and Asian families have replaced them. Nevertheless, the creation of the **Lower East Side Tenement Museum** on Orchard Street (profiled in depth in Part Six), in addition to the more organized promotion of the many family-owned clothing stores in that neighborhood (harking back to its merchant origins), has brought it a certain revived prosperity. The 1887 Moorish Revival **Eldridge Street Synagogue,** on Eldridge Street between Canal and Division streets (☎ 212-219-0888; **www.eldridgestreet.org**), with its lavish stained glass, carved detailing, skylights and "stars," fantastical trompe l'oeil painting that turns plaster to marble, and chandeliers, has been restored to its full beauty and is now being used as a museum as well as a sanctuary; guided tours are available (except Friday and Saturday), and oral histories are welcome. The 1850 Gothic Revival **Beth Hamedrash Hagadol** is the home of the oldest Russian Orthodox Jewish congregation in the United States, founded in 1852. The synagogue, at 60–64 Norfolk Street (☎ 212-674-3330), was actually built as a Baptist Church but converted in 1885.

GREENWICH VILLAGE

THIS IS PROBABLY THE MOST FAMOUS NEIGHBORHOOD in New York, known even to outsiders as "the Village," hotbed of bohemian culture and symbol of the city's artistic and literary history. It was originally covered with large "country houses" belonging to the businessmen from downtown and smaller homes along the riverfront built by marine craftsmen and merchants before it was subdivided.

Its boundaries are Broadway on the east and the Hudson River all the way on the west, Houston Street on the south, and West 14th Street and Union Square on the north. **Washington Square** is at the heart of the Village, and at one time the entire neighborhood was referred to as Washington Square. (Until about the SoHo boom of the 1950s, the area south of Houston toward Spring Street was also considered Village territory.) The blocks between Seventh Avenue and the river are often referred to as the **West Village.**

Because it was developed largely in the late 19th century before the grid system was put in place—the regular grid actually begins at 14th Street, the northern border of the Village—it has a number of diagonals, triangles, and bends that newcomers sometimes find confusing. The part of Greenwich Village east of Sixth Avenue more regularly subscribes to the numbered-street system, but on the west side, most streets have names rather than numbers, and even those few numbers don't behave very predictably: West Fourth Street, for example, seems to move in the usual cross-island direction beneath Washington Square, but almost immediately begins making a series of elbow shifts north, and by the time it gets to the top of the Village, it's nearly gone perpendicular.

Think of the Village map as the left half of an opened fan: The area between Broadway and Sixth Avenue would be the fan's center, with the avenues as fairly upright spines. Seventh Avenue spreads out a little, and beyond that, the main avenues—Hudson Street, Washington Street, and West Street along the Hudson River—all bend a little farther out. (Greenwich Street squiggles a little, like a bent feather, between Washington and Hudson.) By the time the side streets are filled in, you have a series of trapezoids and triangles; it may be hard to negotiate at first, but it gives the area a true village atmosphere.

unofficial **TIP**
This is one area of town where having a street map is really handy—and even then you may get turned around.

Washington Square, at the foot of Fifth Avenue, was one of Manhattan's first prestigious residential neighborhoods, but not immediately. It started out as an Indian territory, which the Dutch quickly snatched away; for a few decades in the mid–17th century, it was a freed-black farming community. (Minetta Lane was named after the creek that ran there, and which is still beneath the street level.) In 1797 the city purchased land near Washington Square for a potter's field, which wound up as a cemetery for many more-prosperous people during the yellow-fever epidemics of the early 19th century. The cemetery was closed in 1825, but by some estimates there are still 20,000 bodies beneath the square.

Washington Square Park was established in 1826, originally as a military parade ground. The Stanford White–designed archway, inspired by the Arc de Triomphe, was erected in 1892; the statues of George Washington were added in 1918. There is also a statue of Giuseppe Garibaldi, sort of the Washington of Italy. The so-called **Hanging Elm,** in the northwest corner, a last reminder of the public executions of the early 19th century, is still hanging in there—at an estimated 330 years old, it's New York's senior arboreal citizen, but, unhappily for legend, it's probably not the one the noose hung from.

Washington Square Park was quickly surrounded by fine Greek Revival town houses; several of the oldest are still standing. Even the mayor's official residence was here, at 8 Washington Square North (the facade is real, but the rest is not). Brothers Henry and William James grew up in the neighborhood; Henry James's *Washington Square* was set at 18 Washington Square North, where his grandmother lived.

James himself, Edith Wharton, and William Dean Howells all lived at various times at No. 1; John Dos Passos was living at No. 3 when he wrote *Manhattan Transfer*—and that's just the square itself.

But there are plenty of celebrity ghosts about. Over time, the money moved north; the Village first became middle-class then somewhat less than that. Town houses were divided into apartments, studio space became cheap, and the Village began to attract a second generation of writers and painters, either poorer or more naturally bohemian in outlook, among them Edna St. Vincent Millay, Walt Whitman, Mark Twain, William Faulkner, Edgar Allan Poe, O. Henry, Louisa May Alcott, Raymond Chandler, Isadora Duncan, Albert Bierstadt, Gertrude Vanderbilt Whitney (who didn't need to scrimp on money, of course), Winslow Homer, Willem de Kooning, Marcel Duchamp, and Edward Hopper.

(The redbrick building at 14 West Tenth Street, where Twain once lived, is more notorious as the home of Joel Steinberg, who battered his companion, Hedda Nussbaum, and beat his adopted daughter, Lisa, to death in 1987.)

Patchin Place, on West Tenth Street just west of Sixth Avenue, a little cluster of rooming houses built in 1848, eventually housed such writers as E. E. Cummings, Theodore Dreiser, and Djuna Barnes.

There was a gentlemen's club at 83 West Third Street where Poe worked on "The Raven." Alcott wrote *Little Women* while living at 130 MacDougal. O. Henry supposedly modeled the scene of "The Last Leaf" on the gate at 10 Grove Street. Hart Crane lived at 45 Grove, and a now-closed tavern called **Marie's Crisis** stood at 59 Grove, where Revolutionary War–era pamphleteer Thomas Paine, author of "The Crisis," died in 1809. (That was before its days as a brothel, presumably.)

James Fenimore Cooper lived at 145 Bleecker Street, and both Willa Cather and Richard Wright occupied 82 Washington Place (though not at the same time, of course). Thomas Wolfe was living at 13 East Eighth Street when he began working on *Look Homeward, Angel;* James Thurber drew, and drank, on Fifth Avenue at Washington Square North. Dylan Thomas famously drank himself to death in the **White Horse Tavern,** on Hudson at West 11th Street (☎ 212-243-9260)—he actually died in St. Vincent's Hospital on West 12th Street, which also supplied Millay with her middle name—and the ghost of Aaron Burr is said to haunt the **One if by Land, Two if by Sea** restaurant at 17 Barrow Street, not because he was poisoned by anyone's cooking (except perhaps his wife's—see the Morris-Jumel Mansion in Washington Heights, page 188) but because he lived in a house on that site.

Ruth McKenney and her sister, Eileen, whose exploits eventually inspired the musical *Wonderful Town,* lived at 14 Gay Street. What is now the **Washington Square Hotel,** formerly the Hotel Earle, has been home to Bob Dylan, Ernest Hemingway, and P. G. Wodehouse, among others. Even Eleanor Roosevelt had a home here for three years, at

29 Washington Square West, while she wrote her memoirs.

It may seen outlandish now, but Washington Square Park very nearly vanished in the 1950s, when city planner Robert Moses wanted to extend Fifth Avenue straight through it. Fortunately, he was prevented (Eleanor Roosevelt was one of the park's defenders), and nowadays the park is alive with **New York University (NYU)** students, aspiring musicians, chess players, dogs on play dates, kids on playground dates, and, on summer evenings, the legendary free Shakespeare performances of the **Gorilla Repertory Company.**

unofficial **TIP**
James Beard, the great American cook and teacher, lived at 167 West 12th Street; his home is now the offices of his foundation and the site of almost nightly celebrity-chef dinners; for information and reservations, call ☎ 212-627-2308 or go to www .jamesbeard.org.

The free Shakespeare is only natural, since Greenwich Village was also home to scores of prominent actors, directors, and playwrights: John Barrymore, Clifford Odets, D. W. Griffith, Kirk Douglas, Judy Holliday . . . some of them already successful, some not.

In fact, the 1873 building at **75½ Bedford Street,** which was Edna St. Vincent Millay's last New York home and was later home to both Barrymore and Cary Grant, is the narrowest building in the city—only 9½ feet wide—built in what was once a passageway. It recently sold for $2.1 million.

The Off-Broadway theatrical scene was born here during World War I, starting with the establishment of the **Cherry Lane Theater** on Commerce Street, founded by St. Vincent Millay in 1924 and still going strong. The **Provincetown Playhouse,** on MacDougal, was Eugene O'Neill's first showcase, and the **Sullivan Street Playhouse** was home for more than 40 years and 17,000 performances of the quintessential Off-Broadway hit *The Fantasticks.* (The Off-Off-Broadway culture was also born here, when in the 1950s the Beats and bohemians decided that even Off-Broadway theaters had become too commercial.)

For most people, the Greenwich Village of their imagination has to do with either literature or music, though visual artists also have had a strong presence here: what is now the **New York Studio School of Drawing, Painting, and Sculpture** on West Eighth Street was the original home of the Whitney Museum, founded in 1914 by Gertrude Vanderbilt Whitney to house her collection of modern art when the Metropolitan Museum declined to accept it. The New York University campus sprawls around Washington Square, and **The New School** and its affiliated **Parsons–The New School for Design** are also here.

And then there were the Beats, aka the beatniks, who in the 1950s turned Greenwich Village into the East Coast pole to the burgeoning Haight-Ashbury district of San Francisco. Jack Kerouac, William Burroughs, and Allan Ginsberg made the Village a literary asphalt jungle. And through a sort of extended family tree, the Village Beats begat the folk music movement of the 1960s, which itself evolved into several other generations of influential songwriting. From Peter, Paul and Mary, Bob Dylan, the Kingston Trio, Joan Baez, the Velvet Underground, Tom Paxton, Phil Ochs, Dave van Ronk, and Eric Andersen (to name a very few), then into the more elaborate literary folk of Laura Nyro, Simon and Garfunkel, Joni Mitchell, and Jackson Browne, Greenwich Village has been a literal byword (it figures in too many song lyrics to count) of popular music. (It also was one of the centers of the blues revival and soul explosion of the late 1960s and '70s.)

If much of the countercultural buzz now centers on Brooklyn or Chelsea, and if the literary crowd has given way to a rather more prosperous TV and Hollywood crowd, the Village is still an active and highly successful arts district.

The Village is also, of course, a famous refuge for gay and lesbian residents, though in recent years many gays have moved north into Chelsea and left the Village to the women. The gay scene historically centered on **Christopher Street;** the **Stonewall Inn,** site of the infamous 1969 police-gays standoff, has gone through periods of closure but is now back at 53 Christopher, facing **Sheridan Square.** (Gay Street, as it happens, was named after a family.) The **Oscar Wilde Bookshop,** at 15 Christopher Street, was believed to be the oldest gay and lesbian bookstore in the world. (It closed in 2009.) At 59 Christopher, what is now the **Kettle of Fish** bar (descended from the Kettle that Bob Dylan frequented) was for many years the Lion's Head, one of the city's most famous literary-journalistic-political hangouts.

unofficial **TIP**
This is a great neighborhood for just walking, because of the mix of 18th- and 19th-century architecture (look for cobblestones on the west side), the ethnic assortment, and the mingling of social classes.

Even if you have only a few minutes, the tiny area around Bedford Street from Christopher to Commerce streets is especially worth seeing. At 102 Bedford is the house called **Twin Peaks,** which looks a little like a Tudor cottage with a Hessian helmet on it; the original 1830 cottage was "done up" in the 1920s by architect Clifford Reed Daily to put a little more fun into the artists' community. The mansard-topped twins at **39 and 41 Commerce Street** around the corner were supposedly built in 1831 by a sea captain for his spinster daughters, who did not speak to each other; the central garden apparently did not bring them closer together, either. On Grove Street just off Bedford is a row of Federal town houses, and between **10 and 12 Grove** is an alley of mid–19th-century workingmen's cottages.

The brick-covered clapboard house at 77 Bedford, the **Isaacs-Hendricks House,** is the oldest in the Village, built in 1799; it's next to the skinny mini–town house mentioned on the previous page.

But perhaps the strangest building in the Village is the redbrick **Jefferson Market Public Library,** on Sixth Avenue at West Tenth Street.

Built in 1877, it was modeled on one of Mad King Ludwig of Bavaria's castles, hiked up at one end with a clock tower and positively pock-marked with arched windows and pointed gables. It was actually a courthouse—and, of all things, it was voted the country's fifth most beautiful building when it was completed.

Although this may seem a little out of character, Greenwich Village is also the spot to find the *Forbes* **Magazine Galleries,** on Fifth Avenue at East 12th (profiled in depth in Part Six), the palace of playthings from the prince of capitalism.

The very northwest corner of the Village, a sort of trapezoid inside Gansevoort, West 14th, Hudson, and Washington streets, has begun to shape its own identity as the **Meatpacking District**—although, as it is where the High Line park begins, it has a sense of belonging more to Chelsea, which of course is all the trend these days. Centered on the site of the late-19th-century landmark Gansevoort Market, it's suddenly chockablock with boutique hotels, designer shops and spas, and cafes so chic and so tiny it's hard to score a reservation.

THE EAST VILLAGE

THOUGH NOT QUITE SO FAMOUS by name as Greenwich Village, the East Village has an equally impressive, if even more erratic, liter-ary and artistic history. Like the Village proper, it was home to wave after wave of countercultures and reactionary artists, from Andy Warhol and Allen Ginsberg to Keith Haring and Jeff Koons (to name a few). And though now perhaps remembered most often as the birth-place of the punk and No Wave music scenes, thanks to the presence of (now-defunct) clubs such as CBGB and Club 57, it was actually the city's first center of psychedelic rock music as well, home to the Fillmore East—"the Church of Rock 'n' Roll"—on Second Avenue and the Electric Circus on St. Mark's Place.

Even earlier in history, it was the first "Broadway" (and the first Off-Broadway), site of one of the city's first opera houses and a major equestrian and circus amphitheater. But by the mid–19th cen-tury, the theatres had been replaced by beer gardens and more vulgar theatrical venues, and gradually the mansions began a slow decline: to boardinghouses and bordellos, then flophouses and slums. So its famous residents, real and imaginary, have ebbed and flowed with its status. Lorenzo da Ponte, who wrote the librettos for Mozart's *Don Giovanni, The Marriage of Figaro,* and *Cosi Fan Tutte,* once lived here; Stephen Foster, by then penniless, died in a Bowery flophouse in 1864 at the age of 37. Theodore Dreiser set a suicide in a similar flop-house in the 1890s-era shocker *Sister Carrie,* Leon Trotsky was living at **77 St. Mark's Place** in 1917, when Czar Nicholas was overthrown; several decades later, poet W. H. Auden moved in, dying there in 1973. The original Bowery Boys were an early and vicious street gang; the later Bowery Boys, also known as the Dead End Kids, were the "stars" of a series of movies about the somewhat cleaned-up slums. A common term for a drunk was a "Bowery bum."

More recently, the East Village served as the background for the musical *Rent*, a restaging of Puccini's *La Bohème* in the time of AIDS. Throughout, however, it has sustained such influential cultural organizations as the **Cooper Union;** the Astor Library, which is now Joseph Papp's **Public Theater;** and the Astor Place Theatre, now home to the **Blue Man Group.**

The East Village, which logically extends east of Greenwich Village from Broadway to the East River between Houston and 14th streets, is topographically far more regular than its sibling: the avenues (here including Avenues A, B, C, and D, known as "Alphabet City," beyond First Avenue) run longitudinally, and the obediently numbered streets, from East First to East 14th, crisscross them more or less latitudinally. (Actually, the East Village used to end at Avenue C; like the Battery, the easternmost part is landfill.) However, it began as part not of Greenwich Village but of the Lower East Side and did not develop its current character until the 1960s.

Socially, the population of the East Village is all over the map: though it was heavily German in the 19th century—home to the largest German community outside Vienna and Berlin—it's now a mix of Indian and Italian restaurateurs, Ukrainian boutiques, art students, street performers, and proto-punks. It's still something of a club scene, though much of the nightlife has moved to Brooklyn, and it is studded with preserved churches and monuments to art movements of earlier days. It is also still a stronghold of the drug culture, though that is much less visible than in the 1970s. But it has many beautiful buildings and important cultural sites, and its history goes back to the days of Nieuw Amsterdam.

> *unofficial* **TIP**
> If you've ever longed to lounge in one of those huge, ornate public baths and saunas, here's the place—the **Russian & Turkish Baths,** at 268 East Tenth between First Avenue and Avenue A (☎ 212-674-9250; www .russianturkishbaths.com), which has been around since 1892. It even has its own Russian-style restaurant. Check ahead: some times are men-only, some women-only, and some coed.

In fact, although it later became a symbol of violence and degradation, the Bowery was originally one of the city's major thoroughfares (George Washington patronized a tavern there) and even after the neighborhood began to deteriorate, was a busy commercial center.

Peter Stuyvesant once owned the lion's share of what is now the East Village, and a fair amount of the island north of there as well (see the section on Gramercy Park, including Madison Square). The western border of the "bouwerie" was Fourth Avenue, which explains why that street becomes known as the Bowery to the south. Stuyvesant's country home was near Tenth and Stuyvesant streets, and he had his own chapel, too, on the site of what is now **St. Mark's Church**

in-the-Bowery on East Tenth at Second Avenue (☎ 212-674-6377; **www.stmarksbowery.org**), which itself goes back to 1799; he was buried in the ground beneath it.

It was still valuable land well into the early 19th century. Parts of the neighborhood, particularly the area just east of Washington Square Park, were once as stylish as that elite neighborhood. The stretch of **Astor Place** between Broadway and Lafayette was inhabited by the richest of the rich in the early 19th century. It was named for John Jacob Astor, the richest man in America, who helped develop it. Astor and some of his equally affluent neighbors purchased an old tavern in 1826 and turned it into the Bowery Theatre; the Bowery Amphitheater opened a few years later. The Astor Place Opera House opened in 1847, but its history was marred by what became known as the Astor Place Riots of 1849, which took place in a time of virulent anti-British sentiment; it started as a quarrel between the paid adherents of two rival actors, one American, one British, and ended in the deaths of 22 people. The original Winter Garden Theatre was here, on Broadway between East Second and Third streets; there, in 1864, the acting Booth brothers—John Wilkes, Edwin, and Junius Brutus—played what is believed to have been their only joint appearance, in *Julius Caesar:* it raised money for the statue of Shakespeare that now stands in Central Park.

In the same area are the Public Theater, originally the Astor Library building, donated by John Jacob Astor and now best known as home of the year-round **Shakespeare Festival,** founded by Joseph Papp, and **The Cooper Union,** the famous free adult educational institution that was the first to accept women and students of all races and religions. Its columned Great Hall, where Lincoln delivered his "right makes might" speech, is still the site of popular public debates. **Colonnade Row,** the homes from 428 to 434 Lafayette Street off Astor Place across from the Public Theater, was known as LaGrange Terrace when the Astors themselves—and the Vanderbilts and Delanos—lived there, along with such temporary celebrity residents as Charles Dickens and William Makepeace Thackeray. Only four of the original nine buildings, and just the facades, survive; one of them is now the **Astor Place Theatre,** home to the Blue Man Group.

> *un*official **TIP**
> If you hear the designation "NoHo," it means "north of Houston," the area around Broadway and Lafayette whose commercial spirit has more in common with the West Village these days than the East.

There are still marks of the area's more-prosperous days of yore. The **Merchant's House Museum** (☎ 212-777-1089; **www.merchants house.com**), just south of the Public Theater at 29 East Fourth Street, is an intact 1830s Greek Revival home with all of its furnishings, paintings, and even books just the way they were when merchant Seabury Tredwell forbade his daughter Gertrude to marry a man he disapproved of. Gertrude then decided never to marry at all.

Sex also used to be an issue at **McSorley's Old Ale House,** which from its founding in 1854 until the 1970s admitted only men; other than that, it's still the same old saloon—complete with a "wanted" poster for John Wilkes Booth, a pair of Houdini's handcuffs, and a legendary array of old wishbones (East Seventh Street near Cooper Square; ☎ 212-474-9148 or **www.mcsorleysnewyork.com**).

Today, the Bowery is beginning to regain its luster. Though the Amato Opera has dissolved, the **Amore Opera** and **Bleecker Street Opera** have opened, both formed by members of the original. And although it's just to the south of Houston Street, the **New Museum of Contemporary Art** is a new landmark on the Bowery skyline.

An odd little spire seems to poke up above Broadway where the street makes a funny little quirk around what was then an apple orchard; the spire leads down to the lovely Gothic Revival **Grace Church** at 802 Broadway (☎ 212-254-2000; **www.gracechurch.org**), designed by St. Patrick's architect James Renwick when he was 23 years old. It has particularly beautiful stained glass in the pre-Raphaelite style, and its moment in the celebrity sun occurred in 1863, when P. T. Barnum staged General Tom Thumb's wedding there.

CHELSEA

IN 1750, WHEN RETIRED MAJOR THOMAS CLARKE, a veteran of the French and Indian Wars, acquired the land from Eighth Avenue to the Hudson River between West 14th and 25th streets, he named it, in what must have seemed a rather ambitious flight of fancy, after one of London's most fashionable districts. For many years, it remained primarily residential and affluent, even when the original estate was subdivided and luxury row houses constructed in the mid–19th century. But then construction began on the elevated Hudson River Railroad along Tenth and Eleventh avenues, and the gradual industrialization of the riverfront caused the residential neighborhood to retreat; by the turn of the 20th century, the westernmost parts of the neighborhood were inhabited by Irish longshoremen who worked the piers and warehouses.

unofficial **TIP**
Richard Rodgers's ballet *Slaughter on Tenth Avenue* and the Marlon Brando classic movie *On the Waterfront* were set in Chelsea, that neighborhood's equivalent of *West Side Story*.

But Chelsea always harbored an intellectual and philosophical culture. Major Clarke's son-in-law, Benjamin Moore, was bishop of the Episcopal Diocese of New York and later president of Columbia College (now Columbia University). Moore's son was Clement Clarke Moore of (though his authorship is now disputed) "A Visit from St. Nicholas ('Twas the Night before Christmas)" fame; but at the time he was renowned as one of the finest Greek and Hebrew scholars in the world, and he followed his father into Columbia, where he taught Greek and Oriental literature.

Chelsea was one of the early theatrical centers (Pike's Opera House, later the Grand Opera House, was a major venue for a century until its demolition in 1960). It was the original Hollywood (Mary Pickford worked out of a studio on West 26th Street), and over the years it has been home to dozens of artists and writers—many famously on the skids, but hugely influential.

Chelsea was an early fashion center and is still home to the **Fashion Institute of Technology (FIT),** on Seventh Avenue at 27th Street (☎ 212-217-4558; **www.fitnyc.edu**), and the fading remnants of the **Fur District** and **Millinery District** above 27th Street. More promisingly, in recent years, the southernmost stretch of Chelsea, especially 14th Street, has become a label-centric boutique strip; see Part Eight, Shopping, for more information.

unofficial **TIP**
For a description of Chelsea's extensive modern-art scene, see the section on "Great Neighborhoods for Shopping" in Part Eight.

If you're interested in fashion and design, stop by the free galleries at FIT, which, like the better-known **Costume Institute** at the Metropolitan Museum, assembles special exhibits that either trace a style through history or showcase designers or collectors and that sometimes detail a technique or material. The galleries are open until 8 p.m. during the week.

The 19-story **Starrett-Lehigh Building,** which occupies the block between 11th and 12th avenues and 26th and 27th streets, was constructed in 1931 as a warehouse and freight terminal for the railroads; the old truck-sized elevator now carries such occupants as Martha Stewart—and her car—directly to the nifty ninth-floor parking spaces.

The redevelopment of Chelsea Piers into a gigantic sports and play complex (see Part Nine, Exercise and Recreation) has spurred the renovation of local warehouses into not only art spaces but also luxury condominiums. Chelsea is also beginning to develop a reputation as a cutting-edge architectural landscape: consider Frank Gehry's design for the **IAC headquarters** across from Chelsea Piers on the West Side Highway between 18th and 19th streets, which looks something like an Issey Miyake pleated dress, and the Jean Nouvel–designed luxury condos alongside that at 19th Street.

Today, Chelsea is generally agreed to extend from Fifth Avenue to West Street (the West Side Highway) on the Hudson and above Greenwich Village from 14th Street north to 34th Street. (A few people, primarily those in the real-estate business, refer to the area below 23rd as "prime Chelsea"; the nicer term for the northern section is "Chelsea Heights.")

Most of Major Clarke's property was inherited by his grandson, Clement Clarke Moore, who in addition to his academic interests was something of a philanthropist. Among his gifts, the public-good component of his commercial development was the land for **The General**

Theological Seminary, on Ninth Avenue between West 20th and 21st streets (☎ 212-243-5150; **www.nyts.edu**). Moore later served three decades as professor of Biblical learning there, which is one reason **St. Mark's Library** now has what is believed to be the largest collection of Latin Bibles in the world. Its West Building is the oldest example of Gothic Revival architecture in the city.

Across Ninth Avenue from The General Theological Seminary is **St. Peter's Episcopal Church** (346 West 20th Street; ☎ 212-929-2390; **www.stpeterschelsea.com**); Moore insisted that it should be built in the style of a classical Greek temple, and the foundation was, but in midconstruction, church officials shifted to the Gothic style then sweeping England.

unofficial **TIP**
Need a break? Stroll through the **Chelsea Market,** on Ninth Avenue between 15th and 16th streets, where some of the city's best bakers, cheese makers, soup brewers, and even noodle makers—the superfusion Buddakan restaurant—lay out their wares.

The elaborate Gothic Revival building that is now the **Serbian Orthodox Cathedral of St. Sava,** at 15–20 West 26th Street (☎ 212-242-9240; **www.stsavanyc.org**), was built as Trinity Chapel. In 1885, Edith Jones, or "Miss Pussy," as she was also known, was married here and emerged as Mrs. Edward Robbins Wharton; she used it as the model for the church in *The Age of Innocence.*

St. John the Baptist (☎ 212-564-9070; **www .padrepioshrine.com**), on West 31st Street just west of Seventh Avenue, is like a geode— nearly obscured by the development around it, especially Penn Station, which dwarfs the five-bell tower. It's an impressive structure nonetheless.

The area around the General Theological Seminary is particularly nice for strolling. The home at Ninth Avenue and West 21st Street with the ornate peaked roof is the oldest home in the neighborhood, built in the 1820s. When Moore subdivided the property in 1830, he required the residential developers to put gardens in front of the homes and trees along the street; the exteriors of the town houses along West 21st Street between Ninth and Tenth avenues are nearly intact, though many of the buildings are now apartments or shops. The Greek Revival row houses along West 20th Street in the same block were originally constructed as middle-class rental units in the late 1930s; notice the cast-iron detailing and the brownstone door frames that became a synonym for upscale Manhattan homes.

The block bounded by West 23rd and 24th and Ninth and Tenth is taken up by the **London Terrace Apartments** (now a co-op). During the Depression, for some speculative reason, developers tried to play on the name by razing the mid-19th-century Greek Revival complex there and replacing it with this Mayfair-wannabe block with a garden in the middle and doormen dressed as London "bobbies." Across

Tenth at 519 West 23rd Street is the former home of the WPA Theatre, one of the best-known Off-Broadway venues; *Little Shop of Horrors* and *Steel Magnolias* were launched here, among others.

Perhaps the most famous address in the neighborhood is the **Hotel Chelsea,** at 222 West 23rd Street between Seventh and Eighth avenues (☎ 212-243-3700; **www.hotelchelsea.com**). At various times, this quite large and surprisingly attractive building was home or hotel to O. Henry, Mark Twain, Thomas Wolfe, Arthur Miller, Tennessee Williams, Brendan Behan, Vladimir Nabokov, Sarah Bernhardt, Dylan Thomas, Virgil Thomson, Jack Kerouac, Bob Dylan, Eugene O'Neill, and assorted touring rock stars; Room 100 is where, in 1978, sometime Sex Pistol Sid Vicious, high on heroin, stabbed his longtime girlfriend, Nancy Spungen. Though the hotel had developed a reputation s something of a high-minded flophouse, it has undergone substantial renovation.

Also on West 23rd Street near Sixth Avenue is the **Masonic Grand Lodge,** which has one of the most elaborate interiors in the city, with gilding, murals, and multiple pipe organs. This Lodge, St. John's No. 1, owns the Bible on which George Washington and several of his successors took the oath of office, though the volume is usually on display at Federal Hall on Wall Street. The lodge building is open for guided tours on weekdays (**www.nymasons.org**).

This neighborhood is also home to three small and particularly special-interest collections: the **Museum of Sex** (27th Street and Fifth Avenue; ☎ 212-689-6337; **mos.dreamhosters.com**), **Tibet House** (22 West 15th Street; ☎ 212-807-0563; **www.tibethouse.org**), and the new **Rubin Museum of Art** at 150 West 17th Street at Seventh Avenue (☎ 212-620-5000; **www.rmanyc.org**), devoted to Himalayan art (profiled in detail in Part Six). The first is a quintessentially American institution, with exhibits that range from the curious and even quaint (fliers for patent medicines, antique underwear, and nickelodeon-style film of pioneering ecdysiasts) to the X-tremely graphic (clips of hard-core films on repeating loops). Not surprisingly, no one under 18 is admitted. Tibet House, on the other hand, is a museum in exile, some 350 pieces of art that staffers hope to return to Tibet when that nation achieves independence.

There's one other area of Chelsea worth strolling through: the **Flower District,** the wholesale flower vendors in the area around Sixth and Seventh avenues between about 23rd and 26th streets.

GRAMERCY PARK AND MURRAY HILL

THIS OLD AND IN MANY CASES WELL-PRESERVED section of Manhattan, which faces Chelsea across Sixth Avenue from 14th street to about 42nd, is one of the city's most attractive, especially to architecture fans, punctuated by squares and parks and baroque white-collar firms. It was the Gilded Age's "uptown," home to society's biggest names (and bank accounts). We do mean "well preserved": of the 100 original residences in just **Murray Hill** that were listed in the 1892 Social Register, more than 60 survive. It is also the area that symbolized the commercial ambitions of the Gilded Age, home to the **Flatiron Building** in the triangle of Fifth Avenue, Broadway, and 23rd Street, which was the world's largest building when it was completed in 1903; the **Metropolitan Life Insurance Building** (now Credit Suisse) at Madison and 23rd, which topped Woolworth by adding a tower in 1909; and the **Empire State Building** (profiled in depth in Part Six), which beat them both to the sky limit in 1931.

In fact, this neighborhood might well be called the Gilded City because of the number of glittering spires in the area, most famously the **New York Life Insurance Building,** on Madison between 26th and 27th streets, designed by Woolworth architect Cass Gilbert and with an octagonal gold stupa on top; the gold-domed 1898 Beaux Arts **Sohmer Piano Building,** now a condo, on Fifth Avenue at 22nd Street; the gargoyle-and-grille-festooned Art Deco **Chrysler Building** at 42nd Street and Lexington Avenue; its gargantuan neighbor, the chromium-, nickel-, and stainless-steel-clad **Socony-Mobil (formerly Standard Oil) Building** at 150 East 42nd; and **St. Vartan,** the "church with the golden dome," on Second Avenue.

Power and influence stalked through this area from **Union Square** up Broadway to **Madison Square,** up Fifth Avenue to the **New York Public Library** and Park Avenue to **Grand Central Terminal.** Union Square, at the intersection of Broadway and Fourth Avenue between East 14th and East 17th streets, is the first of a series of squares marking the diagonal northward progress of Broadway. It began as a potter's field and evolved into a highly desirable residential neighborhood before the Civil War. Frederick Law Olmsted and Calvert Vaux, designers of Central Park, were hired to renovate the square in 1872. Curiously, although it was the site of a huge pro-Union rally shortly after the firing on Fort Sumter, believed to have drawn an unprecedented quarter-million people, and the gathering ground for the first Labor Day parade in 1882, it was named not for any Civil War sentiment or labor dispute but because it was such an important intersection and the transfer station of streetcar lines—a "union station," in effect.

unofficial **TIP**
The term *Midtown* is very loose; by some accounts it begins as far south as 14th Street; other descriptions have it starting at 34th and encompassing Murray Hill. But the essential character of Murray Hill seems to us to be closer to Madison Square Park and Gramercy Park than Times Square. The Public Library certainly owes its allegiance to Gramercy Park, since the bulk of the money for its founding came from the estate of resident Samuel Tilden.

Gramercy Park, the neighborhood centered on the actual Gramercy Park, at the foot of

Lexington Avenue between East 20th and East 21st, was one of the first gated communities, as we would call them now. In the 1830s, developer Samuel Ruggles bought a large chunk of the old Stuyvesant estate that included a creek shaped like a "crooked little knife," or "Crommessie." Ruggles wanted to entice a wealthy patronage, so he filled in the marshy creek area and laid out a London-style park in the heart of his territory, with one adjoining avenue named for the famous Revolutionary War victory and one on the south side called Irving Place after writer Washington Irving. Astonishingly, the square itself is still a private park, the only one in the city—area residents have keys to the lock—and the entire area is a historic district.

Society figures and politicians made their homes here (Union Square was the home of Tammany Hall), and it was near enough to the theater district to attract the most important actors and writers as well. (The **"Block Beautiful"** is simply a well-preserved row of houses along East 19th Street between Irving Place and Third Avenue; theater great Mrs. Patrick Campbell and silent-movie vamp Theda Bara both lived—at various times, of course—at 132 East 19th.)

Edwin Booth, whose statue stands in Gramercy Park, founded the famous **Players Club** on the south side. It was the first "gentlemen's club" in America (though not the kind people speak of now); his partners in the scheme included Mark Twain and Teddy Roosevelt. It's not open to the public, but the exterior alone, a Greek Revival town house going for Baroque, is boggling.

The double brownstone next door to the Players Club was originally the home of Democratic governor and eventually presidential candidate Samuel J. Tilden, who hired Calvert Vaux to redo the interiors, which included John LeFarge stained glass, a vaulted glass dome, turquoise ceiling tiles, and black-walnut woodwork. It's now the offices of the **National Arts Club,** and the gallery space on the ground floor is occasionally open so that nonmembers can glimpse the glories.

Roosevelt himself was a local boy, born on East 20th Street between Park and Broadway. The **Theodore Roosevelt Birthplace** (☎ 212-260-1616; **www.nps.gov/thrb**) had to be reconstructed because the original house was demolished during World War I, but the five rooms of period furniture, memorabilia, teddy bears, and campaign souvenirs are real.

The night-lit clock tower that looks down from Irving Plaza at East 14th is part of the Consolidated Edison—aka **Con Ed**—headquarters;

unofficial **TIP**
Politics makes strange neighbors: Tilden became popular for opposing master skimmer, political fixer, and sometime philanthropist William "Boss" Tweed, whose Tammany Hall was only a block away on East 14th Street (now the **New York Film Academy**). Teddy Roosevelt made his New York name reforming the notoriously corrupt city police force and exposing child slavery on the Lower East Side.

at various times this site held Tammany Hall and the Academy of Music. In fact, before merging with New York Edison, the company was the Consolidated Gas Company of New York, an amalgam of six smaller companies. That, in fact, is why this section of Manhattan was the turf of the Gashouse Gangs; they got the moniker because with so many factories competing to supply the city's lights—most of them along the East River—their employees literally fought for subscribers.

And if you've ever wondered about the name *Tammany,* it, or rather he, was actually Tamanend, a Native American chief who supposedly befriended William Penn. The New York Tammany Society, incorporated in 1789, was originally a Masonic-style fraternity with a Native American twist: 13 "tribes"—for the 13 colonies—with pseudo-Indian ceremonies and titles.

Madison Square Park, between Fifth and Madison avenues and between West 23rd and West 26th streets, was part of the original grid plan of 1811, though only well into the mid–19th century did it become much more than a commons and parade ground. (It also had a turn as a pauper's cemetery—which goes to show that the dead, particularly the poor dead, rarely stand in the way of monied progress.)

Just alongside the park were the first and second **Madison Square Gardens.** (The current behemoth is the fourth.) The second was a palatial exhibition hall-entertainment complex designed by Sanford White; its rooftop garden was where White was shot to death in 1906 by millionaire socialite Harry Thaw, who believed White was having an affair with his showgirl wife, Evelyn Nesbit. The original New York Knickerbockers, the nation's first organized baseball team, played at Madison Square Park. Before it was permanently hoisted into harbor-lighting position, the torch in the upraised hand of the Statue of Liberty was exhibited here as well.

Overlooking Madison Square is the famous clock tower of the old **Met Life Insurance Building,** 384 feet taller than London's Big Ben. In the lobby are a series of historical murals painted by famed children's illustrator N. C. Wyeth. (At press time, access to the lobby was limited.)

A few doors up, at Madison and East 25th, is the **New York State Supreme Court Appellate Division,** believed to be the busiest appellate court in the world (among the former plaintiffs here: Babe Ruth, Charlie Chaplin, Edgar Allan Poe, and Harry Houdini). This building is as astounding as its perp list: the many fine sculptures outside are matched by an interior crammed with extraordinary stained glass, murals as elaborate as those of the Library of Congress, marble stairs, and carved seats, which you can see unless court is in session.

On the east side of Third Avenue is **Sniffen Court,** a beautifully preserved mews of ten Romanesque Revival former carriage houses, built about 1850, at 150–158 East 36th Street.

Murray Hill itself gets its name from colonial merchant Robert Murray, whose country estate it was: it ranges from First to Fifth avenues between 34th and 42nd streets. Legend has it that Mary Murray invited General Howe to tea in 1776, knowing he would be far too polite to refuse, and thus bought Washington time to escape up the island to Fort Tryon.

One of the greatest of the Murray Hill mansions is now a fine museum: the magnificent **Morgan Library & Museum,** at 36th and Madison (profiled in Part Six), which houses an unparalleled collection of illuminated medieval manuscripts, rare books, etchings, musical scores, and prints.

Although they no longer exist, two other neighborhood mansions have a peculiarly New Yorkian history. On the block of Fifth Avenue between West 33rd and West 34th streets stood two of the many Astor family mansions: one belonging to William Waldorf Astor, then the richest man in America; and the other to his aunt, Mrs. William Astor, the Caroline Schermerhorn Astor who ran both New York and Newport societies with an iron glove. A family argument between the two led to William Astor's moving out and putting up a hotel called the Waldorf on his mansion's site. Almost immediately after, his imperious aunt moved out and built a connecting hotel, the Astoria. Despite the estrangement, the two hotels operated as a single company—though with the provision that she could block off the connection at any time—until 1929, when they were demolished in advance of the construction of the Empire State Building, and of the construction of the Park Avenue Hotel still called the **Waldorf-Astoria.**

The Astors (among others) remained loyal to their congregations, and many churches profited by their presence. For instance, **"The Little Church around the Corner,"** at East 29th and Fifth Avenue, officially The Church of the Transfiguration, (☎ 212-684-6770; **www .littlechurch.org**), was given its antique Stations of the Cross by Laura Astor Delano. The church became famous because it buried actors when some more "respectable" churches wouldn't, and it has a collection of theatrically inspired stained glass as well as more traditional religious pieces, some quite old. (The Actors Guild is headquartered upstairs.) Actor Joseph Jefferson gave the church its nickname in 1870 when his colleague George Holland died, and Jefferson is featured in one of the windows as Rip van Winkle, a part he played for 40 years, carrying Holland's body. Another window is a full-length portrait of Edwin Booth by John LaFarge. P. G. Wodehouse was married here and wrote it into the lyrics of a song. In fact, it was such a popular wedding spot that a 1934 *New Yorker* magazine cover showed a newly married couple exiting the church. O. Henry (William Sydney Porter), whose funeral was here—nearly disrupting a wedding—mentioned the church in several short stories. Though small, it's one of the loveliest churches in the entire city, a Gothic beauty filled with elaborate carvings, polychrome, gilding, wrought iron, and a pair of 16th-century Flemish painted panels as well as a fine pipe organ (and boys' choir).

The Gothic Revival **Marble Collegiate Church,** across Fifth Avenue on 29th Street (☎ 212-686-2770; **www.marblechurch.org**), is famous for its large and vivid stained-glass windows, two of them Tiffany, and for former pastor Norman Vincent Peale of *The Power of Positive Thinking* fame.

The **Church of the Incarnation** (☎ 212-689-6350; **www.church oftheincarnation.org**), on Madison Avenue at East 35th, where Delanos (and Roosevelts) and Morgans were parishioners, may be modest on the outside, but its art collection—Louis Comfort Tiffany, William Morris, and Edward Burne-Jones stained-glass windows; Augustus Saint-Gaudens and Daniel French sculptures—is anything but modest. (Its flock might have considered the gold-leaf dome atop **St. Vartan Cathedral,** on Second Avenue between East 34th and East 35th, to be ostentatious, but then St. Vartan is the seat of the Armenian Orthodox Church in the United States.)

MIDTOWN WEST: TIMES SQUARE, THE THEATER DISTRICT, AND BRYANT PARK

MIDTOWN WEST IS TOURIST CENTRAL, so to speak, the most-visited sector of New York City: its entertainment center (highbrow and low-), one of the major cultural centers, a burgeoning retail area, and home to most of the major media outlets, which, come "morning show" time, adds to what is already a major traffic jam. (And if there's an event at the Javits Convention Center, there's an extra influx after dark of off-duty business types.)

Ranging from 42nd Street north to West 59th Street, Columbus Circle, and Central Park South, Midtown West is home to **Broadway, Times Square, Rockefeller Center,** and **Radio City Music Hall.** It also contains some important museums—most notably the **Museum of Modern Art**—as well as the New York Public Library and **Bryant Park,** the city's second-busiest green space.

But that's not nearly a complete list of the neighborhood's cultural landmarks. Give your regards to Broadway, sure—that's "Yankee Doodle Dandy" George M. Cohan on the point of Duffy Square at 45th Street—but remember you to **Herald Square**? Broadway and West 34th. Come and meet those dancing feet? On 42nd Street. How do you get to **Carnegie Hall**? Practice, practice, practice—and walk to West 57th and Sixth Avenue, just around the corner from Broadway. And if you're a fan of pop music anytime from World War II through the MTV era, you have a connection here at the **Brill Building** and the West 48th Street "Music Row." (Sing along, guy: "Boy from New York

City," "Up on the Roof," "On Broadway," "Under the Boardwalk," "Spanish Harlem" . . . and about a thousand others.)

Times Square is the obvious place to start exploring Midtown, not only because the subway station there serves so many lines (and many others are only blocks away), but also because it has its own police station, a fully stocked visitor center, and its own fleet of tourist-information officers. You should probably start by picking up a copy of the neighborhood guide at the **Times Square Information Center** in the old Embassy Theatre, on Seventh Avenue between 46th and 47th streets—it offers tourist services, ATMs, tickets, Internet access, and wheelchair-accessible bathrooms (☎ 212-768-1560; **www .timessquarenyc.org**). You can take a tour of myriad attractions—some historical, some hilarious, and not a few strictly commercial—by showing up at the visitor center at noon on Friday.

Times Square draws more than 20 million visitors a year. This is where the famous ball drops to mark the arrival of the new year, as it has every year for more than a century (except for a couple of blackout years during World War II). It's where the Rockettes kick in chorus line as well as where *A Chorus Line* kicks.

It's also increasingly popular—again—with locals, thanks in part to the 2009 transformation of most of Broadway between Madison Square and Columbus Circle, and particularly the blocks around Times Square, into a pedestrian mall. Hundreds of chairs are set up in the medians, with plenty of benches and cafe tables;

unofficial **TIP**
Those running-light headlines at Fox News, NBC, and Reuters are called "zippers," while the versions tracking the Dow Jones average and NASDAQ figures are correctly referred to as "tickers."

and the now annual simulcast of the Metropolitan Opera's season-opening performance, shown free on the many supersize screens around Times Square, has become a tradition for many.

One of the area's most recognizable newer landmarks is the design-award-winning **TKTS booth** in the pedestrian center at 47th Street, an underlit, all-glass "amphitheater" that turns the crowd into another stage show.

The other candidate for most famous address is **Rockefeller Center,** that TV-friendly complex of 19 Art Deco buildings between Fifth and Seventh avenues and 48th and 51st streets, clustered around the famous plaza-cum-ice-rink and including the eternally family-friendly **Radio City Music Hall,** with its Rockettes and classic revivals. Its facades are virtual museums of sculpture, bas-relief, gilding, mosaics, carvings, and molding; during the Great Depression, construction of the original 14 buildings kept a quarter of a million laborers and artists busy. (For tour information on Rockefeller Center, see Part Six.)

The old **Garment District** is at the south end of the area, which is why some parts of Seventh Avenue have signs reading FASHION

unofficial **TIP**
Just as vibrant as Times Square, though in a more laid-back and less touristy fashion, is **Bryant Park,** on Sixth Avenue between 42nd and 44th streets.

AVENUE—and why design tycoon Peter Nygård has just moved his company's world headquarters from Canada to Times Square. It's also where you'll find the **Diamond District,** on West 47th Street between Sixth and Fifth. (The district, with its wall-to-wall and mall-to-mall shops hawking earrings, rings, and pins, is currently also a gantlet of merchants offering to buy gold and diamonds from those hard hit by the recession.) The Diamond District dates from almost the same era as Rockefeller Center, when the Jewish merchants of Europe began fleeing the increasingly restrictive anti-Semitic laws.

The famous **Rainbow Room** (**www.rainbowroom.com**), on the 65th floor of the tallest building in Rockefeller Center, offers Eve's favorite view of the New York skyline, especially at dusk, but at press time it was closed. Meanwhile, **Top of the Rock** (☎ 877-692-7625 or 212-698-2000; **www.topoftherocknyc.com**), the newly reopened observation deck on the 69th floor, and its even higher walk-up platform, are open to the air in all directions.

But what you see there now is far from what you would have seen in previous centuries, even previous decades. The area started out as a horse farm that belonged to one of George Washington's generals; called Longacre Square, it was home to stables and blacksmiths and the occasional thief. After the turn of the 19th century, it was one of the pastoral neighborhoods bought up and (profitably) developed by John Jacob Astor. It remained a fashionable address for some time, and one of its nicknames, the Tenderloin District, refers to that era, when the area north of Chelsea up to Times Square was considered the prime real-estate location in the city. However, as the city moved north, the district returned to its more questionable character. Until the *New York Times* moved its headquarters to the neighborhood in 1904, it was struggling to regain its position. In the early decades of the 20th century, it became an entertainment center, which also led to its becoming a hot spot for gambling, prostitution, and eventually corruption; once the Depression hit, the seedy elements took control of the entire neighborhood—still called the Tenderloin, but no longer with a particularly classy intonation.

Herald Square was the very center of the venomous red-light and speakeasy district. It was partly the arrival of **Macy's Department Store** in 1902 that gave this area new respectability and encouraged the influx of the newspapers and financial institutions. Nowadays, Herald Square is most famous for serving as the finale stage for Macy's annual Thanksgiving Day Parade, where the arrival of Santa Claus signals the official beginning of the holiday shopping season.

In 1918, as World War I ended, opera superstar Enrico Caruso was staying in the Knickerbocker Hotel, at **6 Times Square** at 42nd, where the Gap store now is. When Caruso heard about the armistice, he came out onto his balcony and sang "The Star-Spangled Banner" and then the Italian and French national anthems.

Even then, the criminal elements lingered in the area. The area from Eighth Avenue west to the Hudson River and from the mid-30s to the upper 50s was known as **Hell's Kitchen,** home to the gang of that name (and many others) long before TV chef Gordon Ramsay came to town. It was also sometimes called Paddy's Market or **Clinton,** the name now coming back into style.

The **Landmark Tavern** at 11th Avenue and 46th Street, open since 1868, was the haunt of local-boy-turned-Hollywood-tough George Raft when he was alive, and still is, according to legend. (And not just Raft: a Confederate soldier and an Irish immigrant girl supposedly haunt the second and third floors, respectively.) And the building at **330 West 45th Street** was formerly the steak house from which in 1930 Judge Joseph Force Crater famously disappeared without a trace.

Nowadays, the strip along 11th and 12th avenues is mostly reduced to auto-body shops and a few X-rated theaters playing off (or off-off) the Broadway name. **Ninth Avenue,** however, particularly through the 40s, is a bazaar of small ethnic restaurants—Brazilian, Jamaican, Afghani, Peruvian, Greek, Turkish, Thai, Moroccan, Japanese, and even Burmese, as well as the relatively tame Italian and Mexican. Not only are these some of the better restaurants in the **Theater District,** but they're also much hipper (where do you think the actors eat?) and a lot less expensive than the bigger and better-known places closer to Broadway. But for pre-theater class, try **Restaurant Row,** the block on West 46th Street between Eighth and Ninth avenues, home to the **Firebird Russian Restaurant, Orso,** celeb spot **Joe Allen Restaurant, B. Smith,** and **Becco,** among others.

Calling Times Square "The Crossroads of the World" may be something of an exaggeration, but considering that 26 million visitors a year come through here, not that much of one. Of course, it's really more than a true square: though centered on the junction of Broadway and Seventh Avenue and 42nd and 43rd streets, what's referred to as Times Square reaches from Sixth to Eighth avenues and from 40th up to at least 47th. (Descriptions continue to expand.)

On the eastern edge of the area, however, especially between Fifth and Sixth avenues, you can still see traces of the neighborhood's golden age. A lot of local property belonged to the very wealthiest families—Rockefeller Center wasn't built on another family's property, obviously—and at one time there were almost more Vanderbilt homes that a cabbie could keep track of.

unofficial **TIP**
"Crossroads of the World" or not, Midtown West is certainly a major crossroads of Manhattan: Several of the large subway transfer points, including 34th Street, Penn Station, Times Square, Rockefeller Center, 42nd Street, 49th Street, and Columbus Circle, are in this area, and so is the **Port Authority Bus Terminal.** The **Lincoln Tunnel,** one end of the nation's first transcontinental highway, runs west from West 38th Street. And at the western edge of the neighborhood is the unlovely but essential West Side Highway.

One block where you can still get a sense of those days is **West 54th Street** between Fifth and Sixth avenues. The houses between 5 and 15 West 54th Street were constructed in the last years of the 19th century for families with such names as Lehman (Philip Lehman, head of that financial family, who commissioned the Beaux Arts residence at 7 West 54th, with its three circular windows and second-floor balcony), Rockefeller (John D. Jr. moved into 13 West 54th when he married Abby Aldrich, so future New York Governor Nelson Rockefeller not only grew up here but also died here), Goodman (John Junius Goodman, first cousin to J. P. Morgan and a banker shrewd enough to have the eastern two-fifths section of the five-bay building made separate so he could rent it out), and Starr (Dr. Moses Allen Starr, the country's most prominent neurologist and sometime colleague of Sigmund Freud.)

Family ties linger: Goodman's son Philip Goodwin and Edward Durrell Stone would go on to design the Museum of Modern Art on 53rd Street. Philip Lehman's son Robert inherited the house and used it as a gallery for the art collection that became the Lehman Wing of the Metropolitan Museum. (Some of the architectural elements of the Lehman House were also incorporated into the Met, but others, including stained glass and fireplace surrounds, have been returned to the renovators.) And if it weren't now MoMa's sculpture garden, 4 West 54th would be John D. Rockefeller's house. The whole block.

When people talk about "Broadway," they rarely mean the actual street; they really mean the Theater District, the less florid term for the old **Great White Way** (Broadway between 42nd and 53rd streets) and its sometimes lower-brow entertainment options. (Though drastically reduced in number, the remnants of Times Square's time as Manhattan's red-light district linger, especially around the edges. However, it's not like New Orleans's Bourbon Street; you won't feel the need to blindfold your underage kids.)

This has been a performance center for decades, and happily many of the older, more-elaborate venues have been preserved. (If you get tickets to a play, look up and around; many of the theaters have elaborate vintage murals, ceiling details, etc.) The latest revival of "legitimate" Times Square can in part be attributed to the Disney Company's meticulous and expensive (reportedly $34 million) 1993 restoration of the historic **New Amsterdam Theatre** on West 42nd Street at Seventh Avenue, once home to the legendary Ziegfeld Follies, as a showcase for its extraordinary adaptation of *The Lion King* (which has moved to the nearby Minskoff Theatre, replaced at the New Amsterdam by *Mary Poppins*).

It wasn't just the New Amsterdam with which Disney contributed to the revival of Times Square. Its first store there, which opened in 1994, was hailed by local officials as proof of the area's cleanup—the replacement of sleazy with Sneezy, so to speak. Though Disney moved out in 2000, it recently returned in even greater glory, taking over much of the old Virgin Megastore site on Broadway for its own character-merchandise megastore and technology showcase.

The **New Victory** across the street was once the neighborhood's most famous burlesque house, the Minsky theater, where such celebrity ecdysiasts as Gypsy Rose Lee ruled the marquee. In a lovely bit of irony, it's now a throwback to the golden age of children's theater.

The **Paramount Building,** at 1501 Broadway between 43rd and 44th streets, was built in 1926 at a cost of $14.5 million, and its illuminated clock tower and 22-foot globe could be seen as far away as New Jersey. It was a premiere (and premier) location, serving as both Paramount Studio's flagship cinema and as a legitimate theater venue. Such first-rank entertainers as Sinatra, the Dorsey Brothers, and Martin and Lewis were booked here, but it was also home to Alan Freed's original *Rock 'n' Roll Show.* Appropriately, it's now a **Hard Rock Cafe.** The baroquely extravagant **Times Square Church** at 237 West 51st Street was built as the Warner Hollywood movie palace in 1930 but quickly transformed into a playhouse—*Jesus Christ Superstar* was housed here, even more appropriately—and is now the site of ecumenical services (☎ 212-541-6300; **www.tscnyc.org**).

And if you love old-fashioned liturgical music, the Sainte-Chapelle (in Paris)–inspired **Church of St. Mary the Virgin,** at 145 West 46th Street just east of Times Square, has a famous pipe organ and choir and hosts concerts by the New York Repertory Orchestra.

kids If you consider **Madame Tussauds** wax museum "entertainment," you can enjoy that here, too, on 42nd between Seventh and Eighth avenues, right next to the **Ripley's Believe It or Not! Odd-itorium.** And just up on 44th Street between Seventh and Eighth is the Discovery Channel's **Times Square Exposition Center,** which stages exhibits on such cable-channel favorites as the *Titanic, Leonardo da Vinci,* and *King Tut.* None of these is inexpensive—adults can expect to spend $25 to $40 per ticket—but compared to theater tickets, that's still something of a bargain.

Theme restaurants are another hallmark of this area: although **B. B. King's Blues Club & Grill** and its **Lucille's Bar & Grill,** just west of Times Square on 42nd Street, actually belong to the owners of the venerable Blue Note club in Greenwich Village and are live-music venues, most are just eateries with souvenir shops, including the Hard Rock, the **ESPN Zone, Planet Hollywood, Mars 2112,** and the 1950s-themed **Ellen's Stardust Diner.**

Even the stores here are like theme parks: The huge **Toys"R"Us** at the corner of Broadway and 44th has a 34-foot-long, animatronic *T. rex* from *Jurassic Park* and a 60-foot-tall indoor Ferris wheel.

But Broadway is only one slice of the entertainment and cultural venues in this neighborhood, both classical and casual. On the "up-town" side of Times Square are many of the more important Off-Broadway venues: the Shriner-Moorish Revival **New York City Center,** on West 55th between Sixth and Seventh avenues (☎ 212-581-1212; **www.nycitycenter.org**), Carnegie Hall (☎ 212-247-7800; **www.carnegie hall.org**), and **Town Hall** (123 West 43rd Street, between Sixth Avenue and Broadway; ☎ 212-840-2824; **www.the-townhall-nyc.org**), famous to Garrison Keillor fans as the Manhattan home of the radio show *A Prairie Home Companion.* The **Brill Building** was the onetime "Broadway" of pop music and the heart of Tin Pan Alley (at 1619 Broadway, between West 49th and West 50th streets). Although the Brill Building may be best known these days for the years when the likes of Neil Diamond, Carole King and Gerry Goffin, Jerry Leiber and Mike Stoller, Burt Bacharach and Hal David, Tommy Boyce and Bobby Hart, Neil Sedaka, and Laura Nyro worked here, it was actually the home of music publishers and composers going back to the big bands of Jimmy Dorsey, Glenn Miller, and Benny Goodman. (For more on the theatrical and classical venues, as well as how to use TKTS, see Part Ten, Entertainment and Nightlife.)

unofficial **TIP**
ABC—which, you may remember, now belongs to The Walt Disney Company—has a sidewalk-view studio in Times Square for *Good Morning America,* while NBC's *Today Show* packs Rockefeller Plaza even when there isn't a live concert.

Several landmarks in this area are named for media companies or figures—Herald Square, Times Square, **The Paley Center for Media,** Bryant Park—and several other media giants have headquarters here. The *New York Times,* which lent its name to Times Square, had to move out of the old tower on the square to larger digs on West 43rd Street early on, but it recently moved back to an extraordinary 650-foot-tall glass tower constructed back in the "old neighborhood" (at 620 Eighth Avenue, between West 40th and West 41st streets), and Reuters built its own glass skyscraper at 3 Times Square (between West 42nd and West 43rd). The Condé Nast magazine group, Reuters, Viacom, and Bertelsmann (the German publisher that has acquired Random House and others) have moved into the "new" Times Square, along with the huge Ernst & Young accounting and auditing firm, Morgan Stanley, Barclays, and other financial institutions. (If you can tear your eyes away from all the running news headlines and other distractions to read the building facades, you'll see many of these names.) Although MTV has left the building, the **Nokia Theater,** on Broadway at 44th Street, on the site of the late, great Astor Plaza cinema, is not only a product showcase but also a nightclub and music venue.

Herald Square is named for the *New York Herald* newspaper building at West 34th, just as Times Square was named for the *New York Times*. And just as Times Square isn't really square, Herald Square is actually a triangle. You could call the neighborhood the "Daily District": **Greeley Square,** another triangle one block south at West 33rd, was named for *New York Tribune* founder Horace Greeley, who made famous the phrase: "Go West, young man, and grow up with the country."

CBS Inc., the famous "Black Rock," is that monolith overshadowing the Paley Center at Sixth Avenue and West 52nd. (The Paley Center is named for longtime CBS CEO William S. Paley.) **NBC** and **MSNBC** famously have studios in Rockefeller Center (as does publishing giant Simon & Schuster); **Fox News** is on Sixth Avenue across the street.

At the top of the hour, make sure to look up at the **James Gordon Bennett Monument** at the north end of Herald Square, with its ten-foot statue of the goddess Minerva and the seven-foot-tall bronze blacksmiths, named Guff and Stuff, who swing their hammers and appear to strike the bell, though they don't actually touch it (there are synchronized mallets to protect the bell). They originally topped the parapet at the New York Herald Building; Bennett was founder and publisher of the paper. They were moved to the monument in 1940.

Midtown West is also home to several of the most important museums in New York City, including the recently (and extravagantly) renovated **Museum of Modern Art** on West 53rd between Fifth and Sixth avenues (☎ 212-708-9400; **www.moma.org**), near the slim and stunning eight-level **American Folk Art Museum** (45 West 53rd Street, between Fifth and Sixth avenues; ☎ 212-265-1040; **www.folkart museum.org**), and a block from The Paley Center for Media on West 52nd (☎ 212-621-6600; **www.paleycenter.org**). MoMA and the Paley Center are profiled in depth in Part Six. The expanded **International Center of Photography** is on Sixth Avenue between 43rd and 44th streets (☎ 212-857-0000; **www.icp.org**). And north of the Javits Convention Center and Lincoln Tunnel, on Pier 86 at the foot of West 46th Street, is the popular **Intrepid Sea, Air & Space Museum** (also profiled in Part Six).

One of the city's most recognizable landmarks—it's a movie backdrop staple—is the **New York Public Library,** on Fifth Avenue at 40th to 42nd streets. The 100-year-old Tennessee-pink-marble lions at the entrance were originally named Leo Astor and Leo Lenox, in honor of library benefactors John Jacob Astor and James Lenox, but they were nicknamed Patience (on the south side) and Fortitude by Mayor

Fiorello La Guardia during the Great Depression, and those names have stuck. The twin fountains are Beauty and Truth, which would please Keats. The building is rich with interior murals, paintings, documents (Jefferson's copy of the Declaration of Independence), and other treasures. The rededicated ceiling of the Gottesman Exhibition Hall sometimes outshines the exhibits. It's a 300-foot-long trompe l'oeil mural that seems to open the room to a classical sky inhabited by angels. And the glories of the great manuscripts and first-editions collection in Room 320 are primarily intellectual. You don't need permission to look around, but if you like, free tours leave from the front desk every day at 11 a.m. and 2 p.m.

Behind the library is the popular **Bryant Park.** But don't miss another architectural marvel facing the park from across 40th Street: now the **Bryant Park Hotel,** it was constructed in 1924 as the headquarters of the **American Radiator and Standard Sanitary Company,** and it looks as much like a radiator as the Chrysler Building does a car. Lavishly decorated in gold (representing fire) and black bricks (representing coal), a mix of Gothic and Deco elements, it lifts a gleaming parapet to the sky and was painted at night by Georgia O'Keeffe in 1927. Appropriately for this newspaper-friendly neighborhood, architect Eliel Saarinen had originally submitted this design to the *Chicago Tribune* for its headquarters competition, but lost.

Also be sure to walk past the **New York City Yacht Club,** at 37 West 44th Street between Fifth and Sixth avenues; its facade is a fantasy on a great oceangoing ship Jack Aubrey might covet. And attorneys must peek inside the **New York City Bar Association** headquarters at 38 West 44th, where you'll see trompe l'oeil busts of some of the city's, and the nation's, great legislators and judges, including Learned Hand, Charles Evans Hughes, Benjamin Cardozo, and Aaron Burr.

MIDTOWN EAST

THIS IS WHAT MIGHT BE THOUGHT OF as Manhattan's genteel getaway, home to many of the city's most famous hotels, the great shopping boulevard of Fifth Avenue, and some of New York's greatest architectural landmarks, spiritual and secular. It's also where many of the city's legendary, and nostalgic-heavy, bars are located, almost worth a toddling tour of their own.

Among the hotel names familiar to literary and libation fans are the **Waldorf-Astoria, New York Palace, St. Regis, Sherry-Netherland, Four Seasons,** and what is arguably New York's most famous temporary address, **The Plaza.**

This is also a living coffee-table book of monumental architecture. Among its landmarks are the lavishly restored Beaux Arts Grand Central Terminal at 42nd and Park Avenue (look up at the constellations winking in the ceiling); the gleaming, Buck Rogers–ish, Art Deco **Chrysler Building,** with its stainless steel "grill" crown and hood-ornament gargoyles saluting the spirit of the automotive age (Lexington at 42nd); the Mies van der Rohe–designed **Seagram Building,** on Park Avenue between East 52nd and East 53rd streets, elegant in its bronze and glass; the equally startling glass razor of the **Lever House** on Park at 53rd; the literally gilded palace—now part of the New York Palace Hotel—that was the **Villard House,** on Madison between 50th and 51st streets; **St. Patrick's Cathedral,** on Fifth at 50th, the largest decorated Gothic-style Catholic cathedral in this country (profiled in Part Six); and the reserved but powerful **United Nations** complex, a perfect architectural metaphor (and one that began undergoing a massive refurbishing and rehabbing in 2007), on the East River at 43rd Street (☎ 212-963-8687; **www.un.org**).

It's not architecture on nearly so grand a scale, but the little-known **General Society of Mechanics and Tradesmen** headquarters at 20 West 44th has not only a replica of the Parthenon frieze on the outside but also a fascinating little lock and vault museum with locks dating back to 4000 BC.

Fifth Avenue along the 40s and 50s and up along Central Park was the site of huge palaces during the Gilded Age, half a dozen belonging to the Vanderbilts alone and nearly as many to the Astors. Although many of the superrich moved farther uptown, among the remaining former houses is the New York Palace Hotel, designed by Stanford White in 1882 as a home with adjoining rental units for journalist, pub-

unofficial **TIP**
At Grand Central Terminal, be sure to peek into the **Campbell Apartment,** above the West Balcony, a 13th-century-Florentine-style hall that was once a luxury office and is now a trendy lounge.

lisher, railroad tycoon, and General Electric founder Henry Villard. (The north section of the hotel was the original offices of Random House books, founded by Bennett Cerf.)

You don't need permission to stroll around **Grand Central Terminal,** but if you'd like to know more about the classical sculptures and other decorations, contact **The Municipal Art Society of New York** (☎ 212-935-3960; **www.mas.org**), which leads tours ($10 suggested donation) Wednesdays at 12:30 p.m.

Step inside the Gothic tower at 60 West 42nd Street, at Vanderbilt Avenue (now called **One Grand Central Place; www.onegrandcentralplace .com**). The chandelier-lit lobby is also home to a statue of Abraham Lincoln—Daniel Chester French's model for the Lincoln Memorial in Washington.

St. Patrick's Cathedral may be the most famous church in the neighborhood, but it's not the only spectacular one. The Byzantine **St. Bartholomew's,** on Park at East 50th, is truly byzantine: part James Renwick, part Stanford White. St. Patrick's is the Gothic giant, but **St. Thomas Church,** just up the street at Fifth and 53rd, is as stubborn as a little David (☎ 212-757-7013; **www.stthomaschurch.org**). It's worth stopping in to admire its fantastic stone reredos, a wall behind the altar of 60 figures that represent Jesus, his apostles, and family, saints, martyrs, prophets, and missionaries. And at the foot of the gallery stairs, to the right as you enter, is an *Adoration of the Magi* believed to be the work of Peter Paul Rubens.

Another striking bit of architecture is **Tudor City,** a complex (40th to 43rd between First and Second avenues) of Henry VIII–style apartments, restaurants, shops, and services built in the 1920s as a sort of early urban-renewal project. (Weirdly, it faces the very modern Le Corbusier **United Nations** building.)

Nearby, on 42nd at Second Avenue, is the **News Building,** former home of the *Daily News.* It was used as the setting for the *Daily Planet* in the *Superman* movies, and there's an inside joke to that: the building has its own "planet," a huge, revolving globe, in the lobby.

There are two exhibition spaces in this area, both related to Japan, but of entirely different character. The **Japan Society,** on East 47th between First and Second avenues (☎ 212-832-1155; **www.japansociety.org**) offers exhibits of antique scroll paintings, textiles, ceramics, arms, and antiques, plus a traditional Japanese garden. On the other hand, the **Sony Wonder Technology Lab** (☎ 212-833-8100; **wondertechlab.sony.com**), on Madison between 55th and 56th, is Japanese technology at its best; this store-cum-showcase has become the city's hippest hands-on playground for both children (who talk with a robot, view the inner workings of the body, and surf the Web) and electronic-trend fashion victims.

Although Fifth Avenue was always a prime address, the stretches closer to the East River were not really "good" territory until well into the 20th century. From Fourth Avenue (before it was Park) to the river lay stockyards and slums; there were railroad yards between Lexington and Madison, where Grand Central is now, and the gashouse, glue factories, prisons, workhouses, and asylums were all on what is now Roosevelt Island in the East River. In fact, what seems to be a series of gardens down the center of Park Avenue actually covers the remnants of the railroad tracks. (Edith Wharton complained of the noise.)

Consequently, there aren't a lot of old neighborhood names attached to this part of the island, but it does have history. **Beekman Place** is a two-block enclave that has been home to such theatrical greats as Lunt and Fontanne, Ethel Barrymore, Irving Berlin, and "Auntie Mame"; climb the steps on 51st Street to the East River promenade between 49th and 51st. **Sutton Place,** the southernmost section of York Avenue, which runs between East 53rd and 59th, was yet another London-style development aimed at the first families, and various of the Morgans and Vanderbilts in their turn lived here. It now contains the residence of the United Nations secretary-general.

In the park between 58th and 59th is a statue of a boar, which may seem strange

unofficial **TIP**
There is a cocktail named the Waldorf: equal parts rye whiskey, absinthe (now legal again), and sweet vermouth with a dash of bitters. An Astoria is a wet martini.

unless you know that it's a copy of *Il Porcellino,* which stands in the market in Florence, Italy; pat its head for luck.

And yes, Simon and Garfunkel fans, that is the **59th Street Bridge,** immortalized in "The 59th Street Bridge Song (Feelin' Groovy)"; it's officially the **Queensboro Bridge.** (It also makes famous cameo appearances in the poster for Woody Allen's *Manhattan* and in F. Scott Fitzgerald's *The Great Gatsby.*) Go under the bridge piers on the Manhattan side and have a look at **Guastavino's** restaurant and banquet facility; the building was a farmer's market at the turn of the 20th century and was designed by the same Spanish architect who created the Grand Central Oyster Bar.

If you have a mind to mix your touring with, um, mixing, consider these famous and lavishly decorated watering holes:

In The Waldorf-Astoria on Park Avenue is the Edwardian-style **Bull and Bear Bar** (enter from Lexington Avenue at 49th Street), which has a pentagonal mahogany bar, an electronic-stock ticker (which replaced the old ticker-tape machine, quieter but no so atmospheric), and the twin bronze "stock market" mascots that came from the old Waldorf at the site of the Empire State Building, back when patrons included not just Diamond Jim Brady and J. P. Morgan but also Bat Masterson and Buffalo Bill Cody.

Although you'll have to walk around the corner, be sure to see the hotel's lobby, truly one of the city's semi-hidden wonders, and not only (though primarily) because of the astonishing Art Deco mosaic in the floor—150,000 pieces—and incredible murals. The nine-foot-tall clock, which was created for the 1893 World's Fair in Chicago, chimes the Westminster Cathedral bells every quarter hour and is ringed with portraits of Queen Victoria, Ben Franklin, and presidents Washington, Lincoln, Grant, and Jackson, among others. The piano on the cocktail terrace is called the Cole Porter piano because when the composer lived here from 1939 to 1964, he frequently entertained friends and friendly passers-by by playing.

The restored **Monkey Bar** in the Hotel Elysée (60 East 54th Street, between Madison and Park avenues), which now belongs to *Vanity Fair* editor Graydon Carter, has two rooms of interest: the original Monkey Bar, with its see-no-evil murals; and the back room, with a modern-but-retro mural by *New Yorker* regular Edward Sorel showing such old-school icons as Fred Astaire, Zelda and Scott Fitzgerald, Dorothy Parker, and Edna Ferber. (Admittedly, the decor somewhat resembles that of a Barnes & Noble cafe, but the drinks are stronger.) This was another popular stop for two-fisted artsy types—Tallulah Bankhead, Ava Gardner, Oscar Levant, Marlon Brando—and Tennessee Williams lived and actually died in the hotel.

The **King Cole Bar** at the St. Regis (2 East 55th Street at Fifth Avenue) is probably best known for its fabulous Maxfield Parrish mural of that jolly old soul—now happily restored and cigar smoke-free—but it also claims to be the place where the Bloody Mary, aka the Red Snapper, was invented. Not only that, but the royal personage is said to have been modeled on John Jacob Astor, who originally commissioned it for his Knickerbocker Hotel over on Times Square—the same Knickerbocker where Caruso serenaded the Armistice Day crowds, and which had one of the bars that claims to have invented the martini—and some people say the artist's joke is that the smirking king has passed some rude bourgeois gas.

After extensive renovation, **The Plaza Hotel,** at the southeast corner of Central Park at Central Park South and Grand Army Plaza, has reopened with a beautifully restored Oak Bar. The Edward Schinn murals have also been restored after decades of smoke damage; the one to the left as you face the bar shows the Vanderbilt mansion that once stood where Bergdorf Goodman is now. (Although she would never have been allowed in the bar, Eloise hangs in glory on the other side of the lobby; pay your respects. And music fans, note: this is where the Beatles stayed on that first U.S. visit in 1964.) The Plaza and The Waldorf-Astoria remain the city's only hotels to have been accorded landmark status by the city's preservation commission.

Though it's just slightly over the theoretical line into the Upper East Side, the Art Deco Sherry-Netherland Hotel on Fifth Avenue at 59th Street has a bar with, if less memorable decor, a more than respectable history: **Harry Cipriani,** New York's original Cipriani and an offshoot of the famous Venetian bar where the Bellini was invented. (The **Four Seasons,** on 57th Street between Madison and Park avenues, takes credit for the martini renaissance; do you need an excuse?)

And although it's a few doors on the west side across Fifth Avenue, no respectable cocktail tour would be complete without a stop at the **Algonquin Hotel,** at 59 West 44th, where such lit-wits as Dorothy Parker, George S. Kaufman, Marc Connelly, Robert Benchley, and Alexander Woollcott met to spar over (mostly) cocktails. You can still have a drink in the Round Table Room, which now sports portraits of those literary lions and lionesses, and imagine the wits of the 1920s gathered around you; but you should also see the Blue Bar, festooned with the Broadway caricatures of legendary *New York Times* cartoonist Al Hirschfeld.

THE UPPER WEST SIDE

THE WEST SIDE JUST ABOVE THE THEATER DISTRICT had never had much identity of its own until fairly recently. There was some port trade—the big cruise ships and liners still use piers in the lower 50s—and some hotel and theater spillover, but not of the better sort. In the early part of the 20th century, it was a respectable if not particularly fashionable district, populated first by Jewish immigrants who had prospered and moved out of the Lower East Side and later by middle-class blacks, who began to be pushed out again by Puerto Rican immigrants and blue-collar white families from Hell's Kitchen. But with the creation of **Lincoln Center for the Performing Arts** (which involved the demolition of San Juan Hill, the Hispanic neighborhood in the West 60s, and the degenerating middle-class houses around it, exactly the area portrayed in *West Side Story,* businesses began to return.

The southeast corner of the area is **Columbus Circle,** where Broadway, Eighth Avenue, and West 59th–Central Park South come together, and where the eponymous Christopher stares out from his 77-foot-high vantage. The gold figure of a goddess on a seashell drawn by three seahorses (on the Central Park side) is a monument to the sailors who died in the explosion of the USS *Maine,* which launched the Spanish-American War. The circle is dominated by the two glass spires of the **Time Warner Center,** which includes the **Shops at Columbus Circle** (see Part Eight) and is home to numerous upscale apartments, restaurants, bars, shops, and the **Mandarin Oriental, New York** hotel. It's not only the new luxury center of Manhattan, but it's also literally the epicenter of New York—the place from which all those mileposts reading __ MILES TO NEW YORK are measured.

The massive **Trump International Hotel & Tower,** which houses the five-star **Jean-Georges** restaurant (profiled in Part Eight), is another tourist attraction in its own right. (Built in 1969 as the Gulf & Western Building and completely redesigned in 1997 for Trump, it's already undergoing a $30 million renovation.) The see-through world globe on Columbus Circle resembles the one at the World's Fair site in Queens, but is smaller. Time Warner's response to TrumpWorld, so to speak, was to install the **Prow Sculpture,** a constantly changing light construction 150 feet tall that tells the time by changing color. It's complemented, so to speak, by the light-filled "seams" of what is now the gleaming white **Museum of Arts and Design.** (That was quite the renovation; when the building was constructed in 1964 as the Hunting-ton Hartford Gallery of Modern Art, it had a curved facade.)

Just up the street, the **Museum of Biblical Art** (Broadway at 61st Street; ☎ 212-408-1500; **www.mobia.org**) mounts surprisingly wide-ranging exhibits of religious art, from traditional to faux and folk, and displays a vast collection of Bibles and scriptural publications.

Lincoln Center and its associated plazas and annexes pretty much take up the area from Columbus Avenue (the extension of Ninth Avenue, remember, not Eighth) and Broadway to Tenth Avenue be-tween West 62nd and West 66th streets. An offshoot gallery of the **American Folk Art Museum** (☎ 212-595-9533; **www.folkartmuseum .org**), on Columbus Avenue between West 65th and 66th, specializes in textiles, furniture, and decorative arts from the 18th century, with particularly nice quilts.

No tourist-savvy city would be complete without an **IMAX** theater these days, and the one at Broadway and 68th, boasts a screen "seven elephants high."

There's plenty of street-side sightseeing around these parts as well. **Alwyn Court** (58th Street and Seventh Avenue) has one of the most fantastic terra-cotta facades in the entire city—designed by the same men who created the Gothic cathedral–look midblock high-rise at **44 West 77th Street,** off Central Park West, and the Loîre Valley castle at **350 West 85th Street.** The darkly Art Deco apartment building at **55 Central Park West** (between 65th and 66th) served as the cinematic battleground between the demon Gozer and the Ghostbusters.

The **Hotel des Artistes,** on West 67th Street at Central Park West, was actually constructed as artists' studios, with two-story spaces designed to take advantage of the daylight (and exterior sculptures for inspiration), but now these are highly prized apartments. Noel Coward, Rudolph Valentino, Alexander Woollcott, Norman Rockwell, Isadora Duncan, and Howard Chandler Christy all lived there; Christy did the murals of romantic nudes in the popular **Café des Artists** in the lobby. (Sadly, at press time, the restaurant was closed and the future of the murals unclear.)

The towered apartment buildings along **Central Park West** date to mostly the 1920s, when building regulations allowed greater height in return for at least partial light (which is why so many New York skyscrapers have those angled or pointed tops). The pretty Art Nouveau building at West 64th and Central Park West is the home of the **New York Society for Ethical Culture** (☎ 212-874-5210; **www.nysec.org**). The **Spanish and Portuguese Synagogue,** on the corner of West 70th Street at Central Park West, though built (with Tiffany windows) only in 1897, is home to the oldest Sephardic Jewish congregation in the city, dating to the arrival in 1654 of fugitives from the Inquisition (☎ 212-873-0300; **www.shearithisrael.org**).

unofficial **TIP**
Another sad social landmark is at 250 West 72nd Street, between Broadway and West End Avenue: the former site of W. M. Tweeds bar, where on New York's Day 1973, schoolteacher Roseann Quinn left with a man who raped her and stabbed her to death, inspiring the book and movie *Looking for Mr. Goodbar.*

As suggested in the "Very Short History" section of Part One, development of the Upper West Side was the stepchild of the Gilded Age. It required the daring of a few developers and the construction of the El up Ninth Avenue to persuade middle-class and professional Manhattanites that it was worth living above Midtown. On the other hand, because the land was a better bargain, many of the apartment buildings and brownstones were more gracious and seemed to have more elbowroom. Broadway, in particular, has a European-boulevard-like spaciousness in this area. Nowadays, it is a popular area for relatively affluent professionals, studded with restaurants, especially along Columbus Avenue.

In its heyday, **Riverside Drive** was the Fifth Avenue of the West Side, with mansions gazing out over their own Frederick Law Olmsted greenery, Riverside Park, instead of Central Park, and with the Hudson River beyond that. Look for the turn-of-the-century **Yeshiva Ketana,** the former Isaac Rice home, at West 89th, for an example.

The construction in the 1880s of the **Dakota** on Central Park West at 72nd Street sparked a luxury apartment building boom. Designed by Plaza Hotel architect Henry Hardenbergh for Singer Sewing Machine heir Edward Clark, it is still probably the most famous apartment building in the city, used as the movie setting of *Rosemary's Baby* (Boris Karloff is said to haunt the building) and now, unfortunately, best known as the home and assassination spot of John Lennon.

The Dakota inspired such other extravagances as the Beaux Arts **Dorilton,** at West 71st and Broadway, and the Belle Époque **Ansonia Hotel,** on Broadway at West 74th, which attracted such musical eminences as Arturo Toscanini, Enrico Caruso, and Leopold Stokowski. William Randolph Hearst was originally satisfied with the view from the top three floors of the 12-story **Clarendon,** on Riverside Drive and West 86th, but after a few years he decided he needed the whole thing and bought it out.

unofficial **TIP**
This is a great area for gargoyles: the **Lucerne Hotel,** at 201 West 79th Street, has a rather frightening monster on the Amsterdam Avenue side and a group of odd swells with handlebar mustaches near the entrance; the **Ansonia** has gnomes and demons all around (as well as turrets and gables); and the **Britannia,** up at 527 West 110th Street, displays ten of the goofiest Gothic creatures ever seen.

The stretch of Central Park West between West 75th and West 77th is a historical district, dating from the turn of the 19th century. The double-towered **San Remo,** between 74th and 75th, is famous as the co-op that turned down Madonna, though several other famous actors and musicians do live here. The same architect, Emery Roth, topped himself by giving the **Beresford,** at West 81st Street, three turrets.

One of the oddest corners is a little gated mews off West 94th Street near West End Avenue known as **Pomander Walk;** although built in 1921, it looks just like a movie set of old London—and in fact, it was modeled after the stage set of a popular play of the time called *Pomander Walk.* So it sentimentally attracted such tenants as Lillian and Dorothy Gish and Humphrey Bogart.

Although the Upper West Side can't rival the East Side's "Museum Mile," it does have several important cultural attractions. The **New York Historical Society** building, on Central Park West between West 76th and West 77th, houses an eclectic collection ranging from American-made fine silver and decorative arts to original watercolors for

John J. Audubon's *Birds of America,* Hudson River School paintings, furniture that marches through the building in chronological order, and a Gilbert Stuart portrait of Washington (☎ 212-873-3400; **www .nyhistory.org**).

kids The **American Museum of Natural History** and the stunning **Rose Center** and **Hayden Planetarium** face Central Park from West 77th Street to 81st (☎ 212-769-5100 or **www.amnh.org;** profiled in depth in Part Six). The **Children's Museum of Manhattan** (☎ 212-721-1234; **www.cmom.org**), one of the city's first institutions to go heavily into interactive exhibits, is on West 83rd Street between Broadway and Amsterdam Avenue.

Symphony Space (☎ 212-864-5400; **www.symphonyspace.org**), which is a cult location both for its Bloomsday marathon readings of *Ulysses* every June 16 and its 12-hour free spring musical marathon, is on Broadway at West 95th Street.

THE UPPER EAST SIDE

THIS IS ARGUABLY THE MOST BEAUTIFUL AREA of Manhattan— fashionable and prosperous almost from the very beginning, and, like the dowager of a good family, remarkably well preserved. It is an area of apartment houses open only to true millionaires (and not always open to them, either) and of the most expensive of boutiques, art and antiques houses, elegant hotels, private clubs, and old-line restaurants, churches, and educational institutions—including, but not limited to, the famed **Museum Mile.**

The riverfront was the original draw; it was an in-town "beach" and resort area in the early 19th century, before bridges made travel to the outer boroughs common. The wealthy, who still lived firmly downtown, built summer homes all the way up the East River to what is now Harlem, boating up- and downtown, taking carriages along the Boston Post Road (Third Avenue) and later riding the El. A huge complex called Jones's Wood filled the whole stretch east of the Post Road from near what is now the Rockefeller University–Cornell University medical center neighborhood in the 60s north to John Jay Park at East 76th; it offered genteel bathing facilities, theatrical entertainments, a beer garden, and parade grounds.

The apartment buildings on the East Side broke ground in several ways: they were so large that even families with whole staffs of servants might share them. (And nowadays, several families can fit within the various subdivisions of one formerly palatial apartment.) The new luxury town houses had elaborate bathrooms, not just water closets. They were fully electrified, not just refitted. And of course they had the immense swath of Central Park for their front yard. Those that had to settle for views of Madison Avenue or Park Avenue offered elaborate lobbies and exterior detail instead: look at the outside of the building on the corner of **East 66th Street and Madison.**

Once Caroline Schermerhorn Astor—the same Mrs. William Astor who single-handedly created "The Four Hundred" and whose feuding with her nephew produced the Waldorf-Astoria Hotel—actually moved all the way up Fifth Avenue as far as 65th Street, the last great millionaires' migration began. Several of their mansions are still visible as museums and cultural institutions, including the extravagant Second Empire **Lotos Club** building, at 5 East 66th just off Fifth Avenue, built by William Vanderbilt's daughter as a wedding present for *her* daughter when she married pharmaceutical tycoon and civil-rights activist William Schieffelin; and the **Frick Collection,** former home of steel boss Henry Clay Frick, on Fifth at East 70th Street.

The Beaux Arts home of banker Henri Wertheim at **4 East 67th** is now the Japanese consul-general's residence. (Astor's own home was torn down to make room for the partially Romanesque, partially Byzantine and Astorially opulent **Temple Emanu-El,** at East 65th and Fifth Avenue, which boasts 60 stained-glass windows and Art Deco mosaics by Hildreth Meière, who also created works at Radio City Music Hall and St. Patrick's Cathedral.)

The Venetian Revival apartment building at **Fifth and East 64th** was once home to Edwin Berwin, who had the coal monopoly for American warships. The four-columned mansion-turned-luxury-condo at **9 East 68th** was built for banker George T. Bliss and was the lifelong home of his daughter Susan, whose art, manuscript, autograph, and book collections benefited the Metropolitan Museum and several major university libraries.

The **Knickerbocker Club** building, on East 62nd at Fifth Avenue, used to have a twin next door; it was home to Mrs. Marcellus Hartley Dodge, a Rockefeller cousin, who filled her five-story mansion with all the stray dogs she could rescue. Next to it is the **810 Fifth Avenue** building, onetime home to William Randolph Hearst, Richard Nixon, and Nelson Rockefeller—penthouse, bomb shelter, and all.

The side-by-side 1890s French Renaissance homes of Oliver Gould Jennings and Henry T. Sloane at **7 and 9 East 72nd Street** became the Lycée Français; they are again town houses. (After Sloane was divorced, he commissioned Cass Gilbert to build the 15-bedroom mansion at **18 East 68th Street;** it went on sale in 2008 for $64 million, but at press time the price was down to a mere $39 million.)

The current headquarters of the **Commonwealth Fund,** at East 75th and Fifth, was built for an heir to a Standard Oil fortune; the Renaissance Revival mansion at **25 East 78th Street** (at Madison Avenue), which is being renovated along with the adjoining mansion as headquarters for the **Bloomberg Family Foundation,** was built for a railroad president. (Mayor Bloomberg himself lives in a separate mansion, a five-story Beaux Arts beauty at **17 East 79th.**)

New York University's **Institute of Fine Arts,** on 78th Street at Fifth Avenue, is housed in what was once the home of American Tobacco founder James Duke, copied from a chateau in Bordeaux; just up Fifth Avenue between 78th and 79th streets is the **French Embassy,** once the home of finance icon Payne Whitney and more recently the site of an apparent Michelangelo sighting, although the Cupid in question has been removed from the lobby and consigned to experts' debates.

(Winston Churchill was seriously injured in 1931 when he stepped out into Fifth Avenue, looking up to find the home of financier Bernard Baruch between 76th and 77th streets, and was struck by a car. A Londoner, he likely forgot which way automobile traffic ran, although critics used it to amplify his reputation for overindulging.)

The Louis XIII–style palace that is now the **Neue Galerie** was built for industrialist-developer William Starr Miller and then became the home of Grace Vanderbilt, widow of Cornelius III (and was bought for the museum by cosmetics heir Ronald Lauder). The **National Academy Museum,** on Fifth at 89th, was originally railroad magnate Archer Huntington's home, and the **Cooper-Hewitt, National Design Museum,** on East 91st at Fifth Avenue, was originally Andrew Carnegie's home (he asked for something "modest and plain"). The French Renaissance **Jewish Museum,** on Fifth Avenue at East 92nd (☎ 212-423-3200; **www.jewishmuseum.org**), was once the homestead of financier Felix Warburg. (Some of these are profiled in Part Six.)

Carnegie may have asked for a simple home, but he was in the minority. Facing the Cooper-Hewitt at 1 East 91st is the last palace of **"Millionaire's Row,"** built for banker Otto Kahn and now the **Convent of the Sacred Heart School;** at No. 7 is the **Burden House,** the home of a Vanderbilt shipping heiress who married a Burden steel scion. It's now a prominent society wedding site; the spiral staircase, centered under a stained-glass dome, is known as "the stairway to heaven." And next to that, at No. 9, is the eight-story Italian Renaissance–style mansion where jazz record producer John Hammond grew up, thanks in part to his own family's Vanderbilt and Sloane connections. The Hammond house is now the Russian consulate.

One of the ex–Mrs. Vanderbilts commissioned the French Revival mansion at **60 East 93rd Street,** between Park and Madison. Flashy Broadway figure and party boy Billy Rose was a millionaire of a lesser sort, perhaps best known as Mr. Fanny Brice, but he lived well enough to afford a great Scottish-romantic mansion of his own across the street at **56 East 93rd** (now part of the Spence School). Even the **Synod of Bishops of the Russian Orthodox Church outside of Russia** at 75 East 93rd, between Park and Madison, was once a private home, the mansion of banker George Baker; its collection of icons is a must-see for devotees of Byzantine and Eastern Orthodox art (by appointment only; ☎ 212-534-1601; **www.russianorthodoxchurch.ws/English**).

Once the Fourth Avenue railroad track was moved underground and paved over to create Park Avenue, the wealthy began to stretch a little farther east.

The houses at 47-49 East 65th Street, between Park and Madison, undergoing renovation to house Hunter College's **Roosevelt House Public Policy Institute,** were donated to the college by Eleanor Roosevelt. Her formidable mother-in-law, Sara Delano Roosevelt, famously commissioned these twin town houses, one for herself and one for the newly married Franklin and Eleanor, with a single entrance and various connecting doors. It was in the fourth-floor front bedroom that FDR endured his long bout with polio, and Eleanor the almost equally paralyzing domination by her mother-in-law.

What is now the **Explorer's Club,** at 46 East 70th, between Madison and Park, was built for Stephen Clark, nephew of the Dakota building Clark, a prominent art and museum figure and founder of the Baseball Hall of Fame in Cooperstown, New York. At **111 East 77th Street,** between Lexington and Park, is the carriage house that belonged to Edith Wharton and her husband when they lived around the corner on Park Avenue. ("Carriage trade" was no joke around here; the **New York School of Interior Design** building, on East 70th between Lexington and Third avenues, was also originally a luxury stable, designed by Cass Gilbert.)

The block of **East 80th Street** between Lexington and Park has three mansions lined up one after another, built for a Whitney (**No. 120**), a Dillon (**No. 124**), and another Astor (**No. 130**).

This is still where the wealthy gather: the 17-story Art Deco building known both as **740 Park Avenue** and **71 East 71st Street** was the childhood home of Jacqueline Bouvier, whose grandfather built it, and it was the final residence of John D. Rockefeller Jr., who lived in a 24-room, 12-bathroom apartment from 1938 to 1960. At various times it has been home to philanthropist Enid Haupt, corporate-buyout king Henry Kravitz, corporate raider Saul Steinberg, Seagram CEO Edgar Bronfman, Time Warner CEO Steven Ross (who built a 24-room, 11-bath apartment of his own), Greek shipping tycoon Spyros Niarchos, Ronald Lauder of Estée Lauder, Ronald Perelman of Revlon, heads of banana and sugar conglomerates, actor Gary Cooper, a few diplomats, and J. Watson Webb, a member of the Vanderbilt family that built the New York Central Railroad.

In fact, there were rumors for years of a secret underground tunnel meant as an escape route from 740 Park to the old Fourth Avenue railroad tracks that then ran under the avenue. The idea was dismissed for decades as an urban myth, but a few years ago a plumbing construction crew discovered a series of ten-by-six-foot, arched brick vaults branching off from the basement. No one has yet determined their original function or who had them built.

Among other buildings with strange histories is the one at **131 East 71st Street,** between Park and Lexington; it was built during the Civil War, but designer Elsie de Wolfe redid the facade in 1910 as a sort of silent advertisement of her own style.

Fifth Avenue is not just Millionaire's Row; it's also the heart of "Museum Mile," that fantastic array of museums and collections ranging more than 20 blocks—more nearly a mile and a half—from the **Metropolitan Museum of Art,** at 82nd Street (☎ 212-535-7710; **www.metmuseum.org**), and the **Goethe-Institut** (☎ 212-439-8700; **www.goethe.de/ins/us/ney/enindex.htm**) and **Neue Galerie** of German and Austrian decorative arts, across the street (☎ 212-628-6200; **www.neuegalerie.org**), past the **Guggenheim** at 89th (☎ 212-423-3500; **www.guggenheim.org**), the **National Academy Museum** at 90th (☎ 212-369-4880; **www.nationalacademy.org**), the **Cooper-Hewitt** at 91st (☎ 212-849-8400; **www.cooperhewitt.org**), and the **Museum of the City of New York,** at 103rd (☎ 212-534-1672; **www.mcny.org**), up to **El Museo del Barrio** at 104th Street (☎ 212-831-7272; **www.elmuseo.org**). Many of these museums are profiled in Part Six.

But there are many other museums and cultural institutions of note in this area, if not right on Fifth Avenue. The **Asia Society** (☎ 212-288-6400; **www.asiasociety.org**), housing the collection of John D. Rockefeller III, is on Park Avenue at East 70th Street. The newly repolished **Whitney Museum of American Art** (profiled in detail in Part Six; ☎ 800-944-8639; **www.whitney.org**) was too aggressively modern for Museum Mile back when it opened in 1966; it juts out in an inverted pyramid over Madison Avenue at East 75th Street. The **Queen Sofía Spanish Institute,** on Park at 68th Street (☎ 212-628-0420; **www.spanishinstitute.org**), showcases great Spanish art in limited exhibits and is an easy hour's visit.

If you enjoy more-commercial art, the **Society of Illustrators,** at 128 East 63rd, east of Park Avenue (☎ 212-838-2560; **www.societyillustrators.org**), exhibits graphic arts, illustrations, and award-winning book jackets.

kids The **Mount Vernon Hotel Museum & Garden,** at 421 East 61st Street, between York and First avenues (☎ 212-838-6878; **www.mvhm.org**), formerly known as the Abigail Adams Smith Museum, is a little bit of pastoral history still visible in the big city. Back when this was several miles "outside" Manhattan, Abigail Adams Smith, the daughter of John Quincy Adams, and her husband, William Smith, planned to build a country estate there, called Mount Vernon in honor of George Washington, under whom William Smith had been a colonel. But they had to sell the land in 1799 without getting much further than building the stone stable, converted into an inn a quarter century later, that is now the museum. It has been furnished in the Federal style, given a period garden, and stocked with antiques. Especially for children, the tour (by costumed members of the Colonial Dames of America, which maintains the house) is fun and a serious change of pace.

The **Park Avenue Armory** (formerly the Seventh Regiment Armory), on Park between East 66th and 67th—the building that looks like an oversize Gothic sand castle—houses many of the city's major art and antiques exhibits, and actually is a piece of art itself. Built in response to Lincoln's call for volunteers by the Seventh New York Regiment, the so-called Silk Stocking Regiment—a roster studded with such names as Vanderbilt, Harriman, Roosevelt, and Livingston—it was part drill hall (a staggering 55,000 square feet of it, based on the original Grand Central Depot shed) and part social club, with 16 reception and great rooms. Among the architects and artists who worked on the project were Louis Comfort Tiffany and Stanford White. It's currently undergoing gradual restoration as an alternative arts space (☎ 212-616-3930; **www.armoryonpark.org**).

Gracie Mansion, the official residence of the mayor of New York and original home of the Museum of the City of New York, is in **Carl Schurz Park**, overlooking the East River at East 88th Street. The mansion's name salutes Scottish immigrant Archibald Gracie, who built a summer home here back in 1799, although an earlier house, called Belview Mansion, is known to have been commandeered by George Washington during the American Revolution and then destroyed by British forces. It has been the mayor's residence only since the days of Fiorello La Guardia—like Lincoln Center, an official residence was the brainchild of Parks Commissioner Robert Moses. (It is open only to official city business.) Carl Schurz, for whom the park surrounding Gracie Mansion is named, was a German immigrant who became editor of the *New York Post,* editorial writer for *Harper's Weekly,* and, after the Civil War, secretary of the interior.

The **92nd Street Y** (☎ 212-415-5500; **www.92y.org**), as the Young Men's and Young Women's Hebrew Association building there is commonly known, is famous for its concerts, readings, and lectures by national and international as well as local artists and writers. (Playhouse 91, the onetime ice house and stable that turned into the premier Off-Broadway venue and home to several of the city's theatrical companies, was in fact on East 91st between First and Second, but sadly has fallen prey to redevelopment fever.)

Madison Avenue is now more commercial than residential, but oh, what commercialism! (For more on Madison Avenue shopping, see "Great Neighborhoods for Shopping" in Part Eight.)

kids Fans of Ludwig Bemelmans' *Madeline* children's books will want to know that the **The Carlyle** hotel's **Bemelmans Bar,** which the author decorated, prepares special dishes for proper young ladies, Saturday and Sunday at 10 a.m. and noon (East 76th Street and Madison Avenue; ☎ 212-744-1600; **www.thecarlyle.com**). Although **Roosevelt Island,** in the East River, is now a residential community, it once held a rather exotic assortment of institutions—lunatic asylums, smallpox hospitals, workhouses, poorhouses, and prisons; it was almost the dark reflection of the wealth of the East Side. (It was once called Welfare Island, as a matter of fact, but of course that word isn't

⌐⌐ anymore.) There are a few historical buildings left, including a lighthouse; and the **Roosevelt Island Tramway,** a 250-foot-high sky ride, crosses over from Second Avenue and 59th Street about every 15 minutes; the four-minute ride costs $2.25, or $4 round-trip (☎ 212-832-4555; **www.rioc.com/tramtransportation.htm**).

A good view of Independence Day festivities comes from the public park on Ward's Island at the south end of Randall's Island in the East River. It faces Scylla Point on the other side of Hell Gate Bridge in Astoria Park, where the Queens Symphony Orchestra accompanies the fireworks there. Ward's Island is accessible by a bike and pedestrian bridge at the east end of 103rd Street. Formerly called Negro Point, the sports facilities are now called Charybdis Playground in tribute (along with Scylla Point) to the monsters of the *Odyssey*. At press time, Ward's Island was undergoing renovation.

unofficial **TIP**
Roosevelt Island is a particularly great place to watch the Fourth of July fireworks.

Several important spiritual shrines are on the Upper East Side, including the **Russian Orthodox Cathedral of St. Nicholas,** at East 97th and Fifth; it looks like the whole Kremlin squashed together, with five onion domes and multicolored tile detailing—Moscow on, if not the Hudson, at least the East River (by appointment only; ☎ 212-289-1915; **www.russianchurchusa.org**). It is also the repository of 34 icons that had been smuggled out of Russia and were about to be sold on the black market when customs officials rescued them; they are estimated to be worth more than $3 million and date to the mid–18th and 19th centuries.

The **Islamic Cultural Center of New York** (☎ 212-722-5234), on Third at East 96th Street, is the spiritual home to the city's Muslims, of whom there may be as many as half a million; it was computer-measured to ensure that it faces directly toward Mecca.

Aside from Fifth Avenue, few old-time neighborhood nicknames persist. **Lenox Hill,** the southern blocks of the area from about 60th to 77th streets between Fifth Avenue and Lexington, was originally farmland belonging to Scots-born merchant Robert Lenox. The old German Hospital was renamed **Lenox Hill Hospital** in 1918 because of anti-German sentiment, and the name stuck. Neighboring **Yorkville,** which runs nearly the length of the Upper East Side from Lexington Avenue over to the river, used to be New York's Germantown from the turn of the 20th century (when many of the Lower East Side families and businesses relocated) until about 20 years ago, but it is now just as much black and Hispanic as European. Actually, the populace wasn't just Germans but also Eastern Europeans and nearly as many Irish, but the German delis and pastry shops, especially around East 86h Street, won out. **Hell Gate** was not a gang hangout but a narrow passage in the East River at Randalls–Wards Island—perhaps a hellish spot for river pilots.

Carnegie Hill, which ranges from the Cooper-Hewitt (Carnegie's mansion) at 91st Street north to the boutique and cafe area of Madison Avenue, is a rapidly upscaling residential neighborhood. But although it begins south of Central Park North, the area above 96th Street and east of Fifth Avenue is still commonly known as **Spanish Harlem** or **East Harlem.** See the next section for more information.

HARLEM, MORNINGSIDE HEIGHTS, AND HAMILTON HEIGHTS

THOUGH OFTEN OVERLOOKED BY TOURISTS, **Upper Manhattan** is filled with important educational institutions, historical sites, and beautiful churches, museums, and 19th-century houses. It's almost as large as Downtown Manhattan, though obviously less densely developed; and, surprisingly, nearly as old. Nieuw Haarlem, as it was called then, was originally—like Lower Manhattan—home to Huguenot-Dutch immigrants who displaced the Native Americans in the early to mid–17th century.

The most famous place name, of course, is **Harlem,** which covers the entire triangle of land north of Central Park North (110th Street) between the Hudson and East rivers.

At the corners of the larger Harlem, however, there are several important neighborhoods. two on either side of Harlem's south end and the other on the northwest corner: **Morningside Heights,** occasionally referred to as **Cathedral Heights** or **Riverside Heights,** begins at the top end of the Upper West Side at Cathedral Parkway (also an extension of 110th Street) and runs north to the diagonal cut of 125th Street between Frederick Douglass Boulevard–Eighth Avenue on the east and Riverside Drive on the west. East Harlem, also known as Spanish Harlem, stretches from the curve of the East River down around the corner of Central Park and Fifth Avenue to about East 96th Street and then around the edges of the Upper East Side's Museum Mile toward 80th Street east to the river. (Depending on your definition, both El Museo del Barrio and the Museum of the City of New York could be considered in Spanish Harlem, but Fifth Avenue and environs are by consensus Upper East Side.)

Hamilton Heights, sometimes referred to as **Harlem Heights,** runs from Morningside Heights north to 155th Street between St. Nicholas Avenue and Riverside Drive. It's named for Founding Father Alexander Hamilton, who spent his last years here on his country plantation; but its best-known locale is probably **Sugar Hill,** which was one of the premier addresses of the late 19th and early 20th centuries, and was where many major literary and music stars of the Harlem Renaissance resided.

(What would be the northeast corner of Harlem, if maps were square, would be the Bronx, near Yankee Stadium.)

These are real heights, or at least ranges of hills that look down on the Hudson River, rising from the Upper West Side to Manhattan's highest natural point at **Fort Washington** in Washington Heights (see following). The 13-block-long **Morningside Park**, for instance, was landscaped along a steep incline that allows for dramatic waterfalls and a series of esplanades and viewpoints.

Among the scholarly centers in Morningside Heights are **Columbia University,** which now stretches from about 114th Street to 124th, plus **Barnard College, Union Theological Seminary, Manhattan School of Music, New York Theological Seminary,** and **Jewish Theological Seminary;** the neighborhood is bookended by the massive **Riverside Church** on its western flank and the extraordinary and still-growing **Cathedral Church of St. John the Divine** on Amsterdam Avenue at 112th (profiled in Part Six). No wonder some residents argued for the name Cathedral Heights.

Riverside Church, at 122nd Street, was another of John D. Rockefeller Jr.'s gifts to the city, a 21-story Gothic beauty inspired by the cathedral at Chartres, France; its carillon of 74 bells was the largest in the world at the time it was built (one bell weighs 20 tons by itself), and the 22,000-pipe organ is one of the largest. Free tours are offered following Sunday services, about 12:15 p.m. (☎ 212-870-6700; **www .theriversidechurchny.org**). (There's a stunning 360-degree view of the city from the observation deck off the bell tower, nearly 400 feet high, but unfortunately at press time it was closed for renovation.)

Among less generally well-known but significant spiritual sites in this neighborhood are **Corpus Christi Church,** on West 121st Street just east of Broadway, where the influential author and Trappist monk Thomas Merton converted to Catholicism; and the more intimate **Church of Notre Dame,** on Morningside Drive at West 114th Street. It contains a replica of the grotto of Lourdes, where a young girl saw visions of the Virgin Mary, and the church is authorized to distribute small bottles of blessed water from Lourdes (☎ 212-866-1500; **www .ndparish.org**).

Before all that, of course, this was pasture and plains. Morningside Heights, especially in the area where Barnard College is now, is where the Battle of Harlem Heights was fought. The main center of Columbia and part of the cathedral grounds were once home to Bloomingdale Insane Asylum.

The **Polo Grounds,** home-away-from-home to generations of New York baseball (and later football) fans, originally was just north of Central Park between 110th and 112th streets and Fifth and Sixth avenues. Though it began as, logically, a polo field, it was converted to a stadium in 1880 for the old New York Metropolitans (Mets) and was later shared by the Mets and New York (baseball) Giants, as well as college baseball and football teams. When city officials decided to remake the street grid north of the park, the new Polo Grounds, named that only for sentiment's sake, was constructed at 155th and Eighth Avenue.

Over the years, the football Giants and the Jets (née Titans) played here, along with (briefly) baseball's Brooklyn Dodgers. The Yankees also played here for a decade before building Yankee Stadium in the early 1920s just across the Harlem River, but there was no "river series." Willie Mays made his famous over-the-shoulder catch here in the 1954 World Series, and one of Babe Ruth's home runs was estimated to have gone 550 feet. It also hosted many Army–Navy football games, championship boxing matches, soccer, Gaelic football, and even a couple of early Thanksgiving Day Harvard–Yale football classics. The current version of the Mets played here while the old Shea Stadium was being built. When the stadium was finally demolished in 1964, it is said that the wrecking crew wore Giants jerseys.

Other sites of interest include the **Nicholas Roerich Museum,** a little south and west of Straus Park at 319 West 107th Street (☎ 212-864-7752; **www.roerich.org**), which houses 200 works of the Russian-born painter as well as frequent concerts and poetry readings.

And if you want to know who's buried in **Grant's Tomb,** walk through Riverside Park to that mosaic-studded mausoleum on the hill near 122nd Street. (The answer, incidentally, is both Grant and his wife, Julia.)

North of Morningside Heights is Hamilton Heights, centered on **City College of New York** (CCNY) and running up to **Trinity Cemetery** at West 155th Street, a four-block-wide strip of nearly six square miles. Among its landmarks are **Dance Theater of Harlem** and the **Harlem School of the Arts,** on the border between the Heights and what might be called Harlem Major.

Hamilton Heights, which has several beautiful blocks of row houses along Convent Avenue between about 141st and 145th streets, was a highly desirable neighborhood for both turn-of-the-19th-century white and early-20th-century black residents, when it was nicknamed Sugar Hill and housed such jazz celebrities as Cab Calloway, Duke Ellington, and Count Basie; writers, including Langston Hughes, Zora Neale Hurston, and Ralph Ellison; and other such prominent African Americans as Sugar Ray Robinson, Paul Robeson, and Thurgood Marshall. It was also home to Richard Rodgers, Lorenz Hart, and Milton Berle.

unofficial **TIP**
The gatehouses at West 113th Street and West 119th streets at Amsterdam Avenue, and at West 135th at Convent Avenue, just west of St. Nicholas Park, are remnants of the old Croton Reservoir system.

The current Hamilton Heights–Sugar Hill Historic District is centered on four blocks of finely preserved row houses, many of them now residences of CCNY faculty and administrators. Hamilton's 1802 Federal house, **The Grange,** originally overlooked the Hudson River, but it has been moved twice, first in 1889 to Convent Avenue, and then a few years ago south to the northwest corner of **St. Nicholas Park.** It has been undergoing restoration to its original design and is scheduled to reopen to the public in 2010 (**www.nps.gov/hagr**).

Our Lady of Lourdes Church, at 142nd Street and Amsterdam, is a true miracle of salvage, having been put together in 1904 from bits of the old National Academy of Design at Park and East 23rd Street, the mansion of department store magnate A. T. Stewart at 34th Street and Fifth Avenue, and the former Madison Avenue apse of St. Patrick's Cathedral, removed to make room for what is now the Lady Chapel.

The blocks of West 138th and 139th from Adam Clayton Powell Jr. Boulevard over to Frederick Douglass Boulevard constitute the **St. Nicholas Historic District,** another group of late-19th-century homes designed by several prominent architects of the day. The neighborhood is also known as **Strivers' Row** because it drew a pre-yuppie-era group of ambitious young professionals.

At the top of St. Nicholas Park at West 141st Street is the famous **Harlem School of the Arts,** which has come to rival the New York High School for the Performing Arts (the model for the school in *Fame*) with its music, dance, and theater classes (☎ 212-926-4100; **www.harlemschoolofthearts.org**).

At the top of Hamilton Heights are **Trinity Cemetery** and **Audubon Terrace,** which face each other across Broadway between West 153rd and 155th streets. This area was once part of the estate of John James Audubon, and the naturalist himself, along with many of those whose names appear repeatedly in these pages—Astors, Schermerhorns, Van Burens, architects Cass Gilbert and Stanford White, and Clement Clarke Moore—are buried at Trinity Cemetery. (Audubon's gravestone is, appropriately, carved with birds.)

Several institutions of more-specialized interest are gathered in a splendid complex at Audubon Terrace, including the **Hispanic Society of America** (☎ 212-926-2234; **www.hispanicsociety.org**), a little-known museum with a fantastic collection of Spanish art by Goya, El Greco, Velázquez, etc.; the **American Numismatic Society** (☎ 212-571-4470; **www.numismatics.org**); and the **American Academy of Arts and Letters,** which mounts periodic exhibitions featuring the works of members (☎ 212-368-5900; **www.artsandletters.org**).

unofficial **TIP**
Surprisingly, when the whole Harlem-Heights area is taken into account, only about 41% of the population is black, and in central Harlem, though blacks make up 60%, only half are native-born.

Audubon Terrace is a sort of family affair itself: architect Charles Pratt Huntington designed the buildings; his philanthropist cousin Archer Huntington donated most of the money and the bulk of the Spanish art collection; and Archer's wife, Anna Hyatt Huntington, sculpted the Cid memorial. (This isn't even the only Huntington museum. Archer Huntington donated his private home on Fifth Avenue for the National Academy Museum and School of Fine Arts.)

Ironically, Harlem, which is both New York's proudest and poorest black neighborhood, was cleared, if not owned, by black slaves and indentured laborers, who blazed the trail that became Broadway all the way up the island. Though most of the area back in the mid–17th century was taken up by the large farms and country estates of the "patroons," as the Dutch landowners were known, the East and Harlem riverfronts were an inevitably ramshackle assortment of immigrants and watermen.

Harlem was a popular upper-middle-class suburb for most of the 19th century, with its own commuter rail system, the New York and Harlem Railroad, to carry businessmen back downtown; but around the turn of the century, things began to go sour. Businesses went bankrupt, buildings emptied, and the continual northward press of development from the wealthier sections of Manhattan drove black and immigrant families into many of the poorer areas.

By the early 20th century, Harlem was the major community for blacks, with all levels of income. The famous Harlem Renaissance of literature, music, and philosophy had a powerful effect on both high art and popular culture, raising Harlem's profile and giving greater force to the growing civil-rights debate. Despite the predations of time, poverty, and unimaginative urban renewal, it's been the center of repeated cycles of boom and bust ever since, with white, black, Hispanic, Caribbean, and Cuban enclaves, now as mixed as ever in its history. One of the new nicknames for the residents of East Harlem and parts of Brooklyn is "Nuyoricans," which refers to New Yorkers of Puerto Rican descent.

In the heart of Harlem proper, historical and artistic, is the area near **Marcus Garvey Park,** between 120th and 125th streets and Madison Avenue toward Malcolm X Boulevard (Lenox Avenue). A city park with playgrounds, pools, an amphitheater, and a community center, it also houses the three-level **Mount Morris Fire Watch Tower,** the last survivor of a squadron of 11 cast-iron towers dating to 1857. (It was once 11 stories tall and used water from the Croton Aqueduct.) Nearby is the **Mount Morris Park Historic District,** another well-preserved area, a Victorian enclave that was dominated by German Jewish families "moving up" from the Lower East Side. It covers about five blocks between Adam Clayton Powell Jr. Boulevard (Seventh Avenue) and Marcus Garvey between West 118th and 124th streets, and there are several proposals for renovating buildings for boutique hotels or bed-and-breakfasts here. **St. Martin's Episcopal Church,** at Lenox and 122nd, may not be as large as Riverside Church, but it has a fine carillon of its own, about 40 bells strong.

unofficial **TIP**
The main shopping strip of Harlem is along Fifth Avenue from Park Avenue to Morningside Drive.

A couple of blocks northwest of the park are the **Studio Museum in Harlem,** west of Lenox Avenue on 125th Street (☎ 212-864-4500; **www.studiomuseum.org**), a small but expanding, select collection of African, African American, and Caribbean fine arts that also offers lectures and educational programs, and the famed **Apollo Theater,** on West 125th between Adam Clayton Powell Jr. and Frederick Douglass boulevards (☎ 212-531-5300; **www.apollotheater.org**), founded as a vaudeville house in 1914 and the major showcase of black talent well into the 1960s. It has been revived, and the Wednesday Amateur Night tradition is as strong and lively as ever. The small but prestigious **National Black Theatre,** at Fifth between 125th and 126th streets (☎ 212-722-3800; **www.nationalblacktheatre.org**), is an increasingly important performing-arts venue.

From here it's a short walk to **Sylvia's,** a soul-food restaurant so famous that its gospel brunch is on many Harlem tours; it's on Malcolm X Boulevard–Lenox Avenue between West 126th and 127th streets (☎ 212-996-0660; **www.sylviassoulfood.com**). Then head straight up the boulevard to West 135th and the **Schomburg Center for Research in Black Culture,** the largest library of African and African American cultural and sociological materials in this country (☎ 212-491-2200; **www.nypl.org/research/sc**).

On Odell Clark Place (West 138th Street) between Malcolm X and Adam Clayton Powell Jr. boulevards is the **Abyssinian Baptist Church,** equally famous for being the onetime pastoral seat of Powell himself and for its gospel choir; its Sunday services draw busloads of tourists from all around the world (☎ 212-862-7474; **www.abyssinian.org**).

WASHINGTON HEIGHTS

THE AREA NORTH OF TRINITY CEMETERY and Audubon Terrace, called Washington Heights, was the area to which Washington's troops retreated during the early battles of the American Revolution. It centers on **Fort Tryon Park** (☎ 212-639-9675; **www.nycgovparks .org;** search for "Fort Tryon"). While the park's official highlights are the remaining defiant bulwark and its overlook, the 66-acre green space offers a far finer overview of Manhattan's original beauty, the Hudson River, and the fine woods and animal life; and it serves as a natural approach to the stunning Cloisters collection of the Met.

The **Morris-Jumel Mansion,** on Jumel Terrace south of West 162nd Street (☎ 212-923-8008; **www.morrisjumel.org**), which dates from 1765, is one of the very few Colonial buildings still standing in New York. It was a summer estate—its grounds stretched from Harlem to the Hudson—belonging to Roger Morris, a prominent Loyalist who had served as aide to General Braddock. Morris refused to act against his former colleague (and rumored rival for the hand of the wealthy Mrs. Morris) Washington, but even so, his estates were confiscated by the Revolutionary state government, and the Morrises returned to England. Washington did in fact sleep here and briefly used it as a headquarters; so, ironically, did Sir Henry Clinton, the British commander. More amazingly, Washington, Jefferson, Hamilton, John Adams, and Adams's son John Quincy Adams met here for lunch in 1790.

The "Jumel" part is equally intriguing: French-Caribbean Creole merchant Stephen Jumel bought the house in 1810 and lavishly remodeled it with the help of his socially ambitious wife, Eliza; she allegedly slept her way through much of New York society, let her husband bleed to death so as to make her a very rich widow, and then married the ruined, aging Aaron Burr—only to divorce him on his deathbed. Her reputation for cold-bloodedness and the house's reputation for reproachful spirits led to its being "cleansed" by a Haitian exorcist a few decades later. Among her furniture is a dolphin chair said to have been purchased from Napoleon.

Swindler Cove Park, where Dykeman Street meets the Harlem River, owes its existence to Bette Midler's New York Restoration Project; it's home to a rowing program intended to provide underprivileged kids with experience and perhaps scholarships (☎ 212-333-2552; **www .nyrp.org**).

Fort Tryon Park, which runs from Broadway to Riverside Drive between West 192nd and Dykeman streets, is only part of the original Cornelius Billings estate; the massive series of arches on Riverside Drive was the "driveway." It was landscaped, like most of New York's great parks, by an Olmsted (Frederick Law Olmsted Jr., son of the designer of Central Park), and it has an incredible assortment of views and gardens. The effect is immediately visible and almost shocking as you get off the A train at 190th Street; although they have not yet been fully restored, the stone terraces down the hillside and the arched entrance to the park seem to bound a different world, a medieval one; it couldn't be a better setting for **The Cloisters.** A 1930s stone gatehouse has been turned into the fine dining **New Leaf Café** (☎ 212-568-5323), serving lunch, dinner, and weekend brunch—again thanks to Midler and (ya gotta have) friends.

kids If your children have read *The Little Red Lighthouse and the Great Gray Bridge,* head to Fort Washington Park at about West 178th Street, and you'll see the lighthouse just below the eastern tower of the George Washington Bridge. Almost due east is High Bridge Park, which runs up Harlem River; the eponymous **High Bridge** is the oldest footbridge between Manhattan and the mainland. Opened in 1848, it stretches across the Harlem River from West 174th Street to the Bronx. It's been closed for decades, but the divine Ms. Midler has also taken up this cause, so stay tuned.

The Cloisters (profiled in depth in Part Six) is the medieval-collection arm of the Metropolitan Museum of Art, constructed from wings of several medieval French and Spanish cloisters that were painstakingly transported from Europe and reassembled here. This is one of New York's premier attractions, gloriously evocative and frequently nearly deserted. Astonishingly, the estate that is now Fort Tryon Park, the Cloisters buildings, and the art and manuscripts of the collection itself were all gifts of philanthropist John D. Rockefeller Jr. He and a few others, including J. Pierpont Morgan and the widow of railroad tycoon E. H. Harriman, also purchased the Palisades across the Hudson River for a state park.

Almost at the other end of the spectrum is the humble **St. Frances Xavier Cabrini Shrine,** on Fort Washington Avenue at 190th Street (☎ 212-923-3536; **www.mothercabrini.org/ministries/shrine_ny.asp**). Mother Cabrini, as she is known, is the patron saint of immigrants, and her remains (with the exception of her head, which is in Rome) are encased within the altar. The miraculous story here is that shortly after her death in 1917, a blind child was touched with a lock of her hair and received sight; naturally, he entered the priesthood. Mother Cabrini was the first American citizen to be canonized, but because she was Italian by birth, Mother Elizabeth Ann Seton can honestly be called the first American-born saint (see the earlier section on Lower Manhattan).

A few blocks from The Cloisters, at Broadway and West 204th Street, is the **Dyckman Farmhouse Museum** (☎ 212-304-9422; **www.dyckmanfarmhouse.org**), the only surviving 18th-century Dutch farmhouse (circa 1783) on the island, authentically fitted out and with a smokehouse and garden as well as a reconstructed Hessian hut.

There are two other sites of interest in Washington Heights: **Yeshiva University,** the oldest Jewish seminary in the country, founded in 1886 (West 185th Street and Amsterdam Avenue; ☎ 212-960-5400; **www.yu.edu**); and the 1930 Loews 175th Street Theatre, now called the **United Palace Theater** (175th Street at Broadway; ☎ 212-568-6700; **www.theunitedpalace.com**), another fantastic movie-palace-turned-church-turned-concert-venue. It was called a "Wonder Palace," which seems appropriate; it looks like a combination of several of the wonders of the ancient world, including Angkor Wat, Hagia Sophia, the Taj Mahal, and the Alhambra. For decades it was the headquarters of the United Church Science of Living Institute, founded by Reverend Ike, who had it lavishly restored. It's now used for concerts and theatrical performances. In January 2010, it hosted the Allman Brothers' annual New York visit, ending the band's legendary 20-year stint at the Beacon Theater.

BROOKLYN

BROOKLYNITES HAVE GOOD REASON TO RESENT all those jokes about accents and Coney Island culture, especially from Manhattanites with a superiority complex—although, these days, that attitude is rightfully in retreat. Brooklyn—originally "Breukelen," Dutch for "broken land," and the name of a city back in the Netherlands—was in fact the first defined city in what is now New York State. It's the most populous borough in the city, with more than 2.5 million residents, and the second largest (after Queens, its Long Island sibling). Even now, if it seceded from the rest of New York, Brooklyn would be the nation's fourth-largest city, with enough famous landmarks, museums, and resorts to make it a destination of its own.

It was the site of the first great battle of the American Revolution, the Battle of Long Island, also known as the Battle of Brooklyn Heights. Although it was a military defeat for Washington, it was something of a tactical victory, as the entire American force managed to slip away from British forces under cover of fog.

Later, however, when the British used foundered ships in Wallabout Bay as prisoner-of-war camps, it gained a more horrific historical tie: more American soldiers died as prisoners there than in all the Revolutionary War battles combined. The **Prison Ship Martyrs' Monument, in Fort Greene Park** (☎ 718-222-1461; **www.nycgovparks.org/parks/ fortgreenepark**), is a 149-foot granite shaft holding up a bronze urn and reached by three flights of 100-foot-wide stone steps; designed by Stanford White, it salutes the 11,000 American patriots who died under notoriously inhumane treatment aboard British prison ships.

Some of the most famous ships in the U.S. Navy were built here, including the Civil War ironclad *Monitor;* the battleship *Maine,* whose mysterious sinking in Havana ignited the Spanish-American War; and the USS *Missouri,* the battleship on which the surrender of Japanese Imperial Forces was tendered and which is now a museum at Pearl Harbor.

Brooklyn has some of the area's trendiest residential and commercial neighborhoods, especially in northwest Brooklyn, which is where many of the tourist-interest areas are and which has pretty much replaced Downtown Manhattan as the hottest arts, dining, and nightlife area of the city. It also has a booming television and film industry.

It's always had a vigorously mixed ethnic population, but these days it has replaced Manhattan as New York's real melting pot, with representatives of nearly 100 different ethnicities. Among the more obvious clusters are the black neighborhood of **Bedford-Stuyvesant,** the "Little Odessa" of **Brighton Beach, Chinatown** in **Flatbush,** and the Vietnamese area of **Sunset Beach,** along with the better-known Italian, Irish, and Orthodox Jewish enclaves throughout the borough. (Some sources put the Jewish population of Brooklyn at 750,000—almost twice that of Tel Aviv.) Nearly a fifth of Brooklynites speak Spanish at home. Brooklyn's other distinct communities include Caribbean families (especially Jamaican and Haitian), African (Nigerian, Senegalese, Ghanian), Middle Eastern and Arabic, Turkish, Georgian, Scandinavian, and Polish.

But this is not the stereotypical immigrant scene; **Boerum Hill** has a quite visible French presence, enough to make Spring Street a sort of mini–cafe society, complete with Bastille Day block party.

The **Brooklyn Museum** (profiled in Part Six), formerly the Brooklyn Museum of Art, is one of the nation's largest public art museums (200 Eastern Parkway; ☎ 718-638-5000; **www.brooklynmuseum.org**); the **Brooklyn Children's Museum** (145 Brooklyn Avenue; ☎ 718-735-4400;

www.brooklynkids.org), which opened in 1899, two years after the art museum, was the first serious arts and education institution in the world designed specifically for children. The 52-acre **Brooklyn Botanic Garden** (1000 Washington Avenue; ☎ 718-623-7200; **www.bbg.org**), also profiled in Part Six, is one of the nation's most beautiful and is a stroll away from the Brooklyn Museum. The **Brooklyn Academy of Music** (30 Lafayette Avenue; ☎ 718-636-4100; **www.bam.org**) and **Bargemusic** (Fulton Ferry Landing near the Brooklyn Bridge; ☎ 718-624-2083; **www.bargemusic.org**) are classical-music venues of the first order (see Part Ten). The new Brooklyn kiosk of **TKTS** sells tickets to not only Broadway and Off-Broadway performances but to music and dance concerts in Brooklyn as well.

unofficial **TIP**
Broadway matinee tickets are sold on the day before the performance at the Brooklyn TKTS booth.

Brooklyn's literary history is as illustrious as Manhattan's: it appears in everything from Arthur Miller's *A View from the Bridge* (revived on Broadway in 2010) to Neil Simon's *Brighton Beach Memoirs* (unsuccessfully revived in 2009); from William Styron's *Sophie's Choice* to Chaim Potok's *The Chosen*; from *Saturday Night Fever* to Spike Lee's *She's Gotta Have It*—and, of course, *A Tree Grows in Brooklyn*. It appears in hundreds of songs and even had its own eponymous band, which topped the *Billboard* charts in the late 1960s.

It has also become a sort of second Harlem, in that it is developing a group of black—American, African, and Caribbean—cultural and social centers that could easily generate another "Renaissance." The Fort Greene area in particular has a number of art galleries, performance spaces, and cafes that sponsor poetry readings. The most prestigious are the **Brooklyn Academy of Music,** familiarly known as BAM; the **Paul Robeson Theater; Museum of Contemporary African Diasporan Arts;** and **BAMcafé,** an outreach project of the Brooklyn Academy of Music.

BAM not only is a respected concert venue and home of the **Brooklyn Philharmonic** but also has its own opera house, the restored **BAM Harvey Theater,** a block down Fulton Street (651 Fulton), and several smaller performance spaces. Its recently restored facade is riotous with cherubs and 22 life-sized lions' heads. And, as the BAM boosters like to point out, its history is every bit as lustrous as Broadway's: Sarah Bernhardt, Edwin Booth, Anna Pavlova, Sergei Rachmaninoff, Carl Sandburg, Winston Churchill, and Enrico Caruso all performed here. Its October-to-December Next Wave Festival is extremely popular.

Nearby, on the corner of Flatbush and Lafayette avenues, is the **Mark Morris Dance Center** (☎ 718-624-8400; **www.markmorrisdance group.org**), which houses the offices and rehearsal spaces of one of the country's most influential modern-dance companies and its dance school, as well as classes for all ages and a wellness center.

The Brooklyn neighborhoods most tourists have heard about when they read about the arts, dining, and music scenes (and those glamorous young actors and musicians) are in northwestern Brooklyn, especially **Brooklyn Heights** and the adjacent areas around the eastern ends of the Brooklyn and Manhattan bridges. The fact that many of the newer residents are from the arts communities that previously frequented TriBeCa, SoHo, NoHo, etc., may explain why Brooklyn is also falling into the acronym habit.

Among the trendiest of neighborhoods are **DUMBO** (**D**own **U**nder the **M**anhattan **B**ridge **O**verpass), **BoCoCa** (an amalgam of **Boerum Heights, Cobble Hill,** and **Carroll Gardens,** a trio of older neighborhoods south of Brooklyn Heights), and **NoGo** (**No**rth of **Go**wanus, the next enclave over).

Park Slope is just south of Gowanus, and **Prospect Heights** is on the north side of **Prospect Park**—which itself adjoins the Brooklyn Botanic Garden and Brooklyn Museum, just east of that. The mini-peninsula southeast of BoCoCa is **Red Hook,** a still-edgy area that is home to cruise-line terminals, emerging artists, a huge new food emporium, a popular craft brewery, Sixpoint Craft Ales (you can't drink on-site, but it's just one reason to go to the great Irish pub Rocky Sullivan's right next door), along with an IKEA store, and several parks offering unobstructed views of the Statue of Liberty. The **Waterfront Museum and Showboat Barge** at Pier 44 (☎ 718-624-4719; **www.waterfrontmuseum .org**) is a renovated century-old barge with an irresistibly eclectic collection of circus paraphernalia and maritime lore, and it also houses performance artists and indie-music concerts.

Northeast of DUMBO, and one bridge up, is **Williamsburg,** logically where the **Williamsburg Bridge** crosses the East River. It was one of the first areas of Brooklyn to attract younger Manhattanites, especially in the arts community, and also one of the first to see skyrocketing rents and redevelopment. It's still home to plenty of art galleries, boutiques, and restaurants, including the famous **Peter Luger Steak House.**

Downtown Brooklyn is south of Brooklyn Heights; Atlantic Avenue is the unofficial border between BoCoCa and Downtown.

The other famous names are the resort areas, especially **Coney Island** and Brighton Beach, at the southern tip of Brooklyn, where the bay opens into the Atlantic Ocean.

(Be careful not to confuse the Broadway in Brooklyn with the Broadway in Manhattan; Brooklyn's runs southeast from the Williamsburg Bridge to Fulton Street near Atlantic Avenue at the edge of Queens. Similarly, Fifth Avenue, and Fourth, and so on are not connected to the avenues of Manhattan but run northeast–southwest roughly parallel to the East River.)

Start exploring Brooklyn by walking across the **Brooklyn Bridge** itself, which offers one of New York's best viewpoints in all directions, and where you are apt to see celebrities and working actors as well as commuters in the pedestrian lanes. Fulton Ferry Landing is

unofficial **TIP**
It's no secret anymore, but one of the nicest views of Manhattan is from the **River Cafe** at the foot of the Brooklyn Bridge; it may be touristy, but it's no trap.

the site of Bargemusic—which is just what it sounds like: chamber music on a floating barge—and beyond that is the **Brooklyn Heights Historic District,** which was not only New York's first bedroom suburb but also its first historic-preservation district. Ranging from the riverfront expressway to about Atlantic Avenue, this area is an amazing pre–Civil War enclave of more than 600 churches and homes (including those of Walt Whitman, Arthur Miller, W. H. Auden, Thomas Wolfe, and Truman Capote). The **Brooklyn Heights Promenade** along the East River has a spectacular view of Manhattan, an almost idyllic grid of community gardens and playgrounds, and a marker for Four Chimneys, where George Washington billeted during the Battle of Long Island.

Just south of the Brooklyn Bridge landing is what is now **Brooklyn Bridge Park,** which offers swimming—not in the river but in a huge "floating pool"—boating, bird-watching, outdoor films in summer, and wireless Internet access.

Despite its name, **DUMBO,** which is threatening to supplant Chelsea as the artists' hangout, just as Chelsea once supplanted SoHo, actually starts underneath the Brooklyn Bridge, includes **Empire–Fulton Ferry State Park** along the waterfront, and extends about six blocks east to Bridge Street. Around the area where the approaches to the Manhattan and Brooklyn bridges nearly meet, an estimated 1,000 artists, musicians, and performers fill 700 lofts in 15 square blocks.

The **Brooklyn Historical Society,** which spotlights local heroes ranging from the Brooklyn Dodgers to *The Honeymooners,* is a little south of DUMBO in the Brooklyn Heights Historic District at Pierrepont and Clinton streets (☎ 718-222-4111; **www.brooklynhistory.org**).

unofficial **TIP**
The stretch of Eastern Parkway between Washington Avenue and Grand Army Plaza, where huge row houses face the Brooklyn Museum, Brooklyn Public Library, Botanic Gardens, and Mount Prospect Park, is Brooklyn's own "Museum Mile."

Another block south, **St. Ann and the Holy Trinity Episcopal Church,** at Montague and Clinton streets, is in need of repair, but its extremely fine stained-glass windows by William Jay Bolton are the oldest set of figural windows made in the United States.

Park Slope, especially the stretch of Fifth Avenue between Ninth and Bergen streets, and **Smith Street** near Carroll Gardens are among the hottest new restaurant and boutique enclaves in any of the five boroughs.

The **Old Stone House,** on Fifth Avenue between Third and Fourth streets (☎ 718-768-3195; **www.theoldstonehouse.org**), is a replica of a 1699 Dutch farmhouse that played a crucial role in the Revolutionary War's Battle of Brooklyn. It later served as the clubhouse for the Brooklyn Dodgers, and during the unofficial World Series of 1889 and 1890, games were played at the site.

Perhaps the most important neighborhood for first-time visitors is the area around **Prospect Park,** at Eastern Parkway and Flatbush Avenue (☎ 718-965-8951; **www.prospectpark.org**). This is the Central Park of Brooklyn, designed by the same men, Frederick Law Olmsted and Calvert Vaux, and with similar facilities and features, These include the **Prospect Park Zoo** (☎ 718-399-7339; **www.prospectparkzoo.com**), which is even larger than the more famous Bronx facility; an antique carousel as fine as Central Park's (and rescued from Coney Island); a mid-19th-century Italianate villa; and a skating rink. It even has its own cemetery, a Friends (Quaker) burial ground, where actor Montgomery Clift is interred.

The northeast boundary of the park adjoins the Brooklyn Botanic Garden grounds, which then lead over to the Brooklyn Museum, which has a collection nearly as comprehensive as the Metropolitan's but far more comprehensible. And serving as a grand foyer to it all is **Grand Army Plaza,** at Plaza Street and Flatbush Avenue, Olmsted and Vaux's grand oval, with its triumphal Soldiers' and Sailors' Arch and a memorial bust of JFK.

kids In addition to these sites, Brooklyn has several other attractions of particular interest to families, including the recently expanded **Brooklyn Children's Museum,** about a mile east of the Brooklyn Museum, and the newly renovated **New York Transit Museum** (☎ 718-694-1600; **www.mta.info/mta/museum**), a bit east of the Brooklyn Heights Historic District at Schermerhorn Street between Court Street and Boerum Place. A former subway station, it now houses a fine collection of vintage cars, signal equipment and signs, old photos, drawings, and subway mosaics that served as directions for the illiterate and for non–English-speaking immigrants. (Not surprisingly, it's very near the Jay Street–Borough Hall subway stop.)

West of Prospect Park in Flatbush, and a little less convenient by public transportation, is the **Wyckoff Farmhouse Museum** (☎ 718-629-5400; **www.wyckoffassociation.org**), which was built in 1652 and added onto until about 1740, making it easily the oldest building in New York and one of the oldest wooden structures in the country. Pieter Claesen, an indentured agent for Peter Stuyvesant, eventually achieved his freedom and bought the estate. His family worked the farm until 1901. It's restored to the 1819 period.

Not everyone likes touring historic cemeteries as much as Eve does, but for those who do, Brooklyn has a lovely one. East of Prospect Park and south of Park Slope is the 478-acre **Green-Wood Cemetery** (☎ 718-768-7300; **www.green-wood.com**), founded in 1838. Its various memorials and sepulchres shelter many of New York's most prominent publishers, artists, politicians, and other notables—Leonard Bernstein, Henry Ward Beecher, Horace Greeley, Samuel Morse, Henry Steinway,

William "Boss" Tweed, Louis Comfort Tiffany, DeWitt Clinton, Theodore Roosevelt Sr., and mobster Joey Gallo among them. It is also home to a statue of Minerva, the Roman goddess of war, whose uplifted arm salutes the Statue of Liberty from atop Battle Hill, the highest point in Brooklyn. The hill figured in the Battle of Long Island, and Minerva is in part a memorial to those who died there. Other sculptures there were created by Augustus Saint-Gaudens and Daniel Chester French.

At the northeast corner of Prospect Heights is the **Vanderbilt Yards** rail terminal, near the junction of Atlantic and Flatbush avenues. A proposal to redevelop the railyard into a mixed-used development called **Atlantic Yards,** including retail space, apartment complexes, offices, parkland, and an arena for the New Jersey Nets basketball team, is still being hotly debated.

Coney Island has appeared in far too many films, books, and songs to mention, and has become synonymous with old-style family amusement parks. It became a beach resort for the well-to-do after the Civil War, a center of horse racing and casino gambling; the first carousel was constructed in 1878, and at one point it was the site of three rival amusement parks. Late in 2009, Mayor Bloomberg announced that the city had acquired Coney Island (for $95.6 million) and would expand the historic district to prevent its being replaced by shopping malls or apartment buildings. The city has said that at least 12 acres would be reserved for amusements within the new 27-acre historic district.

It remains a popular subway ride for locals and tourists alike. The beach itself, and the boardwalk that parallels it, are more than two miles long. **Nathan's Famous** hot-dog stand, which opened on the Coney Island boardwalk in 1916, is still a landmark, and its Fourth of July hot-dog-eating contest has been going strong ever since. The famous wooden **Cyclone** roller coaster was constructed in 1927, was closed in 1968, but was renovated and reopened in 1975. A historical landmark, it is still operating and lent its famous name to the local minor-league baseball team, the Brooklyn Cyclones (also known as the "Baby Mets"). The **B&B Carousel** is being restored and rebuilt. And Ringling Bros. and Barnum & Bailey circus spent the entire 2009 summer season at Coney Island and plan to make it a permanent stop. Coney Island is also the site of a film festival, a seasonal ice rink, several parades—most notably the annual Mardi Gras–style Mermaid Parade, which has been "ruled" by Harvey Keitel, David Johansen, Queen Latifah, and David Byrne, among others—and a small history museum.

The **New York Aquarium** (☎ 718-265-3474; **www.nyaquarium.com**), with its shark tank, SeaWorld-style sea-lion "theater," and hands-on attractions, is also on the boardwalk.

The Miami Beach–like Borscht Boardwalk of Brighton Beach is perhaps another mile to the east. Eat in the melting pot: have a hot dog at the baseball game and a knish later. Or sushi—advertised in Cyrillic letters. Now you know why they call it "Little Odessa by the

Sea." Brighton Beach was developed in the mid–19th century and named after the famous seaside resort town in England. It housed not only upscale hotels but also a large horse-racing track. It was redeveloped as a residential neighborhood in the 1920s when the subway line was completed. After World War II, it was inundated with concentration-camp survivors—relatives of the Jewish American residents—and later those escaping Soviet Union countries. (Manhattan Beach, which adjoins Brighton Beach on the east and faces Rockaway Inlet, is heavily Ashkenazi and Sephardic Jewish and Russian, but is much more affluent than Brighton Beach.)

QUEENS

FOR MOST VISITORS, THERE ARE only two sections of Queens of interest: **Flushing Meadows Corona Park** and **Long Island City.** (Well, that's not quite true: both **LaGuardia** and **JFK International** airports are in Queens, and **Belmont Park** racetrack straddles the Queens–Nassau County line, but in terms of sightseeing, it's a fair assumption.) Fortunately, most important sites are accessible by subway, and in less time than many tourists may think.

Long Island City, although it sounds as if it should be a distant municipality, is just on the other side of Roosevelt Island from the East Side and Upper East Side of Manhattan. And while its reputation as an industrial section lingers, some of those warehouse and factories have been transformed into cultural centers of the first magnitude.

Among them are the **Noguchi Museum,** which used to be a photogravure plant and an adjacent gas station; the Museum of Modern Art–affiliated **P.S. 1 Contemporary Art Center,** named for the onetime public-school building that houses it; the **Fisher Landau Center for Art,** a former parachute-harness factory that now houses an important collection of late-20th-century art; and the **SculptureCenter,** a former trolley-repair shop that was redesigned by Maya Lin.

Even rooftops get repurposed here: **City Ice Pavilion,** a bubble-covered ice-skating rink, is atop a mattress warehouse at 47th Avenue and Van Dam Street (☎ 718-505-6230; **www.cityicepavilion.com**).

The **Noguchi Museum** (33rd Road at Vernon Boulevard; ☎ 718-204-7088; **www.noguchi.org**), across the street from the building where artist and designer Isamu Noguchi lived in the 1960s (now the museum's offices), is one of the few in the world devoted to one man's work, filling 13 galleries with his celebrated lamps, furniture, and theatrical sets, while a gorgeous sculpture garden displays his larger pieces. Many of the benches in the building were made from a 60-foot tree of heaven that until a couple of years ago stood in the heart of the sculpture garden; when it was found to be diseased, museum officials hired artists to use as much of the wood as possible.

P.S. 1 (Jackson Avenue at 46th Avenue; ☎ 718-784-2084; **www.ps1 .org**) houses a large collection of contemporary art and specializes in avant-garde and collaborative exhibitions. It also hosts performance art and concerts.

The three-story **Fisher Landau Center,** at 39th Avenue and 30th Street (☎ 718-937-0727; **www.flcart.org**), houses the 1,100-work modern-art collection (1960 to the present) of collector Emily Fisher Landau; it includes multiple works by Ellsworth Kelly, Cy Twombly, Andy Warhol, and Kara Walker.

And the **SculptureCenter** (Purves Street off Thomson Street; ☎ 718-361-1750; **www.sculpture-center.org**), which has an 80-year history in New York, in 2002 moved from the Upper East Side, where it had been for 50 years, to its current location a few minutes' walk from P.S. 1 and the Noguchi Museum. It has 6,000 square feet of interior galleries and a 3,000-square-foot outdoor exhibition space, and exhibits both emerging and internationally renowned artists.

Although **Astoria** is sometimes referred to as a separate town, it is actually the northern section of Long Island City. Called Hallet's Cove, it was a summer retreat for wealthy New Yorkers well before the Civil War, but town fathers renamed it in an attempt to interest John Jacob Astor, whose summer home was within sight across the East River in Hell Gate. Astor made a token investment, but he never set foot in the place.

The deep-red **Hell Gate Bridge,** between Randall's Island and Astoria, completed in 1916, was the design blueprint for the famous Harbour Bridge in Sydney, Australia. The most famous reason to visit Astoria is the variety of ethnic eateries, especially the Greek and Middle Eastern places. (Although it's not by any means the only sizable group, the ethnic Greek community is one of the largest in the world.) A less famous reason, at least so far, is the **Museum of the Moving Image,** at 35th Avenue and 36th Street (☎ 718-784-0077; **www.movingimage.us**), housed in a building that used to be a working movie studio. And probably only locals know this, but the 330-foot-long swimming pool in Astoria Park, twice the site of Olympic trials, is one of the largest public pools in the country; the two fountains at the east end served as Olympic torches in 1936 and 1964.

kids At the **Museum of the Moving Image**—which includes TV, film, and video—you can dub your own voice into a famous film scene, experiment with animation, provide sound and visual effects, and see classic films screened. The museum is actually part of a larger moviemaking complex: the restored historic **Astoria Studios,** where Valentino, the Marx Brothers, and Gloria Swanson worked in the 1920s and Woody Allen and Martin Scorsese worked in the 1990s. It's a combination of memorabilia, costumes, props, posters, oddities (à la Planet Hollywood), reconstructed sets, and screening rooms. Smaller kids will get a kick out of exhibits that let them "enter" the set—speak through actors' mouths, put their heads on other bodies, and so on. (It's undergoing a substantial renovation and expansion.)

If you plan to go to **Flushing Meadows Corona Park,** expect to spend the day. This is the Central Park of Queens, with its own rowboat lake, ice rink, dual-stage theater, bike rentals, and so on. It also houses the remnants of two World's Fairs (1939–40 and 1964–65), the **New York Hall of Science,** the **Queens Zoo** (☎ 718-271-1500; **www.queenszoo.com**), the **Queens Museum of Art,** the **USTA Billie Jean King National Tennis Center** (☎ 718-595-2420; **www.usta.com/AboutUs/National Tennis Center .aspx**), where the U.S. Open is held, and the Mets' new baseball stadium. Fortunately, it also has its own subway station.

Corona Park is truly a world unto itself—that is, the 140-foot, 350-ton **Unisphere** globe, created for the 1964 World's Fair, still stands at the entrance. (This world, too, we owe to Robert Moses, who dredged out what had been a notorious swamp and rubbish pile—"a valley of ashes," F. Scott Fitzgerald wrote in *The Great Gatsby*—to make a place worthy of an international exhibition.)

The World's Fair site is now a sort of Disney Futurama of the past—what New Yorkers of 70 years ago expected of the 21st century. The "skyscape" is almost a space-scape, full of rocket ships and planets. And like Disney World's backward glimpse at "progress," it reminds us that such marvels as robots, color film, synthetic fabrics, FM radio, and dishwashers were brand new in 1939. Space vehicles, elevated superhighways, and heliports were the hottest draws in 1964. Many of these exhibits have been preserved, along with time capsules, one from each fair, not to be opened for 5,000 years. (The heliport, which has 360-degree views, is now a special-events venue.)

If Brooklyn's Museum of Art is like a miniature Metropolitan, the **Queens Museum of Art** (☎ 718-592-9700; **www.queensmuseum.org**) is like a miniature New York: it was the original New York City Pavilion of the 1939 fair. It houses a huge and detailed scale model (1 inch to 100 feet) of New York, called the Panorama, that was constructed when the building again became the New York City Pavilion for the 1964 fair and is regularly updated to reflect changes in the New York skyline (including the destruction of the Twin Towers, represented by beams of light). It includes all five boroughs, almost 900,000 individual buildings, a 15-inch Empire State Building, 35 bridges, and airplanes that actually "take off" from LaGuardia. The museum also has hundreds of bits of World's Fair memorabilia, such as guidebooks, souvenir plates and pins, board games, and banners. It also has a fine collection of Tiffany glass, reflecting the time when Tiffany's studios were in Queens.

For history buffs, this building also has special significance: it served as the temporary headquarters of the United Nations from 1946 to 1950, and it was here that the nation of Israel was voted into UN membership.

The **New York Hall of Science** (☎ 718-699-0005; **www.nyhallsci.org**) was constructed as the Hall of Education for the 1964–65 World's Fair (and has recently been provided with a 55,000-square-foot addition) but is scrupulously and often astonishingly up to date; it has interactive video stations that store outer-space transmissions, super-TV-size microscope displays, and scores of hands-on demonstrations of light, music, color, and physical properties—not to mention a 3-D spiderweb.

Another attraction in Corona, a few blocks on the other side of the Mets–Willets Point subway stop, might seem more suited to Harlem: **Louis Armstrong's longtime home,** extravagantly decorated in high 1940s style by his fourth wife, Lucille. They lived here together until his death—in his beloved "wall-to-wall" bed (which is very nearly that wide)—in 1971; she continued living here until her death in 1983. Highlights include the custom-built turquoise kitchen appliances, the gold-foil master bathroom, and the portrait of Armstrong by Tony Bennett. The house is on 107th Street between 34th and 37th avenues (☎ 718-478-8274; **www.satchmo.net**).

Incidentally, Astoria isn't the only part of Queens for foodies. A few years ago, the *New York Times* pronounced: "If Manhattan disappeared tomorrow, Queens would become the restaurant capital of the region." The stretch of **Roosevelt Avenue** east of Corona, especially from about 60th Street to 90th Street, is its own sort of world's fare, with Indian, Pakistani, Mexican, Korean, Cuban, Uruguayan, Filipino, Chinese, Thai, and even Texan cooking. **Flushing** has become a multiregional Chinatown-Koreatown, and **Corona** is beefing up with Brazilian *churrascarias*. And yes, there's a subway stop at Roosevelt and 74th Street, on the same 7 line as Flushing Meadows Corona Park. Be sure to carry that Alka-Seltzer.

THE BRONX

THIS OFTEN-OVERLOOKED BOROUGH—the only one of the five that sits on the mainland of the United States—used to be some of the city's thickest woodlands and richest farmland. The name comes from sea captain-turned-landowner Jonas Bronck, who bought 500 acres in the mid–17th century. Sections of the Bronx, particularly **Riverdale,** along the Hudson River toward Westchester County in what might be thought of as the Heights of the Bronx, are still considered prestigious addresses.

But the Bronx gets bad press. Beginning shortly after World War 1, the area was inundated with immigrants, particularly Irish and Italians. During Prohibition, it was the headquarters for many large regional bootlegging operations. In the 1960s, the area began to deteriorate, especially the **South Bronx,** and stories of widespread arson and abandonment gave the borough a bad name. (The fact that **Rikers Island,** New York's main jail and a fixture of television and film, is in the Bronx doesn't help much.)

However, all of the gangster movies in Hollywood should not obscure the fact that some of New York's most famous addresses, and largest parks, are in the Bronx: **Yankee Stadium,** of course, the **Bronx**

Zoo (Fordham Road and Bronx River Parkway; ☎ 718-220-5100; **www.bronxzoo.com**), and the **New York Botanical Garden** (Bronx River Parkway at Fordham Road; ☎ 718-817-8700; **www.nybg.org**). There's also the **Bronx Museum of the Arts; Pelham Bay Park,** the largest green space in New York City; and **Van Cortlandt Park** (Broadway and West 246th Street; ☎ 718-430-1890; **www.nycparks.org**), the city's fourth largest; **Wave Hill,** the Palisades estate whose mansion is now a performing-arts venue; and **The Woodlawn Cemetery,** where the mausoleums are also mansions. (Again, happily, many of these are accessible by public transportation.)

unofficial TIP Although they don't always line up perfectly because of the river bridges, the numbered streets in Harlem and the Bronx are nearly contiguous, so at least you have an idea of the distance and direction you're traveling.

It's also home to numerous colleges and universities, most famously **Fordham,** which is near the Botanical Garden and Zoo, and an increasingly number of Off-Off-Broadway theatrical venues, and it was prominent in the evolution of hip-hop. (Curiously, although it's on the mainland side of the Harlem River, the little town of Marble Hill actually belongs to Manhattan.)

The **Grand Concourse,** which is the great boulevard of the Bronx, modeled on the Champs-Élysées in Paris, runs for four miles from 138th Street at the Harlem River right up to the edge of Van Cortlandt Park. It's lined with hundreds of Art Deco and Art Moderne apartment buildings (several in the neighborhood of the Museum of the Arts have been designated historic sites), and to celebrate its centennial in 2009, a $52 million plan was announced to refit the boulevard with period streetlights, a cobblestone sidewalk, and landscaped medians. **Lou Gehrig Plaza,** which serves as sort of a great gateway from the Grand Concourse to Yankee Stadium at 161st Street, has also been restored. (The elaborate **Lorelei Fountain,** at 161st Street, a memorial to German romantic poet Heinrich Heine, was supposed to have been erected in Midtown Manhattan, but wound up at 164th Street and eventually was moved to 161st.)

unofficial TIP There are subway stops along the Grand Concourse, but remember the "heights"; it's an easy walk downhill to Bronx Park, but you may want to take a bus back uphill, especially after several hours in the park.

Just a few blocks farther up the Grand Concourse, at 165th Street, is the **Bronx Museum of the Arts** (☎ 718 681-6000; **www.bronxmuseum.org**), which specializes in 20th- and 21st-century art, especially Latin American, Asian, and African pieces. Originally a synagogue, it recently completed its second substantial expansion.

And just north of the museum, at 1150 Grand Concourse, is the much-loved Art Moderne **"Fish Building,"** so nicknamed because of the fabulous aquarium mosaic alongside the lobby door and the rounded corners.

East Fordham Road intersects the Grand Concourse at 190th Street; a few blocks east is Fordham University, and beyond that is **Bronx Park,** which houses both the botanical garden and the zoo, the largest such facility in the country. (Both the zoo and garden are profiled in Part Six.)

Just a little north of Fordham Road is East Knightsbridge Road, where you'll find the **Edgar Allan Poe Cottage** (☎ 718-881-8900; **www .bronxhistoricalsociety.org**), where Poe and the dying Virginia lived from 1846 to 1847, and where Poe remained until his own death in 1849. At press time, a new visitor center was nearing completion and the cottage was about to undergo much needed restoration.

Toward the northern edge of the Bronx (and of the subway lines) are several historical estates, most notably the **Van Cortlandt House Museum,** in Van Cortlandt Park (☎ 718-543-3344; **www.vancortlandt house.org**), a restored mid-18th-century mansion used by Washington as one of his headquarters (there was skirmish fire in the yard) and furnished with authentic period Dutch and American pieces as well as Delft ceramics. Van Cortlandt Park is home to the nation's first public golf course and still has a major cricket field.

On the east side, Van Cortlandt Park adjoins **The Woodlawn Cemetery** (☎ 718-920-0500 or 877-496-6352; **www.thewoodlawncemetery .org**), where the very wealthy—Woolworths, Macys, Goulds, Belmonts, Armours, etc.—built eternal homes as elaborate as their temporal ones; get a map at the Webster Avenue entrance.

unofficial **TIP**
Pelham Bay Park is the last stop on the No. 6 subway, and remember, this is a huge park, so wear good walking shoes.

A few blocks on the west of Van Cortlandt Park is **Wave Hill** (☎ 718-549-3200; **www.wave hill.org**), the onetime estate of financier and conservationist George Perkins and at various points home to Theodore Roosevelt, Mark Twain, and Arturo Toscanini. Take one glimpse of its view, over the Hudson River toward the Palisades, and you'll see why Riverdale is still desirable. The mansion is now used for concerts (in the vaulted Armor Hall), art exhibits ranging from sculpture to topiary, and demonstrations; the gardens and grounds are also open, and stunning. (Although Wave Hill isn't close to a subway stop, the organization offers free shuttle service from the Metro North Riverdale train station and the No. 1 subway terminus at 242nd Street.)

At the northeast corner of the Bronx is **Pelham Bay Park** (☎ 718-430-1890; **www.nycgovparks.org**), the largest public space in New York—more than three times the size of Central Park—and one that spreads across both sides of the Hutchinson River. It includes the mile-long **Orchard Beach,** an elaborate complex of playgrounds, sports fields, cafes, and shops; a salt marsh; a wildlife sanctuary; two 18-hole golf courses; and several nature trails. You'll also find the **Bartow-Pell Mansion and Museum,** which has been restored and refurnished to early-19th-century style. The **Bronx Equestrian Center** is on the east side of the bay (☎ 718-885-0551; **www.bronxequestrian center.com**).

Those interested in sailing and whaling might want to visit **City Island,** near the south end of the park, a community of sailing vessels, boatyards (including the manufacturers of several America's Cup champs), marinas, and old-fashioned waterside eateries.

A little-known but historically intriguing site is **St. Paul's Church,** at 897 South Columbus Avenue at South Third Avenue, just outside the Bronx city limits in Mount Vernon (☎ 914-667-4116; **www.nps.gov/ sapa**), a little northwest of Pelham Bay Park. It was built in 1695 as a wooden chapel. In 1758, the retiring minister gave the church a bell from England's Whitechapel Foundry, which also produced the Liberty Bell. When General Washington ordered all the bells in the city melted down for cannon, the parishioners hid it; shortly thereafter, Hessian soldiers tore down the chapel for firewood. It was rebuilt in stone and the bell rehung after the Revolutionary War. Though the bell was originally rung to celebrate the king's birthday on June 4, it is now rung on July 4. The museum has exhibits on historical sites and battles related to the church and hosts occasional reenactments. It's about a ten-minute walk from the No. 5 train's Dyre Avenue stop.

STATEN ISLAND

"I'LL TAKE MANHATTAN / THE BRONX AND STATEN ISLAND, TOO. . . ." Staten Islanders could be forgiven for sometimes feeling as if they were an afterthought, famous primarily as the turnaround point for the Staten Island Ferry. In fact, the story goes that Staten Island would still be part of New Jersey if the Duke of York hadn't put it up as a prize in a sailing contest in 1667. It wasn't even connected to any other borough until the Verrazano-Narrows Bridge between Staten Island and Brooklyn opened in 1964; the country's longest suspension bridge, it's still the only actual point of contact. And Staten Islanders have repeatedly voiced enthusiasm for breaking away from the rest of New York; a 1993 referendum on secession passed by a two-to-one vote.

*uno*fficial **TIP**
To get to Snug Harbor from the ferry terminal, catch the S40 bus.

Despite this apparent sense of independence, or perhaps because of it (too much progress can be a shortsighted thing), Staten Island is the site of several museums worth an excursion, especially for families interested in American history. You can't use a subway for these, of course, but all are accessible by bus from the island side of the Staten Island Ferry—which, remember, is free.

The most important, Staten Island's mini–Museum Mile, is the very all-ages **Snug Harbor Cultural Center and Botanical Garden** at Richmond Terrace and Tyson Street (☎ 718-448-2500; **www.snug-harbor.org**), which was founded in 1833 as a home for "aged, decrepit, and worn-out sailors" (the nation's first) and which served as one, at least in part, for nearly 150 years. It still has several fine Greek Revival structures dating to the 1830s and many Victorian and Italianate buildings. Among its attractions are the **Newhouse Center for Contemporary Art,** which is housed in the old Main Hall, adorned with seafaring-themed stained glass; the **Noble Maritime Collection** (☎ 718-447-6490; **www.noblemaritime.org**), a fabulous art and memorabilia museum that includes the housebaot-turned-studio of artist John Noble; the **Staten Island Children's Museum** (☎ 718-273-2060; **www.statenislandkids.org**), which emphasizes performances as well as science; an arts and sciences museum under construction; and the **Staten Island Botanical Garden,** with its lush orchid greenhouse,

unofficial **TIP**
To reach Historic Richmond Town and the Jacques Marchais Museum, take the S74 bus.

secret garden, Tuscan garden, and the recently completed Chinese scholar's garden, built by local contractors with the assistance of 40 craftsmen from Suzhou. The Botanical Garden also has a fledgling vineyard, which grows Italian varietals as a tribute to Staten Island's large (more than one-third) Italian American population.

kids An even more intriguing complex, and older in part, is **Historic Richmond Town** (☎ 718-351-1611; **www.historicrichmondtown.org**), on Clarke Avenue south of Richmond Road. A re-creation of the island's 19th-century county seat, it includes 27 buildings, many of them original and about half of them open to the public, in a restored "village" something like a Williamsburg of the north. Among the open structures is the 1695 Voorlezer House, once a Dutch Reformed church and the oldest elementary school in the country; the 1839 Bennett House, now called the Museum of Childhood (see the toy room); and the 1840 General Store–post office. Like Williamsburg, Richmond Town is populated by costumed craftspeople and artisans who give demonstrations and sell reproductions as souvenirs in the gift store.

There are also a couple of museums on Staten Island of more specialized interest, including the **Jacques Marchais Museum of Tibetan Art** (☎ 718-987-3500; **www.tibetanmuseum.org**) at 338 Lighthouse Avenue, not far from Historic Richmond Town. "Marchais" was actually Asian art dealer Mrs. Harry Klauber, who built this replica of a Himalayan temple to house her private collection of Buddhas, religious artifacts, and other contemplative figurines. There are life-size stone Buddhas in the garden and what is said to be America's only Bhutanese sand mandala, the multicolored depiction of a deity's palace; visitors have included the Dalai Lama.

Overlooking the Narrows a little north of the Verrazano Bridge is the **Alice Austen House,** on Hylan Boulevard at Lower New York Bay (☎ 718-816-4506; **www.aliceausten.org**), a long, low, gracious cottage built around 1700. Alice, a 19th-century photographer, lived most of her life here and took more than 9,000 photographs of the evolution of New York, but they went almost unnoticed, and at the age of 84, having lost everything in the stock-market crash, she had to move into the poorhouse. Only a year later, she and her work were "discovered" by *Life* magazine, and she was able to spend her last months in a nursing home. Her photos are exhibited in the house on a rotating basis. (Take the S51 bus from the ferry.)

CENTRAL PARK

CENTRAL PARK RANGES 51 BLOCKS, from Central Park South (59th Street) to Central Park North (110th Street), and three east–west avenue blocks, from Fifth to Eighth. It is crossed from east to west in only five places, at roughly 65th, 72nd, 79th, 85th, and 97th streets. Most of the transverse roads have pleasant curves rather than gridlike rigidity, and vehicular traffic is prohibited during the middle of the day and all weekend.

unofficial **TIP**
To see a full list of the attractions, activities, and restroom facilities, go to www.centralparknyc.org.

kids Several of the most famous, and visible, children's attractions are in the southernmost segment of the park, including **Wollman Rink** (restored by Donald Trump; ☎ 212-439-6900; **www.wollmanskatingrink.com**), which during warm weather is transformed into the **Victorian Gardens** amusement park; **the Pond,** a reed-edged sanctuary filled with ducks and other wildlife, curled up in the southeast corner of the park near Grand Army Plaza; the **Central Park Zoo** and **Tisch Children's Zoo** (☎ 212-439-6500; **www.central parkzoo.com**); and the **Carousel** (☎ 212-879-0244; **www.centralpark carousel.com**). A 1908 model with 58 hand-carved horses, south of the 65th Street transverse, the Carousel was moved to Central Park from Coney Island in 1951, replacing a far less attractive merry-go-round.

As you face north, the **Dairy** is to the right of the Carousel, closer to Fifth Avenue. The twin-peaked shed is now the main visitor center (☎ 212-794-6564); Urban Park Rangers (☎ 212-628-2345 or 212-860-1370) sometimes lead tours of the park from here. The **Chess and Checkers House,** a gift of financier Bernard Baruch, is on a rock just southwest of the Dairy. On the other side of the Carousel, across Center Drive, are **Heckscher Playground** and the **softball fields,** which pretty much fill up the southwest part of this section to Columbus Circle.

The frontispiece of the zoo, near where East 64th Street runs into Fifth Avenue, is the medieval-looking **Arsenal** building (☎ 212-360-1311), which originally earned its cannon, but which, in the years since it was built in 1851, has been a weather station, a police station, a menagerie, the original Museum of Natural History, and, finally, headquarters of the Parks and Recreation Department. The original

Central Park

1. *Alice in Wonderland* Statue
2. Arsenal
3. Balto Statue
4. The Bandshell
5. Belvedere Castle
6. Bethesda Terrace & Bethesda Fountain
7. Boathouse Cafe
8. Bow Bridge
9. Carousel
10. Central Park Zoo
11. Charles A. Dana Discovery Center
12. Cleopatra's Needle (The Obelisk)
13. Conservatory
14. Conservatory Garden
15. The Dairy–Visitor Center
16. Delacorte Music Clock
17. Delacorte Theater
18. Diana Ross Playground
19. Hans Christian Andersen Statue
20. Harlem Meer
21. Heckscher Ball Fields
22. Heckscher Playground
23. Henry Luce Nature Observatory
24. *Imagine* Mosaic
25. Jacqueline Kennedy Onassis Reservoir
26. Lasker Rink and Pool
27. Literary Walk
28. Loeb Boathouse
29. The Mall
30. North Meadow Ball Fields
31. Pat Hoffman Friedman Playground
32. The Pool
33. Rustic Playground
34. Shakespeare Garden
35. Spector Playground
36. Summit Rock
37. Swedish Cottage Marionette Theatre
38. Tennis Courts
39. Tisch Children's Zoo
40. Wollman Rink–Victorian Gardens

ⓘ Information
Ⓜ Subway stop

0 ——— 0.2 mi
0 ——— 0.2 km

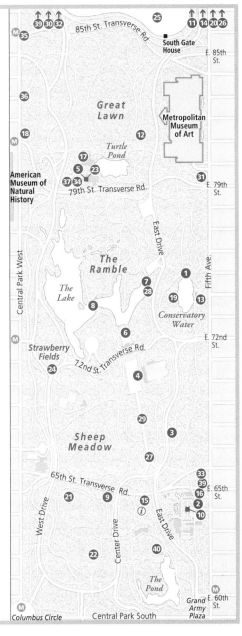

Olmsted-Vaux plans for the park are exhibited here, along with murals in the lobby showing the building's military and museum past.

The Zoo itself was renovated in the late 1980s; the parks department found new homes for the animals that were too large for such a crowded facility, and it constructed more-contemporary, eco-sensitive settings for the animals that were kept. The monkey house is now a real jungle gym, the bats have an eternally nocturnal home, and the reptiles have a swamp that is almost a pre-Olmsted joke.

The **Sheep Meadow,** a pet project of Boss Tweed, is the 15-acre green alongside the Tavern. Nearby are the immaculate **Bowling Green** and **Croquet Field,** where top-ranked competitive collegiate and professional teams play. Just to the right of the Sheep Meadow and Bowling Green, running just about down the middle of this second rung of the park's ladder, is a popular roller-skating strip.

Alongside the skaters is the **Mall,** a 40-foot-wide formal promenade flanked by quadruple rows of American elms that form a sight line of ten blocks all the way up to **Belvedere Castle** atop **Vista Rock.** The lower stretch is also known as **Literary Walk** because it's lined with sculptures and busts of famous writers and composers: Shakespeare (the one the three Booth brothers raised funds for), Beethoven, Robert Burns, Sir Walter Scott, et al.

The band shell there, the second on the site, is no longer used; summer concerts are now held on the adjoining playground, **Rumsey Field,** which, in case you need a good meeting point, is the one with the statue of Mother Goose. Facing the old band shell across Terrace Drive (the 72nd Street transverse) is **Bethesda Terrace,** a fountain setting at the edge of **The Lake** that offers a grand view of the **Ramble** (see next page). The statue atop the fountain represents "The Angel of the Waters," from a story in the Gospel of John that says the touch of an angel gave healing powers to a Bethesda pool in Jerusalem. The Lake, which is about one-third of the way up the park, is the second-largest body of water in the park, pinched together in the middle and crossed by Vaux's 60-foot-high, cast-iron **Bow Bridge.**

Around the west end of the 72nd Street transverse, within sight of the Dakota apartment building on Central Park West, where John Lennon lived and was murdered in 1980, is **Strawberry Fields,** Yoko Ono's memorial to Lennon, her husband. The mosaic, reading "Imagine," was a gift from the city of Naples, Italy, and the "peace garden" includes plants from 161 nations.

At the upper edge of the Lake on the east side is **Loeb Boathouse,** which houses **The Boathouse** cafe (☎ 212-517-2233; **www.thecentral parkboathouse.com**), one of Manhattan's most popular scenic eateries for locals as well as tourists. It's also Central Park's romance central, with a Venetian gondola; you can take a 30-minute ride from an Italian-trained gondolier for about $30 and canoodle in style.

kids A little to the east of Loeb Boathouse near Fifth Avenue is an unconnected, smaller lake called **Conservatory Water,** where the **Kerbs Model Boathouse** houses the miniature yachts that, as any *Stuart Little* fan can tell you, race every Saturday afternoon in summer. You don't even have to bring your own; you can rent one at $10 for a half hour.

Around Conservatory Water are the statues of the **Mad Tea Party** (from *Alice's Adventures in Wonderland*) and **Hans Christian Andersen.** The Mad Tea Party was the gift of publisher George Delacorte, who also donated the animal-fair clock at the zoo; he is said to have been the model for the Mad Hatter himself, though the likeness is somewhat exaggerated. Andersen's only permanent audience is a bronze bird (and some live ones that seem pretty steady), but his memorial is the gathering place for story time on Saturdays at 11 a.m.

To the west of Bethesda Terrace is the **Cherry Hill** overlook, which offers a view of the Mall, the Lake, and the **Ramble,** a 37-acre stretch of woods and wildflower gardens that is a haven for birds and bird-watchers alike.

On the western shore of the Lake is the **Ladies Pavilion,** an elaborate Victorian filigreed-iron gazebo set in a carefully crafted miniature woodland landscape (one of Olmsted's favorite projects).

Across from the Ramble, in the middle of the 79th Street transverse, is **Vista Rock** and its crowning glory, **Belvedere Castle,** a somewhat smaller but impressive replica of a Scottish stone castle—turrets, terraces, and such—that was meant to be just part of the decor back in Olmsted and Vaux's day. Today it houses the **Henry Luce Nature Observatory,** which arranges family tours and programs (☎ 212-772-0210), and a branch of the **National Weather Service** that has information on wildlife. The roof offers a splendid view of the park.

Just on the west side of the castle near Winter Drive are the **Swedish Cottage,** a marionette theater originally built for the Philadelphia Exposition of 1876, and the **Shakespeare Garden,** all of whose trees and flowers are mentioned in Shakespeare's works. Visible across Belvedere Lake to the northwest is the **Delacorte Theater,** the 2,000-seat site of the popular summer Shakespeare in the Park shows—yet another gift from George Delacorte. To the northeast you can see **Cleopatra's Needle,** which, despite its popular nickname, was actually built by Pharaoh Thutmose III in 1450 BC. The obelisk was presented by the Khedive of Egypt to the city of New York in 1879.

Beyond Cleopatra's Needle, along Fifth Avenue from East 81st to 84th streets, is the **Metropolitan Museum of Art.** And the great green oval in the center of the park from **Turtle Pond** nearly to the 85th Street transverse is the 55-acre **Great Lawn.** At least, now it's a lawn. It started as a reservoir; then it was the site of Central Park's Hooverville, as Depression-era shantytowns were called. In the mid-1930s,

Robert Moses, the great public-works developer, created the Great Lawn. After the city installed eight ball diamonds in the 1950s, it became brown and hard-packed from overuse, but later resodded and regulated, it has been the venue for several famous concerts, including Simon and Garfunkel's 1981 performance, which drew a crowd of half a million, the even larger "No Nukes" show a year later, and Luciano Pavarotti's recital in 1993. It is also where the Metropolitan Opera and the New York Philharmonic stage their summer concerts.

The 85th Street transverse the geographic waistline of the park. Above it is the 106-acre **Jacqueline Kennedy Onassis Reservoir,** by far the largest of the park's half-dozen bodies of water, which takes up most of the area between the 85th and 97th Street transverses. It dates back to the original Croton reservoir system of 1862 and was in active use until 1991. The trail around the reservoir is a popular jogging route. The remaining corner of this section, northwest of the reservoir, is where the tennis courts are.

North of the 97th Street transverse are the large **North Meadow,** which has one of the park's newest sports and recreation centers; and the smaller, still pastoral **East Meadow,** which even for some city dwellers seems to be the end of the park. However, there are more gardens and even some historic sites above about 105th Street. The **Conservatory Garden**—actually three formal gardens (and no conservatory building)—includes a "secret garden," with an appropriate statue of Dickon and Mary (characters from the book of that name); the entrance gate, from the Cornelius Vanderbilt estate in Midtown, is on Fifth Avenue between 104th and 105th.

Behind the Conservatory Garden is **the Mount,** which is now bare but once held a tavern (later a convent!) from which Washington's men held off the British. It looks down on **McGowan's Pass** at East 106th Street and beyond the pass to the former site of a pair of 1812 forts (now identified by markers only). Look for the blockhouse below East Drive (about West 109th Street) south of the Adam Clayton Powell Jr. Boulevard entrance.

At the opposite end of the park from Wollman Rink is **Lasker Rink,** another ice-skating rink, which becomes a wading pool in summer. Because of its location, this rink is cheaper and generally less crowded than Wollman.

Finally, at the top of the park beyond the **Harlem Meer** lake is **Charles A. Dana Discovery Center,** once the boathouse and now an outpost of the Urban Park Rangers, dedicated to environmental issues. Borrow a fishing pole and put your feet up.

Oh, that circle at the northeast corner? It's named for James Frawley, whose construction company built the Manhattan and Queensboro bridges, but the statue of the pianist and his instrument, held up by nine nude Muses, depicts Duke Ellington.

PART SIX

SIGHTSEEING, TOURS, *and* ATTRACTIONS *in* DEPTH

LET YOUR FINGERS DO *the* WALKING . . . FIRST

THE NICE THING ABOUT SIGHTSEEING is that you can do it at your own pace, lingering over what intrigues you, gazing appreciatively at what pleases you, and pushing right on past what stirs not a flicker of interest. In New York, you can tour by land, sea, air, bicycle, horse-drawn carriage, or helicopter. You can see historic spots or literary haunts, cathedrals or courts, authentic remnants or virtual realities. (And you can pay nothing, something, or, well, a lot.)

There's no question that these famous skylines are impressive; that's why we've listed some of the best and highest viewpoints in the city in this chapter. But we believe that, ultimately, you can see New York best if you get right down to street level. New York is particularly well suited to walking tours, and that's why we recommend you consider it a neighborhood at a time.

As you can see from our own walking tours in Part Five, New York's Neighborhoods, there are sights and scenes of everywhere in the five boroughs. Even in Part Eight, Shopping, we've combined souveniring in the most important neighborhoods with a little background flavor and a few landmarks so you can enjoy the city's historical riches while plundering its boutiques. So keep your eyes open and your schedule a little loose. We've done our best to guide you around, but trust us—we haven't begun to cover the possibilities.

On the other hand, we know that not everybody prefers do-it-yourself tours. Some people find it a bit distracting to try to read directions and anecdotes while walking, and others use packaged tours as a quick way of getting a mental map of the area.

So we've outlined some categories of special interest, considered family dynamics, and suggested a few specialized tours you might want to try. We've also listed some of the most reputable guided-tour companies around. These are by no means complete lists; tourism is a boom industry in New York, and you'll see flyers for new tours every month.

We also realize that New York is not one-size-fits-all. Walking is wonderful if you're young and fit, but if your party includes children or seniors, build in a timely stop in a park; or split the touring day into "shifts" so that, if necessary, those with less stamina can head back to the hotel while the others continue. Schedule the attractions everyone wants to see first, the could-be-missed intermediate ones later, and the only-for-fanatics excursions last. And set a time and a clearly understood place to regroup.

> *unofficial* **TIP**
> Although described in Part Five, some of the most important museums, historic houses, zoos, and parks are covered in more detail in the attraction profiles at the end of this chapter.

(Lunch works well as an automatic time limit, especially for family groups with multiple agendas. No matter how absorbed a teenager gets in a particular exhibit, there are few things that can override a kid's stomach alarm, even a *T. rex* skeleton.)

STRETCHING YOUR SIGHTSEEING DOLLAR

AS WE SAID, THE TOUR BUSINESS in New York is booming, and there's a good reason: it's quite profitable. With museum and attraction tickets regularly hovering around the $20 mark, and attraction operators increasingly savvy about selling "express access" and other add-ons, the cost can quickly mount. So you should decide on your priorities—are you willing to pay $25 in addition to the $20 entry fee just to go to the front of the security lines at the **Empire State Building,** knowing you'll also have to pay $15 to go up to the 102nd-floor observatory? (For a 12-year-old, that means a $14 ticket becomes $45, and probably $60.) Time really is money here.

Obviously you'll have to pay for some things, so you should look to offset that by taking advantage of freebies, and of whatever packages and bargains you can. That's one reason we've provided so many walking tours of our own in Part Five; we're grateful you bought this book, and we'd like to help you out in return.

Because they're often organized by nonprofit or cultural groups, many tours are free or very affordable. The *New York Times* Friday Weekend section lists not only museum exhibits, family attractions, and concerts but also special-interest tours scheduled for that weekend, often remarkably eccentric—the homes of famous salsa musicians, for instance. We've

> *unofficial* **TIP**
> Be sure to check into "categorical" discounts. Many museums, parks, and attractions offer discounts for AAA members, veterans, or students. Hotels may offer AAA, AARP, or other discounts. Members of the military may even get in free, but in some cases an ID isn't enough; you have to be in uniform.

listed a few free or less-expensive options under "Guided Walking (Mostly) Tours" following.

Actually, although a few museums do have required ticket prices, a surprising number—including the **Metropolitan Museum of Art** and the **American Museum of Natural History**—only "suggest" you pay their posted admission prices. We believe you should support these fine institutions, but if it really will strain your wallet to pay $60 for a family of four to visit the dinosaurs, give what you can.

Many of the major museums and gardens or zoological parks have a free evening or "pay what you wish" hours (also listed on page 215). Not only that, but many also have cut back on admission prices in recent years.

If you expect to make repeat visits, a membership might be a bargain. For example, admission to the Museum of Modern Art is $20 per adult, but a year's membership with unlimited free entrance, is $75, so in four visits (or even four days), you've saved $5. And guest tickets are $5 to members, so for a couple, those four visits would cost $95 instead of $160. It just depends on your passion for the arts.

Similarly, a $124 family membership to the Wildlife Conservation Society covers a year's admission for two adults and all children under 18 to the **Bronx Zoo,** *and* the zoos in **Central Park, Prospect Park,** and Queens, plus the **New York Aquarium** and 16 **Bronx Zoo** attraction tickets. One-day tickets for two adults and two kids for one day at the Bronx Zoo alone would cost $52, except on freebie Wednesday. (On the other hand, the Bronx Zoo's admission is also "suggested." Consult your conscience.)

If you decide to take one of the big-name tours—the most popular being the harbor cruises to **Ellis Island** and the **Statue of Liberty,** and the **open-air bus tours**—see if there are package tickets of any sort: you won't find two-for-one, probably, but a combo ticket will be less than the two individually.

The most elaborate versions of these package deals, and the best if you are serious about getting into a lot of the major landmarks, are the various citywide tour "passes." These allow you to pay according to the number of sites you want to visit and/or the number of days you want the pass to be valid. You'll have to do some calculating in advance; on the face of it, a $75 pass that gets you into 55 attractions across all five boroughs, including most of the major art museums, historic homes, and zoos, sounds like a steal—and that doesn't count the discounts at **Macy's** and for the harbor cruises—but how much can you do in one day? A somewhat more realistic time frame, three days, doubles the cost, and so on.

Nevertheless, even single-day passes can be substantial cost-cutters if you're a die-hard sightseer. (Remember those $20-plus tickets?) Three big companies offer multiaccess tickets of this type. The **New York**

Pass (☎ 877-714-1999; **www.newyorkpass.com**), which we used as the previous example, includes admission to 55 sites and discounts at an additional two dozen retail and tour options; a week's pass is $190 for adults and $150 for children ages 2 to 12.

The **Explorer Pass** (☎ 800-887-9103; **www.smartdestinations.com**) allows you to decide how many places you want to go and charges by the visit. You can choose from more than 30 attractions and tours, paying for admission to three, five, seven, or ten of them. The pass is good for 30 days from the time it's first used, which might be especially helpful if New York is the jumping-off point for, say, a tour of Long Island wineries or the Hudson River Valley. Passes range from $48 to $140 for kids and from $70 to $210 for adults, but the Web site sometimes has discount offers.

unofficial **TIP**
Even tour companies have slow seasons. In January, a $190 weeklong pass was available for $155.

New York City Pass (☎ 888-330-5008; **www.citypass.com**) allows access to six sites for $79 ($59 ages 13 to 17). This is, as the pricing suggests, a little more in the adult and teen style: the attractions include the **American Museum of Natural History,** the **Guggenheim,** the **Metropolitan** and the **Museum of Modern Art,** the (yes) **Empire State Building,** and a choice of a harbor cruise or a ferry to Ellis Island and the Statue of Liberty. This pass is good for nine days.

All three of these "passes" include guidebooks with more coupons and express-line access to a few attractions, and can be picked up a various locations around the city.

It's not just big attractions that come in bargain packages. **Big Onion Tours,** one of the city's best walking-tour companies, has a frequent-walker incentive program (see page 219). Ask your tour operator if it offers any special incentives.

If you prefer your attractions one at a time, there are plenty of discount coupons for museums, sightseeing options, and even Broadway shows; though these coupons are usually for shows that have been around a little longer, that doesn't mean you've seen them—or don't want to see them again. And those coupons pop up in a surprising variety of ways. The sightseeing map you pick up in one of the visitor centers may have a 10% coupon off up to two tickets to the **Intrepid Sea, Air & Space Museum.** A promotional flyer for **South Street Seaport,** picked up in a rack of attraction brochures at a train station, included a $6 discount for the (fairly expensive) Bodies exhibit then at the Seaport complex. So read the back, sides, and fine print of any flyer you see. At least you may get a "free gift."

You don't have to do this in advance; in addition to the visitor centers, listed in Part Two, Planning Your Visit, many hotels have racks of brochures, and the hotel concierge may have a few special offers in the desk drawer.

But don't fall into the "if it's cheaper, it's better" trap, either. It's a bargain only if you really want it. For instance, a 72-hour pass on one of those on-off tour buses may be only $10 more than the 48-hour version, but are you actually using the bus for transportation between **Harlem** and the **Battery**? Do you want to see all those sights (from a distance)? And even if you do, how many are that much of a walk from a subway or bus line? A daylong MetroCard Fun Pass is $8.25, and a weeklong unlimited pass only $27—half that if you're age 65 or older. Even if your bus tour includes a ticket to the Empire State Building, how much could you save by walking or riding the subway?

unofficial **TIP**
When surfing tour Web sites, be sure to check the dates (or enter 2010 in the search line); many references are outdated. Several offer tours of the Ground Zero site, for instance, which has been closed off for some time.

Also, while a helicopter tour of the area may offer a different perspective on the Statue of Liberty, if you combined it with a harbor cruise, will you see enough of a difference to be happy with spending the extra money? You might—we just suggest you pay close attention to the details. But personally, we prefer our views to come with a cocktail and sunset; see the list of "Best Views" below.

CATEGORIES AND RECOMMENDATIONS

kids **BEST CHILDREN'S FARE**

American Museum of Natural History (UPPER WEST SIDE)

Bronx Zoo (THE BRONX)

Central Park

Coney Island and the New York Aquarium (BROOKLYN)

Forbes Magazine Galleries (GREENWICH VILLAGE)

Hayden Planetarium–Rose Center for Earth and Space (UPPER WEST SIDE)

IMAX theater, AMC Loews Lincoln Square 13 (UPPER WEST SIDE)

Intrepid Sea, Air & Space Museum (MIDTOWN WEST)

Museum of the City of New York (UPPER EAST SIDE)

New York Aquarium (BROOKLYN)

New York City Fire Museum (SOHO)

New York City Police Museum (LOWER MANHATTAN)

New York Hall of Science (QUEENS)

New York Transit Museum (BROOKLYN)

Roosevelt Island Tramway (UPPER EAST SIDE)

Sony Wonder Technology Lab (MIDTOWN EAST)

Staten Island Ferry (LOWER MANHATTAN)

BEST VIEWS

Battery Gardens restaurant (LOWER MANHATTAN)

Beekman Tower Hotel, Top of the Tower restaurant (MIDTOWN EAST)

Dream Hotel Ava Bar (MIDTOWN WEST)

Empire Hotel Rooftop Bar (MIDTOWN WEST)

Empire State Building (GRAMERCY PARK)

Mandarin Oriental, New York hotel Lobby Lounge (**UPPER WEST SIDE**)

Marcel at Gramercy Baboon Lounge (**GRAMERCY PARK–MURRAY HILL**)

Metropolitan Museum of Art Roof Garden Café (**UPPER EAST SIDE**)

New York Marriott Marquis Times Square hotel View Restaurant (**MIDTOWN WEST**)

The Ritz-Carlton New York, Battery Park, Rise bar (**LOWER MANHATTAN**)

The River Café (**BROOKLYN**)

Top of the Rock (**MIDTOWN EAST**)

ETHNIC AND "ROOTS" EXHIBITS

Ellis Island Immigration Museum (**LOWER MANHATTAN**)

Japan Society (**MIDTOWN EAST**)

The Jewish Museum (**UPPER EAST SIDE**)

Lower East Side Tenement Museum (**LOWER EAST SIDE**)

El Museo del Barrio (**UPPER EAST SIDE**)

The Italian American Museum (**LOWER EAST SIDE**)

Museum of Chinese in America (**LOWER EAST SIDE**)

Museum of Jewish Heritage (**LOWER MANHATTAN**)

National Museum of the American Indian (**LOWER MANHATTAN**)

Rubin Museum of Himalayan Art (**GRAMERCY PARK**)

SMALLER, LESS-CROWDED MUSEUMS OF NOTE

Asia Society and Museum (**UPPER EAST SIDE**)

The Cloisters (**WASHINGTON HEIGHTS**)

The Frick Collection (**UPPER EAST SIDE**)

Hispanic Society of America Museum and Library (**UPPER WEST SIDE**)

New York Historical Society (**UPPER WEST SIDE**)

Neue Galerie for German and Austrian Art (**UPPER EAST SIDE**)

FREE (*or Pay What You Wish*)
MUSEUM HOURS

Asia Society and Museum, Friday, 6–9 p.m. (*except July 4–Labor Day*)

Bronx Museum of the Arts, Friday, 11 a.m.–8 p.m.

Bronx Zoo, Wednesday, 10 a.m.–4:30 p.m.

Brooklyn Botanic Garden, Tuesday, 8 a.m.–4:30 p.m.; Saturday, 10 a.m.–noon; Tuesday–Friday, mid-November–February; Fridays for seniors

Brooklyn Museum, first Saturday of the month, 5–11 p.m.

The Frick Collection, Sunday, 11 a.m.–1 p.m. (*pay what you wish*)

Guggenheim Museum, Saturday, 5:45–7:45 p.m. (*pay what you wish*)

International Center of Photography, Friday, 5–8 p.m. (*pay what you wish*)

Jewish Museum, Saturday, 11 a.m.–5:45 p.m.

Museum of Arts & Design, Thursday, 6–9 p.m. (*pay what you wish*)

Museum of the City of New York, Sunday, 10 a.m.–noon

Museum of Jewish Heritage— A Living Memorial to the Holocaust, Wednesday, 4–8 p.m.

Museum of Modern Art, Friday, 4–8 p.m.

Museum of the Moving Image, Friday, 4–8 p.m.

New Museum of Contemporary Art, Thursday, 7–9 p.m.

New York Botanical Garden, Wednesday, 10 a.m.–6 p.m., and Saturday, 10 a.m.–noon

New York Hall of Science, Friday, 2–5 p.m., and Sunday, 10–11 a.m. (*except July and August*)

South Street Seaport Museum, third Friday of the month, 5–9 p.m.

Whitney Museum of American Art, Friday, 6–9 p.m. (*pay what you wish*)

TOURING OPTIONS

PACKAGE TOURS

THERE ARE EASILY MORE THAN 1,000 LICENSED TOUR GUIDES in New York, and, unfortunately, many more unlicensed ones. And no wonder: the city draws 30 million visitors every year, and the numbers keep going up. That's good news and bad—good because you as a tourist have a huge number of tours and guides to choose from, and bad because it can be difficult to differentiate between the worthwhile and the time-consuming.

Frankly, we're not enthusiastic about most packaged mass tours. We think it's more rewarding to select the attractions you're truly interested in and go on your own or with a more intimate group. After all, most of the "sights" on those sightseeing tours are so famous you already know what the outside looks like, and a lot of the time that's all you'll see out the window, anyway. And you're a lot more likely to end the day feeling, just as you did in the morning, that Manhattan is a large, crowded, and loud place.

Besides, there are several drawbacks to these overview tours. For one thing, simply loading and off-loading passengers at every stop— not to mention dealing with traffic—takes up a substantial portion of the time you are supposedly sightseeing. A more recent twist is that many neighborhoods, from **SoHo** to Harlem, are complaining about tour-bus traffic and the noise and pollution created by idling vehicles. Commercial traffic is already banned around some areas, most notably **Washington Square.**

However, if you plan to return frequently, getting an idea of the landscape might be an advantage. Many of the longer tours include a meal, which may be a relief for those with sticker and/or map shock. Those with limited walking power might prefer to stay on the bus in any case. Those shy about sidewalk adventures may find security in numbers. And you can hear a lot of history and (fairly basic) humor in a single dose, if that's what you like.

The quickest computer check will bring up many possibilities, so we'll give you a sense of the options (and representative prices).

Among the biggest names in the business is **Gray Line Tours,** which has conventional buses and a newer fleet of eco-friendly (low-emission) and wheelchair-accessible double-decker buses, as well as trolleys. It remains one of the most reliable packaged-tour operators. (If you delve a little deeper into what looks like other tour fleets, you'll find that Gray Line is the bottom line.) You can spend from two hours to the whole day in the tour company's care, see the whole island or just a district or two, and get picked up from many major hotels as well as from Gray Line's headquarters on Eighth Avenue between 47th and 48th streets and from Times Square (☎ 800-669-0051; **www.newyorksightseeing .com**). A nice feature is that Gray Line's hop-on, hop-off tickets are good for two days, so you can spread your tour out if you don't want to make the whole circuit at once. Adult tickets are $88, kids' $65. (For another $11 apiece, you can spread the tour out over three days.) Gray Line can pick you up from the airport as well.

Harbor cruises lasting about 90 minutes and offering views of the Statue of Liberty and the downtown skyline are offered by **Statue Cruises** (☎ 877-523-9849; **www.statuecruises .com**), among others. Statue Cruises leave from either **Battery Park,** at the foot of Manhattan, or **Liberty State Park,** across the river in New Jersey; a single ticket entitles you to leave from one and disembark at the other side, but only once. (That is, you can't just use it as a round-trip ferry between Noo Yawk and Joisey.) The basic reserved tickets for adults are $12 and for kids $5, plus $3 for access to the state's crown and additional charges for audio tours. Pay attention to all the caveats: for instance, if you board after 2 p.m., you will only be able to visit either the Statue or the Ellis Island museum. If tickets aren't available for your day of choice in advance, there are usually tickets at the boarding points.

unofficial **TIP**
Many tour companies have guides who can speak several foreign languages—useful if you or your friends would be more comfortable with such options.

kids **NY Waterway Tours** (☎ 800-533-3779; **www.nywaterway .com**) offers a number of harbor tours, but perhaps most intriguing is the *Yankee Clipper* cruise to Yankee Stadium, on a food-and bar-equipped ship that cruises up to the stadium and heads back 30 minutes after the last out. (No, it's not really a clipper; the name is just a tribute to Yankees legend Joltin' Joe DiMaggio.) Tickets for this floating tailgate party are $22 for adults and $18 for ages 3 to 11. The *Clipper* leaves from Pier 78 (West 38th Street at the Hudson River).

World Yacht, which offers dinner cruises (about $100 to $112, plus cash bar), brunch (about $60), or cocktail cruises ($39 to $49, including drinks), leaves from Pier 81 (41st Street) and goes down the west side of the island (☎ 800-498-4270; **www.worldyacht.com**).

Rocks Off Concert Cruises (☎ 212-571-3304; **www.rocksoff.com**) are floating warm-weather music shows with cash bar and bathrooms leaving from 23rd Street and the East River. Tickets cost about $20 to $35, and shows range from hip-hop to classic country rock to alt-thrash to jazz to, well, karaoke and tribute bands (hey, for $20 . . .).

A ramped-up version of the harbor tour, for the thrill-ride generation, is a *Beast,* 145-seat speedboats painted with *Jaws*-style grins and cranking out (canned) rock 'n' roll music to spice up a 30-minute wet and (fairly) wild tour available daily on the hour, May through September, leaving from Pier 83 at West 42nd Street ($23, $17 kids;

☎ 212-563-3200; **www.circleline42.com**). This is one of the few cruises that requires passengers to be at least 40 inches/100 centimeters tall.

For romantics and sailing buffs, the 80-foot Gilded Age–style schooners **Adirondack** and **Imagine** go the windy route around Lady Liberty with (among other options) a "City Lights" after-dark tour featuring Champagne or beer (**Chelsea Piers** near West 22nd Street; ☎ 646-336-5270 or **www.sail-nyc.com**).

If you really want to make a splash, consider a happy-hour cruise on the **Shearwater** (☎ 212-619-0885 or **www.shearwatersailing.com**), an 82-foot Art Deco sailing yacht that offers warm-weather sunset cruises ($48, beer and wine included) or late-night sails for $50 (open bar is $20 or $30 extra, depending on whether you want basic or "premium" drinks), plus Sunday Champagne brunch tours for $79 ($39 for children ages 12 and under). The **Shearwater** docks at the **North Cove Marina** on the Battery, just another reason to stroll there.

If you want a bird's-eye view of the harbor, you can take a helicopter tour, but it'll cost you: a 10-minute flight is $150 a person, plus another $30 in "passenger fees"; a private copter is $1,000 (☎ 800-542-9933; **www.libertyhelicopters.com**), but it's a great proposal set-up.

More fun than a simple harbor cruise is the **Circle Line**, tour, a surprisingly entertaining, three-hour, 39-mile circumnavigation of Manhattan. The ships, all former Coast Guard cutters or Navy landing craft, leave from Pier 83 at West 42nd Street and head down the Hudson past the Statue of Liberty, back up the East River along the old Upper East Side, and through Spuyten Duyvil Creek ($34 adults, $29 seniors, $21 children; ☎ 212-563-3200; **www.circleline42.com**).

GUIDED WALKING (MOSTLY) TOURS

AS WE'VE SAID, WE THINK WALKING TOURS, either independent or guided, are the best way to see New York. Just use a little common sense. Many guided walking tours are weather-dependent, so be sure to ask how to confirm whether the tour is on if the skies darken. The big companies are full-time, but smaller groups and personal guides may have more limited schedules. Most walking tours offered through museums or similar organizations are on weekends, as are most of the specialty tours—remember to check the Friday *New York Times*—though you can often arrange in advance for a weekday tour.

unofficial **TIP**
Tips are appreciated by some guides but declined by others, particularly those affiliated with non-profit agencies; ask when you call.

Some of the best things in life really are free, even in New York. The **Urban Park Rangers** frequently lead walking tours through Central Park and other green areas in all five boroughs, and the guides are as family-friendly as the price. For a schedule, see **www.nycgovparks.org** (click on "about," then "divisions").

The **Times Square Exposé** walking tours have great guides, too—professional actors, in fact. The free tour starts at noon on Fridays, rain or shine, at the **Times Square Information Center** (☎ 212-768-1560; **www.timessquarenyc.org**) on Seventh Avenue between 46th and 47th streets.

If you want to set up a more personalized tour, or one with a specialized focus, contact **Big Apple Greeter,** which, with a month's notice, can put you in contact with a knowledgeable companion (☎ 212-669-8159; **www.bigapplegreeter.org**). This is an astounding program; escorts are volunteers, and the buddy-system tour, arranged through the Manhattan borough president's office, is free (though it would be nice if you brought along a little souvenir from your hometown). At last count, the volunteers spoke 22 languages among them.

You can take a free, one-hour guided tour of the main **New York Public Library** building on Fifth Avenue and 42nd Street, like its neighbor **Grand Central Terminal** a gem of Beaux Arts design, at 11 a.m. and 2 p.m. Monday through Saturday and 2 p.m. Sunday; tours of exhibits start at 12:30 and 2:30 p.m. Monday through Saturday and 3:30 p.m. Sunday (☎ 212-869-8089; **www.nypl.org**).

Members of the Municipal Arts Society lead tours of Grand Central itself every Wednesday at 12:30 p.m.; there's a $10 suggested donation, but as we've said, if you're really short . . . (☎ 212-935-3960; **www.mas.org**). Alternatively, although his custom tours are much more expensive (about $100 an hour), veteran guide **Justin Ferate** leads one free tour every week: inside and out around Grand Central, including such other landmarks as the **Chrysler Building.** Tours leave at 12:30 Fridays from the sculpture garden at the southwest corner of 42nd Street and Park Avenue, across from Grand Central. As to those custom tours, take them seriously; Ferate wrote the tour guide license exam for the city (☎ 212-223-2777; **www.justinsnewyork.com**).

You can pay to take a guided tour of **Rockefeller Center** (see page 222), but you can also pick up a brochure for a self-guided tour at the desk in the lobby of the GE Building, better known as 30 Rock. Don't miss the mini-museum of the complex on the concourse.)

Of course, most tour guides are trying to make a living at this. Even so, there are some good and budget-friendly operators out there.

Among the best is **Big Onion Walking Tours.** ("Long before it was dubbed the Big Apple, those who knew New York City called it the Big Onion," advises the brochure.) Most of the Big Onion tours cover the historically polyglot **Lower East Side,** but others explore Gramercy Park and Union Square, historic Harlem, the East Village, Brooklyn Heights and the Brooklyn Bridge, gay and lesbian New York, "Revolutionary New York," TriBeCa, and other locations.

Big Onion (☎ 212-439-1090; **www.bigonion.com**) was the brainchild of two history scholars, Seth Kamil and Ed O'Donnell. They and a staff of graduate students from NYU and Columbia University—many now professors—bring to life the eras of Tammany Hall, tenements, sweatshops, flophouses, and ethnic gang struggles. You can even sign up for the "Multiethnic Eating Tours," in which you nosh on a pickle, swipe a dumpling, and savor fresh mozzarella as you go. Tours cost $15 for adults, $12 for seniors, students, and active military personnel (plus $5 for the noshes). Even better, you don't have to make reservations. You can just show up, and if you buy a "frequent walker" card for $75 (five tours), a sixth tour is free; the card is good for a year.

For 46 years, Astoria native **Howard Goldberg** has been leading folks around Greenwich Village, Hell's Kitchen, "Marilyn Monroe's Manhattan," "The World of Edith Wharton," and almost anywhere else for the same price—$5, not even adjusted for inflation. Call him (☎ 212-265-2663), and he'll tell you what's on the calendar or arrange to meet you. Goldberg leads all tours himself, rain, snow, or shine.

NYU and New School for Social Research professor **Joyce Gold** has been leading her walking tours of Five Points, Hell's Kitchen, Chelsea, and Greenwich Village for more than 20 years, and most recently has taken on the Meatpacking District and High Line Park. Public tours are $15 ($12 for seniors ages 62 and older). Like Goldberg, Gold leads them, all rain or shine (☎ 212-242-5762; www.nyctours.com).

Lower East Side native and three-decade Garment Center veteran Michael Kaback combines walking tours of his old neighborhoods with insider anecdotes, tastings, and—especially around the Fashion District—unscheduled sales stops. As his Web site says, better bring cash ($20; ☎ 212-370-4214 or www.mikesnyctours.com).

Brooklynite Linda Sarrel of **Rent A New Yorker Tours** is a not-quite-free Big Apple Greeter; she offers both public and private itineraries by request (from $15; ☎ 212-982-9445 or www.rentanewyorker.com).

Part neighborhood tour, part literary gossip fest: the **Dorothy Parker Society** literary-legend tours, two hours of acid wit leaves from, naturally, the Algonquin Hotel ($15 to $35; www.dorothy parker.com).

Even more specialized neighborhood tours with an emphasis on architecture—gargoyles, Carnegie Hill, "turn-of-the-century Manhattan,"—can be had from former Parks Department supervisor Albert Pommer of **New York City Cultural Walking Tours** ($15; www .nycwalk.com).

Tourists, like armies, travel on their stomachs. At least some do, and several guides and companies will lead you on **culinary tours** around Chinatown and the Lower East Side, the Village, Chelsea Market, Astoria, sushi bars, beer bars, even chocolate boutiques. Tours cost $50 to $70, but that includes noshing and lunch; among them are **Foods of New York** (☎ 212-209-3370; www.foodsofny.com), **City Food Tours** (☎ 212-535-TOUR; www.cityfoodtours.com), **Ahoy New York** (☎ 518-332-4386; www.ahoyny.com), and **New York Drinking Buddies** (☎ 646-330-5878; www.nydrinkingbuddies.com).

The **Slice of Brooklyn Pizza Tour** buses visitors around the landmarks of the borough, including movie locations, battle markers, celebrities' homes, and two local dining favorites (one thin-crust, one thick). The pizza had better be primo; the four-and-a-half-hour tour is $75 for adults, $65 for kids; (☎ 212-209-3370; **www.bknypizza.com**).

If you want to work off some calories instead of spending extra on them, **Bike the Big Apple** works the outer boroughs, including a broader section of Brooklyn (☎ 877-865-0078; **www.toursbybike.com**). (See other bike companies in Part Nine, Exercise and Recreation.)

If you wonder what it would be like to run the New York Marathon (not), you can sign up for a guided run along one of 12 routes, up to 13-plus miles, with a licensed and exceptionally fit partner from **City Running Tours.** You pick the pace, the sights, the time of day—and for $60 (for the first six miles, $6 per mile beyond that), you get a T-shirt, too (☎ 877-415-0058 or 646-216-9989; **www.cityrunning tours.com**). Bring three friends and get a discount.

A lot of people see New York every day, on screen, and there are increasingly specialized tours for both TV and movie buffs. **On Location Tours** leads channel surfers past such buildings as the Jeffersons' high-rise, the West Village site of *Friends,* the Huxtables' Brooklyn brownstone—actually in Greenwich Village—40 sights featured on *The Sopranos,* Carrie Bradshaw's favorite cupcake bakery, and the Soup Nazi's kitchen, along with some very familiar-looking courthouses. Tours are two to four hours ($38–$44; ☎ 212-209-3370; **www .screentours.com** or **www.sceneontv.com**). And if you don't know what **Kramer's Reality Tour** is, you're not a *Seinfeld* fan and don't need to call (☎ 800-KRAMERS or **www.kennykramer.com;** three hours for $39.50).

If you're interested in historical sites in Harlem and in African American culture, particularly jazz, gospel, and soul (as in food), contact **Harlem Spirituals** (prices start at $55 for adults and $39 for children ages 5 to 11; food is additional; ☎ 800-660-2166; **www.harlemspirituals .com**), which offers tours in a half-dozen languages. **Harlem Your Way** (☎ 800-382-9363; **www.harlemyourwaytours.com**) has a range of tours from $25 ("Sights and Sounds of Harlem") to $75 ("Champagne safaris to the Apollo Theater") and up (the $95 gospel brunch).

BACKSTAGE AND BEHIND THE SCENES

In addition to the free tours mentioned previously, there are several landmarks in town that draw back the curtain for visitors.

Two of the best insider tours in the city are at **Lincoln Center.** Backstage tours of the **Metropolitan Opera House** are led by members of the Opera Guild from October through June at 3:30 p.m. weekdays and 10:30 a.m. on Sundays except on dress rehearsal days ($15 for adults, $8 for full-time students under age 29; ☎ 212-769-7020 or **www.operaed.org**). The general Lincoln Center tour explores at least three theaters in the complex, and though there is no backstage involved, it comes with enthusiastic background info and the nicest kind of gossip. You may even get to hear a bit of rehearsal. Tours run between 10:30 a.m. and 4:30 p.m., depending on the day, and venues vary according to rehearsal and set construction ($15 for adults, $12 for seniors and students, and $8 for children 11 and under; ☎ 212-875-5350 or **www.lincolncenter.org**).

The **Radio City Music Hall Stage Door Tour** lasts about an hour, shows off the wonderful Art Deco interior, and usually includes a personal appearance by at least one Rockette. Tours leave daily every half hour from 11 a.m. to 3 p.m.; adults $18.50, seniors 62 and older $15, children ages 12 and under $10 (**www.radiocity.com**).

While you're in the neighborhood, check into the **NBC Studio Tour,** which includes network history, a tour of technical equipment, and famous studio sets. The tour starts from the **NBC Experience Store** at Rockefeller Plaza and 49th Street every 15 to 30 minutes from 8:30 a.m. to 5:30 p.m. Monday through Saturday and 8:30 a.m. to 4:30 p.m. Sundays. An NBC page leads the 70-minute tour (adults $19.25, seniors and children ages 6 to 12 $16.25; **www.nbcuniversalstore.com**).

Rockefeller Center itself, that landmark of Deco idealism, offers a 75-minute tour that includes many vintage murals, mosaics, gardens, and statuary. Tours begin every two hours starting at 10 a.m. at the NBC Experience Store (adults $12, seniors and children ages 6 to 12 $10; ☎ 212-664-7174 or **www.rockefellercenter.com**).

Madison Square Garden is both a famous sports arena—home to the Knicks, the Rangers, and the Liberty—and a famous rock arena, not to mention the site of circuses, tournaments, and general craziness. Go behind the scenes to the locker rooms, see the **WaMu Theater,** and meet, if not a Rockette, at least a team dancer. Hour-long tours are available every day on the half hour from 11 a.m. to 3 p.m. (adults $18.50, seniors 62 and older $15, children age 12 and under $12; ☎ 212-465-6080; **www.thegarden.com**).

Finally, many museums, including the **American Museum of Natural History** and **Metropolitan Museum of Art,** offer highlights; check the in-depth profiles below for details.

An **ABUNDANCE** of **RICHES**

OKAY, NOW THAT YOU'VE SKIMMED the neighborhood profiles in Part Five and the lists of sightseeing recommendations earlier in this chapter, you've probably settled on a few places that really interest you or your group. The following are more in-depth descriptions of some of the most important attractions throughout the city that may add to your enjoyment or help you winnow down the selection even further. After all, if you're faced with only a few hours, choosing among the museums in the Upper East Side alone might come down to whether you prefer Asian, European, or American art—or even ancient, medieval, or modern.

unofficial **TIP**
Don't budget time just to see an attraction; build in extra for standing in line, going through security, checking your coat, stopping at restrooms, etc.

We try to estimate how long it will take to see the collection or building in any reasonable sense, although of course you must factor in both the extent of your own interest and your stamina. We've also tried to gauge the degree to which a particular attraction might interest visitors of different ages and backgrounds, so that members of a group might be able to divide up within a neighborhood and see things to their particular liking. Again, these are all suggestions; if a particular teenager is boat- or book-crazy, she may score an otherwise two-star attraction as a four.

Although New York is committed to making all public attractions accessible in time, certain sites (wildlife trails, historic-house museums) are going to have more limited access than others. We have specifically addressed wheelchair access, but we may refer to other disability aids. (Audio tours and captioning for films, for example, are common.) In most cases, the only animals allowed are service animals.

And because we pointed out that many of these admission prices are "suggested," and you can choose to pay less, you should note that if you choose to buy tickets in advance online, you will be paying not only that suggested amount but also a service charge of several dollars. On the other hand, you won't have to stand in line; it's up to you.

ATTRACTION PROFILES

kids **American Museum of Natural History** ★★★★★

APPEAL BY AGE	PRESCHOOL ★★½	GRADE SCHOOL ★★★½	TEENS ★★★★
YOUNG ADULTS ★★★★	OVER 30 ★★★★		SENIORS ★★★★

Central Park West at 79th Street, Upper West Side; ☎ **212-769-5100; IMAX** ☎ **212-769-5200; www.amnh.org**

Type of attraction Popular and wide-ranging scientific and research collection. **Nearest subway station** 81st Street–Museum of Natural History or 79th Street. **Admission** Suggested donation $16 adults, $12 seniors and students, $9 children ages 2–12; additional charge for some special exhibits. *Admission to either IMAX or planetarium:* $20 adults, $16.50 seniors and students, $11 children. *All-areas admission:* $32 adults, $24.50 students and seniors, $20 children. **Hours** Daily,

Continued on page 230

Uptown Attractions

1. American Museum of
   Natural History
2. Cathedral Church of
   Saint John the Divine
3. Cooper-Hewitt, National
   Design Museum
4. El Museo del Barrio
5. The Frick Collection
6. Guggenheim Museum
7. Jewish Museum
8. Metropolitan Museum
   of Art
9. Museum of the City of
   New York
10. Whitney Museum of
    American Art

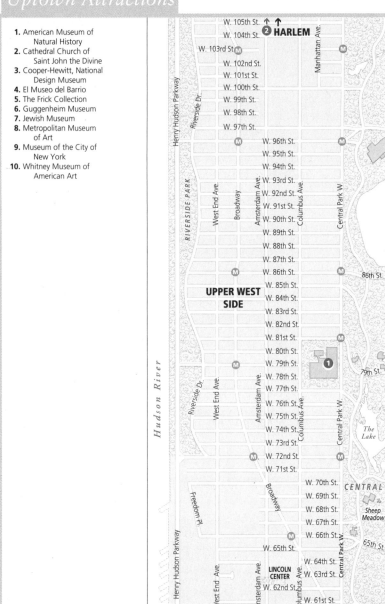

M Subway stop

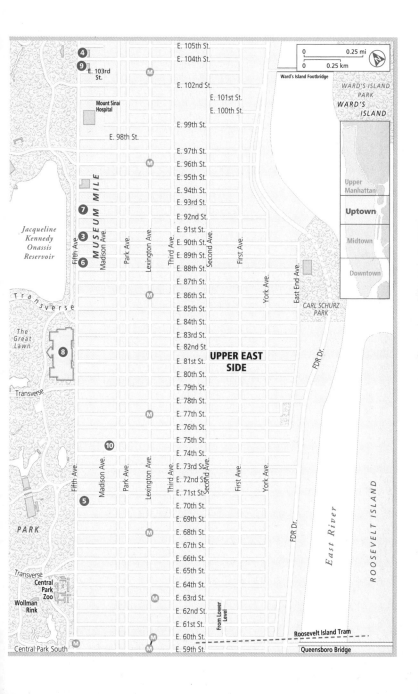

Midtown Attractions

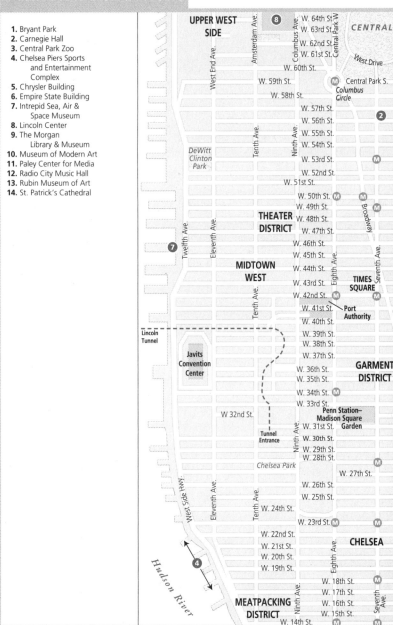

1. Bryant Park
2. Carnegie Hall
3. Central Park Zoo
4. Chelsea Piers Sports
   and Entertainment
   Complex
5. Chrysler Building
6. Empire State Building
7. Intrepid Sea, Air &
   Space Museum
8. Lincoln Center
9. The Morgan
   Library & Museum
10. Museum of Modern Art
11. Paley Center for Media
12. Radio City Music Hall
13. Rubin Museum of Art
14. St. Patrick's Cathedral

Downtown Attractions

Ganesvoort St.
Horatio St.
Jane St.
W. 12th St.
Bethune St.

W. 12th St.
W. 11th St.
W. 10th St.
W. 9th St.
W. 8th St.
Waverly Pl.

University Pl.
Broadway
Fourth Ave.
Third Ave.
E. 11th St.
E. 10th St.
E. 9th St.

Greenwich Ave.
Waverly Pl.
Sixth Ave.
Eighth Ave.
Fifth Ave.

E. 9th St.
Wanamaker
E. 8th St.
Astor Pl.
Lafayette
St. Mark's Pl.
E. 7th St.
E. 6th St.
E. 5th St.
E. 4th St.
E. 3rd St.
E. 2nd St.
E. 1st St.

Stuyvesant

Second Ave.

GREENWICH VILLAGE

Bank
W. 11th St.
Perry
Charles
W. 10th St.
Christopher
Barrow
Morton
Leroy
Clarkson

Bleecker
W. 4th St.
Grove
Jones
Cornelia
Commerce
Bedford
Carmine
Downing
Seventh Ave. S.

Washington
Pl.
W. 4th St.
W. 3rd St.

MacDougal
Sullivan
Thompson
La Guardia

Bond
Bleecker
Gt. Jones

NOHO

E. Houston

SOHO

Prince

NOLITA

Bowery
Chrystie
Forsyth
Allen

Rivington

Delancey

W. Houston
King
Charlton
Vandam
Spring
Dominick
Broome

Greenwich St.
Washington
Varick St.
Sixth Ave.
W. Broadway
Wooster
Greene
Mercer

Spring
Broome
Grand
Crosby
Lafayette

Mott
Mulberry
Elizabeth
Kenmare

LITTLE ITALY

Elizabeth
Mott
Mulberry
Baxter
Hester
Bayard
Canal
Bowery
Eldridge

Holland Tunnel

Canal
Watts
Desbrosses
Vestry
Laight
Hubert
West St.
Beach

Howard
Canal
Lispenard
Walker
White
Franklin
Leonard
Worth

Centre
Cortlandt

TRIBECA

N. Moore
Franklin
Harrison
Jay

Hudson
W. Broadway
Thomas
Duane
Reade
Chambers
Warren

Duane
Reade
Chambers

CHINATOWN

Henry
Madison
Division
Catherine

(3)
(14)
(7)

Chambers St.
Murray
Park Pl.
Barclay
Vesey

Greenwich St.

City Hall
Park Row
Spruce
Beekman
Ann

Frankfort
Dover
Pearl
Water
Front

Robert F.
Wagner Pl.

(15)
(9)

World Financial Center

World Trade Center Site Ⓜ

Battery
Park
City

South End Ave.

Cortlandt
Liberty
Cedar
Albany
Carlisle
Rector

Church
Greenwich St.
Trinity Pl.
Broadway
Nassau

John
Maiden
Platt
Liberty
Cedar
Pine

William
Cliff
John
Fletcher
Maiden

Fulton

Pier 17

(10)

(8)
(12)
(13)

Rector Pl.
W. Thames
Pl.
J. P. Ward
Morris
2nd Pl.
1st Pl.

Wall St. Ⓜ
Exchange Pl.
FINANCIAL DISTRICT
Beaver
S. William
Stone
Pearl
Broad
Bridge
Whitehall
State

Pier 16

Water
Front
South Street Viaduct

Vietnam
Veterans
Plaza

(6)

Pier 6

South
Gardens **(5)** Battery Pl.

(1)

Hudson River

Upper
Manhattan

Uptown

Midtown

Downtown

Ⓜ Subway stop
Ⓜ Closed indefinitely

0   1/4 mi
0   0.25 km

(2)
(11) ←

Brooklyn–Battery Tunnel ——

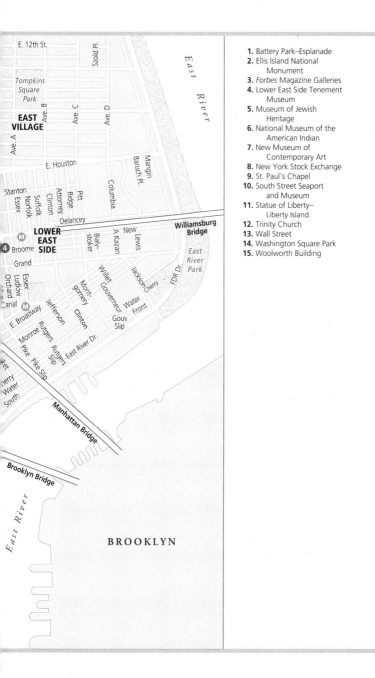

1. Battery Park–Esplanade
2. Ellis Island National Monument
3. *Forbes* Magazine Galleries
4. Lower East Side Tenement Museum
5. Museum of Jewish Heritage
6. National Museum of the American Indian
7. New Museum of Contemporary Art
8. New York Stock Exchange
9. St. Paul's Chapel
10. South Street Seaport and Museum
11. Statue of Liberty–Liberty Island
12. Trinity Church
13. Wall Street
14. Washington Square Park
15. Woolworth Building

New York City Attractions by Type

TYPE AND NAME | NEIGHBORHOOD | AUTHOR'S RATING

CHURCHES

Cathedral Church of St. John the Divine | **Heights-Harlem** | ★★★

St. Patrick's Cathedral | **Midtown East** | ★★½

St. Paul's Chapel | **Lower Manhattan** | ★★★½

Trinity Church | **Lower Manhattan** | ★★★

FAMOUS BUILDINGS

Empire State Building | **Gramercy Park** | ★★½

MONUMENTS

Ellis Island National Monument | **Lower Manhattan** | ★★★★★

Statue of Liberty–Liberty Island | **Lower Manhattan** | ★★★★★

MUSEUMS

American Museum of Natural History | **Upper West Side** | ★★★★★

Brooklyn Museum | **Brooklyn** | ★★★★½

The Cloisters | **Washington Heights** | ★★★★

Cooper-Hewitt, National Design Museum | **Upper East Side** | ★★★

Forbes Magazine Galleries | **Greenwich Village** | ★★★½

The Frick Collection | **Upper East Side** | ★★★★★

Guggenheim Museum | **Upper East Side** | ★★★½

Intrepid Sea, Air & Space Museum | **Midtown West** | ★★★

Continued from page 223

10 a.m.–5:45 p.m.; closed Thanksgiving and Christmas. **When to go** Weekdays. **Wheelchair access** Very good (ramp access at 81st Street); assisted listening for theaters. **Special comments** The Children's Discovery room is one of the best of its kind, and there are treasure hunts and fun facts online you can download in advance. **Author's rating** Thanks to the museum's careful combination of adult and family-style exhibits, this will keep a whole group occupied as long as you can stand, literally; ★★★★★. **How much time to allow** 2–4 hours.

DESCRIPTION AND COMMENTS This is a museum that inspires a passionate loyalty from tourists and locals alike. Its dioramas of Alaska and Africa and the evolutionary progress of humans; the huge, magnificent, and famous dinosaur skeletons; the live-butterfly conservatory, which has become an annual feature; the iconic blue whale; and the glittering array of gemstones (worth an estimated $50 million and including the famous Star of India sapphire) are the sort of exhibits we all seem to remember, but better. The recently spiffing-up of the 77th Street lobby

TYPE AND NAME | NEIGHBORHOOD | AUTHOR'S RATING

MUSEUMS (CONTINUED)

Jewish Museum | **Upper East Side** | ★★★½

Lower East Side Tenement Museum | **Lower East Side** | ★★★½

Metropolitan Museum of Art | **Upper East Side** | ★★★★★

The Morgan Library & Museum | **Midtown East** | ★★★★★

El Museo del Barrio | **Upper East Side** | ★★★½

Museum of the City of New York | **Upper East Side** | ★★★

Museum of Jewish Heritage | **Lower Manhattan** | ★★★★

Museum of Modern Art | **Midtown East** | ★★★★★

National Museum of the American Indian | **Lower Manhattan** | ★★★

New Museum of Contemporary Art | **Lower East Side** | ★★½

The Paley Center for Media | **Midtown East** | ★★★

Rubin Museum of Art | **Gramercy Park** | ★★★½

South Street Seaport and Museum | **Lower Manhattan** | ★★

Whitney Museum of American Art | **Upper East Side** | ★★★★

PARKS AND GARDENS

Bronx Zoo | **Bronx** | ★★★★★

Brooklyn Botanic Garden | **Brooklyn** | ★★★

New York Botanical Garden | **Bronx** | ★★★½

included a restoration of another icon, the century-old, 63-foot Great Canoe of the Pacific Northwest Native Americans.

The stunning Rose Center for Earth and Space is a visible "universe"— a 95-foot glass cube enclosing a "floating" sphere that is the Hayden Planetarium itself. The computer-assisted effects are as far beyond old star-light projections as *Star Wars* wizardry is compared to *King Kong.* A Guggenheim-style ramp holds interactive displays, models, etc. Adjoining exhibits discuss the evolution of the universe and the likelihood of extra-terrestrial life. The four statues atop the columns outside on Central Park West represent Lewis and Clark, Daniel Boone, and John J. Audubon.

TOURING TIPS A general highlights tour begins at 10:15 and 11:15 a.m., and 12:15, 1:15, 2:15, and 3:15 p.m.; meet on the second floor between the rotunda and the Hall of African Mammals. Staffers are available for questions in the fossil, gem, and Rose Center exhibits. The museum has several cafes, one geared toward adults, and snack carts.

NYC Attractions by Neighborhood

ATTRACTION NAME | DESCRIPTION | AUTHOR'S RATING

LOWER MANHATTAN, WALL STREET, AND THE BATTERY

Ellis Island National Monument
Re-creation of immigrants' first contact with America | ★★★★★

Museum of Jewish Heritage
Re-creation of Jewish culture of the last century | ★★★★

National Museum of the American Indian (The George Gustav Heye Center)
Part art collection, part anthropology lesson | ★★★

St. Paul's Chapel | **Small pre-Revolutionary church | ★★★½**

South Street Seaport and Museum
Historic district and maritime museum | ★★

Statue of Liberty–Liberty Island | **America's symbol of freedom | ★★★★★**

Trinity Church | **Gothic Revival church from mid–19th century | ★★★**

CHINATOWN, LITTLE ITALY, AND THE LOWER EAST SIDE

Lower East Side Tenement Museum
Reconstructed early-20th-century slum | ★★★½

New Museum of Contemporary Art | **Avant-garde and 21st-century art | ★★½**

GREENWICH VILLAGE

Forbes Magazine Galleries
Fantastic collection of toys (for both kids and adults) | ★★★½

GRAMERCY PARK AND MADISON SQUARE

Empire State Building | **Landmark tower with famous view | ★★½**

Rubin Museum of Art
First-rate collection of ½imalayan art and icons | ★★★½

MIDTOWN WEST, TIMES SQUARE, AND THE THEATER DISTRICT

Intrepid Sea, Air & Space Museum | **Mini-fleet of retired military vessels | ★★★**

MIDTOWN EAST

The Morgan Library & Museum
Medieval and Renaissance books and drawings | ★★★★★

Museum of Modern Art
Premier collection of modern and contemporary art and design | ★★★★★

ATTRACTION NAME | DESCRIPTION | AUTHOR'S RATING

MIDTOWN EAST (CONTINUED)

The Paley Center for Media | **Combination archives and rerun haven** | ★★★

St. Patrick's Cathedral | **Largest Catholic cathedral in U.S.** | ★★½

UPPER WEST SIDE

American Museum of Natural History
Popular and scientific collection | ★★★★★

UPPER EAST SIDE

Cooper-Hewitt, National Design Museum
International design and design art | ★★★

The Frick Collection | **18th- and 19th-century art in mansion** | ★★★★★

Guggenheim Museum | **20th-century European art** | ★★★½

Jewish Museum | **Ancient Judaica and Jewish art** | ★★★½

Metropolitan Museum of Art
One of the greatest museums in the world | ★★★★★

El Museo del Barrio | **Pan-American Hispanic art and culture** | ★★★½

Museum of the City of New York
Specific and often unusual collection of city history | ★★★

Whitney Museum of American Art | **20th-century American art** | ★★★★

MORNINGSIDE HEIGHTS, HAMILTON HEIGHTS, AND HARLEM

Cathedral Church of St. John the Divine | **Vast Episcopal cathedral** | ★★★

WASHINGTON HEIGHTS

The Cloisters | **Premier medieval-art collection** | ★★★★

BROOKLYN

Brooklyn Botanic Garden
Landscaped park with Japanese garden and greenhouse | ★★★

Brooklyn Museum | **Cultural artifacts and fine art** | ★★★★½

THE BRONX

Bronx Zoo | **Famous old-fashioned zoo** | ★★★★★

New York Botanical Garden | **Gardens and greenhouse complex** | ★★★½

kids **Bronx Zoo** ★★★★★

| APPEAL BY AGE | PRESCHOOL ★★★ | GRADE SCHOOL ★★★★ | TEENS ★★★★½ |
| YOUNG ADULTS ★★★★★ | | OVER 30 ★★★★★ | SENIORS ★★★★ |

Bronx River Parkway at Fordham Road, the Bronx; ☎ 718-367-1010; www.bronxzoo.com

Type of attraction Famous old-fashioned zoo transformed for modern times. **Nearest subway station** West Farms Square–East Tremont Avenue. **Admission** Suggested donation $15 adults, $13 age 65 and older, $11 ages 3–12. **Hours** April through October: Monday–Friday, 10 a.m.–5 p.m.; weekends and holidays, 10 a.m.–5:30 p.m.; November through March: daily, 10 a.m.–4:30 p.m. **When to go** Weekdays. **Wheelchair access** Very good; all buildings accessible. The Web site has extensive information on disability aids. **Special comments** Wednesday, pay what you wish. **Author's rating** One of the best of its kind, and a quintessential New York experience. It gives Disney World's Animal Kingdom a run for a fraction of the money; ★★★★★. **How much time to allow** 3–4 hours.

DESCRIPTION AND COMMENTS   The Beaux Arts main buildings date from the turn of the 20th century and are wonderful examples of fantastic architecture (the monkey house has playful animals around the edge of its roof; the former big-cat house has lions and tigers around the frieze). These are being refitted as exhibit centers; the zoo is moving quickly toward replacing all the old cage-type enclosures with naturalistic ones divided by "continent," including a wildlife marsh, savannah area (giraffes, wild dogs, zebras, lions), and Wild Asia mini-zoo with a glass-enclosed tropical rain forest, elephant plain, tiger hillside, and encircling monorail. More than 4,300 creatures live here, representing 775 species.

The Congo Gorilla Forest is six and a half acres with 300 primates and 75 species of other animals and birds, such as okapi, red river hogs, and hornbills; 1,500 plants (400 varieties) that took a decade of cultivation; 11 waterfalls; 55 artificial trees; mist machines; and sound effects. Like the nearby **New York Botanical Garden,** the zoo goes all-out for kids from Thanksgiving past New Year's, staying open until 9 p.m. and filling the park with animal-shaped light "trees" and sculptures, with a special focus on reindeer and other seasonal topics. The hands-on **Children's Zoo** is great, but it may be a madhouse on weekends.

TOURING TIPS   The zoo is closer to the subway (No. 5) than to the train (Metro Line to Fordham), or take an express BxM11 bus from Madison Avenue at 26th, 54th, and 99th streets to Gate B. It returns to several stops along Fifth Avenue. The zoo is worth a trip year-round, because while summer is easier, winter allows views of snow leopards and tigers, polar and brown bears, and other such beasts. If the weather is bitter, you can explore indoor environments, including a reptile house and a bat house. If you can make a day of it, the zoo adjoins the New York Botanical Garden; see the next profile. The zoo has one year-round restaurant and several seasonal cafes as well as picnic areas; BYO food but not liquor.

Brooklyn Botanic Garden ★★★

APPEAL BY AGE	PRESCHOOL ½	GRADE SCHOOL ★★	TEENS ★★½
YOUNG ADULTS ★★★★★		OVER 30 ★★★½	SENIORS ★★★

Washington Avenue at Eastern Parkway, Brooklyn; ☎ 718-623-7200; www.bbg.org

Type of attraction Landscaped park with Japanese garden and greenhouse complex. **Nearest subway station** Prospect Park or Eastern Parkway–Brooklyn Museum. **Admission** $8 adults, $4 seniors and students with ID; children age 11 and under free. **Hours** *November–mid-March:* Tuesday–Friday, 8 a.m.–4:30 p.m.; Saturday and Sunday, 10 a.m.–4:30 p.m.; closed Monday (except Martin Luther King Jr. Day and Presidents Day), Thanksgiving, Christmas, and New Year's Day. *Mid-March–October:* Tuesday–Friday, 8 a.m.–6 p.m.; Saturday and Sunday, 10 a.m.–6 p.m.; closed Monday (except Memorial Day, Labor Day, and Columbus Day). **When to go** Anytime. **Wheelchair access** Good; all buildings accessible, some paths unsuitable. Some wheelchairs available. **Special comments** Free admission on Tuesday and 10 a.m.–noon on Saturday, and on all weekdays mid-November–February. Seniors also get free admission every Friday. **Author's rating** ★★★. **How much time to allow** 1–1½ hours.

DESCRIPTION AND COMMENTS Even if you only walk through the grounds on your way from Prospect Park or the subway to the **Brooklyn Museum,** it's worth a few minutes to look into the greenhouses, particularly the lily-pond room, the mini–rain forest (which includes several promising medicinal trees), and the bonsai garden; and it's absolutely essential to see the Japanese Tea Garden, with its many small pleasures and twists. (It was the first Japanese garden in an American public park.) If possible, see this in late April or May, when the thousands of Japanese cherry trees blossom (as they do more famously in Washington, D.C.), along with nearly 80 magnolias. Among other popular areas are the rose garden, the hands-on discovery garden, the Brooklyn celebrity garden (something like a greener Hollywood Walk of Fame), and the fragrance garden, which is heavily perfumed and has Braille labeling.

TOURING TIPS The Brooklyn Botanic Garden and Brooklyn Museum (see next profile) offer combination tickets with a small discount. There is a cafe on-site, but no picnicking.

Brooklyn Museum ★★★★½

APPEAL BY AGE	PRESCHOOL ★½	GRADE SCHOOL ★★	TEENS ★★★
YOUNG ADULTS ★★★★		OVER 30 ★★★★½	SENIORS ★★★★

Eastern Parkway at Washington Avenue, Brooklyn; ☎ 718-638-5000; www.brooklynmuseum.org

Type of attraction World-class collection of cultural artifacts and fine art. **Nearest subway station** Eastern Parkway. **Admission** Suggested donation $10 adults, $6 students and seniors (some special exhibits extra); children under age 12 accompanied by an adult free. **Hours** Wednesday–Friday, 10 a.m.– 5 p.m.; 1st Saturday of every month, 11 a.m.–11 p.m.; other Saturdays, 11 a.m.– 6 p.m.; Sunday, 11 a.m.–6 p.m.; closed Monday and Tuesday and Thanksgiving, Christmas, and New Year's Day. **When to go** Anytime. **Wheelchair access** Very good; only some period rooms inaccessible. Some wheelchairs available. ASL tours require 3 weeks' advance notice (☎ 718-501-6150). **Special comments** Free Internet access throughout; free admission first Saturday of each month, 5–11 p.m. **Author's rating** A more schedule-friendly and, in some ways, a more user-friendly mirror of the Met; ★★★★½. **How much time to allow** 2–4 hours.

DESCRIPTION AND COMMENTS Only in a city that already boasted the Metropolitan Museum of Art could the Brooklyn Museum be so often overlooked. (And if Brooklyn hadn't been absorbed into New York City, the original plans for the museum might have been fulfilled, which would have made it the largest in the world, just as the city would have been larger than Manhattan.) Its collections may be a little smaller, but they're no less well exhibited; in fact, the Met can be so overwhelming that many tourists, especially the less tour-hardened, find the Brooklyn Museum nicer (and it's certainly less crowded). Its Egyptian and African holdings and the 19th-century American and European (particularly French) collections are world-renowned, and it has its own complex of 28 reconstructed rooms from the New York area going back to the 17th century and up to the Gilded Age (more Rockefeller Moorishness).

But it has particular strengths in less-familiar areas as well, including the art of Native American peoples, spectacular Persian paintings, and a smallish but exquisite gallery of Korean art. The museum's definition of "prints" should set a new dictionary standard: from Dürer woodblocks to Whistler lithographs, from Toulouse-Lautrec posters to Cassatt portraits, Winslow Homer engravings, and Picasso line drawings. In the past few years, the museum has also hosted several blockbuster exhibits, including *Monet in the Mediterranean,* Judy Chicago's *Dinner Party,* and *In the Light of Italy: Corot and Early Open-air Painting.* Oh, and there's a 30-foot replica of the Statue of Liberty in the sculpture garden.

TOURING TIPS There is a nice little cafe on the ground floor. The first Saturday of each month offers late-night music and wine. Also, check the schedule of the **Brooklyn Academy of Music** (☎ 718-636-4100; **www.bam.org**), which is only a pleasant walk or a couple of subway stops back toward Manhattan; you might be able to top off your day with a concert. The museum offers free gallery tours at different times, generally early afternoon; check the Web site or call for information.

Cathedral Church of St. John the Divine ★★★

APPEAL BY AGE			
PRESCHOOL ½	GRADE SCHOOL ★★		TEENS ★★
YOUNG ADULTS ★★★½	OVER 30 ★★★½		SENIORS ★★★

Amsterdam Avenue at 112th Street, Heights-Harlem; ☎ 212-316-7540; www.stjohndivine.org

Type of attraction Vast (though unfinished) Episcopal cathedral. **Nearest subway station** Cathedral Parkway (110th Street). **Admission** Suggested donation $3. **Hours** Monday–Saturday, 7 a.m.–6 p.m.; Sunday, 7 a.m.–7 p.m. unless there's a concert. **When to go** Weekdays, midmorning or afternoon to avoid disrupting services. **Wheelchair access** Very good; entrance ramp on 113th Street. Only "vertical" tours inaccessible. **Special comments** Try to hook up with one of the tours; there's so much going on. **Author's rating** The continued ambitions (aspirations?) of the builders are somehow moving, the adherence to traditional building methods even more so. The vertical tour is one of the city's best moments; ★★★½. **How much time to allow** 1½–2 hours.

DESCRIPTION AND COMMENTS   After more than a century, this almost symbolically style-embracing cathedral is still only two-thirds complete, and it may take most of a second century and half a billion dollars to finish it. Part Romanesque and part Gothic; a little Spanish, a little French, a little Italian, when finished, it will be the largest cathedral in the world—as large as Notre Dame plus Chartres. There's a scale model in the gift shop that shows how at least the front half, from tower to tower, will look. Builders are trying to stick to real medieval methods. Until recently, the stone blocks were being carved out just as they had been centuries ago (some Harlem students apprenticed under imported British master masons), and there are no steel supports. The portals were cast by the man who cast the Statue of Liberty; the so-called temporary dome has lasted nearly 90 years. Be sure to look closely at the stone carvings atop the columns and friezes. They're not all solemn; some feature famous New York landmarks and creatures.

Inside, the "melting pot" philosophy has been extended to religion: the various chapels salute other major religions and ethnic groups, and the justly famous concerts and lectures are as often secular as sacred. One of the most popular events of the year is the annual Memorial Day concert by the **New York Philharmonic;** another is the famous blessing of the animals on the feast of St. Francis, the first Sunday in October, which each year attracts hundreds of not only dogs and cats but also exotic birds, snakes, and even a zoo animal or two.

TOURING TIPS Hour-long highlights and "spotlight" tours ($6, $5 seniors and students) are offered Tuesday through Saturday at 11 a.m. and 1 p.m., Sunday at 2 p.m. The "vertical tour" (Saturday noon and 2 p.m.; $15) is the best, including a rooftop view and close-up stained-glass views; these are limited to 20 people age 12 and older; go to the Web site or call ☎ 866-811-4111.

The Cloisters   ★★★★

APPEAL BY AGE	PRESCHOOL ★	GRADE SCHOOL ★★	TEENS ★★½
YOUNG ADULTS ★★★	OVER 30 ★★★		SENIORS ★★★

**Fort Tryon Park, Washington Heights; ☎ 212-523-7710;
www.metmuseum.org**

Type of attraction Premier medieval-art collection in historical setting. **Nearest subway station** 190th Street. **Admission** Suggested donation $20 adults, $15 seniors, $10 students; children ages 11 and under (with adult) free. **Hours** Sunday and Tuesday–Thursday, 9:30 a.m.–5:30 p.m.; Friday and Saturday, 9:30 a.m.–9 p.m. (9:30 a.m.–4:45 p.m. November through February); closed Monday (except holidays), New Year's Day, Thanksgiving, Christmas. **When to go** Weekdays. **Wheelchair access** Limited; some wheelchairs and audio aids free. **Special comments** A ticket covers both the Metropolitan Museum of Art (including main building) and The Cloisters on the same day. **Author's rating** It was a stroke of genius (and immeasurable Rockefeller philanthropy) to build a period home for part of the Metropolitan's medieval-art collection; ★★★★. **How much time to allow** 1½–2½ hours.

DESCRIPTION AND COMMENTS This fantastic assemblage of stone, with its serenely beautiful and stylistically otherworldly saints, stained glass, prayer-eroded blocks, and entombed crusaders, is like a dream. You're not even surprised to find, hanging on one wall, the frequently reproduced pictures of the hunting of the unicorn. Or the almost-as-familiar illuminated *Belles Heures* of the Duc de Berry. The cloisters of the title—five of them, taken from the ruins of French monasteries dating from the 12th through the 15th centuries, plus a 12th-century Spanish apse and a Romanesque chapel—have been fitted together on two levels, so that you can actually stroll through them as the residents did. (They are actually organized chronologically, so you sort of circle from the Romanesque period, about 1000, to the Gothic era, circa 1500.) The stone block benches of the chapter house are curved with the long erosion of centuries of use. One of the cloister gardens has been planted to match the courtyard garden seen in one of the huge tapestries, another with the herbs and medicinal plants of the Middle Ages. There is an air- and light-conditioned room of jewels, enamels, reliquaries, and manuscripts (this is one of those museums where a penlight might be helpful). There are also sculptures and altarpieces and a rare and extremely fine early-15th-century triptych of the Annunciation by Robert Campin of Tournai.

The Cloisters frequently offers free gallery tours (generally at noon and 2 p.m.), lectures—some of them aimed at students—and wonderfully atmospheric concerts; go to the Web site or call for schedules.

TOURING TIPS The museum itself is as wheelchair-accessible as such a building can be (there is an elevator down by the security desk), but patrons with disabilities would be well advised to spring for a cab, at least from the 175th Street subway station, which is accessible. Or take the M4 bus, which, though notoriously slow, stops right at the museum entrance; once you get to the museum itself, call security (☎ 212-650-2211) for assistance. There is a small cafe on the lower level, but it's open only May through September.

Cooper-Hewitt, National Design Museum ★★★

APPEAL BY AGE	PRESCHOOL ½	GRADE SCHOOL ★★	TEENS ★★
YOUNG ADULTS ★★★	OVER 30 ★★★		SENIORS ★★

East 91st Street and Fifth Avenue, Upper East Side; ☎ 212-849-8400; www.cooperhewitt.org

Type of attraction Collection of international design and design art. **Nearest subway station** 96th Street or 86th Street. **Admission** $11 adults, $5 seniors and students; children age 11 and under free. **Hours** Monday–Friday, 10 a.m.– 5 p.m.; Saturday, 10 a.m.–6 p.m.; Sunday, noon–6 p.m.; closed Thanksgiving, Christmas, and New Year's Day. **When to go** Midafternoon. **Wheelchair access** Very good; some wheelchairs available. **Special comments** This is a branch of the Smithsonian Institution; members get in free. **Author's rating** The strength of the museum's appeal to younger visitors depends heavily on the special exhibits on view at the time, but adults will probably always find something to like; ★★★. **How much time to allow** 1–1½ hours.

DESCRIPTION AND COMMENTS This was originally the "modest" home of Andrew Carnegie (one of the first private structures in the city with an elevator, incidentally); the two families whose names are linked in the museum's name collected textiles, jewelry, glassware, silver, furniture, and artisan paper from all over the world. Although the museum's collection as a whole is quite large, only a small fraction is on view at one time, but there may be several different exhibits coexisting; for example, most of one whole room may be given over to a lineup of six or eight intriguing chairs, while the library and the hallway may serve as a "rogue's gallery" of lettering styles.

This has one of the most intriguing museum shops in the city, with a lot of clever, attractive, and convenient writing implements, clocks and calculators, and other utensils.

TOURING TIPS Free highlights tours leave from the Great Hall at noon and 3 p.m. weekdays, 12:30 and 2 p.m. Sunday. There is a nice light-fare cafe with some outdoor seating.

Ellis Island
National Monument ★★★★★

| APPEAL BY AGE | PRESCHOOL ½ | GRADE SCHOOL ★★★ | TEENS ★★★ |
| YOUNG ADULTS ★★★★ | | OVER 30 ★★★★★ | SENIORS ★★★★ |

New York Harbor, Lower Manhattan; ☎ 212-363-3200; www.nps.gov/ elis (for ferry tickets, ☎ 877-523-9849 or www.statuecruises.com)

Type of attraction Re-creation of immigrants' first contact with America. **Nearest subway station** Bowling Green or South Ferry. **Admission** Free (ferry tickets $5–$12). **Hours** Daily, 9 a.m.–5:15 p.m. (last ferry at 4 p.m.); extended hours during summer and on some holidays; closed Christmas. **When to go** Weekdays. **Wheelchair access** Ferries, museum, and grounds accessible; some wheelchairs available; ASL tours require 3 weeks' notice (☎ 212-363-3200 or TTY 212-363-8343). **Special comments** Access may depend on weather; elevators are sometimes out of service. **Author's rating ★★★★★. How much time to allow** 1½–2 hours.

DESCRIPTION AND COMMENTS Few museums can have an association for as many Americans as this one; by some estimates, half of the nation's population has roots here. From 1892 to 1954, when the processing center was abandoned, as many as 10,000 immigrants per day, a total of more than 12 million, stumbled off often-wretched boats into the waiting lines of Ellis Island, where they were examined, cross-examined (whether or not they could speak English), quarantined, frequently rechristened, and just as frequently turned away. And that total would be higher if the station hadn't been used to house German POWs during World War II. Many arrivals were children or orphans; the first immigrant to set foot on the island, on New Year's Day 1892, was 15-year-old Annie Moore.

Visitors follow the immigrants' route, entering through the main baggage room and up to the high-vaulted and intentionally intimidating Registry and then the bluntly named Staircase of Separation. Astonishingly, these historic rooms can be rented out for catered events. Exhibits include the stark dormitories and baggage, dozens of rooms full of poignant photos and oral histories, video clips and dramatic presentations, and a thousand individual remembrances of home—crucifixes, jewelry, clothing, family heirlooms—donated by the families of those who passed through. The 1898 main building has been magnificently restored at a cost of more than $150 million, from the copper roofing to the rail station–style glass-and-wrought-iron entranceway; plans for the other buildings are uncertain. The American Immigrant Wall of Fame lists half a million names, including the grandfathers of presidents from Washington to Kennedy, whose descendants contributed to the restoration. (You can contribute too—from $150 to $1,000; **www.wall ofhonor.org.**) Except for the very youngest, who may get tired in the long lines, almost everyone will be taken with this experience—not only the older visitors, who remember the melting-pot era best, but also those school-age visitors for whom multiculturalism is a daily affair. First- and second-generation Americans will be especially affected.

TOURING TIPS Statue Cruises picks up and lets off at the Battery and Liberty State Park in New Jersey. Although reserved tickets bought in advance can include passes to the Statue of Liberty monument, flex tickets, good for three days, do not; those passes are first-come, first-served. Note that the visiting time suggested previously is only for this museum, not for the ferry passage or visiting the Statue of Liberty. The audio tour here is unusually good. Cafe on-site.

kids Empire State Building ★★½

APPEAL BY AGE	PRESCHOOL ★	GRADE SCHOOL ★★½	TEENS ★★★½
YOUNG ADULTS ★★★½		OVER 30 ★★★½	SENIORS ★★★½

350 Fifth Avenue (at West 34th Street), Gramercy Park;
☎ **212-736-3100; www.esbnyc.com**

Type of attraction Landmark tower with famous view. **Nearest subway station** 34th Street. **Admission** $20 adults and teens, $14 children ages 6–12 and seniors 62 and older, $13 children ages 6–11; military members in uniform and children age 5 and under free. Includes the 86th-floor observatory; $15 extra for the 102nd-floor observation deck. **Hours** Daily, 8 a.m.–2 a.m. (last elevator ascends at 1:15 a.m.). **When to go** After dark. **Wheelchair access** The lobby and 86th floor are wheelchair-accessible. **Special comments** Some small children may find this scary. **Author's rating** The lobby is great, and the observation deck provides a nice view, but it's not the only choice. And because this is squarely on many bus-tour routes, it can be very crowded; ★★½. **How much time to allow** 30–45 minutes.

DESCRIPTION AND COMMENTS There are two observation decks: one on the 86th floor, a glass-enclosed viewing area surrounded by open-air decks (from which, promoters say, you can see ships 40 miles out at sea); and an entirely enclosed one on the 102nd level, near the top of the spire, whose range, on the legendary clear day, is supposed to be 80 miles. The decks are open until 2 a.m., when the view is even nicer and, oddly, less vertiginous than during the day. The tallest building in the city, it's 1,454 feet (counting the transmitters and all; the 102nd-floor observatory is 1,224 feet up). It took a year and 45 days to build, required 10 million bricks, and weighs 365,000 tons. There are 1,860 steps, as veterans of the annual race up can attest, and 73 elevators. King Kong wasn't really here, of course, but the tower was struck by a fogbound bomber back in 1945 just above the 78th floor, and it's still struck by lightning as many as 500 times a year. It has hosted more than 90 million visitors in its time, more than 3.5 million every year. The exterior lights—always on, to avoid a second plane crash—are color-coded on holidays and special occasions: red, white, and blue on Independence Day; green for St. Patrick's; pink for Gay Pride Day; and so on. Once it was lit blue to honor Frank "Ol' Blue Eyes" Sinatra.

The recently restored lobby is a three-story Art Deco marvel; the futuristic ceiling murals—showing the solar system as a vast gold-and-aluminum machine—have been revealed (actually reproduced, as the originals were badly damaged). The building houses other attractions as well, including exhibits and memorabilia from the movie *King Kong* and several simulated adventures, something like IMAX movies with motion.

TOURING TIPS There are two restaurants and a sushi bar on-site. Tickets are sold on the concourse level below the main lobby; you don't have to use the tickets the same day you buy them. Security checks here are among the strictest in the city, and you must pass through security before getting into the ticket-buying queue unless you purchase advance tickets.

kids *Forbes* Magazine Galleries ★★★½

APPEAL BY AGE	PRESCHOOL ★★★	GRADE SCHOOL ★★★★	TEENS ★★★
YOUNG ADULTS ★★★	OVER 30 ★★★		SENIORS ★★★½

62 Fifth Avenue (at 12th Street), Greenwich Village; ☎ 212-206-5548; www.forbesgalleries.com

Type of attraction Fantastic collection of toys: tin soldiers, model boats, and antique games, collected by Malcolm Forbes Sr. **Nearest subway station** 14th Street–Union Square or 14th Street (F and V trains). **Admission** Free, but limited numbers admitted per day. **Hours** Tuesday–Saturday, 10 a.m.–4 p.m., (Thursdays reserved for group tours); closed Sunday and Monday, Fourth of July, Thanksgiving, Christmas, and New Year's Day. **When to go** Before lunch if there are children in the party, after if not. **Wheelchair access** Very good. **Special comments** Children 15 and under must be accompanied by an adult, and no more than 4 children per adult are allowed. **Author's rating** Quite the enviable escape, and a nostalgic wonder trip; ★★★½. **How much time to allow** 1–1½ hours.

DESCRIPTION AND COMMENTS If you think you've seen toy soldiers before, think again. The more than 12,000 flat and 3-D tin figures arranged in dioramas here—not just soldiers of every historical period and nation, but also cowboys and Indians, Aztecs and Spaniards, knights and ladies, and many others—are only about one-tenth of Malcolm Forbes's collection. The room built to match the famous "counterpane" illustration from Robert Louis Stevenson's *A Child's Garden of Verses* has a glass bubble above the dummy figure, allowing visitors to become the "child" in the picture. This labyrinth of galleries begins with a series of cases holding more than 500 vintage toy boats (not model boats, an interesting distinction) arranged in flotillas against a background of etched-glass Art Deco panels from the ocean liner *Normandie*; it continues with a collection of period and special-edition Monopoly sets, trophies, sporting awards, and rotating exhibits of presidential memorabilia, including Nixon's letter of resignation and models of Washington's headquarters at Yorktown and Jefferson's bedroom at Monticello.

TOURING TIPS This can be so exhilarating for kids that they get a little loud, while the tight space and highly focused lighting can be tiring for some older visitors. Also note that the galleries are occasionally closed on regular viewing days; call ahead. There is no cafe on-site.

The Frick Collection ★★★★★

| APPEAL BY AGE | PRESCHOOL ★½ | GRADE SCHOOL ★½ | TEENS ★★ |
| YOUNG ADULTS ★★★½ | OVER 30 ★★★★ | | SENIORS ★★★★ |

1 East 70th Street (at Fifth Avenue), Upper East Side; ☎ 212-288-0700; www.frick.org

Type of attraction Collection of 18th- and 19th-century art in a gracious mansion. **Nearest subway station** 68th Street–Hunter College. **Admission** $18 adults, $12 seniors (62 and over), $5 students; children under 10 not admitted. **Hours** Tuesday–Saturday, 10 a.m.–6 p.m.; Sunday, 11 a.m.–5 p.m.; closed Monday and holidays. **When to go** Weekdays; pay-what-you-wish Sunday. **Wheelchair access** Extremely good (ramp on 70th Street just left of main entrance); assisted-listening devices available. **Author's rating** A personal favorite, glorious in both setting and collection; ★★★★★. **How much time to allow** 1½–3 hours.

DESCRIPTION AND COMMENTS This is both a stunning house museum and a first-class collection, small by Met standards but studded with exquisite portraits (Whistler, Goya, El Greco, Titian, Vermeer, Sargent, Holbein, Rembrandt, Reynolds), landscapes (Turner, Constable), marbles, and murals (Fragonard and an entire boudoir's worth of Boucher panels painted for Madame de Pompadour). Then there's the enamel Limoges miniatures, the garden court with its lily pond, the ghost of the pipe organ (the pipes are still there, in the hallway, though the works are gone), all those Oriental rugs (you are looking down, aren't you?), and just a smattering of fine furniture left from the days when steel magnate Henry Clay Frick and his family lived here. Several of the galleries have just been repainted and paintings rearranged, adding to their beauty.

TOURING TIPS This is two blocks from the **Asia Society** collection at 70th and Park (☎ 212-288-6400; **www.asiasociety.org**), which is a fine match of temperament and pacing even if it is a world away in art. There is no restaurant on-site. Audio tours are available in several languages.

Guggenheim Museum ★★★½

| APPEAL BY AGE | PRESCHOOL ½ | GRADE SCHOOL ★★ | TEENS ★★ |
| YOUNG ADULTS ★★★½ | OVER 30 ★★★ | | SENIORS ★★★ |

Fifth Avenue at 89th Street, Upper East Side; ☎ 212-423-3500; www.guggenheim.org

Type of attraction Fine collection of 20th-century European art. **Nearest subway station** 86th Street. **Admission** $18 adults, $15 seniors and students;

children age 11 and under free. **Hours** Saturday–Wednesday, 10 a.m.–5:45 p.m.; Friday, 10 a.m.–7:45 p.m.; closed Thursday. **When to go** Anytime. **Wheelchair access** Very good; companion to guest in manual wheelchair admitted free. ASL tours and tours for visually impaired offered free, 6–8 p.m., third Monday of the month (☎ 212-360-4355). **Special comments** Fridays, 5:45–7:45 p.m., pay what you wish. Though the spiral ramp seems good for wheelchairs and keeps kids interested, it can be hard on the legs. **Author's rating** ★★★½. **How much time to allow** 1½–3 hours.

DESCRIPTION AND COMMENTS   This is one of those museums more famous for its architecture than for its collection. Frank Lloyd Wright's upwardly expanding six-floor spiral, like a squared-off chambered nautilus (it's been called ruder things), frames the Great Rotunda and looks up to an often brilliantly lit glass dome; the exhibits fill the walls of the long ramp and lead off into the chambers. Among the permanent exhibits are major pieces by Klee, Picasso, Kandinsky, Chagall, and Modigliani; the museum also has a fine selection of Impressionists, including works by Monet, Renoir, and Van Gogh.

   Though in the shadow of the giant Museum of Modern Art collection, the Guggenheim, which has more European works, forms a strong duet with the **Whitney Museum of American Art.** (Also, it reaches back a little further into the 19th century.) Guggenheim was aggressive in collecting avant-garde and new talent, and that was the reputation the museum was supposed to have, although it has been criticized for "maturing."

TOURING TIPS   The new, upscale Wright restaurant stays open until 11 p.m. Thursday–Saturday. Free tours are interesting but irregular; check the Web site in advance.

kids Intrepid Sea, Air & Space Museum   ★★★

APPEAL BY AGE	PRESCHOOL ★½	GRADE SCHOOL ★★★½	TEENS ★★★
YOUNG ADULTS ★★★		OVER 30 ★★★	SENIORS ★★★½

Pier 86, West 46th Street at 12th Avenue, Midtown West;
☎ **212-245-0072 or 877-957-7447; www.intrepidmuseum.org**

Type of attraction Mini-fleet of retired Navy and Coast Guard vessels, including the World War II aircraft carrier *Intrepid*. **Nearest subway station** 42nd Street or 50th Street. **Admission** $22 adults; $13 seniors and college students; $17 children ages 3–17; military personnel, veterans, and children under age 3 free. Simulator rides and tours additional; various combination tickets available. **Hours** *April–September*: Monday–Friday, 10 a.m.–5 p.m.; Saturday, Sunday, and holidays, 10 a.m.–6 p.m.; *October–March:* Tuesday–Sunday and holidays, 10 a.m.–5 p.m.; closed Monday except some holidays. Last admission 1 hour before closing. **When to go** Early or immediately after lunch. **Wheelchair access** Good, albeit limited. **Special comments** Although much of the museum is wheelchair-accessible, several areas, including the *Growler* submarine and the Concorde, are not; other areas (particularly staircases) may be difficult for older visitors, small children, or the claustrophobic. Note that the ticket office closes at 4 p.m. **Author's rating** This is really a sort of amusement-park-cum-elephant-graveyard, and for those with a real interest (or experience) in naval history, it's a 4- or even 5-star attraction. But don't underestimate the time required if you intend to tour all the various vessels and exhibits. And there can be waiting lines for the guided tours. Better pick your spots; ★★★. **How much time to allow** 2–4 hours.

DESCRIPTION AND COMMENTS This complex includes half a dozen vessels and a mix of guided and self-guided tours. The centerpiece is, of course, the aircraft carrier *Intrepid,* which has a 900-foot flight deck on which sit 30 real planes dating from the 1940s to the 1990s (including an A12 Blackbird spy plane), the era of wars in which the *Intrepid* served. Visitors can wander through the bridge and most of the corridors and may well spend, as staffers estimate, three hours on the carrier alone. In addition to the vessels, such as the guided-missile submarine *Growler,* the Vietnam-era destroyer escort *Slater,* the Coast Guard lightship *Nantucket,* the SS *Elizabeth* research ship, and the fleet destroyer *Edson,* there are a variety of quirky exhibits focusing on space flight, underwater exploration, rockets, the sort of personal mementoes that sailors collect, and so on. And true to theme park rules, it now has several simulator thrill rides, part of its $115 million restoration, which have amped the teenage appeal.

TOURING TIPS There are several cafes in the complex. Although interiors are air-conditioned and heated, you will be spending some time outside, so dress accordingly.

Jewish Museum ★★★½

APPEAL BY AGE	PRESCHOOL ½	GRADE SCHOOL ★★	TEENS ★★★
YOUNG ADULTS ★★★½	OVER 30 ★★★½		SENIORS ★★★★

Fifth Avenue at 92nd Street, Upper East Side; ☎ 212-423-3200; www.jewishmuseum.org

Type of attraction Surprisingly rich collection of ancient Judaica and Jewish art. **Nearest subway station** 96th Street. **Admission** $12 adults, $10 seniors 65 and older, $7.50 students; children age 11 and under free. **Hours** Saturday–Tuesday, 11 a.m.–5:45 p.m.; Thursday, 11 a.m.–8 p.m.; Friday 11 a.m.–4 p.m.; closed Wednesday and New Year's Day, Martin Luther King Jr. Day, Thanksgiving, and major Jewish holidays. **When to go** Anytime. **Wheelchair access** Very good; some wheelchairs available (☎ 212-423-3213). **Special comments** Free admission on Saturday. Extensive accessibility information on the Web site, or call ☎ 212-423-3225. **Author's rating** One becomes so accustomed to seeing Christian relics and even Asian religious art that the age and variety of these ruins and sacred objects are startling; ★★★½. **How much time to allow** 1–2 hours.

DESCRIPTION AND COMMENTS This fine collection, now moving toward its centennial, centers on a permanent exhibition about the Jewish experience—religious and secular—that ranges back 4,000 years. Among its works are temple facades from Sumer, wall paintings of biblical battles,

Torah covers and crowns, fine art and sculpture, candelabras, flatware, manuscripts, and portraits of Jewish Americans. Downstairs is a gallery used for special exhibitions.

Like many of the fine specialized museums in the city, this was originally a mansion, and the two-level, wood-paneled library, which is filled with fine arks and altars and ceremonial items and holds an almost pulpitlike spiral staircase, is a beauty. There is also a family exhibit area designed for children and parents to visit together. Incidentally, the stonework in the rear extension was done by the same masons who are working on the Cathedral Church of St. John the Divine (see page 237).

TOURING TIPS There is a cafe in the basement. Spotlight tours leave from the lobby at various times during the day.

Lower East Side Tenement Museum ★★★½

APPEAL BY AGE	PRESCHOOL ½	GRADE SCHOOL ★★	TEENS ★★
YOUNG ADULTS ★★★	OVER 30 ★★★		SENIORS ★★★

90 Orchard Street (the actual tenement building is 97 Orchard), Lower East Side; ☎ 212-431-0233 or 866-811-4111; www.tenement.org

Type of attraction Reconstructed early-20th-century slum. **Nearest subway station** Delancey or Grand Street. **Admission** $20 adults, $15 seniors 65 and older and students; children age 5 and under free. **Hours** Gallery 90, the office and shop, is open 10 a.m.–6 p.m. Tours begin 10:30 a.m.–5 p.m. daily. **When to go** Weekdays. **Special comments** Museum can been viewed by guided tours only; each tour requires a ticket. Exact hours vary; reserve in advance if possible. **Author's rating** The only way to understand 12 people living in 1 room is to see it; ★★★½. **How much time to allow** 1–1½ hours.

DESCRIPTION AND COMMENTS In 1903, city officials reported that there were at least 2,200 people, most of them immigrants, packed into the single block bounded by Orchard, Delancey, Broome, and Allen streets, in buildings such as this 1863 tenement, restored in the main to turn-of-the-20th-century conditions (it had no water, heat, or toilets until 1905). One apartment was left just as it was found in 1988, having been abandoned for about 50 years; another was restored to the (relatively) comfortable state it was in when the Gumpertz family lived there in 1878. The Levines used their apartment as a garment factory. The museum puts together changing exhibits portraying the life of the neighborhood. Incidentally, this is not, as some people may think, a "Jewish museum"—it's very hybridized. The newest tour features the Irish immigrant Moore family, which lost a child in 1869.

TOURING TIPS The museum also offers 90-minute neighborhood heritage tours that don't enter the tenement but make a nice complement. All tours can be conducted in foreign languages. There is no cafe on-site, but it's a short walk to either Katz's Deli on East Houston or the Little Italy of Mulberry Street, so you can stick with the theme.

Metropolitan Museum of Art   ★★★★★

APPEAL BY AGE	PRESCHOOL ★½	GRADE SCHOOL ★★½	TEENS ★★★
YOUNG ADULTS ★★★★★	`OVER 30 ★★★★★		SENIORS ★★★★★

Fifth Avenue between 80th and 84th streets (entrance at 82nd), Upper East Side; ☎ 212-535-7710; www.metmuseum.org

Type of attraction One of the greatest museum collections in the world. **Nearest subway station** 86th Street. **Admission** Suggested donation $20 adults, $15 seniors, $10 students; children age 11 and under free. **Hours** Sunday and Tuesday–Thursday, 9:30 a.m.–5:30 p.m.; Friday and Saturday, 9:30 a.m.–9 p.m.; closed Monday except holidays. **When to go** Friday and Saturday evenings for dining and music; call ☎ 212-570-3949 for special-events schedule. **Wheelchair access** Very good (enter at Fifth Avenue and 81st Street); some wheelchairs available. **Special comments** Extensive accessibility information on the Web site. **Author's rating** We could visit this every time we were in New York and never feel as if we had seen it all; ★★★★★. **How much time to allow** 1½–5 hours.

DESCRIPTION AND COMMENTS   The figures are almost unbelievable: 3.5 million pieces of art, some dating back more than 5,000 years, representing every culture in the world; 32 acres of exhibit space; 5 million visitors a year. It was founded in 1870 by New York's leading philanthropists and city boosters, who intended it to rival the great museums of Europe and prove New York the equal of any Old World center—and they were willing to pony up to make it happen. Their plan worked, too.

You can't see it all, so pick a century, a style, or a special exhibit and start there. Or pick a centerpiece. For example, the American wing gently spirals down past Tiffany glass and Arts and Crafts pieces to the neoclassical sculpture in the garden court; the Temple of Dendur, which was erected by Augustus, has been reconstructed in a chamber of glass at the end of the Egyptian wing (a thank-you from the nation of Egypt for the United States's help in rescuing monuments threatened by the Aswan Dam). The Astor Court, a replica of a Ming Dynasty–era scholar's garden created by artisans from Suzhou, China, using traditional techniques, is the jewel at the heart of the Asian art department on the second floor. Many of the Greek and Roman pieces are housed in a gallery that resembles a glass-roofed Roman villa, and the adjoining rooms are real villas with frescos rescued from Mount Vesuvius lava. The South Asian collection of Buddhist and Hindu sculpture is fabulous (and less well known, so rarely crowded). Or you could luxuriate in medieval art, including ornately carved altarpieces and icons; all-American painting; or entirely reinstalled rooms—art, furniture, and all—from the Lehman town house on West 54th Street. And these are just the permanent exhibits. The Metropolitan continually hosts or initiates special collections of blockbuster art from other countries or by great masters.

There are several areas that even small children will like, including the Egyptian mummies and the Temple of Dendur; the "knights" in all kinds of glittering armor; the musical instruments; and the furnished rooms (like playhouses). Depending on the exhibit, they may also get a kick out of the Costume Institute downstairs, which owns 45,000 pieces of clothing dating back to the 17th century. There's a playground just outside, to the south, for emergencies.

As if it weren't impressive enough, the Met has added a huge new expanse along the south end facing Central Park, including a Roman Court, and is constantly renovating galleries.

TOURING TIPS There are several places to eat, including an upscale cafe off the American wing and the wine bar on the roof in the sculpture garden. The gift shop is famous; you could decorate your whole house with its high-quality prints and posters. The Metropolitan also administers The Cloisters (see page 238); admission covers both on the same day.

Tours offering overviews of the exhibits are conducted in Italian, Spanish, French, Japanese, Korean, Portuguese, Russian, Mandarin, and German as well as English. Tours leave from the Great Hall; times vary. Staffers are also available at the fossil, gem, and Rose Center displays.

The Morgan Library & Museum ★★★★★

APPEAL BY AGE	PRESCHOOL ★	GRADE SCHOOL ★★	TEENS ★★½
YOUNG ADULTS ★★★	OVER 30 ★★★★		SENIORS ★★★

225 Madison Avenue (at East 36th Street), Midtown East;
☎ **212-685-0008; www.morganlibrary.org**

Type of attraction World-class collection of medieval and Renaissance illuminated manuscripts, rare books, and master drawings. **Nearest subway station** 33rd Street. **Admission** $12 adults, $8 seniors 65 and older, students, and children ages 13–16; children age 12 and under free. **Hours** Tuesday–Thursday, 10:30 a.m.–5 p.m.; Friday, 10:30 a.m–9 p.m.; Saturday, 10 a.m.–6 p.m.; Sunday, 11 a.m.–6 p.m.; closed Monday and Thanksgiving, Christmas, and New Year's Day. **When to go** Weekdays; late afternoon. **Special comments** There are child-friendly areas, but some special exhibits, say of children's books and illustrations, might have even higher appeal for young visitors. **Author's rating** As admitted medieval-history freaks and bibliophiles to boot, we think this is an incredible collection, and it's usually not very crowded; ★★★★★. **How much time to allow** 1½–3½ hours.

DESCRIPTION AND COMMENTS Legendary financier J. P. Morgan may have been giving himself aristocratic airs when he built this Renaissance palace of a home, but he and his collection must have been a perfect fit for this warm, otherworldly complex. Gold and full-color manuscripts, Old

Master drawings, ancient seals, musical manuscripts, gilt and enamel bindings, the most delicate of red-chalk sketches, the almost illegibly tiny handwriting of the Brontë children, Mozart's own scores, Gutenberg's Bible, Voltaire's briefcase, Dickens's cigar case—the rotating pleasures of this museum are perhaps specialized, but they are certainly superior. And the recent renovation—which doubled the exhibit space, joined the two older buildings with a four-story atrium, and provided the reading room with a jewel of a translucent roof—makes it almost irresistible. The sheer number of books will fill you with envy, and the glorious murals, wood-work, and plaster detailing will do the same.

TOURING TIPS Like many upscale museums these days, the Morgan has both a less-formal cafe that serves lunch, Friday dinner, and, appropriately, tea, and a quite nice new dining room that serves lunch and weekend brunch. So true book-lovers can make quite a day of it. Admission to the McKim rooms (the "old" section, the libraries and rotunda), a real trea-sure, is free Tuesday, 3 to 5 p.m.; Friday, 7 to 9 p.m.; and Sunday, 4 to 6 p.m. Historical and exhibit tours daily; call ☎ 212-685-0008.

El Museo del Barrio ★★★½

APPEAL BY AGE	PRESCHOOL ★	GRADE SCHOOL ★★	TEENS ★★★
YOUNG ADULTS ★★★½		OVER 30 ★★★★	SENIORS ★★★½

Fifth Avenue at 104th Street, Upper East Side; ☎ 212-831-7272; www.elmuseo.org

Type of attraction Smallish but distinguished collection of Pan-American Hispanic art and culture. **Nearest subway station** 103rd Street. **Admission** Suggested donation $6 adults, $4 seniors and students; children age 11 and under free. **Hours** Wednesday–Sunday, 11 a.m.–6 p.m.; closed Monday and Tuesday, and Fourth of July, Thanksgiving, Christmas, and New Year's Day. **When to go** Midafternoon. **Wheelchair access** Good (enter between 104th and 105th streets). **Special comments** Admission free third Saturday of the month; seniors free on Wednesday. **Author's rating** Its cultural message is pointed without being at all preachy; ★★★½. **How much time to allow** 1–2 hours.

DESCRIPTION AND COMMENTS Once a small, slightly dowdy facility, El Museo recently reopened after an extensive face-lift (a stunning glass facade and steel-wrapped courtyard) and much-needed expansion and mod-ernization (coinciding with its 40th anniversary). Exhibits often focus on thematic issues, such as dream symbols or regional development, com-bining, religious carvings, textiles, prints, paintings, vintage photographs, pre-Columbian artifacts, and contemporary art.

TOURING TIPS Free gallery tours Saturdays at 3 p.m. in Spanish, 4 p.m. in English. El Museo also hosts some concerts, films, and readings; check the Web site for a calendar of events. The new cafe offers classic Latin American and Caribbean fare.

kids Museum of the City of New York ★★★

APPEAL BY AGE	PRESCHOOL ★★½	GRADE SCHOOL ★★★	TEENS ★★
YOUNG ADULTS ★★★		OVER 30 ★★★	SENIORS ★★★

Fifth Avenue at 103rd Street, Upper East Side; ☎ 212-534-1672; www.mcny.org

Type of attraction Historical collection that shines specific and often unusual lights on city history. **Nearest subway station** 103rd Street. **Admission** Suggested donation $9 adults, $4 seniors and children, $20 families; children age 12 and under free. **Hours** Tuesday–Sunday, 10 a.m.–5 p.m.; closed Monday except holidays. **When to go** Anytime. **Wheelchair access** Very good. **Special comments** Admission is free on Sundays from 10 a.m. to noon. **Author's rating** An underappreciated and less-crowded pleasure; ★★★. **How much time to allow** 2–3 hours.

DESCRIPTION AND COMMENTS This might be the sort of museum in which families could split up to see different wings and then regroup—say, at the huge, mezzanine-level model of what the museum will look like once its vast wing addition is built. The rotating exhibits are often quirky and fascinating, focusing on such topics as the long tradition of circuses in New York (the theme music included a snippet from the PBS show *Washington Week,* perhaps a joke on media circuses!), the building of the Empire State Building and some of the art that it has inspired, New York's master developer Robert Moses, political campaigns, and the Broadway tradition, complete with posters and recordings. And there are some fine examples of native craftsmanship, furniture, household items, and such. In the basement is a mini–fire museum and a selection of antique city maps. Two of the best exhibits are the toys—including novelty banks, fire trucks and trains, tin soldiers and animals, and a series of dollhouses from the 18th, 19th, and even early 20th centuries—and the reconstructed Moorish-fantasy bedroom and dressing room from John D. Rockefeller's demolished mansion at 5th and 51st. (You'll spot a matching room in the Brooklyn Museum.) Just look at the stenciled canvas ceiling over the sleigh bed, or the woodwork in the dressing room, decorated with appropriate implements such as scissors and combs and mirrors worked in mother-of-pearl.

Like many other New York museums, this one is partway through a significant expansion designed to elevate its profile in both senses; the two-story glass addition is not only stunning but also intentionally contemporary. The 1832 mansion is also getting a face-lift. During the renovation, certain areas of the museum may be closed.

Museum of Jewish Heritage—
A Living Memorial to the Holocaust ★★★★

APPEAL BY AGE	PRESCHOOL ½	GRADE SCHOOL ★★★	TEENS ★★★
YOUNG ADULTS ★★★★	OVER 30 ★★★★		SENIORS ★★★★★

36 Battery Place, Lower Manhattan; ☎ 646-437-4200; www.mjhnyc.org

Type of attraction Re-creation of Jewish culture over the last century—that is, before, during, and after the Holocaust. **Nearest subway station** Bowling Green or South Ferry. **Admission** $12 adults, $10 seniors, $7 students; children age 12 and under free. **Hours** Sunday–Thursday, 10 a.m.–3:30 p.m.; Friday, 10 a.m.–2:30 p.m. during Daylight Saving Time, 10 a.m.–1 p.m. during Standard Time and on the eve of Jewish holidays; closed Saturday, Jewish holidays, and Thanksgiving. **When to go** Anytime. **Wheelchair access** Good. **Special comments** Admission is free on Wednesdays from 4 to 8 p.m. **Author's rating** This seems to hit seniors (who remember the bad times) and teenagers (who may not previously have really understood the Holocaust) the hardest; ★★★★. **How much time to allow** 2–3½ hours.

DESCRIPTION AND COMMENTS This carefully orchestrated collection, which begins in a subtle key, crashes into the Holocaust, and climaxes in a visual paean to the future and specifically to the United States, is subtitled "A Living Memorial to the Holocaust," with emphasis on the "Living." It has a gentler, more affirmative tone than the larger U.S. Holocaust Memorial Museum in Washington, D.C. Instead of placing visitors in the character of victims, as the Washington site does, this museum tries to include all visitors, Jewish and not, by emphasizing the importance of tradition and faith. And while the Washington memorial is almost entirely focused on the Holocaust itself, this collection also speaks to the recovery of Judaism and the state of Israel—a happier present and future. The key to its mission is in the dual message carved in the wall of the foyer: "Remember . . . NEVER FORGET." And right next to it: "There is hope for the future."

The lower floor (one moves from the bottom up) spotlights the richness of Jewish family life in the late 19th and early 20th centuries, with clothing and artifacts from holidays and special occasions, such as a gorgeous silver-and-silk bride's headdress and belt. (Wherever possible, the photograph of the item's owner—victim or survivor—is shown with it.) One of the most spectacular items is a hand-painted Sukkah mural, almost byzantine in its detail, showing life in Budapest in the 1920s and 1930s, along with biblical scenes and family portraits created by an untrained kosher butcher.

The second story focuses on the Holocaust itself, with thousands of photos of the executed (posted on the stall-like wooden slabs that symbolize the boxcars that carried Jews to the concentration camps);

toys and mementos of both escapees and victims; and a salute to those such as Raoul Wallenberg and the now-famous Oskar Schindler who helped Jews escape the Nazis. The third floor, the post-Holocaust era, culminates in a glass-walled expanse, almost blinding after all that granite darkness, that looks directly out upon icons of Jewish freedom: the Statue of Liberty, Ellis Island, and the railroad terminal on the New Jersey shore from which many immigrants began their new lives. It packs quite an emotional wallop.

The special-events wing has a balcony that has an installation of boulders with trees growing in them.

TOURING TIPS   The kosher cafe has a view of the Statue of Liberty.

Museum of Modern Art   ★★★★★

APPEAL BY AGE	PRESCHOOL ½	GRADE SCHOOL ★★	TEENS ★★
YOUNG ADULTS ★★★	OVER 30 ★★★★		SENIORS ★★★

11 West 53rd Street (between Fifth and Sixth avenues), Midtown East;
☎ **212-708-9400; www.moma.org**

Type of attraction Premier collection of modern and contemporary art and design. **Nearest subway station** Fifth Avenue–53rd Street. **Admission** $20 adults, $16 seniors, $12 students; children 16 and under free. **Hours** Monday, Wednesday, Thursday, Saturday, and Sunday, 10 a.m.–5:30 p.m. (open until 8 p.m. the 1st Thursday of each month and every Thursday in July and August); Friday, 10:30 a.m.–8 p.m.; closed Tuesday, Thanksgiving, and Christmas Day. **When to go** Weekdays, Friday afternoons. **Wheelchair access** Very good; some wheelchairs available. Free audio tours for the visually impaired, plus free ASL-interpreted gallery talks at 1:30 p.m. the 4th Sunday of the month. **Special comments** Admission is free Friday, 4–8 p.m. **Author's rating** Challenging and often difficult, but fascinating—the world's leading modern-art collection, just as advertised. ★★★★★. **How much time to allow** 2–4 hours.

DESCRIPTION AND COMMENTS   Following its $850 million renovation (with admission prices to match), this icon of American art and design is bigger—630,000 square feet over six floors—brasher, and more breathtaking than ever. First-timers may be surprised at how many of these great paintings and prints they already "know," because so many of the most famous and frequently reproduced 20th-century works hang here, by the Impressionists Cubists, Pop Artists, and so on. (Stop by the main desk and ask for the self-guided tour; it points up many of these "greatest hits," including Van Gogh's *The Starry Night,* Monet's *Water Lilies*—centerpiece of its own gallery—and Picasso's *Les Demoiselles d'Avignon.*) A soaring six-floor glass atrium and repeated glimpses of the sculpture garden blur the line between art and nature-as-art, and even art-as-nature. As might be guessed by the sight of the 1945 Bell "bug-eyed" helicopter suspended over a walkway, MoMA is also famous for its vetting of industrial and commercial design, from automobile bodies to typewriters, architectural models to appliances, even watches; Movado's most famous face, the one with a single dot at the 12, is called "the Museum Watch" because MoMA approved of it so highly. There are two shops in the main building and a large design store across the street, featuring jewelry, home accessories, and disabled-friendly utensils.

TOURING TIPS   Gallery tours Wednesday–Monday, 11:30 a.m. and 1:30 p.m., leaving from the second-floor atrium. Call and ask about film screenings, or check the local press; the museum's collection of films tops 10,000. The restaurant, the Modern, is a full-fledged member of Danny Meyer's group (Gramercy Tavern, Union Square Cafe, etc.).

 ## National Museum of the American Indian (The George Gustav Heye Center)   ★★★

APPEAL BY AGE	PRESCHOOL ★½	GRADE SCHOOL ★★★	TEENS ★★★
YOUNG ADULTS ★★½		OVER 30 ★★★	SENIORS ★★½

Old U.S. Custom House, 1 Bowling Green (near State and Whitehall streets), Lower Manhattan; ☎ 212-514-3700; nmai.si.edu

Type of attraction Part art collection, part anthropology lesson. **Nearest subway station** Bowling Green, Whitehall, Broad Street, or South Ferry. **Admission** Free. **Hours** Daily, 10 a.m.–5 p.m. (till 8 p.m. on Thursday); closed Christmas. **When to go** Anytime. **Wheelchair access** Good (enter to the right of the grand staircase); some wheelchairs available. **Author's rating** There is beautiful work here, and surprising (to many Americans) diversity, but it may run into a generational guilt gap; it captures many children's attention faster than their parents'; ★★★. **How much time to allow** 1–1½ hours.

DESCRIPTION AND COMMENTS   This is a branch of the Smithsonian Institution, and, not surprisingly, its captions and clarity of information are first-rate. It includes artifacts not only from the more familiar (from TV and movies) Plains Indians but also from the Aztec, Olmec, Mayan, northwestern, and even Siberian tribes. There are often demonstrations of weaving or music in the center area, which children will enjoy. They'll also enjoy some of the temporary exhibits, ranging from American Indian skateboarding culture to a history of the importance of the horse.

TOURING TIPS   Don't overlook the Beaux Arts Custom House itself, with its exterior sculptures of metaphoric goddesses by Daniel Chester French representing Asia (the meditative one), America (the optimistic one), Europe (with the vestiges of her empire), and Africa (unawakened). Well, it was pre-PC. No on-site dining.

New Museum of Contemporary Art   ★★½

APPEAL BY AGE	PRESCHOOL ★★	GRADE SCHOOL ★★	TEENS ★★½
YOUNG ADULTS ★★½		OVER 30 ★★★	SENIORS ★★

235 Bowery, Lower East Side; ☎ 212-219-1222; www.newmuseum.org

Type of attraction Cutting-edge collection of contemporary art. **Nearest subway station** Lower East Side–Second Avenue. **Admission** $12 adults,

$10 seniors, $8 students; ages 18 and under free. **Hours** Wednesday, Saturday, and Sunday, noon–6 p.m.; Thursday and Friday noon–9 p.m.; closed Monday and Tuesday, except holidays, and Thanksgiving, Christmas, and New Year's Day. **When to go** Midweek; weekends to visit the Sky Room. **Special comments** Free admission Thursday, 7–9 p.m. **Author's rating** Avant-garde can translate as ironic or even arch, and because much of what's on exhibit at any time is temporary, it's somewhat hit-or-miss; this is probably more for the serious art lover; ★★½. **How much time to allow** 1–2 hours.

DESCRIPTION AND COMMENTS　This is a museum that you will either love or shrug off. Many installations are extremely clever, a few jejune; some are minimalist and a few just minimal. The structure itself is a little like that, simultaneously imposing—a glittery, teetering pile of expensive gift boxes floating on a glass lobby—and a little SoHo nostalgic, with concrete floors and flat white walls. One of the staircases is 50 feet long and barely wide enough for two visitors. And while many of the pieces on display are large, the space is relatively limited. On the other hand, the museum was built for a bargain $50 million, a fraction of what MoMA's renovation cost, and that may partly explain the more afford-able ticket price.

TOURING TIPS　Free highlights tours Wednesday through Friday, 12:30 p.m., and Saturday and Sunday, 12:30 and 3 p.m. Free iPod audio tours avail-able. Self-guided tour materials $20 with online reservation, or call ☎ 212-219-1222, ext. 235. The seventh-floor Sky Terrace has panoramic views of Lower Manhattan. The cafe partakes of the new-Bowery vibe: restaurant supply store chic meets Japanese cool.

New York Botanical Garden　★★★½

APPEAL BY AGE	PRESCHOOL ★★★	GRADE SCHOOL ★★★½	TEENS ★★½
YOUNG ADULTS ★★★	OVER 30 ★★★		SENIORS ★★★★

Bronx River Parkway at Fordham Road, the Bronx; ☎ 718-817-8700; www.nybg.org

Type of attraction Half "natural," half formal gardens with dazzling greenhouse complex. **Nearest subway station** Bedford Park Boulevard. **Admission** Grounds only, $6 adults, $5 adult Bronx residents, $3 seniors and students, $1 children ages 2–12; all-access tickets, $20 adults, $18 seniors and students, $8 children 2–12. **Hours** Tuesday–Sunday, 10 a.m.–6 p.m.; closed Monday, except holidays, and Christmas. **When to go** Midweek. **Special comments** Free admission on Wednesday and 10 a.m.–noon Saturday. **Author's rating** Restful and restorative, and particularly family-friendly; definitely a four-star attraction for gardeners and for kids at holiday time; ★★★½. **How much time to allow** 1½–4 hours.

DESCRIPTION AND COMMENTS　Within this 250-acre spread are a 40-acre forest with a variety of short but pretty trails through the sorts of hardwoods New York State had in abundance back in the last days of the Mohicans, and more than two dozen specialty gardens, among them a seasonal rose garden, a cherry valley, a picnic area, a giant water-lily pond, a rock garden, orchid houses, a mini-maze, and an herb garden. The star is the Enid A. Haupt Conservatory, the glorious Crystal Palace–style greenhouse complex, which encloses both upland and lowland rain forests (with mezzanine-level walkway), deserts from the Americas and Africa, and special collections. The garden's children's fare is first-rate, with special "treasure map" guides to the conservatory gardens, a hands-on adventure garden, family plant-your-own areas, and the like, plus there are a wide variety of special programs, children's walking tours, and demonstrations. It even offers a houseplant first-aid hotline: ☎ 718-817-8681, weekdays 9:30 a.m.–12:30 p.m.

The gardens make a surprisingly buoyant addition to a December holidays trip. The plants inside the conservatory are covered in lights, as are many outdoor trees; a huge model-train exhibition winds through landscapes based on both imaginary and real New York scenes; and special family concerts and performances are scheduled.

TOURING TIPS There are free guided tours, but times vary; call ☎ 718-817-8700 for specific dates. The garden is actually about eight blocks from the Bedford Park subway stop, and though it's downhill on your way there, it's a hard uphill return; take the Bx26 bus. However, Metro North commuter trains (☎ 800-638-7646 or 212-532-4900; **www .mta.info**) run from Grand Central right to a Botanical Garden stop a stone's throw from the side entrance in about 20 minutes.

There is a full-service cafe between the conservatory and the trainside gate, and a lighter cafe in the visitor center.

The Paley Center for Media (formerly The Museum of Television & Radio) ★★★

| APPEAL BY AGE | PRESCHOOL ★½ | GRADE SCHOOL ★★★ | TEENS ★★★ |
| YOUNG ADULTS ★★★ | | OVER 30 ★★★½ | SENIORS ★★½ |

25 West 52nd Street, Midtown East; ☎ 212-621-6600 for information, ☎ 212-621-6800 for schedule; www.paleycenter.org

Type of attraction A combination archives and rerun haven. **Nearest subway station** 47th–50th streets–Rockefeller Center or Fifth Avenue–53rd Street. **Admission** Suggested donation $10 adults, $8 seniors and students, $5 children age 13 and under. **Hours** Wednesday–Sunday, noon–6 p.m.; theaters only, Thursday until 8 p.m.; closed Monday and Tuesday, New Year's Day, Fourth of July, Thanksgiving, and Christmas. **When to go** Anytime. **Wheelchair access** Very good. **Special comments** Listening-assist devices available at the front counter; closed-captioning decoders in the library. Note that the age-group appeal may vary depending on the day's screenings. **Author's rating** Although it's a lot easier to download or rent old TV shows than it used to be, this is still fascinating, and the rare films shown are a delight. In fact, you can download a surprising number of clips and sound recordings, many contemporary, from the Web site; ★★★. **How much time to allow** 2–2½ hours.

DESCRIPTION AND COMMENTS Five floors of exhibits, various-sized screening theaters, and a radio listening room.

Not so famous as most of New York's older museums, this is nevertheless a fine attraction, and one with strong interest for all ages. In fact, with its ongoing screenings on various floors, through which visitors are welcome to sit for as long or as short a time as they like, this is channel surfing to the max. In a single afternoon, for example, you might be able to see rare footage of Sinatra's "Rat Pack" in action, a segment of *The George Burns and Gracie Allen Show,* Jackie Kennedy taking CBS for a tour of the White House, a full-length Wallace and Gromit Claymation adventure, bits of *Sesame Street* and *Fraggle Rock,* a semi-serious documentary on the evolution of sci-fi TV, and a segment of (the original) *Miami Vice.* The hallways are filled with changing exhibits on such topics as journalists and special-effects makeup. Screenings begin at noon each day.

You can take a guided tour (offered only a couple of times a day; call the schedule line), but the real treasure trove is the library, for which you need time-specific tickets (available at the front counter). You cruise the museum's library on computer, picking segments from 140,000 radio and TV programs and even TV and radio advertising, and then you are sent to a private booth to screen (or hear) your selections.

TOURING TIPS There is no cafeteria.

Rubin Museum of Art   ★★★½

| APPEAL BY AGE | PRESCHOOL ★★½ | GRADE SCHOOL ★★½ | TEENS ★★½ |
| YOUNG ADULTS ★★★ | | OVER 30 ★★★★ | SENIORS ★★★★ |

150 West 17th Street, Gramercy Park; ☎ 212-620-5000; www.rmanyc.org

Type of attraction Collection of fine Himalayan art. Nearest subway station 18th Street, 14th Street (1, 2, 3), or 14th Street (F, V). Admission $10 adults, $7 seniors and students, $2 college students with ID; children 12 and under free. Hours Monday and Thursday, 11 a.m.–5 p.m.; Wednesday, 11 a.m.–7 p.m.; Friday, 11 a.m.–10 p.m.; Saturday and Sunday, 11 a.m.–6 p.m.; closed Tuesday and Thanksgiving, Christmas, and New Year's Day. When to go Anytime. Wheelchair access Very good; some wheelchairs available. Extensive accessibility information on Web site. Special comments Free 7–10 p.m. Friday; free to seniors first Monday of the month. Author's rating A special-interest collection, but a fine one; ★★★★½. How much time to allow 1½–2 hours.

DESCRIPTION AND COMMENTS This astonishing collection of more than 1,700 paintings, sculptures, and textiles from the mountainous tribes of Tibet, Nepal, Bhutan, Mongolia, China, India, and Pakistan was assembled over 30 years by New Yorkers Donald and Shelley Rubin, who fell in love with a painting of White Tara, guide of pilgrims, that they saw in a window. (Astonishingly, they didn't make their first actual trip to Tibet until 2002.) The museum, six years and $160 million in the renovation, is housed in the old Barney's department store, and the spiral staircase design has been retained; but now, open and airy, it reflects the Buddhist concept of rising through stages of enlightenment to the nirvana of the fifth-floor gallery.

Exhibits tend to emphasize paintings of Buddhas, demons, avatars, and protectors, many of them brilliantly colored, which may entice younger children who see them as cartoons or anime art. (A step-by-step "coloring" exhibit explains how the ritualized paintings are created.) A few children may find some of the demons a little scary, but most will be fascinated by the exotic, masklike features.

TOURING TIPS   The cafe offers light Asian-fusion fare and a menu of boutique teas. The gift shop stocks lovely belts, beaded skullcaps, strings of gumball-sized turquoise beads, ring boxes, carpets, even cabinets.

For those particularly interested in this field, **Tibet House,** which has its own galleries of art and sculpture and a small bookshop, is an easy walk away at 22 West 15th Street (☎ 212-807-0563; **www.tibethouse.org**).

St. Patrick's Cathedral   ★★½

APPEAL BY AGE	PRESCHOOL ½	GRADE SCHOOL ★★	TEENS ★★
YOUNG ADULTS ★★½	OVER 30 ★★★		SENIORS ★★★

Fifth Avenue between 50th and 51st streets, Midtown East;
☎ 212-753-2261; www.saintpatrickscathedral.org

Type of attraction The largest decorated Gothic-style Catholic cathedral in the United States. **Nearest subway station** 47th–50th Street–Rockefeller Center or 51st Street. **Admission** Free. **Hours** Daily, 6:30 a.m.–8:45 p.m. **When to go** Late morning or midafternoon to avoid interrupting services. **Wheelchair access** Good. **Author's rating** Although this clearly has greater resonance for Catholic visitors, it is quite beautiful and well worth a visit for anyone, if only as a rest between other attractions. If you can combine your visit with an organ recital or other music, it's even better; ★★. **How much time to allow** 30–45 minutes.

DESCRIPTION AND COMMENTS   This cathedral was designed by James Renwick before the Civil War; but it was not until 1888 that the 330-foot spires were completed; the Stations of the Cross won a prize in the religious-art competition at the 1893 Chicago World's Fair. This looks almost as much like a fairy-tale castle as a cathedral, it's full of spires and arches and stained glass. Among the highlights are its huge and transporting organ (nearly 8,000 pipes) and the 26-foot Rose Window, both right over the main Fifth Avenue entrance; the Pietà in the rear near the Lady Chapel, which has its own set of gorgeous stained-glass windows; and the all-bronze baldachin that protects the high altar. Altogether there are 70 stained-glass windows, more than half from Chartres and Nantes.

TOURING TIPS So much of the cathedral's power comes from the windows that sunlight (or reflected snow) really makes a difference; try to avoid going on a rainy day. Walk-in tours are offered many days; check the Web site for schedules.

St. Paul's Chapel   ★★★½

APPEAL BY AGE	PRESCHOOL ½	GRADE SCHOOL ★★	TEENS ★★
YOUNG ADULTS ★★★	OVER 30 ★★★		SENIORS ★★★

Broadway at Fulton Street, Lower Manhattan; ☎ 212-233-4164; www.saintpaulschapel.org

Type of attraction Small, remarkably peaceful pre-Revolutionary church. **Nearest subway station** Cortlandt or Fulton Street. **Admission** Free; donations requested for concerts. **Hours** Monday–Friday, 10 a.m.–6 p.m.; Saturday, 8 a.m.–3 p.m.; Sunday, 7 a.m.–3 p.m. **When to go** Anytime. **Special comments** George Washington's private pew and a few artifacts are preserved here. **Wheelchair access** Limited. **Author's rating** ★★★★. **How much time to allow** 30 minutes.

DESCRIPTION AND COMMENTS   You might almost walk right by this little church without noticing it; it's besieged by construction. But it's a blessing in its own right—warmly though simply painted, the wood lit by Waterford crystal chandeliers, and President Washington's box unobtrusively roped off. It dates from the mid-1760s, and in one of those ironies of history, is purely Georgian—the style named for the kings New Yorkers would shortly renounce. It's modeled on St. Martin-in-the-Fields in London's Trafalgar Square and, like St. Martin's, often hosts concerts. It's one of the very few buildings to have survived the great fire of 1776, not to mention 9/11. In fact, it became a special sanctuary for rescue workers and support staff in the horrific days following the attacks.

Although it's open only on the third Thursday of the month from 4 to 6 p.m., St. Paul's Labyrinth offers a half-hour's calm amid the crush.

TOURING TIPS Don't enter, as most people do, right off Broadway; that's actually the altar end. Walk around the yard (the cemetery once reached all the way to the river, providing a much grander setting) and come in at the "rear"; the effect is much more dramatic.

kids South Street Seaport and Museum   ★★

APPEAL BY AGE	PRESCHOOL ½	GRADE SCHOOL ★★	TEENS ★★
YOUNG ADULTS ★★★★	OVER 30 ★★★		SENIORS ★★

Water Street between John Street and Peck Slip, Lower Manhattan; general information ☎ 212-732-7678; www.southstreetseaport.com (museum ☎ 212-748-8600; www.southstreetseaportmuseum.org)

Type of attraction Combination historic district, shopping mall, and maritime museum. **Nearest subway station** Fulton Street. **Admission** *Museum:* $8 adults,

$6 seniors and students, $4 children ages 5–12. **Hours** *Mall:* Monday–Saturday, 10 a.m.–7 p.m.; Sunday, 11 a.m.–6 p.m. *Museum:* November–March: Friday–Sunday, 10 a.m.–5 p.m.; Monday, Schermerhorn Row Galleries only open, 10 a.m.–5 p.m.; closed Tuesday–Thursday; April–October: Tuesday–Sunday, 10 a.m.–6 p.m.; closed Monday. **When to go** Anytime. **Wheelchair access** Good. **Special comments** Restaurants and bars may be open later. Free museum programs third Friday of the month, 5–9 p.m. **Author's rating** ★★. **How much time to allow** 1½–4 hours.

DESCRIPTION AND COMMENTS   This is sort of a miniature theme park, covering 11 square blocks (some of them cobblestone) of real and reproduced seafaring New York. (It's a Rouse development, like Boston's Faneuil Hall and Baltimore's Harborplace.) In its heyday, the first half of the 19th century, it was so busy that South Street was nicknamed the "street of sails." But once steamships took over, the deeper-water piers on the Hudson River side gradually drew ship traffic away from this area. The old Pilothouse is now the visitor center, where you pick up the free guide maps; the old Pier 17 is a food court and shopping mall. One of the nicest stretches, in terms of architectural preservation, is Schermerhorn Row—Federal-style warehouses on the south side of Fulton Street between Front and South streets dating from the very early 19th century. (Expansion has uncovered such unique artifacts as Gaelic graffiti.) They were later used as hotels and shops and are now boutiques and restaurants.

Quite frankly, most of the good stuff here is free: the view from Pier 17; the sight of craftsmen building and restoring small boats; and the view of the Brooklyn Bridge, which took 13 years to build and the lives of 20 of the 600 workers, many from the bends. (John Roebling, who designed it, had his foot crushed in a freak accident on the pier here just before construction was to begin in 1869 and died three weeks later.) The best reason to buy the museum ticket is to tour the tall ships anchored there: the 1911 *Peking,* one of the largest sailing ships ever built, and the three-masted *Wavertree* of 1885. If you want to take a harbor tour from here, on the schooner *Pioneer* (March to November only), you can either make reservations up to two weeks in advance (☎ 212-748-8590) or take a chance on unreserved tickets at 10 a.m. Other commercial cruises also leave from here.

One of the old buildings has been turned over to long-term exhibits (for example, Bodies), but tickets are additional, and pricey.

TOURING TIPS   Walk to the corner of Peck Slip and Front Street and look at the mural on the Con Ed substation; it's a trompe l'oeil painting of the Brooklyn Bridge. Also look for the lighthouse at the intersection of Fulton and Water streets. A memorial to the 1,500 passengers of the *Titanic* who perished in the 1912 catastrophe, it originally overlooked the harbor from the Seamen's Church but was moved here in 1976.

Statue of Liberty–Liberty Island ★★★★★

APPEAL BY AGE	PRESCHOOL ★	GRADE SCHOOL ★★★½	TEENS ★★★½
YOUNG ADULTS ★★★★½		OVER 30 ★★★★★	SENIORS ★★★★★

New York Harbor, Lower Manhattan; ☎ 212-363-3200; ticket and ferry information ☎ 877-523-9849; www.statueofliberty.org or www.nps.gov/stli (for ticket and ferry information, www.statuecruises.com)

Type of attraction America's premier symbol of freedom. **Nearest subway station** Bowling Green or South Ferry. **Admission** No entrance fee; ferry tickets are $12 adults, $10 seniors ages 62 and over, $5 children ages 4–12; children age 3 and under free. Crown access $3. **Hours** Daily, 9:30 a.m.–5 p.m. (last ferry at 3 p.m.); extended hours during summer and on some holidays; closed Christmas. **When to go** Weekdays. **Special comments** Its Independence Day 2009 re-opening was reason for celebration. Unfortunately, at press time, the elevator from ground level up to the museum was going to be out of service for some time; check the Web site. **Author's rating** It does pack an emotional punch, and if you can walk the stairs (for the time being), it's worth the wait to look out the Crown; ★★★. **How much time to allow** 1½–4 hours.

DESCRIPTION AND COMMENTS This most famous symbol of liberty is also a reminder of the revolutionary fervor required to create it. It was a gift from the republic of France, a massive feat of art (sculpted by visionary Frédéric-Auguste Bartholdi, who used his mother as the model for that stern yet merciful face) and engineering (erected by Gustave Eiffel of that landmark tower in Paris). It was formally unveiled on October 28, 1886, and restored for its centennial at a cost of $70 million plus $2 million for the fireworks. However, the torch had corroded so badly that a replica, covered in 24-carat gold, was put in its place; the original is in the lobby.

There are four stations, so to speak: the outside of the base, engraved with Emma Lazarus's poem *The New Colossus* ("Give me your tired, your poor . . ."); the exhibit hall inside the base, with its record of Bartholdi's 17-year struggle and the many patriotic and commercial uses his figure has been put to; the observation decks at the top of the pedestal; and the view from the crown—the crowning touch, so to speak. Bartholdi's title for the massive sculpture was *Liberty Enlightening the World,* and the crown's seven rays represent the seven continents and the seven seas.

While you're waiting, you can ponder the numbers: The statue itself is a little more than 150 feet tall, twice that counting the pedestal and base, and it weighs 156 tons—31 tons of which represent the copper sheeting that covers the frame. There are 354 steps from the pedestal up into the crown, the equivalent of 22 stories. And don't feel bad about your own nose; hers is four and a half feet long.

TOURING TIPS Note that the last ferries leave Lower Manhattan at 3 p.m. (The only consolation for having to wait until late in winter is that you'll see the Manhattan skyline begin to light up. Cafe on-site.

Trinity Church ★★★

APPEAL BY AGE	PRESCHOOL ½	GRADE SCHOOL ★	TEENS ★★
YOUNG ADULTS ★★½	OVER 30 ★★★		SENIORS ★★★

Broadway at Wall Street, Lower Manhattan; ☎ 212-602-0872; www.trinitywallstreet.org

Type of attraction Fine Gothic Revival church from the mid–19th century. **Nearest subway station** Wall Street or Rector Street. **Admission** Free. **Hours** Monday–Friday, 7 a.m.–6 p.m.; Saturday, 8 a.m.–4 p.m.; Sunday, 7 a.m.–4 p.m.; free tours daily at 2 p.m. For group tours, call ☎ 212-602-0872. **When to go** Midafternoon; Tuesday–Wednesday evenings for bell ringing. **Special comments** A lovely short respite for the weary tourist. **Author's rating ★★★**. **How much time to allow** 30 minutes.

DESCRIPTION AND COMMENTS This church, as much as any other single edifice, is responsible for the Gothic Revival craze of the 19th century; its balance of interior extravagance (carved wood, stained glass, and ornate stone) and exterior restraint (itself a metaphor for religious faith) is striking. Actually, this is the third church on this site: the first was built in 1698 and burned in the conflagration of 1776, and the second was razed in 1839. The brass doors are a tribute to Ghiberti's Gates of Paradise at the Duomo in Florence and serve as a memorial to John Jacob Astor III. A 15th-century altar and early Renaissance triptych are in the baptistry, and, amazingly, the stained-glass windows were made on-site, in a shed out back. The 280-foot steeple pointed unrivaled to heaven until the late 19th century. Even surrounded by the towers of international finance, it has a certain obdurate confidence.

Romantics take note: this is where founding Federalist and dueling victim Alexander Hamilton is buried, along with inventor Robert Fulton and other luminaries. The father of poet Clement Clarke Moore was rector here, and every December there is a dramatic reading of "The Night before Christmas."

TOURING TIPS This is a wonderful place to hear music. There are vocal concerts Thursdays at 1 p.m., and bell-changing rehearsals Tuesday and Wednesday at 6:30 to 8:30 p.m. and before and after 11:45 a.m. Sunday service. There are also organ concerts; check listings for special events.

Whitney Museum of American Art ★★★★

APPEAL BY AGE	PRESCHOOL ½	GRADE SCHOOL ★★½	TEENS ★★★
YOUNG ADULTS ★★★	OVER 30 ★★★½		SENIORS ★★★½

Madison Avenue at 75th Street, Upper East Side; ☎ 800-944-8639 or 212-570-3676; www.whitney.org

Type of attraction World-class collection of 20th-century American art. **Nearest subway station** 77th Street. **Admission** $18 adults, $12 college students and ages 62 and older; ages 18 and under free. **Hours** Wednesday–Thursday,

11 a.m.–6 p.m.; Friday, 1–9 p.m.; Saturday and Sunday, 11 a.m.–6 p.m.; closed Monday and Tuesday. **When to go** Anytime. **Wheelchair access**: Good; some wheelchairs available. Silent ASL tours first Saturday of the month (☎ 212-570-7789). **Special comments** Pay what you wish Friday, 6–9 p.m. **Author's rating** More ingratiating than it appears from the outside; ★★★★. **How much time to allow** 2½–3 hours.

DESCRIPTION AND COMMENTS   There is much to be said for an insider's eye, and because the Whitney was founded by sculptor Gertrude Vanderbilt Whitney, its collection of modern American art in many opinions rivals the international collection of the Museum of Modern Art. (She founded a new museum when the prestigious and no doubt somewhat pompous Metropolitan turned down her offer to donate her whole collection.)

Compared to some of the city's more traditional museums, this inverted concrete pyramid seems a little forbidding, though now that there is the staggered-box New Museum as well, this seems more play- ful. Which is appropriate: this is a collection with a great deal of humor. Though it has many serious and dark pieces as well, it may surprise you how interested younger patrons may be in the cartoonlike Lichtensteins or robust Thomas Hart Bentons, the boxing art of George Bellows, Warhol's post-advertising art and other familiar elements of Pop Art, O'Keeffe's flowers, or the superrealistic Hopper paintings—or even many of the brilliantly colored abstracts. The famous Calder assemblage called *Circus* that used to be mounted just inside the main entrance has been moved upstairs; it is still the only piece on permanent display.

TOURING TIPS   There are free gallery tours at irregular hours; check the Web site. At press time, a restaurant by Danny Meyer's Union Square group was under construction on the lower level.

PART SEVEN

DINING *and* RESTAURANTS

NYC EATS:
Everything, Anything, All the Time

TALK ABOUT THE MELTING POT: New York's the 1,000-burner stove. With food on offer from every part of the globe, presented on everything from paper plates to porcelain platters, New York boasts myriad culinary delights. But whether it's comparing chorizo with andouille or arguing about where to find a decent *dosa*, obsession with food and the chefs who prepare it is as much a New York tourist attraction as the Statue of Liberty—and quite possibly a tourist *trap*. Therefore, it's best to know the guidelines:

- **Don't judge an establishment by its tabletop.** Some of the tastiest food is served on Formica, while mediocrity can be hidden with an expanse of starched linen. Price doesn't necessarily reflect quality, and many mid-range restaurants tend to be the weakest link in the dining spectrum.
- **Understand the difference between fad and revolutionary gastro-delights.** Foie gras–stuffed burgers were a fad; sushi, although still trendy, is here to stay and is currently opening the door for various other types of Japanese fare to be appreciated. Similarly, tapas are an *it* dining experience and will probably manage to survive once the wave of fashion subside. The point is that diners should beware of overdressed and overhyped menu items, unless the chef is known for being particularly experimental and opts to serve anchovy sorbet with barbecued sweetbreads.
- **Remember that less is (very often) more.** Fine food doesn't have to be intricate; it just needs the freshest ingredients served with flair.
- **Know the playing field.** Manhattan alone has more than 4,000 restaurants, and the range of food and flavors is exhilarating. The array of indigenous kitchens testifies to the range of people who have chosen

to settle on the New York shores. Feel safe in the knowledge that if you have a yearning for artichokes or crave a zucchini pie, you'll find your dish and please your taste buds somewhere in the metropolis.

- **Make the effort to go the extra mile to find the best dim sum** (Flushing, Queens), an amazing falafel (Atlantic Avenue, Brooklyn), or real pierogi (Greenpoint, Brooklyn). For a quick culinary tour, visit Sunset Park, Brooklyn, for Chinese, Vietnamese, and Mexican. If you're in town between May and September, visit the soccer fields in Red Hook, Brooklyn, on the weekend to savor some of the best home-cooked Honduran, Mexican, and other Latin American–inspired dishes. Bedford-Stuyvesant has soul food and renowned roti (**Ali's Roti Shop,** 1267 Fulton Street; ☎ 718-783-0316). Indian food can be found not just on East Sixth Street but also in the "Curry Hill" area between East 26th and East 33rd streets, along Third, Lexington, and Park avenues in Manhattan, and in Jackson Heights in Queens. You can find tasty Italian throughout the city, but Staten Island, not generally a mecca for discerning gourmets, is considered by natives to have a few exceptional Southern Italian establishments; the same can be said for areas in the Bronx, including Arthur Avenue.

unofficial **TIP**
For specific advice on far-flung underground dining and opinions on every type of food imaginable, consult the bulletin boards at **www.chowhound.com.**

- **Above all:** Enjoy your food, and come back to New York for seconds.

This chapter provides some insight and reviews a few highlights, but if you'd like more information, check the *Village Voice* (**www .villagevoice.com**), *Time Out* (**newyork.timeout.com**), and *New York* magazine (**www.nymag.com**) reviews, or the Dining Out section in the Wednesday edition of the *New York Times.* Also try **www.citysearch .com, www.urbanspoon.com,** and **www.yelp.com.**

PICKLES *or* PANACHE

A TRIP TO THE BIG APPLE ISN'T COMPLETE without tasting quintessential New York fare, such as a bagel, a slice of pizza, or a hot dog, as well as reserving a table at a fashionable and/or established kitchen. Our definition of "fashionable" doesn't include the spots that survive purely on the whim of the fickle. Rather it encompasses the enviable combination of excellent food, a pleasing ambience, and a steady flow of people, many of whom may be famous, which gives the place an added mystique. People wait months to get a reservation at renowned chef Thomas Keller's **Per Se** (10 Columbus Circle; ☎ 212-823-9335; **www.perseny.com**); the food is sublime, creative, and impeccably presented. Although it's not as difficult a spot to get a seat in, **Le Périgord** (405 East 52nd Street; ☎ 212-755-6244;

www.leperigord.com), one of the last bastions in New York City of traditional French cuisine, has maintained its level of food and service for years. As for New York landmarks, restaurants that have stood the test of time include the **Four Seasons** (99 East 52nd Street; ☎ 212-754-9494; **www.fourseasonsrestaurant.com**), **21 Club** (21 West 52nd Street; ☎ 212-582-7200; **www.21club.com**), and **Keens Steakhouse** (72 West 36th Street; ☎ 212-947-3636; **www.keens.com**).

At the other end of the spectrum, but just as important, are the staples of New York snacks, light meals, or brunches. If you can, try a New York bagel. **H & H Bagels** (2239 Broadway; ☎ 212-595-8003; **www.hhbagels.com**), a perennial NY favorite, is great, as is **Murray's Bagels** (500 Sixth Avenue; ☎ 212-462-2830; **www.murraysbagels.com**), offering delicious, hand-rolled bagels from plain to "everything," with cream cheese and lox, otherwise known as smoked salmon. Hot dogs can be had at many a stand, but traditionalists like to go to **Nathan's Famous** hot dogs on the pier at Coney Island in Brooklyn (1310 Surf Avenue; ☎ 718-946-2202; **www.nathansfamous.com**). Besides bagels, some of the Eastern European selections include knishes—that is, potato pies (**Yonah Schimmel's,** 137 East Houston Street; ☎ 212-477-2858; **www.knishery.com**)—pickles (**Pickle Guys,** 49 Essex Street; ☎ 212-656-9739; **www.nycpickleguys.com**), and whitefish salad (**Sable's Smoked Fish,** 1489 Second Avenue; ☎ 212-249-6177; **sablesnyc.rapidorders.com;** and **Russ & Daughters,** 179 East Houston Street; ☎ 212-475-4880; **www.russanddaughters.com**). For another New York dining experience, have lunch at a coffee shop and wash it down with a milk shake or chocolate egg cream (seltzer, milk, and chocolate syrup). You'll feel the fast New York pace, and if you're lucky, you'll get a pleasantly churlish New Yorker as a waiter. If the bill is more than $27 for two people, then it's not a typical coffee shop.

HOT SPOTS

FASHIONABLE, AS DEFINED PREVIOUSLY, can sometimes mix with hot spot, but we find that some New York hot spots are more about the hype and the clientele than the food. That said, as the NY restaurant business is very competitive, an experienced and/or famous chef does wonders for the reservation line.

Minetta Tavern (113 MacDougal Street; ☎ 212-475-3850; **www.minettatavernny.com**), a favorite haunt of writers from the 1930s and '40s, languished in recent years on a block of New York University bars and cheap eats until Keith McNally of **Balthazar** (see page 292) fame stepped in, shined its surfaces, updated its menu, and turned on the PR machine. Scoring a

unofficial **TIP**
New York is awash with food carts, most indistinguishable from the next. But for those on the run and in the know, a few stand out. If there's a line, there's a reason. Just have a look at the masses waiting to eat from the legendary halal cart on 53rd and Sixth. Heck, it's even spawned a fan site (**www.53rdand6th.com**).

reservation is now a chore. Grand and glittering seafood palaces are not a thing of the past, as evidenced by **Marea** (240 Central Park South; ☎ 212-582-5100; **www.marea-nyc.com**), the expensive and quickly celebrated new venture from Michael White. One place that has managed to sustain its early magnetic appeal is **The Modern,** restaurateur Danny Meyer's dining gem at the Museum of Modern Art (9 West 53rd Street; ☎ 212-333-1220; **www.themodernnyc.com**), where the chef was the recipient of the 2009 James Beard Foundation Award for best New York City chef. David Chang, who can do no wrong in many meat-lovers' eyes, has expanded his imaginative **Momofuku** (**www.momofuku.com**) empire to include **Noodle Bar** (171 First Avenue), **Ssäm Bar** (see Momofuku Ssäm Bar, page 331), **Ko** (163 First Avenue), **Milk Bar** (207 Second Avenue), and **Má Pêche** at Chambers hotel. If you'd like to dine in stylish hotels, we can also recommend dinner at **Asia de Cuba** at Morgans (237 Madison Avenue; ☎ 212-726-7755; **www.chinagrillmgt.com**) and **The Standard Grill** at the The Standard Hotel (846 Washington Street; ☎ 212-645-4100; **www.thestandardgrill.com**).

WHERE'S THE BEEF?

THE POPULARITY OF THE ATKINS DIET has waned, but steak houses are still enjoying the renaissance that Atkins helped kindle. **Peter Luger Steak House** (see page 342) is a favorite, its no-nonsense waitstaff serving some of the best porterhouse in the country. Wolfgang Zweiner, former headwaiter at Peter Luger's, has opened two of his own places, both simply called **Wolfgang's Steakhouse** (4 Park Avenue, ☎ 212-889-3369; and 409 Greenwich Street, ☎ 212-925-0350; **www.wolfgangssteakhouse.com**). The meat, other food, and ambience are outstanding. Another meat institution is **Old Homestead Steak House** (56 Ninth Avenue; ☎ 212-242-9040; **www.theoldhomesteadsteakhouse.com**), where the jury is still out as to whether it matches or surpasses the others in its meaty merits, but it *is* the place to get a Kobe beef hamburger. After renovating, **Aretsky's Patroon** (160 East 46th Street; ☎ 212-883-7373; **www.patroonrestaurant.com**) altered the menu to add more than just steak, but it still has a good meaty base and a rooftop terrace for cigar smokers. For a very masculine Midtown chophouse, try **Ben Benson's Steakhouse** (123 West 52nd Street; ☎ 212-581-8888; **www.benbensons.com**). For meat with a South American flavor, try Brazilian *rodizio* at **Churrascaria Plataforma** (see page 303).

THE DRESS CODE: SILK OR SNEAKERS

IT'S SAID THAT ANYTHING GOES IN NEW YORK, and in many cases, this is true. However, some establishments expect people to abide by a certain decorum that requires a jacket; we've noted where this is the case. Also, some places have jackets and occasionally ties on hand to loan, so as not to turn away business. Dressy casual to casual and/or funky are usually the norm for most of our profiled restaurants. However, should you be dining in one of these places on business, then your own sense of the importance of the meeting should dictate your clothing.

RESERVATIONS?

AT THE HOTTEST TABLES IN TOWN, reservations are still determined by who you are or who you know, especially if you're looking to sneak in at the last minute. Yet we are happy to report that many of New York's finest restaurants have gotten a little more democratic in their reservations policies. The days of battling busy signals and surly hosts and hostesses are (mostly) over, thanks to **www.opentable .com.** A Web site dedicated to finding and placing reservations, it currently features 800 Manhattan restaurants, with more added every day. Simply search by restaurant name, neighborhood, or cuisine, and then pick the date and time you would like to dine. If your preferred hour or day is not available, the site allows you to find the closest time you can be accommodated. *Note:* The site allows you to book no more than 30 days in advance, and the most popular spots will fill up almost immediately. If you miss your chance, check back periodically, as cancellations will put some tables back into play. And remember, there are still plenty of restaurants that don't take reservations at all, and many small eateries that don't even have Web sites.

WHERE TO FIND A DEAL FOR A MEAL

TRUE TO THE ENTREPRENEURIAL SPIRIT, many NY restaurants, eager to attract a hungry crowd, offer some super deals at lunch or dinner for pre-theater and prix-fixe meals. Two of the best prix-fixe lunches in town are at **Jean-Georges** (see page 318), offering a superb dining experience for $28 in the Nougatine dining area, and **Chennai Garden** (see page 303), providing a $6.95 buffet of wonderfully fresh and tasty kosher vegetarian Indian food. During January and June, many top restaurants sign up to be part of the twice-a-year, citywide Restaurant Week, which allows lucky diners to eat lunch, dinner, or both at first-rate restaurants for a fixed price. Look for ads, and check **www.nycvisit.com** for more info.

The RESTAURANTS

OUR FAVORITE NEW YORK RESTAURANTS

THIS SURVEY OF MORE THAN 100 of New York's niftiest nosheries covers a wide spectrum of price categories, global origins, and New York neighborhoods, including tried-and-true oldies, popular trendies, offbeat ethnics, and local favorites. We give an overall impression of food and mood and what it will cost. Don't be surprised if some of our menu recommendations are not available on a particular day; many New York restaurants change their menus often to take advantage of ultra-fresh seasonal offerings. And though we've worked overtime to ensure the freshness of our opinions (places were checked at the very last minute before publication), do bear in mind that restaurants are works in progress. They're not static and are essentially moving targets.

We've developed detailed profiles for the best and most interesting restaurants in town. Each profile features an easily scanned heading that allows you to check out the restaurant's name, cuisine, star rating, cost, quality rating, and value rating.

CUISINE The more entrenched imported cuisines are fragmenting— French into bistro fare and even Provençal, "new Continental" into regional American and "eclectic"—while others have broadened and fused: Spanish and South American into Nuevo Latino, for instance. In some cases, we use a broad classification but clarify the fare with additional description.

OVERALL RATING This encompasses the entire dining experience: style, service, and ambience as well as the taste, presentation, and quality of the food. Five stars is the highest rating possible. Four-star restaurants are exceptional, three-star restaurants well above average. Two-star restaurants are good. One star indicates an average restaurant that demonstrates an unusual capability in some area—for example, an otherwise unmemorable place that has great barbecued chicken.

PRICE This provides a comparative sense of the cost of a complete meal: for our purposes, an entree with a side and soup or salad. Appetizers, desserts, drinks, and tips are excluded.

Inexpensive	$20 or less per person
Moderate	$21–$40 per person
Expensive	$40–$75 per person
Very expensive	More than $75 per person

QUALITY RATING Food quality is rated on a scale of one to five stars, five being the best. If you want the best food available, and cost isn't an issue, you need look no further than the quality ratings.

VALUE RATING If, on the other hand, you are looking for both quality and value, then you should check the value rating. The value ratings are defined as follows:

★★★★★	Exceptional value; a real bargain
★★★★	Good value
★★★	Fair value; you get exactly what you pay for
★★	Somewhat overpriced
★	Significantly overpriced

NEIGHBORHOOD This designation will give you a general idea of where each profiled restaurant is located. We've divided New York into the following neighborhoods:

Financial District

SoHo and TriBeCa

Chinatown, Little Italy, and the Lower East Side

Greenwich Village

The East Village

Chelsea

Union Square

Gramercy Park and Madison Square

Midtown West, Times Square, and the Theater District

Midtown East

Upper West Side

Upper East Side

Morningside Heights, Hamilton Heights, and Harlem

Brooklyn

Queens

The Bronx

PAYMENT We've listed the type of payment accepted at each restaurant using the following code: AE equals American Express (Optima), CB equals Carte Blanche, D equals Discover, DC equals Diners Club, MC equals MasterCard, and V equals Visa.

WHO'S INCLUDED Restaurants in New York open and close at an alarming rate. So, for the most part, we have tried to confine our list to establishments with a proven track record over a substantial period of time. The exceptions here are the newer offspring of the demigods of the culinary world—these places are destined to last, at least until our next update. Newer or changed establishments that demonstrate staying power and consistency will be profiled in subsequent editions. Also, the list is highly selective. Failure to include a particular place does not necessarily indicate that the restaurant is not good, only that it was not ranked by us to be among the best in its genre. Detailed profiles of individual restaurants follow in alphabetical order at the end of this chapter.

The Best New York Restaurants

TYPE AND NAME	OVERALL RATING	PRICE	QUALITY RATING	VALUE RATING
AMERICAN				
Cookshop	★★★★	Exp	★★★½	★★★½
Gramercy Tavern	★★★½	Exp	★★★★	★★★
Blue Water Grill	★★★	Mod	★★★★	★★★★
Blue Ribbon	★★★	Mod	★★★½	★★★★
Penelope	★★½	Inexp	★★★	★★★★
EJ's Luncheonette	★★	Inexp	★★★½	★★★½
Gray's Papaya	★½	Inexp	★★★½	★★★★★
AMERICAN SOUTHWEST				
Mesa Grill	★★★	Exp	★★★½	★★★
ASIAN				
Zen Palate	★★½	Inexp	★★★½	★★★★
AUSTRIAN				
Café Sabarsky	★★★★	Mod/exp	★★★½	★★★
BARBECUE				
Dinosaur Bar-B-Que	★★★	Mod	★★★½	★★★★½
BELGIAN				
BXL Café	★★★	Mod	★★★	★★★
Petite Abeille	★★½	Inexp	★★★★	★★★★½
BISTRO				
Artisanal	★★★½	Mod/exp	★★★★	★★★
Tartine	★★★	Inexp	★★★★	★★★½
Pastis	★★½	Mod	★★★½	★★★
BRAZILIAN				
Churrascaria Plataforma	★★★	Mod	★★★★	★★★★
BRITISH				
The Spotted Pig	★★★½	Mod/exp	★★★★	★★★½
Tea & Sympathy	★★★	Inexp/mod	★★★½	★★★
CHINESE (SEE ALSO DIM SUM)				
Ping's	★★★★	Mod	★★★★½	★★★★½
Shun Lee West, Shun Lee Café	★★★½	Mod/exp	★★★★	★★★★
Joe's Shanghai	★★★	Mod	★★★★½	★★★★★

TYPE AND NAME	OVERALL RATING	PRICE	QUALITY RATING	VALUE RATING
CHINESE *(CONTINUED)*				
Grand Sichuan International	★★★	Mod	★★★★	★★★★★
CREOLE				
Stan's Place	★★★	Inexp/mod	★★★	★★★
CUBAN				
Margon Restaurant	★★	Inexp	★★★½	★★★★★
DIM SUM (SEE ALSO CHINESE)				
Ping's	★★★★	Mod	★★★★½	★★★★½
ETHIOPIAN				
Meskerem	★★★	Inexp/mod	★★★½	★★★½
FRENCH				
Le Bernardin	★★★★½	Very exp	★★★★	★★★
Jean-Georges	★★★★½	Exp	★★★★½	★★★
Eleven Madison Park	★★★★	Exp	★★★★½	★★★★
Veritas	★★★★	Exp	★★★★½	★★★★
Il Buco	★★★★	Exp	★★★★½	★★★
Café Boulud	★★★½	Exp	★★★★½	★★★½
Balthazar	★★★½	Mod/exp	★★★★	★★★★
Degustation	★★★½	Mod/exp	★★★★	★★★★
Bouchon Bakery	★★★	Inexp/mod	★★★½	★★★★½
Les Halles	★★½	Mod/exp	★★★½	★★★
La Boîte en Bois	★★½	Mod	★★★½	★★★★
GREEK				
Kefi	★★★½	Inexp/mod	★★★★	★★★★½
Molyvos	★★★½	Exp	★★★★	★★★★
Symposium	★★★	Inexp/mod	★★★½	★★★★
INDIAN				
Tabla	★★★★	Exp	★★★★½	★★★★
Tamarind	★★★½	Exp	★★★★	★★★
Chennai Garden	★★★	Inexp	★★★½	★★★★
Jackson Diner	★★½	Inexp/mod	★★★½	★★★★★
IRISH				
Molly's Pub & Restaurant	★★★	Mod	★★★★	★★★★

The Best NY Restaurants (continued)

TYPE AND NAME	OVERALL RATING	PRICE	QUALITY RATING	VALUE RATING
ITALIAN				
Il Buco	★★★★	Exp	★★★★½	★★★
Piccola Venezia	★★★★	Exp	★★★★½	★★★
Sfoglia	★★★★	Exp	★★★★½	★★★★
Scarpetta	★★★★	Exp	★★★★½	★★★★½
Noodle Pudding	★★★★	Mod	★★★★	★★★½
Babbo	★★★½	Exp	★★★★	★★★★½
Il Mulino	★★★½	Exp	★★★★½	★★★★½
Pó	★★★½	Mod	★★★★	★★★★
The Spotted Pig	★★★½	Mod/exp	★★★★	★★★½
Osteria del Circo	★★★	Exp	★★★★	★★★
Paola's	★★★	Mod/exp	★★★★	★★★★
Piccolo Angolo	★★★	Mod	★★★★	★★★½
Becco	★★★	Mod	★★★½	★★★★★
Orso	★★★	Mod	★★★½	★★★
Gigino	★★½	Mod	★★★	★★★½
JAPANESE				
Nobu	★★★★	Exp	★★★★½	★★★
Sachiko's on Clinton	★★★★	Mod/exp	★★★½	★★★
Tomoe Sushi	★★★½	Mod	★★★★	★★★★
Soba-ya	★★★½	Inexp/mod	★★★½	★★★★
Sushi-Ann	★★★½	Exp	★★★★	★★★★
Menchanko-Tei	★★	Inexp	★★★½	★★★★
JEWISH DELI				
Mr. Broadway Kosher Deli	★★★	Mod	★★★★	★★★★★
2nd Ave Deli	★★½	Mod	★★★★	★★★
KOREAN				
Momofuku Ssäm Bar	★★★★½	Mod/exp	★★★★½	★★★★
Woo Chon	★★★	Mod	★★★★	★★★★
Mandoo Bar	★★	Inexp	★★★	★★★★★
LATIN AMERICAN				
Calle Ocho	★★★	Mod	★★★★	★★★½
Café con Leche	★★½	Inexp	★★★★	★★★★★

TYPE AND NAME	OVERALL RATING	PRICE	QUALITY RATING	VALUE RATING
MALAYSIAN				
Fatty Crab	★★★	Mod/exp	★★★★	★★★
Penang	★★½	Mod	★★★½	★★★
Jaya Malaysian	★★	Inexp	★★★½	★★★★½
MEDITERRANEAN				
Picholine	★★★★	Exp	★★★★½	★★★
The Tree House Restaurant	★★	Inexp/mod	★★★½	★★★½
MEXICAN				
Rosa Mexicano	★★★	Mod	★★★★	★★★
Mexicana Mama	★★★	Mod	★★★½	★★★
MIDDLE EASTERN				
Sahara East	★★½	Mod	★★★★	★★★★
MOROCCAN				
Café Mogador	★★½	Mod	★★★★	★★★★★
NEW AMERICAN				
The River Café	★★★★★	Very exp	★★★★★	★★★★½
Blue Hill	★★★★	Exp	★★★★½	★★★★
Union Square Café	★★★★	Exp	★★★★½	★★★★
Gotham Bar & Grill	★★★½	Exp	★★★★	★★★
PIZZA				
Patsy's Pizza	★★★	Inexp	★★★★½	★★★★★
Kesté	★★★	Mod	★★★★	★★★½
Otto	★★★	Mod	★★★★	★★
RUSSIAN				
Firebird	★★★	Exp	★★★★	★★★★
Petrossian	★★★	Exp	★★★½	★★★
SCANDINAVIAN				
Aquavit	★★★★½	Very exp	★★★★★	★★★½
SEAFOOD				
Le Bernardin	★★★★½	Very exp	★★★★	★★★
Atlantic Grill	★★★★	Exp	★★★★	★★★½
Oceana	★★★½	Exp	★★★★½	★★★
Blue Water Grill	★★★	Mod	★★★★	★★★★

The Best NY Restaurants (continued)

TYPE AND NAME	OVERALL RATING	PRICE	QUALITY RATING	VALUE RATING
SPANISH				
Il Buco	★★★★	Exp	★★★★½	★★★
Degustation	★★★½	Mod/exp	★★★★	★★★★
STEAK				
Peter Luger Steak House	★★★½	Exp	★★★★	★★★★
Les Halles	★★½	Mod/exp	★★★½	★★★
TEAROOM				
Lady Mendl's Tea Salon	★★★	Mod	★★★★	★★★
THAI				
My Thai	★★★★	Inexp	★★★★½	★★★★
Pam Real Thai Food	★★½	Inexp	★★★	★★★★½
Jasmine	★★½	Mod	★★★	★★★
VEGETARIAN				
Candle Cafe	★★★½	Inexp/mod	★★★★	★★★½
Pure Food and Wine	★★★	Exp	★★★½	★★½
Gobo	★★½	Mod	★★★½	★★★
Zen Palate	★★½	Inexp	★★★½	★★★★
VIETNAMESE				
New Pasteur	★★★½	Inexp	★★★★	★★★★★
Baoguette	★★	Inexp	★★★	★★★★½

New York Restaurants by Neighborhood

FINANCIAL DISTRICT
Gigino
Les Halles

SOHO AND TRIBECA
Balthazar
Blue Ribbon
Nobu
Petite Abeille

CHINATOWN, LITTLE ITALY, AND THE LOWER EAST SIDE
Jaya Malaysian
Joe's Shanghai
New Pasteur
Sachiko's on Clinton

GREENWICH VILLAGE
Babbo
Baoguette
Blue Hill
Fatty Crab
Gray's Papaya
Gobo
Gotham Bar & Grill
Il Mulino
Kesté
Meskerem
Mexicana Mama
Otto
Pastis
Petite Abeille
Piccolo Angolo
Pó
The Spotted Pig
Tartine
Tea & Sympathy
Tomoe Sushi

THE EAST VILLAGE
Baoguette
Café Mogador
Degustation
Il Buco
Momofuku Ssäm Bar
Sahara East
Soba-ya

CHELSEA
Cookshop
Grand Sichuan
Scarpetta

UNION SQUARE
Pure Food and Wine
Rosa Mexicano
Union Square Cafe

GRAMERCY PARK AND MADISON SQUARE
Artisanal
Baoguette
Blue Water Grill
Chennai Garden
Eleven Madison Park
Gramercy Tavern
Lady Mendl's Tea Salon
Les Halles
Mesa Grill
Molly's Pub & Restaurant
Penelope
Petite Abeille
Tabla
Tamarind
Veritas

(CONTINUED ON NEXT PAGE)

NY Restaurants by Neighborhood (cont'd)

MIDTOWN WEST, TIMES SQUARE, AND THE THEATER DISTRICT

Aquavit
Becco
BXL Café
Churrascaria Plataforma
Firebird
Gray's Papaya
Joe's Shanghai
Le Bernardin
Margon Restaurant
Menchanko-Tei
Meskerem
Molyvos
Oceana
Mr. Broadway Kosher Restaurant
Orso
Osteria del Circo
Pam Real Thai Food
Petrossian
Zen Palate

MIDTOWN EAST

Mandoo Bar
Menchanko-Tei
Rosa Mexicana
2nd Ave Deli
Sushi-Ann
Woo Chon

UPPER WEST SIDE

Bouchon Bakery
Café con Leche
Calle Ocho
EJ's Luncheonette
Fatty Crab
Gray's Papaya
Jean-Georges

Kefi
La Boîte en Bois
Penang
Picholine
Rosa Mexicana
Shun Lee West, Shun Lee Café

UPPER EAST SIDE

Atlantic Grill
Café Boulud
Café Sabarsky
Candle Cafe
EJ's Luncheonette
Gobo
Jackson Diner
Jasmine
Paola's
Penang
Saigon Grill
Sfoglia

MORNINGSIDE HEIGHTS, HAMILTON HEIGHTS, AND HARLEM

Dinosaur Bar-B-Que
Patsy's Pizza
Symposium Greek Restaurant

BROOKLYN

Blue Ribbon
Noodle Pudding
Peter Luger Steak House
The River Café
Stan's Place

QUEENS

Joe's Shanghai
My Thai
Piccola Venezia
Ping's

THE BEST . . .

The Best Brunch

- **Flatbush Farm** 76 St. Mark's Avenue, Brooklyn; ☎ 718-622-3276; www.flatbushfarm.com
- **Good Enough to Eat** 483 Amsterdam Avenue; ☎ 212-496-0163; www.goodenoughtoeat.com
- **Penelope** (see page 341)
- **Prune** 54 East First Street; ☎ 212-677-6221; **www.prunerestaurant.com**
- **Tartine** (see page 364)
- **Zoë** 90 Prince Street, ☎ 212-966-6722; **www.zoerestaurant.com**

The Best Burgers

- **Burger Joint** 119 West 56th Street (in Le Parker Meridien Hotel); ☎ 212-708-7414; **www.parkermeridien.com/eat4.php**
- **Corner Bistro** 331 West Fourth Street; ☎ 212-242-9502; cornerbistro.ypguides.net
- **Cozy Soup & Burger** 739 Broadway; ☎ 212-477-5566; www.cozysoupnburger.com
- **Joe Allen** 326 West 46th Street; ☎ 212-581-6464; www.joeallenrestaurant.com
- **Molly's Pub & Restaurant** (see page 329)
- **P. J. Clarke's** 915 Third Avenue; ☎ 212-317-1616; **www.pjclarkes.com**
- **Royale** 157 Avenue C; ☎ 212-254-6600

The Best Chinatown Restaurants

- **Grand Sichuan** 125 Canal Street; ☎ 212-625-9212
- **Joe's Ginger** 25 Pell Street; ☎ 212-285-0999; **www.joeginger.com**
- **Joe's Shanghai** (see page 318)
- **Mandarin Court** 61 Mott Street; ☎ 212-608-3838
- **New Pasteur** (see page 332)
- **Nha Trang Centre** 87 Baxter Street; ☎ 212-233-5948
- **Great N. Y. Noodle Town** 28 Bowery; ☎ 212-349-0923

The Best Cozy Tearooms

- **Alice's Tea Cup** 102 West 73rd Street, ☎ 212-799-3006; 156 East 64th Street, ☎ 212-486-9200; 220 East 81st Street, ☎ 212-734-4832; www.alicesteacup.com
- **Cha-An Tea Room** (Japanese) 230 East Ninth Street; ☎ 212-228-8030; www.chaanteahouse.com
- **Lady Mendl's Tea Salon** (see page 321)
- **Tea & Sympathy** (see page 360)

Continued on page 285

Midtown, Chelsea, Flatiron District, and

◆ **DINING**
1. Aquavit
2. Artisanal
3. Baoguette
4. Becco
5. Blue Water Grill
6. Bouchon Bakery
7. BXL
8. Chennai Garden
9. Churrascaria Plataforma
10. Cookshop
11. Eleven Madison Park
12. Firebird
13. Grand Sichuan International
14. Gramercy Tavern
15. Gray's Papaya
16. Jean-Georges
17. Lady Mendl's Tea Salon
18. Le Bernardin
19. Les Halles
20. Mardoo Bar
21. Margon Restaurant
22. Menchanko-Tei
23. Mesa Grill
24. Meskerem
25. Molly's
26. Molyvos
27. Mr. Broadway Kosher Deli
28. Oceana
29. Orso
30. Osteria del Circo
31. Pam Real Thai
32. Penelope
33. Petite Abeille
34. Petrossian
35. Picholine
36. Pure Food and Wine
37. Rosa Mexicano
38. Scarpetta
39. 2nd Ave Deli
40. Sushi-Ann
41. Tamarind
42. Tabla
43. Union Square Café
44. Veritas
45. Woo Chon
46. Zen Palate

● **NIGHTLIFE**
47. Bongo
48. Campbell Apartment
49. Carolines
50. Flatiron Lounge
51. Hudson Bar
52. O'Flaherty's Ale House
53. P. J. Clarke's
54. Rodeo Bar
55. Rudy's
56. Sakagura
57. Slate
58. Swing 46
59. The Ginger Man
60. Top of the Tower

Gramercy Park Dining and Nightlife

Uptown Dining and Nightlife

◆ **DINING**
1. Atlantic Grill
2. Café Boulud
3. Café con Leche
4. Café Sabarsky
5. Calle Ocho
6. Candle Café
7. EJ's Luncheonette
8. Fatty Crab
9. Gobo
10. Gray's Papaya
11. Jasmine
12. Kefi
13. La Boîte en Bois
14. Paola's
15. Penang
16. Rosa Mexicana
17. Saigon Grill
18. Sfoglia
19. Shun Lee West,
    Shun Lee Café

⬤ **NIGHTLIFE**
20. Café Carlyle
21. Club Macanudo
22. Smoke

Ⓜ Subway stop

HARLEM

UPPER WEST SIDE

Henry Hudson Parkway

Riverside Dr.

RIVERSIDE PARK

West End Ave.

Broadway

Amsterdam Ave.

Columbus Ave.

Central Park W.

Manhattan Ave.

American Museum of Natural History

Hudson River

Riverside Dr.

Freedom Pl.

LINCOLN CENTER

Columbus Circle

CENTRAL

The Lake

Sheep Meadow

Central Park South

W. 105th St.
W. 104th St.
W. 103rd St.
W. 102nd St.
W. 101st St.
W. 100th St.
W. 99th St.
W. 98th St.
W. 97th St.
W. 96th St.
W. 95th St.
W. 94th St.
W. 93rd St.
W. 92nd St.
W. 91st St.
W. 90th St.
W. 89th St.
W. 88th St.
W. 87th St.
W. 86th St.
W. 85th St.
W. 84th St.
W. 83rd St.
W. 82nd St.
W. 81st St.
W. 80th St.
W. 79th St.
W. 78th St.
W. 77th St.
W. 76th St.
W. 75th St.
W. 74th St.
W. 73rd St.
W. 72nd St.
W. 71st St.
W. 70th St.
W. 69th St.
W. 68th St.
W. 67th St.
W. 66th St.
W. 65th St.
W. 64th St.
W. 63rd St.
W. 62nd St.
W. 61st St.
W. 60th St.
W. 59th St.

86th St.
79th St.
65th St.

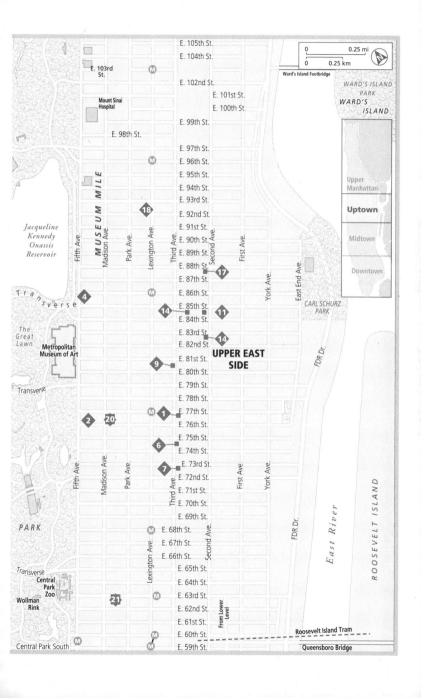

Financial District, Tribeca, Chinatown, and Little Italy Dining

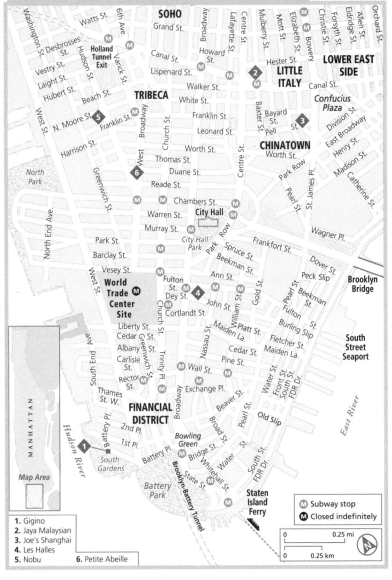

1. Gigino
2. Jaya Malaysian
3. Joe's Shanghai
4. Les Halles
5. Nobu
6. Petite Abeille

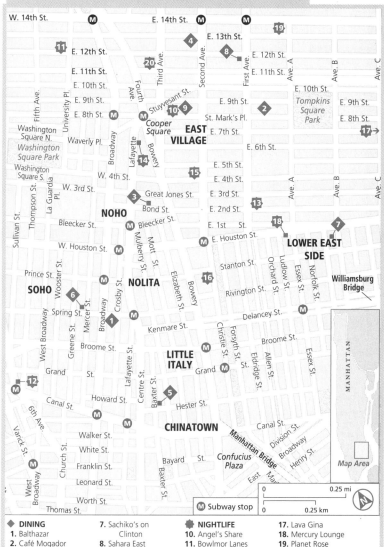

Lower East Side, Soho, Nolita, and East Village Dining and Nightlife

♦ DINING
1. Balthazar
2. Café Mogador
3. Il Buco
4. Momofuku Ssäm Bar
5. New Pasteur
6. Penang
7. Sachiko's on Clinton
8. Sahara East
9. Soba-ya

♣ NIGHTLIFE
10. Angel's Share
11. Bowlmor Lanes
12. The Bubble Lounge
13. D.B.A.
14. Joe's Pub
15. KGB
16. Kush

17. Lava Gina
18. Mercury Lounge
19. Planet Rose
20. Webster Hall

Ⓜ Subway stop

Greenwich Village Dining and Nightlife

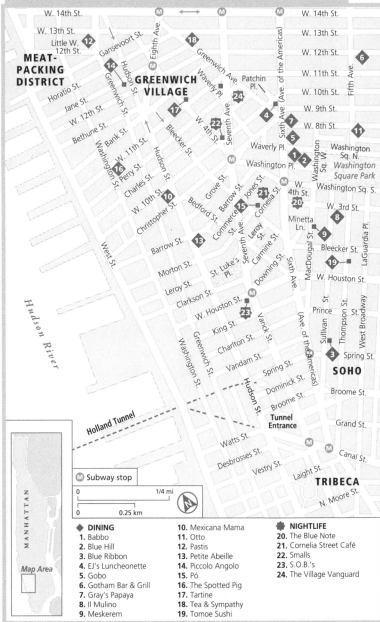

● DINING
1. Babbo
2. Blue Hill
3. Blue Ribbon
4. EJ's Luncheonette
5. Gobo
6. Gotham Bar & Grill
7. Gray's Papaya
8. Il Mulino
9. Meskerem
10. Mexicana Mama
11. Otto
12. Pastis
13. Petite Abeille
14. Piccolo Angolo
15. Pó
16. The Spotted Pig
17. Tartine
18. Tea & Sympathy
19. Tomoe Sushi

● NIGHTLIFE
20. The Blue Note
21. Cornelia Street Café
22. Smalls
23. S.O.B.'s
24. The Village Vanguard

Ⓜ Subway stop

0   1/4 mi
0   0.25 km

MANHATTAN

Map Area

Continued from page 277

The Best Delis

- **Barney Greengrass** 541 Amsterdam Avenue; ☎ 212-724-4707;
  www.barneygreengrass.com
- **Ben's Best** 96-40 Queens Boulevard, Rego Park, Queens;
  ☎ 718-897-1700; **www.bensbest.com**
- **Carnegie Deli** 854 Seventh Avenue at 55th Street;
  ☎ 212-757-2245, 800-334-5606; **www.carnegiedeli.com**
- **Fine & Schapiro** 138 West 72nd Street; ☎ 212-877-2721;
  www.fineandschapiro.com
- **Katz's Deli** 205 East Houston Street; ☎ 212-254-2246; **www.katzdeli.com**
- **Mr. Broadway Kosher Restaurant** (see page 329)
- **2nd Ave Deli** (see page 352)

The Best Family Dining

- **Barking Dog Luncheonette** 150 East 34th Street, ☎ 212-871-3900;
  1453 York Avenue, ☎ 212-861-3600; 1678 Third Avenue, ☎ 212-831-1800
- **Chat 'n' Chew** 10 East 16th Street; ☎ 212-243-1616
- **Churrascaria Plataforma** (see page 303)
- **City Crab** 235 Park Avenue South; ☎ 212-529-3800;
  www.citycrabnyc.com
- **La Bonne Soupe** 48 West 55th Street; ☎ 212-586-7650;
  www.labonnesoupe.com
- **Popover Cafe** 551 Amsterdam Avenue; ☎ 212-595-8555;
  www.popovercafe.com

The Best Fireplaces

- **The Black Sheep Bar** 583 Third Avenue at 38th Street; ☎ 212-599-3476;
  www.blacksheep.nv.switchboard.com
- **I Trulli** 122 East 27th Street; ☎ 212-481-7372; **www.itrulli.com**
- **La Ripaille** 605 Hudson Street; ☎ 212-255-4406; **www.laripailleny.com**
- **Molly's Pub & Restaurant** (see page 329)
- **The Place** 310 West Fourth Street; ☎ 212-924-2711;
  www.theplaceny.com
- **Savoy** 70 Prince Street; ☎ 212-219-8570; **www.savoynyc.com**
- **Vivolo** 140 East 74th Street; ☎ 212-737-3533; **vivolo.vivolonyc.com**

The Best Gardens

- **Barbetta** 321 West 46th Street; ☎ 212-246-9171;
  www.barbettarestaurant.com
- **Barolo** 398 West Broadway; ☎ 212-226-1102; **www.nybarolo.com**
- **The Boathouse** Central Park Lake, East 72nd Street and Park Drive North;
  ☎ 212-517-2233; **www.thecentralparkboathouse.com**
- **Gascogne** 158 Eighth Avenue (between 17th and 18th streets);
  ☎ 212-675-6564; **www.gascognenyc.com**

- **I Coppi** 432 East Ninth Street; ☎ 212-254-2263; **www.icoppinyc.com**
- **Le Jardin Bistro** 25 Cleveland Place (between Kenmare and Spring streets); ☎ 212-343-9599; **www.lejardinbistro.com**
- **Le Refuge** 166 East 82nd Street; ☎ 212-861-4505; **www.lerefugenyc.com**
- **Sahara East** (see page 350)
- **Shake Shack** Madison Square Park (at Madison Avenue and 23rd Street); ☎ 212-889-6600; **www.shakeshacknyc.com**

The Best Legends and Landmarks

- **The Algonquin Hotel** 59 West 44th Street; ☎ 212-840-6800; **www.algonquinhotel.com** (stick to the lobby bar)
- **Grand Central Oyster Bar** Grand Central Terminal, Lower Level; ☎ 212-490-6650; **www.oysterbarny.com**
- **Peter Luger Steak House** (see page 342)
- **Pete's Tavern** 129 East 18th Street; ☎ 212-473-7676; **www.petestavern.com**
- **P. J. Clarke's** 915 Third Avenue; ☎ 212-317-1616; **www.pjclarkes.com**
- **Rao's** 455 East 114th Street; ☎ 212-722-6709; **www.raos.com**
- **Sylvia's** 328 Lenox Avenue; ☎ 212-996-0660; **www.sylviassoulfood.com**
- **White Horse Tavern** 567 Hudson Street; ☎ 212-243-9260

The Best Night-owl Prowls

- **Blue Ribbon** Closes 4 a.m. (see page 295)
- **Café Noir** 32 Grand Street; ☎ 212-431-7910; **www.cafenoirny.com;** closes 4 a.m. on weekends
- **Cafeteria** 119 Seventh Avenue; ☎ 212-414-1717; 24 hours
- **Corner Bistro** 331 West Fourth Street; ☎ 212-242-9502; **cornerbistro.ypguides.net;** closes 4 a.m.
- **'inoteca** 323 Third Avenue, ☎ 212-683-3835, closes 3 a.m.; 21 Bedford Street, ☎ 212-989-5769, closes 2 a.m.; 98 Rivington Street, ☎ 212-614-0473, closes 3 a.m.; **www.inotecanyc.com**
- **Lucky Strike** 59 Grand Street; ☎ 212-941-0772; **www.luckystrikeny.com;** closes 2:30 a.m. on weekends
- **Sahara East** Closes 4 a.m. on weekends (see page 350)
- **The Spotted Pig** Closes 2 a.m. (see page 355)
- **Veselka** 144 Second Avenue (at Ninth Street); ☎ 212-228-9682; **www.veselka.com;** 24 hours
- **Woo Chon** Closes at 2 a.m. most days (see page 363)

The Best Pizza

- **Artichoke Basille's Pizza & Brewery** 328 East 14th Street; ☎ 212-228-2004; **www.artichokepizza.com**
- **Arturo's** 106 West Houston; ☎ 212-677-3820
- **Di Fara Pizza** 1424 Avenue J, Brooklyn; ☎ 718-258-1367; **www.difara.com**

- **Grimaldi's Pizzeria** 19 Old Fulton Street (under the Brooklyn Bridge), Brooklyn; ☎ 718-858-4300; **www.grimaldis.com**
- **John's of Bleecker Street** 278 Bleecker Street; ☎ 212-243-1680; **www.johnsbrickovenpizza.com**
- **Kesté** (see page 320)
- **La Pizza Fresca Ristorante** 31 East 20th Street; ☎ 212-598-0141; **www.lapizzafresca.com**
- **Lombardi's** 32 Spring Street; ☎ 212-941-7994; **www.firstpizza.com**
- **Patsy's Pizza** (see page 340)
- **Sal & Carmine's Pizza** 2671 Broadway; ☎ 212-663-7651

The Best Raw Bars

- **Aquagrill** 210 Spring Street; ☎ 212-274-0505; **www.aquagrill.com**
- **Atlantic Grill** (see page 290)
- **Blue Ribbon** (see page 295)
- **Blue Water Grill** (see page 296)
- **Docks Oyster Bar & Seafood Grill** 633 Third Avenue; ☎ 212-986-8080; **www.docksoysterbar.com**
- **Grand Central Oyster Bar** Grand Central Terminal, Lower Level; ☎ 212-490-6650; **www.oysterbarny.com**
- **Redeye Grill** 890 Seventh Avenue; ☎ 212-541-9000; **www.redeyegrill.com**

The Best Romantic Dining

- **August** 359 Bleecker Street; ☎ 212-929-4774; **www.augustny.com**
- **King's Carriage House** 251 East 82nd Street; ☎ 212-734-5490; **www.kingscarriagehouse.com**
- **Mas** 39 Downing Street; ☎ 212-255-1790; **www.masfarmhouse.com**
- **One if by Land, Two if by Sea** 17 Barrow Street; ☎ 212-255-8649; **www.oneifbyland.com**
- **The River Café** (see page 349)

The Best Steak Houses

- **BLT Steak** 106 East 57th Street; ☎ 212-752-7470; **www.bltsteak.com**
- **Churrascaria Plataforma** (see page 303)
- **Peter Luger Steak House** (see page 342)
- **Sparks Steak House** 210 East 46th Street; ☎ 212-687-4855; **www.sparkssteakhouse.com**
- **Strip House** 13 East 12th Street; ☎ 212-328-0000; **www.striphouse.com**
- **Wolfgang's Steakhouse** 4 Park Avenue, ☎ 212-889-3369; 409 Greenwich Street, ☎ 212-925-0350; **www.wolfgangssteakhouse.com**

The Best Sushi

- **Japonica** 100 University Place; ☎ 212-243-7752; **www.japonicanyc.com**
- **Sushi of Gari** 402 East 78th Street, ☎ 212-517-5340; Sushi of Gari 46, 347 West 46th Street, ☎ 212-957-0046; Gari, 370 Columbus Avenue, ☎ 212-362-4816; **www.sushiofgari.com**

- **Sushi Yasuda** 204 East 43rd Street; ☎ 212-972-1001; **www.sushiyasuda.com**
- **Tomoe Sushi** (see page 361)

The Best Ultra-cheap Meals (under $10)

- **Azuri Café** 465 West 51st Street; ☎ 212-262-2920; **www.azuricafe.com**
- **Bouchon Bakery** (see page 297)
- **Cosmic Cantina** 101 Third Avenue; ☎ 212-420-0975
- **Defonte's** 261 Third Avenue at East 21st Street; ☎ 212-614-1500; **www.defontesofbrooklyn.com**
- **Excellent Dumpling House** 111 Lafayette Street; ☎ 212-219-0212
- **Gray's Papaya** (see page 314)
- **Roomali** 97 Lexington Avenue; ☎ 212-679-8900; **roomali.tripod.com**

The Best Vegetarian

- **Angelica Kitchen** 300 East 12th Street; ☎ 212-228-2909; **www.angelicakitchen.com**
- **Candle Cafe** (see page 302)
- **Caravan of Dreams** 405 East Sixth Street; ☎ 212-254-1613; **www.caravanofdreams.net**
- **Gobo** (see page 311)
- **HanGawi** 12 East 32nd Street; ☎ 212-213-0077; **www.hangawirestaurant.com**

The Best Views

- **Gigino at Wagner Park** (see page 310)
- **The River Café** (see page 349)
- **Terrace in the Sky** 400 West 119th Street; ☎ 212-666-9490; **www.terraceinthesky.com**
- **Top of the Tower Bar & Lounge at Beekman Tower Hotel** 3 Mitchell Place (49th Street and First Avenue); ☎ 212-980-4796; **www.thebeekmanhotel.com**
- **The Water Club** The East River at 30th Street; ☎ 212-683-3333; **www.thewaterclub.com**

RESTAURANT PROFILES

Aquavit ★★★★½

| SCANDINAVIAN | VERY EXPENSIVE | QUALITY ★★★★★ | VALUE ★★★½ |

65 East 55th Street, Midtown East; ☎ 212-307-7311; **www.aquavit.org**

Reservations Necessary. **When to go** Anytime. **Entree range** Prix-fixe dinner, 3-course menu, $84 per person; chef's tasting menu, $105 per person ($170 with wine pairing); seasonal tasting menu, $65 per person; 3-course prix-fixe dinner in cafe, $35; prix-fixe lunch in cafe, $24; lunch tasting menu in dining room, $58;

Sunday brunch (smorgasbord), $48; à la carte lunch, $12–$26. Note that cafe is cheaper (see below). **Payment** All major credit cards. **Service rating** ★★★★. **Friendliness rating** ★★★★½. **Bar** Full service, many house-made aquavits. **Wine selection** Very good. **Dress** Dressy casual to business and elegant (no sneakers or shorts). **Disabled access** Yes. **Customers** Businesspeople, curious foodies without a budget, New York elite. **Hours** Monday–Thursday, noon–2:30 p.m. and 5:30–10:30 p.m.; Friday, noon–2:30 p.m. and 5:15–10:45 p.m.; Saturday, noon–2:30 p.m. (cafe only) and 5–10:45 p.m.; Sunday, noon–2:30 p.m. (brunch) and 5:30–10:30 p.m. (dining room only). Chef's tasting menus served until 10 p.m.

SETTING AND ATMOSPHERE   Not as lovely as the original site (no more waterfall), but larger and more user-friendly for chefs and diners alike. The main dining room is simple and clean in its Scandinavian decor, with a muted cream, brown, and wood color scheme, plus fresh orchids. There's no natural light, and some argue that tables are a bit too close together, but the cafe is cheaper and worth a try. Keep in mind, though, that the cafe kitchen is separate from the main dining room's; it's supervised by the executive chef, and a little bit of overlap can be found.

HOUSE SPECIALTIES   Herring plate (various herring preparations served with Carlsberg beer and aquavit); lobster roll; gravlax; hot smoked arctic char; braised beef cheeks.

OTHER RECOMMENDATIONS   Swedish meatballs; sage-roasted chicken; venison loin; arctic circle.

SUMMARY AND COMMENTS   Swedish chef Marcus Samuelsson, who won the James Beard Foundation accolade as Best Chef in New York City for 2003, has taken Aquavit to new levels of culinary prowess. If it weren't for the prices, we'd recommend a few return visits to try the tasting menu as well as some of the selections from the prix-fixe. House-made aquavits can accompany the fish appetizers perfectly; selections include pear, vanilla, and black peppercorn, cloudberry, and citrus flavors. Presentation of all dishes is creative.

Artisanal ★★★½

BISTRO-FROMAGERIE   MODERATE/EXPENSIVE   QUALITY ★★★★   VALUE ★★★

2 Park Avenue (entrance on 32nd Street), Gramercy Park and Madison Square; ☎ **212-725-8585; www.artisanalbistro.com**

Reservations Recommended, but first come, first served at a few tables by the bar. **When to go** Anytime. **Entree range** $20–$36; prix-fixe lunch and dinners available. **Payment** All major credit cards. **Service rating** ★★★. **Friendliness rating** ★★★. **Bar** Full service. **Wine selection** Extensive. **Dress** Business casual. **Disabled access** Yes. **Customers** Regulars, couples, professionals. **Hours** Monday–Friday, 11:45 a.m.–11 p.m.; Saturday, 11 a.m.–5 p.m. (brunch) and 5–11 p.m.; Sunday, 11 a.m.–5 p.m. (brunch) and 5–10 p.m.

SETTING AND ATMOSPHERE   A large, bustling dining room with high ceilings, large windows, and happy diners. There's an upscale bistro-brasserie ambience and a buzz in the air, which can often be almost too loud. If you're looking for intimacy, go somewhere else. That said, there's something quite romantic about sharing fondue for an entree and dessert.

HOUSE SPECIALTIES Cheese, fondue, and wine.

OTHER RECOMMENDATIONS Chocolate fondue; cassoulet; side of spinach gratin with Parmesan; three-cheese onion soup; "chicken under brick."

SUMMARY AND COMMENTS The great thing about Artisanal is that you don't need to have a full meal: you can come in anytime and have a cheese and wine flight combination for $27. These pairings of three notable cheeses and wines from around the world carry colorful names such as Ancient Tradition, Magic of Blues, and Sinful Experience. Fried fish-and-chips at $20 are hardly worth it, so opt for other dishes. Even if you are already cheese savvy, take advantage of the *fromager* to ask him or her about the more than 200 cheeses. A cheese plate takes on new meaning after you discuss your options and realize that a good way to go about selecting a five-cheese platter is to include "a goat, a cow, a sheep, a blue, and a Cheddar." Fondue can be ordered in two sizes and a choice of varying cheese, herb, and oil-infusion combinations. There's always a fondue of the day. If you need something sweet besides a cheese plate, try the chocolate fondue or the tarte tatin with the Cheddar-cheese crust.

Atlantic Grill ★★★★

SEAFOOD	EXPENSIVE	QUALITY ★★★★	VALUE ★★★½

**1341 Third Avenue (between 76th and 77th streets), Upper East Side;
☎ 212-988-9200; www.brguestrestaurants.com**

Reservations Highly recommended. **When to go** Anytime. **Entree range** $20–$32. **Payment** All major credit cards. **Service rating** ★★★★½. **Friendliness rating** ★★★½. **Bar** Full service. **Wine selection** Decent. **Dress** Business, casual chic. **Disabled access** Yes. **Customers** Locals, fish and raw-bar lovers, professionals. **Hours** Monday–Wednesday, 11:30 a.m.–4 p.m. and 5–11 p.m.; Thursday and Friday, 11:30 a.m.–4 p.m. and 5–11:30 p.m.; Saturday, 11:30 a.m.–4 p.m. and 4:30–11:30 p.m.; Sunday, 10:30 a.m.–4 p.m. (brunch) and 4:30–10 p.m.

SETTING AND ATMOSPHERE Stylish yet unimposing. Behind the front bar are two dining areas. The first is roomier, with banquettes along the walls and tables in the center; the second is narrower and full of tables. There is a pervasive positive buzz of activity and conversation in the air.

HOUSE SPECIALTIES Oysters and clams from the raw bar; nori-wrapped tuna; grilled mahimahi.

OTHER RECOMMENDATIONS Anything from the sushi bar; chopped salad; shrimp-and-lobster spring roll; Scottish salmon.

SUMMARY AND COMMENTS An Upper East Side favorite and perennially consistent for fresh fish and enjoyable dining. That said, if you're interested in a quiet setting, this is not the place. Banquettes can be intimate, but the restaurant is usually full, so noise levels are high. The sushi rolls are

scrumptious, and the daily special roll is often worth trying. The efficient waitstaff aims to please, but be mindful of the zealous wine and
water pouring, which results in overfilled glasses and what appears to
be a need for another bottle before the main course arrives. Sidewalk
dining available when weather allows.

Babbo ★★★★

ITALIAN	EXPENSIVE	QUALITY ★★★★½	VALUE ★★★★

**110 Waverly Place (between MacDougal Street and Sixth Avenue),
Greenwich Village; ☎ 212-777-0303; www.babbonyc.com**

Reservations A must. **When to go** Anytime you can get a reservation. **Entree range**
$19–$35; 8-course pasta-tasting menu, $69; 8-course traditional tasting menu, $75.
Payment All major credit cards. **Service rating** ★★½. **Friendliness rating** ★★★.
Bar Full service. **Wine selection** Lots of Italian; ask for recommendations; fairly
priced. **Dress** Casual to dressy (no flip-flops or tank tops). **Disabled access** Main
dining room and restrooms. **Customers** Locals, professionals, celebrities. **Hours**
Sunday, 5–11 p.m.; Monday–Saturday, 5:30–11:30 p.m.

SETTING AND ATMOSPHERE Formerly home to James Beard favorite Coach
House, this bilevel Greenwich Village space was thoroughly updated to
house Mario Batali's innovative Italian cooking. The main room is dressed
comfortably in soft yellow, with banquettes along the walls and a center
table proudly displaying a beautiful bouquet of flowers. A majestic staircase splits the back of the room and leads up to a more serene second
floor with white walls and a grand skylight. The main room brims with
energy; upstairs tends to be quieter and more relaxed.

HOUSE SPECIALTIES Marinated fresh sardines; warm tripe parmigiana; pappardelle Bolognese; grilled lamb chops; saffron panna cotta.

OTHER RECOMMENDATIONS Beef-cheek ravioli with crushed squab livers; two-
minute calamari, Sicilian lifeguard style; linguine with clams; assortment
of gelati and sorbetti; cheesecake.

SUMMARY AND COMMENTS Power team "Molto" Mario Batali and Joseph
Bastianich are responsible for more than half a dozen of New York's most
notable restaurants (**Bar Jamon, Casa Mono, Del Posto, Esca, Lupa,
OTTO**), and many believe Babbo is the crown jewel in their empire. The
room is raucous, and an open table comes up about as often as Halley's
Comet, but it's worth the wait for Batali's fearless food. Batali pushes the
limits of traditional Italian cooking, using ingredients that most diners
shun, such as anchovies, calf's brains, and beef cheeks. More of it works
than doesn't, but figuring it out is all the fun. For starters, Batali smartly
tempers fresh, silvery anchovies with dusky summer beans, and normally
bland tripe gets a healthy dose of character from a spicy tomato sauce.
But certain pastas can be disappointing. Avoid such excessively rich
preparations as duck-liver ravioli, buried in an overly sweet, overbearing,
hoisinlike sauce; also, the beef-cheek ravioli may be too much for some.

Balthazar ★★★½

FRENCH   MODERATE/EXPENSIVE   QUALITY ★★★★   VALUE ★★★★

80 Spring Street (between Broadway and Crosby Street), SoHo;
☎ 212-965-1414; www.balthazarny.com

Reservations Recommended. **When to go** Anytime. **Entree range** $17–$42.
Payment All major credit cards. **Service rating** ★★★. **Friendliness rating** ★★★.
Bar Full service and usually full. **Wine selection** Good and not overpriced; heavy on
French options; house wine by the carafe is drinkable and inexpensive. **Dress** Chic—
upscale or down. **Disabled access** Yes. **Customers** The trendy, celebrities, locals.
Hours Monday–Thursday, 7:30–11:30 a.m., noon–5 p.m., and 5:45 p.m.–midnight.;
Friday, 7:30–11:30 a.m., noon–5 p.m., and 5:45 p.m.–1 a.m.; Saturday, 8–10 a.m.
(Continental only), 10 a.m.–4 p.m. (brunch), and 5:45 p.m.–1 a.m.; Sunday, 8–
10 a.m. (Continental only), 10 a.m.–4 p.m. (brunch), and 5:30 p.m.–midnight.

SETTING AND ATMOSPHERE   Keith McNally, his advisers, and a fortune in francs
(or dollars) turned what had been a leather store into a fabulous fac-
simile of a Paris brasserie that looks as though it has nestled on this East
SoHo street for years. Outside, red awnings mark the spot; inside,
uneven old-gold–ocher walls, peeling mirrors, a tiled floor, a pewter-
topped bar, and paper-covered bistro tables set the trendy stage.

HOUSE SPECIALTIES   Balthazar salad; steak au poivre; steak frites; braised
short ribs; *brandade de morue* (pureed salt cod); warm goat-cheese-and-
caramelized-onion tart; whole roast free-range chicken.

OTHER RECOMMENDATIONS   Duck confit; roasted halibut; duck shepherd's pie;
caramelized banana–ricotta tart.

SUMMARY AND COMMENTS   Though not quite the place to see and be seen as
when it first opened, Balthazar has more than held its own as a New York
hot spot thanks to its laid-back, lively atmosphere and solid bistro fare.
Such bistro classics as steak frites and steak au poivre remain stellar, and
garlicky brandade will have you coming back for more. Prices are surprisingly reasonable, but reservations are still hard to come by, so try to go
for an upbeat and satisfying late lunch. If you can stand the wait, experience a super brunch. The adjacent Balthazar Bakery offers an excellent
selection of tasty breads, pastries, and sandwiches.

Baoguette ★★

VIETNAMESE SANDWICHES   INEXPENSIVE   QUALITY ★★★   VALUE ★★★★½

61 Lexington Avenue (between 25th and 26th streets), Gramercy Park
and Madison Square, ☎ 212-532-1133; 120 Christopher Street (at
Bedford Street), Greenwich Village, ☎ 212-929-0877; 37 St. Mark's Place
(between Second and Third avenues), East Village, ☎ 212-380-1487;
www.baoguettecafe.com

Reservations Not accepted. **When to go** Lunch or late night. **Entree range** $5–
$8. **Payment** Cash only. **Service rating** ★. **Friendliness rating** ★★. **Bar** None.

Wine selection None. **Dress** Anything goes. **Disabled access** For takeout only. **Customers** Office workers, students, sandwich aficionados. **Hours** *Lexington Avenue:* Monday–Saturday, 11 a.m.–8 p.m.; Sunday, noon–5 p.m. (delivery only); *Christopher Street:* daily, 11 a.m.–11 p.m.; *St. Mark's:* Sunday–Thursday, 11 a.m.–midnight; Friday and Saturday, 11 a.m.–2 a.m.

SETTING AND ATMOSPHERE   Aside from counter seats and a few small tables at the East Village location, there's nowhere to set up camp, nor would you want to. The smell is so strong inside, you'll probably prefer to wait in line on the sidewalk and take your sandwich to go.

HOUSE SPECIALTIES   Baoguette banh mi; catfish banh mi.

OTHER RECOMMENDATIONS   BBQ chicken banh mi; sloppy bao banh mi; there are also bun noodles and salads, but they're nothing special.

SUMMARY AND COMMENTS   Forget sky-high pastrami. Forget the Italian hero. New York's current favorite sandwich now comes from an unlikely place: Vietnam. *Banh mi* are Vietnamese sandwiches that combine French baguettes, pickled veggies, pâté, herbs, and various (and sometimes surprising) cuts of meat. Pulled pork, duck liver, and cilantro aren't commonly thought of as compatible, but they make up Baoguette's signature sandwich, and the taste has been known to astound newcomers and convert doubters. Countless places sell banh mi now, but Baoguette's prices, locations, and sheer quality are hard to beat. As this is being written, Baoguette is planning new locations in Midtown East, the Lower East Side, and the Financial District. Almost as good are **Banh Mi Saigon Bakery** (138 Mott Street, ☎ 212-941-1541) and **Nicky's** (150 East Second Street, ☎ 212-388-1088; **www.nickyssandwiches.com**), which could be credited with starting New York's banh mi craze.

Becco ★★★

ITALIAN	MODERATE	QUALITY ★★★½	VALUE ★★★★★

355 West 46th Street (between Eighth and Ninth avenues), Midtown West, Times Square, and the Theater District; ☎ 212-397-7597; www.becco-nyc.com

Reservations Recommended; a must before theater. **When to go** Anytime. **Entree range** $20–$35; prix-fixe pasta lunch, $17.95; prix-fixe pasta dinner, $22.95. **Payment** All major credit cards. **Service rating** ★★★. **Friendliness rating** ★★★. **Bar** Full service. **Wine selection** Good; there's a sizable list for only $25. **Dress** Casual, theater. **Disabled access** None. **Customers** Pre- and post-theater, tourists, locals. **Hours** Sunday and Monday, noon–3 p.m. and 5–10 p.m.; Tuesday, Thursday, and Friday, noon–3 p.m. and 5 p.m.–midnight; Wednesday, 11:30 a.m.–3 p.m. and 5 p.m.–midnight; Saturday, 11:30 a.m.–2:30 p.m. and 5 p.m.–midnight.

SETTING AND ATMOSPHERE   This thriving Restaurant Row–er is thronged with theatergoers. The narrow dining area in the front, with its beamed ceilings, has a few touches that suggest a country inn, but tables are so close together that the happy din can become daunting. The upstairs dining room, away from the noise and constant bustle, is a much better bet for a civilized dining experience.

HOUSE SPECIALTIES *Sinfonia di pasta* (unlimited servings of three pastas that change daily); antipasto of grilled, marinated veggies and fish; homemade fruit sorbets.

OTHER RECOMMENDATIONS Osso buco with fava beans; swordfish; Italian stuffed peppers; rack of lamb.

SUMMARY AND COMMENTS You get a lot for your lire at this popular Theater District trattoria run by the Bastianich family, which also runs the famed **Felidia** (243 East 58th Street, between Second and Third avenues; ☎ 212-758-1479; **www.felidia-nyc.com**). The pastas are almost always homemade and usually surprisingly good; you'd be hard-pressed to find a better deal in the city. Entrees are good but for the most part unspectacular. Stick with the all-you-can-eat pastas, and use the money you save on entrees to order a couple of extra bottles from the wine list.

Blue Hill ★★★★

NEW AMERICAN	EXPENSIVE	QUALITY ★★★★½	VALUE ★★★★

75 Washington Place (between Sixth Avenue and Washington Square West), Greenwich Village; ☎ 212-539-1776; www.bluehillfarm.com

Reservations Essential. **When to go** Dinner. **Entree range** $30–$36. **Payment** All major credit cards. **Service rating** ★★★★½. **Friendliness rating** ★★★½. **Bar** Full service. **Wine selection** Good choices, with more than 25 by the glass. **Dress** Elegant casual. **Disabled access** 3 steps down to enter. **Customers** Foodies, couples, locals. **Hours** Monday–Saturday, 5:30–11 p.m.; Sunday, 5:30–10 p.m.

SETTING AND ATMOSPHERE Hidden just below street level in a former speakeasy, it resists the temptation to embrace the darkness. White walls and linens, backlit banquettes, and long strips of recessed lighting bathe the space in an understated elegance. The main dining room fits only 55, and even though you're unlikely to be bumping shoulders, seats at the banquettes make for closer quarters than some may like. The bar is small, but deep and friendly, and a light and airy garden room in the back is available for private functions. The servers are honest and knowledgeable, if a bit serious.

HOUSE SPECIALTIES The menu changes daily, depending on what's in season. Recent favorites include: veal with Klaas Martens' emmer and quinoa; Berkshire pig; morning farm egg; chocolate bread pudding.

OTHER RECOMMENDATIONS Stone Barns pastured chicken; venison; sweet potato ravioli; marinated beets.

SUMMARY AND COMMENTS Sustainability and "locavore" menus may be in vogue, but Blue Hill does something undeniably authentic: it grows its own food. For ten years, Stone Barns and Blue Hill Farm, the restaurant's agricultural centers in the Hudson Valley and Berkshires, have been providing this "slow food" mecca with seasonal ingredients that executive chef and co-owner Dan Barber renders into new American classics. The menu changes daily, but not on whims. The vegetables are served only at their peaks and paired with meats that have been raised or caught in as humane a manner as possible. Sauces are used judiciously, allowing delicately cooked cuts (the veal practically melts) to show their full flavor. Fruits and vegetables are never overcooked and can be enjoyed with minimal embellishment—a simple bowl of grape tomatoes. The Manhattan venue is actually an offshoot of the Barber family's Hudson Valley restaurant, Blue Hill at Stone Barns, one of the few places in New York State outside the city that can hold its own against the Manhattan juggernauts.

Blue Ribbon ★★★

ECLECTIC AMERICAN	MODERATE	QUALITY ★★★½	VALUE ★★★★

97 Sullivan Street (near Spring Street), SoHo and TriBeCa, ☎ 212-274-0404; 280 Fifth Avenue (between First Street and Garfield Place), Brooklyn, ☎ 718-840-0404; www.blueribbonrestaurants.com

Reservations Only for parties of 5 to 8. **When to go** Dinner only. **Entree range** $20–$35; $125 for the signature paella. **Payment** All major credit cards. **Service rating** ★★★. **Friendliness rating** ★★★. **Bar** Full service. **Wine selection** Interesting. **Dress** Anything goes. **Disabled access** Yes, but very crowded. **Customers** Locals, hipsters, night owls. **Hours** *SoHo:* daily, 4 p.m.–4 a.m.; *Brooklyn:* Monday–Thursday, 5 p.m.–midnight.; Friday, 5 p.m.–2 a.m.; Saturday, 4 p.m.–2 a.m.; Sunday, 4 p.m.–midnight.

SETTING AND ATMOSPHERE This smallish, square, noisy, and dark SoHo room is a magnet for young and not-so-young trendoids, but it's not the decor that draws them. If you can see through the throng at the bar, you'll find a wall of painted, dark red brick; dark red, plush banquettes; and one large, semicircular enclosure seating five or more, with a few interestingly odd paintings and closely spaced tables. In Brooklyn, there's more breathing room and a bigger oyster bar. Much of the noise emanates from the local kids who accompany Mom and Dad out for a bite, so skip this locale if your tolerance for tots is limited.

HOUSE SPECIALTIES Fried chicken with collard greens and mashed potatoes; whole steamed flounder; anything from the raw bar; chocolate Bruno; banana split.

OTHER RECOMMENDATIONS Roast duck; sweet and spicy catfish; hanger steak with wild mushrooms and onion rings; French fries; crème brûlée. Skip such "favorites" as the pupu platter and paella.

SUMMARY AND COMMENTS The original location is the happening place in the happening SoHo scene. Open until 4 a.m., it attracts a late-night crowd, local chefs included, but it's jammed from 8 p.m. on. Expect to wait at least one hour, and very possibly more, to sample chef Eric Bromberg's eclectic menu. Hanging out here is fun; the crowd is anything but dowdy.

The Brooklyn location is less of a late-night scene, but just as fun and frenetic and only four blocks from Prospect Park. If the waiting game at the SoHo location is not for you, go north up Sullivan Street and see if you can get into **Blue Ribbon Sushi** (119 Sullivan Street; ☎ 212-343-0404), Blue Ribbon's hip Japanese sibling restaurant. You can also try Blue Ribbon's downtown wine bar (34 Downing Street; ☎ 212-691-0404), its Midtown sushi bar and grill (308 West 58th Street; ☎ 212-397-0404), or, of all things, its Brooklyn bowling alley (61 Wythe Avenue, Brooklyn; ☎ 718-963-3369; **www.brooklynbowl.com**), where comfort food is served alongside 16 lanes of elegant kitsch.

Blue Water Grill ★★★

AMERICAN-SEAFOOD	MODERATE	QUALITY ★★★★	VALUE ★★★★

31 Union Square West (at 16th Street), Gramercy Park and Madison Square; ☎ 212-675-9500; www.brguestrestaurants.com

Reservations Recommended. **When to go** Anytime. **Entree range** $19–$30. **Payment** All major credit cards. **Service rating** ★★★. **Friendliness rating** ★★★. **Bar** Full service. **Wine selection** Not particularly exciting, but not bad either. **Dress** Casual. **Disabled access** In main dining room. **Customers** Professionals, locals, tourists. **Hours** Monday–Thursday, 11:30 a.m.–4 p.m. and 5–11 p.m.; Friday and Saturday, 11:30 a.m.–4 p.m. and 5 p.m.–midnight; Sunday, 10:30 a.m.–4 p.m. (brunch) and 5–11 p.m.

SETTING AND ATMOSPHERE Big, breezy, and beautiful, this converted 1904 bank, with its vaulted marble ceilings, marble walls, and high columns, is the epitome of laid-back and casual. Perfect-for-warm-weather seating is available outside just above street level, and during dinner you can listen to jazz while you eat downstairs. But the best seats in the house are the banquettes in the balcony of the main dining room.

HOUSE SPECIALTIES Maryland crab cakes with lobster mashed potatoes; big-eye tuna; blackened swordfish; warm molten chocolate cake.

OTHER RECOMMENDATIONS Jumbo sea scallops; chilled shellfish sampler; warm lobster salad; sweet potato–crabmeat hash; crème brûlée.

SUMMARY AND COMMENTS Whenever out-of-towners visit, New Yorkers invariably take them here, and for one simple reason: Blue Water Grill knows how to make people happy. With its cool setting, casual atmosphere, friendly service, and something-for-everyone menu at prices that won't empty your wallet, Blue Water executes the game plan for success to perfection. At the fresh raw bar, choose from the extensive and user-friendly list of oysters, each with a quick description and those for beginners marked conveniently with asterisks. Owner Steve Hanson has repeated his formula for success at uptown sibling **Ocean Grill** on the Upper West Side (384 Columbus Avenue at 78th Street; ☎ 212-579-2300; **www.brguestrestaurants.com**) and **Atlantic Grill** on the Upper East (see page 290).

Bouchon Bakery ★★★

FRENCH BAKERY   INEXPENSIVE/MODERATE   QUALITY ★★★½   VALUE ★★★★½

**10 Columbus Circle (third floor of Time Warner Center),
Upper West Side; ☎ 212-823-9366; www.bouchonbakery.com**

Reservations Not accepted. **When to go** Lunch. **Entree range** $10–$20 (less at the bakery counter). **Payment** All major credit cards. **Service rating** ★★★★. **Friendliness rating** ★★★★. **Bar** Beer and wine only. **Wine selection** Small but nice. **Dress** Casual. **Disabled access** Yes. **Customers** Shoppers, office workers, tourists. **Hours** Monday–Saturday, 11:30 a.m.–9 p.m.; Sunday, 11:30 a.m.–7 p.m. Bakery counter opens daily at 8 a.m.

SETTING AND ATMOSPHERE Just one floor below Thomas Keller's redoubtable and astoundingly expensive Per Se, this cafe and bakery counter (also Keller creations) could easily be missed. Glass walls are all that separate it from the upscale-mall atmosphere, and a giant Samsung sign overhead suggest that this is just some glorified food court. But not many food courts have Central Park views and critic-approved food.

HOUSE SPECIALTIES Cookies; tarts; pastries; quiche of the day; tuna niçoise sandwich; wagyu beef brisket on rye.

OTHER RECOMMENDATIONS Muffins; fresh-baked breads; Bibb lettuce salad; focaccia; cashew-butter-and-jelly sandwich; ham-and-cheese sandwich.

SUMMARY AND COMMENTS Finding a good lunch around Columbus Circle can be a tricky endeavor. There are plenty of options, but those not in the mood for an expense account–fueled feast or a cafeteria-style quick bite are left shrugging their shoulders. Bouchon Bakery fills the void. The baked sweets are clearly the stars here, but sandwiches, quiche, and focaccia should not be overlooked. Opt for sit-down service, and linger with a glass of wine. Better yet, buy a few items from the less-expensive bakery counter, and head out to the park.

BXL Cafe ★★★

BELGIAN BISTRO-BEER BAR   MODERATE   QUALITY ★★★   VALUE ★★★

**125 West 43rd Street (between Broadway and Seventh Avenue),
Midtown West, Times Square, and the Theater District;
☎ 212-768-0200; www.bxlcafe.com**

Reservations Recommended. **When to go** Anytime. **Entree range** $10–$17 (lunch); $12–$24 (dinner). **Payment** All major credit cards. **Service rating** ★★★. **Friendliness rating** ★★★. **Bar** Full service. **Wine selection** Small. **Dress** Casual. **Disabled access** Good. **Customers** Expat Belgians, theater crowd, businesspeople. **Hours** Daily, 11:30 a.m.–11.30 p.m.; brunch: weekends, 11.30 a.m.–4 p.m.; bar open most nights until 2 a.m.

SETTING AND ATMOSPHERE Small, cozy bistro and bar. The decor reflects the authentic ambience of a Belgian bistro in a small town. The decoration:

huge pictures of the Belgian kings from Leopold I all the way to present-day King Albert II. The only lady joining the illustrious group is Queen Astrid, nicknamed the "Snow Princess," whose death in a 1935 car accident triggered Princess Diana–style mourning in Belgium.

HOUSE SPECIALTIES Steamed mussels and frites; Flemish stew cooked with beer; croquettes with gray North Sea shrimp; classic steak tartare.

OTHER RECOMMENDATIONS Near Times Square, this is a great place for a pre-show dinner. The bar features 10 Belgian beers on tap and another 20 in bottles. On the must-try list: Delirium Tremens and a triple-fermented Chimay Cinq Cents. Both are available on draft.

SUMMARY AND COMMENTS Good brasserie fare combined with decent prices at a top location. The restaurant is small, and lunch can be a noisy affair. The all-you-can-eat mussels nights every Sunday and Monday ($20; includes one Stella Artois) are a steal. A new Midtown location, **BXL Cafe East** (210 East 51st Street, between Second and Third avenues; ☎ 212-888-7782), offers a revised beer and food menu in a brighter, airier room.

Café Boulud ★★★½

FRENCH	EXPENSIVE	QUALITY ★★★★½	VALUE ★★★½

20 East 76th Street (between York and First avenues), Upper East Side; ☎ 212-772-2600; www.danielnyc.com

Reservations Required. **When to go** Anytime. **Entree range** $22–$44; dinner tasting menu, $89. **Payment** All major credit cards. **Service rating** ★★★★½. **Friendliness rating** ★★★★. **Bar** Full service. **Wine selection** Extensive and reasonably priced. **Dress** Nice casual–dressy. **Disabled access** Yes. **Customers** Businesspeople, locals. **Hours** Tuesday–Thursday, noon–2:30 p.m. and 5:45–10:30 p.m.; Friday, noon–2:30 p.m. and 5:45–11 p.m.; Saturday, 5:45–11 p.m.; Sunday and Monday, 5:45–10:30 p.m.

SETTING AND ATMOSPHERE Fresh from a face-lift that added new upholstery and fixtures, two additional dining rooms, and an adjoining bar (Bar Pleiades), Daniel Boulud's eponymous cafe has been designed to evoke Paris of the 1930s. Mahogany and marble, a subdued color palette, Asian-inspired touches, communal tables, and private, banquette-lined alcoves combine to make this casually elegant dining writ large. The atmosphere is more at ease than you might expect from such an Upper East Side establishment. There's a respectful (relative) hush within the restaurant, which allows diners to talk at low to normal decibels and yet not be heard at the next table. Eat outside during warm weather.

HOUSE SPECIALTIES The menu is divided into four sections: La Tradition, La Saison, Le Potager, and Le Voyage. La Tradition focuses on classic French dishes; La Saison concentrates on what's fresh in the market; Le Potager celebrates the vegetable (good choices for vegetarians); and Le Voyage highlights a chosen world cuisine and creates dishes within the genre. Le Voyage selections change monthly, and the others vary depending on the market and the chef. Some offerings have included lobster and seafood bisque; peeky-toe–crab salad; roasted-beet-and-pear salad; roasted chicken with potatoes and bacon; and steamed wild striped bass.

OTHER RECOMMENDATIONS Poached pear; warmed madeleines; raw and cooked tuna with beans, potatoes, and quail egg; roasted monkfish.

SUMMARY AND COMMENTS In the space formerly housing Daniel Boulud's three-star Michelin-rated signature restaurant **Daniel** (now at 60 East 65th Street; ☎ 212-288-0033; **www.danielnyc.com**), Café Boulud is designed to be more casual than its predecessor, yet to maintain high-quality offerings. The food is clearly fresh and undoubtedly delicious, but not superb. The chefs seem to excel when working with fish, seafood, or vegetables, but meat dishes can disappoint. However, with each month bringing a new variation or a different flavor inspired by a new destination, the meat or chicken might be transformed into something very special. The choice of breads—such as sourdough, pumpkin seed, and olive—also varies depending on the chef's whim and the availability of ingredients. Service is well paced and professional. Desserts are a little overly sweet except for the poached pear in wine sauce. The fresh, hot madeleines served at the table in a linen funnel at the end of the meal are a lovely treat. Take advantage of the lunch menu before you commit to a hefty bill at dinner.

Café con Leche ★★½

DOMINICAN	INEXPENSIVE	QUALITY ★★★★	VALUE ★★★★★

**424 Amsterdam Avenue (between 80th and 81st streets),
Upper West Side; ☎ 212-595-7000**

Reservations Accepted Monday–Wednesday only. **When to go** Anytime; especially for bargain weekday lunch specials. **Entree range** $10–$20. **Payment** All major credit cards. **Service rating** ★★½. **Friendliness rating** ★★★. **Bar** Full service. **Wine selection** Limited. **Dress** Casual. **Disabled access** Small step up; restrooms not accessible. **Customers** Locals. **Hours** Daily, 11 a.m.–11 p.m.; weekend and holiday brunch, 10 a.m.–4 p.m.

SETTING AND ATMOSPHERE This sunny cafe looks like any old joint from outside, but the interior is a pleasant surprise: a pizzazzy, updated coffee shop with a colorful, tropical look (carnival masks, silver trim on bright yellow walls).

HOUSE SPECIALTIES The *pernil asado* (roast pork) is intense, amazingly rich stuff; delicious, revisionist *chicharron de pollo* (chunks of on-bone chicken) are herbaceous and expertly deep-fried with a batter that's more St. Louis than San Juan. Black-bean soup is awesome, with good, crunchy onions, and *sancocho* (a ubiquitous, thick Dominican soup), a frequent special, is even better—an intense, golden-brown broth, clearly the product of long, careful cooking, with lovingly prepared root vegetables and a few chunks of pork. Beans and rice, served in appealing decorative bowls, are quite good (the rice is never dry here), and both the *tostones* (starchy green plantains) and *maduros* (sweet ripe plantains) are skillfully fried.

OTHER RECOMMENDATIONS The condiments almost steal the show; there's a sensational hot sauce with incendiary flecks of black, green, and red and an innocent-looking thick, white dressing that looks like sour cream but is actually potent garlic sauce—great on toasted bread. On the other hand, the surprisingly light *mofongo* (fried mash of plantains, pork, and garlic) comes with a fatally overwrought gravy, and the Cuban sandwiches taste too cleaned-up—not compressed or garlicky enough for the flavors to come together.

SUMMARY AND COMMENTS Café con Leche is the diametrical opposite of those trendy, Pan-Latino fusion places. It has solid Dominican-coffee-shop credentials: the salsa recordings are what the staff wants to hear, not "Latin atmosphere"; the roast pork is rich and garlicky; and the cooks shmoosh the bread slices when they toast them. Their innovative touches—for example, that frothy puree of a garlic sauce replacing the standard emulsion of garlic chunks and oil—have grown organically from serious tradition. There's a second Café con Leche farther up Amsterdam Avenue (at number 726), but it's nowhere near as good.

Café Mogador ★★½

MOROCCAN	INEXPENSIVE	QUALITY ★★★★	VALUE ★★★★★

101 St. Mark's Place (near First Avenue), East Village; ☎ 212-677-2226; www.cafemogador.com

Reservations Accepted (necessary Wednesdays). **When to go** Anytime (arrive by 8 p.m. for the Wednesday-night belly dancing). **Entree range** $9–$17. **Payment** All major credit cards. **Service rating** ★★★. **Friendliness rating** ★★. **Bar** Beer and wine only. **Wine selection** House. **Dress** Casual. **Disabled access** Very poor. **Customers** Local. **Hours** Daily, 9 a.m.–1 a.m.; weekend brunch, 9 a.m.–4 p.m.

SETTING AND ATMOSPHERE Mogador looks less Moroccan than a standard-issue East Village bohemian cafe. It's a casual space below street level with tiny tables, faux oil lamps, and ceiling fans.

HOUSE SPECIALTIES Several flavors of *tagine* (a thick stew made with chicken or lamb, served over rice or couscous); *bastilla* (sweet and savory chopped chicken in flaky pastry) containing real saffron; homemade baklava; and fresh-squeezed, pulpy lemonade, served with a mint leaf.

OTHER RECOMMENDATIONS Anything from the appetizer plates.

SUMMARY AND COMMENTS If you're a fan of Moroccan cooking—or are looking for an authentic experience—stay away. This East Village cafe doesn't purport to serve the Real Deal. But it's not fake tourist fodder, either—it's honest Moroccan-American food, as if made from hand-me-down recipes from someone's great-grandmother. The little appetizer plates (you'll be shown a trayful of selections) are tempting, simple things such as spicy sliced carrots, peppery garlic potatoes, and long-stewed chicken livers. As with the rest of the menu, all are pleasing but none attention-grabbing; this is more everyday food than a special-occasion eat.

Café Sabarsky ★★★★

AUSTRIAN   MODERATE/EXPENSIVE   QUALITY ★★★½   VALUE ★★★

1048 Fifth Avenue (at East 86th Street), Upper East Side;
☎ **212-288-0665; www.wallse.com**

Reservations Not necessary. **When to go** Mid–late afternoon. **Entree range**
$13–$28. **Payment** All major credit cards. **Service rating** ★★★½. **Friendliness
rating** ★★★. **Bar** Beer and wine only. **Wine selection** Very small. **Disabled
access** Yes. **Dress** Casual chic. **Customers** Locals, ladies who lunch, gallery
viewers. **Hours** Monday and Wednesday, 9 a.m.–6 p.m.; Thursday–Sunday,
9 a.m.–9 p.m.; breakfast served 9–11 a.m.; closed Tuesday.

SETTING AND ATMOSPHERE A perfect place to have either a late lunch or a
coffee-and-dessert break on an autumn or winter afternoon. The cafe
has a typical Viennese coffeehouse feel, with newspapers on wooden
sticks, marble-topped tables, dark wood, and an impressive selection of
cakes displayed on one side of the space.

HOUSE SPECIALTIES Green-pea soup; spaetzle with mushrooms and sweet
corn; sausage with sauerkraut; Sacher torte; apple strudel.

OTHER RECOMMENDATIONS Matjes herring sandwich; trout crepes; Gugelhupf
(marble cake).

SUMMARY AND COMMENTS Set in a beautiful stone building that is part of the
Neue Galerie, a gallery dedicated to German and Austrian art, the cafe
exudes refinement. Even when the space is full, which is often, it never
seems noisy. While the savory lunch dishes conceived by chef Kurt
Gutenbrunner are delicious, the main attractions are his sweet pastries,
which pair wonderfully with a coffee of one's preference. The presentation of the coffee on a silver tray with accompanying glass of water is as
much true to Viennese style as is the decor. If you go before or after the
lunch rush (noon to 1:45 p.m.), you'll be less likely to have to wait for a
table. Cabaret evenings combined with a prix-fixe dinner sometimes
occur—call for information. If you'd like to try more of Chef Gutenbrunner's
dishes, check out **Wallsé** (344 West 11th Street at Washington Street;
☎ 212-352-2300; **www.wallse.com**). Keep in mind that **Café Fledermaus**
is a recent addition to the Neue Galerie and is downstairs from Café
Sabarsky—same food, different ambience.

Calle Ocho ★★★

NUEVO LATINO   MODERATE   QUALITY ★★★★   VALUE ★★★½

**446 Columbus Avenue (between 81st and 82nd streets),
Upper West Side;** ☎ **212-873-5025; www.calleochonyc.com**

Reservations Recommended. **When to go** Anytime. **Entree range** $21–$29.
Payment All major credit cards. **Service rating** ★★★. **Friendliness rating** ★★★.
Bar Full service. **Wine selection** Heavy on Spanish, Argentinean, and Chilean. **Dress**

Casual, hip. **Disabled access** Dining room, yes; restrooms, no. **Customers** Locals, trendies. **Hours** Monday–Thursday, 6–11 p.m.; Friday, 6 p.m.–midnight; Saturday, 5 p.m.–midnight; Sunday, 11:30 a.m.–3 p.m. (brunch) and 5–10 p.m.

SETTING AND ATMOSPHERE The front area, a colorful bar and lounge with its own singles scene, is highlighted by a Technicolor wall of brightly lit circles. The cavernous main dining room has the look and feel of a fancy airplane hangar, and may be just as loud. Bottom line: Downtown is uptown at this happening spot. *Cool* and *fun* are the operative words.

HOUSE SPECIALTIES Puerto Rican rum–glazed jumbo shrimp with crispy onions and avocado salsa; Maine-lobster seviche.

OTHER RECOMMENDATIONS Sweet-corn *arepa;* lobster empanada; beans and rice; yuca fries.

SUMMARY AND COMMENTS Calle Ocho has sass and style, lively presentation, and a brash blending of flavors. Appetizers are clearly the highlight here. Lobster empanadas come with green papaya seaweed slaw and mirasol peppers. Puerto Rican rum–glazed shrimp, the best of the lot, are big, bold, and fantastic. Entrees lack the same impact, though spicy adobo-rubbed pork loin is more than respectable, and carnivores will savor the Cuban-style sirloin. Fish entrees, such as the red snapper, try too hard and come up short. The *churros* (elongated doughnut-type desserts) are made to order and are a prime dessert choice. This is a super place for a date.

Candle Cafe ★★★½

VEGETARIAN-VEGAN   INEXPENSIVE/MODERATE   QUALITY ★★★★   VALUE ★★★½

1307 Third Avenue (between 74th and 75th streets), Upper East Side;
☎ **212-472-0970; www.candlecafe.com**

Reservations Not necessary. **When to go** Anytime. **Entree range** $12–$20. **Payment** All major credit cards. **Service rating** ★★★½. **Friendliness rating** ★★★★. **Bar** A few organic beers. **Wine selection** A few organic reds and whites. **Dress** Casual and/or funky. **Disabled access** Yes. **Customers** Regulars, locals, vegans, herbivores, and even closeted carnivores. **Hours** Monday–Saturday, 11:30 a.m.–10:30 p.m.; Sunday, 11:30 a.m.–9:30 p.m.

SETTING AND ATMOSPHERE Except for off-peak times, Candle Cafe is often full of people and good vibes. The juice bar, with a good view of the vast selection of ripe fruits and veggies, dominates the entrance. Pro-veggie reading material is available at the bar. Kids who like their greens will find plenty here to satisfy.

HOUSE SPECIALTIES Anything from the juice bar; Aztec salad (barbecued, grilled tempeh, pumpkin seeds, mixed greens, quinoa, black beans, corn, and red onions); ginger-miso stir-fry.

OTHER RECOMMENDATIONS Carrot-ginger dressing; corn bread; chocolate cake; daily wraps; many of the daily specials; tofu club.

SUMMARY AND COMMENTS Don't let the vegan label scare you away. The food here is organic, sustainable, and often so well executed that you might not even miss the meat. Daily specials include combinations such as lemon-parsley ravioli with artichoke filling served with spinach in a roasted tomato–truffle sauce, and cumin-seed-crusted tofu with eggplant and chickpea masala, coconut brown basmati rice, and lemon-date chutney. Call beforehand to check the daily specials. You can also stop here for a quick smoothie or fresh fruit or vegetable juice. Staff members are knowledgeable and not militant about their food predilections, which makes for a calm dining experience, even when the place is packed. Candle Cafe has been so successful that it opened another, slightly more formal space, Candle 79, not far away at 154 East 79th Street (corner of Lexington Avenue); ☎ 212-537-7179, **www.candle79.com.**

Chennai Garden ★★★

INDIAN-KOSHER-VEGETARIAN   INEXPENSIVE   QUALITY ★★★½   VALUE ★★★★

129 East 27th Street (near Lexington Avenue), Gramercy Park and Madison Square; ☎ 212-689-1999

Reservations Not necessary. **When to go** Lunch. **Entree range** $8–$16. **Payment** All major credit cards. **Service rating** ★★★½. **Friendliness rating** ★★★. **Bar** Beer and wine only. **Wine selection** Very small. **Dress** Casual. **Disabled access** None. **Customers** Locals, ethnic, regulars, vegetarians. **Hours** Monday–Friday, 11:30 a.m.–3 p.m. (buffet lunch) and 5–10 p.m.; Saturday and Sunday, noon–10 p.m.

SETTING AND ATMOSPHERE Perhaps the lack of atmosphere is what enables the food to be sold at such low prices. There's nothing wrong with the decor; it's simply not a factor—but that's okay, because the focus is definitely the food.

HOUSE SPECIALTIES *Dosai* (rice-and-lentil-flour crepes), including one with onions and potatoes, masala, and butter; *chana saag* curry (spinach and chickpea).

OTHER RECOMMENDATIONS Buffet lunch; *lassi*; coconut chutney; *samosa*.

SUMMARY AND COMMENTS Chennai Garden caught the attention of the *New York Times* within months of its opening and has gained a steady following ever since. How it manages to produce freshly prepared, natural and/or organic and flavorful South Indian fare at such low prices is both a mystery and a blessing. The buffet lunch is so popular that there's no danger of food sitting too long or becoming stale—plus, it's kosher!

Churrascaria Plataforma ★★★

BRAZILIAN   MODERATE   QUALITY ★★★★   VALUE ★★★★

316 West 49th Street (between Eighth and Ninth avenues), Midtown West, Times Square, and the Theater District; ☎ 212-245-0505; www.churrascariaplataforma.com

Reservations Recommended. **When to go** Avoid weekend dinner rush; probably too heavy for lunch. **Entree range** Prix-fixe for $57 ($36 for lunch); children

under age 5, free; ages 5–10, $20. **Payment** All major credit cards. **Service rating**
★. **Friendliness rating** ★★★. **Bar** Full. **Wine selection** Decent. **Dress** Casual.
Disabled access Restrooms not accessible. **Customers** Tourists, professionals (at
lunch), pre-theater. **Hours** Daily, noon–midnight.

SETTING AND ATMOSPHERE Enormous space, dominated by a monster salad
bar at center. Desserts and cocktails are dispensed by beautiful young
waitresses wheeling carts. The place is brightly lit, with refined, understated decor, but amid all the swirling meat and trips to the salad bar,
who's paying attention? Sound level is high at peak times.

HOUSE SPECIALTIES All-you-can-eat meat, with all the trimmings (including
gigunda Brazilian salad bar and good fried stuff).

OTHER RECOMMENDATIONS The *caipirinha* is the traditional accompaniment: a
cocktail of *cachaça* (a spirit similar to rum) and lots of fresh lime.

ENTERTAINMENT AND AMENITIES Live Brazilian music Friday and Saturday nights.

SUMMARY AND COMMENTS *Rodizio* is a Brazilian tradition where all-you-can-eat
roast meats are brought to your table by skewer-bearing waiters. It's all
very ritualized in Brazil, and this is the only one of a rash of local rodizios
that observes all the rituals (it's also the only one that's Brazilian owned
and run). You're served the traditional plates of fried yuca, French fries,
batter-fried bananas, and particularly good fried polenta. Management
hopes you'll fill up on this cheap stuff, as well as the extensive salad bar
(vegetarians will be more than sated: tons of salads, vegetables, and even
a few entrees in their own rights), but hold out for the meat. Pace yourself
carefully as more than a dozen cuts come around. The best thing of all
doesn't come unless you ask for it, though: unbelievably delicious black
beans, made from specially imported, small, and silky legumes. Spoon
farofa (garlicky toasted yuca flour) over them. If all the meat doesn't give
you a coronary, the service will; confused and incompetent waiters take
their cue from the managers, who pompously stroll through in suits and
ties, scanning the room for trouble spots and summarily ignoring your
desperate pleas for service, dessert, or the check. Bad service also extends
to the reservations line—if you're staying at the Belvedere Hotel, get a
concierge to reserve for you.

Cookshop ★★★★

AMERICAN	EXPENSIVE	QUALITY ★★★½	VALUE ★★★½

**156 Tenth Avenue (at 20th Street), Chelsea; ☎ 212-924-4440;
www.cookshopny.com**

Reservations Recommended. **When to go** Anytime. **Entree range** $24–$36. **Payment**
All major credit cards. **Service rating** ★★★★½. **Friendliness rating** ★★★★. **Bar** Full
service. **Wine selection** Good. **Dress** Casual chic. **Disabled access** Yes. **Customers**
Foodies, locals, the environmentally conscious. **Hours** Monday–Friday, 8 a.m.–3 p.m.
and 5:30–11:30 p.m.; Saturday, 11 a.m.–3 p.m. (brunch) and 5:30–11:30 p.m.; Sunday,
11 a.m.–3 p.m. (brunch) and 5:30–10 p.m.

SETTING AND ATMOSPHERE "Cookshop" refers to private homes in the 1800s where chefs served simple meals using primarily what was available on their own land. The welcoming, knowledgeable staff and understated decor of stone floors and an open kitchen recall this tradition well. Floor-to-ceiling windows and a corner location make this an ideal place for watching the hustle and bustle of Chelsea.

HOUSE SPECIALTIES Hudson Valley rabbit; house sausage; Montauk squid.

OTHER RECOMMENDATIONS Dandelion salad; pasture-raised burger; rotisserie-roasted chicken; fish smoked in-house.

SUMMARY AND COMMENTS Chef-owner Marc Meyer and his wife, Vicki Freeman, opened this green-market hot spot in 2005. Cookshop was one of the first New York City restaurants to focus on not just seasonal, but also local and sustainable ingredients. Meat, fish, and seafood, whether Catskill duck or Montauk squid, are organic and humanely raised or caught. Simple, health-conscious preparations allow diners to enjoy the freshness of each dish, such as Atlantic porgy cooked in a massive stone oven, rotisserie-roasted Hudson Valley baby chicken, and grilled Berkshire pork chop. As a surprisingly flavorful accompaniment with many meals, Cookshop serves a variety of local greens, including bitter dandelions, crisp purslane, and others more commonly considered "weeds." The beer list focuses on regional microbrews, but the wine menu offers surprisingly few domestic options. Brunch is popular, and the restaurant recently began serving breakfast on weekdays from 8 to 11 a.m. You may also like to visit Marc and Vicki's less-expensive sister restaurant, **Five Points,** in the East Village (31 Great Jones Street; ☎ 212-253-5700; **www.five pointsrestaurant.com**).

Degustation ★★★½

SPANISH-FRENCH TAPAS   MODERATE/EXPENSIVE   QUALITY ★★★★   VALUE ★★★★

295 East Fifth Street (between Bowery and Second Avenue), East Village; ☎ 212-979-1012

Reservations Recommended. **When to go** Dinner only. **Entree range** Small plates, $6–$16; 5- and 10-course tasting menus, $50 and $75. **Payment** All major credit cards. **Service rating** ★★★★. **Friendliness rating** ★★★★½. **Bar** Beer and wine only. **Wine selection** Good. **Dress** Hip, casual. **Disabled access** None. **Customers** Foodies, chefs, couples. **Hours** Monday–Saturday, 6–11 p.m.; closed Sunday.

SETTING AND ATMOSPHERE At first glance it seems like a cozy wine bar, with soft lighting, lacquered wood, and stone walls. While there is plenty of good wine to be had, the attraction is actually the chefs and the food, which is chopped, mixed, cooked, and presented to the 16 diners (maximum capacity) at the horseshoe-shaped counter around the kitchen.

HOUSE SPECIALTIES The menu is continually changing, but fine preparations of eggs, sardines, croquettes, sweetbreads, quail, and pork belly—not to mention the signature "cheese steak"—are frequent specials.

SUMMARY AND COMMENTS With no Web site and no online booking, this minuscule tapas bar prides itself on being a whispered favorite among foodies. It's a good thing too, because with so few seats, trying to score a reservation has the potential to cause a lot of frustration. Call a week or two in advance, and you should be all right. On weeknights, walk-ins tend to find a spot without much waiting. Any wait, however, is worth it for the innovative and alluring parade of plates you will encounter. This isn't traditional Spanish tapas. It combines French, Asian, and other traditions with modern techniques (for example, blowtorches). Skip ordering plates on your own and go for the five- or ten-course tasting menus. You won't get twice as much food with the ten-course menu, but you will get a fuller picture of the chefs' unique offerings. Just trust them and let the bites come out in the order they determine. The room is designed for singles and couples, not groups.

Dinosaur Bar-B-Que ★★★

BARBECUE	MODERATE	QUALITY ★★★½	VALUE ★★★★½

646 West 131st Street (between Broadway and Riverside Drive), Morningside Heights, Hamilton Heights, and Harlem; ☎ 212-694-1777; www.dinosaurbarbque.com

Reservations Recommended for large parties or at peak hours. **When to go** Anytime. **Entree range** $10–$24. **Payment** All major credit cards. **Service rating** ★★★. **Friendliness rating** ★★★★. **Bar** Full service. **Wine selection** Limited; stick with beer. **Dress** Anything you don't mind getting stained with sauce. **Disabled access** Yes. **Customers** Locals, rowdy young men, barbecue enthusiasts. **Hours** Monday–Thursday, 11:30 a.m.–11 p.m.; Friday and Saturday, 11:30 a.m.–midnight; Sunday, noon–10 p.m.

SETTING AND ATMOSPHERE A neon sign greets you as you enter the raucous room, designed as warehouse-meets-roadhouse. Vintage biker paraphernalia, B-movie posters, and other artifacts of roadside Americana adorn the walls. Bathrooms are covered head-to-toe in graffiti, and the bar is perpetually swarmed. Dinosaur opened only in 2004, so many of the grungier elements are definitely forced, but the heart is in the right place, and the tattoos on the cooks and servers are undoubtedly real.

HOUSE SPECIALTIES Jumbo barbecue chicken wings; pork ribs; Big Ass Pork Plate; pulled-pork sandwich; barbecue baked beans; Syracuse-style salt potatoes.

OTHER RECOMMENDATIONS Drunken Spicy Shrimp; Creole Spiced Deviled Eggs; coleslaw.

ENTERTAINMENT AND AMENITIES Live blues on Friday and Saturday nights.

SUMMARY AND COMMENTS After conquering Syracuse and Rochester, pit master John Stage decided to test the notoriously dangerous waters of New York City barbecue with his third Dinosaur venue. It would be foolish to say any New York barbecue joint is as authentic as what you would find in Memphis, Kansas City, or Dallas, but that's beside the point. What

Dinosaur does right is provide a vibrant and bustling place in Harlem to enjoy well-smoked and -seasoned meats along with cold beers and live blues. The chicken wings, pulled pork, and pork ribs are consistent favorites, while the beef brisket can be hit or miss. Many of the meats come dripping with Dinosaur's signature sauce (sold in many grocery stores) and even the salad comes topped with slices of bacon. Detractors think the sauce is too sweet, but most can't get enough of it.

In recent years, barbecue restaurants, some no more than glorified roadside stands, have been springing up all over the city. Everyone has a favorite, with candidates including **RUB BBQ** (208 West 23rd Street between Seventh and Eighth avenues; ☎ 212-524-4300; **www.rubbbq .net**), **Daisy May's BBQ** (623 11th Avenue at 46th Street, ☎ 212-977-1500; **www.daisymaysbbq.com**), **Hill Country** (30 West 26th Street between Broadway and Sixth Avenue, ☎ 212-255-4544; **www.hill countryny.com**), and **Blue Smoke** (116 East 27th Street between Park and Lexington avenues, ☎ 212-447-7733; **www.bluesmoke.com**). Thankfully, Dinosaur is less dedicated to trend than it is to providing good food and good times. And even though it's off the beaten path, it's right around the corner from Fairway, the legendary market where New York gourmands go to find just about anything. We suggest taking a cab, especially at night. The surrounding area beneath the Riverside Drive Bridge can be dark and desolate once the sun sets.

EJ's Luncheonette ★★

AMERICAN	INEXPENSIVE	QUALITY ★★★½	VALUE ★★★½

447 Amsterdam Avenue (between 81st and 82nd streets), Upper West Side, ☎ 212-873-3444; 1271 Third Avenue (at 73rd Street), Upper East Side, ☎ 212-472-0600

Reservations Not accepted. **When to go** Anytime. **Entree range** $7–$14; appetizers, $4–$9. **Payment** Cash only. **Service rating** ★★★. **Friendliness rating** ★★★. **Bar** Beer only. **Wine selection** Limited; a few house wines. **Dress** Casual. **Disabled access** Good. **Customers** Locals and local children. **Hours** Daily, 8 a.m.–11 p.m., but hours vary slightly by location.

SETTING AND ATMOSPHERE Think *Happy Days*. These luncheonettes could just as well be on Main Street in Small Town, USA—straight-up 1950s "Dinersville" all the way, from the blue-and-white vinyl booths with Formica tables to the counter with blue-topped stools.

HOUSE SPECIALTIES Buttermilk or multigrain flapjacks with a dozen different toppings; ditto for the buttermilk or bran Belgian waffles; Caesar salad; EJ's club sandwich; great home fries; Stewart's root beer float.

OTHER RECOMMENDATIONS Mac and cheese; grilled tuna club with wasabi; chicken salad; chicken Reuben. Check the specials and the kids' menu.

SUMMARY AND COMMENTS This New York standby packs it in with people of all ages: solo diners, couples, and families small and large. They come for the large portions, kid-friendly atmosphere, and good, familiar food.

There may be a wait, but service is so fast that once you sit down, you'll be out before you can sing "Blueberry Hill." Great place for breakfast or weekend brunch, but watch out for those weekend crowds.

Eleven Madison Park ★★★★

FRENCH	VERY EXPENSIVE	QUALITY ★★★★½	VALUE ★★★★

11 Madison Avenue (at Madison Square Park), Gramercy Park and Madison Square; ☎ **212-889-0905; www.elevenmadisonpark.com**

Reservations Essential. **When to go** Anytime. **Entree range** 3-course prix-fixe dinner, $88; 7-course tasting menu, $125; 11-course tasting menu, $175; prix-fixe lunch, $28; lunch tasting menu, $68. **Payment** All major credit cards. **Service rating** ★★★★½. **Friendliness rating** ★★★★. **Bar** Full service. **Wine selection** Excellent. **Dress** Business casual or dressy. **Disabled access** Yes. **Customers** Businesspeople, groups out for special occasions. **Hours** Monday–Friday, noon–2 p.m. and 5:30–10 p.m.; Saturday 5:30–10 p.m.; closed Sunday.

SETTING AND ATMOSPHERE   Housed in the former Met Life North Building, Danny Meyer's restaurant at Madison Square Park is surely one of the most awe-inspiring dining rooms in the city. This Art Deco wonder has ceilings that reach to the heavens. Tones of olive and ochre weave their way along the terrazzo floor and walls. Floral and topiary arrangements are tastefully distributed, but are secondary to the view of the park through the massive windows. Diners sit on black banquettes, at tables set with crisp white tablecloths. It's big, it's bright, and it's glorious.

HOUSE SPECIALTIES   Suckling pig; foie gras; gnocchi; Nova Scotia lobster; slow-poached egg with pork cheek; chocolate caramel tart.

OTHER RECOMMENDATIONS   Sea urchin; peeky-toe crab; Dover sole; chicken for two; strawberry sorbet.

SUMMARY AND COMMENTS   Since opening in 1998, Eleven Madison Park has always been a destination restaurant for expensed lunches and celebratory dinners, but in recent years it has stepped up its game and now ranks among the city's very best. The credit can go to the Daniel Humm, a Swiss-born chef who ditched the New American cuisine of his predecessors, took traditional French flavors, and applied modern cooking techniques. The prix-fixe lunch is an amazing deal for the food and the atmosphere, but if you want to try the suckling pig and get the full experience, come for dinner and splurge on the tasting menu.

Fatty Crab ★★★

MALAYSIAN-INSPIRED	MODERATE/EXPENSIVE	QUALITY ★★★★	VALUE ★★★

643 Hudson Street (between Gansevoort and Horatio streets), Greenwich Village, ☎ **212-352-3592; 2170 Broadway (at West 77th Street), Upper West Side,** ☎ **212-296-2722; www.fattycrab.com**

Reservations Not accepted at West Village location; recommended for Upper West Side. **When to go** Anytime. **Entree range** $14–$40 (depending on market price of crab). **Payment** All major credit cards. **Service rating** ★★½. **Friendliness rating** ★★★. **Bar** Full service. **Wine selection** A small, eclectic, overpriced selection. **Dress** Casual, trendy. **Disabled access** Better at Upper West Side location. **Customers** Hipsters, locals, couples. *Hours* *Greenwich Village:* Monday–Thursday, noon–midnight; Friday, noon–2 a.m.; Saturday, 11 a.m.–2 a.m. (brunch until 4 p.m.); Sunday, 11 a.m.–midnight (brunch until 4 p.m.); *Upper West Side:* Monday–Friday, 11:30 a.m.–3:30 p.m. and 5 p.m.–midnight; Saturday, 11 a.m.–midnight (brunch until 4 p.m.); Sunday, 1–10:30 p.m. (brunch menu only).

SETTING AND ATMOSPHERE Those looking for a raucous night out with a few friends need not settle for substandard pub grub to get the evening going. Both locations of Fatty Crab offer lively settings and lively food. The music pumps, and the waiters are a bit too cool for school, but if you're in the right mood, it can be a blast. The West Village location is essentially a tiny neighborhood bar that has been converted into a hip, Asian-inspired eatery. The uptown location is bigger, a bit more polished, a little less cluttered, but just as loud.

HOUSE SPECIALTIES Chili crab; watermelon pickle and crispy pork; fatty duck; green mango salad.

OTHER RECOMMENDATIONS Steamed buns; whole fish; fatty dog (i.e. homemade sausage, not Rover!), curried bacon sandwich; short-rib *rendang.*

SUMMARY AND COMMENTS Watching your fat? Not the biggest fan of spice? Eating without utensils give you the willies? Then avoid this place at all costs. While not the effortless culinary gems the owners would like to think they are, these two trendy hot spots do a couple of things very well. They shoot for big, bold flavors and score on most counts. They also know what to do with a big hunk of fat. The watermelon and crispy pork salad is evidence of both of these facts, and is not to be missed. Many rave about the signature chili crab, but most would also agree it costs too much for what you actually get. The service here can be spotty, food comes out as soon as it's ready, and they show you the door the moment you're done. But while you're there, get your hands a little dirty, have a few of their signature cocktails, and forget that diet.

Firebird ★★★

RUSSIAN	EXPENSIVE	QUALITY ★★★★	VALUE ★★★★

365 West 46th Street (between Eighth and Ninth avenues), Midtown West, Times Square, and the Theater District; ☎ 212-586-0244; www.firebirdrestaurant.com

Reservations Recommended. **When to go** Anytime. **Entree range** $20–$38 (lower range includes hefty appetizers that are almost as filling as an entree); prix-fixe, $50; 5-course tasting menu, $90; 8-course tasting menu, $120. **Payment** All major credit cards. **Service rating** ★★★. **Friendliness rating** ★★★. **Bar** Full service, with a selection of more than 40 vodkas. **Wine selection** Good, with some surprisingly low-priced choices. **Dress** Upscale casual, Theater District dressy. **Disabled access** Yes. **Customers** Theatergoers, locals, tourists.

Hours Tuesday, 11:45 a.m.–2:30 p.m. and 5–9 p.m.; Wednesday–Saturday, 11:45 a.m.–2:30 p.m. and 5–11 p.m.; Sunday, 5–9 p.m.; closed Monday.

SETTING AND ATMOSPHERE Two spruced-up brownstones stand behind gilt-edged gates manned by a Cossack-costumed sentry. No, you're not really in imperial St. Petersburg, but you're close. The fabulously over-done, charmingly ornate interior, with eight rooms and two pretty bars, is decorated with chandeliers, lushly patterned carpets, Fabergé-ish objects, Russian wall hangings, ballet costumes, and ancient books.

HOUSE SPECIALTIES Wild-mushroom-and-three-grain soup; buckwheat blini with sour cream; lightly smoked salmon; grilled, marinated rack of lamb; tea-smoked duck breast; Siberian *pelmeni.*

OTHER RECOMMENDATIONS Kasha–wild mushroom salad; roasted-eggplant caviar; *karsky shashlik;* salmon baked in puff pastry; poached sturgeon.

SUMMARY AND COMMENTS Firebird prides itself on exacting detail—the china was specially designed, the waitstaff garbed by Oleg Cassini—and on serving the authentic cuisine of czarist Russia in an ambience of equal authenticity. Best of all, it's fun; you actually hear people say "Wow!" when they walk in. Firebird is a wonderfully theatrical stop in Theater District dining.

Gigino at Wagner Park ★★½

ITALIAN	MODERATE	QUALITY ★★★	VALUE ★★★½

20 Battery Place (at Robert F. Wagner Jr. Park), Financial District;
☎ **212-528-2228; www.gigino-wagnerpark.com**

Reservations Suggested. **When to go** On a sunny day. **Entree range** $15–$38. **Payment** All major credit cards. **Service rating** ★★★½. **Friendliness rating** ★★★½. **Bar** Full service. **Wine selection** Not bad. **Dress** Business casual. **Disabled access** Yes. **Customers** Locals, businesspeople, tourists. **Hours** Daily, 11:30 a.m.–10 p.m.

SETTING AND ATMOSPHERE There aren't many ground-level dining establishments in New York that boast fantastic views at such reasonable prices. Though you feel as if you're bound to go subterranean once you walk in, the narrow entrance opens to a medium-sized space with a huge window overlooking New York Harbor and the Statue of Liberty. For those unlucky enough to be seated with their backs to the window, a mirror (positioned just above eye level so you won't see your own face with your mouth full) provides a similar view. During warmer weather, parts of the window open onto a patio where alfresco dining takes place.

HOUSE SPECIALTIES Gazpacho; grilled calamari; homemade chicken sausage; spaghetti del padrino.

OTHER RECOMMENDATIONS Angel-hair pasta with shrimp, broccoli, and peppers; farfalle Isabella; Esotica salad; calamari fritti.

SUMMARY AND COMMENTS The food, although certainly tasty, is not the best Italian available, but the trade-off is a lovely view. If it's too cold to dine outside, get a table against the wall opposite the big window.

Gobo ★★½

| VEGAN-VEGETARIAN | MODERATE | QUALITY ★★★½ | VALUE ★★★ |

1426 Third Avenue (at East 81st Street), Upper East Side, ☎ 212-288-4686; 401 Sixth Avenue (between Waverly Place and West Eighth Street), Greenwich Village; ☎ 212-255-3902; www.goborestaurant.com

Reservations Not necessary. **When to go** Anytime. **Entree range** $8–$21. **Payment** All major credit cards. **Service rating** ★★★½. **Friendliness rating** ★★★. **Bar** Interesting selection of organic wines and beers. **Wine selection** Limited. **Dress** Casual chic. **Disabled access** Yes. **Customers** Locals, vegans, vegetarians, and curious carnivores. **Hours** *Sixth Avenue:* daily, 11:30 a.m.–10:30 p.m.; *Third Avenue:* daily, noon–11 p.m.

SETTING AND ATMOSPHERE The atmosphere is decidedly noncrunchy and not tie-dyed; rather, Gobo attracts health-conscious and eco-aware types who can afford stylish organic cotton clothing and French lentil truffle soup. "Green" also applies to the color scheme: light green, cream, and pale wood. The focal point on the main wall is a beautifully polished portion of a tree trunk.

HOUSE SPECIALTIES Green-tea noodles with vegan bolognese; *konnyaku*; nori-wrapped tofu in red Thai curry sauce.

OTHER RECOMMENDATIONS Five-spice tofu rolls with mango puree; scallion pancakes; spinach-wrapped pan-seared dumplings.

SUMMARY AND COMMENTS Gone are the days when meatless food was equated with tasteless cubes of tofu thrown over a bowl of overcooked vegetables. The newer Upper East Side location for Gobo opened in 2004, and the chef de cuisine, Yuki Chen—creator of many of the Zen Palate (see page 364) dishes—has extended the food influences to include Pan-Asian tastes of Malaysia, Japan, Thailand, India, and Vietnam. The fresh-juice and herbal-drink list is useful for knowing which elixir will ease which malaise. The vegan chocolate cake dusted with green tea is surprisingly tasty considering it contains no butter.

Gotham Bar & Grill ★★★½

| NEW AMERICAN | EXPENSIVE | QUALITY ★★★★ | VALUE ★★★ |

12 East 12th Street (between University Place and Fifth Avenue), Greenwich Village; ☎ 212-620-4020; www.gothambarandgrill.com

Reservations Recommended. **When to go** Anytime. **Entree range** $30–$50; 3-course prix-fixe lunch, $25. **Payment** All major credit cards. **Service rating** ★★. **Friendliness rating** ★★. **Bar** Full service. **Wine selection** Very good. **Dress** Business, dressy, casual chic. **Disabled access** None. **Customers** Businesspeople, locals. **Hours** Monday–Thursday, noon–2:15 p.m. and 5:30–10 p.m.; Friday, noon–2:15 p.m. and 5:30–11 p.m.; Saturday, 5–11 p.m.; Sunday, 5–10 p.m.

SETTING AND ATMOSPHERE This lofty space has been tamed by sophisticated alterations: grand, fabric-draped overhead lighting fixtures, tables on varying levels, ocher columns, teal trim, bountiful bouquets of flowers on pedestals and on the imposing bar. All is dimly lit and austerely opulent.

HOUSE SPECIALTIES Soft-shell crab; seafood salad; rack of lamb; New York steak; Gotham chocolate cake.

OTHER RECOMMENDATIONS Chilled corn soup; Muscovy duck with foie gras; miso-marinated black cod; fruit soufflés.

SUMMARY AND COMMENTS Chef Alfred Portale, a major influence on New American cuisine and mentor to many of its now-successful practitioners, continues to turn out reliable and memorable food. His soaring, structured presentations seem perfectly suited to the impressive room in which they are served.

Gramercy Tavern ★★★½

AMERICAN   VERY EXPENSIVE   QUALITY ★★★★   VALUE ★★★

42 East 20th Street (between Broadway and Park Avenue South), Gramercy Park and Madison Square; ☎ 212-477-0777; www.gramercytavern.com

Reservations Essential in the main dining room. **When to go** Anytime. **Entree range** Prix-fixe lunch, $55; prix-fixe dinner, $86; tasting menu, $112 (vegetarian, $92). **Payment** All major credit cards. **Service rating** ★★★. **Friendliness rating** ★★. **Bar** Full service. **Wine selection** Excellent; many available by the full glass or 3-ounce tasting glass. **Dress** Anything goes; jacket suggested in the main dining room. **Disabled access** Yes. **Customers** Businesspeople, locals, celebs. **Hours** Monday–Thursday, noon–2 p.m. and 5:30–10 p.m.; Friday, noon–2 p.m. and 5:30–11 p.m.; Saturday, 5:30–11 p.m.; Sunday, 5:30–10 p.m.

SETTING AND ATMOSPHERE Lovely and inviting—flowers in profusion deck the entry, spill over a table near the open grill, ornament the dining spaces, even bloom in the restrooms. Floor-to-ceiling windows front the tavern room, with its big, black-topped bar, and boldly colored paintings of fruits and vegetables brightening the upper walls. The light fixtures in the more formal, cathedral-ceilinged dining rooms go from early-American copper sconces to trendy glass buckets; the decorations follow suit with a few American primitive portraits, a quilt, and large metal starfish. Somehow it all works well together.

HOUSE SPECIALTIES Smoked trout; tuna tartare with cucumber vinaigrette; beef sirloin; rack of pork and braised belly; individual nectarine tatin.

OTHER RECOMMENDATIONS Marinated shrimp salad; roasted cod; rack of veal and braised deckle; chocolate pudding; selection of cheeses.

SUMMARY AND COMMENTS Danny Meyer, the man who brought you Union Square Cafe, Eleven Madison Park, and Tabla (see profiles), teamed with chef and *Top Chef* host Tom Colicchio to open this Gramercy-area winner in 1994. Gramercy, with Michael Anthony now running the kitchen, has the same comfortable atmosphere and agreeable service that make Union Square Cafe such a hit; the surprise lies in the food, which is more adventurous than that of its older sibling. The seafood fondues, an occasional theme at Gramercy, consistently please beyond expectation, and the meat entrees shine, especially the roasted sirloin. Desserts are good but not memorable, so a selection of fine cheeses may be the way to go here. For a more informal and less expensive alternative, try the equally pleasing Tavern Room up front.

Grand Sichuan International ★★★

CHINESE	MODERATE	QUALITY ★★★★	VALUE ★★★★★

229 Ninth Avenue (at 24th Street), Chelsea; ☎ 212-620-5200; www.thegrandsichuan.com

Reservations Accepted. **When to go** Anytime. **Entree range** $10–$18. **Payment** All major credit cards. **Service rating** ★★. **Friendliness rating** ★. **Bar** Beer and wine only. **Wine selection** Small. **Dress** Casual. **Disabled access** Good, but tight path to restrooms. **Customers** Locals. **Hours** Daily, 11:30 a.m.–11 p.m.

SETTING AND ATMOSPHERE To all appearances a generic "nice" Midtown Chinese place with track lighting, elegant, shiny little black chairs, and nice tablecloths. Only the huge informational-pamphlet-cum-textbook, unfurled across the length of the front window, tells you that this is not just another mediocre joint for gringo moo shu. Foodie passersby stop and gape at the menu as if it were a Christmas window at Macy's.

HOUSE SPECIALTIES Terrific spicy Sichuan (Szechuan) cuisine with some other hard-to-find regional dishes from Hunan and Shanghai, and even a small selection of "Mao's Home Cooking" culled from the former leader's little black book of favorite recipes. You can't go wrong if you stick with hot-and-spicy stuff and the fancier exotic specialties (borrow the informational pamphlet and choose from the more-extolled items); avoid the duller-sounding and more clichéd offerings (chow fun or egg rolls, for example, are wrong orders, and your taste buds will be punished accordingly). Don't miss tea-smoked duck, the spicy double-cooked pork, or any of the Shanghai "red cooking" dishes. Dan dan noodles with chile sauce is a popular starter that will get the peppery fires going.

SUMMARY AND COMMENTS Sichuan cuisine is spicy, hearty, and oily. Complaining about the greasiness of, say, Sichuan twice-cooked pork is like objecting to the wetness of soup. So . . . don't come here if you're on a diet. The aforementioned pamphlet—a thick swath of information written in great, enthusiastic detail—makes a super guide to the restaurant's offerings. Unfortunately, you won't have much time to read it—despite Grand Sichuan's relatively upscale Midtown decor, the rushed service is strictly Chinatown-style. GSI has four other nominal locations: 19–23 St. Mark's Place (at East Eighth Street), ☎ 212-529-4800; 15 Seventh Avenue South (near Leroy Street), ☎ 212-645-0222; 125 Canal Street (at Chrystie Street), ☎ 212-625-9212; 227 Lexington Avenue (between 33rd and 34th streets), ☎ 212-679-9770; **www.grandsichuan.com.** Different owners and styles, but good food all around.

kids Gray's Papaya ★½

AMERICAN	INEXPENSIVE	QUALITY ★★★½	VALUE ★★★★★

**2090 Broadway (at 72nd Street), Upper West Side, ☎ 212-799-0243;
539 Eighth Avenue (at 37th Street), Midtown West, Times Square,
and the Theater District, ☎ 212-904-1588; 402 Sixth Avenue (at Eighth
Street), Greenwich Village, ☎ 212-260-3532**

Reservations Not necessary. **When to go** Anytime. **Entree range** Less than $10.
Payment Some loose change. **Service rating** ★. **Friendliness rating** ★½. **Bar**
None. **Wine selection** Only if grape juice counts. **Dress** Pretty much anything, or
nothing at all. **Disabled access** Drive-through accessibility. **Customers** Anybody
and everybody (except vegetarians). **Hours** Daily, 24 hours.

SETTING AND ATMOSPHERE Cheery and cheap old-school orange counters,
white tile, paper fruits hanging from the ceiling; decor is not exactly a
priority here. Although it's not a place to bring kids for a sit-down meal,
the food here is cheap and cheerful enough to satisfy a child who needs
a quick fix and is prepared to nosh either standing up or alfresco.

HOUSE SPECIALTIES Hot dog; hot dog with mustard; hot dog with sauerkraut;
hot dog with sautéed onions; hot dog with mustard, sauerkraut, and
sautéed onions. You get the idea. Gray's toasts its buns for a crispier hot-
dog experience.

SUMMARY AND COMMENTS New York wouldn't be New York without hot
dogs, and Gray's is a New York institution. Although prices go up every
couple of years, hot dogs are still only $1.50 a pop, and the "Recession
Special" is by far the best deal in town at $4.50 for two dogs and a drink.
The franks are grilled to perfection, leaving the skin crisp and locking in
the flavor, and like all good wieners, they come regular or well done.

Il Buco ★★★★

FRENCH-SPANISH-ITALIAN	EXPENSIVE	QUALITY ★★★★½	VALUE ★★★

**47 Bond Street (between Lafayette Street and the Bowery);
☎ 212-533-1932, East Village; www.ilbuco.com**

Reservations A must. **When to go** Anytime. **Entree range** $20–$50. **Payment**
All major credit cards. **Service rating** ★★★. **Friendliness rating** ★★. **Bar** Full
service. **Wine selection** Carefully selected collection of unusual (but savvy)
choices. **Dress** Expensive informal. **Disabled access** Good. **Customers** Locals.
Hours Monday, 6 p.m.–midnight; Tuesday–Thursday, noon–4 p.m. and 6 p.m.–
midnight; Friday and Saturday, noon–4 p.m. and 6 p.m.–1 a.m.; Sunday, 5 p.m.–
midnight.

SETTING AND ATMOSPHERE A former antiques store, woody, atmospheric Il
Buco has an old European farmhouse feeling quite unlike that of any
other spot in the city. You eat at rough, candlelit tables surrounded by
old furnishings and knickknacks. It's tremendously romantic in its
rustic way.

HOUSE SPECIALTIES Changing seasonal menu, but risottos, grilled octopus, homemade sausages, pastas, flourless chocolate cake, and plum cake are delicious fixtures.

ENTERTAINMENT AND AMENITIES The wine cellar allegedly was the inspiration for Edgar Allan Poe's story "The Cask of Amontillado," and it's got atmosphere galore; have a peek.

SUMMARY AND COMMENTS Il Buco's cooking incorporates French, Italian, and Spanish influences, and the chef shows considerable command in all three culinary languages, but with a distinctive (though not trendy) style. Not widely known, Il Buco is nonetheless much loved by a discerning few, and the smallish place fills up most nights. This is an especially good locale for special occasions—long tables can be reserved either in the middle of the main room or in a rear alcove.

Il Mulino ★★★½

ITALIAN	EXPENSIVE	QUALITY ★★★★½	VALUE ★★★★½

86 West Third Street (between Sullivan and Thompson streets), Greenwich Village; ☎ 212-673-3783; www.ilmulino.com

Reservations Highly recommended. When to go Anytime. Entree range $30–$60. Payment All major credit cards. Service rating ★★★. Friendliness rating ★★★. Bar Full service. Wine selection Good. Dress Upscale, business suits. Disabled access Yes. Customers Businesspeople, locals. Hours Monday–Friday, noon–2:30 p.m. and 5–11 p.m.; Saturday, 5–11 p.m.; closed Sunday.

SETTING AND ATMOSPHERE Low-key elegance and low-key lighting prevail from the small, pretty bar in the front to the single perfect rose and heavy white cloths on each table. Tall potted plants separate the dining room from the entrance; the ceiling is mercifully soundproofed, and the walls that are not exposed brick are covered in soft, feathery wallpaper. Service is unobtrusively attentive.

HOUSE SPECIALTIES Check the daily specials; carpaccio; spaghettini carbonara; fillet of beef with caper sauce; rolled veal braised in wine, cream, and wild mushrooms; veal chop.

OTHER RECOMMENDATIONS Spaghettini with clams; spicy veal with anchovies, capers, and mushrooms; chicken in white wine; capellini Il Mulino.

SUMMARY AND COMMENTS Don't confuse this with the franchise offshoots: many New Yorkers consider Il Mulino the best Italian restaurant in the city, and with good reason. Complimentary appetizers, including delicious fried zucchini, superb salami, spicy bruschetta, and scrumptious chunks off the biggest slab of Parmigiano-Reggiano you've ever seen will have your stomach running up the white flag before you've even ordered. The pastas, such as the rich capellini Il Mulino and perfect spaghettini carbonara, prove addictive, and the veal, in any of its preparations, is excellent. One thing's certain—you won't leave here hungry. Finish your meal with a bang by taking in a glass of the potent house-made grappa.

Jackson Diner ★★½

| INDIAN | INEXPENSIVE/MODERATE | QUALITY ★★★½ | VALUE ★★★★★ |

37–47 74th Street (between Madison and Park avenues), Queens; ☎ 718-672-1232; www.jacksondiner.com

Reservations Not necessary. **When to go** Anytime. **Entree range** $10–$22. **Payment** Cash only. **Service rating** ★★½. **Friendliness rating** ★★★. **Bar** Full service. **Wine selection** Limited. **Dress** Casual. **Disabled access** 2 steps into restaurant; no steps for restrooms. **Customers** Locals, ethnic, spice lovers. **Hours** Sunday–Thursday, 11:30 a.m.–10 p.m.; Friday and Saturday, 11:30 a.m.–10:30 p.m.

SETTING AND ATMOSPHERE   In brief: there is no atmosphere! A large, high-ceilinged room filled with no-nonsense tables and chairs. Banquet hall also available.

HOUSE SPECIALTIES   Shrimp curry with coconut and spices; lentil cakes (*idly*) and other variations of Southern Indian pancakes and crepes; *sag paneer* (spicy spinach and homemade cheese cubes); *murg lajwab* (chicken cooked with tomatoes, ginger, and cilantro).

OTHER RECOMMENDATIONS   Lentil soup (*mulligatawny*); *baignan bhurta* (eggplant with onions, ginger, and tomatoes); *dal diwan* (yellow lentils with coriander and cumin); tandoori mixed grill.

SUMMARY AND COMMENTS   So many of the dishes here hit the spot and tantalize the taste buds—assuming you appreciate Indian spice blends. This is not a place for the weak-hearted. Although you're allowed to choose from mild through medium to hot, it seems that the chef feels a lot more comfortable farther up the spicy scale.

Jasmine ★★½

| THAI | MODERATE | QUALITY ★★★ | VALUE ★★★ |

1619 Second Avenue (at 84th Street), Upper East Side; ☎ 212-517-8854

Reservations Not accepted. **When to go** Anytime. **Entree range** $7–$18. **Payment** All major credit cards. **Service rating** ★★½. **Friendliness rating** ★★½. **Bar** Beer and wine only. **Wine selection** Limited. **Dress** Casual. **Disabled access** Yes. **Customers** Locals. **Hours** Monday–Saturday, noon–10 p.m.; Sunday, 1–10 p.m.

SETTING AND ATMOSPHERE   Dark, candlelit with lots of dark red wood and some Southeast Asian touches. Nicer than most neighborhood Thai places, but certainly won't inspire any glossy magazine spreads with its decor.

HOUSE SPECIALTIES   Steamed shrimp dumplings with garlic-ginger sauce; *pad see yu* (chow fun noodles with chicken or beef, Chinese broccoli, and eggs); spicy basil chicken with peppers, onions, and chile paste; *gaeng panang* (Thai red curry with coconut milk).

OTHER RECOMMENDATIONS   *Po pia* (spring rolls); *tom kha gai* (spicy Thai coconut-milk soup); pad thai noodles; *khao pad supparot* (coconut fried rice with chicken topped with ground peanuts and fried onions); *goong phao* (grilled jumbo prawns with house special chile sauce); green curry chicken; Thai iced tea or iced coffee.

SUMMARY AND COMMENTS Serving the best Thai on the Upper East Side, this neighborhood favorite draws crowds for its well-prepared food and spicy change of pace. Though its menu is small, there's enough to choose from, and the things the restaurant does, it does very well. Start with one of the soups or excellent steamed shrimp dumplings. Don't miss the *gaeng panang* with beef or the green curry with chicken. Pad thai and other noodle and rice dishes are above average, and to douse the flames in your mouth there's nothing better than soothing Thai iced tea or yummy Thai iced coffee.

Jaya Malaysian ★★

MALAYSIAN	INEXPENSIVE	QUALITY ★★★½	VALUE ★★★★½

**90 Baxter Street (between Walker and Bayard streets),
Chinatown, Little Italy, and the Lower East Side; ☎ 212-219-3331**

Reservations Not necessary. **When to go** Anytime. **Entree range** $5–$16. **Payment** All major credit cards. **Service rating** ★★½. **Friendliness rating** ★★½. Bar Beer only. **Wine selection** None. Dress Casual. **Disabled access** None. Customers Ethnic, locals. Hours Daily, 11 a.m.–10:30 p.m.

SETTING AND ATMOSPHERE The storefront looks a little tacky, and it hardly convinces you that you've arrived at a place that serves authentic Malaysian food. Don't let the outside deter you; the restaurant is a fair size and can easily seat large groups. The "decor" consists of bamboo light fixtures, a wooden mesh ceiling, and one wall of painted plaster with seashells, rocks, dried sea creatures, and vegetation.

HOUSE SPECIALTIES Stingray in lotus leaf; shrimp with dried-chile paste; various *laksas* (noodles in curried broth with chicken, shrimp, seafood, or tofu); *chendor* (shaved ice with coconut, red beans, and green jelly).

OTHER RECOMMENDATIONS Thai-style fish cake; bean curd stuffed with cucumber and bean sprouts; lemongrass jumbo shrimp; carp with ginger-garlic sauce; Malaysian iced coffee; lychee iced tea.

SUMMARY AND COMMENTS Try to get here early because the place is full by 7:30 p.m., and the noise level can really rise. The menu is extensive, with everything from standard fried rice to more-adventurous dishes such as crispy pork intestines. If this cuisine is new to you, try a shrimp, squid, or fish dish with curry, chile, and/or garlic. The stingray in lotus leaf is incredibly succulent, but it has a weird smell attributed to the leaf. It's also worth trying a selection of appetizers. Ask your waiter for some suggestions. If you need a shot of caffeine, end the meal with an iced coffee—the condensed milk makes it heavenly. Jaya has another branch on the Upper West Side, but that location has a limited menu.

Jean-Georges ★★★★½

| FRENCH | EXPENSIVE | QUALITY ★★★★½ | VALUE ★★★ |

**1 Central Park West (at 60th Street) in the Trump International Hotel &
Tower, Upper West Side; ☎ 212-299-3900; www.jean-georges.com**

Reservations Required. **When to go** Anytime. **Entree range** $29–$35; prix-
fixe lunch, $29; prix-fixe dinner, $98; chef's tasting menu, $148. **Payment** Most
major credit cards. **Service rating** ★★★★. **Friendliness rating** ★★★. **Bar** Full
service. **Wine selection** Excellent; good range of prices from $22 to $1,000.
Dress Jacket required for men; dressy. **Disabled access** Yes. **Customers** Locals.
Hours Monday–Thursday, noon–2:30 p.m. and 5:30–11 p.m.; Friday and
Saturday, 5:15–11 p.m.; closed Sunday.

SETTING AND ATMOSPHERE Restaurant designer Adam Tihany has kept this
large dining room simple and spare with subdued tones of beige and
gray. The huge windows let in sun and sky and views of Central Park
during the day; at night, the lights of Columbus Circle and Central
Park South twinkle in the distance, and the gargantuan globe that sits
outside the Trump International Tower takes on extra prominence. The
overall feeling is more cool than cozy, but definitely elegant.

HOUSE SPECIALTIES Foie gras brûlée; lobster tartine; roasted sweetbreads;
baked arctic char; Parmesan-encrusted chicken; chocolate soufflé with
warm raspberries and vanilla ice cream.

OTHER RECOMMENDATIONS Sea scallops in caper-raisin emulsion with caramelized cauliflower; broiled squab with corn pancake; steamed black
sea bass; rhubarb tart with rhubarb crème glacé.

SUMMARY AND COMMENTS Jean-Georges, given four stars by the *New York
Times,* is the eponymous jewel in Jean-Georges Vongerichten's culinary
crown—he also owns JoJo, Matsugen, Perry St, Spice Market, and
Mercer Kitchen. This is where Vongerichten concentrates on his innovative, intensely flavored French cuisine. The food is superb, as is the
service; each dish is finished at your table, and this kind of attention is
rare indeed. Jean-Georges was a New York sensation from the moment
it opened, and reservations are hard to come by, but try. The sleeker
Nougatine cafe, the front room and bar of the restaurant, serves breakfast as well as lunch and dinner. Entrees are less expensive there, and the
atmosphere is somewhat less formal.

Joe's Shanghai ★★★

| CHINESE | MODERATE | QUALITY ★★★★½ | VALUE ★★★★★ |

**9 Pell Street (between Mott Street and the Bowery), Chinatown,
Little Italy, and the Lower East Side, ☎ 212-233-8888; 24 West 56th
Street (between Fifth and Sixth avenues), Midtown West, Times Square,
and the Theater District, ☎ 212-333-3868; 136-21 37th Avenue,
Flushing, Queens, ☎ 718-539-4429; www.joeshanghairestaurants.com**

Reservations Only for parties of 10 or more. **When to go** During off-hours (between 2:30 and 5:30 p.m. or after 9:30 p.m.) to avoid wait. **Entree range** $10–$13. **Payment** Cash only. **Service rating** ★★★. **Friendliness rating** ★★★. **Bar** Beer only, and a limited variety. **Wine selection** BYOB. **Dress** Casual. **Disabled access** Queens good, Manhattan fair (1 step to dining room). **Customers** Locals, foodies. **Hours** *Pell Street:* daily, 11 a.m.–11 p.m.; *56th Street:* Monday–Friday, 11:30 a.m.–3 p.m. and 5–10:30 p.m.; Saturday, 11:30 a.m.–10:30 p.m.; Sunday, 1–10:30 p.m.; *Queens:* Monday–Thursday, Sunday, 11 a.m.–11 p.m.; Friday and Saturday, 11 a.m.–midnight.

SETTING AND ATMOSPHERE Several notches up from a Chinatown-style no-frills cafe, always busy but comfortable. The big tables are shared, but that's part of the ritual.

HOUSE SPECIALTIES Crabmeat steamed buns; stewed pork balls; shredded pork with pickled-cabbage soup; anything with mushrooms; shrimp-fried rice cake; hot-and-sour soup; pork shoulder (with honey glaze); Shanghai fried flat noodles; shredded-turnip shortcakes; soya (mock) duck.

SUMMARY AND COMMENTS By all means, start with the crabmeat steamed buns, amazing soup-filled dumplings that New Yorkers go wild over. Wait for them to cool a bit, then delicately (don't puncture—you'll lose the soup!) transfer a dumpling to a spoon into which you've pooled a bit of soy-ginger sauce and a dab of hot sauce. Nibble a hole in the skin, suck the soup, then down the dumpling. The shiitake mushrooms are great here, and the stewed pork balls are the lightest meatballs you've ever tasted, in a succulent sauce. Don't order typical Chinese restaurant fare, though—try to stick with the Shanghai specialties. Ask the harried but affable waiters for tips, or ask about good-looking dishes passing by. You can also check out **Joe's Ginger** from the same owners (25 Pell Street; ☎ 212-285-0999; **www.joeginger.com**).

Kefi ★★★½

GREEK	INEXPENSIVE/MODERATE	QUALITY ★★★★	VALUE ★★★★½

505 Columbus Avenue (at 84th Street), Upper West Side;
☎ **212-873-0200; www.kefirestaurant.com**

Reservations Not accepted. **When to go** Anytime. **Entree range** $10–$18. **Payment** Cash only. **Service rating** ★★★½. **Friendliness rating** ★★★. **Bar** Full service. **Wine selection** A few nice Greek choices. **Dress** Casual. **Disabled access** Yes. **Customers** Locals, couples, Natural History Museum visitors. **Hours** Tuesday–Thursday, noon–3 p.m. and 5–10 p.m.; Friday and Saturday, noon–3 p.m. and 5–11 p.m.; Sunday, 11 a.m.–3 p.m. (brunch) and 5–10 p.m.; closed Monday.

SETTING AND ATMOSPHERE While the original Kefi was cramped and intimate, it has recently relocated and is now an Upper West Side behemoth. The entrance would be a quaint restaurant on its own, with its stone floors, hanging lanterns, and line of small tables opposite the long, thin bar and massive wooden wine shelf. The upstairs dining room features thatched chairs and long blue banquettes, and the ceiling is a lattice of painted beams. The white walls are decorated with Greek earthenware, rustic shutters, and paintings. Down the back stairs are two more rooms. The first resembles the main dining room but with an earthier color palette. The second room is arguably the coziest even though, with its stone floors and hanging baskets, it's designed to evoke a Greek porch.

HOUSE SPECIALTIES Selection of spreads; meatballs; grilled sardines; glazed cuttlefish; sheep's milk dumplings; pork souvlaki; walnut cake with walnut ice cream.

OTHER RECOMMENDATIONS Crispy cod; flat pasta with pulled, braised rabbit; sheep-milk ravioli; grilled branzino with potato, olive, and tomato; braised lamb shank.

SUMMARY AND COMMENTS When the owners of the stylish Greek restaurant Onera shut it down to rethink the menu, they came up with Kefi, a decidedly more sedate and traditional Greek restaurant. The idea was to do Greek standards, but do them so well that they would seem new—and not to charge very much. But that doesn't mean having gyros for dinner: rabbit, octopus, and cuttlefish are on the menu, and don't worry if you don't know much about Greek wine; there is a foolproof selection. Even though Kefi is fairly large, it's almost always packed. It's also just a few blocks from the American Museum of Natural History. So plan ahead if you want to combine a trip to both.

Kesté ★★★

NEAPOLITAN PIZZA MODERATE QUALITY ★★★★ VALUE ★★★½

271 Bleecker Street (between Jones and Cornelia streets), Greenwich Village; ☎ 212-243-1500; www.kestepizzeria.com

Reservations None. When to go Anytime. Entree range $9–$19. Payment All major credit cards. Service rating ★★★. Friendliness rating ★★★. Bar Beer and wine only. Wine selection Small Italian selection. Dress Casual. Disabled access Difficult; room is thin, tables are cramped. Customers Locals, tourists, students. Hours Monday–Saturday, noon–3:30 p.m. and 5–11 p.m.; Sunday, noon–3:30 p.m. and 5–10 p.m.

SETTING AND ATMOSPHERE Basically a tiny pizza cafe, though not without its charm. A finely crafted stone wall evokes the Neapolitan nostalgia of the owners. A seat in the front gives you a view onto the scramble of Bleecker Street. A seat in the back offers a peek at the roaring oven and the talented pie artists. In bad weather, come early or late, 'cause while the staff is gregarious and jovial, they'll be quick to shuffle you to the sidewalk if tables aren't available.

HOUSE SPECIALTIES Pizza: kesté; margherita; mast'nicola; pizza del re.

OTHER RECOMMENDATIONS It all depends on your taste. Many pies come with cured meats (salami, prosciutto, etc.), and a handful are vegetarian friendly. All are delicious.

SUMMARY AND COMMENTS This is *not* the place for a New York slice. The Italian owners are re-creating pizza as it was originally conceived hundreds of years ago in Naples. The cheese is made from buffalo milk. Toppings are often barely cooked. An artisanal wood-burning oven, brought to a temperature of 800 degrees Fahrenheit, flash-fires the delicious concoctions in less than a minute, lending both a crunchiness and gooeyness to the crust. The dough is thick, but filled with pockets of air, making it surprisingly fluffy. Some complain that the pizzas are "wet," but that's the style, and it would be a shame to overcook the sauce. Ordering one pie per person and sampling from each is the way to go, and you're likely to find that no one will leave hungry.

La Boîte en Bois ★★½

FRENCH	MODERATE	QUALITY ★★★½	VALUE ★★★★

75 West 68th Street (Central Park West and Columbus Avenue), Upper West Side; ☎ 212-874-2705; www.laboitenyc.com

Reservations Recommended. **When to go** Anytime. **Entree range** $20–$27. **Payment** AE, MC, V. **Service rating** ★★★. **Friendliness rating** ★★★. **Bar** Full service. **Wine selection** Good range, good prices. **Dress** Casual. **Disabled access** None. **Customers** Loyal locals, Lincoln Center attendees. **Hours** Sunday–Thursday, 11:30 a.m.–10:30 p.m.; Friday and Saturday, 11:30 a.m.–11 p.m.

SETTING AND ATMOSPHERE This cute, cozy, hole-in-the-wall bistro takes you from the sidewalks of Manhattan right into the French countryside. It's only a few blocks from Lincoln Center, and thus a pre-concert favorite.

HOUSE SPECIALTIES Lamb stew; homemade pâté; breast of duck with wild rice; seafood crepe with tomato coulis; praline mousse.

OTHER RECOMMENDATIONS Pan-roasted chicken with herbs; pot-au-feu de poisson; veal scaloppine with wild mushrooms; crème brûlée.

SUMMARY AND COMMENTS Popular with concertgoers in the know, this small space can get quite crowded, but by 7:45 p.m. it clears out and quiets down. The pre-theater menu runs to $40 and is available from 5 to 7 p.m. The bread is wonderfully warm and tasty and the service personal and attentive, but the menu needs updating, and the food, though decent, could use some fresh legs.

Lady Mendl's Tea Salon ★★★

TEAROOM	MODERATE	QUALITY ★★★★	VALUE ★★★

56 Irving Place (between 17th and 18th streets in The Inn at Irving Place), Gramercy Park and Madison Square; ☎ 212-533-4466; www.ladymendls.com

Reservations Accepted. **When to go** Anytime. **Entree range** $35 prix-fixe. **Payment** All major credit cards. **Service rating** ★★. **Friendliness rating** ★★★½. **Bar** Beer, wine, Champagne, port, sherry. **Wine selection** Very small. **Dress** Nice casual. **Disabled access** None. **Customers** Hotel guests, locals. **Hours**

Monday–Friday, seatings at 3 p.m. and 5 p.m.; Saturday and Sunday, seatings at noon, 2:30 p.m., and 5 p.m.

SETTING AND ATMOSPHERE This tearoom, in the pricey Inn at Irving Place, aims for an upscale English boardinghouse look. Unlike some of the Midtown hotel teas, this room—equipped with a working fireplace—is whisper-quiet.

HOUSE SPECIALTIES A five-course tea, with all the usual fixings: crustless sandwiches of cucumber and smoked salmon; pâtés; warm scones; clotted cream; jams; tarts; and chocolate mousse cake, all served with a pot of tea per guest.

ENTERTAINMENT AND AMENITIES People-watching; The Inn at Irving Place is an exclusive hotel, so high-powered and celebrity guests are common.

SUMMARY AND COMMENTS The food is nearly irreproachable; sandwiches are properly fussy, scones (perhaps the best item) taste homemade, and chocolate mousse cake is far better than the usual. There is a wide selection of teas and herbal infusions—all fancier than on-the-shelf brands—and each guest is served from one of the handsome antique pots collected by the owners. As you'd expect at a proper tea, everything's served on bone china. This is a very popular place for bridal and baby showers.

Le Bernardin ★★★★½

FISH, FRENCH	VERY EXPENSIVE	QUALITY ★★★★	VALUE ★★★

155 West 51st Street (between Sixth and Seventh avenues), Midtown West, Times Square, and the Theater District; ☎ 212-554-1515; www.le-bernardin.com

Reservations Required. **When to go** Anytime. **Entree range** Prix-fixe dinner, $109; 7-course tasting menu, $135; 8-course chef's tasting menu, $185; prix-fixe lunch, $68. **Payment** All major credit cards. **Service rating** ★★★★. **Friendliness rating** ★★★★. **Bar** Full service. **Wine selection** Excellent. **Dress** Dressy; jackets required for men. **Disabled access** Yes. **Customers** Businesspeople, locals. **Hours** Monday–Thursday, noon–2:30 p.m. and 5:30–10:30 p.m.; Friday, noon–2:30 p.m. and 5:30–11 p.m.; Saturday, 5:30–11 p.m.; closed Sunday.

SETTING AND ATMOSPHERE Formal elegance, without arrogance, suffuses this grand space, and the clientele dresses and acts accordingly—this is a luxurious setting for truly upscale dining. Blue-gray walls, adorned with fine classic maritime paintings in ornate frames, rise to a teak ceiling. Small roses top tables handsomely set and graciously spaced.

HOUSE SPECIALTIES The menu changes frequently, but recent favorites include yellowfin-tuna carpaccio; lemon-splashed slivers of fluke; warm lobster timbale; seared rare hamachi over sweet cherry tomato, and portobello escabeche. (In an effort to speed the recovery of endangered species, Le Bernardin does not serve Chilean sea bass, grouper, shark, swordfish, sailfish, or wild bluefin tuna.)

OTHER RECOMMENDATIONS Spanish mackerel tartare with osetra caviar; shaved geoduck clam with wasabi and soy-ginger dressing; peeky-toe crab with green tomatoes and preserved lemon; barbecued eel, sautéed black trumpet mushrooms, and chive blossoms; poached skate with caramelized baby fennel ragoût; lobster tail with shrimp sambal sauce and roasted mangoes; pan-roasted codfish.

SUMMARY AND COMMENTS Flawless fish, flawless service. Another New York candidate for number one—whether restaurant, fish restaurant, or French restaurant—thanks to star chef Eric Ripert, who has reached the same glorious gastronomic heights as Gilbert Le Coze, his renowned predecessor. Steamed black bass is one of the best dishes in Manhattan; with soft citrus notes and fresh coriander that gives it an Indian edge, its subtle complexity will have you shaking your head in disbelief that food could ever be this good. To ease the stress of picking your own dishes, it might be best to go with one of the tasting menus. They may be ridiculously expensive, but if ever there was a place to justify such an expense, this is it. Ripert also consulted on the menu for **Geisha** (33 East 61st Street, between Madison and Park avenues; ☎ 212-813-1113; **www.geisharestaurant.com**).

Les Halles ★★½

| FRENCH BISTRO, STEAK | MODERATE/EXPENSIVE | QUALITY ★★★½ | VALUE ★★★ |

**411 Park Avenue South (between 28th and 29th streets),
Gramercy Park and Madison Square, ☎ 212-679-4111;
15 John Street (between Broadway and Nassau Street), Financial District,
☎ 212-285-8585; www.leshalles.net**

Reservations Recommended. **When to go** Anytime. **Entree range** $19–$29. **Payment** All major credit cards. **Service rating** ★★. **Friendliness rating** ★★★. **Bar** Full service. **Wine selection** Well chosen; some good values. **Dress** Casual. **Disabled access** Yes. **Customers** Locals, professionals. **Hours** *Park Avenue:* daily, 7:30 a.m.–midnight; *John Street:* Monday–Friday, 7:30 a.m.–midnight; Saturday and Sunday, 11:30 a.m.–midnight.

SETTING AND ATMOSPHERE Don't expect a quiet, romantic evening for two at either location of this boisterous French bistro–butcher shop. Patrons are packed elbow to elbow like, dare we say, cattle, and the noise quotient is high. Both rooms have a familiar, well-worn feel, with dozens of posters and photos lining the walls in Gramercy and simple mirrors downtown. Throw in some cigarette smoke, and you might as well be in Paris. (Oh, wait, they banned smoking in France too!)

HOUSE SPECIALTIES Endive salad with apples, walnuts, and Roquefort cheese; steak frites; *boudin aux pommes* (blood sausage, caramelized apples); onglet (hanger steak); warm chocolate-and-banana tart.

OTHER RECOMMENDATIONS *Tarte alsacienne* (caramelized-onion tart); home-made rillettes; steak tartare; *moules marinières* (mussels steamed in white wine); rib-eye steak; fresh apple tart with vanilla ice cream.

SUMMARY AND COMMENTS Les Halles proves that predictability can be a good thing. If you're in the mood for a dependable bistro menu and train-terminal atmosphere, Les Halles should be your call. Appetizers are winsome, lose some. Steaks here may not be up to par with those at Peter Luger's or any of the city's other big-name establishments, but they're good for what they are, and at $23, the steak frites are a great deal. They come with every steak and are delicious.

Mandoo Bar ★★

| KOREAN DUMPLING BAR | INEXPENSIVE | QUALITY ★★★ | VALUE ★★★★★ |

2 West 32nd Street (at Fifth Avenue), Midtown East; ☎ 212-279-3075

Reservations Not accepted. **When to go** Lunch. **Entree range** $5–$10. **Payment** AE, MC, V. **Service rating** ★★. **Friendliness rating** ★★. **Bar** Beer and wine only. **Wine selection** Limited. **Dress** Casual. **Disabled access** Yes. **Customers** Koreans, office workers, shoppers. **Hours** Daily, 11:30 a.m.–10 p.m.

SETTING AND ATMOSPHERE When you enter this popular Koreatown lunch spot, you may find yourself hypnotized by watching the dumpling makers standing at the front window, furiously churning out colorful morsels. Too bad the rest of the room isn't as eye-catching. The long, thin space is clean and basic, with tile floors and lacquered wood tables and benches. The staffers like to shuffle diners in and out, and with the prices Mandoo charges, you can't blame them.

HOUSE SPECIALTIES *Goon mandoo*; kimchi *mandoo; pajeon; chapchae.*

OTHER RECOMMENDATIONS *Mool mandoo*; combo *mandoo; mandoo* ramen; *bibimbap.*

SUMMARY AND COMMENTS Every meal begins with the requisite complimentary bowl of radish kimchi that the servers will toss in front of you almost as soon as you sit. Whether you like your *mandoo* (Korean dumplings) steamed, boiled, or fried and with or without meat, you'll find something to satisfy your tastes. The dough is color-coded (guess what?—the green ones are vegetarian), so you'll know what you're eating if you order a combo platter. If you don't care for dumplings at all, the restaurant also serves nice interpretations of Korean favorites *chapchae* and *bibimbap.* A couple of blocks from Macy's on the eastern edge of Koreatown, Mandoo Bar may not be as authentic as other Korean spots in the neighborhood, but it's an excellent place for a quick and cheap bite. For other adventures in "Seoul food," you may want to try **HanGawi** (12 East 32nd Street, between Fifth and Madison avenues; ☎ 212-213-0077; **www.hangawirestaurant.com**), **Kunjip** (9 West 32nd Street, on the same block as Mandoo Bar; ☎ 212-216-9487; **www.kunjip.net**), and **Woo Chon** (see page 363).

Margon Restaurant ★★

CUBAN CAFETERIA   INEXPENSIVE   QUALITY ★★★½   VALUE ★★★★★

136 West 46th Street (between Sixth and Seventh avenues),
Midtown West, Times Square, and the Theater District;
☎ **212-354-5013; www.margonrestaurant.net**

Reservations Not accepted. **When to go** Quick lunch. **Entree range** $6–$10 (breakfast, $3–$7). **Payment** Cash only. **Service rating** ★★½. **Friendliness rating** ★★★. **Bar** None. **Wine selection** None. **Dress** Casual. **Disabled access** None. **Customers** Locals, businesspeople. **Hours** Monday–Friday, 6 a.m.–5 p.m.; Saturday, 7 a.m.–2:30 p.m.; closed Sunday.

SETTING AND ATMOSPHERE A harshly lit, bare-bones, hustle-your-tray-through-the-line basement cafeteria.

HOUSE SPECIALTIES Roast chicken; octopus salad; rice and beans; fried plantains. All the standard-issue Latino-luncheonette fare, but good!

SUMMARY AND COMMENTS If you need to catch a quick lunch in Midtown, this place will get you in and out in a jiffy (don't sweat long lines; they move quickly), but patrons' fast-shoveling forks belie the high quality of the food. Everything's very fresh and made with care. There are precious few Latin lunch counters left in this part of town, and friendly, efficient Margon is a proud bastion.

Menchanko-Tei ★★

JAPANESE   INEXPENSIVE   QUALITY ★★★½   VALUE ★★★★

43–45 West 55th Street (between Fifth and Sixth avenues), Midtown
West, Times Square, and the Theater District, ☎ **212-247-1585;**
131 East 45th Street (between Lexington and Third avenues),
Midtown East, ☎ **212-986-6805; www.menchankotei.com**

Reservations *45th Street:* accepted; *55th Street:* only for parties of 5 or more. **When to go** Avoid the 1 p.m. rush. **Entree range** $9–$14. **Payment** All major credit cards. **Service rating** ★★★★. **Friendliness rating** ★★. **Bar** Full service, with several sakes, Japanese beers, and such spirits as *shochu*. **Wine selection** House. **Dress** Nice casual. **Disabled access** Difficult at both branches (restrooms are not accessible). **Customers** Locals and local workers. **Hours** *45th Street:* Monday–Thursday, 11:30 a.m.–11:30 p.m.; Friday, 11:30 a.m.–midnight; Saturday, 11:30 a.m.–11 p.m.; Sunday, 11:30 a.m.–10:30 p.m.; *55th Street:* Monday–Thursday, Saturday, and Sunday, 11:30 a.m.–11:30 p.m.; Friday 11:30 a.m.–midnight.

SETTING AND ATMOSPHERE Noodles are taken very seriously here, and the dignified decor immediately signals that this ain't no fooling around. The 55th Street Menchanko-Tei has low ceilings, wood floors, some cursory Oriental tchotchkes, a low bar in front of an open (sparkling) kitchen, and a long line of tables for two and four (there's also a more peaceful dining room in back, painted a friendly mustard yellow). The

45th Street branch is airier and more Western, with higher ceilings and a small dining spillover area upstairs near the restrooms.

HOUSE SPECIALTIES Several variations on souply themes: *menchanko* itself is an egg-noodle soup of profound delicacy; additions can include miso, hot pickled vegetables, or fish balls. A kitchen-sink version called *tokusei menchanko* is dominated by chunks of fresh, flaky salmon. There are two ramen soups, both topped with a succulent slice of *yakibuta* pork: white broth (gingery and simple) and a soy-based version. *Zousui* soups are made with rice rather than noodles; kimchi zousui is particularly good, homey, and quite spicy from the hot, pickled cabbage. Nagasaki Saraudon is frizzy, thin, fried noodles with a sweetish seafood sauce; Nagasaki Chanpon is the same, but in soup.

OTHER RECOMMENDATIONS There are a handful of non-noodle options, few of them in a class with the soups. *Oden* are small appetizer plates; check out *kinchaku*—a deliciously exotic cake of fried tofu stuffed with sticky rice paste in a soothing broth-sauce. There are also side orders such as *yakibuta* (pork), *menma* (tender bamboo shoots with a slightly caramelized flavor), or kimchi (hot, pickled cabbage). Ask for some *yuzu-kosho*—a red-pepper paste flavored with yuzu fruit—to spoon into the soups. A fuller menu is served nights at the 55th Street location.

SUMMARY AND COMMENTS Fans of the film *Tampopo* will feel at home here in NYC's best Japanese noodle-soup restaurant, where noodles are made with great care for a discerning clientele. These loyal customers come often; the 55th Street branch will sell regulars a full bottle of booze to keep on reserve (they have three months to drain it). Soups are served in heavy iron kettles, with a wooden ladle for transference to your bowl. Slurp loudly (silent noodle-scarfing is an insult to the chef), but get out quickly; despite the deliciousness, the well-appointed decor, the polite service, and the nonbargain prices (soups run as high as $13), this type of restaurant is considered fast food, so lingering is discouraged. Another great noodle place is **Soba-ya** (see page 354).

Mesa Grill ★★★

AMERICAN-SOUTHWEST   EXPENSIVE   QUALITY ★★★½   VALUE ★★★

102 Fifth Avenue (between 15th and 16th streets), Gramercy Park and Madison Square; ☎ 212-807-7400; www.mesagrill.com

Reservations Recommended. **When to go** Anytime. **Entree range** $21–$35; appetizers, $11–$15. **Payment** All major credit cards. **Service rating** ★★★. **Friendliness rating** ★★. **Bar** Full service, with 20 different kinds of tequila. **Wine selection** Good. **Dress** Casual; some business attire at lunch; no jacket required. **Disabled access** Yes, downstairs. **Customers** Locals, businesspeople. **Hours** Monday–Thursday, noon–2:30 p.m. and 5:30–10:30 p.m.; Friday, noon–2:30 p.m. and 5:30–11 p.m.; Saturday, 11:30 a.m.–2:30 p.m. (brunch) and 5–11 p.m.; Sunday, 11:30 a.m.–3 p.m. (brunch) and 5:30–10:30 p.m.

SETTING AND ATMOSPHERE Substantial columns, painted with bands of southwestern colors, hold up the two-story ceiling. The lime-green-and-yellow walls sprout tin lighting fixtures, and the banquettes are covered in a kitschy "Hi-Ho Silver" design. All this is to let you know that you're in for spicy Southwestern fare. The tables are close, and the noise level can rear up and buck like a bronco.

HOUSE SPECIALTIES Shrimp-and-roasted-garlic corn tamale; spicy salmon tartare with plantain croutons and cilantro oil; grilled red snapper; spice-rubbed pork tenderloin.

OTHER RECOMMENDATIONS Barbecued pork quesadilla; crispy squid; barbecued duck with blue corn pancake; pan-roasted striped bass; miniature ice-cream sandwiches.

SUMMARY AND COMMENTS Food Network mainstay Bobby Flay has pizzazz aplenty, and this smart venue is the perfect place for him to strut his Southwestern stuff. Every dish has a spicy regional accent—even the romaine salad has red-chile croutons, the red snapper is crusted with blue-corn tortillas, and there's blue corn again in the biscotti. The appetizers are especially interesting and pretty on their Fiesta Dinnerware plates, and the main courses are large enough to satisfy the hungry cowboys in the cookhouse, though some of the combos can be a little over the top. Flay aficionados can also sample his more far-ranging takes on our domestic cuisines at **Bar Americain** (152 West 52nd Street; ☎ 212-265-9700; **www.baramericain.com**).

Meskerem ★★★

ETHIOPIAN	INEXPENSIVE/MODERATE	QUALITY ★★½	VALUE ★★★½

124 MacDougal Street (between Bleecker and West Third streets), Greenwich Village, ☎ 212-777-8111; 468 West 47th Street (between Ninth and Tenth avenues), Midtown West, Times Square, and the Theater District; ☎ 212-664-0520

Reservations Not required except for large groups; the Village location doesn't take reservations. When to go Anytime. Entree range $9–$20. Payment MC, V. Service rating ★★★½. Friendliness rating ★★★★. Bar Full service. Wine selection Very small, but does include Ethiopian honey wine. Dress Casual. Disabled access No for Village, yes for Midtown. Customers Locals, ethnic, regulars. Hours Daily, noon–10:30 p.m.

SETTING AND ATMOSPHERE Cheery, casual, and almost always full of happy people sharing food and looking almost guilty for not having to use utensils. Ethiopian artifacts, and cloths can be found in both locations.

HOUSE SPECIALTIES *Shero wat* (ground chickpeas with ground red pepper–berbere sauce); *yebeg alecha* (lamb with ginger, garlic, and curry); *kitfo* (chopped beef with butter and ground-chile-pepper sauce, served rare or raw); *miser wat* (lentils with garlic, onions, and berbere sauce).

OTHER RECOMMENDATIONS *Timatim* salad (tomatoes, onions, scallions, peppers);

Meskerem combination dish with beef, lamb, and vegetables prepared in various ways.

SUMMARY AND COMMENTS This is an ideal place for at least four people with clean hands. That way you can try several dishes and have them all placed before you, collectively, on a huge, circular platter. Then everyone gets to dig in on one plate using the *injera* (slightly sour, spongy, flat, soft bread made from an Ethiopian grain called *tef*) as the tool to collect, scoop, and place food into your mouth (or that of a friend's). Utensils are available. Order one vegetarian combo entree plus two to three meat entrees to get a full spectrum of tastes. You can wait by the bar (although it's quite small) for your table and order an Ethiopian honey wine as an aperitif.

Mexicana Mama ★★★

MEXICAN	MODERATE	QUALITY ★★★½	VALUE ★★★

525 Hudson Street (between Charles and West 10th streets), Greenwich Village; ☎ 212-924-4119

Reservations Not accepted. **When to go** Anytime. **Entree range** $12–$19. **Payment** Cash only. **Service rating** ★★★. **Friendliness rating** ★★★. **Bar** Stick with beer and margaritas. **Wine selection** Limited. **Dress** Casual. **Disabled access** Extremely cramped; bathroom up step through kitchen. **Customers** Locals, couples, barhoppers. **Hours** Tuesday–Sunday, noon–11 p.m.; closed Monday.

SETTING AND ATMOSPHERE This place is tiny. A bench and a short row of tables run along one wall, while the servers struggle to move back and forth from the open kitchen in the rear. The few sidewalk seats (in good weather) don't really ease congestion. Decor is limited to the fruit-printed plastic tablecloths and the heavily painted blue walls, where the main hangings are folding chairs. This all gives it a south-of-the-border, hole-in-the-wall vibe, which is probably why some complain the food is too expensive.

HOUSE SPECIALTIES *Ensalada mexicana*; guacamole; burritos; tacos with chile-roasted pork; margaritas.

OTHER RECOMMENDATIONS Taquitos; chorizo quesadillas; chicken mole; chiles rellenos.

SUMMARY AND COMMENTS One of the most important aspects of high-quality Mexican food is the freshness of the ingredients. The variety of home-made salsas and the perfectly textured corn tortillas prove that Mexicana Mama knows this. An authentic mole sauce is harder to achieve than many realize, and Mama gets the subtleties right here. This is certainly not Tex-Mex or Mexican of the fast-food variety. It isn't necessarily what you might find in Mexico. It is, however, worth the slightly inflated prices for the inventive combinations of sauces, grilled and roasted meats, and fresh-picked fruits and veggies. A new, slightly larger location, **Mexicana Mama Centro** (47 East 12th Street, between Broadway and University Place; ☎ 212-253-7594), is not far away if you find the wait for a table unbearable.

Mr. Broadway Kosher Restaurant ★★★

JEWISH DELI   MODERATE   QUALITY ★★★★   VALUE ★★★★★

1372 Broadway (between 37th and 38th streets), Midtown West, Times Square, and the Theater District; ☎ 212-921-2152; www.mrbroadwaykosher.com

Reservations Accepted. **When to go** Anytime. **Entree range** $6–$30. **Payment** All major credit cards. **Service rating** ★★★. **Friendliness rating** ★★★. **Bar** Beer and wine. **Wine selection** Small (kosher). **Dress** Casual. **Disabled access** Fair. **Customers** Locals, professionals. **Hours** Monday–Thursday, 10 a.m.–10 p.m.; Friday, 10 a.m.– 3 p.m.; Sunday, 11 a.m.–10 p.m.; closed Saturday and all Jewish holidays.

SETTING AND ATMOSPHERE   From the front this looks like just another of the area's many kosher fast-food spots, but the rear is classic Jewish deli, a bustling cavern with darting waiters, tables crammed with pickles and coleslaw, and regulars who look as if they eat a lot of pastrami trying to squeeze through the tight floor plan.

HOUSE SPECIALTIES   Garlicky baba ghanoush; potato knishes; couscous; kasha *varnichkes* (oniony buckwheat with bow-tie noodles); deep-fried potato pancakes; French fries; chicken soup with matzo balls; falafel; *derma* (rich, spicy stuffing in sausage casing); fried "Moroccan cigars" (pastry flutes stuffed with minced meat); homemade gefilte fish.

OTHER RECOMMENDATIONS   There's a terrific self-service Middle Eastern salad bar up front for takeout or dining in.

SUMMARY AND COMMENTS   Mr. Broadway Kosher Deli & Restaurant is known by many names: it's also Me Tsu Yan Kosher Chinese Restaurant and Chez Lanu, serving North African dishes. The confluence of cuisines makes for some strange culinary juxtapositions, from customers smearing hummus on their hot dogs to the Moroccan couscous served with a homely piece of Eastern European roast chicken riding on top. For both Middle Eastern and deli specialties, Mr. Broadway is a winner. Corned beef is, of course, of paramount importance in a Jewish deli; Mr. Broadway's is good and well cut but perhaps a bit too lean (everything's a tad lighter than usual here; perhaps it's the Sephardic influence). Chinese dishes—*glatt* kosher, like everything else—are handily available for those for whom real Chinese isn't an option.

Molly's Pub & Restaurant ★★★

IRISH PUB FOOD   MODERATE   QUALITY ★★★★   VALUE ★★★★

287 Third Avenue (between 21st and 22nd streets), Gramercy Park and Madison Square; ☎ 212-889-3361; www.mollysshebeen.com

Reservations Limited. **When to go** Anytime. **Entree range** $12–$22. **Payment** All major credit cards. **Service rating** ★★½. **Friendliness rating** ★★. **Bar** Full service. **Wine selection** Small. **Dress** Casual. **Disabled access** Fair. **Customers** Locals. **Hours** Monday–Saturday, 11 a.m.–4 a.m.; Sunday, noon–4 a.m.

SETTING AND ATMOSPHERE Classic Irish pub; woody and snug, complete with fireplace. Lots of booths and tables (the largest, a round table seating eight, is handy for after-work get-togethers).

HOUSE SPECIALTIES Cheeseburgers; shepherd's pie; chicken potpie; respectable steak; mashed potatoes; most fried items.

OTHER RECOMMENDATIONS Avoid specials; stick with the main menu. Ask for fried onions on your cheeseburger (they're sensational), and request the special walnut dressing on your salad.

SUMMARY AND COMMENTS The area has plenty of generic Irish bar-restaurants to choose from, but this one is the standout. Typical pub food is grand (best cheeseburgers and shepherd's pie in Manhattan), and Molly's transcends type with such touches as a surprisingly worthy bread basket and fresh (gasp!), not overcooked vegetable sides.

Molyvos ★★★½

GREEK	EXPENSIVE	QUALITY ★★★★	VALUE ★★★★

871 Seventh Avenue (between 55th and 56th streets), Midtown West, Times Square, and the Theater District; ☎ 212-582-7500; www.molyvos.com

Reservations Recommended. **When to go** Anytime. **Entree range** $22–$38. **Payment** All major credit cards. **Service rating** ★★★. **Friendliness rating** ★★★★. **Bar** Full service; excellent ouzo selection. **Wine selection** Good; especially interesting Greek selections. **Dress** Business, casual. **Disabled access** Fair; three steps to the dining room. **Customers** Businesspeople, locals. **Hours** Monday–Thursday, noon–3 p.m. and 5:30–11:30 p.m.; Friday, noon–3 p.m. and 5:30 p.m.–midnight; Saturday, noon–3 p.m. and 5 p.m.–midnight; Sunday, noon–11 p.m.

SETTING AND ATMOSPHERE An airy, comfortable Greek taverna with a bright front room and substantial bar that lead into a large, somewhat dimmer, main dining room. Greek key panels top stenciled planks; the terra-cotta sponged walls are dotted with black-and-white photos of Molyvos (the town), and all is accented with Hellenic objects, plates, amphorae, glass bottles, and the capital of a marble column.

HOUSE SPECIALTIES Marinated lamb shanks; *moussaka;* grilled baby octopus; *meze;* shrimp *saganaki;* wood-grilled whole fish; *loukoumades* (dessert fritters with honey sauce).

OTHER RECOMMENDATIONS Cabbage *dolmades;* grilled jumbo prawns; ocean blackfish *plaki;* toasted almond vanilla cake.

SUMMARY AND COMMENTS With Molyvos, John Livanos, also owner of Oceana (see page 335), pays homage to his hometown on the Greek island of Lesbos. The mouthwatering *mezedes* (little bites), such as *tzatziki* and grilled, marinated sardines, alone can make a meal, but don't limit yourself, or you could miss out on such great dishes as grilled baby octopus. Smoky and packed with flavor, the octopus needs little else to satisfy. The superfast service and great food make this an excellent stop either before or after a concert at Carnegie Hall.

Momofuku Ssäm Bar ★★★★½

KOREAN-INSPIRED AMERICAN   MOD/EXP   QUALITY ★★★★½   VALUE ★★★★

207 Second Avenue (at 13th Street), East Village; ☎ 212-254-3500; www.momofuku.com

Reservations Not accepted, unless as a group you're ordering *bo ssäm* (whole pork butt). **When to go** Anytime. **Entree range** $12–$32. **Payment** All major credit cards. **Service rating** ★★★½. **Friendliness rating** ★★★★. **Bar** Beer and wine only. **Wine selection** Small but good. **Dress** Casual. **Disabled access** Yes. **Customers** The trendy, foodies, off-duty chefs, absolutely no vegetarians. **Hours** Sunday–Thursday 11:30 a.m.–3:30 p.m. and 5 p.m.–midnight; Friday and Saturday, 11:30 a.m.–3:30 p.m. and 5 p.m.–2 a.m.

SETTING AND ATMOSPHERE The eponymous bar stretches along one edge of the long, narrow room. Everything is sleek and efficient. Right angles reign. The floors are stone, the walls and ceilings are wood paneled, and the chairs are simple black stools. It's lively, a little loud, and a lot of fun.

HOUSE SPECIALTIES *Bo ssäm* (must reserve in advance); steamed pork buns; roasted brussels sprouts; country ham; pan-roasted, dry-aged rib eye.

OTHER RECOMMENDATIONS BBQ rib sandwich; pickles; crispy pig's head.

SUMMARY AND COMMENTS The first thing people ask is, "What exactly is a ssäm?" Momofuku's Web site currently defines it as "anything that is encircled or wrapped," but when David Chang, the 2008 winner of the James Beard Best New York City Chef award, opened his always-evolving, Korean-inspired, pork-obsessed restaurant, that Korean burrito—a sumptuous combination of meat or tofu mixed with kimchi, rice, mushrooms, sprouts, and/or onions, then topped with hoisin sauce and wrapped in flour pancakes—was pretty much the only thing the place sold. But everyone assumed Chang had more tricks up his sleeve, and now Momofuku Ssäm boasts one of the most eclectic menus around, and the only ssäm you'll find is bo ssäm: a whole pork shoulder served with oysters and kimchi. It must be reserved online in advance, and to have any hope of finishing it, you'll need six to ten people. Of late, the menu has added more seafood, including a raw bar, but it's the meat that people come here for, not to mention experiments in offal (beef tendon or pig's head anyone?). Chang first came to prominence with **Momofuku Noodle Bar** (171 First Avenue, between 10th and 11th streets; ☎ 212-777-7773; **www.momofuku.com**), which gets raves for its fried-chicken dinner. The restaurateur's newest ventures, **Momofuku Ko** (163 First Avenue; same phone and Web site as above) and **Momofuku Milk Bar** (207 Second Avenue), are just as popular. Ko is considered the masterpiece of the bunch, but it's tiny, and the only way to get a seat for its two- to three-hour tasting menu is to log in to the Web site at 10 a.m. exactly one week before the date on which you wish to dine, then hope your keyboard fingers are faster than local foodies'. Good luck!

My Thai ★★★★

| THAI | INEXPENSIVE | QUALITY ★★★★½ | VALUE ★★★★ |

8347 Dongan Avenue, Elmhurst, Queens; ☎ 718-476-6743

Reservations Accepted. **When to go** Anytime. **Entree range** $7–$23. **Payment** Cash only. **Service rating** ★★★★. **Friendliness rating** ★★★. **Bar** None. **Wine selection** None. **Dress** Casual. **Disabled access** Small step in; tight route to accessible restroom. **Customers** Thai locals, questing aficionados. **Hours** Sunday–Thursday, noon–11 p.m.; Friday and Saturday, noon–11:30 p.m.

SETTING AND ATMOSPHERE A warm, well-lit, immaculate little dining room, with a few unusual Thai products on display. Certainly not elegant, but invitingly bright and cheery in this neighborhood of inexpensive holes-in-the-wall. Comfortable seating.

HOUSE SPECIALTIES Start with *larb* (pronounced "lab"), ground pork with plenty of red onion, mint, lime, and pepper. All noodle dishes are wonderful, particularly pad thai, which is fresh and focused, not sweet and gunky. Chinese broccoli with crispy pork cracklings is amazing, and you can't go wrong with the curries. Specials of the day (often smoky, marinated pieces of roast chicken or Manila clams in a succulent brown sauce) are always good. Iced tea (served in a tall glass with milk) is bright orange, aromatic, and slightly smoky; Thai iced coffee is as rich and delicious as melted ice cream.

OTHER RECOMMENDATIONS Soups are good, not great; skip the stuffed chicken wings. For dessert, My Thai offers "toast": thick-cut white bread carefully toasted and spread with butter and a light sprinkling of sugar (and, optionally, a light drenching of condensed milk), which is a far cry from the stuff served with eggs in diners. There are also shaved-ice desserts (choose from a large bar of toppings, including various beans, jellies, syrups, and squiggly things).

SUMMARY AND COMMENTS My Thai is one of the few Thai restaurants in town patronized by a largely Thai clientele. There is a battle among ethnic food devotees as to which is more important: authenticity or great flavor. This place offers both. Throw in friendly, sincere service by a family staff that clearly takes great pride in what it's doing, and you have an unbeatable combo. The restaurant is a quick walk from the R-V subway (Elmhurst Avenue stop). Nearby and just as great is **Ping's** (see page 346) for Cantonese, and a couple of stops closer to Manhattan on the R-V train is **Sripraphai** (64-13 39th Avenue, ☎ 718-899-9599), the Thai wonder of Woodside.

New Pasteur ★★★½

| VIETNAMESE | INEXPENSIVE | QUALITY ★★★★ | VALUE ★★★★★ |

85 Baxter Street (between Walker and Bayard streets), Chinatown, Little Italy, and the Lower East Side; ☎ 212-608-3656 or 212-608-4838

Reservations Suggested. **When to go** Avoid the peak hours of 8–10 p.m. **Entree range** $5–$19. **Payment** All major credit cards. **Service rating** ★★★. **Friendliness rating** ★★½. **Bar** Beer and wine. **Wine selection** House. **Dress** Casual. **Disabled access** Fair. **Customers** Ethnic, locals, foodies. **Hours** Daily, 11 a.m.–10 p.m.

SETTING AND ATMOSPHERE Spare storefront with little decoration to detract from the memorable cooking. Be prepared to share tables.

HOUSE SPECIALTIES Any of the *phos* (beef-based noodle soups); barbecue beef (with vermicelli or on its own); shrimp rolls; fried spring rolls; barbecue-shrimp rolls on sugarcane; iced coffee.

SUMMARY AND COMMENTS Year in and year out, homely New Pasteur (formerly Pho Pasteur) outclasses all new Vietnamese start-ups with no-nonsense, first-class cooking. The barbecue beef is a marvel of gastronomic engineering, an entire beefy symphony compressed into each small nugget (wrap them in lettuce leaves, along with mint, cucumber slices, sprouts, and carroty fish sauce; the Vietnamese eat almost everything this way). If New Pasteur is full, as it often is, head up the block and around the corner to larger and more upscale **Nha Trang Centre** (148 Centre Street; ☎ 212-941-9292), whose food is nearly as good.

Nobu ★★★★

JAPANESE	EXPENSIVE	QUALITY ★★★★½	VALUE ★★★

105 Hudson Street (at Franklin Street), SoHo and TriBeCa;
☎ **212-219-0500; www.myriadrestaurantgroup.com**

Reservations Absolutely necessary. **When to go** Anytime. **Entree range** $28–$35; multicourse "omakase," chef's choice, $100 and up for dinner, $60 and up for lunch; sushi and sashimi à la carte, $3–$13. **Payment** All major credit cards. **Service rating** ★★★. **Friendliness rating** ★★★. **Bar** Full service. **Wine selection** Okay, but sipping sake might be better. **Dress** Business, casual. **Disabled access** Fair; call in advance to arrange. **Customers** Locals, businesspeople, celebs, ethnic. **Hours** Monday–Friday, 11:45 a.m.–2:15 p.m. and 5:45–10:15 p.m.; Saturday and Sunday, 5:45–10:15 p.m.

SETTING AND ATMOSPHERE Birch-tree columns, blond wood, high, copper-leafed ceiling, plush banquettes, a wall of black river stones, and a large sushi counter are all part of the stunningly original million-dollar decor. Just as stunning are the number of well-known faces to be seen.

HOUSE SPECIALTIES The "omakase" tasting dinner; toro tartare with caviar; black cod with miso; sea urchin in spinach; yellowfin sashimi with jalapeño; squid "pasta" with garlic sauce.

OTHER RECOMMENDATIONS Broiled toro with spicy miso; shrimp and lobster with spicy lemon sauce; salmon tartar with caviar; sea urchin tempura; toro *to-ban yaki*.

SUMMARY AND COMMENTS No doubt, Nobu is one of the most exciting eateries in New York—it's not the place to order simply sushi. Chef Nobuyuki

Matsuhisa's brilliant, innovative menu is as striking as the decor and considered by some to be the city's best Japanese food, by others to be just the city's best food. The menu is huge, with more than a hundred small and medium-size dishes—a grazer's paradise. Reservations are hard to come by, but you can get the same food without the formality at **Nobu Next Door.** This spot doesn't take reservations, so you may wait up to an hour to get a table. Next Door is a bit more casual than the original but has many of the same menu items, including unforgettable toro tartare with caviar and everybody's favorite, black cod with miso. You'll even find a few noodle dishes for good measure, something big brother lacks (though you can hardly call Nobu lacking). Although some claim that the service suffers because of its larger size, **Nobu Fifty Seven** (40 West 57th Street, between Fifth and Sixth avenues; ☎ 212-757-3000; **www.myriad restaurantgroup.com**) features all of Nobu's now-classic flavor combinations with the addition of a wood-burning oven and hibachi table.

Noodle Pudding ★★★★

ITALIAN	MODERATE	QUALITY ★★★★	VALUE ★★★½

38 Henry Street, Brooklyn; ☎ 718-625-3737

Reservations Not accepted. **When to go** Dinner. **Entree range** $9–$40. **Payment** Cash only. **Service rating** ★★★★. **Friendliness rating** ★★★★. **Bar** Full service. **Wine selection** Very good. **Dress** Casual. **Disabled access** Yes to space; no to bathroom. **Customers** Locals, regulars from far and wide. **Hours** Tuesday–Thursday, 5:30–10:30 p.m.; Friday and Saturday 5:30–11 p.m.; Sunday, 5–10 p.m.; closed Monday.

SETTING AND ATMOSPHERE The minimal signage just hints at the restaurant's existence, but look hard enough, and once you see happy diners comfortably ensconced in a dark wooden interior, simply furnished with wooden tables and a bar at the front of the space, you have probably found the spot. Acoustics are poor, so when the space is crowded, it's a bit noisy, but not offensively so.

HOUSE SPECIALTIES Homemade gnocchi with sage butter; osso buco; panna cotta of varying flavors; daily fish specials.

OTHER RECOMMENDATIONS *Strozzapretti* with ricotta and eggplant; calamari fritti; risotto of the day; polenta.

SUMMARY AND COMMENTS Divulging the existence of Noodle Pudding is tantamount to admitting where you've hidden a family treasure: the family (read: locals) will not be happy. But the secret is out, and the locals may need to wait just a bit longer for a table. Service is very personable and efficient, and each table is always presented with warmed ciabatta and decent olive oil. The food is consistently delicious, which explains why the place is such a local favorite. During warm weather the front window opens completely for a feel of alfresco dining.

Oceana ★★★½

SEAFOOD   EXPENSIVE   QUALITY ★★★★½   VALUE ★★★

1221 Sixth Avenue (at 49th Street), Midtown West, Times Square, and the Theater District; ☎ 212-759-5941; www.oceanarestaurant.com

Reservations Recommended. **When to go** Anytime. **Entree range** $26–$48. **Payment** All major credit cards. **Service rating** ★★★. **Friendliness rating** ★★★. **Bar** Full service. **Wine selection** Excellent. **Dress** Smart casual. **Disabled access** None. **Customers** Businesspeople, locals. **Hours** Monday–Thursday, 11 a.m.– 3 p.m. and 5–11 p.m.; Friday and Saturday, 11 a.m.–3 p.m. (brunch on Saturday) and 5 p.m.–midnight; Sunday, 11 a.m.–3 p.m. (brunch) and 4–10 p.m.

SETTING AND ATMOSPHERE Oceana relocated and expanded in 2009 from an East Side town house to Rockefeller Center, but it retained its nautical theme. While the old location evoked the interior of a yacht, the new one brings you closer to the deck, with a sprawling dining room highlighted by tall, partially curtained windows looking out on 49th Street. White-clothed tables, fabric banquettes, and booths are spread generously over the wood floors, while a marble raw bar and custom-designed lobster tank elegantly display the fresh catches. In summer it adds outdoor tables and four rooms, including the six-seat Chef's Table, are available for private dining.

HOUSE SPECIALTIES Oysters; fluke tartare; taro-wrapped pompano; halibut saltimbocca; grilled market fish; doughnut platter.

OTHER RECOMMENDATIONS Stinging-nettle soup with yogurt panna cotta; house-cured gravlax; grilled swordfish; sea scallops à la plancha; chocolate chip–pecan "cookie" bar.

SUMMARY AND COMMENTS In case you couldn't tell from the name, Oceana serves fish, and serves it well. Chef Ben Pollinger, who was recently awarded three stars by the *New York Times,* continues the restaurant's tradition of borrowing from a variety of global cuisines to turn seafood into something surprising and eclectic. The clientele mainly consists of what you would expect to see on a grand ocean vessel—men in suits— but don't be put off by the members-only vibe. All will find the service generous and the desserts top-notch.

Orso ★★★

NORTHERN ITALIAN   MODERATE   QUALITY ★★★½   VALUE ★★★

322 West 46th Street (between Eighth and Ninth avenues), Midtown West, Times Square, and the Theater District; ☎ 212-489-7212; www.orsorestaurant.com

Reservations Necessary at least a week in advance. **When to go** Anytime. **Entree range** $24–$30. **Payment** MC, V. **Service rating** ★★★. **Friendliness rating** ★★★. **Bar** Full service. **Wine selection** Italian only; house wine by the carafe is serviceable and well priced. **Dress** Casual. **Disabled access** None. **Customers** Theatergoers, theater people, locals. **Hours** Monday, Tuesday, Thursday, and Friday, noon–11:45 p.m.; Wednesday, Saturday, and Sunday, 11:30 a.m.–11:45 p.m.

SETTING AND ATMOSPHERE This star of Restaurant Row opens through a narrow, low-ceilinged bar area to a vaulted back room, where the open kitchen is fronted by a counter topped with large flower pots heaped with bread and lemons. Modesty prevails, the lights are low, adornment is limited to framed black-and-white photos, and, *grazie Dio,* there is soundproofing so that you can hear your companions and snatches of theatrical gossip from neighbors.

HOUSE SPECIALTIES This menu changes daily, but there are always wonderful thin-crusted pizzas; pasta with porcini mushrooms; grilled vegetable plate; calf's liver with onions.

OTHER RECOMMENDATIONS Ultra-thin pizza bread with oil and rosemary; arugula salad; pasta with broccoli rabe; gelato.

SUMMARY AND COMMENTS Orso has been a winner for more than 20 years, and it's still hard to get a reservation—so if this is your pre-theater destination, book well ahead (reservations are taken up to one month in advance). The northern Italian dishes are expertly and authentically prepared, the waiters are cordial, the setting is relaxed, theater folk actually eat here, and prices are fair.

Osteria del Circo ★★★

ITALIAN **EXPENSIVE** **QUALITY ★★★★** **VALUE ★★★**

120 West 55th Street (between Sixth and Seventh avenues), Midtown West, Times Square, and the Theater District; ☎ 212-265-3636; www.osteriadelcirco.com

Reservations Recommended. **When to go** Anytime. **Entree range** $27–$45; appetizers, $11–$30. **Payment** All major credit cards. **Service rating ★★★**. **Friendliness rating ★★★**. **Bar** Full service; serves a top-notch Negroni. **Wine selection** Very good. **Dress** Midtown mélange of business and smart casual. **Disabled access** Yes. **Customers** Businesspeople, locals, tourists. **Hours** Monday, 11:30 a.m–2:30 p.m. and 5:30–10:30 p.m.; Tuesday–Friday, 11:30 a.m–2:30 p.m. and 5:30–11:30 p.m.; Saturday, 5:30–11:30 p.m.; Sunday, 5–10:30 p.m.

SETTING AND ATMOSPHERE From the tentlike red and yellow swaths of cloth that adorn the high ceiling to the trapeze ladder with hanging monkeys over the bar, designer Adam Tihany set out to create an atmosphere of fun—and he succeeded. The festive aura elicits smiles and childlike anticipation for the main attraction: Mama Maccioni's food.

HOUSE SPECIALTIES Egi's ravioli; *zuppa alla frantoiana* (Tuscan 30-vegetable soup); crème brûlée; *bomboloncini* (custard-, chocolate-, and raspberry-filled doughnuts).

OTHER RECOMMENDATIONS *Cacciucco* (Tuscan fish soup); any of the thin-crust pizzas; warm bread pudding.

SUMMARY AND COMMENTS It's hard not to enjoy yourself at this Midtown Italian hot spot, run by Sirio Maccioni's (Le Cirque) three sons. The room is spacious, the mood is festive, and everyone seems happy to be there. Outdoor seating is popular in the summer months. The food, however, can be hit or miss. The yellowfin-tuna tartare is a bland mush, held together, barely, by tender white beans on top. On the other hand, Egi's ravioli (a must-order), stuffed with spinach, bitter greens, and sheep's milk ricotta, comes with a choice of sauces but works best with the butter-sage. The many choices also include a three-course prix-fixe menu for $28 at lunch or $38 at dinner (5:30 to 6:30 p.m. and 9:30 to close) and several dishes for two. Desserts steal the show. The list is among the largest and best in the city, and the warm bread pudding topped with caramelized pecans is blissful and addictive.

Otto ★★★

PIZZERIA-ENOTECA	MODERATE	QUALITY ★★★★	VALUE ★★

1 Fifth Avenue (corner of Eighth Street), Greenwich Village;
☎ **212-995-9559; www.ottopizzeria.com**

Reservations Recommended. **When to go** Anytime. **Entree range** $8–$15. **Payment** All major credit cards. **Service rating** ★★★. **Friendliness rating** ★★½. **Bar** Full service. **Wine selection** Extensive Italian. **Dress** Casual and hip. **Disabled access** Yes. **Customers** Professionals, fashionistas, locals. **Hours** Daily, 11:30 a.m.–midnight; pizza served all day.

SETTING AND ATMOSPHERE Although the space is large, it doesn't seem cavernous, in part due to the partitions and the red, burgundy, and brown colors along with the wooden furniture and floor. It's far from cozy, but it is warm and sleek. Noise levels can be overwhelming when it's packed.

HOUSE SPECIALTIES Otto Lardo pizza (yep—paper-thin strips of pork fat and fresh rosemary over a pizza crust) and other pizza specials; gelato—all flavors; seasonal hot chocolate; fennel-and-*bottarga* pizza (fennel, fish roe, two cheeses, and tomato); Italian wine.

OTHER RECOMMENDATIONS *Funghi misti* (mixed mushrooms); *ceci bottarga* (fried chickpeas with fish roe); figs *agrodolce*.

SUMMARY AND COMMENTS Mario Batali opened Otto in spring 2003, and it became, instantly, a controversial hit. The controversy is not about the pizzas (although the Otto Lardo pizza reached cult status in months), but more about the antipasti and whether Otto can justify charging $4 to $25 for small to "grande" portions of various cuts of ham, seafood, cheese, olives, and various salads. We think the portion size is a bit undersized, but many of the dishes are well executed with subtle tastes worth trying in spite of the poor cost–size ratio. The knowledgeable sommelier is on hand to discuss Italian wine accompaniments. As you wait for your table in the bar, we'd suggest indulging in a flight of wine for tasting. The gelato has already been graced with well-deserved awards; the olive oil, coffee, and hazelnut *stracciatella* flavors are superb.

Pam Real Thai Food ★★½

| THAI | INEXPENSIVE | QUALITY ★★★ | VALUE ★★★★½ |

404 West 49th Street (between Ninth and Tenth avenues), Midtown West, Times Square, and the Theater District; ☎ 212-333-7500

Reservations Not accepted. **When to go** Anytime. **Entree range** $6–$10. **Payment** Cash only. **Service rating** ★★. **Friendliness rating** ★½. **Bar** Limited selection of beer, wine. **Wine selection** House. **Dress** Casual. **Disabled access** Difficult restroom access. **Customers** Locals, pre-theater, ethnic. **Hours** Sunday–Thursday, 11:30 a.m.–11 p.m.; Friday and Saturday, 11:30 a.m.–11:30 p.m.

SETTING AND ATMOSPHERE While not completely spartan, the decor of the cramped dining room doesn't add much to your dining experience. The small wooden tables, linoleum floors, drop-panel ceilings, and cushioned black chairs are not far from what you would find in a cafeteria. The walls are olive-green and faux marble with framed portraits, laudatory reviews, and Thai tourism posters providing the only eye candy.

HOUSE SPECIALTIES *Hae kern;* crispy-duck *yum;* panang curry; fried whole red snapper with chile sauce; *pad kra prow.*

OTHER RECOMMENDATIONS *Som tum* (green-papaya salad); *yum koon chiang* (pork-sausage salad); pad thai; duck with chile sauce.

SUMMARY AND COMMENTS *Quick, reasonably authentic,* and *affordable* are the operative words here. Service, while not rude, is brisk and impersonal. The servers shuffle diners in and out as the waiting line stretches into the street. People come back not only for the astoundingly low prices, but also because owner Pam Panyasiri has faithfully reproduced the dishes of her Bangkok home. If your taste buds can't handle a little heat, avoid anything on the menu marked with chile peppers. The cooks' idea of hot is indeed on the high end of the spectrum (though not as hot as some Thai enthusiasts would wish). Because of the lines, Pam has opened a venue around the corner called **Pam Thai Encore** (402 West 47th Street; ☎ 212-315-4441). It features the same menu, and because it doubles as a gallery, the interior design is decidedly more hip.

Paola's ★★★

| NORTHERN ITALIAN | MODERATE/EXPENSIVE | QUALITY ★★★★ | VALUE ★★★★ |

1295 Madison Avenue (at 92nd Street), Upper East Side; ☎ 212-794-1890; www.paolasrestaurant.com

Reservations Recommended. **When to go** Dinner only. **Entree range** $20–$40. **Payment** AE, MC, V. **Service rating** ★★★. **Friendliness rating** ★★★. **Wine selection** Good; a bit pricey. **Dress** Casual. **Disabled access** Fair. **Customers** Locals. **Hours** Monday–Saturday, 1–4 p.m. and 5–11 p.m.; Sunday, 1–10 p.m.

SETTING AND ATMOSPHERE In a lobby corner of the Hotel Wales, Paola's is a lively addition to the Carnegie Hill neighborhood of the Upper East Side. (The restaurant thrived for more than ten years in a smaller space eight blocks south.) Wood-paneled walls are matched with lofty tin ceilings, and various hues of yellow and orange can be found in the paint, drapes, and floral arrangements. When the restaurant fills up, the noise level can rise, but at dinnertime the staff lowers the lights, draws the curtains, and strives for the cozy and romantic.

HOUSE SPECIALTIES   Mussels marinara (the best in Manhattan); crispy artichokes; *taglierini* with chanterelle mushrooms and shaved black truffles; veal scaloppine; ricotta cheesecake.

OTHER RECOMMENDATIONS   Mozzarella with red peppers, tomatoes, and basil; roasted beets with goat cheese, toasted hazelnuts, and watercress; pappardelle with duck ragu; potato gnocchi.

SUMMARY AND COMMENTS   A cut or two above a neighborhood trattoria, this Upper East Side Italian restaurant is worth the trip. The service is solicitous, and the food is authentic, homey, and very comforting. Chef-owner Paola Marracino has changed the menu very little over the years, and it's obvious she knows what she's doing with appetizers. Pastas are first-rate, especially the stuffed variety, such as ravioli and tortelloni.

Pastis ★★½

FRENCH BISTRO   MODERATE   QUALITY ★★★½   VALUE ★★★

9 Ninth Avenue (at Little West 12th Street), Greenwich Village;
☎ 212-929-4844; www.pastisny.com

Reservations Recommended. **When to go** Anytime. **Entree range** $18–$38. **Payment** All major credit cards. **Service rating** ★★★. **Friendliness rating** ★★★½. **Bar** Full service, very popular. **Wine selection** Decent. **Dress** Casual for day; chic at night. **Disabled access** Accessible in front room and bathrooms. **Customers** Locals, trendies, celebrities. **Hours** Monday–Wednesday, 8 a.m.–1 a.m.; Thursday, 8–2 a.m.; Friday, 8–2:30 a.m.; Saturday, 10 a.m.–4:30 p.m. (brunch) and 6 p.m.–2:30 a.m.; Sunday, 10 a.m.–4:30 p.m. (brunch) and 6 p.m.–1 a.m.

SETTING AND ATMOSPHERE   Large restaurant with an airy, crisp, bistro-French feel. Mirrors, brass, wood, and tile are the predominant materials used to decorate the expanse. Brunch and lunchtime bring a more relaxed feel to the restaurant, but come nighttime, the glitz shines in all its glory, and the front room with the bar becomes very crowded.

HOUSE SPECIALTIES   Steak frites with béarnaise sauce; onion soup; *croque monsieur; croque madame;* crêpes suzette.

OTHER RECOMMENDATIONS   *Gratin dauphinois;* skate; mussels; niçoise salad; omelet.

SUMMARY AND COMMENTS   Pastis is not a place noteworthy for its food (though the coffee is excellent), but it has a high glamour factor, particularly at night, while sibling Balthazar (see page 292) seems to have a better grip on food but has lost its hold on Pastis-bound celebrities. Come for a drink, get a feel for the place, and then decide if you'd like to tackle dinner here in another outfit. The food is standard, but brunch is fun if you order a drink and munch on the bread basket, a croque monsieur, or an omelet. One favorite beverage is L'Orchidée Verte, which consists of pastis, mint, and water. The bathrooms have a Continental style; men and women wash their hands together in a troughlike sink but use separate toilets. In warm weather, sit outside, where it feels a bit more relaxed.

Patsy's Pizza ★★★

| PIZZERIA | INEXPENSIVE | QUALITY ★★★★½ | VALUE ★★★★★ |

2287 First Avenue (between 117th and 118th streets), Harlem; ☎ 212-534-9783

Reservations Not necessary. **When to go** Anytime. **Entree range** Whole pizzas, $12–$21 (with 3 toppings). **Payment** Cash only. **Service rating** ★★. **Friendliness rating** ★★. **Bar** Full service (Friday and Saturday only). **Wine selection** Limited. **Dress** Casual. **Disabled access** Good. **Customers** Locals, foodies. **Hours** Daily, 11 a.m.–midnight.

SETTING AND ATMOSPHERE The room with the oven (where you order) is harshly lit but permeated with the collective spirit of three quarters of a century of great pizza, not to mention the pile of coal. Next door, the restaurant has friendly but amateurish waiter service.

HOUSE SPECIALTIES Fantastic, unpretentious brick-oven pizza by the slice from an ancient coal-burning oven.

SUMMARY AND COMMENTS Though this is the only top-notch brick-oven pizzeria that will serve slices, you should really get a whole pie; order slices—from pizzas that have been sitting—and you may face less-crusty crust, though the taste is still tops. The neighborhood is far uptown, in Spanish Harlem, so taxi in after dark. *Note:* The other Patsy's Pizzas in Manhattan have merely licensed the name; they're not recommended.

Penang ★★½

| MALAYSIAN | MODERATE | QUALITY ★★★½ | VALUE ★★★ |

127 West 72nd Street (between Columbus and Amsterdam avenues), Upper West Side; ☎ 917-441-4791; www.penangusa.com

Reservations Only for parties of 6 or more. **When to go** Anytime. **Entree range** $11–$23. **Payment** AE, MC, V. **Service rating** ★★★. **Friendliness rating** ★★★. **Bar** Full service. **Wine selection** Limited, but the beers on tap seem to be the beverage of choice. **Dress** Casual. **Disabled access** Yes. **Customers** Locals, ethnic. **Hours** Sunday–Thursday, noon–10:45 p.m.; Friday and Saturday, noon–11:45 p.m.

SETTING AND ATMOSPHERE The cavernous "lounge" is low on lights and high on decibels. Dark wood and slick, angular surfaces dominate. Oil lamps flicker on black tables, but don't really cast any additional illumination on the brick or blue-painted walls.

HOUSE SPECIALTIES *Masak nenas* (chicken or beef with fresh pineapple chunks and lemongrass, served in a pineapple shell); *roti canai* (Indian flat bread with curry dipping sauce); chicken with shredded mango and peppers served in a mango shell; spiced, deep-fried whole red snapper.

OTHER RECOMMENDATIONS Penang clay pot noodles with seafood; Malaysian *nasi goreng;* fried taro stuffed with seafood; beef *rendang*.

SUMMARY AND COMMENTS Malaysia, the crossroads of the food world, incorporates into its cooking the best culinary qualities of nearby India, China, Thailand, and Vietnam, along with some European touches from the British colonizers. Though Penang has suffered from expansion and sometimes-spotty food, it remains a viable venue for Malaysian cooking in Manhattan. Appetizers outshine entrees, so load up on those, especially the *roti canai:* warm, ultra-thin, ribbony bread that you tear up and dip into positively addictive chicken-and-potato curry sauce. **Nyonya** (194 Grand Street between Mott and Mulberry streets; ☎ 212-334-3669 and 212-334-6701), by the same owners, has a wider selection of more obscure and authentic Malaysian dishes (try the Hainanese chicken rice and *mee siam*).

Penelope ★★½

AMERICAN-COMFORT FOOD   INEXPENSIVE   QUALITY ★★★   VALUE ★★★★

159 Lexington Avenue (at 30th Street), Gramercy Park and Madison Square; ☎ 212-481-3800; www.penelopenyc.com

Reservations Not accepted. When to go Lunch and brunch. Entree range $8–$15. Payment Cash only. Service rating ★★★. Friendliness rating ★★★★½. Bar Beer and wine only. Wine selection Limited. Dress Casual. Disabled access Three steps up to enter. Customers Locals, office workers, shoppers. Hours Daily 8 a.m.–midnight.

SETTING AND ATMOSPHERE This bright cafe has the feel of a farmhouse kitchen, complete with mismatched chairs and aproned staff. Clipped on a clothesline near the entrance is proof of dedicated customers and staff—handwritten thank-you notes, glowing reviews, and even a calendar with employees of the month.

HOUSE SPECIALTIES Arugula salad with warm chicken meatballs and pesto; mac and cheese; Ellie's spinach pie; BBLT (double bacon, lettuce, tomato on sourdough); Nutella French toast; vanilla or chocolate cupcakes with a variety of frostings.

OTHER RECOMMENDATIONS Spinach and beet salad; chicken potpie; grilled three cheese with Swiss, Fontina, and white American; magic bar.

SUMMARY AND COMMENTS In an area packed with curry joints, Penelope's comfort food stands out. While the menu contains few surprises, the warm chicken meatballs are a delectable combination of savory and spicy. The popular meatballs are also available à la carte or on a sandwich. Salads are filling enough, but the accompanying bread makes them a full meal. The wine list is limited, but many options are available by the glass. Penelope cooks all of its desserts in house, so it's hard to resist ordering something from the display of brownies, carrot cake, and hearty pies. Breakfast is available during the week until 11:45 a.m., and brunch is served on Saturday and Sunday from 8 a.m. to 4 p.m. The reasonable prices and friendly staff make this beyond popular, so plan for a wait at peak lunch times and on weekends.

Peter Luger Steak House ★★★½

STEAK HOUSE   EXPENSIVE   QUALITY ★★★★   VALUE ★★★★

178 Broadway (at Driggs Avenue), Brooklyn (Williamsburg); ☎ 718-387-7400; www.peterluger.com

Reservations Required for dinner. **When to go** Anytime. **Entree range** $32–$42. **Payment** Cash only. **Service rating** ★★★. **Friendliness rating** ★★★. **Bar** Full service, proud of its "oversized drinks." **Wine selection** Fair. **Dress** Casual. **Disabled access** Yes. **Customers** Locals, businesspeople, tourists. **Hours** Monday–Thursday, 11:45 a.m.–9:45 p.m.; Friday and Saturday, 11:45 a.m.–10:45 p.m.; Sunday, 12:45–9:45 p.m.

SETTING AND ATMOSPHERE Just over the Williamsburg Bridge in Brooklyn, this 120-year-old landmark steak house is as plain as its menu. Scrubbed wooden tables, scrubbed wooden floors, a few beer steins, and crusty veteran waiters (who are actually very nice) are staples. This is the way a steak house should be.

HOUSE SPECIALTIES USDA prime dry-aged (on the premises) porterhouse steak; creamed spinach; Luger's German fried potatoes; apple strudel with whipped cream.

OTHER RECOMMENDATIONS Double-thick loin lamb chops; steak sandwich; Luger-burger; French fries; thick sliced bacon; cheesecake.

SUMMARY AND COMMENTS What's a trip to New York City without a trip to the city's best steak house? Okay, so maybe Luger's isn't in "the city," but it's close enough and more than worth the cab fare. Start with a thick strip of bacon—it's greasy, it's fatty, and it's good. But don't have too many strips, because you're going to need all the stomach room you can spare for that porterhouse, a huge cut of meat for two. Watch as the waiter pours the excess meat juices and melted butter over the perfectly cooked slices. Then take one bite of the tender, moist meat, and you'll know why many will never go to another steak house again.

Petite Abeille ★★½

BELGIAN LUNCHEONETTE   INEXPENSIVE   QUALITY ★★★★   VALUE ★★★★½

134 West Broadway (at Duane Street), SoHo and TriBeCa, ☎ 212-791-1360; 466 Hudson Street (at Barrow Street), Greenwich Village, ☎ 212-741-6479; 401 East 20th Street (at First Avenue), Gramercy Park and Madison Square, ☎ 212-727-1505; 44 West 17th Street, Gramercy Park and Madison Square, ☎ 212-727-2989; www.petiteabeille.com

Reservations Not accepted. **When to go** Anytime. **Entree range** $10–$17. **Payment** All major credit cards. **Service rating** ★★. **Friendliness rating** ★★★.

Bar Full service (except for Hudson Street location). **Wine selection** Limited. **Dress** Casual. **Disabled access** Good; staff helps with step. **Customers** Locals, businesspeople, expat Belgians. **Hours** Monday–Friday, 8 a.m.–11 p.m.; Saturday and Sunday, 9 a.m.–11 p.m. (brunch until 4:30 p.m.).

SETTING AND ATMOSPHERE Decor is different in each Petite Abeille; what is consistent is the European flair, good food, and friendly service.

HOUSE SPECIALTIES Waffles (unadorned, per Belgian tradition); Flemish-style carbonade (savory beef stew cooked in abbey beer); *stoemp de carrote* (ultra-homey carrot-flecked mashed potatoes); mussels.

OTHER RECOMMENDATIONS Brunch omelets are tasty and fluffy, while coffee and cappuccino tend to be spot-on.

ENTERTAINMENT AND AMENITIES Once a month, the 20th Street location hosts a jazz night. Call for details.

SUMMARY AND COMMENTS It's hard to decide whether you're eating in a good restaurant masquerading as a cheap lunchroom or whether this is simply a super-high-quality lunchroom. Don't expect gastronomic miracles, just skillfully cooked Belgian comfort food at unbeatable prices. Monday is half-price-Belgian-beer night; Tuesday is half-price-wine night; Wednesday is all-you-can-eat-mussels night; and Thursday is lobster night. Petite Abeille is child-friendly for its bright, colorful, and casual atmosphere; volumes of Belgian comic-strip hero Tintin and his adventures are at hand for the reading pleasure of young and old.

Petrossian ★★★

RUSSIAN	EXPENSIVE	QUALITY ★★★½	VALUE ★★★

182 West 58th Street (at Seventh Avenue), Midtown West, Times Square, and the Theater District; ☎ 212-245-2214; www.petrossian.com

Reservations Recommended. **When to go** Anytime. **Entree range** $27–$40. See below for prix-fixe options. **Payment** All major credit cards. **Service rating** ★★★. **Friendliness rating** ★★★. **Bar** Full service. **Wine selection** Very good, especially the Champagne by the glass. **Dress** Upscale; jackets and ties. **Disabled access** None. **Customers** Businesspeople, ladies who lunch, caviar cravers. **Hours** Monday–Friday, 11:30 a.m.–3 p.m. and 5:30–11:30 p.m.; Saturday, 11:30 a.m.–3:30 p.m. (brunch) and 5:30–11:30 p.m.; Sunday, 11:30 a.m.–3:30 p.m. (brunch) and 5:30–10:30 p.m.

SETTING AND ATMOSPHERE Only one block from Carnegie Hall, this dimly lit caviar cave is nestled in a corner of the Alwyn Court. Art Nouveau lovelies grace the mirrors behind the polished granite bar. The dining area, mirrored, small, and darkly elegant, is appointed in rose, black, and well-buffed wood.

HOUSE SPECIALTIES Caviar! Beluga, sevruga, osetra, and so on, served with toast or blini and crème fraîche; "teasers," an assortment of smoked fish appetizers with a touch of foie gras.

OTHER RECOMMENDATIONS Borscht with piroshki; foie gras salad; steamed lobster; tropical fruit and vodka sorbets.

SUMMARY AND COMMENTS You can blow a big budget on the caviar, but don't be intimidated—you can also dine surprisingly well on the $25 prix-fixe lunch, which includes a glass of fine Champagne, or the $35 prix-fixe dinner ($47 if you want a 12-gram taste of caviar), graciously served throughout the evening. Brunch, too, is excellent. The adjoining cafe offers caviar, foie gras, smoked fish, breads, pastries, and tarts to go, as well as table service for breakfast, lunch, or snacks.

Piccola Venezia ★★★★

ITALIAN	EXPENSIVE	QUALITY ★★★★½	VALUE ★★★

42-01 28th Avenue (at 42nd Street), Astoria, Queens; ☎ 718-721-8470; www.piccola-venezia.com

Reservations Necessary. When to go Avoid lunch (same menu, same stratospheric prices). Entree range $20–$45. Payment All major credit cards. Service rating ★★★. Friendliness rating ★★★★. Bar Full service. Wine selection Extensive; mostly Italian. Dress Elegant casual to dressy. Disabled access Good. Customers Politicians, movie stars, and neighborhood folks who've been eating here for decades. Hours Monday–Friday, 11:30 a.m.–11 p.m.; Saturday, 4:30 p.m.–midnight; Sunday, 2–10:30 p.m.

SETTING AND ATMOSPHERE Spirited conviviality amid Old World graciousness. This is a real class joint, from the top-quality table linens to the marble paneling and uniformed waiters, and it's filled to the rafters meal after meal with celebratory eaters. Venetian scenes decorate the walls; the management is actually Istrian—from a part of the former Yugoslavia that was once under Venetian rule.

HOUSE SPECIALTIES Excellent veal, especially the oversize veal porterhouse. Don't miss *fusi* (a twisty Istrian pasta), with either grappa sauce or a traditional Istrian veal sauce. Fried calamari, roasted peppers, tricolore and house salad, tripe, chicken campagnola (basically, chicken Marsala with mushrooms), osso buco, and oniony sautéed Venetian liver are all dependably first-rate. With seafood, stick to specials (and ask your waiter for help). Specials not to miss: venison, rabbit, seafood pasta with onions, veal valdestano, and Istrian sauerkraut soup. Ask nicely and you may be granted some of these off-menu faves: roast loin of pork, scallops casino, stuffed artichokes, and shrimp or clams in vodka sauce.

OTHER RECOMMENDATIONS This was once a regular neighborhood restaurant that over the years has grown exorbitant. So while the plainer preparations are perfectly fine, they may not taste as sensational as their price tag. Avoid potential disappointments, such as the two lobster-tail selections (whole lobster—lobster fra diavolo, for example—is much more interesting), cold antipasto plate, minestrone soup, and filet mignon. And definitely skip the ho-hum desserts.

ENTERTAINMENT AND AMENITIES Valet parking.

SUMMARY AND COMMENTS Piccola Venezia, the most senior of several Astoria Istrian-Italians, has a fanatically devoted clientele. These folks know the waiters (old pros all) and count on them for guidance on matters of pesto freshness, seafood quality, and such. The staff may not go the extra mile for fresh faces, so unless you manage to establish a particular rapport with your waiter, stick with the above suggestions, the accumulated insights of several knowledgeable insiders.

Piccolo Angolo ★★★

ITALIAN	MODERATE	QUALITY ★★★★	VALUE ★★★½

621 Hudson Street (at Jane Street), Greenwich Village;
☎ **212-229-9177; www.piccoloangolo.com**

Reservations Recommended. **When to go** Dinner only. **Entree range** $18–$30; pastas, $14–$22. **Payment** MC, V. **Service rating** ★★★. **Friendliness rating** ★★★. **Wine selection** Limited, mostly Italian; hold out for the inexpensive, homemade "house" wine. **Dress** Casual. **Disabled access** None. **Customers** Locals. **Hours** Tuesday–Thursday, 5–11 p.m.; Friday and Saturday, 5–11:30 p.m.; Sunday, 4–10 p.m.

SETTING AND ATMOSPHERE This storefront West Village classic is small, loud, and crowded, but that doesn't stop a steady stream of fans from huddling in the doorway while they wait to be seated.

HOUSE SPECIALTIES Fettuccine with porcinis; linguine with white clam sauce; lobster canneloni; rack of lamb with Marsala and mushrooms.

OTHER RECOMMENDATIONS Cold seafood antipasto; shrimp fra diavolo; grilled portobello mushrooms; eggplant rollatini; ricotta cheesecake.

SUMMARY AND COMMENTS This place is family-run in the best sense. Renato Migliorini and his son, Peter, welcome customers and worry over the pint-sized kitchen, which somehow manages to turn out enough traditional, "home-cooked" Italian food to satisfy the full house expecting to be fed. When Papa lists the ample array of daily specials, it sounds more like a fast recitative from a Verdi opera. Listen closely; he's loath to repeat, and these are the dishes to eat. Try to resist the irresistible garlic bread—you'll need room for the reasonably priced, large portions.

Picholine ★★★★

MEDITERRANEAN	EXPENSIVE	QUALITY ★★★★½	VALUE ★★★

35 West 64th Street (between Columbus Avenue and Central Park West),
Upper West Side; ☎ **212-724-8585; www.picholinenyc.com**

Reservations Recommended. **When to go** Anytime. **Entree range** 3 courses, $92 ($12 for an additional course); tasting menu, $125 ($210 with wine pairing); prix-fixe, $58. **Payment** All major credit cards. **Service rating** ★★★. **Friendliness rating** ★★★. **Bar** Full service. **Wine selection** Interesting selections in a good range of prices. **Dress** Business, dressy, upscale casual; jacket required.

Disabled access Yes. **Customers** Locals, businesspeople, Lincoln Center patrons. **Hours** Tuesday–Thursday, 5–10 p.m.; Friday and Saturday, 5–11:45 p.m.; closed Sunday and Monday.

SETTING AND ATMOSPHERE East Side elegance on the West Side, with silk-shaded wall lamps, chandeliers hanging from ornate ceilings, brocade banquettes, and some well-distributed mirrors and modern paintings. The "picholine" (a small, green olive) theme appears on the plates, while lavender and white soften the edges of this windowless room.

HOUSE SPECIALTIES The menu changes seasonally, but recent favorites have included warm Maine lobster; foie gras, black mission figs, duck "prosciutto," and purslane; polenta, tuna, and truffle toast "bacon and eggs"; loin of lamb; baked-to-order warm chocolate tart.

OTHER RECOMMENDATIONS Scallop sashimi with watermelon relish; wild-mushroom and rabbit risotto; day-boat seafood selection; cheesecake mousse napoleon.

SUMMARY AND COMMENTS This is by far the best restaurant on the Upper West Side, and chef Terrance Brennan's Mediterranean-influenced French fare would more than hold its own on the East Side as well. The menu is simply divided into "preludes," "day boats," and "the land." Warm Maine lobster is absolutely sensual, and, if it's available, Brennan's perfectly balanced dish known as "bacon and eggs" is an absolute must. There's no shortage of good food here, and the knowledgeable and pleasant staff will be happy to steer you in the right direction. Even desserts are excellent, but who needs sugar when you have that incredible cheese cart running around the room? After all, Brennan also owns Artisanal (see page 289). Maître d'fromage Max McCalman chooses about 50 cheeses from Picholine's cheese cave and sets about the room, offering suggestions for enthralled patrons and enthusiastically describing each cheese. In fact, a late-night stop for wine and cheese after a concert at Lincoln Center makes for a wonderful end to an evening.

Ping's ★★★★

CHINESE	MODERATE	QUALITY ★★★★½	VALUE ★★★★½

83-02 Queens Boulevard, Elmhurst, Queens; ☎ 718-396-1238

Reservations Accepted. **When to go** Before noon for dim sum; otherwise, anytime. **Entree range** $19 and up. **Payment** All major credit cards. **Service rating** ★★★★. **Friendliness rating** ★★★½. **Bar** Beer and wine only. **Wine selection** House. **Dress** Nice casual. **Disabled access** Good (if the dim sum carts can get around, so can you!). **Customers** Local Chinese and questing Occidentals. **Hours** Daily, 8 a.m.–3:30 p.m. (dim sum) and 3:30–11 p.m.

SETTING AND ATMOSPHERE Despite its bleak Queens Boulevard location, Ping's is an elegant, upscale Hong Kong banquet hall, with red velvet, gold tassels, and a wall of sparkling fish tanks. In spite of the grand decor (and suavely attired staff), many patrons come quite casually dressed.

HOUSE SPECIALTIES Very skillful and schooled renditions of classic Hong Kong dishes, plus the best Peking duck in town. Try the exquisitely fresh and delicate scallops in shell, whole sea bass (prepared in a variety of ways), snow pea pod leaves served with egg, any of the shellfish, pretty much anything on the specials menu, and the more ambitious-sounding offerings on the regular menu. Even less-ambitious dishes such as humble seafood panfried noodles are prepared with uncommon flair and served with great pizzazz.

OTHER RECOMMENDATIONS Outstanding dim sum each morning, perhaps the city's best (it's crowded on weekends, but the selection is also wider). Don't miss the awesome roast-pork triangles (*xia siu so,* pronounced "cha sill sew"), with ultra-flaky pastry and rich, tender barbecue filling. For dessert, buns decorated with a yellow spiral, stuffed with potent, coconut-spiked egg custard.

ENTERTAINMENT AND AMENITIES Free parking (whew!) in a lot across the side street. Don't forget to have your ticket stamped by the cashier.

SUMMARY AND COMMENTS The kitchen's elegance and flair belie the reasonable prices of many menu items. But while it's possible to make out quite well with noodles or chicken 'n' cashew nuts here, don't waste your trip (or the kitchen's great skill) by bargain hunting. This is a special-occasion place for exotic shellfish, rare baby vegetables, and fancy whole-fish preparations. For especially special occasions, Ping's will put together a banquet meal (sky's the limit, pricewise; negotiate with a manager, and be sure to carefully specify your party's squeamishness about unfamiliar ingredients). Service is excellent, with English-speaking managers in slick gray suits constantly walking the floor and offering help.

The best Chinese food is in Queens these days, and Elmhurst—fast morphing into the city's fourth Chinatown—is quite accessible (a ten-minute taxi ride once over the 59th Street Bridge, or take the E-F subway to Roosevelt Avenue and switch to the local G-R to the Grand Avenue stop). For other superb eats in this area, see the profile for **My Thai.**

Pó ★★★½

ITALIAN	MODERATE	QUALITY ★★★★	VALUE ★★★★

31 Cornelia Street (between Bleecker and West Fourth streets), Greenwich Village; ☎ 212-645-2189; www.porestaurant.com

Reservations A must. **When to go** Dinner only. **Entree range** $15–$23. **Payment** AE, MC, V. **Service rating** ★★★. **Friendliness rating** ★★★. **Bar** Beer and wine. **Wine selection** Limited, but good and fairly priced. **Dress** Casual. **Disabled access** Fair. **Customers** Locals, aficionados from the boroughs and the burbs. **Hours** Monday and Tuesday, 5:30–11 p.m.; Wednesday and Thursday, 11:30 a.m.–3 p.m. and 5:30–11 p.m.; Friday and Saturday, 11:30 a.m.–3 p.m. and 5:30–11:30 p.m.; Sunday, 11:30 a.m.–3 p.m. and 5:30–10 p.m.

SETTING AND ATMOSPHERE A thimbleful of space with hardly a dozen tables, creamy buff walls, and the patterned tin ceiling characteristic of old

Village buildings. Mirrors above the banquettes are the sole decoration, but the feeling is warm, informal, and inviting.

HOUSE SPECIALTIES White-bean ravioli with balsamic vinegar and brown butter; guinea hen with butternut squash and scallion *fregula;* terrine of dark chocolate, amaretti, and *vin santo* with espresso caramel.

OTHER RECOMMENDATIONS Coach Farm goat-cheese truffle with balsamic onions, roasted peppers, and tapenade; linguine with clams, pancetta, and hot chiles; grilled lamb sirloin with *merguez*, white beans, and preserved lemons; Campari-grapefruit sorbetto.

SUMMARY AND COMMENTS The decor is not the draw here—it's the very well-prepared, often inventive Italian food. The tradition began with former celeb chef Mario Batali and has since continued. Excellent white bean bruschetta, good bread, and olive oil come to the table to whet your appetite, but don't overnibble; you'll need the room for what follows. If choosing is too taxing, try the six-course tasting menu for $52 (entire table only). The prices are as unpretentious as the setting; ditto for the service—helpful and friendly without fuss. It's perhaps not as well kept a West Village secret as many of its repeat patrons would like: so plan ahead for this one. If you can't get a table in advance at this location, try making a reservation at the popular Brooklyn location (276 Smith Street, near Sackett Street; ☎ 718-875-1980).

Pure Food and Wine ★★★

VEGAN-RAW	EXPENSIVE	QUALITY ★★★½	VALUE ★★½

54 Irving Place, Union Square; ☎ 212-477-1010; www.purefoodandwine.com

Reservations Recommended. **When to go** Warm weather. **Entree range** $23–$39; prix-fixe $69. **Payment** All major credit cards. **Service rating** ★★★½. **Friendliness rating** ★★★½. **Bar** Wine, cider, and sake cocktails. **Wine selection** Well-chosen organics. **Dress** Trendy, no leather. **Disabled access** Yes. **Customers** Vegans, the health-conscious, curious carnivores. **Hours** Sunday–Monday, 5:30–10 p.m.; Tuesday–Saturday, 5:30–11 p.m.

SETTING AND ATMOSPHERE The wonderful stone patio and garden draw as many people as the organic, raw food. The space can be enclosed during bad weather, but there's also nothing wrong with eating inside, where the red and wood-paneled walls complement the small wooden tables and plush fuchsia chairs. It's a bit more formal than your typical vegan restaurant, but it's also a lot pricier. The small but elegant wood bar is a friendly place to wait for your table and sample organic wine.

HOUSE SPECIALTIES Zucchini-and-Roma-tomato lasagna; white-corn tamales with raw cacao mole; caper lemon roasted chanterelle mushroom.

OTHER RECOMMENDATIONS Asparagus sushi rolls with mirin-soaked forest mushrooms; sea-vegetable salad; Thai coconut noodles in red coconut curry; chocolate–passion fruit tart; strawberry shortcake Napoleon.

SUMMARY AND COMMENTS The raw-food movement certainly hasn't gone mainstream, and likely never will, but it has a shining example of its potential in Pure Food and Wine. The magic number here is 118. Nothing at the restaurant is heated to more than 118 degrees. Of course, a menu entirely dependent on fruits, vegetables, mushrooms, and legumes changes from season to season. A five-course tasting menu is available, and the young staff is always happy to help with selections. Proprietor Sarma Melngailis's beauty and marketing savvy often overshadow her greatest contribution to the New York dining scene—making raw, vegan cuisine fun, diverse, and subtle. She's also made it expensive, but your heart and conscience are worth it, right?

The River Café ★★★

| NEW AMERICAN | VERY EXPENSIVE | QUALITY ★★★★★ | VALUE ★★★★½ |

1 Water Street, Brooklyn; ☎ 718-522-5200; www.therivercafe.com

Reservations Necessary, unless you wish to have drinks or order à la carte in the Terrace Room; call in advance to see if the room is booked. **When to go** Anytime. **Entree range** Prix-fixe 3-course dinner, $98; 6-course tasting menu, $125; à la carte lunch menu, $23–$30. **Payment** All major credit cards. **Service rating** ★★★★½. **Friendliness rating** ★★★★. **Bar** Full service. **Wine selection** Extensive; more than 500 selections. **Dress** Dressy for women, jacket required for men in main dining room; less formal in Terrace Room. **Disabled access** Yes. **Customers** Couples, loyal and deep-pocketed regulars, professionals, anyone celebrating extra-special occasions. **Hours** Monday–Saturday, noon–3 p.m. and 5:30–11 p.m.; Sunday, 11:30 a.m.–3 p.m. (brunch) and 5:30–11 p.m.

SETTING AND ATMOSPHERE It's hard to find restaurants with better views, and there's not even any elevation involved. The restaurant is directly on the waterfront on the Brooklyn side of the East River, almost under the Brooklyn Bridge. Romantic and elegant in the evening, and inspiring (and a bit cheaper) during the day. At the risk of belaboring the point, we'll mention that this may be one of the top ten places in New York for marriage proposals, wedding celebrations, and anniversary meals.

HOUSE SPECIALTIES Maine lobster (seasonal preparations); rack of lamb; chocolate marquise Brooklyn Bridge dessert.

OTHER RECOMMENDATIONS Venison loin; most of the daily specials, especially the creative appetizers; the Roquefort cheese soufflé is a decent vegetarian option but can sometimes err on the heavy side.

SUMMARY AND COMMENTS Unlike other spots that may have great settings but mediocre food, the River Café excels in food and service—it's well worth a splurge on all levels. This is the place where several famed chefs once reigned, including Larry Forgione and David Burke; Brad Steelman is currently at the helm. If the Terrace Room isn't booked, and you don't feel like paying for a full meal, enjoy some wine and an appetizer or two.

Rosa Mexicano ★★★

MEXICAN	MODERATE	QUALITY ★★★★	VALUE ★★★★

**1063 First Avenue (at 58th Street), Midtown East, ☎ 212-753-7407;
61 Columbus Avenue (at 62nd Street), Upper West Side, ☎ 212-977-
7700; 9 East 18th Street (between Fifth Avenue and Broadway),
Union Square, ☎ 212-533-3350; www.rosamexicano.com**

Reservations Recommended. **When to go** Dinner only. **Entree range** $19–$28.
Payment All major credit cards. **Service rating** ★★. **Friendliness rating** ★★★.
Bar Full service; emphasis on margaritas, especially the pomegranate variation.
Wine selection Limited. **Dress** Casual. **Disabled access** Yes. **Customers**
Locals, ethnic, tourists. **Hours** *First Avenue:* Monday, 5–10:30 p.m.; Tuesday–
Thursday, 5–11:30 p.m.; Friday and Saturday, 4–11:30 p.m.; Sunday, 4–10:30
p.m.; *Columbus Avenue:* Sunday and Monday, 11:30 a.m.–10:30 p.m.; Tuesday–
Saturday, 11:30 a.m.–11:30 p.m.; *18th Street:* Sunday–Wednesday, 11:30 a.m.–
10:30 p.m.; Thursday–Saturday, 11:30 a.m.–11:30 p.m.

SETTING AND ATMOSPHERE It's always fiesta time here. Colorful cutout banners flutter from the dark rose ceilings over dusty rose adobe walls, star
lighting fixtures twinkle, potted ferns add a little greenery, and traditional copper plates contribute some elegance to the table settings.

HOUSE SPECIALTIES Guacamole; *enchiladas de mole poblano; alambres de camarones* (grilled, skewered marinated shrimp).

OTHER RECOMMENDATIONS Seviche of tuna and shrimp; *menudo* (tripe stew);
enchiladas de pato (duck with a green mole sauce); *crepas camarones*
(crepes filled with shrimp in a pasilla-chile sauce).

SUMMARY AND COMMENTS Above and beyond the usual Tex-Mex fare, this
mini-chain is closer to authentic, classic Mexican cuisine than almost any
other place in New York. Be sure to order the made-to-order-at-your-
table guacamole; it has become a renowned signature dish. The color and
dash of the food and the setting are guaranteed to lift your spirits, even
before you down a few divine frozen margaritas.

Sachiko's on Clinton ★★★★

JAPANESE	MODERATE/EXPENSIVE	QUALITY ★★★½	VALUE ★★★

**25 Clinton Street (between Stanton and Houston streets), Chinatown,
Little Italy, and the Lower East Side; ☎ 212-253-2900;
www.sachikosonclinton.com**

Reservations Not necessary. **When to go** Anytime. **Entree range** $12–$32;
5-course omakase, $35; 6-course omakase, $65. **Payment** All major credit cards.
Service rating ★★★½. **Friendliness rating** ★★★★. **Bar** Sake, beer, special
cocktails. **Wine selection** Very small. **Dress** Casual chic. **Disabled access** Yes.
Customers Locals, ethnic, sushi lovers. **Hours** Sunday, Tuesday, and Wednesday,
5:30 p.m.–midnight; Thursday–Saturday, 5:30 p.m.–1 a.m.; closed Monday.

SETTING AND ATMOSPHERE   No ceremony needed, as Sachiko's gives off an air of quiet confidence. A lovely back garden and patio provide dining in decent weather. Indoor diners can either sit at the smallish sushi bar or choose among several tables in two adjacent spaces.

HOUSE SPECIALTIES   *Gomadofu* (blend of sesame and kuzu root powder); soba with duck soup; kushiage; sake cocktails.

OTHER RECOMMENDATIONS   Anything from the sushi bar; *sasazushi* (bamboo-leaf-wrapped sushi); soba salad.

SUMMARY AND COMMENTS   The sushi is wonderfully fresh, but there's plenty on the menu for those not interested in raw sea life. The *kushiage*, a variety of meat or vegetables dipped in *panko* (light bread crumbs), fried, and often placed on skewers, is special and can't be found in many New York kitchens. Service is very attentive, and, if you're lucky, you might meet Sachiko herself, who talks proudly to diners about the cuisine.

Sahara East   ★★½

MIDDLE EASTERN	MODERATE	QUALITY ★★★★	VALUE ★★★★

184 First Avenue (between 11th and 12th streets), East Village;
☎ **212-353-9000**

Reservations Recommended. **When to go** Warm weather. **Entree range** $10–$13. **Payment** Cash only. **Service rating** ★½. **Friendliness rating** ★★★★. **Bar** Beer and wine. **Wine selection** Small. **Dress** Casual. **Disabled access** Poor (big step at front door). **Customers** Locals, ethnic. **Hours** Sunday–Thursday, 11 a.m.–1 a.m.; Friday, 11 a.m.–3 a.m.; Saturday, 11 a.m.–4 a.m.

SETTING AND ATMOSPHERE   A narrow little cafe, but pass through to the large garden in back, decorated with lights and hanging knickknacks.

HOUSE SPECIALTIES   Falafel; grape leaves; *fattoush* (salad with pita croutons); lamb or chicken shish kebab; lamb or chicken couscous.

OTHER RECOMMENDATIONS   *Shisha* (aromatic tobacco available in 65 flavors), smoked from hookahs.

ENTERTAINMENT AND AMENITIES   Live music Friday and Saturday, 9 to 11:30 p.m.

SUMMARY AND COMMENTS   This place is most fun when crowded, so one must weigh speed against ambience when choosing a time to eat here (busy nights are Thursday through Sunday). On nice, clear evenings, the garden fills up until late, and the perfumed shisha smoke wafts as snakily as the music. Older Middle Eastern guys and East Village hipsters blend effortlessly into the scene, and it feels wonderful to be a part of it all. On these busy kitchen nights, stick with the dishes we've listed, and you'll do fine. If, however, food is more important to you than setting, go on off-nights, and ask the friendly chef about the day's specials.

Scarpetta ★★★★

ITALIAN	EXPENSIVE	QUALITY ★★★★½	VALUE ★★★½

355 West 14th Street, Chelsea; ☎ 212-691-0555; www.scarpettanyc.com

Reservations Essential. **When to go** Dinner. **Entree range** $22–$36. **Payment** All major credit cards. **Service rating** ★★★★½. **Friendliness rating** ★★★★. **Bar** Full Service. **Wine selection** Very good, with excellent Italian choices. **Dress** Elegant casual. **Disabled access** Yes. **Customers** Businesspeople, foodies, trendy. **Hours** Monday–Thursday, 5:30–11 p.m.; Friday and Saturday, 5:30 p.m.–midnight; Sunday, 5:30–10:30 p.m.

SETTING AND ATMOSPHERE The white-marble floor and matching marble bar announce this is no mom-and-pop Italian. The main dining room is modern, but not harsh. Angled mirrors mounted on the wall provide the waitstaff with a bird's-eye view, so servers quickly refill a drained drink or fold a wayward napkin. What people will remember most is the triangular glass roof that retracts in nicer weather and fills the space with fresh air. For even more fresh air, sidewalk seats are available.

HOUSE SPECIALTIES Mozzarella in *carozza;* spaghetti *pomodoro;* moist roasted *capretto* (baby goat); venison or veal chops; Amedei chocolate cake; anything with tomatoes or polenta.

OTHER RECOMMENDATIONS House-made chips (at bar); braised short ribs; duck and foie gras ravioli; black cod with tomatoes; banana *budino.*

SUMMARY AND COMMENTS Simplicity is what people rave about at the Meatpacking District's finest Italian restaurant, the latest from Scott Conant, who achieved fame at Alto and L'Impero. Freshly made pastas are silkier than you might have thought possible, made even silkier by foie gras, tenderly cooked meats, and delicate seafood. The spaghetti pomodoro, which is "just" noodles with tomatoes and basil, surprises even the most jaded foodie. The creamy polenta is worth buying on its own, but it's also the perfect accompaniment to a veal or venison chop. Steep prices and the well-heeled crowd may intimidate some, but the staff is welcoming, and the food is extremely comforting.

2nd Ave Deli ★★½

JEWISH DELI	MODERATE	QUALITY ★★★★	VALUE ★★★

162 East 33rd Street (near Third Avenue), Midtown East;
☎ 212-689-9000; www.2ndavedeli.com

Reservations Not accepted. **When to go** Anytime. **Entree range** $10–$26. **Payment** All major credit cards. **Service rating** ★★★. **Friendliness rating** ★★★. **Bar** Wine and beer. **Wine selection** Limited kosher. **Dress** Casual. **Disabled access** Good. **Customers** Locals, tourists. **Hours** Sunday–Thursday, 6 a.m.–midnight; Friday and Saturday, 7–4 a.m.; closed Jewish holidays.

SETTING AND ATMOSPHERE No, it's on Second Avenue anymore; that legendary location closed in 2006. It's smaller and more polished now, but it's still a classic deli, with kvetching meat slicers and comfortable booths in abundance. Kids will like the simple, tasty soups and sandwiches.

HOUSE SPECIALTIES Free, pungent health salad; great, smooth chopped liver; authentic matzo ball soup; knishes; *derma* (rich stuffing—here with globs of paprika—in sausage casing); *cholent* (an ultra-slow-cooked meat-and-potato stew); sweet, orangey stuffed cabbage; homemade applesauce. There's much debate over the corned beef; it's very lightly "corned," but this allows more beefy flavors to emerge.

OTHER RECOMMENDATIONS Skip dessert; the deli may be open Friday nights and Saturdays, but it's kosher nonetheless, and desserts made with dairy substitutes aren't worth the calories.

ENTERTAINMENT AND AMENITIES The deli will ship food anywhere.

SUMMARY AND COMMENTS You'll find better consistency at **Mr. Broadway Kosher Restaurant** (see page 329), but it has none of the history and little of the soul of this very traditional place.

Sfoglia ★★★★

ITALIAN	EXPENSIVE	QUALITY ★★★★½	VALUE ★★★★

1402 Lexington Avenue (at 92nd Street), Upper East Side;
☎ **212-831-1402; www.sfogliarestaurant.com**

Reservations Essential. **When to go** Anytime. **Entree range** $24–$32. **Payment** AE, MC, V. **Service rating** ★★★★½. **Friendliness rating** ★★★★. **Bar** Full service. **Wine selection** Excellent. **Dress** Smart casual. **Disabled access** Yes. **Customers** Foodies, locals, those with second homes on Nantucket. **Hours** Sunday and Monday, 5:30–11 p.m.; Tuesday–Saturday, noon–2:30 p.m. and 5:30–11 p.m.

SETTING AND ATMOSPHERE Husband-and-wife team Ron Suhanosky and Colleen Marnell-Suhanosky have done an excellent job re-creating the cozy atmosphere of their first Sfoglia restaurant, a true gem on the island of Nantucket. This tiny corner trattoria is always crowded and certainly not the place to throw a party. For an evening of lively conversation and entree-swapping among two to four people, it's ideal. Wood floors, antique tables, cushioned benches, chandeliers, painted brick walls, and a marble bar all add up to give it a classy but entirely unpretentious feel.

HOUSE SPECIALTIES The menu changes bimonthly, but recent favorites include antipasti plate; pappardelle bolognese; chicken al mattone; ricotta gnocchi; fruit tart.

OTHER RECOMMENDATIONS Spaghetti with figs, hazelnuts, and ricotta salata; braised short ribs; roasted orata fillets; corn risotto.

SUMMARY AND COMMENTS Sfoglia flew under the radar for a little while after opening, and that was just fine by Upper East Siders who adored the first version while summering in Nantucket. These days, thanks to rapturous press and limited seating, dinner books up weeks in advance, but the reasonable prices and heavenly food are worth the wait. This is another of the recent green-market restaurants, but its staff is less interested in impressing you with ingredients than it is with evoking "memories of

Sunday at Grandma's." A place named after the Italian word for an uncut sheet of pasta can't be ashamed to wear its heart on its sleeve.

Shun Lee West, Shun Lee Café ★★★½

CHINESE   MODERATE/EXPENSIVE   QUALITY ★★★★   VALUE ★★★★

43 West 65th Street, Upper West Side; ☎ 212-595-8895 or
212-769-3888 (Café); www.shunleewest.com

Reservations Recommended. **When to go** Anytime. **Entree range** $15–$47; in the Café, most entrees are $16–$25. **Payment** All major credit cards. **Service rating** ★★. **Friendliness rating** ★★. **Bar** Full service. **Wine selection** Good. **Dress** Dressy, business; casual in the Café. **Disabled access** Yes. **Customers** Locals, businesspeople, Lincoln Center patrons. **Hours** Monday–Saturday, noon–midnight; Sunday, noon–10:30 p.m.

SETTING AND ATMOSPHERE Dark and dramatic: large silver-white dragons with little red eyes chase each other across black walls above luxurious black banquettes and black floors, and soft halogen lighting flatters the complexion. Silver-white monkeys swing over the small bar in the entrance, where you are greeted by tuxedoed maître d's. This is a snazzy take on the Chinese scene, and the clientele seems to revel in it.

HOUSE SPECIALTIES Sichuan wonton; steamed dumplings; beggar's chicken (order 24 hours in advance); Grand Marnier prawns; Cantonese sausage with Sichuan sausage; dim sum (Café only).

OTHER RECOMMENDATIONS Sliced duckling with young gingerroot; lobster in black-bean sauce; rack of lamb, Sichuan-style.

SUMMARY AND COMMENTS High-style chinoiserie with high-style Chinese cooking to match make this an upscale Lincoln Center favorite. Some of the same excellent food is available in the more casual Café, which has its own entrance, for a lot less. The Café, black and white checked from floor to ceiling, also offers very good dim sum from wandering carts and abrupt but rapid service.

Soba-ya ★★★½

JAPANESE   INEXPENSIVE/MODERATE   QUALITY ★★★½   VALUE ★★★★

229 East Ninth Street (between Second and Third avenues), East Village;
☎ 212 533-6966; www.sobaya-nyc.com

Reservations None. **When to go** Anytime. **Entree range** $10–$20. **Payment** All major credit cards. **Service rating** ★★★½. **Friendliness rating** ★★★. **Bar** Beer and sake. **Wine selection** None. **Dress** Casual-trendy. **Disabled access** None. **Customers** Locals, ethnic, those in search of good soba and broth. **Hours** Daily, noon–3:50 p.m. and 5:30–10:30 p.m.

SETTING AND ATMOSPHERE Down a few steps, you enter a square room filled with wooden tables and chairs. Across from the till is a display of traditional netsuke figurines. A sit-down counter bar is in the far corner.

HOUSE SPECIALTIES Anything with soba (buckwheat) or udon noodles accompanied with fresh scallions in a vegetable, meat, or fish broth (the extra ingredients vary depending on which broth you choose).

OTHER RECOMMENDATIONS *Goma ae* (spinach with sesame sauce); tempura; extensive sake selection.

SUMMARY AND COMMENTS Although it's possible to order sashimi, one tends not to come here for sushi, but for other types of Japanese fare, especially the noodle soups. A whole bowl is easily a meal, so relax and enjoy the whole slurping experience. During peak dinner times, you may have to wait for a table, but it's worth it. Service is fast, and the staff is helpful in talking you through any menu confusion.

The Spotted Pig ★★★½

BRITISH-ITALIAN GASTROPUB   MOD/EXP   QUALITY ★★★★   VALUE ★★★½

350 West 11th Street (at Greenwich Street), Greenwich Village;
☎ **212-620-0393; www.thespottedpig.com**

Reservations Not accepted. **When to go** Anytime. **Entree range** $17–$32. **Payment** All major credit cards. **Service rating** ★★★. **Friendliness rating** ★★★½. **Bar** Full service. **Wine selection** Excellent. **Dress** Casual. **Disabled access** Small step up; accessible bathroom; crowded. **Customers** Locals, young foodies, the occasional celebrity. **Hours** Monday–Friday, noon–2 a.m.; Saturday and Sunday, 11 a.m.–2 a.m. (brunch served until 3 p.m.).

SETTING AND ATMOSPHERE The pig hanging above the entryway is just a preview of the recurring motif. Inside, the brick pillars and walls are covered with framed pictures and statues of pigs (along with other artistic tributes to meat and produce). Specials are written on a large mirror that dominates the back wall and gives the small room added depth. An inviting bar lies opposite the upholstered booths and small wooden tables. Diners sitting on short, comfortable stools can look at the crowd inside, or outside through the wall of windows. An upstairs room is used to accommodate bigger crowds, but you will want to try to dine near the bar. At night, the room glows with a warmth you would expect from a traditional English pub.

HOUSE SPECIALTIES Sheep's ricotta gnudi; char-grilled burger with Roquefort cheese and shoestrings; seared squid with cilantro butter.

OTHER RECOMMENDATIONS Duck egg with lamb's tongue; devils on horseback; smoked haddock chowder; Hampshire pork belly.

SUMMARY AND COMMENTS When The Spotted Pig received a coveted single star in Michelin's first *Red Guide* to New York, many among the food literati cried foul. What had this humble little gastropub done to deserve the honor? What chef–co-owner April Bloomfield has done is create a simple, appealing menu combining English and Italian sensibilities. Order the burger and shoestring fries, but don't ask for ketchup. The Roquefort cheese topping the meat, and the garlic and rosemary on the mountain of fries, provide plenty of flavor. The restaurant doesn't take reservations, but if there are lines (guaranteed on weekends), put your name in, and the staff can usually predict how long the wait will be, leaving you the option of grabbing a drink around the corner on Hudson Street or sitting at the bar. To make it a true pub experience, order one of the bar's two hand-drawn cask ales. Ubiquitous in England, they're surprisingly hard to find in Manhattan.

Stan's Place ★★★

CREOLE	INEXPENSIVE/MODERATE	QUALITY ★★★	VALUE ★★★

411 Atlantic Avenue (between Bond and Nevins streets), Brooklyn;
☎ **718-596-3110; www.stansplacerestaurant.com**

Reservations Not necessary. **When to go** Anytime. **Entree range** $10–$16. **Payment** Cash only. **Service rating** ★★★½. **Friendliness rating** ★★★★. **Bar** Beer and wine. **Wine selection** Small. **Dress** Casual. **Disabled access** Yes. **Customers** Locals, ethnic, regulars. **Hours** Monday–Thursday, 10 a.m.–10 p.m.; Friday and Saturday, 10 a.m.–11 p.m.; Sunday, 10 a.m.–4 p.m.

SETTING AND ATMOSPHERE This New Orleans–style cafe has an open, airy warmth. The high-ceilinged space has a small balcony in the back and a long coffee-dessert bar in the front. Dark wooden tables line the sides of the space, and there are a few tables in the middle.

HOUSE SPECIALTIES Creole café; chicory au lait; cheese grits; saffron bouillabaisse; catfish po'boys; Cajun scrambled eggs.

OTHER RECOMMENDATIONS Fried chicken; chicken-and-andouille jambalaya; *boudin blanc;* crab cakes.

SUMMARY AND COMMENTS Although much of the brunch menu has food preceded by the word *Cajun,* some would call the dinner dishes more Creole. We'll say that whatever one calls it, the fare is tasty. Tabasco is served with breakfast eggs, and the cheese grits are wonderfully smooth and savory. Weekend brunch is a great time to bring the kids. The New Orleans ties are strong here, as shown in the aftermath of Hurricane Katrina, when Stan's wasn't able to place orders; its supplies were all back home. The chicory au lait is good, but the Creole café is made from chicory and real coffee beans for a special taste. The beignets available are fresh, but a bit too stodgy compared with their Southern counterparts. Stan's sometimes has live music on Thursday nights.

Sushi-Ann ★★★½

JAPANESE	EXPENSIVE	QUALITY ★★★★	VALUE ★★★★

38 East 51st Street (between Madison and Park avenues), Midtown East;
☎ **212-755-1780; www.sushiann.com**

Reservations Recommended. **When to go** Anytime. **Entree range** $20–$65; sushi available à la carte. **Payment** All major credit cards. **Service rating** ★★.

Friendliness rating ★★★. **Bar** Beer, wine and sake only. **Wine selection** Minimal. **Dress** Casual, business. **Disabled access** None. **Customers** Ethnic, businesspeople, locals. **Hours** Monday–Friday, noon–2:45 p.m. and 6–10 p.m.; Saturday, 5:30–9:30 p.m.; closed Sunday.

SETTING AND ATMOSPHERE Startlingly simple, sharp-angled, and bright, with off-white and light-wood walls, and light-wood tables. Understated Japanese floral arrangements add spots of vibrant color here and there, and a large, 20-seat sushi bar, staffed by six sushi chefs and jammed with Japanese businessmen at lunch, forms the centerpiece.

HOUSE SPECIALTIES Special deluxe *bento* boxes; special *makimoto;* sea-urchin hand roll, spicy codfish sushi, Japanese mackerel sushi, and anything else on the à la carte sushi list.

OTHER RECOMMENDATIONS Cooked sushi assortment (good for sushi beginners); *chirashi* (assorted fish fillets on vinegar-seasoned rice); sushi deluxe (an assortment of fresh and cooked items).

SUMMARY AND COMMENTS Celestial sushi and sashimi draw praise and crowds. Formerly called Sushisay, this is an excellent Midtown choice for the freshest of fresh fish. Order the preselected assortments, or make individual selections from the extensive à la carte list of sushi and hand rolls. The ambience and service are friendly; the high prices reflect the location.

Symposium Greek Restaurant ★★★

GREEK	INEXPENSIVE/MODERATE	QUALITY ★★½	VALUE ★★★★

544 West 113th Street (between Broadway and Amsterdam Avenue), Morningside Heights, Hamilton Heights, and Harlem; ☎ 212-865-1011

Reservations Recommended. **When to go** Anytime you have a yen for a stuffed grape leaf. **Entree range** $8–$20. **Payment** MC, V. **Service rating** ★★★★. **Friendliness rating** ★★★★½. **Bar** Limited. **Wine selection** Small, but includes Greek selections (besides ouzo) and sangria. **Dress** Casual. **Disabled access** None. **Customers** Regulars, Columbia University staff and students, ethnic. **Hours** Daily, noon–10:30 p.m.

SETTING AND ATMOSPHERE The main dining room has a tavern feel, with closely arranged, dark wooden tables, a few booths, a wood floor, paintings on the walls, and a low ceiling. A feeling of dining community pervades: everyone is there to have a good time and eat good Greek food. The enclosed garden practically doubles the number of tables. Two trees have grown to a considerable height and girth there (the trees' canopies are way above the enclosure's roof).

HOUSE SPECIALTIES Mixed appetizer plate (especially the stuffed grape leaves, *taramasalata,* and eggplant dip); shish kebab (lamb and vegetables on a skewer); moussaka.

OTHER RECOMMENDATIONS Pastitsio (baked pasta and ground meat); vegetarian moussaka; spanakopita (spinach-and-feta pie).

SUMMARY AND COMMENTS It's clear that the owners (it's family-run) have a lot of confidence when the only route to the enclosed garden is through the kitchen. Symposium has been around for almost 40 years and proclaims that it serves genuine Greek cuisine, which we can't dispute. The best bet is to order the Symposium salad for the table so you can sample a mixture of dips with a few olives and delectable stuffed grape leaves; warm pita bread accompanies the dish. The spinach pie is the right combination of spinach and feta, but sometimes the phyllo dough is not as crunchy as it could be. The vegetarian moussaka is pretty decent as well. Plenty of space, a casual atmosphere, and a friendly and welcoming staff make Symposium kid-friendly.

Tabla ★★★★

INDIAN FUSION	EXPENSIVE	QUALITY ★★★★½	VALUE ★★★★

11 Madison Avenue (at 25th Street), Gramercy Park and Madison Square; ☎ 212-889-0667; www.tablany.com

Reservations Recommended for main dining room. **When to go** Anytime. **Entree range** 3-course prix-fixe dinner, $59; 6-course tasting menu, $89 (vegetarian option, $79). **Payment** All major credit cards. **Service rating ★★★**. **Friendliness rating ★★★**. **Bar** Full service. **Wine selection** Well chosen for food; fairly priced. **Dress** Casual or better. **Disabled access** Bread bar, yes; dining room, no. **Customers** Locals, businesspeople, ethnic. **Hours** Monday–Wednesday, noon–2 p.m. and 5–9 p.m.; Thursday–Friday, noon–2 p.m. and 5:30–10:30 p.m.; Saturday, 5:30–10:30 p.m.; Sunday, 5–9 p.m.

SETTING AND ATMOSPHERE A beautiful crimson wood staircase separates two levels of space, each with its own distinct personality. The upstairs dining room is formal but hip, buzzing with excitement and alive with voluptuous colors—a perfect setting for the meal that follows. The street-level Bread Bar is more casual and doesn't require reservations.

HOUSE SPECIALTIES Goan-spiced crab cake; rice-flaked crisped halibut; eggplant-stuffed braised Vidalia onion; vanilla-bean *kulfi*.

OTHER RECOMMENDATIONS Crispy pork terrine; slow-cooked wild striped bass; tapioca-crusted soft-shell crabs.

SUMMARY AND COMMENTS Danny Meyer, king of New York's New American establishments **Gramercy Tavern** and **Union Square Cafe** (see profiles), has tackled Indian fusion, and this may well be the best of the bunch. Meyer hired Floyd Cardoz, a native of India, to literally add some spice to an increasingly predictable cuisine, and Cardoz took him at his word, using ingredients such as kokum, cumin, tamarind, and tapioca to breathe new life into dishes such as crab cake, foie gras, and fettuccine. Even the tandoori breads come in flavors such as buckwheat honey and horseradish. Though fusion is often a failed experiment, Tabla manages to pull it off with style. But be warned: Tabla is not for everybody; some people love it, while others hate it, though everyone agrees the vanilla-bean kulfi is one of the best desserts in Manhattan. Lunch upstairs can be a bit of a disappointment because of meager portions, so go for the awesome Bread Bar downstairs instead.

Tamarind ★★★½

INDIAN	EXPENSIVE	QUALITY ★★★★	VALUE ★★★

41–43 East 22nd Street (between Park Avenue and Broadway), Gramercy Park and Madison Square; ☎ 212-674-7400; www.tamarinde22.com

Reservations Recommended. **When to go** Anytime. **Entree range** $16–$35. **Payment** All major credit cards. **Service rating** ★★★½. **Friendliness rating** ★★★★½. **Bar** Full service. **Wine selection** Good, with varied prices. **Dress** Smart casual, chic, or business. **Disabled access** Yes. **Customers** Businesspeople, regulars, foodies on expense accounts. **Hours** Sunday–Thursday, 11:30 a.m.–3 p.m. and 5:30–11:30 p.m.; Friday and Saturday, 11:30 a.m.–3 p.m. and 5:30–midnight.

SETTING AND ATMOSPHERE This restaurant has a lot of style and warmth, with large windows at the front, a skylight in the back, a fully stocked and well-appointed bar, a glass-enclosed kitchen, modern chairs, white-linen tablecloths, and freshly cut orchids on each table. You can eat at a table across from the bar in the narrow section of the restaurant, or you can sit at a table that opens out into a larger space toward the back. Private round tables are available around the periphery of the open room.

HOUSE SPECIALTIES Tandoori scallops; lobster masala; lamb shank; *murgh kolhapuri* (chicken with peppercorns); crab soup; other tandoori items.

OTHER RECOMMENDATIONS Rosemary *naan;* lemon rice; *luckhnow ki bhajia* (incredibly crisp and light fritters with spinach, banana, and cheese); *bhagarey baigan* (eggplant with coconut, sesame, and peanut sauce); shrimp in coconut sauce with mustard seeds, ginger, and curry leaves).

SUMMARY AND COMMENTS When it opened in 2001, Tamarind earned its culinary stripes almost immediately thanks to the freshness of the ingredients. The meats are as tender as the homemade cheese cubes, which melt in the mouth. Presentation excels with the appetizers more than with the entrees; the succulent tandoori scallops are served in a fried potato lattice cup that has become a signature dish. For a variety of chutneys and spices, try the vegetarian *thali.* Desserts range from chocolate soufflé to *gulab jamun* (pastry with dried milk and honey). The owner and manager are proud of their venture and are often seen schmoozing among the diners. The tearoom next door offers a wider selection of teas, desserts, and sandwiches in a more casual setting.

Tartine ★★★

FRENCH BISTRO	INEXPENSIVE	QUALITY ★★★★	VALUE ★★★½

**253 West 11th Street (corner of West Fourth Street), Greenwich Village;
☎ 212-229-2611**

Reservations Not accepted. **When to go** Anytime. **Entree range** $9–$19.
Payment Cash only. **Service rating** ★★. **Friendliness rating** ★★. **Bar** BYOB.
Dress Casual. **Disabled access** For outside tables. **Customers** Locals. **Hours**
Monday–Friday, 9 a.m.–4 p.m. and 5:30–10:30 p.m.; Saturday and Sunday, 10:30
a.m.–4 p.m. (brunch) and 5:30–10:30 p.m.

SETTING AND ATMOSPHERE This cute corner bistro on a pretty West Village
street attracts lots of locals. There's usually a line waiting for the ten
Formica-topped tables squeezed into the small, exposed-brick interior
or for space in the outside cafe (weather permitting).

HOUSE SPECIALTIES Desserts—*dacquoise, tarte tatin à la mode,* custard-filled
fruit tarts—are all made on the premises and are top-notch; *salade
basquaise;* grilled salmon with citrus vinaigrette; *croque monsieur* made
with brioche; beef mignonette aux poivres with frites.

OTHER RECOMMENDATIONS Tart du jour; beet-and-endive salad; daily specials.

SUMMARY AND COMMENTS Basic bistro fare at very fair prices, the added saving of BYOB, and the cozy setting make Tartine a very popular place.
Appetizers are hit-or-miss. Go with one of the salads or check out the
daily specials, and skip the escargots. Save room for desserts, though,
especially the tarte tatin à la mode, served warm with caramelized
apples. Service can be either charming or indifferent. Saturday and
Sunday brunch at $15 is a great deal and very tasty.

Tea & Sympathy ★★★

BRITISH	INEXPENSIVE/MODERATE	QUALITY ★★★½	VALUE ★★★

**108 Greenwich Avenue (between 12th and 13th streets), Greenwich
Village; ☎ 212-989-9735; www.teaandsympathynewyork.com**

Reservations Not accepted. **When to go** Anytime. **Entree range** $12–$19.
Payment AE, MC, V. **Service rating** ★★★½. **Friendliness rating** ★★★★. **Bar** No,
but lots of tea. **Wine selection** BYOB. **Dress** Casual or avant-garde. **Disabled access**
Yes, but not for restroom. **Customers** Regulars, locals, homesick Brits, occasional
celebs. **Hours** Monday–Friday, 11:30 a.m.–10:30 p.m.; Saturday–Sunday, 9:30 a.m.–
10:30 p.m.; Sunday dinner, $28, served after 1:30 p.m. until it sells out.

SETTING AND ATMOSPHERE As you might guess from the name, this is a cozy,
square room with ten small tables and a 22-seat capacity. A chalkboard
lists the daily desserts, teas, and entree specials. On the walls hang items
of British kitsch, including caricatures of famous British icons, old-fashioned
posters advertising British products, and shelves of mismatched china.
The small kitchen is visible over the dessert case.

HOUSE SPECIALTIES Full afternoon tea, served anytime and including a variety of finger sandwiches, scones with clotted cream and jam, and assorted cakes and cookies; shepherd's pie; bangers and mash; rhubarb crumble with custard; Sunday dinner (choice of roast beef, lamb, or chicken, Yorkshire pudding, potatoes, and vegetables).

OTHER RECOMMENDATIONS Victoria sponge cake; baked beans on toast; Welsh rarebit (Cheddar with mustard on toast); Stilton-and-walnut salad with beets; chicken-and-leek pie; tuna melt. The macaroni falls a little short.

SUMMARY AND COMMENTS Because of the small size and addictive and delicious comfort food, it's not uncommon to have to wait outside for a table. Nicky, the owner, is often seen wandering between the restaurant and the chippery next door, making sure that customers are satisfied. She refuses to allow people to take a table unless everyone in the group is present; a few more of "Nicky's Rules" are displayed prominently on the front-door window. There aren't many places in NYC where you can find hot ribena and a Scotch egg on the menu. The afternoon tea is super and costs $35; if there are certain sweet things you don't like, let the server know beforehand so the selection can reflect your preferences. If you'd prefer fish-and-chips, the **A Salt & Battery** chip shop (☎ 212-691-2713; **www.asaltandbattery.com**) next door is also owned by Nicky.

Tomoe Sushi ★★★½

JAPANESE-SUSHI   MODERATE   QUALITY ★★★★   VALUE ★★★★

172 Thompson Street (between Houston and Bleecker streets), Greenwich Village; ☎ 212-777-9346

Reservations Not accepted. When to go Anytime. Entree range $17–$36. Payment Cash or AE. Service rating ★★. Friendliness rating ★★★. Bar Beer and sake. Wine selection Stick to sake and beer. Dress Very casual. Disabled access None. Customers Ethnic, locals. Hours Monday, 5–11 p.m.; Tuesday–Saturday, 1–3 p.m. and 5–11 p.m.; Sunday, 5–10 p.m.

SETTING AND ATMOSPHERE The quintessential Village hole-in-the-wall with a few Japanese touches—lantern lights, prints on the wall, and a small sushi bar that seats a lucky five people at a time. Tomoe is about as big as the upper right-hand section of a bento box, but that's part of its charm.

HOUSE SPECIALTIES Anything from the sushi bar; *toro* (fatty tuna); *hamachi* (yellowtail) belly; fresh salmon; *amaebi* (sweet shrimp).

OTHER RECOMMENDATIONS Going to Tomoe for anything but raw fish is like going to a concert only for the opening act. The *shumai* are standard, and the *zaru* soba are subpar and much better elsewhere (try **Soba-ya**—see page 354).

SUMMARY AND COMMENTS Tomoe gives the phrase "fresh off the boat" new meaning. The sushi and sashimi here are wonderfully fresh, clean, and delicious. Pieces are big but not so unwieldy that you can't fit the whole thing in your mouth comfortably. Buttery toro will melt in your mouth, and the huge king crab legs are so sweet and juicy you'll start to hear waves crashing around your eardrums. Tomoe boasts a great selection and reasonable prices, but you might stand up to an hour, and it would be worth every minute.

Union Square Cafe ★★★★

NEW AMERICAN   EXPENSIVE   QUALITY ★★★★½   VALUE ★★★★

21 East 16th Street (between Union Square and Fifth Avenue), Union Square; ☎ 212-243-4020; www.unionsquarecafe.com

Reservations Recommended. **When to go** Anytime. **Entree range** $24–$36. **Payment** All major credit cards. **Service rating** ★★★★. **Friendliness rating** ★★★★. **Bar** Full service. **Wine selection** Excellent, both by the bottle and by the glass. **Dress** Casual, business. **Disabled access** Fair. **Customers** Locals, businesspeople. **Hours** Sunday–Thursday, noon–2 p.m. and 5:30–10 p.m.; Friday and Saturday, noon–2 p.m. and 5:30–11 p.m.

SETTING AND ATMOSPHERE Dining spaces—a few steps down, a small flight up—with creamy beige walls, dark green chair rails, vibrant modern paintings, a mural of many merry maidens (*The Women of USC*), and bright bunches of fresh flowers. The cherry-wood floors and a long, dark wooden bar add to the warm, welcoming ambience. All is stylish without trying too hard.

HOUSE SPECIALTIES Hot garlic potato chips; black-bean soup; calamari; grilled, marinated filet mignon of tuna; warm banana tart with honey-vanilla ice cream.

OTHER RECOMMENDATIONS Roasted duck breast; peach potpie. For lunch: yellowfin tuna burger with creamy cabbage slaw and the USC burger.

SUMMARY AND COMMENTS For more than 20 years, Union Square Cafe has been one of New York's most desired dining destinations. But when Union Square Cafe is billed as New York's best restaurant, it's not for the food but for the overall experience. Owner Danny Meyer and chef Michael Romano have set the standard for flawless, informed, amiable service as well as dependable, usually delicious New American food.

Veritas ★★★★

FRENCH   VERY EXPENSIVE   QUALITY ★★★★½   VALUE ★★★★

43 East 20th Street (between Park Avenue South and Broadway), Gramercy Park and Madison Square; ☎ 212-353-3700; www.veritas-nyc.com

Reservations Necessary. **When to go** Anytime. **Entree range** Prix-fixe 3-course dinner, $85; 5-course tasting menu, $110; 9-course tasting menu, $145. **Payment** All major credit cards. **Service rating** ★★★. **Friendliness rating** ★★★. **Bar** Full service. **Wine selection** Unbelievable and incredibly reasonable. **Dress** Dressy casual, business. **Disabled access** Yes. **Customers** Locals, businesspeople, oenophiles. **Hours** Monday–Saturday, 5:30–10:30 p.m.; Sunday, 5–10 p.m.

SETTING AND ATMOSPHERE This small, one-room space has an elegant, modern look but a thoroughly comfortable feel. The room is decorated simply, with colorful, handblown glass objets d'art set smartly into random spaces in the wall. Check out the bathrooms and the very cool sinks.

HOUSE SPECIALTIES Smoked foie gras; salad St. Jacques; wagyu fillet.

OTHER RECOMMENDATIONS Lamb degustation; lobster nage; Barbary duck breast.

SUMMARY AND COMMENTS When people think of Veritas, they think of wine. The size of a small bible, the wine list runs the gamut and has something for everyone, including a surprising number of quality bottles in the $25-to-$40 range. But because of that reputation, people might not go there to eat, and that would be a shame, because Veritas turns out some of the best food in the city. Despite the Ivy League–evoking name and the dedication to oenophilia, Veritas goes out of its way to keep things down to earth. Twenty-five-dollar bottles still bring out the top-of-the-line stemware. The wine list is great, but the food's even better.

Woo Chon ★★★

KOREAN	MODERATE	QUALITY ★★★★	VALUE ★★★★

8–10 West 36th Street (near Fifth Avenue), Midtown East;
☎ 212-695-1342; www.woochon.com

Reservations Accepted. **When to go** Anytime. **Entree range** $12–$28. **Payment** All major credit cards. **Service rating** ★★★. **Friendliness rating** ★½. **Bar** Beer and wine only. **Wine selection** Very limited. **Dress** Nice casual or better. **Disabled access** Good. **Customers** Korean businessmen, aficionados. **Hours** Monday–Saturday, 10:30 a.m.–2 a.m.; Sunday, 10:30 a.m.–midnight.

SETTING AND ATMOSPHERE Two levels: a rather intense downstairs space (spotlighted and dramatically appointed with lacquered calligraphy, dark wood, and Asian ink prints) and a slightly more laid-back upstairs room.

HOUSE SPECIALTIES Attention centers on the great *bulgolgi*: rib eye prepared on the grill set into each table. Unfortunately, the tableside grills are outfitted for gas flame rather than glowing coals, but Woo Chon's awesome marinade—so delicious the restaurant bottles the stuff for sale—and top-quality meat easily compensate. *Kalbi* (beef short ribs) are equally recommended. *Panchan,* the traditional gratis assortment of little vegetable and fish starter plates, is unparalleled in its freshness. *Yookgaejang* (a restorative, spicy beef soup) and *dduk guk* (a hearty dumpling soup) are both good choices, as are rice and noodle dishes. Also try *gooksoo,* a lot like Japanese shabu-shabu. Special feasts may be ordered 48 hours in advance (bring a group and reserve a private room for the full effect).

SUMMARY AND COMMENTS Management's haughty manner has unfortunately been adopted by many of the waiters. As in many Korean restaurants, the menu stretches well beyond its strengths in an effort to please a broad audience, so stick with the recommended dishes and avoid stews (*jigae*), intricate seafood or vegetable preparations, and homier items—this is no grandma kitchen.

Zen Palate ★★½

VEGETARIAN-ASIAN **INEXPENSIVE** **QUALITY ★★★½** **VALUE ★★★★**

663 Ninth Avenue (at 46th Street), Midtown West, Times Square, and the Theater District; ☎ 212-582-1669; www.zenpalate.com

Reservations Only for 6 or more. **When to go** Anytime. **Entree range** $8–$10; $2.50–$9 for pastas and soups. **Payment** All major credit cards. **Service rating** ★★★. **Friendliness rating** ★★. **Bar** None. **Wine selection** No liquor license; BYOB. **Dress** Casual. **Disabled access** Yes. **Customers** Ethnic, locals. **Hours** Monday–Saturday, 11:30 a.m.–10:30 p.m.; Sunday, noon–10 p.m.

SETTING AND ATMOSPHERE This laid-back joint offers pockets of peace with soft ocher walls and clouds on the ceiling.

HOUSE SPECIALTIES Vegetable dumplings; spinach linguine salad with sesame-peanut dressing; eggplant in garlic sauce.

OTHER RECOMMENDATIONS Basil moo-shu rolls; stir-fried fettuccine; fresh-squeezed vegetable juice.

SUMMARY AND COMMENTS An inexpensive oasis for noncarnivores, but you don't have to be a vegetarian to get the good karma and good vibes that come with the more-than-soul-satisfying cuisine here. The veggie variations are flavorfully inventive, and some are surprising in their intensity.

PART EIGHT

SHOPPING

KEEPING *your* EYES
on the PRIZE *(and the Price)*

IT'S ALMOST REDUNDANT to talk about a shopping guide to **Manhattan.** In fact, it's almost impossible *not* to shop in a city whose souvenirs—miniature Statues of Liberty, Empire State Buildings, (little) Big Apples—are so instantly familiar. There are Fifth Avenues in a million cities, but no dedicated follower of fashion will mistake that New York street for any other. Nearly every tony hotel lobby now comes complete with a fancy gift shop, if not a couple of name-brand boutiques. And then there are the street vendors, the shopping marts, the jewelry malls, the flea markets. . . . In fact, if you're not careful—even if it's exactly what you have in mind—you could find yourself spending your whole visit, and more than your budget, haphazardly acquiring things. That seems like a waste in more ways than one. When every city you visit seems filled with the same stores and labels—and you'll see them all here a number of times—New York is a treasure trove of specialty items, one-of-a-kind gifts, and real connoisseur's delights. We can't list them all, but we've picked out some we particularly like.

And as usual, we've tried to pick out ways that you can combine your shopping expeditions with explorations of neighborhoods, which have much nicer views than all those prepackaged malls. Sure, this is prime window-shopping territory, and you can can see and buy a little of almost everything just by wandering around; but, intriguingly, communities of merchants have evolved that offer great walking tours, so if you know what sort of purchases you want to make, you can comparison-shop for hours and see history at the same time.

Longing to amble through art galleries? You could spend your whole visit in **Chelsea.** Designer couture? **Fifth Avenue,** of course, but also **upper Madison Avenue** and the increasingly brand-name **SoHo.** Or show you're hip to the up-and-coming designers as well as the world-famous, and head for **NoLita.** And if you really want a kitchen that will have your Food Network–addict friends in a frenzy, head for the **Bowery.** (Yup, you heard us.)

For more-single-minded collectors, we've included a selection of stores and purveyors specializing in specific goods. Rare books, black ties, vintage rock 'n' roll—you want it, we got it.

ALL TOGETHER NOW:

Department Stores, "Malls," and Flea Markets

THE BIG NAMES

WE'RE NOT BY ANY MEANS SUGGESTING that you settle for department-store shopping in New York, but sometimes traveling is a matter of so many gifts, so little time. In that case, you need a lot of options at one address. Besides, some stores in New York are so famous in and of themselves that they almost qualify as tourist attractions.

The best-known names in department-store shopping in Manhattan are the alphabet soup–ers: ABC, the four Bs—Barneys, Bergdorf Goodman, Bloomingdale's (Bloomie's for short), and Bendel—and Century 21, plus Lord & Taylor, Macy's, and Saks.

unofficial **TIP**
If you want to get that souvenir stuff out of the way in a hurry, you might want to hustle through those company-logo superstores; see "Brand Loyalty," page 372.

ABC Carpet and Home (☎ 212-473-3000; www.abchome.com) is so big it lolls over two buildings, 881 and 888 Broadway, between East 18th and East 19th streets. It not only deals in furniture, antiques, clothes, gifts, lighting, and so on, but it also has two cafes (open quite late), a bakery, and a chocolate shop, the first Michel Cluizel boutique outside Paris.

Barneys' original Chelsea store has become the transcendent Rubin Museum of Art, but the uptown Barneys, a $100 million Midtown megastore on Madison Avenue at East 61st (☎ 212-826-8900; www.barneys.com), is more than compensation.

The B&G logo of **Bergdorf Goodman** (☎ 800-558-1855; www.bergdorfgoodman.com) has been at the cornerstone of Fifth and 57th, both literally and metaphorically, for generations, and while so many stores are cutting back on either prices or service, Bergdorf is booming. It has a whole men's store, **Bergdorf Goodman Men,** dedicated to the best in ready-to-wear couture, on the opposite side of the street. Bergdorf is so dependable that should you suddenly discover that the dinner you're invited to is black tie, you can call the gender-appropriate store to dispatch a personal shopper to your hotel with an armful of outfits for you to try on. (It also has some of the city's most elaborate and inventive window displays at holiday time.)

Bloomingdale's is the designer version of a department store, and it looks it. Everything is name-brand, from Polo to Petrossian (yes, there's a caviar stand). Two locations: Lexington Avenue at East 59th Street (☎ 212-705-2000; **www.bloom ingdales.com**) and Broadway at Spring Street in SoHo (☎ 212-729-5900).

Henri Bendel remains a temple for the haute and the ultra-hip (712 Fifth Avenue, between 55th and 56th streets; ☎ 800-423-6335; **www.henribendel.com**). Start with cosmetics on the ground floor and work your way upstairs through jewelry and accessories to evening wear.

Although it's put together like a department store, TriBeCa's **Century 21** has set a whole new standard for bargain-hunting, something like a really great flea market and designer sale under permanent cover. Discounts on big-name labels here can reach 80% (Cortlandt Street between White and Walker; ☎ 212-227-9092; **www.c21stores.com**).

Lord & Taylor is the oldest specialty-clothing shop in the country and still a standard (Fifth Avenue between 38th and 39th streets; ☎ 212-391-3344; **www.lordandtaylor.com**).

Macy's, which every TV veteran knows is on Herald Square, may be a giant—it covers more than a million square feet—but aside from the flagrantly discounted Century 21, it's the most moderately priced of the bunch. Perhaps its merchandise is on the conventional side, but it covers nearly all the bases, from kitchen goods (and carry-out) in the basement to antiques on the ninth floor, and from haircuts to pedicures. And its rather stubborn nostalgia is fairly represented by that famous Thanksgiving Day Parade (Broadway between West 34th and 35th streets; ☎ 212-695-4400; **www.macys.com**).

Saks Fifth Avenue (☎ 212-753-4000; **www.saksfifthavenue.com**) is just where you'd expect it to be, on Fifth Avenue, between 49th and 50th streets next to **St. Patrick's Cathedral.** This is an old-money outlet with an old-money outlook on fashion, jewelry, fine foods, and even lunch; the Café SFA on the eighth floor has views of the cathedral and Rockefeller Center across the street.

Although it isn't of the same in-crowd stature as Century 21, **Loehmann's** gets a nod, if only because this discount-clothing chain is a New York original; it started out of Frieda Loehmann's Brooklyn brownstone back before Prohibition. The flagship on Seventh Avenue at 16th Street makes for an intriguing counterpoint to the big-name boutiques moving into Chelsea (see "Great Neighborhoods for Shopping," page 373).

Our personal favorite is much less famous and on the expensive side, but it's so beautifully appointed that it's worth a look. **Takashimaya** (Fifth Avenue between East 54th and 55th streets; ☎ 212-350-0115 or 800-753-2038; **www.ny-takashimaya.com**), in a fine six-story town house, begins with a tea shop in the basement and rises through gifts, men's, women's, and home-furnishings displays to a superb florist and urban-gardening boutique. One visit and you'll have a whole new respect for interior design.

MALLS AND ALL

WE CERTAINLY DON'T SUGGEST YOU GO LOOKING FOR a shopping mall in Manhattan (especially as the streets are already full of Banana Republic, J.Crew, Gap, and other chain stores). If you must run off a quick list, however, there are a couple of shopping towers ("malls" in the city are more likely to be vertical than horizontal) that won't be far from your path.

Manhattan's version of a supermall is **The Shops at Columbus Circle,** in the Time Warner Center at the southwest corner of Central Park. This seven-story honeycomb of some 40 stores includes **A/X Armani Exchange, Hugo Boss, Bose, Stuart Weitzman, Sisley, Eileen Fisher, Thomas Pink, Coach, J.Crew, Benetton, Tourneau, Davidoff, bebe, FACE Stockholm, Aveda, L'Occitane, J. W. Cooper,** and more, plus a huge **Whole Foods Market.** It also houses several of the city's most expensive restaurants, such as Thomas (French Laundry) Keller's **Per Se,** Japanese celebrity chef Masa Takayama's **Masa** and **Bar Masa,** former Windows on the World chef Michael Lomonaco's **Porter House** steak house, **Bouchon Bakery, Stone Rose** lounge, and a branch of the TriBeCa fave **Landmarc** as well as **Jazz at Lincoln Center** complex.

The **Manhattan Mall,** at Sixth Avenue and 33rd Street, has about 120 shops on nine levels, including the huge new flagship of **JCPenney, Express, Victoria's Secret,** a typical food court, and a useful, brochure-heavy visitor center. Even handier, it's right next to Macy's.

The over-the-top **Trump Tower,** on Fifth Avenue between 56th and 57th streets, looks like a reality-series backdrop (which, actually, it is), a glittery pink-marble-and-mirrors blingfest with waterfalls to boot. Half-condo, half-mall—the three-level, 46,000-square-foot **Gucci** flagship store is just stop number one—with a six-floor marble atrium, it's a tourist attraction in itself, especially given that Donald Trump's $100-million penthouse triplex, *The Apprentice* boardroom, and the suites used by that reality show's contestants are also here.

Rockefeller Center, just off Fifth Avenue between 49th and 50th streets, also has a mini-mall (featuring **Cole Haan, Movado, Kenneth Cole, Coach, Brookstone, Banana Republic,** and **J.Crew**) that you can tour while admiring the Plaza display of the moment, the skating rink, the Deco buildings, *Today* show guests, and other diversions.

unofficial **TIP**
South Street Seaport also has a branch of the **TKTS** booths, where you can purchase discount tickets for Broadway shows.

The renovated **South Street Seaport,** one of the showpieces of the built-up Lower Manhattan area just south of the Brooklyn Bridge at Water Street, is now an attractive, if somewhat predictable, mini-mall of shops (**Abercrombie & Fitch, J.Crew, Gap, Guess**), restaurants, and marine-history souvenir stores.

The most attractive one-stop shopping destination for now is the renovated **Grand Central Terminal,** on Park Avenue between 42nd and 44th streets, which has more than 120 boutiques, service stores, coffee shops, and carryouts. And of course, it also has several serious restaurants to choose from, including **Michael Jordan's The Steakhouse N.Y.C.,** with its view of the Grand Concourse; a mezzanine bar; the famed **Grand Central Oyster Bar;** the third-floor cocktail lounge in the long-neglected **Campbell Apartment,** built in the 1920s as a private office and modeled on a 13th-century Florentine palazzo; and a trendy faster-food and trattoria concourse on the lower level, complete with fish and meat markets.

But chances are you only have to get off the elevator to find plenty of immediate attractions; most luxury hotels have stores in the lower levels. The newly refurbished **Plaza Hotel,** for instance, has 25 mini-boutiques, including the art-book and print dealer **Assouline;** jewelers **Kenneth Jay Lane, Maurice,** and **Good Fortune Ten Thousand Things; MCM** bags; custom shirtmakers **Seize Sur Vingt;** and **Plaza Beauty,** stocked with the sort of hard-to-find beauty products—selected by celebrity hairdresser Joel Warren, whose salon is here—that only the very in-the-know will know to desire.

FLEA MARKETS

WHAT WOULD SHOPPING IN MANHATTAN BE without a visit to the flea markets? Of course, we mean semi-pro shopping—not the sort of amateur souveniring you can do anywhere, but spot, dash, and bargain stuff. Frequently there are serious antiques dealers as well (see more on antiques centers later in this section), but with flea markets, you need to be a little more careful about provenance and aging.

unofficial **TIP**
Don't expect dealers to accept credit cards, although a few whose merchandise is particularly expensive (antique furniture, for example) might. In general, expect cash and carry to be the order of the day.

Some flea markets are regularly scheduled, some are more impromptu (especially in good weather), and a few are more like block parties with vendors involved, especially downtown. The Weekend section of the *New York Times* (**www.nytimes .com**) may mention some special fairs; also check the classifieds.

The most famous, the original, the **Annex Antiques Fair and Flea Market,** has now merged with the **Hell's Kitchen Flea Market.** It operates every Saturday and Sunday on West 39th Street between Ninth and Tenth avenues, with up to 170 vendors. A $1 shuttle bus runs between there and the two-story **Antiques Garage** at 112 West 25th Street, between Sixth and Seventh avenues. From there it's a short walk to the **West 25th Street Market,** along West 25th Street between Broadway and Sixth Avenue. All are run by the same people, and all open Saturday and Sunday at 9 a.m., with the Garage closing at 5 p.m. and the street markets closing at 6 p.m. (☎ 212-243-5343; **www.hells kitchenfleamarket.com**).

Unless you're a flea-market veteran, you may find it easier to grasp the opportunities at the somewhat smaller **SoHo Antiques Fair and Flea Market,** which sets up Saturdays and Sundays from 9 a.m. to 5 p.m. at the corner of Broadway and Grand. **GreenFlea** (☎ 212-239-3025; **www.greenfleamarkets.com**) operates a Saturday market (closed during the coldest months) from 11 a.m. to 7 p.m. at Greenwich Avenue and Charles Street (near Sixth Avenue) in Greenwich Village, and an indoor–outdoor Sunday market, open year-round, from 10 a.m. to 5:30 p.m. at **Public School 44** on Columbus Avenue at West 77th Street. The upscale flea market at **Public School 183** on East 66th Street between First and York avenues (Saturday only, 6 a.m. to 6 p.m.) also includes a farmers market.

ONE-STOP SHOPPING:
Museum Shops and Theme Stores

ART-IFACTS: THE MUSEUM SHOPS

IF YOU'RE SICK OF THE COOKIE-CUTTER GIFT LIST, treat yourself to a mall of the mind, so to speak. Along two straight lines, one on the East Side and the other in Midtown, are clusters of the smartest—meaning chic and brainy—shops, each a little different and each, so to speak, of museum quality.

The first line, of course, is along **Museum Mile,** that stretch of Fifth Avenue between 82nd and 104th streets along which nine major collections are assembled. All have some sort of gift shop, but it's fair to say that the **Met Store** in the **Metropolitan Museum of Art** at 82nd (☎ 212-570-3894; **www.metmuseum.org**) has one of the most stunning collections anywhere: replica jewelry, Egyptiana, art-design scarves, notepaper, reproductions of classic posters, decorative glass, books, T-shirts, desk accessories, card cases, calendars, vases, reproduction statuary, Impressionist umbrellas, Munch and Dalí wristwatches, and even rugs. Check out some of the art being sold on consignment upstairs. The Met has become a mini-chain: there are outposts in Rockefeller Center, Macy's, South Street Seaport, and even at **LaGuardia** and **JFK** airports—handy if you forget someone on the gift list.

The shop at the **Neue Galerie,** at 86th Street (☎ 212-994-9496; **www.neuegalerie.org**), is a magnet for lovers of turn-of-the-20th-century European design, with reproductions of Loos lighting, Bauhaus tea services, Josef Hoffman silver, and more.

The **Jewish Museum,** on Fifth Avenue at 92nd Street (☎ 212-423-333; **www.thejewishmuseum.org**), has a small but striking collection of jewelry, menorahs, and scarves, many with designs adapted from religious or historical works.

The **Cooper-Hewitt, National Design Museum,** at 91st Street (☎ 213-849-8355; **www.cooperhewitt.org**), is design central for those whose taste in silver, platters, and small personal and office items such as pens, bath luxuries, salt and pepper shakers, and coasters tends to an earlier, more sensual age than the cooler **Museum of Modern Art** (MoMA) collection (this is, after all, the former Carnegie mansion). If you like a more post-modern look, step into the shop at the **Guggenheim Museum,** at 89th Street (☎ 800-329-6109; **www.guggenheimstore.org**), and peruse the posters, notepapers, jewelry, and textiles.

A short stroll away are **The Frick Collection** (Fifth Avenue and 70th Street; ☎ 212-547-6848; **www.frick.org**), with lovely stationery, post-cards, and notebooks; and the **Whitney Museum of American Art** store (Madison Avenue and 75th Street; ☎ 212-570-3614; **www.whitney .org**), with its sometimes elegantly spare, sometimes witty assort-ment of ties, toys, and other home and closet whimsy.

On Columbus Circle, the **Museum of Arts & Design** has one of the finest art-gift shops in town (☎ 212-299-7777; **thestore.madmuseum .org**). Though the selection is not large, the jewelry is particularly attractive, sometimes spectacular, and often hilarious. Although the elegant glassworks, handbags, and jewelry can hit high price notes, there are plenty of fun bargain items: wrapping tape imprinted with a measuring tape's inches, light-up postcards of Times Square, Kyo-cera ceramic kitchen knives, and build-your-own kaleidoscopes.

Several museum shops are within easy walking distance of each other in Midtown. The **MoMA Design Store** (44 West 53rd Street, between Fifth and Sixth avenues; ☎ 212-767-1050; **www.moma.org**) has for good reason inspired one of the great mail catalogs. Every one of these prod-ucts—glassware, pens, kids' flatware, vases, photo frames, even watches and ties—has passed such muster with the museum's design mavens that it has become part of the permanent collection. And, smart as these items are, they are frequently great bargains: among our personal favorite acquisitions include spiral-twist stretch bracelets, something like Slinkys for the wrist, for $8 to $12.

The **MoMA Design and Book Store** (across the street in the lobby of the main museum building at 11 West 53rd Street; ☎ 212-708-9700) stocks more than 6,000 coffee-table books, catalogs, and high-quality paperbacks, as well as educational videos, software, art posters, cal-endars, and so on. For downtowners, there's another MoMA shop in SoHo at 81 Spring Street, between Broadway and Crosby Street (☎ 646-613-1367).

Once squeezed into a niche near Lincoln Center, the coolly elegant **American Folk Art Museum,** in the same block of West 53rd Street as MoMA (☎ 212-265-1040, ext. 124; **www.folkartmuseum.org**), now has eight stories to display its fine collection of naive and faux-naïf art—plus a shop full of books and handcrafted gifts.

Just around the corner on 52nd Street between Fifth and Sixth avenues is **The Paley Center for Media** (☎ 212-621-6600; **www.paley center.org**), which has a small store ideally suited to those whose kids (or spouses) still have crushes on Mary Tyler Moore or Captain Kirk:

videos, T-shirts, posters, vintage radio shows—stocking stuffers with character, so to speak.

The **New Museum Contemporary Art,** on Bowery between Houston and Prince streets (☎ 212-219-1222; **www.newmuseum.org**) stocks artist-designed home furnishings, jewelry, lamps, and smart and unusual baby gifts.

For friends with special interests, these museum shops can be real treasures: The **International Center of Photography** at Sixth Avenue and 43rd Street (☎ 212-857-9725; **www.icp.org**) is the only museum in the city that collects and exhibits only photographs; its calendars, prints, and coffee-table books are first-rate. The **Museum of the City of New York** has such urban memorabilia as stickball sets and vintage posters (Fifth Avenue at 103rd Street; ☎ 212-534-1672; **www.mcny .org**). The **Metropolitan Opera Shop** in Lincoln Center, on Amsterdam (10th) Avenue between West 62nd and West 65th streets (☎ 212-580-4090; **www.metoperafamily.org**), stocks not only great records and biographies but also diva (and danseur) T-shirts, mugs, and the sort of unabashed art-lover's accessories that fill PBS catalogs.

The shop at the **National Museum of the American Indian** (☎ 212-514-3766; **nmai.si.edu**), in the old Custom House near Battery Park, has Native American music and meditation tapes, beadwork kits, and turquoise jewelry of the sort that is once again popular with young people, plus T-shirts, arrowheads, and reproductions of famous paintings of the West.

For those who love ethnic accessories, the **Rubin Museum of Art,** dedicated to Himalayan works, has beautiful jewelry, purses, cabinets, and rugs (West 17th Street at Seventh Avenue; ☎ 212-620-5000, ext. 350; **www.rmanyc.org**). Vaguely exotic jewelry, shawls, inlaid boxes, and leather-bound goods are among the attractions at the **Dahesh Museum of Art** shop, on East 52nd Street between Park and Madison avenues (☎ 212-759-0606; **www.daheshmuseum.org**). And the **Asia Society**'s **AsiaStore** (Park Avenue between 70th and 71st streets; ☎ 212-327-9217; **www.asiastore.org**) stocks not only adult and children's books on Asian culture, cooking, language, and design but also toys, jewelry, teapots, chopsticks, Indonesian carvings, and unusual paper goods.

BRAND LOYALTY: THEME STORES

THE 1990S GAVE BIRTH TO A WHOLE NEW BOOM in merchandising: stores specializing in movie and television tie-ins, corporate brand names, celebrity properties, and so on. If your kids long for these sorts of souvenirs, there are several along almost any major tour route.

kids Young ladies who have become "moms" to one of the various American Girl dolls may have tea (or pizza) with their child by visiting the **American Girl Place** at Fifth Avenue and 49th Street (☎ 877-247-5223; **www.americangirl.com**) in the third-floor cafe: a $24 three-course lunch isn't much of a splurge for a $100 doll.

For slightly older trendinistas, the huge **Diesel** "planet"—the fourth in that denim megastar's galaxy, after Hong Kong, Tokyo, and Milan—boasts 700 styles of denim, plus watches, bags, accessories, and the like (Fifth at 54th; ☎ 212-755-3555; **www.diesel.com**). The three-figure-sneaker set will glory in the multistory **Niketown,** on 57th east of Fifth (☎ 212-891-6453; **www.nike.com**), and the **NBA** store, on Fifth at 52nd (☎ 212-515-6221; **www.nba.com/nycstore**).

Though several **Original Levi's Stores** can be found around the city, the showcase branch is on Broadway, in Times Square at 44th Street (☎ 212-944-8555; **www.levisstore.com**). But that's nothing compared with the four-story **Toys"R"Us** store across Broadway (☎ 646-366-8800 or 800-869-7787; **www.toysrus.com/timessquare**), with its 60-foot-high Ferris wheel and Lego versions of the Empire State and Chrysler buildings. The **ESPN Zone,** on Broadway at 42nd Street, is like a living page of box scores with a built-in menu and playground (☎ 212-921-3776; **www.espnzone.com/newyork**). The **NBC Experience Store** in Rockefeller Center is stocked with T-shirts, mugs, and caps from *The Tonight Show, Saturday Night Live,* and other entertainments.

The newest versions of catalog stores are electronics boutiques, most notably the **Sony Style Store,** on Madison Avenue at 56th Street (☎ 212-833-8800; **www.sonystyle.com**); the **Porsche Design Store,** on Madison near 59th Street, which includes not only autos but also such über-lifestyle accoutrements as Ferragamo luggage (☎ 212-308-1786; **www.porsche-design.com**); and the stunning glass cube on Fifth Avenue between 58th and 59th streets that marks the site of the first 24-7 **Apple Store** (☎ 212-336-1440; **www.apple.com/retail**).

And because more and more restaurants have their own in-house merchandise stores, check out the **Jekyll & Hyde Club** (Sixth Avenue and 57th; ☎ 212-541-9505; **www.jekyllandhydeclub.com**), **Planet Hollywood** (Broadway and 45th; ☎ 212-333-7827; **www.planethollywood.com**), and the **Hard Rock Cafe** (1501 Broadway between 43rd and 44th; ☎ 212-343-3355; **www.hardrock.com**).

Of course, if your particular brand loyalty lies with a famous designer, you're headed uptown, so see the following sections on Fifth Avenue and Madison Avenue.

GREAT NEIGHBORHOODS *for* SHOPPING

WINDOWS ON THE WORLD: FIFTH AVENUE

A VERY FEW STREETS have stores and window displays so famous that they don't even need city names attached. Rodeo Drive. The Champs-Élysées. Via Veneto. And Fifth Avenue.

Fifth Avenue was nicknamed "Millionaires' Row" at the turn of the century, when the Vanderbilts, Astors, and Goulds all built palaces for themselves along the road, and it's never quite given up that expensive spirit. A few of the 19th-century mansions are still standing, and the churches of the area give you an idea of the luxury such tycoons expected even in their houses of worship. (Remember that Fifth Avenue is the east–west dividing line, and don't let addresses on the numbered streets confuse you. **Cartier,** on Fifth at East 52nd Street, faces **Juicy Couture,** at West 52nd.)

To get a sense of both the retail and historical beauties of Midtown, start 49th Street and head north on Fifth Avenue toward Central Park. On your left sits **Rockefeller Center,** which fills the blocks between Fifth and Sixth avenues and West 48th and 51st streets and incorporates **Radio City Music Hall** and the **NBC Studios.** Notice the gilded gods of industry on the facades.

Across the street is **Saks Fifth Avenue,** and in the next block is **St. Patrick's Cathedral,** which was designed by James Renwick Jr. and completed in 1878. Above that, you'll see **Armani A/X, Jimmy Choo, H.Stern, Versace,** and the elaborate facade of the famous jeweler **Cartier** at the corner of East 52nd, one of the few turn-of-the-20th-century mansions still intact. (Legend has it that the original owner traded the house to Pierre Cartier for a string of pearls.) Walk on past **Rolex, St. John, Brooks Brothers, Ermenegildo Zegna,** and **Ferragamo.**

The French Gothic **St. Thomas Church,** at the corner of Fifth and 53rd, was completed in 1913; the **University Club,** at 54th, was built in 1899 by Charles McKim (a partner of Stanford White's) in imitation of Italian *palazzi.* McKim also designed what is now the **Banco de Napoli** across the street. The **Fifth Avenue Presbyterian Church,** built in 1875, was where the Roosevelts, Auchinclosses, and Wolcotts worshipped, helping give it the reputation of having the city's most influential congregation.

Now the credit-card boutiques begin to thicken: **Fendi, Zara, Takashimaya,** and **Gucci** around East 54th; **Pucci, Hugo Boss, Henri Bendel,** and **Prada.** The huge, new all-glass **Giorgio Armani** flagship store at 56th is four floors and 43,000 square feet, enough to hold all of his various lines plus a bar and restaurant.

This is one of the major bling junctions in the country. **De Beers,** the first name in diamonds (it invented the phrase "A diamond is forever"), has opened an American flagship store at Fifth and 55th (☎ 212-906-0001; **www.debeers.com**); one of its neighbors is **Wempe,** the biggest name in authorized Rolex sales. **Harry Winston,** diamond designer to the rich and famous, is on Fifth at West 56th, and the other three famous "Four Carat" neighbors, **Tiffany, Van Cleef & Arpels,** and **Bulgari,** are all at the intersection of 57th, along with **Mikimoto** and **Piaget.** And while **Omega** may not be Rolex, its new boutique at 56th has a museum collection, including JFK's 1960 18K timepiece, that makes it worth a stop.

Above 57th, look for **Louis Vuitton, Burberry, Chanel,** and **Fendi. Norma Kamali** is just around the corner on 56th.

Bergdorf Goodman and **Bergdorf Goodman Men** fill the blocks from West 57th to 58th. And as you get near the bottom of Central Park, where Fifth meets 58th Street, look over to your right and you'll see **FAO Schwarz,** one of the most famous toy stores in the world, the flagship **Apple Store,** and the outdoor "set" of the *CBS Early Show.*

CLOTHING ON THE HIGH SIDE: THE EAST SIDE

IF YOU LOVE THAT COUTURE LOOK but don't have time to fly to Paris or Rome, relax. These days, the signs along Madison Avenue from the 60s to the 90s read like satellite transmissions from Europe's runway centers, with just enough American and international designer boutiques to keep you grounded.

Start walking east along 57th Street from Fifth Avenue, and you will see the signs for **Louis Vuitton, Christian Dior, Chanel, Yves Saint Laurent, Montblanc, Burberry, Coach,** and another **Prada.** Turn left at the corner onto Madison and you'll see **Tourneau,** one of a handful of Manhattan branches of that high-end watch temple, and **Sermoneta,** where you can get gloves fancy enough to frame that expensive timepiece.

> *unofficial* **TIP**
> Don't think you need to hit all these areas; you'll see the same names, even the big ones, two or three times around town—and in the major department stores.

Here's a sampling of what you'll see in the next ten blocks of Madison Avenue: **Emporio Armani, DKNY, Lara Marks, Anne Klein,** the **Calvin Klein** flagship at East 60th, custom shirtmaker **Borrelli** and Italian shoemaker **Tod's, Hermès, Raymond Weil, Luca Luca, Ivanka Trump, Anne Fontaine, Lalique and Haviland, Thos. Moser, Shanghai Tang, David Yurman, Jimmy Choo, Krizia, Valentino, BCBG Max Azaria, Paul & Shark** (the nautically minded Italian sportswear company), **Porsche, Baccarat, Fratelli, Jil Sander, Bulgari, Oscar de la Renta, Fred Leighton, Nicole Miller** (who is to ties as the *New Yorker* is to cartoons), the nearly as popular **Robert Talbott, Emanuel Ungaro, Kenzo, Moschino, Davide Cenci, Issey Miyake,** and **Frette,** producer of the finest Martha-and-then-some Italian linens.

The fur starts to fly around here: **Dennis Basso** may not be a household name, but if you're a diva the likes of Liza or Janet or Diana, you might be buying his over-the-top fur creations (Madison between 65th and 66th; ☎ 212-794-4500; **www.dennisbasso.com**). Just below 64th, **J. Mendel** (☎ 212-832-5830; **www.jmendel.com**) has taken up the challenge of draping Beyoncé and J.Lo in luxury.

Some of these shops are almost sightseeing destinations. At the northwest corner of West 65th and Madison, the **Giorgio Armani** boutique is a stunning white four-story showplace that resembles the National Gallery's East Building. **Isaac Mizrahi** has a new store at the corner of 67th Street that houses all of his various lines together. **Dolce & Gabbana,** at Madison and 69th, is 7,000 square feet of recently renovated, retro-rococo chic. And **Ralph Lauren** has four floors of Polo clothing, accessories, and home luxuries in a massive 1890s French

Renaissance Revival mansion on the west side of Madison between 71st and 72nd streets, along with a whole second building full of baby and kids' Polo, plus his weathered-look RRL line.

Feel like window-shopping for another ten blocks? Above 68th Street are the complete ready-to-wear collections of **Alessandro Dell'Acqua, Cartier, Oilily, Calypso Christiane Celle, Max Mara, Malo** (the European cashmere king), **Donna Karan, Chloé,** and yet another **Prada** boutique. If you're crazy for natural fibers or custom-woven linens, it's dueling designer labels: the Italian **Pratesi** versus the French **D. Porthault.** Next in succession, on Madison between 70th and 71st streets, are the marquees of ex–Gucci head designer **Tom Ford, Christian Dior, Jimmy Choo, Morgane le Fay, Vera Wang, Eileen Fisher, Sonia Rykiel,** and **Santoni,** of handmade-Italian-footwear fame. Keep going past **Carolina Herrera, Michael Kors, Larry Gargosian,** and **Missoni.** Nor is that nearly the end of the strip—in fact, the stores will hold out longer than your feet are likely to.

Not surprisingly the Upper East Side has also spawned a cluster of "pre-owned fashion" boutiques: see the section on consignment and vintage clothing in "Specialty Shopping," page 384. Also see the sections on shopping on the Lower East Side and NoLita.

CLOTHING ON THE HIP SIDE: SOHO AND LITTLE ITALY

FASHION- AND/OR BARGAIN-CONSCIOUS VISITORS have a great reason to explore the SoHo area, even aside from the street theater.

Retro, nouveau, haute, and so-so, SoHo and surroundings are big boutique territory, so much so that locals quite frequently describe it as having "fallen" (as in the rise and fall of the bohemian empire) or sold out. (Admittedly, having the Guggenheim Museum SoHo turn into a Prada superstore is a serious blow for boho.) You're as likely to see those same suburban-mall-chain names (**Victoria's Secret, Eddie Bauer, Club Monaco,** and, yes, **J.Crew**) here as anywhere else in town.

unofficial **TIP**
SoHo shops and names, even the big ones, play musical addresses so often that you may have to wander around to find again that great find you found before. And remember that weekends are prime wandering time, so quite a few SoHo shopkeepers close on Monday.

Still, if it is a shopping mall, it's one in a beautiful setting, and with people-watching that can't be beat (and better bars than most).

If you don't mind walking in circles, exploring SoHo can be fun, but you can stay relatively well oriented by picking a few streets to concentrate on, at least to stat.

For example: along and just off Mercer from Grand Street north to West Houston, you see such familiar names as **Yohji Yamamoto, Vivienne Tam, Hugo Boss, Kate Spade, Marc Jacobs, Ted Baker London,** and milliner **Kelly Christy.** Down near Grand, **Pearl River** stocks decorating imports of the sort the original Pier 1s used to: Asian scrolls, oversized birdcages, parasols, and lantern lights.

Jack Spade, the men's store founded by Kate's husband (whose name is actually Andy), is on Greene Street, along with the likes of **Anna Sui, Louis Vuitton, Jill Stuart, Moss, Nicole Miller, Kirna Zabête** (a smart and eclectic collection of independent designers), and custom shirtmakers **Seize sur Vingt.** Greene Street also houses one of two SoHo shoe stores that footsore tourists might want to look into: **Glory Chen** (☎ 212-677-2938; **www.joychen.com**), between Prince and Houston streets, showcases footwear that is both striking and comfortable from designer Joy Chen and others.

West Broadway offers plenty of familiar uptown names, including **Emporio Armani, Oska, Max Azria, Oilily, Dolce & Gabbana, Elie Tahari, DKNY, Missoni, Links of London, Ralph Lauren, Tommy Hilfiger, Eileen Fisher, Sportmax** (the upscale-casual line from Max Mara), and **Coach.** This is where you'll find the other intriguing shoe store: **Onesole,** between Prince and Spring (☎ 212-219-8595; **www.onesole .com**), which offers comfortable wedge sandals with interchangeable snap-on tops, so that one pair of shoes becomes a wardrobe.

One of SoHo's big draws always was the size of the former warehouses, and it still is—only not so much for artists anymore. However depressing it might be to some residents as evidence of SoHo's transformation from counterculture to couture counter, the huge **Prada** flagship at Broadway and Prince Street (☎ 212-334-8888; **www.prada.com**) is another of those near-destination buildings: a $40 million, 23,000-square-foot loft with computers in the racks, stadium seating in the shoe department, and handbags in the elevators. (And after all, before it was the Guggenheim, the six-story, 160,000-square-foot loft served John Jacob Astor II as a garment-manufacturing and retailing complex.)

Even that's not the standard for space: the global flagship store of **Uniqlo,** a half-block down Broadway between Prince and Spring streets (☎ 917-237-8811; **www.uniqlo.com**), is the Japanese version of the Gap, only bigger—36,000 square feet—and much, much cooler. Even cooler than that, literally, is the 4,600-square-foot **Burton** boutique, which specializes in high-tech, brand-name ski equipment, accessories, clothing, and knickknacks—and even has a "cold room" where you can test the chill factor (Spring and Mercer streets; ☎ 212-966-8070; **www.burton.com**).

If you have a craving for something more individual, here are some other SoHo shops we like: **Carrol Boyes** (186 Prince Street, between Wooster and Greene streets; ☎ 212-334-3556; **www.carrolboyes online.com**) designs metal housewares and utensils of unusual wit and competence. **Morgane Le Fay** is Liliana Ordas's splendidly mysterious cave of dresses and capes (67 Wooster Street, between Spring and Broome; ☎ 212-219-7672; **www.morganelefay.com**). **Tokidoki** (176 Spring Street, between Thompson Street and West Broadway; ☎ 212-334-6021; **www.tokidoki.it**) stocks bold anime-graphic skateboards and bags. **Evolution** delves into the animal kingdom (look under "Bones" in "Specialty Shopping," page 385). And **Marisa Perry**

(154 Prince, between West Broadway and Thompson; ☎ 212-566-8977; **www.marisaperry.com**) makes exquisite jewelry, including custom wedding rings, that are worth the close-up.

And although the home-decor shops are being squeezed by the clothing boutiques (and you aren't likely to be looking for an Italian Modern sofa, unless you're about to move to the city), there's plenty of free style education to be had via showroom windows. (Check out the latest in Japanese toilets at the **TOTO Gallery** at 25 Mercer.)

With Broadway below Houston becoming such a big retail draw—besides **Prada, Uniqlo,** and **Puma** there's **Bloomingdale's, Old Navy, Adidas, Ann Taylor, Guess, H&M, Dean & DeLuca, Victoria's Secret, Swarovski,** etc., etc.—it's not surprising that the not-so-franchise-famous boutique designers are starting to look for space on the other side of the avenue in NoLita and Little Italy (and even the Lower East Side; see next section). In fact, the expansion has led to the strip between Broadway and Lafayette, which used to be considered Little Italy, being "annexed" into SoHo, while Little Italy—which is shrinking as Chinatown swells—has been split into the old section and NoLita above Kenmare.

The main commercial streets in NoLita are **Mott and Elizabeth streets,** but boutiques here change hands and names pretty quickly, so this is the sort of area you need to be willing to hunt through. However, there are a couple of names savvy fashionistas may want to visit. Even if you confine yourself to the one square block bounded by Prince, Mott, Elizabeth, and Houston, you'll see plenty of them.

Sigerson Morrison (Kari Sigerson and Miranda Morrison) is a must for Carrie Bradshaw wannabes—unless you already have kid-leather pumps the color of a swashbuckler's wine and velvet loafers for your dinner jacket. The bigger store is at 28 Prince Street between Elizabeth and Mott (☎ 212-219-3893; **www.sigersonmorrison.com**), while the original location at 242 Mott just above Prince is now the home of the secondary collection, **Belle by Sigerson Morrison** (☎ 212-941-5404; **www.bellenyc.com**).

Project Runway also-ran Emmett McCarthy's retro-chic dress-and-coat sets are the stars of **EMc2** on Elizabeth (he's generous enough to stock his former rivals' best as well). Also on Elizabeth are **Me&Ro,** for funky one-of-a-kind jewelry, sportswear icon **Tory Burch,** and the top-to-bottom (bed linens to blouses) designs of **Erica Tanov.** On Prince is **INA,** a prime source for designer consignments and sell-offs; and on Mott check out **Lugo** shirts, **Jaalber** jewelers, **INA Men,** and the ethnic-print, modern-look **Calypso Christiane Celle.**

unofficial **TIP**
Speaking of Carrie Bradshaw: *Sex and the City* wardrobe stylist **Patricia Field**'s own oversized "closet" is at 302 Bowery, just above Houston (☎ 212-966-4066; **www.patriciafield.com**).

NoLita has also become a treasure trove of high-end designer consignment stores and vintage boutiques. Also on Mott, check out **Use Your Head,** which not only offers consignments from Dior, Valentino, Christian Lacroix,

Gianfranco Ferré, and others, but also donates the proceeds to organizations that help the homeless. Almost shoulder to shoulder with Use Your Head are the ultra-modern **VeKa** and **Blue** bridal salons, and the celeb-conscious **Second Time Around** couture consignment store—all just above Prince on Mott Street.

If you can't find what you're looking for there, then check out **Resurrection,** one of New York's most famous vintage-clothing stores, at Mott just below Prince; its clients tend to be the first-name variety (Paris and Nicole, Lisa Marie, Posh). Also flip through the eponymous fare at **Frock** on Elizabeth south of Spring Street. There's more vintage to be seen the Lower East Side; read on.

CLOTHING ON THE BARGAIN SIDE: THE LOWER EAST SIDE

THE LOWER EAST SIDE WAS FAMOUS FOR YEARS as the place bargains were best; serious shoppers flew in to gawk along **Orchard Street,** where previous-season department-store and even designer wear could be had for, well, if not a song, then no more than that plus an extra chorus or two. These days, with sales so much more common and outlet malls thriving, the trek is a little lower on some visitors' itineraries, but the merchants of the neighborhood, now being more aggressively promoted as the Historic Orchard Street Bargain District, have banded together to raise their profile again. (The new Lower East Side slogan: LES Is More.) So if you do have that bargain bug—and, after all, how many of your office mates can tell last year's classics from this year's?—head east from SoHo into this evocative old section. (If you pick up the group's "Go East!" guide and punch out the ID card, you're eligible for even deeper discounts or extra items from many of the retailers.) To avoid getting disoriented in all this retail abundance, stop by the offices of the **Lower East Side Visitor's Office,** at 70 Orchard Street between Grand and Hester streets (☎ 866-224-0206; **www.lowereastsideny.com**).

unofficial **TIP**
When shopping on the Lower East Side, it's best to go with the established stores; many of the sidewalk vendors are hawking bootleg or counterfeit goods. And don't flash your cash too carelessly; if nothing worse, you'll be mobbed by insistent shopkeepers.

Hundreds of businesses in this neighborhood are still family owned, and with just a little imagination (and maybe a stop at the **Lower East Side Tenement Museum** or other historic landmark), you'll be able to see it as it was when the pushcart and peddler era was melding into the wholesale world—especially if you go on a Sunday, when a lot of the area streets are blocked off for pedestrian traffic and turned into open-air vendor markets. And you'll definitely still hear the rhythms of the Yiddish that millions of Eastern European Jews stamped on the bargaining patter of the vendors, even though the community's ethnicity now ranges from South American to Southeast Asian. (Stand too long staring into one store's windows, and a rival shopkeeper from across the street is likely to chase you down.)

unofficial **TIP**
Consult stores' Web
sites before you go;
many observant Jewish
shopkeepers close early
on Friday afternoon to
attend Sabbath services,
remain closed Saturday,
and reopen Sunday.

You may also find 19th-century echoes in some stores' cash-only policies (though this is becoming less common) and the haggling over prices you may experience every once in a while. If you like the hurly-burly of contact-sport shopping, this is the place.

Although not all the stores are actually on Orchard, you might think they were, especially the corset-and-bra stores—some of which have served generations of women—and leather outlets. Probably the biggest shopping draws for out-of-towners, however, are the stores boasting classic labels.

Among the places for women to see a lot in a little time is **Giselle Sportswear** (143 Orchard Street, near Rivington; ☎ 212-673-1900; **www.giselleny.com**), four floors of discounted European labels such as Valentino and Escada. For men, it's the three floors of big-name men's fashions (including Burberry, Brioni, Versace, and Ferré) at **Jodamo International** (Grand Street at Orchard; ☎ 212-219-1039; **www.jodamointernational.com**) and the almost-as-extensive collection at the 50-year-old **Global International** (62 Orchard; ☎ 212-219-1039), which offers free alterations. For men who prefer the Japanese designers, **First Among Equals,** at 177 Orchard, is the hot spot (☎ 212-253-2202; **www.firstamongequalsnyc.com**). And for tuxedos for men or women, try **Ted's Formal Wear** (155 Orchard; ☎ 212-966-2029; **www.tedsrocktshirts.com**).

Exotic-leather-shoe freaks, hit **Cellini Uomo** (59 Orchard; ☎ 212-219-8657; **www.celliniuomousa.com**), **Cougar Italian Fashion** (96 Orchard; ☎ 212-475-0692), or **Michele Olivieri** (118 Orchard; ☎ 212-388-1095; **www.moshoes.com**).

For luggage, try **Altman** (135 Orchard; ☎ 212-254-7275; **www.altmanluggage.com**). For fur, shearling, and leather coats, look into **Arivel** at 150 Orchard (☎ 212-673-8992) or **VIP** at 194 (☎ 212-477-1083; **www.vipleathergallery.com**). Actually, you can't escape the leather shops on Orchard Street, but in spite of their plenitude, keep an eye for quality; walk around before you buy, or at least try to bargain a little.

On the other hand, there's just one place for umbrellas, **Salwen's** (45 Orchard Street; ☎ 212-226-1693), because if you don't hear Irving Salwen play Yiddish folk songs on the guitar, you haven't really gotten the Lower East Side experience.

That SoHo chic-boutique wave is headed east, so keep your eyes peeled for iconoclastic designers setting up temporary shop. Good examples of incipient sticker shock are **international playground** at 186 Orchard (**www.internationalplayground.com**), a pop-up designer gallery, showroom, and occasional party venue, and **Kaight** (83 Orchard), which stocks only eco-friendly and green designers from the U.S. and U.K. (☎ 212-680-5630; **www.kaightnyc.com**).

Thanks also to trend-tide, even the lower Lower East Side—that is, Orchard and Ludlow streets below Delancey toward Canal—is becoming a youth-oriented bar-and-boutique area. Some spots are retro-hip, with overtones of funk and psychedelia as well as hip-hop and a little ethnic flavor; others are treasure troves of small, progressive European and local designers.

There's one other style that's increasingly accessible on the Lower East Side: high-end vintage. Among the most reputable purveyors are **Daha** (175 Orchard; ☎ 212-388-1176), **David Owens** (154 Orchard; ☎ 212-677-3301), **Frock** (170 Elizabeth Street; ☎ 212-594-5380; **www.frocknyc .com**), and **Resurrection** (217 Mott Street; ☎ 212-625-1374; **www.resurrectionvintage.com**).

unofficial **TIP**
If you drop by **Katz's Deli** at Ludlow and East Houston streets (☎ 212-254-2246; **www.katzdeli .com**) any Sunday at 11 a.m. from April through December, you can hook up with a free, two-hour shopping tour. (If Katz's looks particularly familiar to you, it's probably because the most famous scene in *When Harry Met Sally*—the, uh, loud one— was shot here.)

ART GALLERIES AND CREEPING CHIC: CHELSEA

WHILE "STARVING" IS NOT A REQUIRED ATTRIBUTE for an artist, those romanticized financial straits do help explain why it's the run-down areas that harbor artists—until the hip factor drives the rents up. And, as SoHo went HighHo, Chelsea began to supplant it as the center for both established art dealers and up-and-comer galleries.

What goes around, yadda-yadda-yadda, and this still-edgy neighborhood, presently in the grip of busy hotel, restaurant, and retail developers, is beginning to battle for the art-scene buzz with Brooklyn's DUMBO strip. And there is still a sort of "onward and uptown-ward with the arts" movement, as the *New Yorker* might say. After the closing of the Guggenheim's downtown branch, the **Dia Center for the Arts**—which arguably sparked the whole SoHo-to-Chelsea art migration when it moved to West 22nd Street—decamped to look for new digs uptown. **The Museum for African Art** left SoHo for Queens in 2005, but plans to move into a new building along Museum Mile on the Upper East Side in 2011. (The **New Museum of Contemporary Art** opened in neither SoHo nor Chelsea, but in NoLita, on the Bowery between Houston and Prince.)

But with an estimated 300 galleries, Chelsea is, at least for now, New York's art central. (The *New York Times* has taken to listing "Galleries: Chelsea," "Galleries: 57th Street," and "Galleries: Elsewhere.") And after five years in exile, the Dia Center has announced that it will move back to Chelsea in 2012 and build a new museum at one of its old exhibit sites on West 22nd Street.

The easiest way to take in some of the major ones is to stroll back and forth between Tenth and Eleventh avenues along the streets from West 20th to West 27th, stopping at the **Chelsea Art Museum** in a renovated 1850 warehouse at 556 West 22nd and Eleventh. If you

unofficial **TIP**

Make a pub part of your Chelsea art crawl: the comfy, battered old **Half King Bar & Restaurant** (Tenth Avenue and West 23rd Street), owned by author Sebastian Junger, war correspondent–novelist Scott Anderson, and film producer–director Nanette Burstein, offers not only good food and drink but also Monday-night readings and "magazine nights" with prominent journalists.

have specific artists in mind, you can do some advance research at **www.chelseagalleries.com.**

In fact, with all the ongoing upscaling, you could make a sort of all-in-one tour of Manhattan here, with some boutique-label shopping and lunch in the **Meatpacking District,** a tour of the new **High Line** elevated park, and then as much gallery-viewing as you can manage.

Start by strolling across West 14th between Ninth Avenue and Washington Street—the heart of the Meatpacking District—and you'll see the boutique sign for rock-star-child-cum-design-star **Stella McCartney** side by side with **Mossimo** and **Matthew Williamson.** An amalgam of Miu Miu, Jil Sander, Prada, Fendi, and other designers can be found at **Jeffrey New York,** while former Vivienne Westwood designer Sonya Rubin and ex–Armani designer Kip Chapelle have merged into **Rubin Chappelle.** When you get to the corner of Washington, you'll see the half-old, half-skylit warehouse that is the flagship store of wrap-dress queen (and onetime actual princess) **Diane von Furstenberg** (☎ 646-486-4800; **www.dvf.com**).

At this point, if you look up, you'll realize that you are beneath abandoned elevated railroad tracks, now the **High Line Park.** There are entrances every couple of blocks starting from Gansevoort Street and extending (at press time) to 20th Street. (The park will eventually stretch 30th Street; for information, go to **www.thehighline.org.** This is the coolest way to traverse the streets from the Meatpacking District to the heavy arts scene, so pick a watering hole along Washington or 13th Street, and then head up to the High Line and strike out toward 20th—passing beneath **The Standard** hotel and enjoying dozens of stunning views—and then walk down and start gallery-surfing.

Just to give you an idea: in the 500 stretch of West 21st Street, you'll see **Tanya Bonakdar, Paula Cooper, Matthew Marks, Yvon Lambert,** and **Casey Kaplan.**

unofficial **TIP**

Chelsea galleries used to be open on Sunday, but many are now shifting to Saturday-only weekend hours. Be sure to check ahead if you have weekend wandering in mind.

Former Cooper Gallery directors **Christopher D'Amelio** and **Lucien Terras** now have their own eponymous gallery around the corner on West 22nd Street, along with Lisa Spellman's **303 Gallery,** two more Matthew Marks galleries, **Max Protetch, Ameringer | McEnery | Yohe, Sonnabend, Sikkema Jenkins,** and one of two **PaceWildenstein** galleries in Chelsea. The four-story structure that was the Dia Center's former main building, at 535 West 22nd Street, now houses the galleries of **Yancey Richardson, CRG, Friedrich Petzel,** and **Julie Saul,** among others.

And on West 24th are the fourth **Matthew Marks** marquee, **Fredericks & Freiser, Mary Boone, Marianne Boesky, Mary Reed Kelley, Zach Feuer, Bruce Silverstein,** and more; on 26th are **Sara Meltzer, James Cohan, Mitchell-Innes & Nash, Barry Friedman, Lombard-Freid, George Adams, Galerie Lelong, Stephen Haller,** and **Tony Shafrazi.** And this is just for starters.

COOKWARE & CHANDELIERS: THE BOWERY

THE BOWERY IN NOLITA has long been known as the restaurant-supply district, but in recent years, with the craze for Food Network–worthy home-cooking displays and professional-grade gadgets, many of the old resale centers are now going blade-to-bowl with boutiquelike stores stocked top to bottom with stainless-steel freezers and glass-front butcher's refrigerators, enameled casseroles and eight-burner gas stoves, espresso machines, and supersized Cuisinarts.

Just walk along Bowery between Houston and Kenmare, and you see everything from trendy giant whisks to five-foot-tall commercial mixers. (The decor of celeb chef Daniel Boulud's **DBGB Kitchen & Bar** at 299 Bowery [☎ 212-933-5300; **www.danielnyc.com**] is a sort of tribute to this overstocked realm of classic culinary equipment.) Some stores also deal in such other restaurant paraphernalia as bar stools, shakers, and countertops.

unofficial **TIP**
It's a little bit of a walk from here, but **Fishs Eddy,** on Broadway at 19th Street (☎ 212-420-9020; **www.fishs eddy.com**), has overstocked, deaccessioned, and leftover lots of plates, glassware, and platters from restaurants, hotels, and sometimes even ships.

Keep walking down Bowery past Kenmare to about Grand, and you'll see the whole history of high-fashion lighting hanging from shop windows: huge crystal chandeliers, sconces, standing lamps, and high-tech track lighting . . . some pieces with shades like acrobats and others looking like stars going nova. There are fixtures made of chrome, gilt, carved wood, and wrought iron; lamps in pastels or Mondrian squares, neon-trimmed, or with multipsychedelic brilliants. You'll see painted animals, Asian obi shades, Baroque bar lamps, fake and real Tiffany, and just plain oddities. It's a hoot.

Not only is the name of Daniel Boulud's **DBGB,** on Bowery just above Houston, partly a pun on the seminal punk-scene CBGB club, but the **John Varvatos** store at 315 Bowery is actually in the old CBGB space. The shop (☎ 212-358-0315; **www.johnvarvatos .com**) offers not only clothing but also vintage records, punk posters, even free live music—sometimes from CBGB vets.

SPECIALTY SHOPPING

IF YOU'RE A COLLECTOR or are shopping for someone who is, you can almost certainly find in New York whatever it is that's being collected. Whole volumes have been devoted to shopping here, and we ain't just talking the phone book. But unless buying stuff is your life or you plan to move to town permanently, you can get bogged down. This is a sort of biggest-and-broadest list, with gifts for everyone from the bookworm to the bling babe to the boss who has everything.

ANTIQUES It would be impossible to pick the finest antiques dealers in a city like this, so we've mentioned only a few and their specialties. Don't overlook the auction houses, especially **Christie's,** which has a 24-hour hotline for auction information (20 Rockefeller Plaza; ☎ 212-636-2000; **www.christies.com**); **Sotheby's** (York Avenue at East 72nd Street; ☎ 212-606-7000; **www.sothebys.com**); **Doyle** (175 East 87th; ☎ 212-427-2730; **www.doylenewyork.com**); **Phillips de Pury & Company** (450 West 15th; ☎ 212-440-1200; **www.phillipsdepury.com**); **Bonhams** (580 Madison Avenue; ☎ 212-644-9001; **www.bonhams .com/newyork**); and **Swann Auction Galleries,** which specializes in rare books and prints (104 East 25th Street; ☎ 212-254-4710; **www .swanngalleries.com**). These and other reputable firms advertise previews and auctions in the *New York Times* and the *New Yorker*.

If you like just to walk in and out of shops to see what catches your eye, the area around East 60th Street between Second and Third avenues is treasure alley. Check the **Chelsea Antiques Building,** at 110 West 25th Street (☎ 212-929-0909), which has 150 dealers spread over three floors, or **The Manhattan Art and Antiques Center,** with 100 galleries of Asian, African, American, and European works (1050 Second Avenue between 55th and 56th streets; ☎ 212-355-4400; **www.the-maac.com**). **Showplace Antique + Design Center** houses 100 dealers on two huge floors (40 West 25th Street; ☎ 212-633-6063; **www.nyshowplace.com**), but it's something of an offshoot of its neighboring flea market, and most galleries are open only on weekends.

Among the specialists is **Eileen Lane,** who refurbishes Deco, Biedermeier, antique Swedish, and alabaster chandeliers and sconces; she also appraises and consults, so make an appointment to visit her Brooklyn warehouse (62 18th Street, second floor; ☎ 212-475-2988; **www.eileenlaneantiques.com**). For truly haute Southwest, look into **Rabun & Claiborne Antiques,** which specializes in late-19th-century Latin American antiques and collectibles (115 Crosby Street; ☎ 212-226-5053).

And **Les Pierre Antiques** in Greenwich Village continues the legacy of the (late) Pierres Deux—Pierre Moulin, who has been described as the Julia Child of French Provincial decor, and his partner, Peter LeVec (369 Bleecker Street; ☎ 212-243-7740; **www .lespierreinc.com**).

ARCHITECTURAL REMNANTS As is obvious from the number of full-time cable channels devoted to renovations, the thirst for recycled and vintage decor is deep. Etched-glass doors, Deco lighting fixtures, oversized marble tubs, wrought-iron gates, and even the occasional elevator box are on display at **Urban Archaeology** in TriBeCa (143 Franklin Street; ☎ 212-431-4646) and uptown (239 East 58th Street; ☎ 212-371-4646; **www.urbanarchaeology.com**). Brooklyn's **Architectural Salvage Warehouse,** in the Williamsburg area (337 Berry Street; ☎ 718-388-4527), was established by the New York Landmarks Preservation Commission to supply historically minded New Yorkers (you don't have to show identification) with doors, mantels, wrought iron, chandeliers, and so on. The trick is that you'll have to arrange your own shipping. Also check out **Demolition Depot** in Harlem (216 East 125th Street, between Second and Third; ☎ 212-860-1138; **www.demolitiondepot.com**).

ASIAN ART AND ANTIQUES For Japanese woodblocks, contact **Ronin Gallery** (425 Madison Avenue, at 49th; ☎ 212-688-0188; **www.roningallery.com**) or **Joan B. Mirviss, Ltd.** (39 East 78th Street, between Madison and Park, fourth floor; ☎ 212-799-4021; **www.mirviss.com**), which also handles paintings and antiques. New Orleans's prominent Asian art and textiles specialist **Diane Genre** shows in New York several times a year; call ☎ 504-595-8945 for an appointment, or see **www.dianegenreorientalart.com. Art of the Past** (1242 Madison Avenue, between 89th and 90th; ☎ 212-860-7070; **www.artofthepast.com**) specializes in Southeast and Central Asian art and antiques. For Chinese art and porcelains, visit the **Ralph M. Chait Galleries** (724 Fifth Avenue, between 56th and 57th, tenth floor; ☎ 212-397-2818; **www.rmchait.com**). **The Chinese Porcelain Company** handles both antique and contemporary art as well as Vietnamese and Cambodian pieces (475 Park Avenue; ☎ 212-838-7744; **www.chineseporcelainco.com**). And **Robert Turley** has a huge collection of Korean and Himalayan art and antiques at his Chelsea store (40 West 25th Street, between Fifth and Sixth; Friday through Sunday or by appointment, ☎ 917-675-1369, **www.koreanartandantiques.com**).

AUTOGRAPHS Forget those mall stores with their preframed sports photos and replicated signatures. Head to the East Side to **James Lowe** (by appointment, 30 East 60th Street, between Madison and Park; ☎ 212-759-0775) or **Kenneth W. Rendell** (989 Madison Avenue, between 76th and 77th; ☎ 800-447-1007 or 212-717-1776; **www.kwrendell.com**) for authentic signed letters, manuscripts, photographs, and other documents. Inquire about searches for specific autographs or professional evaluations if you have items to insure or sell.

kids **BONES** Since the auctioning of Sue the *T. rex* at Sotheby's, bones have become big business. Actually, they already were starting to be, but for most tourists, the skeletons, teeth, fossils, and anatomical charts at **Maxilla & Mandible** will be a revelation (451 Columbus Avenue, between 81st and 82nd; ☎ 212-724-6173; **www.maxillaandmandible.com**). It's just around the corner from the **American Museum of Natural History,** where dinosaurs are truly king, Rex or no, so this is a natural for kids' day. M&M owner Harry Galiano used to work at the museum, in fact, and his museum-quality merchandise is impeccably treated.

In SoHo, look into **The Evolution Store,** which also has a fascinating assortment of bugs, skulls, horns, feathers, shells, and fossils—plus T-shirts to match (120 Spring Street, between Greene and Mercer streets; ☎ 800-952-3195; **www.evolutionnyc.com**).

BOOKS Manhattan is crammed with general-interest bookstores, of course, including the glorious old flagship **Barnes & Noble** in Union Square—and believe us, you've never seen a B&N like this one (105 Fifth Avenue; ☎ 212-675-5500; **www.bnnewyork.com**). Opened in 1932, this Barnes & Noble wears a sign that boasts, not improbably, that it's "the biggest bookstore in the world," and it's far from the cookie-cutter bestseller boutique that most people know.

Uptown is a haven for fine antique, rare, used, and specialty bookshops. **Rizzoli** (31 West 57th, between Fifth and Sixth; ☎ 212-759-2424 or 800-522-6657; **www.rizzoliusa.com**) is one of the prettiest stores in town as well as a treasure trove of collector's editions and art and design books. **Argosy Books** (116 East 59th Street, between Park and Lexington; ☎ 212-753-4455; **www.argosybooks.com**) has six floors of maps, posters, antiquarian books, political cartoons, and autographs.

Fifth and Madison avenues offer a virtual treasure map of rare books. Look for **Bauman Rare Books** (535 Madison Avenue, between 54th and 55th, ☎ 212-751-0011 or 800-992-2862; **www.baumanrarebooks.com**); **James Cummins** (699 Madison Avenue, between 62nd and 63rd, seventh floor; ☎ 212-688-6441; **www.jamescumminsbookseller.com**); **Imperial Fine Books** (790 Madison Avenue, between 66th and 67th, second floor; ☎ 212-861-6620 or 877-861-6620; **www.imperialfinebooks.com**), which occasionally mounts exhibitions of its bound beauties; **Ursus Books** (981 Madison, between 76th and 77th, ☎ 212-772-8787; **www.ursusbooks.com**); and **Crawford Doyle** (1082 Madison Avenue near 81st; ☎ 212-288-6300). Closer to the Fifth Avenue strip are the elegant new outpost of **Assouline,** in the Plaza Hotel overlooking the lobby with a view of Central Park, stacked with hard-to-find art books, prints, event programs, photographs, and fine botanical illustrations (☎ 212-593-7236; **www.assouline.com**), and **Martayan Lan** (70 East 55th Street, sixth floor; ☎ 212-308-0018 or 800-423-3741; **www.martayanlan.com**).

The most famous secondhand-book store in New York is the **Strand** in Greenwich Village (828 Broadway at 12th Street; ☎ 212-473-1452; **www.strandbooks.com**), which has an estimated 18 miles of shelves with books at rock-bottom prices, plus some first editions, autographed copies, and serious rare books (on the third floor) for those on lavish budgets. (It was here the Strand that one collector purchased the boundary papers for Washington, D.C., signed by then–Secretary of State Thomas Jefferson.)

Manhattan's last surviving for-profit gay bookstore is **Bluestockings,** on the Lower East Side (172 Allen Street; ☎ 212-777-6028; **www.bluestockings.com**). **Housing Works Bookstore Cafe** at 126 Crosby Street in SoHo (☎ 212-334-3324; **www.housingworks.org**) has 45,000 books and records (and wine and light fare), the proceeds from which go to provide housing and assistance for homeless persons living with HIV and AIDS. It often hosts special concerts or appearances by gay artists and comics.

Biography Bookshop in Greenwich Village is just what it sounds like, incorporating not only straight biographies but also diaries, children's versions, and biographical fiction (400 Bleecker Street; ☎ 212-807-8655). Just off Times Square, **Drama Book Shop** (250 West 40th Street; ☎ 212-944-0595; **www.dramabookshop.com**) is the place to go for titles on the performing arts.

Books of Wonder in Chelsea is the sort of children's bookstore you never grow out of, one where authors and illustrators pop in for pleasure as well as for autographings (18 West 18th Street; ☎ 212-989-3270; **www.booksofwonder.com**). **Printed Matter Bookstore** (195 Tenth Avenue, between West 21st and 22nd, ☎ 212-925-0325; **www.printedmatter.org**) is a nonprofit outlet for fine and largely affordable books designed and produced by artists, often by hand.

With home-style fare back in vogue, you may be furrowing your brow for just that particular zucchini-casserole recipe. **Joanne Hendricks Cookbooks** is heaven for culinary wannabes, including those who remember their moms working out of treasures that have long been out of print (488 Greenwich Street; ☎ 212-226-5731; **www.joannehendrickscookbooks.com**). **Bonnie Slotnick** has thousands of volumes—her West Village store is so full you can't get in—but you call and "browse" on the phone (163 West Tenth Street; ☎ 212-989-8962; **www.bonnieslotnickcookbooks.com**). An even larger selection, 13,000 titles both in and out of print, is available at **Kitchen Arts and Letters,** the brainchild of former Harper & Row editor Nachum Waxman (1435 Lexington Avenue, between 93rd and 94th; ☎ 212-876-5550; **www.kitchenartsandletters.com**).

Kinokuniya, long based at Rockefeller Plaza, sells books on Japanese food, culture, art, martial arts, and fine literature in both English and Japanese. Its new store on Avenue of the Americas at Bryant Park is three stories tall and far more international in scope—a veritable Asian Barnes & Noble (1073 Sixth Avenue near 40th Street; ☎ 212-869-1700 or **www.kinokuniya.com**).

If you're a Sherlockian or murder-procedural fan, you should head to the **Mysterious Book Shop** of Baker Street Irregular Otto Penzler (58 Warren Street, between Church and West Broadway;

☎ 212-587-1011; **www.mysteriousbookshop.com**); or find your Watson at **Partners & Crime** (44 Greenwich Avenue, near Charles; ☎ 212-243-0440; **www.crimepays.com**). Science-fiction fans head to the **Forbidden Planet** (840 Broadway; ☎ 212-473-1576; **www.fpnyc.com**). For comic books, head down to **St. Mark's Comics,** which carries underground, limited-edition, and other hard-to-find works (11 St. Mark's Place, between Second and Third; ☎ 212-598-9439; **www.stmarks comics.com**). There's another St. Mark's Comics in Brooklyn, at 148 Montague Street (☎ 718-935-0911).

BRIDAL GOWNS Here, the first (and second) name in wedding designs is **Vera Wang** (991 Madison Avenue, at 77th; ☎ 212-628-3400; **www .verawangonweddings.com**). Also on the Upper East Side is the salon of English designer **Jane Wilson-Marquis** (42 East 76th Street; ☎ 212-452-5335; **www.janewilsonmarquis.com**), who specializes in nontraditional and superromantic gowns. Both strongly suggest advance appointments. For downtown style, try **Mika Inatome** (93 Reade Street, Suite 2; ☎ 212-966-7777 or 800-758-7518; **www.mikainatome.com**) or **Mary Adams The Dress** (31 East 32nd Street, Number 904, between Madison and Park avenues; ☎ 212-473-0237; **www.maryadamsthedress.com**). The **Bridal Garden** has a great selection of couture and designer gowns, many donated by designers and boutiques, the sale of which benefits educational programs in needy neighborhoods (also by appointment only; 54 West 21st Street, ninth floor; ☎ 212-252-0661; **www.bridalgarden.org**). In fact, if you don't mind playing Secondhand Rose, you should also peruse the listings in "Consignment and Vintage Clothing," lower right.

CHEESECAKE It's unlikely that the debate about which is *the* original New York–style cheesecake will ever be settled, but probably the two top contenders are **S&S Cheesecake** in the Bronx (222 West 238th Street; ☎ 718-549-3388; **www.sscheesecake.com**); and **Junior's** (**www.juniorscheesecake.com**), which makes what it calls "the world's most fabulous cheesecake." The original Junior's is in Brooklyn (386 Flatbush Avenue; ☎ 718-852-5257) but also has outposts in Times Square (West 45th between Broadway and Eighth Avenue) and Grand Central Terminal (lower-level dining concourse, plus a carryout near Track 36, so you can eat on the run).

CHOCOLATE AND CONFECTIONS Designer desserts? But of course! And downtown is designer-dessert heaven. One look at the petits fours at **Ceci-Cela** (55 Spring Street in NoLita, ☎ 212-274-9179; **www .cecicelanyc.com**) or the 200 chocolates in 25 flavors that Kee Ling Tong sets out at **Kee's Chocolates** (80 Thompson Street, at Spring; ☎ 212-334-3284; 452 Fifth Avenue, inside HSBC; ☎ 212-525-6099; **www.keeschocolates.com**), and you'll never settle for grocery-store candy again. **Vosges Haut Chocolat Boutique,** on Spring at Greene (☎ 212-625-2929; **www.vosgeschocolate.com**) and also on Madison at 82nd (☎ 212-717-2929), mixes exotic spices and holistic infusions into its bonbons. The **Chocolate Bar,** in the West Village

(19 Eighth Avenue; ☎ 212-366-1541; **www.chocolatebarnyc.com**) offers candy-themed clothing and accessories as well as delectables. Among celebrity confection stands are **Jacques Torres,** SoHo's own see-it-made Willy Wonka (350 Hudson Street at King Street; ☎ 212-414-2462; 285 Amsterdam Avenue between 73rd and 74th streets; ☎ 212-787-3256; and in Brooklyn's DUMBO at 66 Water Street, ☎ 718-875-9772; **www.mrchocolate.com**); and **Dylan's Candy Bar,** the quirky confectionery, fashion, and beauty emporium owned by Dylan Lauren, Ralph's daughter (Third Avenue at 60th Street; ☎ 646-735-0078; **www.dylanscandybar.com**).

CHOPSTICKS Asian food is so popular now that maybe you (or your friends) are sick of those cheap—and ecologically unfriendly—disposable chopsticks. For high-end, calligraphy-inscribed, gold-leafed, inlaid, ox-bone, ebony, and otherwise wow-factor implements a sushi-crazy bride and groom will never forget, head to Chinatown's outpost of Beijing-based **Yunhong Chopsticks** at 50 Mott Street between Pell and Bayard streets (☎ 212-566-8828; **www.happychopsticks.com**).

CLASSIC RECORDS Elvis fans in particular should check out the fine selection in vintage vinyl, particularly rock and roll, R&B, and soul—in 45 and 78 rpm as well as 33—at **Strider Records,** in Greenwich Village (22 Jones Street; ☎ 212-675-3040; **www.striderrecords.com**). **Rebel Rebel** in the West Village (319 Bleecker Street, between Christopher and Grove; ☎ 212-989-0770) has more recent releases (and hometown punk) on CD as well as vinyl. For early and rare jazz records, books, and CDs, try **Jazz Record Center** (236 West 26th, between Seventh and Eighth avenues; ☎ 212-675-4480; **www.jazzrecordcenter.com**). **Academy Records** emphasizes classical, jazz, and rock (12 West 18th Street, between Fifth and Sixth; ☎ 212-243-3000; **www.academy-records.com**). If you need a turntable to play those discs, head to **J&R Music,** near City Hall Park (23 Park Row; ☎ 800-805-1115), which stocks both analog and digital versions.

CONSIGNMENT AND VINTAGE CLOTHING This is one town where resale is still high fashion, so you really can get designer clothing at department-store prices. A lot of the consignment shops, not surprisingly, are Uptown. **Roundabout** new and resale couture center offers such names (right off the Avenue) as Galliano, Hermès, Pucci, D&G, Dior, Chloé, Missoni, Oscar de la Renta, and Balenciaga at half-off and more (East 72nd at Madison; ☎ 646-744-8009). Big-name evening dresses are the hottest items at **Designer Resale** (324 East 81st Street, between First and Second; ☎ 212-734-3639; **www.designerresaleconsignment.com**) and **Encore** (1132 Madison Avenue, between 84th and 85th; ☎ 212-879-2850; **www.encoreresale.com**). In the same general area are **Michael's** (1041 Madison Avenue, second floor, between 79th and 80th; ☎ 212-737-7273; **www.michaelsconsignment.com**), which specializes in bridal and bridesmaids' gowns; **Elle W** (Lexington at 64th; ☎ 212-472-0191; **www.ellew.com**); **Tatiana** (767 Lexington

Avenue; ☎ 212-755-7744); and **Gentlemen's Resale** (322 East 81st Street, between First and Second avenues; ☎ 212-734-2739; **www.gentlemens resaleclothing.com**).

The **Sloan-Kettering Memorial Thrift Shop** at Third Avenue and 81st Street benefits the hospital (☎ 212-535-1250; **www.mskcc.org**—click on "How to Help," then "Thrift Shop").

Farther downtown, you can slide into **Riflessi's** for Armani, Ermenegildo Zegna, and Cerutti, and in sizes up to 60XL (260 Madison Avenue; ☎ 212-679-4875). (Look also at the previous sections on shopping in SoHo and NoLita.)

The first name in vintage chic, of course, is SoHo's **Harriet Love,** author of the best-selling guide to the stuff and maven of the store that outfitted onetime employee Cyndi Lauper (126 Prince Street, between Greene and Wooster; ☎ 212-966-2280). **Cherry** might be the second name; you might even find Cyndi's seconds there (40 West 25th Street; ☎ 212-924-1410; **www.cherryboutique.com**).

What Goes Around Comes Around, also in SoHo, stocks more than 60,000 vintage pieces, from designer to denim (351 West Broadway, between Broome and Grand; ☎ 212-343-1225; **www.nyvintage.com**).

Mary Efron (68 Thompson Street; ☎ 212-219-3090) goes the classic route: Dior, Bergdorf Goodman, and the like. Also check out **Screaming Mimi's,** in NoLita (382 Lafayette Street, between Great Jones and Fourth; ☎ 212-677-6464; **www.screamingmimis.com**) and **Stella Dallas** (218 Thompson, near Bleecker; ☎ 212-674-0447). **De Leon Collection** specializes in vintage accessories, especially couture handbags, scarves, clutches, and more (40 West 25th Street in the Showplace Antique + Design Center; ☎ 212-675-1574).

INA (21 Prince Street; ☎ 212-334-9048) and **INA Men** (19 Prince Street; ☎ 212-334-2210; **www.inanyc.com**) assemble recent-collection Prada, Helmut Lang, Joseph, etc. at cut-rate prices. Also look into **New and Almost New** (166 Elizabeth Street, between Spring and Kenmare; ☎ 212-226-6677; **www.newandalmostnew.com**) and **Yu** (151 Ludlow Street; ☎ 212-979-9370) to score Yohji Yamamoto and Comme des Garçons on the rebound.

COSMETICS AND SKIN CARE Nobody cares more about facial products and cosmetics than Big Apple women (and men); the city is packed with outposts of Aveda, MAC, Sephora, FACE Stockholm, Origins, and the like, not to mention an ever-increasing list of exotic and celebrity-list day spas. For one-stop choices, try **Sephora** (Midtown, Union Square, and several other locations; **www.sephora.com**), which allows you to experiment with more than 200 brands; **Saks Fifth Avenue,** whose first floor is almost entirely cosmetic-centric; or **Bergdorf Goodman,** which carries several cult lines of cosmetics from other countries, such as Japan's Kanebo and Paris's Yon-Ka, as well as the Spa to Go goods from top resorts. (It's also home to the **Susan Ciminelli Day Spa** on the ninth floor.)

If you're tired of trying to find (or refind) that perfect lipstick, check out **Giella Custom Blends** at Henri Bendel on Fifth and 65th (☎ 212-904-7969; **www.giella.com**). It can custom-blend lipsticks or glosses—powders, blushes, eye shadows, etc.—to your specifications. Two lipsticks, $54. Matching something you always loved but can't find anymore: priceless. Or you can get a makeup consultation from the ready-to-wear collection. If you left that old favorite at home, just go to Bendel and ask for one of the mail-back packages.

However, for the quintessential New York experience, visit **Kiehl's Since 1851** (109 Third Avenue, between 13th and 14th streets; ☎ 212-677-3171; **www.kiehls.com**), which, as the name makes clear, has been a Manhattan staple for more than a century and a half. It's still owned and operated by the same family and still making its body treatments, shampoos, and skin-care items by hand from all-natural ingredients. How famous is it? There's a branch in the über-uptown Shops at Columbus Place (☎ 212-799-3438).

While most high-end spas serve both sexes, men get their (spa) day alone at **Nickel** (77 Eighth Avenue, at 14th Street; ☎ 212-242-3203; **www.nickelspanyc.com**), the first U.S. branch of a Parisian pair of spas. **Paul Labrecque's Gentleman's Salon** has three locations, including 66 East 55th Street in the CORE: club (☎ 212-988-78160; **www .paullabrecque.com**); and longtime Wall Street in-secret **John Allan's** now has four Manhattan locations: downtown, TriBeCa, Midtown, and Saks Fifth Avenue (**www.johnallans.com**). Ultra-premium shaving products are available—along with the shave itself—at **The Art of Shaving** in Midtown (373 Madison Avenue, at 46th; ☎ 212-986-2905; **www.theartofshaving.com**) and in **Bloomingdale's** at 59th and Lexington Avenue. (Its other locations, at The Shops at Columbus Circle, Grand Central Terminal, and East 62nd Street at Lexington, have the goods but not the barber.)

DECORATIVE ARTS With all the revived interest in imperial Russia, Fabergé, and so on, it's fascinating to step into **A La Vielle Russie** at the southeast corner of Central Park (781 Fifth Avenue, at West 59th; ☎ 212-752-1727; **www.alvr.com**), which has been selling Russian enamels, icons, porcelain, fine jewelry, and, yes, Fabergé, since the Romanovs were in power.

If it's early-20th-century style you seek, you can indulge your craving for American and European Art Deco at **DeLorenzo Gallery** (956 Madison Avenue at 75th; ☎ 212-249-7575; **www.delorenzogallery .com**). Tiffany and other Art Nouveau classics are a house specialty at **Macklowe Gallery** (667 Madison Avenue; ☎ 212-644-6400; **www .macklowegallery.com**).

FINE ARTS If, despite all that Chelsea (see page 381) has to offer, you prefer to stick to Midtown, you can spend a lot of time amid the old, fine, and famous art galleries between 56th and 57th streets and Park and Sixth avenues, particularly at the **Fuller Building** (41 East 57th

Street at Madison Avenue), home to more than two dozen galleries. Among the most prominent 57th Street galleries are **PaceWildenstein** (32 East 57th Street; ☎ 212-421-0835; **www.pacewildenstein.com**); **Marian Goodman** (24 West 57th Street; ☎ 212-977-7160; **www.marian goodman.com**); **David Findlay Jr.** (in the Fuller Building), where you may spot a John Singer Sargent; **Zabriskie Gallery** (Fuller Building), whose photo collection includes Man Ray and Marcel Duchamp); and a branch of the international **Marlborough Gallery** (40 West 57th Street; ☎ 212-541-4900; **www.marlboroughgallery.com**).

FURS Although the highest-end designer and celebrity furriers are uptown (see "Clothing on the High Side: The East Side," page 375), the traditional center of the retail fur trade in Manhattan was **Seventh Avenue** between 28th and 29th streets in Chelsea, a neighborhood often called (a little grandly) the Fur District. Among the most reliable names still in the neighborhood are **G. Michael Hennessy** (345 Seventh Avenue, between 29th and 30th streets, Number 5; ☎ 212-695-7991) and **Frederick Gelb,** also at 345 Seventh Avenue, 19th floor (☎ 212-239-8787; **www.fredgelbfurs.com**).

But the greatest bargain, especially for the nonrich and the unknown, is **Ritz Furs** on the ninth floor of the same building at 345 Seventh Avenue (☎ 212-265-4559; **www.ritzfurs.com**), which buys, refits, and reconditions estate-sale furs, turns antique coats into linings or novelty coats, and sometimes just offers nice but not premium new coats at half price or even lower. It'll buy its own coats back, too, although at a very much lower price and only if the fur is still in very good condition; so you can keep trading up.

GOURMET FOODS *Gourmet* is in the stomach of the beholder, and perhaps it's stretching a point to put New York's signature noshes here—but then, they are "signatures." Among the most famous bagel shops are **H&H Bagels** on Broadway at 80th Street (☎ 212-595-8003; **www.hhbagels.com**), which makes the larger, lighter version; and **Murray's,** in Greenwich Village (Sixth Avenue between 12th and 13th streets; ☎ 212-462-2830; **www.murraysbagels.com**) and Chelsea (Eighth Avenue, between 22nd and 23rd), and 646-638-1335), and **Daniel's** (569 Third Avenue, between 37th and 38th; ☎ 212-972-9733; **www.daniels bagelnyc.com**), which make the chewier style.

Among other beloved noshes of note: **Yonah Schimmel Knish Bakery** (137 East Houston Street, near Forsyth; ☎ 212-477-2858; **www.knishery .com**); the 80-year-old **Streit's Matzos** on Rivington, near Suffolk (☎ 212-505-7650; **www.streitsmatzos.com**); and **Kossar's Bialys** (367 Grand, near Essex; ☎ 212-473-4810; **www.kossarsbialys.com**), the oldest baker of that Polish cousin of a bagel.

Russ & Daughters (179 East Houston, between Allen and Orchard streets; ☎ 212-475-4880; **www.russanddaughters.com**) specializes in smoked and cured salmon and herring and caviar. **Petrossian** is the most famous name in mail-order caviar, and for good reason, but its uptown cafe (West 58th Street at Seventh Avenue; ☎ 212-245-2214;

www.petrossian.com) is like a Moorish palace. On the East Side, try **Caviar Russe** (Madison between West 54th and 55th streets; ☎ 212-980-5908; **www.caviarrusse.com**), a smaller but even more "bazaar" spot where the other specialty is sushi.

For those who consider Cheddar the vanilla of cheeses, New York is *quel fromage!* heaven. Check out the tasting menus at **Artisanal** (East 32nd Street and Park Avenue; ☎ 212-725-8585; **www.artisanal bistro.com**), **Ideal Cheese** (942 First Avenue at 51st Street; ☎ 212-688-75779; **www.idealcheese.com**), or **Murray's Cheese** in Greenwich Village (254 Bleecker Street; ☎ 212-234-3289) and Grand Central Terminal (☎ 212-922-1540; **www.murrayscheese.com**). Don't worry about smelling up your suitcase; the shops ship.

If you like all your temptations under one roof, New York's most famous names in food are **Zabar's** and **Dean & DeLuca.** Zabar's, on the Upper West Side, goes to show you what a serious Jewish deli can be, especially when it grows to be 20,000 square feet (Broadway at 80th Street; ☎ 212-787-2000; **www.zabars.com**). D&D, the Bloomie's of food, is on Broadway at Prince in SoHo (☎ 212-226-6800; **www .deananddeluca.com**) and on Madison Avenue at 85th Street (☎ 212-717-0880). It also has several cafe locations, including Rockefeller Center, The Shops on Columbus Circle, and Times Square (46th Street between Seventh and Eighth).

In addition, there are **Chelsea Market,** on Ninth Avenue between 15th and 16th streets (☎ 212-243-6005; **www.chelseamarket.com**), an 800-foot arcade of vendors and producers, and the **Essex Street Market,** at Essex and Delancey streets on the Lower East Side. Fifteen thousand square feet of meats, cheeses, desserts—even a barbershop.

HATS There may be a number of places to find good hats these days, but for serious Uptown style, there's only one name: Bunn. He was born in Trinidad, worked for years in Brooklyn, and about ten years ago moved to Harlem, where he has "crowned" such stars as Aaron Neville and Alicia Keys: **Hats by Bunn,** 2283 Adam Clayton Powell Jr. Boulevard (Seventh Avenue; ☎ 212-694-3590; **www.hatsbybunn.com**). If you're more Midtown than very Uptown, try **J. J. Hat Center,** Fifth Avenue at 32nd Street; ☎ 212-239-4368; **www.jjhatcenter.com**).

For women, it's **Kelly Christy** (37 Spring Street, SoHo; ☎ 212-965-0686) or **Leah C. Couture Millinery** (124 West 30th, between Sixth and Seventh, second floor; ☎ 212-947-3505; **www.leahc.com**).

JEWELRY Bling falls right between the "Bronx is up and the Battery's down," not just physically but metaphorically. The most eye-bulging pieces, already set with precious and semi-precious stones, are in an even more glittery row along Fifth Avenue between 55th and 57th streets, including **Tiffany & Co.** (☎ 212-755-8000; **www.tiffany.com**), **Harry Winston** (☎ 212-245-2000; **www.harry winston.com**), **Bulgari** (☎ 212-315-9000; **www.bulgari.com**), **De Beers**'s new flagship (☎ 212-906-0001; **www.debeers.com**), and **Van Cleef &**

Arpels (in the Bergdorf Goodman building; ☎ 212-644-9500; **www .vancleef-arpels.com**).

Bergdorf also carries some pieces from **Verdura,** which has outfitted everyone from Cole Porter and Greta Garbo to Princess Di. You can peruse the showroom yourself; it's at 745 Fifth Avenue on the 12th floor (☎ 212-758-3388; **www.verdura.com**). The New York branch of London's venerable **S. J. Shrubsole** is on 57th Street at Park Avenue (☎ 212-753-8920; **www.shrubsole.com**), and **Cartier** is only a few blocks away at Fifth Avenue and 52nd Street (☎ 212-753-0111; **www.cartier .com**) and on Madison Avenue at 69th Street (☎ 212-472-6400).

If you prefer your diamonds more straight up, you have to cruise the **Diamond District,** a continuous wall of glittering store windows and mini-malls along 47th Street between Fifth and Sixth avenues, traditionally operated by Orthodox Jewish and (increasingly) Middle Eastern dealers, where somehow if you cannot find just the setting you want, it can be made in about 24 hours.

If you want the one-of-a-kind look without the Indian-curse pedigree or the Shah of Iran price tag, visit **Reinstein/Ross,** Susan Reinstein's boutiques in SoHo (122 Prince Street; ☎ 212-226-4513; **www.reinsteinross.com**) and the Upper East Side (29 East 73rd; ☎ 212-772-1901), or **Me&Ro,** the Robin Renzi–Michele Quan shop in NoLita (241 Elizabeth Street; ☎ 212-237-9215; **www.meandrojewelry.com**). For custom-made pieces—and fine art as well—go to **Belenky Brothers,** still in family hands after more than a century in SoHo (91 Grand Street, near Greene; ☎ 212-674-4242; **www.belenky.com**). Or check out **Stuart Moore,** also in SoHo (128 Prince Street, between Wooster and West Broadway; ☎ 212-941-1023; **www.stuartmoore.com**).

For fine and unique cufflinks as well as bracelets, brooches, and such, head to **Seaman Schepps,** 100 years old and thriving (485 Park Avenue, near 58th; ☎ 212-753-9520; **www.seamanschepps.com**).

And, although in other times it would have been a hush-hush affair to sell old or estate jewelry, it's big business now. Check with **Doyle & Doyle** (that is, sisters Elizabeth and Irene) estate jewelry on the Lower East Side (189 Orchard Street; ☎ 212-677-9991; **www.doyledoyle.com**); **Andrew & Peter Fabrikant,** on Fifth Avenue at 46th Street, eighth floor (☎ 212-557-4888; **www.fabon5th.com**); or resale specialists **Circa,** on Madison Avenue between 48th and 49th (☎ 212-486-6019; **www.circa jewels.com**).

MUSICAL INSTRUMENTS More than a dozen specialty instrument, sheet music, and repair shops line Times Square's "Music Row," aka 48th Street. It's worth a stroll even if you're not in the market. Manny's Music, formerly at 156 West 48th Street, may have been the first music superstore; it had the signed photos of customers from Benny Goodman and Charlie Parker to Jimi Hendrix and Eric Clapton to prove it. However, Manny's was surrounded (literally) and finally absorbed by the various showrooms of **Sam Ash** (155 West

48th Street; ☎ 212-719-2625; **www.samash.com**), where the signature include Muddy Waters and Peter Frampton. For a selection of fine acoustic guitars, try **Matt Umanov,** in Greenwich Village at 273 Bleecker Street, between Morton and Cornelia (☎ 212-675-2157; **www.umanovguitars.com**). For guitar repairs, try **30th Street Guitars,** at 236 West 30th Street, between Seventh and Eighth; ☎ 212-868-2660; **www.30thstreetguitars.com**). And if you can't play anything but air guitar, spin around to **Colony Music Center,** at 49th Street and Broadway (☎ 212-265-2050; **www.colonymusic.com**); it has a huge collection of karaoke selections as well as sheet music. (Incidentally, that happens to be the old Brill Building, the temple of Tin Pan Alley.)

unofficial **TIP**
If you need a safe-but-not-ugly place to keep your baubles, check out **Traum Safe** (946 Madison Avenue near 74th; ☎ 212-452-2565; **www.traumsafe.com**), and see just how slick custom custody can be.

The **Steinway & Sons** store at 109 West 57th Street (☎ 212-246-1100; **www.steinwayhall.com**) is as much museum as shop, and it's not alone: even the rankest amateur would recognize the names on the violins and cellos at **Gradoux-Matt Rare Violins** (31–33 East 28th Street, 212-582-7536; **www.gradouxmattrareviolins.com**). For less-common international string and percussion instruments, try **Music Inn World Instruments** in the Village (169 West Fourth Street, near Jones Street; ☎ 212-243-5715).

PHOTOGRAPHY Cindy Sherman is just one of the big names whose work can be found at **Metro Pictures** in SoHo (519 West 24th Street, between Tenth and Eleventh; ☎ 212-206-7100; **www.metropictures gallery.com**), and hours of browsing won't begin to exhaust the fine options at **Laurence Miller Gallery** (20 West 57th Street between Fifth and Sixth; ☎ 212-397-3930; **www.laurencemillergallery.com**) or the museum store of the International Center of Photography (Sixth Avenue at 43rd Street; ☎ 212-857-9725; **www.icp.org**). Although it's really a little farther south in TriBeCa than its name suggests, the **Soho Photo Gallery** is the oldest, most comprehensive co-op in the country (15 White Street; ☎ 212-226-8571; **www.sohophoto.com**). The **Aperture Foundation** in Chelsea (547 West 27th Street, near Eleventh; ☎ 212-505-5555; **www.aperture.org**) publishes some of the most influential and striking books and magazines in the industry.

kids **TOYS** Everyone knows **FAO Schwarz** (Fifth Avenue and 58th Street; ☎ 212-644-9400; **www.fao.com**) and **Toys"R"Us,** which has actually bought FAO Schwarz (see "Brand Loyalty: Theme Stores," page 372). But more uncommon stuff is at the imaginative **Dinosaur Hill** in the East Village (306 East Ninth Street; ☎ 212-473-5850; **www.dinosaurhill.com**), which is intentionally hard to find, like a fairy-tale treasure; look for the name set in marbles in the sidewalk. And if a trip to the *Forbes* Magazine Galleries (see page 242) leaves you longing for vintage tin soldiers and such, go up to

Burlington Antique Toys in the basement of 1082 Madison Avenue, between 80th and 81st streets (☎ 212-861-9708).

VINTAGE POSTERS, PRINTS, AND CARTOONS The only complete collection of Toulouse-Lautrec advertising posters belongs to *Wine Spectator* and *Cigar Aficionado* tycoon Marvin Shanken. Unfortunately, unless you're invited to his office, you won't be able to see them. But you can pick up a few items almost as rare at **La Belle Epoque** on the Upper West Side (Columbus Avenue at 73rd Street; ☎ 212-362-1770; www.la-belle-epoque.com); or **Ross Art** (532 Madison Avenue at 54th; ☎ 212-223-1525; www.rossartgroup.com). **Arader Galleries,** which has two Madison Avenue galleries, one at 72nd and the other at 78th, specializes in Audubon aquatints and centuries-old maps (www.aradergalleries.com).

WATCHES Counterfeit Rolexes, Piagets, and Movados are all over town, and for $25 or $30 they can be a fun souvenir, although whether they'll run for 24 hours or 24 months is a matter of pure chance. So is whether the hands will work, incidentally. For guaranteed models of those luxury names—the ones that shout platinum! titanium! white gold!—visit **Tourneau** (www.tourneau.com), whose double-page ads in the *Times* and various luxury magazines are whole catalogs in themselves. In fact, it's practically an avenue in itself, with stores along Madison Avenue at 52nd (☎ 212-758-6098) and 57th (☎ 212-758-7300) as well as at West 34th and Seventh Avenue (☎ 212-563-6880) and in The Shops at Columbus Circle (☎ 212-823-9425). Tourneau owns so many watches that a company official estimated it would take a whole week for the staff to reset all the timepieces to match daylight saving time. For more unusual vintage timepieces and clocks, try **Fanelli Antique Timepieces** (790 Madison Avenue, near 66th Street, Suite 202; ☎ 212-517-2300) or **Aaron Faber Gallery** (666 Fifth Avenue, between 52nd and 53rd; ☎ 212-586-8411; www.aaronfaber.com).

Fine watches require equally fine caretaking, so if your Cartier or Rolex is being uncharacteristically cranky, take it to the experts at **Swiss Watch Repair Center** (60 East 42nd Street, Suite 2328; ☎ 212-696-0153; www.swisswatchrepaircenter.com), **Jacob Khalif,** in the Diamond District at 10 West 47th Street (Booths 21–22; ☎ 212-398-2333), or the nearby **Master of Time** (15 West 47th Street, Booth 8; ☎ 212-354-8463; www.mastersoftime.com).

WINES Sherry-Lehmann's inventory is famous, and not by accident; it's probably the largest in the world. The catalogs, which come out every couple of months, make great souvenirs and gifts as well (505 Park Avenue between 59th and 60th streets; ☎ 212-838-7500; www.sherry-lehmann.com). But for atmosphere, and for a wine bar right next door, try **Morrell & Company,** at 1 Rockefeller Plaza (☎ 212-688-9370 or 800-969-4637; www.morrellwine.com), one of Manhattan's best-respected shops (and host of frequent free tastings).

PART NINE

EXERCISE *and* RECREATION

DOUBLE *your* PLEASURE, DOUBLE *your* FUN

A FEW YEARS AGO IT WOULD HAVE SEEMED SILLY to put a chapter on exercise in a vacation guide—particularly a guide to New York. But most of us at the *Unofficial Guides* are into some form of exercise, if only as a matter of self-preservation. It reduces stress, helps offset those expense-account and diet-holiday meals (no, it's not true that food eaten on vacation has no calories), and even ameliorates some of the effects of jet lag. Even more importantly, we've discovered that jogging, biking, and just plain walking are among the nicest ways to meet a city on its own turf, so to speak; and we're happy to see that more and more travelers feel as we do. Besides, workout gear takes up relatively little room and, at least until that step class, may double as walking-about wear. If you're caught short, there are always T-shirts and shorts to be had on the street, and probably at the gym.

In addition, New York's exercise clubs in are often on the front lines of workout trends. If you've read about Pilates or capoeira or some other new routine, this is the place to try it.

If you're an outdoor type, consider the seasonal weather at that time of year. when you're packing. In the summer, when it can be not only hot but also extremely humid, plan to exercise early in the day or in the first cool of the evening; it's also a good idea to pack bug spray. Better yet, double up and get some of those sunscreen packets with repellent built in.

unofficial **TIP**
If you're staying in one of the ritzier hotels, such as **The New York Palace**, the fitness center may have T-shirts and even shoes you can borrow for your workout, further lightening your load.

Viewing holiday decorations lights up cold-weather jogging, if the sidewalks aren't slick, but be sure to pack a water-resistant layer.

Remember that first-aid kit: we go nowhere without sports-style adhesive strips, ibuprofen or some other analgesic, petroleum jelly, and a small tube of antiseptic. And consider doubling your socks.

CHELSEA PIERS *and* CENTRAL PARK

THE REDEVELOPMENT of the old **Hudson River** pier area between 17th and 23rd streets into the **Chelsea Piers Sports and Entertainment Complex** (☎ 212-336-6666; **www.chelseapiers.com**) may have cost millions, but it sure is bringing the money back in now: it's a sports theme park, and if you can afford it, you can spend the whole day. Among its attractions is one of those Japanese multilevel golf driving ranges with 52 stalls and a 200-foot fairway, plus a fully computerized "driving cage" with automatic tee-up; two indoor ice rinks; a huge field house with basketball, batting cages, gymnastics bars, and the like; a 40-lane bowling alley; and a mega–workout club, the **Sports Center at Chelsea Piers,** with a running track, boxing ring, pool, 10,000-square-foot rock-climbing wall, and weight-training areas (day pass $50). Spend the whole day.

unofficial **TIP**
Chelsea Piers also houses a spa for postworkout massages and manicures, waxes, and other indulgences, plus a sundeck and a huge brewpub (☎ 212-336-6440; **www .chelseabrewingco.com**) for more-liquid rewards.

Central Park is where outdoor sports meets spectacle—ultimate Frisbee, softball, flag football, baseball, even bocce. There are rowboats and rental bikes at **Loeb Boathouse** (☎ 212-517-2233; **www .thecentralparkboathouse.com**); wall climbing around 97th Street; tennis courts; croquet and British-style "bowls" near West 69th and petanque near the erstwhile Tavern on the Green; swimming; catch-and-release fishing; and ice-skating.

If you're fond of **folk dancing,** you'll find plenty of partners on Sunday afternoons near the East 79th Street entrance toward Turtle Pond. Or take a free **tango** lesson and then dip till you trip Saturday evenings near the Shakespeare statue.

For information on other areas to play, go to **www.centralpark.com** or **www.nycgovparks.org**. Also read the in-depth description of Central Park in Part Five, New York's Neighborhoods.

WORKING OUT

WORKOUT CLUBS AND GYMS

NEW YORK IS SO body-conscious that you can try out almost anything—at any time, 24-7.

Among the hottest workout clubs—the ones always written up in fitness magazines—are **Sports Center at Chelsea Piers** (see facing page), the **Crunch Fitness** clubs (open 24 hours weekdays at 404 Lafayette Street, ☎ 212-614-0120; for ten other Manhattan locations, see **www.crunch.com**); **Equinox Fitness** (**www.equinoxfitness.com**), with 17 clubs in Manhattan, including its flagship at The Shops at Columbus Circle (☎ 212-871-0425); and **Reebok Sports Club/NY** (160 Columbus Avenue at 67th Street; ☎ 212-362-6800 or **www.thesportsclubla.com**). You'll need to go with a member to get into either Equinox Fitness or Reebok Sports Club, but $25 is the ticket for **Printing House Fitness + Squash Club** in the West Village (421 Hudson Street, at St. Luke's Place; ☎ 212-243-7600 or **www.phfrc.com**), which besides offering 60 classes a day ranging from Pilates and yoga to spinning and boxing, offers massage, 360-degree views, and a rooftop pool and sundeck.

Yoga is incredibly hot here; look in at the branch of Hollywood's **Golden Bridge Yoga** at Centre Street and Grand (☎ 212-343-8191; **www.goldenbridgeyoganyc.com**), or visit **www.yogaalliance.com** for other studios.

Even hotter is **Pilates,** and the most cutting-edge studio, where traditional Pilates meets modern medical research, is **IM=X Pilates** at Madison and 39th Street (☎ 212-997-5550; **www.imxpilates.net**). The introductory session is free, so you can learn the mechanics.

There are 21 branches of the **YMCA** (**www.ymcanyc.org**) in the city, including the **Vanderbilt YMCA** at 224 East 47th Street, between Second and Third avenues (☎ 212-912-2500; one-day pass for $25), which also has guest rooms. The **West Side YMCA** is the largest branch, with two pools, basketball and volleyball, racquetball and squash, massage rooms, free weights, and more included in a $20 daily pass (5 West 63rd Street; ☎ 212-875-4100).

Serious bodybuilders should check out the **19th Street Gym** in Chelsea (22 West 19th Street, between Fifth and Sixth; ☎ 212-415-5800; **www.19thstreetgym.com**); a one-day pass is $25.

WALKING

CONSIDERING HOW STRONGLY WE'VE URGED you to do your touring on foot, you may have already guessed that we find not agony but ecstasy in da feet. It's almost impossible not to enjoy the sidewalks of New York, and it's unfortunate that many of its most beautiful sections, particularly downtown, have been so reduced to the tour-stop circuit that most tourists never experience them.

unofficial **TIP**
To combine a workout with a quintessential New York experience, take a class at the **Alvin Ailey American Dance Theater Extension school** at West 55th and Ninth Avenue,. All classes are walk-up and start at $16.50, with discounts for multiple classes. Go to **www.alvin ailey.org** for schedules and information.

The most obvious walking area, of course, is Central Park, where you can stick to the seven-mile **Outer Loop,** the four-mile **Middle Loop** (from 72nd Street south), or the mile-and-a-half reservoir track; but it's even more fun to just take whatever asphalt trails attract you. You can't really get lost—some part of the outer world's skyline is almost always visible, and you'll come back across the main road several times—but there is always something new to discover that way: statues (have you found the **Mad Tea Party** yet?), lakes, ornate old bridges, gingerbread-trimmed buildings, the carousel, flower beds, dancing dogs, tiny transmitter-driven sailboats reminiscent of *Stuart Little,* chess players, stages, and so forth.

The Esplanade, which runs about a mile from **Battery Park** along the Hudson River to **Battery Park City,** is one of the prettiest greenways in the area, and it has the added benefit of being divided part of the way so that walkers don't have to contend with bladers or bikers. (That's also true of the **High Line** in Chelsea, but it's not really good for pacing, just for stretching your legs.)

Another popular park for walkers is **Riverside Park,** on the Upper West Side between West 72nd and 158th streets. If you're really interested in seeing the natural sights, you can turn out of Central Park along the main crossroads at West 86th, at 97th, or even at the top of the park—110th Street–Cathedral Parkway—and go west four blocks to the Hudson and Riverside Park, which is another four miles long.

RUNNING AND JOGGING

IF YOU HADN'T ALREADY GUESSED that Central Park is also runners' central, a quick glance will convince you. Central Park Drive has a dedicated biking–running lane (see mileage loops above), and the road is closed to traffic from 10 a.m. to 3 p.m. every weekday—except, please note, during the holidays, when the traffic crush is too heavy—and all weekend, starting at 7 p.m. Friday. Runners are there at most any (daylight) hour, especially on weekends; feel free to join the pack. For group therapy, call the **New York Road Runners** (☎ 212-860-4455; **www.nyrrc.org**), or hook up with its regular runs: about 6:30 a.m. and 6:30 p.m. weekdays and 10 a.m. Saturdays and Sundays. Meet at the club at 9 East 89th Street (between Madison and Fifth avenues), or catch up at the starting point, just inside the park at Fifth and 90th.

Another popular stretch for runners, as it is for walkers, is **Riverside Park** by the Hudson River, discussed in the preceding section. There is another two-mile stretch along the **Hudson Promenade** in the Village near the piers at the foot of Christopher Street; there's a track along the East River between the **Queensboro Bridge** and **Gracie Mansion;** Brooklyn's **Prospect Park** has a three-and-a-half-mile trail that begins near the boathouse entrance. If you'd like a short but sharp and visually stunning interval run, take the mile-long **Brooklyn Bridge** over and back, and consider the view of the Manhattan skyline a reward for chugging over that high curve.

BIKING AND BLADING

NOT SURPRISINGLY, CENTRAL PARK IS A HUGE DRAW for recreational bikers, and several companies offer park-related tours. For example, **Central Park Bike Rentals** (250 West 49th Street, between Seventh and Eighth avenues; ☎ 347-713-0013, **www.centralparkbike rent.com**), which offers discounts on advance Web site reservations, is near Times Square but will deliver your bike almost anywhere you choose. It also offers guided bike tours and pedicab tours of the park. **Bite of the Apple Central Park Bike Tours** leaves from 310 West 55th, between Eighth and Ninth (☎ 212-541-8759; **www.centralparkbike tour.com**). **Bike Rental Central Park** is closer to **Columbus Circle** on West 57th Street near Ninth (☎ 212-664-9600; **www.bikerentalcentralpark .com**). It offers mountain bikes, comfort bikes, tandems, and baby trailers, and all bikes come with a map, helmet, basket, chain lock, etc. **Bike Central Park**—seeing a pattern here?—is even closer, at 221 West 58th, between Seventh Avenue and Broadway, a block south of the park. It also offers a full range of models as well as pedicab tours (☎ 212-969-9729; **www.bikecentralpark.com**). **Pedal Pusher Bike Shop** is on the Upper East Side (1306 Second Avenue, between 68th and 69th; ☎ 212-288-5592 or 877-257-9437; **www.pedalpusherbikeshop .com**). Or you can rent bikes right at the **Loeb Boathouse,** which is in Central Park near East 74th Street (☎ 212-517-2233; **www.thecentral parkboathouse.com**).

If you want to spend more time touring downtown, check with **Bike and Roll** (☎ 866-736-8224; **www.bikeandroll.com/newyork**), which has pickup locations right next to the **Statue of Liberty** ferry terminals, and at Pier 84 (at West 43rd near the **Intrepid Sea, Air & Space Museum**), at **South Street Seaport,** and on **Governor's Island** as well as in Central Park. On the Lower East Side, try **Frank's Bike Shop** (553 Grand Street, near Lewis; ☎ 212-533-6332; **www.franksbikes.com**), which also rents folding bikes that could be just the thing for hop-on, hop-off touring. **Metro Bicycles** also has a half-dozen locations all around Manhattan (**www.metrobicycles.com**).

Central Park is the place for recreational biking not only for its beauty but also because it has a designated biking–jogging lane that stretches about seven miles. (See the preceding section, "Running and Jogging," for auto-free hours.) You must stick to the road, however; no impromptu mountain or trail riding allowed. If you'd like to see the park by moonlight, and you're in town on the last Friday of the month, wheel over to

unofficial **TIP**
In the summer of 2009, **Bike and Roll** worked with city officials to make bikes available for use by the public for three-hour periods at its South Street Seaport site; officials hope to fund the program again in 2010.

Columbus Circle at 10 p.m. Or you can take the Riverside Park path from West 110th Street to West 72nd and continue down the bike lane through **Hudson River Park** all the way to Battery Park City. Both the **Five Borough Bicycle Club** (☎ 212-932-2300, ext. 115; **www.5bbc.org**) and the **New York Cycle Club** (**www.nycc.org**) organize group rides on weekends.

If you're more into blades, either ice or inline, **Blades** (**www.blades .com**) has locations downtown (659 Broadway, between Bleecker and Third; ☎ 212-477-7350) and on the Upper West Side (West 72nd between Broadway and Columbus; ☎ 212-787-3911).

kids The most famous ice rink in New York is, of course, the one at **Rockefeller Plaza.** It's also the costliest: adults pay $15.50 to $19, depending on the day of the week and how close it is to the holidays; seniors and kids under age 11 pay $9.50 to $12.50—not including the $9 skate rentals (☎ 212-332-7654; **www.therinkat rockefellercenter.com**). On the other hand, there's a special "engagement package" here, complete with flowers, Champagne toasts, and a five-minute private skate, so if you're looking for something romantic, it's open till midnight on weekends.

In contrast, skating is free at another popular Midtown rink, **The Pond at Bryant Park,** between Fifth and Sixth avenues and 40th and 42nd streets (☎ 866-221-5157 or 212-382-2953; **www.thepondat bryantpark.com**); if you need skates, that's $12, and The Pond is also open late.

At Central Park's **Wollman Rink,** adults skate for $9.50 or $12 on weekends; kids skate for $4.75/$5 (☎ 212-439-6900; **www.wollman skatingrink.com**). **Lasker Rink** is a less-famous and less-expensive rink for roller- and ice-skating at the northern end of the park (☎ 917-492-3857; **www.wollmanskatingrink.com/main_lasker.htm**); here, adults skate for $4.50 and kids and seniors for $2.25.

Riverbank Skating Rink, at Riverside Drive and 145th Street, charges $5 for adults, $3 for children; skate rental is $5 (☎ 212-694-3642; **nysparks.state.ny.us/parks**—select "Riverbank State Park"). For group skates and lessons, contact **Sky Rink** (☎ 212-336-6100; **www .chelseapiers.com**) at Chelsea Piers, which offers lessons and a little pickup hockey as well.

If you are a serious blader, into semi-guerilla sorts of expeditions, contact the **Night Skates,** who meet at various sites around town, including Columbus Circle, **Union Square,** and skate shops (ask at a shop for information, or check **www.weskateny.org**). Also look over the biking and running routes mentioned in the preceding sections.

OTHER RECREATIONAL SPORTS

DESPITE THE SUCCESS OF NEIL SIMON'S *Brighton Beach* trilogy, many tourists are surprised to discover that New York has beaches, and that several are easily accessible by subway: the **Rockaways,** by the A train; **Orchard Beach,** in Pelham Bay Park at the terminus of the 6 Line; **Coney Island,** by the B, D, F, or N; and **Brighton Beach** itself, by the D or Q. (Surfers, note: There's a section of the Rockaways set aside year-round for surfing only.)

Only a few hotels have **swimming pools**—The Peninsula, Hotel Gansevoort, and Soho House among them—so if lapping is your thing, check into Chelsea Piers (see page 398) or **Asphalt Green,** another of those we-do-it-bigger sports facilities, with an Olympic-size (50-meter) pool, indoor and outdoor tracks, a cutting-edge gym, etc. A day pass ($10 to $35) gets you into both the pool and the gym, but access to the pool for nonmembers is limited (York Avenue at 90th Street; ☎ 212-369-8890; www.asphaltgreen.org).

If **tennis** is your racquet, the city parks department operates many courts in every borough that you can use for $7 an hour (two hours for doubles), but you need a permit (☎ 212-360-8133; www.nycgov parks.org; click on "Permits & Services"), and you have to sign up on a first-come, first-served basis. Among the nicest are the 26 clay and 4 asphalt courts in Central Park, and the 10 clay and 10 hard at Riverside Park. The rather more expensive ($90 an hour for nonmembers) **Manhattan Plaza Racquet Club** has five courts on the roof—there's a bubble in bad weather—at 450 West 43rd Street; ☎ 212-594-0554; www.manhattanplazaracquetclub.com).

Horseback riding through Central Park is legendary, but, unfortunately, the old days of riding straight over from an Upper West Side stable are over. However, the **Riverdale Equestrian Center** at **Van Cortlandt Park** in the Bronx will make arrangements to bring your mount to the North Meadow Recreation Center and guide you on the bridle path. Trail rides cost $100 per person per hour; contact the center at ☎ 914-633-0303 or go to www.riverdaleriding.com. There are also other outer-borough trails; for information on these, go to www.nycgov.parks.org/facilities/horseback.

You'll see **rock climbing** in Central Park—it's called Rat Rock, and it's near Fifth Avenue around 62nd Street—but if you want something tougher, drop $15 at the **Manhattan Plaza Health Club** (482 West 43rd Street, near Tenth Avenue; ☎ 212-563-7001; www.mphc.com), or check the gyms mentioned previously.

Pickup softball, basketball, and **volleyball** are visible all over town, but the competition is really tough, especially when it comes to B-ball: just watch a few minutes outside the cages at West Fourth and Sixth Avenue near **Washington Square,** famous as the original stomping

unofficial **TIP**
The big thrill, of course, is playing at the USTA's **Billie Jean King complex** in Queens, home of the U.S. Open. Though the stadium courts are pros-only, the others are open to the public 18 hours a day, seven days a week, 11 months out of the year, for $20–$62 an hour. For reservations (accepted 48 hours in advance), call ☎ 718-760-6200.

grounds of Dr. J. There are more than a dozen golf courses in the city, but if you wish to waste most of a day in New York leaning over a little white ball, you're on your own.

Kayakers should check out **Manhattan Kayak Company** at Pier 66 (☎ 212-924-1788; **www.manhattankayak.com**), **New York Kayak Company** at Pier 40 (☎ 800-KAYAK99; **www.nykayak.com**); or the **Downtown Boathouse** at Pier 26 (☎ 646-613-0375 or 646-613-0375; **www.downtownboathouse.org**); they'll take you "around town" in a whole new fashion.

The **Hudson River Park Trust,** which maintains the entire stretch of the West Side from the tip of the Battery up to 59th Street as a park, allows **fishing** at several places, including the Battery; Pier 46, at Charles Street in the West Village; and Pier 96, at 56th Street. In fact, during the summer, it provides free fishing poles, reels, bait, and even a lesson for participants of all ages; call ☎ 212-627-2020 or visit **www.hudsonriverpark.org.**

There is one **bowling alley** in the **Port Authority Bus Terminal** (550 Ninth Avenue, between West 40th and 41st streets; ☎ 212-268-6909; **www.leisuretimebowl.com**) and one near Union Square, the retro-funky **Bowlmor Lanes** (110 University Place, between East 12th and 13th streets; ☎ 212-255-8188; **www.bowlmor.com**).

But for a once-in-a-lifetime experience, make like the man on the flying trapeze: **Trapeze School New York** is on top of Pier 40, at the end of Houston Street (with views of the Statue of Liberty, Ellis Island, and the river). Call ☎ 212-242-TSNY or go to **newyork.trapezeschool.com.**

SPECTATOR SPORTS

NEW YORK'S PRO SPORTS TEAMS are legendary and seemingly legion; it's no wonder that Madison Square Garden is a cable network as well as a venue. However, this is one time when "New York" means all five boroughs, and more—namely, New Jersey and Long Island.

Both NFL teams, the **New York Giants** and the **New York Jets,** play "at home" in New Jersey, at the new $800 million, 82,500-seat **Meadowlands Stadium,** which has been carefully constructed to give them equal status. (The extravagant interior light scheme will change colors depending on which team is playing, turning green for the Jets and blue for the Giants.) But tickets are almost impossible to get unless you're visiting friends with connections (or you're willing to pay a high price to a scalper). However, if you feel like making a stab at it, you can call the Meadowlands box office at ☎ 201-935-3900 or visit **www.meadowlands.com.** You can also see if there are any odd seats left with **Ticketmaster** at ☎ 800-745-3000 or **www.ticketmaster.com,** or you can check the newspaper classified ads or **StubHub!**

(☎ 866-788-2482; **www.stubhub.com**) for tickets or ticket-resale pack-agers. And if you do score a ticket—or one for a concert or other special event expected to draw at least 50,000 fans—you can take advantage of the new Meadowlands station on the **NJ Transit** rail sys-tem, which runs out of Penn Station on event days, with shuttle-bus service for smaller events: ☎ 973-275-5555 or **www.njtransit.com.**

The **New York Red Bulls** (formerly the MetroStars) have departed the Meadowlands for a huge, state-of-the-art facility in nearby Harri-son, New Jersey, which is accessible by public transit from Manhattan (the PATH train from World Trade Center station) as well as Hobo-ken and Newark. For tickets, go to **redbull.newyork.mlsnet.com.**

One of the region's two NBA teams, the **New Jersey Nets,** is at home at the Meadowlands' **Izod Center,** though there is a proposal to relocate the team to Brooklyn (☎ 201-935-8500; **www.njnets.com**).

One of the three metro-area NHL teams, the **New Jersey Devils,** has already moved into new digs at the Newark Prudential Center (☎ 973-757-6000; **www.newjerseydevils.com**). Another NHL team, the **New York Islanders,** is actually in New York—at Long Island's Nassau Coliseum—but east of New York City in Uniondale, and it takes both the Long Island Rail Road (to Uniondale) and then a bus (N70, 71, or 72) to get there, so only fanatics need apply (☎ 516-501-6700; **islanders.nhl.com**). On the other hand, the Islanders did win four straight Stanley Cup titles in the 1980s.

But you don't have to leave town to score. If you've never seen baseball live, you've never seen baseball. (And you'll never see base-ball fans the way you'll see them in New York, for good or evil.) **Yankee Stadium**—the fancy new 52,000-seat replacement for the House that Ruth Built—is in the Bronx; hence the team nickname "Bronx Bombers." It's an easy subway ride to the 161st Street–Yankee Stadium station. (*Hint:* Transfer to the D line at Columbus Circle or 125th Street, because it's an express during peak times.) Do not take a taxi; it's not only about 20 times more expensive, but it might also take you 5 times longer to get there. Besides, you'd miss an essential part of the experience: joining the fan crowd. You can also take a direct Metro-North shuttle from **Grand Central Station** to the new Yankees–East 153rd Street Station. (There will be a hotel on-site, and parking, but at $25 a space . . .) Call the box office at ☎ 718-293-6000 or Ticketmaster at ☎ 212-307-7171, or visit **www.yankees.com.** Get there early enough to wander around and check out the plaques beyond the outfield saluting Mickey Mantle, Babe Ruth, Lou Gehrig, Joe DiMaggio, and

unofficial **TIP**
One-hour tours of Yan-kee Stadium are offered at midday most days dur-ing the season, though if the team is in town the locker rooms will not be open; for timed tickets and info, go to **www .yankees.com.**

others. (Some of these memorials used to be actually in play, but cooler heads prevailed.)

The **New York Mets'** new stadium, **Citi Field,** was constructed right alongside the Mets' old Shea Stadium and has the same easy subway access. (Its design partly echoes the Dodgers' old Ebbets Field, and a statue of the number "42" inside the entrance honors Brooklyn Dodgers great Jackie Robinson, who wore that number and who in 1947 broke the color barrier in major-league baseball.) Citi Field is in Queens, in **Flushing Meadows Corona Park.** Take the 7 line subway (you can get it from Grand Central or 42nd Street–Times Square, among other stops) right to the Mets–Willets Point Station; or take an 18-minute ride on the Long Island Rail Road from Penn Station. You can quite possibly walk up and get tickets, but it might be better to call the stadium box office at ☎ 718-507-8499 or visit **www.mets.com.**

Both the NHL **New York Rangers** and the NBA **New York Knicks** call Madison Square Garden home. Unfortunately for tourists, they both have strong followings, so tickets are problematic. Call ☎ 212-465-6000 for Rangers info, ☎ 212-465-6741 for the Knicks, or Ticketmaster at ☎ 212-307-7171 (**www.ticketmaster.com**), or see **rangers .nhl.com** or **www.knicks.com.**

You can also catch women's pro-basketball games; the **WNBA New York Liberty** also tends the Garden (☎ 212-564-9622; **www.wnba .com/liberty**). So do the **Golden Gloves** boxing cards in January and February and college basketball's **National Invitation Tournament** in March and sometimes early April. For any of these events, contact the Garden box office (☎ 212-465-6741; **www.thegarden.com**) or Ticketmaster (☎ 212-307-7171; **www.ticketmaster.com**).

Horse racing has a long and aristocratic tradition in New York, and though the crowds may be more democratic these days, the thoroughbred bloodlines are as blue as ever. You can take the subway (Far Rockaway A) to **Aqueduct Race Track** in Queens from mid-October to May (☎ 718-641-4700; **www.nyra.com**) or the Long Island Rail Road's Belmont Special from Penn Station to **Belmont Park** (☎ 516-488-6000; **www.nyra.com/Belmont**) from May through July and again from Labor Day to mid-October. (In between, the very old-style racing circuit moves upstate to hallowed Saratoga Springs.) The **Belmont Stakes,** the third jewel of the Triple Crown, is run the first or second Saturday in June.

PART TEN

ENTERTAINMENT *and* NIGHTLIFE

LIGHTS, TICKETS, ACTION . . .

IT'S HARD TO BEAT THE SCOPE AND BREADTH of entertainment options in NYC. If you haven't already figured it out, there are countless events, free or otherwise, occurring every single day and night. Modern, classical, tap, jazz, international, and experimental dance; jazz, classical, rock, blues, alternative, and hip-hop music; light and dramatic opera; performance art; street busking; and of course theater—legitimate, semi-legitimate, and comedy—are presented in all areas and many venues. Musicians perform in the subway, on the sidewalk, and in the parks.

So where to start? It helps to break down the options. Consider the area of town where you're staying (or would like to visit), your budget, the type of entertainment that tickles you, how late you're prepared to stay out, and, obviously, ticket availability. If you're treating the whole family, you also need to consider the suitability of the subject matter, the length of the performance, any fright factors, and so on. The annual "home stand" of the **Big Apple Circus** at **Lincoln Center** is a major draw, but it's very up-close and personal, so if anybody in the party has coulraphobia—the infamous fear of clowns—you'll regret the investment.

Once you've weighed these factors, you can peruse the listings and eliminate or focus on some of the possibilities. For the latest information, check either the Web sites or the papers, including *Time Out* (**newyork.timeout.com**), the *Village Voice* (**www.villagevoice.com**), the online arts and culture *L Magazine* (**www.thelmagazine.com**), the *New Yorker* (**www.newyorker.com**), and *New York* magazine (**www.nymag .com**). The *New York Times* (**www.nytimes.com**) has an extensive Arts & Leisure section, which expands over the weekend for some of the latest previews and reviews. (At press time, the *Times* was considering charging for online content, but casual readers would likely be able to sample it before subscribing, so you could still check the marquees.) The latter part of this chapter profiles more than 40 club and bar options that can be enjoyed either before or after your chosen diversion, or can even be the main entertainment of the night.

Finally, don't underestimate the value of spontaneity. If you can't get tickets to one thing, you might end up going to something you like even better. Ask people for suggestions, and by "people" we mean the hotel concierge, the Times Square restaurants' staffs (they hear a lot of post-theater chatter), and the folks next to you in the TKTS line; they may already have seen a show you're wondering about. Almost everything here is at a pro level, so it's a good place to try out a genre you know nothing about. Who knows? You might turn out to be the first opera buff on your block.

TICKETS THE EASY WAY

SURE, THERE'S A CERTAIN CACHET to having opening-night seats for a big performance. But often with big-time events, such seats are taken up by the press, luminaries, and those with connections and/ or deep pockets—not to mention an expensive wardrobe. Here are some useful numbers and Web sites, and ways you can avoid going bankrupt in the process of pursuing hot tickets.

If you decide to buy tickets in advance, you'll probably deal with one of the two main ticket-handling agencies for New York theatrical, sports, and concert events: **Ticketmaster** (☎ 800-745-3000, 866-448-7849, or 212-307-7171; **www.ticketmaster.com**) or **Telecharge** (☎ 800-432-7250 or 212-239-6200; **www.telecharge.com**). The individual performing-arts companies (**Metropolitan Opera, New York City Ballet,** etc.) and such venues as **Carnegie Hall** and **New York City Center** sell tickets to their performances online (see "The Big Tickets," page 412).

If you have an American Express gold, platinum, or Centurion card, call ☎ 800-448-8457 or visit **www.americanexpress.com** to see if any special promotional seats are available (this usually applies only to hot new shows).

There are plenty of ticket resellers that are sort of corporate scalpers; they "find" tickets to sold-out shows either by buying in bulk or buying tickets already sold by the box office. (Look under "Tickets" in the Yellow Pages, or do a Web search.) This is a sort of gray market: all the tickets are guaranteed authentic, but you may be paying extra, and you will certainly face handling charges. And these days, the ticket agencies and the resellers are getting hard to tell apart: eBay owns **StubHub!,** for instance, and Ticketmaster owns **TicketsNow.**

Still, if money's no object, if you don't have the patience or leisure to deal with the big, automated phone-charge networks yourself, or if time is at a premium, they are easy and reliable sources. Among the more reputable firms are **Prestige Entertainment** (☎ 800-243-8849; **www.prestigeentertainment.com**) and **Manhattan Entertainment** (☎ 212-382-0633; **www.manhattanentertainment.com**).

TICKETS THE ECONOMY WAY

IT AIN'T CHEAP PUTTIN' ON A SHOW, as those old movies used to point out, and ticket prices reflect the costs. Whether the venue is **Off-Off-Broadway** or the **Metropolitan Opera House,** salaries and rent need to be paid; costumes, lights, and props need to be rented, borrowed, made, and/or insured; and publicity needs to be generated. Chances are that a ticket for an Off-Off-Broadway production won't cost more than $20 and will more likely be $5 to $12. However, the bigger the event, the more expensive, and tickets for some events can be, easily, upwards of $100 before a handling or scalping fee is even added. An average **Broadway** or Lincoln Center ticket costs about $80, though in recent years ticket prices have unabashedly risen to at least twice that. But that shouldn't put you off one of the great adventures of New York; theater deals do exist.

The first place to start is **TKTS** (**www.tdf.org**), a branch of the **Theatre Development Fund,** which has outlets in **Times Square, South Street Seaport,** and **Downtown Brooklyn.** This nonprofit arts organization has persuaded most of the major Broadway and **Off-Broadway** venues to offer same-day tickets (in some cases, next-day) to their shows for 25% to 50% off, plus a $4 surcharge; the only trick is that you have to go in person and take your chances on getting into a show you want to see.

Or another. The best idea is to have three alternatives, in order of preference, already in your head; that way, if your first choice is sold out when you finally make it up to the sales window, and there are only obstructed or nosebleed seats for your second choice, you'll still have something else to go for.

Show up well in advance. TKTS is no secret to residents or tourists, and even though the official lines don't form until an hour before the windows open, the formidable informal queues, especially at the Times Square booth, coagulate at least an hour before that.

The main TKTS outlet is at the north end of the Times Square area at 47th and Broadway, a row of ticket windows beneath a fabulous underlit red amphitheater of scene-watching bleachers in the traffic island officially called **Duffy Square.** The shows for which tickets are available that day are listed on electronic boards at either side of the kiosk; it's usually lit at least an hour early, or you can study it while in line.

Windows at the Times Square location open at 3 p.m. and stay open until 8 p.m. (which just gives you time to sprint for the theater door) Monday and Wednesday through Saturday; open at 2 p.m. and close at 8 p.m. on Tuesday; and open from 3 p.m. until a half hour before curtain time on Sunday. These are all sales times for evening performances only; for matinee performances, you must be in line between 10 a.m. and 2 p.m. on Wednesday and Saturday, and between 11 a.m. and 3 p.m. on Sunday. (Tickets for evening shows are not

unofficial **TIP**
You can't buy musical tickets at the drama window, so if your top two choices are a Shakespeare play and *Chicago*, you'd best split up, get into both lines, and keep in touch by cell phone.

sold during the matinee sales hours, and vice versa.)

You should also be aware that there are two separate queues at the Times Square TKTS, one (the longer one, with more ticket windows) that sells tickets to musicals, and another, on the west side of the steps, that handles only nonmusical plays.

The South Street Seaport TKTS outlet is at John and Front streets. Hours are 11 a.m. to 6 p.m. Monday through Saturday and 11 a.m. to 4 p.m. Sunday. (The booth has been open on Sundays only during warm months.) At this location, matinee tickets are sold the day before rather than the day of: Wednesday matinee tickets are sold on Tuesday, Saturday matinee tickets on Friday, and Sunday matinee tickets on Saturday.

The newest TKTS booth is at **MetroTech Center** in Brooklyn, at Jay Street and Myrtle Avenue. It's accessible by several subway lines and only a block or so from the **Brooklyn Marriott,** a popular convention site. It's open Tuesday through Saturday from 11 a.m. to 6 p.m. except 3 to 3:30. As at South Street Seaport, matinee tickets are sold the day before.

Although until recently TKTS required cash or traveler's checks, it now accepts credit cards as well its own gift certificates, available in $25, $50, and $100 denominations—great stocking stuffers for theater fans. Gift certificates are available at the booths; at ☎ 212-912-9770, ext. 374; or at **www.tdf.org**.

The Theatre Development Fund also offers discount voucher packages—currently four for $36—for smaller Off-Off-Broadway and alternative venues; again, go to **www.tdf.org**. (As TDF reminds you, it's important to call the theater and make sure the vouchers are good on that night.)

While you're standing in line—actually, before you even get there—

unofficial **TIP**
A few shows (at press time, these included *Hair, Rock of Ages,* and *In the Heights*) have lotteries for tickets that are discounted or in special seating areas; call individual theater box offices for information.

you are likely to see young actors and actresses, often in costume, touting various shows and handing out discount coupons. (*Chicago* and *Cabaret* hawkers in particular are famous for their outfits, as were the performers of both sexes wearing Princess Leia–style honey-bun wigs while promoting Carrie Fisher's *Wishful Drinking*.) If you are interested in one of the longer-running shows rather than a new hit or don't care so much which show you see, look for discount coupons (some coupons are known as "twofers," that is, two for one) at the various NYC & Company branches and stalls (**www.nycgo.com**).

You'll also hear plenty of offers from the street sellers who wander up and down outside the TKTS lines offering tickets to popular shows, including some that aren't on the TKTS marquee. These are not "cast members," but the more old-fashioned sort of semi-scalpers. The street sellers will be out as soon as potential buyers hit Times Square—that is, by about 11 a.m.

This is something of a gamble; although in our experience these have been legitimate tickets, there have been instances when people have shown up at the theater with computer-generated fakes or even tickets that had been reported lost, replaced by the theater, and then resold either online or on the street. In any case, if the person sell-ing won't show you an ID, *walk*. And you need to be quite sure you understand whether the seat is partly obscured, right up front (if you tend to get a crick in your neck) or way in the back (if you have any hearing problems). If you do know where the seat is, it can be fine; as an experiment, Eve bought a ticket to *Hair* that was slightly obscured but in the second row and found herself the recipient of two flowers, three kisses, a guitar pick, and an invitation (happily accepted) to join the onstage dance party.

Matinees are generally less expensive than eve-ning performances, although tickets to Wednesday matinees are harder to come by because it's a big locals day; it was always popular with Manhat-tan ladies who lunched before the show, and later became so with senior citizens because matinees are less expensive and the city's less frantic than over the weekend. You're also more likely to score a ticket if you can go at an off-peak time, such as Monday (though many theaters are dark then), Tuesday (another day the principals might choose to rest), or after the holidays.

unofficial **TIP**
A tip for solo travel-ers, parties who don't have the same tastes, or couples who don't mind sitting apart for a couple of hours: single tickets that someone can't use or that fell between ticket purchases are the most common.

More strategies: Go directly to the box office of the show you want to see with cash or a credit card and avoid the handling charge; this also frequently allows you to look at a seating chart and pick the best ticket available. There might even be some really good tickets turned in by patrons who could not use them: New Yorkers, having such a long theatrical tradition, are good about that.

Broadway shows, Lincoln Center, and Carnegie Hall have nightly cancellation lines that form about 90 minutes before the curtain rises. It's also common for theaters (and sports venues as well) to release their own unneeded house seats at the end of the afternoon. Such tickets, if available, are released shortly before curtain and are a real coup to acquire. (You may even luck into a free ticket, if a kind soul approaches you in line to offer an extra one.) Obviously there's no guarantee of getting a seat by depending on the kindness of strang-ers, but what's to lose but another few minutes?

Other ways to see a show on the cheap include standing-room-only (SRO) tickets, discounted student prices (you'll need your ID, of course), and what are now called "rush" tickets (discounted

unofficial **TIP**
If you must miss a show that you already had tickets for, don't just give up and dispose of the tickets. Many theaters will replace them with day-of-show tickets depending on availability.

tickets usually sold only the day of the show and in many case only to students). Like turn-ins, these are available at the theater's box office only, usually starting about two hours in advance of the curtain. (SROs can be uncomfortable, but some people will probably leave at intermission, and you may be able to take their seats.) Each theater has its own policies about what seats might be available; many require cash. Expect to stand in line.

You might consider tickets to previews (full-dress run-throughs of shows that have not officially opened yet and are still being polished), which are frequently cheaper, or even a rehearsal—say, of the **New York Philharmonic** (see next section).

Some cultural institutions have discounts for students, senior citizens, and members of the military or first responders, but be sure to carry ID when you seek tickets.

Finally, if you travel to New York frequently, consider joining an online club that helps you get discounted tickets. It works something like frequent-flier plans; in exchange for the membership fee, these clubs alert you to special offers, package deals, and in some cases same-day discounts. Read the fine print; in one case, the "half-price" ticket saving was offset by the cost of the membership. In many cases, these are shows that have been open for many years, in which case discount vouchers are available from a variety of sources.

PERFORMING ARTS

THE BIG TICKETS: LINCOLN CENTER, CARNEGIE HALL, ETC.

"LIVE FROM LINCOLN CENTER" is almost an understatement. Since the mid-1960s, the **Lincoln Center for the Performing Arts** (**www.lincolncenter.org**) has been home to New York's most prestigious companies, an almost incomprehensible (and redundantly rich) lineup of artists, including the **New York Philharmonic,** both the **Metropolitan Opera** and the **New York City Opera,** the **New York City Ballet** and **American Ballet Theater,** such popular series as the **Mostly Mozart Festival, Midsummer Night Swing,** and **Big Apple Circus,** Wynton Marsalis's **Jazz at Lincoln Center Orchestra** (now housed down the block in a brilliant three-stage complex at the **Time Warner Center**), the **Chamber Music Society,** the **Film Society of Lincoln Center,** and the prestigious **Juilliard School** and **School of American Ballet.** Lincoln Center draws more than 5 million patrons a year. Even if you only worked your way through all its programs and never set foot on Broadway, you could still fill up most of a week.

The six-building complex, a cluster that looks out toward Broadway and Columbus Avenue between West 62nd and 65th, includes five theatrical venues: the great opera house—known universally to opera fans as "the Met," just as the Metropolitan Museum is "the" Met to art fans—the beautifully renovated **Alice Tully Hall** for recitals and concerts; the sibling legitimate theaters the **Vivian Beaumont** and the **Mitzi Newhouse**; and the **David H. Koch Theater** (formerly the New York State Theater); plus several recital halls, an outdoor band shell, and the **New York Public Library for the Performing Arts** (including the **Bruno Walter Auditorium** concert hall). And if that weren't impressive enough, ongoing renovations estimated at $1.5 billion continue to give venues face-lifts and improved acoustics. Peripheral venues include the **Gerard W. Lynch Theatre** and **LaGuardia Concert Hall,** just a block or so off-campus, and the **Jazz at Lincoln Center** complex at the Time Warner Center.

The New York Philharmonic is in residence at Avery Fisher Hall from September through June. Open rehearsals during the season normally run from 9:45 a.m. until about 12:30 p.m. on various days of the week. Tickets are $16 (plus handling fees where applicable). Call ☎ 212-875-5656 or see **www.nyphil.org.** (Students should check for $12 rush tickets up to 10 days before concert dates. Seniors should check for day-of rush tickets by calling ☎ 212-875-5656.)

The Metropolitan Opera House, with its crystal chandeliers and Chagall murals, is worth a tour of its own (see Part Six). The Met (**www.metfamily.org**) holds the stage from mid-September into May; the American Ballet Theater (**www.abt.org**) has been using it the rest of the year and sometimes performs at New York City Center (see next section).

The David H. Koch Theater, on the south side of the opera house, was designed by Philip Johnson and looks it, with its sequential entrances like layers of architectural curtains drawing back, its gilded ceiling, and its five banks of balconies. (That curtain of gold beads has 8 million parts.) The New York City Ballet (**www.nycballet.com**) is in residence from around Thanksgiving through February (*The Nutcracker* pretty much fills up the schedule until January) and again from April through June. The New York City Opera (**www.nycopera .com**), under the direction of Gerard Mortier, performs July through November.

The Eero Saarinen–designed Vivian Beaumont Theater, next to the opera house behind the reflecting pool with the Henry Moore sculpture, is shining after a $5 million renovation. It's what might be called a Broadway stage off Broadway, having staged what most people think of as Broadway's *The Light in the Piazza* and *South Pacific.* Under the Beaumont is the smaller (only 300 seats) and more cutting-edge Mitzi Newhouse Theater, which is the venue long known as the Forum (for both: **www.lct.org**).

Alice Tully Hall, which has just completed its own $1.2 billion modernization, is the home of the **Chamber Music Society of Lincoln Center** (**www.chambermusicsociety.org**) and often hosts concerts by Juilliard students; it turns cinematic in fall for the **New York Film Festival** at the **Walter Reade Theater** upstairs (**www.filmlinc.org**).

Although they are not so well publicized, the Juilliard School has its own opera company, jazz orchestra, baroque consort, and frequent solo and dance concerts.

kids The wide plaza in front of the Metropolitan Opera House, on the 62nd Street side of Lincoln Center, is called **Damrosch Park** and is the winter home (under a tent, of course) of the Big Apple Circus as well as various fine-arts and crafts shows during the year. It's also where the **Guggenheim Bandshell** is located and where free concerts, dance programs, and family shows organized by **Lincoln Center Out of Doors** pop up in August; watch the papers.

OTHER MAJOR VENUES

FEW CONCERT HALLS HAVE ATTRACTED as many legends (and jokes, of course) as **Carnegie Hall** (154 West 57th Street, near Seventh Avenue; ☎ 212-247-7800; **www.carnegiehall.org**), and no wonder: Tchaikovsky conducted the premiere concert; the New York Philharmonic played here in the heydays of Mahler, Toscanini, Stokowski, and Bernstein; and a concert date here has for the past century been recognized as a mark of supreme artistry. Nowadays it hosts pop concerts as often as classical, but its astonishing acoustics and displays of memorabilia make it a genuine experience. Its newer, $50 million, 599-seat underground venue, **Zankel Hall,** is a more intimate space that hosts such artists as Yo-Yo Ma, Emmylou Harris, Emanuel Ax, the Juilliard String Quartet, the New World Symphony, and Mitsuko Uchida.

Nearby is **New York City Center** at 130 West 56th Street (☎ 212-581-1212; **www.nycitycenter.org**), which hosts touring shows, dance performances, and concerts. (The Moorish-Spanish facade is a hint that it was originally a Shriners' temple.)

Most people think of **Radio City Music Hall** only at holiday time, when the "world-famous Rockettes" and the equally famous "Mighty Wurlitzer" kick into high gear. But this Modernist Art masterpiece, lavishly decorated with gold foil, marble, cork, Bakelite, and aluminum, is still the world's largest indoor theater. It's equipped to handle films (it has hosted more than 700 premieres), stage shows, and concerts. Its schedule regularly includes a broad range of big-name acts: the Allman Brothers, Celtic Woman, Riverdance, New Kids on the Block, and the like (☎ 212-307-7171; **www.radiocity.com**).

The new **Baryshnikov Arts Center** in Hell's Kitchen (450 West 37th Street; ☎ 646-731-3200; **www.bacnyc.org**) promises to be one of the most influential alternative performance spaces; its **Jerome Robbins Theater** is home to not only the **Baryshnikov Dance Company** but also the **Wooster Group** avant-garde theatrical troupe, free chamber-music concerts, and film series, among other attractions.

Three other frequently star-studded venues are worth watching (and not hard to get to): The **Brooklyn Academy of Music** (☎ 718-636-4100; **www.bam.org**), affectionately known as BAM, hosts film, theater, dance, opera, and music from local and international companies, including the **Brooklyn Philharmonic. Aaron Davis Hall,** on the campus of the **City College of New York** at West 135th Street and Convent Avenue, is a two-stage venue that brings in well-known jazz and pop performers (☎ 212-281-9240, ext. 19 or 20; **www.harlemstage.org**). And although it might take a train transfer, the **New Jersey Performing Arts Center in Newark** (☎ 800-GO-NJPAC; **www.njpac.org**) stages many major international ballet, opera, and dance touring companies, not to mention world-class jazz and classical concerts.

BROADWAY, OFF-BROADWAY, AND OFF-OFF-BROADWAY

WHEN THE LIGHTS GO OUT on Broadway, which happened most recently in November 2007 for a stagehands' strike, people around the world know. A large number of theaters were already operating in the area when the arrival of the New York Times Building in 1904 changed the name of the former Longacre Square to Times Square. More than a century later, despite razings and redevelopment, renovations and relocations, there are still some four dozen theaters that can lay claim to the "Broadway" moniker.

The "official" Broadway theater district spans a 14-block stretch with a southern boundary at West 41st Street, where the **Nederlander** stands, to the northern boundary at Broadway and West 54th, where the **Roundabout Theater at Studio 54** sits. (Only a half-dozen theaters have literal Broadway addresses: the **Minskoff,** at 45th Street; the **Marquis,** at 46th; the **Palace,** stretching out off 47th; **Circle in the Square** and the **Winter Garden,** at 50th; and, of course, the **Broadway,** at 53rd Street. All other theaters are east or west of this stretch.)

"Off-Broadway" in one sense did actually refer to theaters not in that district; in fact, the Greenwich Village theatrical movement was in part a revolt against the "establishment." But not only is the term increasingly loose, but the importance of a "Broadway" address also is to some extent a matter of publicity, and the spiritual line between some on-Broadway and Off-Broadway venues is getting fuzzier. Many of the more "uptown" Off-Broadway houses have pretty much been assimilated, whereas the downtown Off-Broadway troupes, many of whom may once have been rather antiestablishment, are threatening to mellow into the high-culture circuit. And theaters such as the **Playwrights Horizons** (416 West 42nd Street; ☎ 212-564-1235; **www.playwrightshorizons.org**) and **Roundabout** (227 West 42nd Street; ☎ 212-719-1300; **www.roundabouttheatre.org**), despite their Great White Way addresses, have Off-Broadway attitudes.

The **Manhattan Theater Club** produces shows on and off Broadway, often simultaneously.

Among the best-known Off-Broadway venues are the ambitious **Minetta Lane Theater** (18 Minetta Lane; ☎ 212-420-8000); **Cherry Lane Theatre**, founded by Edna St. Vincent Millay (38 Commerce Street; ☎ 212-989-2020; **www.cherrylanetheatre.org**); the **Classic Stage Company** (136 East 13th Street, ☎ 212-677-4210, ext. 10; **www.classicstage .org**); the **Lucille Lortel Theatre** (121 Christopher Street; ☎ 212-924-2817; **www.lortel.org**); the **Vineyard Theatre** (108 East 15th Street; ☎ 212-353-0303; **www.vineyardtheatre.org**); the **Atlantic Theater Company** (336 West 20th Street; ☎ 212-691-5919; **www.atlantictheater .org**); the **Joyce Theater** (175 Eighth Avenue at West 19th; ☎ 212-691-9740; **www.joyce.org**), which also showcases many dance troupes; Joseph Papp's six-hall **Public Theater,** in the onetime free library near **Astor Place** (425 Lafayette Street; ☎ 212-539-8500; **www.publictheater .org**), and the **Astor Place Theatre** across the street, home of **Blue Man Group**'s wildly creative multimedia extravaganzas (434 Lafayette; ☎ 800-BLUEMAN; **www.blueman.com**); **Players Theatre**, near **Washington Square** (115 MacDougal Street; ☎ 212-475-1449; **www.theplayers theatre.com**); and **Union Square Theatre** (100 East 17th Street and Park Avenue; ☎ 212-505-0700).

Similarly, Off-Off-Broadway refers less to an address (generally downtown, though it may be Village, East Village, SoHo, or Brooklyn) than to a mind-set. It used to imply experimental or avant-garde productions, satires, debut productions, and sometimes just deeply serious art, and to a great extent it still does. But sometimes productions that are destined (or at least intended) to make their way to Broadway get their final editings here. Among the most visible are the **Manhattan Theater Club** (**Friedman Theatre,** 261 West 47th Street, ☎ 212-239-6200), and **Stage I and II** at New York City Center, 130 West 56th Street, ☎ 212-581-1212; **www.mtc-nyc.org**); the multimedia-minded **Kitchen** (512 West 19th Street; ☎ 212-255-5793; **www.thekitchen.org**); **Ohio Theatre** in SoHo (66 Wooster Street; ☎ 212-966-4844; **www.sohothink tank.org**); the four-stage **Theater for the New City** (155 First Avenue; ☎ 212-254-1109; **www.theaterforthenewcity.net**) and nearby **Performance Space 122** in the East Village (150 First Avenue at East Ninth; ☎ 212-352-3101; **www.ps122.org**); and **New York Theatre Workshop** (79 East Fourth Street; ☎ 212-460-5475; **www.nytw.org**). For more listings, check the newspapers and Web sites mentioned previously.

SOMETHING FOR FREE?

IT MAY BE HARD TO BELIEVE, but New York does have free theater. The most famous is **Shakespeare in the Park.** Central Park's **Delacorte Theater** is the summer home to the company that otherwise holds forth at the **Papp Public Theater** near Astor Place. It's a matter of principle, or at least of sentiment, for some of the biggest stars of stage and screen to do their stints in the open air: Patrick Stewart, Andre

Braugher, Kevin Kline, Anne Hathaway, and Michelle Pfeiffer have all trod the B(o)ards here.

Tickets are given out on a first-come, first-served basis at the Delacorte Theater beginning at 1 p.m. the day of show, but you'd better be there long before that. You can double your chances of getting in by sending an ally down to the Papp box office, at 425 Lafayette Street (☎ 212-539-8500; **www.publictheater.org**) between 1 and 3 p.m.; only two tickets per person, but that's better than none. Furthermore, on selected dates, tickets will be distributed in each of the five boroughs; visit **www.publictheater.org** for details.

As mentioned, every summer, **Lincoln Center Out of Doors** hosts free concerts of all types and dance parties, many with lessons beforehand. And the smaller outdoor Shakespeare groups that play in places such as Washington Square and **Riverside Park** are local favorites.

You may even be surprised by the quality of the free subway entertainment. Although some performances aren't officially sanctioned, the MUNY (Music Under New York) program of the MTA (Metropolitan Transit Authority) allows musicians to perform "legally" and grants them a special banner to prove that they have gone through the application process and passed a competitive audition. More than 100 sanctioned acts, individuals or ensembles, perform more than 150 times, somewhere in the subway system, each week. **Times Square** and **Union Square** are usually fixed spots. See **www.mta.info/mta/aft/muny.** Impromptu free entertainment is common during the summer in many New York parks.

OTHER PERFORMANCE VENUES

AS MENTIONED EARLIER, the **New York City Ballet** calls Lincoln Center home, but that is far from the only premier dance troupe that plays Manhattan. The **American Ballet Theatre** (☎ 212-477-3030; **www.abt.org**) and the **Alvin Ailey American Dance Theater** (☎ 212-405-9000; **www.alvinailey.org**) use New York City Center; other companies book the **Joyce Theater.**

Major rock, pop, reggae, soul, and country concerts are apt to be held, like most everything else, in **Madison Square Garden** (☎ 212-465-MSG1; **www.thegarden.com**), but other popular concert venues include MSG's smaller annex, the **WaMu Theater;** the **Orpheum,** in the East Village (126 Second Avenue; **www.stomponline.com**), longtime home of the rousingly percussive show *Stomp;* the revived **Apollo Theater** (West 125th Street and Frederick Douglass Boulevard; ☎ 212-531-5305; **www.apollotheater.org**); the **Hammerstein Ballroom** at **Manhattan Center Studios** (311 West 34th Street; ☎ 212-279-7740; **www.mcstudios.com**); **Symphony Space** (2537 Broadway, at 95th; ☎ 212-864-5400; **www.symphonyspace.org**); and **Roseland Ballroom** (239 West 52nd Street; ☎ 212-247-0200; **www.roselandballroom.com**).

After a $15 million restoration, the **Beacon Theatre** (Broadway and 74th Street; ☎ 212-465-6500; **www.beacontheatre.com**) is back in a big way, hosting major concerts as it has for more than 80 years; it's also to be one of Cirque du Soleil's extended-play homes in the city. And if rock dinosaurs are your generation, but not quite your taste, more mainstream names in dance, music, and performance, ranging from Garrison Keillor to Yes, Judy Collins to Ballet Folklórico de México, show up at **Town Hall** (123 West 43rd Street; ☎ 212-840-2824; **www.the-townhall-nyc.org**).

CAMERAS AND CLOSE-UPS

IF YOU'RE INTERESTED in one of the television talk or talk-and-entertainment shows, you most likely need to try to get tickets ahead of time—at least six or eight weeks. In the case of *Saturday Night Live,* it's a matter of seasons rather than weeks. Tickets for the whole taping season are awarded by lottery every August. E-mail requests are accepted that month only at **snltickets@nbcuni .com**—and even then winners get only two seats for a randomly selected date. (There have been rumors that this is more for show than for the show, but hey, that's show biz.) For ticket information, call ☎ 212-664-3056 or see **www.nbc.com/Footer/Tickets** (*note:* Web address is case-sensitive).

Most seats are a little easier to score, but almost all requests should be sent in several months in advance. (For *Live with Regis and Kelly,* the wait can be a year!) Of course, if you regularly watch the shows, you probably already know this. (What happens if your favorite personality gets canceled in the meantime? It probably means his name is not Jay Leno.)

Most shows limit not only the number of tickets you can get, but also how often you can get them—once every six months is not unusual. You should also be aware that most shows have age limits (and even if they don't, kids won't be allowed without adults).

On the other hand, nobody likes empty chairs, even a couple, to show up on camera. So if you're still longing for that wild and crazy *SNL* moment, and you feel lucky, go over to **Rockefeller Plaza** no later than 7 on Saturday morning, stand around on the sidewalk on 49th Street between Fifth and Sixth avenues (where the NBC STUDIOS marquee is), get your face on television in the background of the **Today** show, and keep an eye on the 49th Street entrance to 30 Rockefeller Plaza. By about 9:15 a.m., not every week and with no guarantees, a few standby tickets to **Saturday Night Live** (either the dress rehearsal at 8:30 p.m. or the live taping at 11:30) may be passed out. If you do get in, prepare to arrive by 7:15 p.m. for the dress rehearsal or 10:45 p.m. for the taping.

unofficial **TIP**
A standby ticket to any of these shows does *not* guarantee you a seat; it just improves your chances.

Being an NBC show, **Late Night with Jimmy Fallon** also distributes tickets by request. Standby tickets are handed out at about 9 a.m. on taping days at the 49th Street entrance (one ticket per person). Any tickets left are taken to the NBC Studio Tour desk, on the second floor of the NBC Experience store. However, it's best to call the ticket line (☎ 212-664-3056) the night before to make sure there is actually going to be a show—sometimes tapings take place several days in advance of their air dates, and during certain weeks the show is dark. If you want to be one of those music fans hanging over the bleachers behind the special guests, you can enter a special online sweepstakes at **www.latenight withjimmyfallon.com.**

The Daily Show with Jon Stewart tapes Monday through Thursday starting at 5:45 p.m. at 513 West 54th Street (between Tenth and Eleventh avenues). Call ☎ 212-586-2477 for information, but at press time tickets were being distributed only online through **www.thedaily show.com.**

More-daytime-oriented fans can try for standby tickets for **The View** by going to ABC Studios, at 320 West 66th Street (near West End Avenue) at the audience-entrance door between 8:30 a.m. and 10 a.m. Seating is first come, first served—but be warned: the ladies have become so popular that there's a one- to two-year wait for tickets, and sometimes the show distributes more tickets than the studio can hold. Sort of like an airline.

As mentioned, **Live with Regis and Kelly** also has a year's wait. If you want to try, call ☎ 212-456-1000, or see the mailing address at **bventertainment.go.com/tv/buenavista/regisandkelly.** For day-of standby tickets, go to the studio, at 7 Lincoln Square (on the southeast corner of Columbus Avenue and 67th Street), but be sure to arrive by 7 a.m. to get a standby number. Audiences enter for warm-up at 8 a.m. or the taping at 9 a.m.

The Martha Stewart Show tapes three times a week (generally Tuesdays, Wednesdays, and Thursdays at 10 a.m. and 2 p.m.). You'll have to go to Martha's Web site (**www.marthastewart.com**) well in advance to get confirmed seats—because of the erratic schedule, you name a week you'd like to come, though you can specify a preference for the day of the week or ask to be part of a special-interest audience. (This is one of the few shows that allow larger groups to apply for tickets.) Or you can go to Chelsea Television Studios at 221 West 26th Street, between Seventh and Eighth avenues, about two hours before showtime and hope for an opening. Can't get in? You can always go shopping in her on-site store.

Emeril Lagasse tapes *Emeril Live* at the Food Network's Chelsea studios at 75 Ninth Avenue (between 15th and 16th streets) on a somewhat erratic schedule, usually in bursts of a couple of weeks several times a year; these tapings, and the lottery for tickets, are obviously intended for serious fans, so they're announced via the Food Network Web site (**www.foodnetwork.com/emeril-live**) and newsletter. But if you're a serious fan, you probably already subscribe. . . .

Or you can just horn in on the alfresco audiences for the morning shows: **Good Morning America** (on the east side of Broadway, between 43rd and 44th streets) and **Today** (in Rockefeller Plaza, on 49th Street between Fifth and Sixth avenues). But even here, depending on the day's guests, and especially if the special musical guest is going to be performing outdoors, you had better plan to show up *waaaay* early. This is no exception.

NEW YORK NIGHTLIFE

IF YOU'D LIKE TO BE AN ACTIVE PARTICIPANT in your evening's events as opposed to an audience member, then you'll need to do a bit of bar- or club-hopping. This can be fun or tiresome depending on the distances between your chosen destinations, but you're bound to have some sort of an adventure—on foot, in a taxi, or on the subway—between venues. Consider doing a little research before you get to town if you'd like to see a performance at a bar or club; *Time Out* magazine (**newyork.timeout.com**) has the most comprehensive listings; **www.sheckys.com** is a good supplementary resource.

To wet your whistle, we suggest places that offer good beer, sake, sumptuous cocktails, jazz, rock, cabaret, country, alternative sounds, comedy, cigars, hookah pipes, and literary discussions. It's just a taste of the possibilities, but a good place to start.

For those who still smoke and aren't quite sure how to drink and puff simultaneously in public since the New York smoking ban of 2003, we offer a few options: If you'd like something stronger than a hookah pipe at **Kush** (see page 444), then you can opt for cigars at **Club Macanudo** (see page 438) and the **Velvet Cigar Lounge** (80 East Seventh Street; ☎ 212-533-5582; **www.velvetcigars.com**). For cigarettes and a taste of Art Deco, try **Circa Tabac** (32 Watts Street; ☎ 212-941-1781; **www.circatabac.com**).

We hope that with this bit of insider advice you'll be motivated to do some regular New York City night-owl exploration. We look forward to seeing you on the dark side. . . .

JAZZ

JAZZ MAY HAVE ORIGINATED IN NEW ORLEANS, but for decades New York has been the center of the jazz universe. If you have even the slightest interest in this style, you'll want to check out one or two of the following clubs; be prepared to stay up late, especially if you'd like to catch a jam session.

See profiles for **Village Vanguard, Smoke, Blue Note,** and **Smalls.**

CLEOPATRA'S NEEDLE (2485 Broadway at 92nd Street; ☎ 212-769-6969; **www.cleopatrasneedleny.com**) has live music nightly and jam sessions Wednesday through Saturday, 11:30 p.m. or midnight until 2:30 or 3 a.m.; $10 minimum per person.

55 BAR (55 Christopher Street; ☎ 212-929-9883; **www.55bar.com**) is a no-nonsense Greenwich Village joint with music that's often surprisingly good. Two-drink minimum. Open daily until 4 a.m.

FAT CAT BILLIARDS (75 Christopher Street; ☎ 212-675-6056; **www .fatcatmusic.org**) offers jazz, pool, Ping-Pong, and chess. Jam sessions nightly at 12:30 a.m. on weekdays and 1:30 a.m. on weekends.

IRIDIUM (1650 Broadway at 51st Street; ☎ 212-582-2121; **www.iridium jazzclub.com**), with its over-the-top ultra-modern decor, is a trippy exception to the rule that jazz is often played in drab spaces.

SWEET RHYTHM (88 Seventh Avenue South; ☎ 212-255-3626; **www .sweetrhythmny.com**) was formerly the jazz-only Sweet Basil, but it now hosts world music with a bit of jazz thrown in.

ZINC BAR (82 West Third Street; ☎ 212-477-9462; **www.zincbar.com**) is a great place to watch some amazing musicians in an intimate setting. Occasional impromptu audience participation occurs during performances. It's also cozy for a tête-à-tête with drinks. Open very late!

ROCK AND ALTERNATIVE

ROCK CLUBS IN MANHATTAN fit mostly into three categories. There are the bar venues that host big-name acts for big cover charges—places such as **The Fillmore New York at Irving Plaza** (17 Irving Place; ☎ 212-777-6800; **www.irvingplaza.com**), **The Bowery Ballroom** (6 Delancey Street; ☎ 212-533-2111; **www.boweryballroom.com**), **Terminal 5** (610 West 56th Street; ☎ 212-665-3832; **www.terminal5nyc .com**), and **Roseland Ballroom** (239 West 52nd Street; ☎ 212-247-0200; **www.roselandballroom.com**). Then there are the showcase places where newly signed bands preen for industry insiders—like **Southpaw** (125 Fifth Avenue, Brooklyn; ☎ 718-230-0236; **www.spsounds.com**) and **Mercury Lounge** (see page 446). At the bottom of the ladder are the vanity clubs, such as **Kenny's Castaways** (157 Bleecker Street; ☎ 212-979-9762; **www.kennyscastaways.net**), where amateurish weekend warriors and ambitious start-ups play short sets.

The country's best bar bands have long played their hearts out in nearby New Jersey and Long Island (remember the origins of Southside Johnny, Bruce Springsteen, the Rascals, and so on), but Manhattan, right between those two areas, has few groups (or venues to present them) dedicated to entertaining a bar. The showcasing kids angle more for record-label attention than for a grooving good time for the house crowd, and an evening in one of the name venues means buying expensive tickets and standing amid rapturous crowds; you're basically at a concert, not hanging out in a bar.

unofficial **TIP**
If you just want to have a beer and listen to pro-quality local guys who play live for a living—a real bar band—you're in the wrong place.

If you don't mind your rock filtered through other influences, **Rodeo Bar** (see page 448) presents good, professional rockabilly and alt-country bands. **Hank's Saloon** (46 Third Avenue at Atlantic Avenue, Brooklyn; ☎ 347-227-8495; **www.hankssaloon.com**) offers country music and a divey saloon vibe. Here are some other venues:

ARLENE'S GROCERY (95 Stanton Street; ☎ 212-995-1652; **www.arlenes grocery.net**) has cover charges on Friday, Saturday, and sometimes Sunday; price is dependent on the event. Considered a prestigious showcase for indie bands; medium to heavy rock; rock karaoke on Mondays at 10 p.m. and open mic on Saturday afternoons.

THE BITTER END (147 Bleecker Street; ☎ 212-673-7030; **www.bitterend .com**) has been around for decades, hosting some great and not-so-good music. Worth a visit just for the tradition it represents.

CRASH MANSION (199 Bowery; ☎ 212-982-0740; **www.crashmansion .com**) hosts "Between a Rock and a Hard Place," a showcase of hip young bands on Friday nights in a basement club that avoids the grunge of typical rock venues.

KNITTING FACTORY (361 Metropolitan Avenue, Brooklyn; ☎ 347-529-6696; **ny.knittingfactory.com**) was a legendary downtown club for alternative music, featuring everything from klezmer to thrash. Rents skyrocketed, and relocation to Brooklyn was inevitable. It's still a nice venue for seeing eclectic bands, but nostalgists complain.

LIVING ROOM (154 Ludlow Street; ☎ 212-533-7237; **www.living roomny.com**) charges no cover; one-drink minimum. Medium rock to folk with focus on singer-songwriters.

MAXWELL'S (1039 Washington Street, Hoboken, New Jersey; ☎ 201-653-1703; **www.maxwellsnj.com**) may be in (gasp!) New Jersey, but it's one of the area's finest rock clubs. Take the 15-minute ride on the 126 bus from Port Authority to Hoboken, and get off at 12th Street, a block from the stage where Bruce Springsteen's *Glory Days* video was filmed and REM, Nirvana, and Beck all cut their teeth. Today, indie-rock fans thrill to see their favorites up close in a venue that barely holds 200. There's a menu of decent comfort food.

SIDEWALK CAFE (94 Avenue A; ☎ 212-473-7373; **www.sidewalkmusic .net**) no cover, two-drink minimum. The premier venue for anti-folk music, a mutating genre which combines the sensibilities of folk, punk, and rock. Avoid Monday's open-mic night.

South of Houston Street, the music is often edgier and more experimental.

DANCING

DESPITE WEIRD CABARET LAWS prohibiting dancing in bars unless they're licensed, dancing is alive and well in NYC. Clubs, both underground and mainstream, abound and satisfy all musical and stylistic tastes. Herein lies the rub—some of the best beats are spun by DJs who travel and host club parties at various venues; some stationary clubs have nonstop style, but not always the best music, as hip takes precedence over harmonics. We won't list the DJ parties, because they often change, but *Time Out* magazine (**newyork .timeout.com**) has a good weekly clubs section listing. As for the trendy clubs, we'll give you an intro, but blink and they may already be passé.

Cielo (18 Little West 12th Street; ☎ 212-645-5700; **www.cieloclub .com**), in the still-hot Meatpacking District, takes dancing and DJs seriously, but this you can appreciate only once you get past the bouncers. **Love** (179 MacDougal Street; ☎ 212-477-5683; **www.music islove.net**) lives up to its name by virtue of its sound system, which dancers absolutely adore, though this is not a glitzy place by any stretch of the imagination. The recently renovated **Sullivan Room** (218 Sullivan Street; ☎ 212-252-2151; **www.sullivanroom.com**) bills itself as one of New York's few showcases for "underground" DJs, and that's not just because it's located in a dark and sultry basement.

Other clubs include the African-themed **Cain** (544 West 27th Street; ☎ 212-947-8000; **www.cainnyc.com**) and **Pacha** (618 West 46th Street; ☎ 212-209-7500; **www.pachanyc.com**), the import from party-weary Ibiza. Also try **Element** (225 East Houston; ☎ 212-254-2200; **www.elementny.com**) and **Hiro** (371 West 16th Street; ☎ 212-242-4300; **www.hiroballroom.com**) at **The Maritime Hotel.**

For salsa dancing in a setting more down-home than glossy, choices include nightspots such as **S.O.B.'s** (see page 452); or warm, artsy **Nuyorican Poets Cafe** (236 East Third Street; ☎ 212-780-3286; **www.nuyorican.org**). There's also **LQ** (511 Lexington Avenue in the Radisson Lexington Hotel; ☎ 212-593-7575; **www.lqny.com**). Yet another option is **Swing 46** (see page 452).

CABARET

SOME OF NEW YORK'S WORTHY cabaret bars include **Joe's Pub** (see page 443), and, notably, **Feinstein's at Loews Regency** (540 Park Avenue; ☎ 212-339-4095; **www.feinsteinsattheregency.com**), featuring namesake-owner Michael Feinstein and

unofficial **TIP**
For more info on NYC cabaret, check out **www .svhamstra.com, www .cabaretexchange.com,** and **www.cabaret.org.**

other legends. Old standbys (and we mean *old;* some of the following have been in operation for decades) include **The Duplex** (61 Christopher Street at Seventh Avenue; ☎ 212-255-5438; **www.theduplex .com**), the **Oak Room** (see "Hotel Bars," page 426), **Don't Tell Mama** (343 West 46th Street; ☎ 212-757-0788; **www.donttellmamanyc.com**), and **Café Carlyle** (see page 436).

IRISH

IRISH PUBS ARE A SAFE BET for finding good beer, pub grub, and fine *cráic*. You may even get some live music, complete with a fiddle or two. The following are of particular interest:

AN BEAL BOCHT CAFE (445 West 238th Street; Riverdale, Bronx; ☎ 718-884-7127; **www.anbealbochtcafe.com**) offers great music from Wednesday through Saturday; it's a trek to get to, but it serves the best Guinness of all (warm fire, too).

MONA'S (224 Avenue B; ☎ 212-353-3780), an ultra-dive, serves cheap beer and hosts Monday-night jam sessions starting at 10:30 p.m.

MR. DENNEHY'S (63 Carmine Street; ☎ 212-414-1223; **www.mr dennehys.com**) has a relaxed atmosphere, a fine menu of pub grub, and plenty of "footie" (soccer) on the telly.

PADDY REILLY'S (519 Second Avenue; ☎ 212-686-1210) has music nightly.

SWIFT HIBERNIAN LOUNGE (34 East Fourth Street; ☎ 212-227-9438; **www.swiftnycbar.com**) has music on Tuesdays, poetry readings on the fourth Monday of the month, and great beer to boot.

FINE DRINKS

ONE OF THE BEST THINGS ABOUT NEW YORK is the substantial number of people who seek out the best food and drink with an obsessive zeal and passion. Mind you, the city has a plethora of corner bars where Bud Light is drunk unrepentantly. But for those on a mission to enjoy only the finest drinks, there are zillions of places whose selections will astound. And for those who aren't professional bon vivants, the true believers populating these bars will gladly help clueless novices. New Yorkers may be rude and blasé, but once they start enthusing, it's hard to keep 'em down.

unofficial **TIP**
The New York City Beer Guide provides exhaustive annotated listings of pubs, tastings, and local microbrews online at **www.nycbeer.org.**

The best bars and restaurants for good beer:

BLIND TIGER ALE HOUSE (281 Bleecker Street at Jones Street; ☎ 212-462-4682; **www.blindtigeralehouse.com**) has the most beers on tap per square foot in the city, in addition to two hand-pumps, a gravity cask, and an impressive collection of bottles.

THE BROOKLYN BREWERY (79 North 11th Street; ☎ 718-486-7422; **www.brooklynbrewery.com**) in **Williamsburg** offers free brewery tours on Saturday at 1, 2, 3, and 4 p.m. Worth a visit.

BURP CASTLE (41 East Seventh Street; ☎ 212-982-4576; **burpcastlenyc .wordpress.com**) is all about beer, and the bartenders are dressed in monks' robes to ensure a reverential feeling toward the brew.

CAFÉ DE BRUXELLES (118 Greenwich Avenue; ☎ 212-206-1830; **www .cafebruxellesonline.com**) fries great pommes frites and offers a small but smart selection of Belgian bottles.

d.b.a.: See page 439.

EAR INN (326 Spring Street; ☎ 212-226-9060; **www.earinn.com**) is one of the city's oldest bars and a nice little bohemian cafe with especially good Guinness.

THE GATE (321 Fifth Avenue, Brooklyn; ☎ 718-768-4329; **thegate brooklyn.blogspot.com**) has an extensive, ever-changing list of taps, outdoor seating, and a diverse clientele, and is just a few blocks from **Prospect Park.**

THE GINGER MAN: See page 441.

McSORLEY'S OLD ALE HOUSE (15 East Seventh Street; ☎ 212-474-9148; **www.mcsorleysnewyork.com**) is a tourist fave with "old New York" ambience and mediocre beer swilled alongside rambunctious fraternity boys.

OLD TOWN BAR (45 East 18th Street; ☎ 212-529-6732; **www.oldtown bar.com**) has a halfway-decent beer selection plus great, traditional ambience.

PECULIER PUB (145 Bleecker Street; ☎ 212-353-1327; **www.peculier pub.com**) is expensive and incredibly mobbed with college kids on weekends, but the selection is amazing.

SPUYTEN DUYVIL (359 Metropolitan Avenue, Brooklyn; ☎ 718-963-4140; **www.spuytenduyvilnyc.com**) offers a superb array of brews both bottled and on tap. The atmosphere is friendly and just a tad cool-kitsch.

THE STAG'S HEAD (252 East 51st Street; ☎ 212-888-2453; **www .thestagsheadnyc.com**) focuses on American microbrews and pub grub.

VOL DE NUIT (148 West Fourth Street; ☎ 212-979-2616; **www .voldenuitbar.com**) is tucked away inconspicuously just a block from **Washington Square Park** and features a full menu of Belgian beers, including a good selection from Trappist breweries.

WATERFRONT ALE HOUSE (540 Second Avenue; ☎ 212-696-4104; and 155 Atlantic Avenue, Brooklyn; ☎ 718-522-3794; **www.waterfront alehouse.com**) has an excellent tap selection with some ultra-rare specials and good pub food.

HEARTLAND BREWERY's many locations (35 Union Square West, ☎ 212-645-3400; 127 West 43rd Street, ☎ 646-366-0235; 350 Fifth Avenue (in the **Empire State Building**), ☎ 212-563-3433; 93 South Street Seaport, ☎ 646-572-2337; and 1285 Sixth Avenue at 51st Street, ☎ 212-582-8244; **www.heartlandbrewery.com**) and **Chelsea Brewing Company** (Pier 59, Chelsea Piers; ☎ 212-336-6440; **www.chelseabrew ingco.com**) are half-decent microbreweries but very popular.

JAPANESE AND SAKE

THERE ARE TWO LOCI OF JAPANESE CULTURE in Manhattan: the East Village, where hip bohemian Japanese kids live and hang out, and Midtown, where a more suit-and-tie crowd has its bars and restaurants, many private. In the East Village is **Decibel** (240 East Ninth Street; ☎ 212-979-2733; **www.sakebardecibel.com**), a knickknack-filled haven in a very cool little basement space where you can talk and drink any of tons of sakes from your choice of unique cups. You can also try plum wine or a lychee martini. For other Japanese-flavored nightlife, see profiles for **Angel's Share** and **Sakagura** (pages 429 and 449).

HOTEL BARS

SOME OF THE MOST ELEGANT BARS in town are in hotels. These are places where beer takes a back seat to the gin, mojitos, and martini hybrids.

THE ALGONQUIN (59 West 44th Street; ☎ 212-840-6800; **www.algon quinhotel.com**) was built in 1902 and was where the famed Algonquin Round Table was formed. Authors who met daily to drink and wax witty over lunch included Dorothy Parker and Robert Benchley. The hotel is full of good drinking options: there's the famous **Oak Room,** scene of seasonal cabaret shows, as well as the elegant and relaxing lobby bar and the woody, clubby Blue Bar.

BAR 44 at the **Royalton Hotel:** See page 429.

THE CARLYLE HOTEL (35 East 76th Street; ☎ 212-744-1600; **www.the carlyle.com**) contains not only the famous **Café Carlyle** (see page 436) but also **Bemelmans Bar,** which features tinkling piano and a clubby atmosphere with watercolors on the walls. Bemelmans also offers Madeline's tea on Saturday and Sunday, with seatings at 10 a.m. and 12:30 p.m.

GRAND BAR & LOUNGE at the **Soho Grand Hotel** (310 West Broadway; ☎ 212-965-3000; **www.sohogrand.com**) has a very atmospheric lounge area, all inside the hotel lobby; very hip.

HUDSON BAR: See page 442.

MONKEY BAR at the **Hotel Elysée** (60 East 54th Street; ☎ 212-308-2950; **www.elyseehotel.com**) is anything but restrained and stuffy; it attracts an exuberant crowd, and laughter—sometimes even singing, if you get there late enough—drowns out clinking glasses.

MORGANS BAR at **Morgans** hotel (237 Madison Avenue; ☎ 212-686-0300; **www.morganshotel.com**) serves up attitude, romantic atmosphere, and pricey but good mixed drinks below the hotel lobby. Alternatively, above on street level, Morgans hotel's **Asia de Cuba** (☎ 212-726-7755) has a very popular but small bar as well as a lively, stylish restaurant. Try the martinis.

TOP OF THE TOWER BAR & LOUNGE at the **Beekman Tower Hotel:** See page 453.

THE VIEW RESTAURANT at the **New York Marriott Marquis** hotel (1535 Broadway; ☎ 212-704-8900; **www.theviewny.com**) is the only revolving bar in New York, so there's never a static vantage point. Don't eat the food.

SEX

THE BIG APPLE OFFERS MANY OPPORTUNITIES to either sow your wild oats or have a great time in places that don't flaunt the pickup vibe. For those who want to try out some smooth moves on strangers, there are ample choices. Try **Bounce Restaurant & Sports Lounge** (1403 Second Avenue; ☎ 212-535-2183; **www.bounceny.com**); **Asia de Cuba** (see facing page); **Tao** (42 East 58th Street; ☎ 212-888-2288; **www.taorestaurant.com**); **People Lounge** (163 Allen Street; ☎ 212-254-2668; **www.peoplelounge.com**); **Divine Bar** (244 East 51st Street, ☎ 212-319-9463; 236 West 54th Street, ☎ 212-265-9463; **divinebar .ypguides.net**); **The Bubble Lounge** (see page 435); and the chic and grown-up **King Cole Bar** at **The St. Regis New York** (2 East 55th Street; ☎ 212-753-4500; **www.stregis.com**) for power pickups.

For those looking for something a little racier, fancy strip clubs such as **Scores** (536 West 28th Street; ☎ 212-868-4900; **www.scoresny .com**), **Penthouse Executive Club** (603 West 45th Street; ☎ 212-245-0002; **www.penthouseexecutiveclub.com**) and **VIP Club** (20 West 20th Street; ☎ 212-633-1199; **www.thevipclubnyc.com**) offer super examples of plastic surgery gone wild (and very steep bar tabs).

Beware of such clip joints as **Legz Diamond** (622 West 47th Street; ☎ 212-977-3200; **www.legzny.com**), many of which pass out promotional flyers on Midtown streets; these are full-nudity places that bypass restrictions by serving no alcohol. Your cranberry juice will cost you dearly, and talkative women hired by the bar will attempt to pressure you into buying them even more outrageously priced drinks.

GAY NIGHTLIFE

THE LATEST SCENES CHANGE AT A DIZZYING PACE; widely available publications such as *Time Out* (**newyork.timeout.com**) and the *New York Blade* (**www.nyblade.com**) are good sources for information, as is the **Lesbian, Gay, Bisexual & Transgender Community Center** (208 West 13th Street; ☎ 212-620-7310; **www.gaycenter.org**). The following are some spots with longevity.

The granddaddy of all piano bars is **Don't Tell Mama** (343 West 46th Street; ☎ 212-757-0788; **www.donttellmamanyc.com**). **The Stonewall Inn** still stands at 53 Christopher Street (it's gone through several incarnations since the infamous 1969 riots; ☎ 212-488-2705; **www .thestonewallinn.net**). A walk down Christopher Street and environs will reveal a plethora of clubs and bars. **The Monster** (80 Grove Street; ☎ 212-924-3558; **www.manhattan-monster.com**) has an upstairs piano bar for an older crowd, plus a downstairs mirrored disco that's more of a pickup joint. The crowd's diverse, and while things can get silly, it's always fairly tasteful and safe.

Barrage (401 West 47th Street; ☎ 212-586-9390) and **Splash Bar New York** (50 West 17th Street; ☎ 212-691-0073; **www.splashbar.com**) have good pickup potential.

On the Upper East Side: the **Townhouse Bar of New York** (236 East 58th Street; ☎ 212-754-4649; **www.townhouseny.com**) is a place where Young Men Who Want to Meet Guys Who Wear Coats and Ties meet guys who wear coats and ties who want to meet Young Men Who Want to Meet Guys Who Wear Coats and Ties.

Eagle NYC (554 West 28th Street; ☎ 646-473-1866; **www.eaglenyc .com**) is the popular reincarnation of New York's most famous leather bar. Lesbian hangout **Henrietta Hudson** (438 Hudson Street; ☎ 212-924-3347; **www.henriettahudson.com**) has live bands and DJs. **Eastern Bloc** (505 East Sixth Street; ☎ 212-777-2555; **www.eastern blocnyc.com**) is small and draws a rowdy, beer-drinking, jeans-and-T-shirt crowd.

Sugarland (221 North Ninth Street, Brooklyn; ☎ 718-599-4044) is Williamsburg's hottest new gay bar, with monthly lesbian parties and a varied clientele on most nights. **Cubby Hole** (281 West 12th Street; ☎ 212-243-9041; **www.cubbyholebar.com**) is a more intimate fixture on the lesbian scene that's been around for more than 15 years.

Also outside Manhattan, check out **Excelsior Bar** (see page 440) and **Ginger's** (see page 442), both in Park Slope, Brooklyn.

COMEDY

COMEDY CLUBS ARE OFTEN LOOKED DOWN UPON by Manhattanites as strictly for tourists (or worse, for "bridge-and-tunnelers"—the derisive name for suburbanites drawn to the island for weekend entertainment). But if you must indulge in such shamefully uncosmopolitan pleasures, there are a few nationally known clubs, plus some intriguing cutting-edge comedy venues, where you can both yuk it up and feel hip.

The best mainstream clubs are **Carolines** (see page 437), **Gotham Comedy Club** (208 West 23rd Street; ☎ 212-367-9000; **www.gotham comedyclub.com**), and the **Comic Strip Live** (1568 Second Avenue; ☎ 212-861-9386; **www.comicstriplive.com**). Gotham feels serious and intimate—upscale but no baloney or showbiz touches, just a room with mic and audience. The Comic Strip, best on weekends, is even less slick. Celebs are fairly common at the Monday-night showcase at the Comic Strip, but otherwise the show's very hit-or-miss. Those three get the best-known acts and have the most upscale ambience. Beware of "new talent nights" at the big clubs: audiences paying a hefty cover with a two-drink minimum often see not the brightest young talent but those newcomers who've promised club owners they'll pack the club (and thus its coffers) with friends and family. **Laugh Lounge** (151 Essex Street; ☎ 212-614-2500; **www.laughloungenyc.com**) is a relative newcomer and boasts that it's the only comedy club on the Lower East Side. **The Com-edy Cellar** (117 MacDougal Street; ☎ 212-254-3480; **www.comedy cellar.com**) and **Stand-Up NY** (236 West 78th Street; ☎ 212-595-0850; **www.standupny.com**) are also worth visiting.

Other places offering comedic sketches and improv stylings are the **Upright Citizens Brigade Theatre** (307 West 26th Street; ☎ 212-366-9176; **www.ucbtheatre.com**) and its spin-off, **People's Improv Theater** (154 West 29th Street; ☎ 212-563-7488; **www.thepit-nyc .com**). Chances are you won't be disappointed, and performances are fairly inexpensive.

NIGHTCLUB PROFILES

Angel's Share

SECRET-HIDEAWAY COCKTAIL OASIS

8 Stuyvesant Street (second floor), East Village; ☎ 212-777-5415

Cover None. **Minimum** None. **Mixed drinks** $12–$16. **Wine** Bottles, $25–$60. **Beer** $6–$18. **Dress** Elegant casual or anything black. Dressing up is fine, but don't be flashy. **Specials** None. **Food available** Small menu of excellent Korean-Japanese snacks; great fried oysters. **Hours** Daily, 7 p.m.–2:30 a.m.

WHO GOES THERE 25 to 45; the beautiful, the hipsters, and the bohemian East Village Japanese.

WHAT GOES ON You go up steps with pink-neon banisters, turn left through the sushi restaurant, and open an unmarked door to enter a mega-atmospheric little den of hip urbanity. Inside are suave young bartenders crafting cocktails with single-minded intensity, soothing jazz played over a fine sound system, a few romantic tables with great views, and a bar filled with an interesting, intelligent, attractive clientele. Martinis are awesome, as are gimlets and fresh-fruit daiquiris (not too sweet), plus you'll find wonderful selections of spirits such as whiskey and bourbon—there's not a single dumb bottle in the room. Service is classy but utterly unpretentious. While the original mix-ologists have moved on to the equally swanky **B Flat** (277 Church Street; ☎ 212-219-2970; **www.bflat.info**), the bristling intensity of the current bartenders still electrifies the place; it's the ideal choice for an intelligent date. The "no standing" rule can make it frustratingly difficult to get in (especially on crowded weekends).

SETTING AND ATMOSPHERE A narrow sliver with a bar on one side and a dra-matic view up Third Avenue through tall, draperied windows on the other. A huge mural of an Asian angel baby sets the tone of elegance with a sardonic twist. Tables are mostly for two—this isn't a destination for groups.

IF YOU GO Fridays and Saturdays, you may find Japanese jazz duos strum-ming in a cramped corner, but the stereo is far more pleasing (yet another reason to avoid weekend prime time).

Bar 44 at Royalton Hotel

SWANKY BUT STRANGELY COZY HOTEL-LOBBY BAR

44 West 44th Street, Midtown West; ☎ 212-944-8844; www.brasseriefortyfour.com

New York Nightclubs by Neighborhood

NAME	DESCRIPTION
SOHO AND TRIBECA	
The Bubble Lounge	Champagne bar
S.O.B.'s	Latin and world music/dance nightclub
CHINATOWN, LITTLE ITALY, AND THE LOWER EAST SIDE	
Kush	Funky Moroccan-themed bar
GREENWICH VILLAGE	
The Blue Note	Jazz club
Bowlmor Lanes	Hip bowling with attitude
Cornelia Street Café	Intimate performance cafe
Smalls	Jazz club for cool cats
The Village Vanguard	Jazz club
THE EAST VILLAGE	
Angel's Share	Secret hideaway cocktail oasis
d.b.a.	Mecca for ultra-high-quality drinks
Joe's Pub	Lush nightclub
KGB	Socialist-themed literary bar
Lava Gina	Offbeat music and drink bar
Mercury Lounge	Rock showcase
Planet Rose	Kitschy karaoke lounge
Cornelia Street Café	Intimate performance cafe
CHELSEA	
Bongo	Trendy hangout/oyster bar
Slate	Sophisticated pool hall and lounge
GRAMERCY PARK AND MADISON SQUARE	
Flatiron Lounge	Chic cocktail lounge
The Ginger Man	Giant-sized beer bar

Cover None. **Minimum** None. **Mixed drinks** $15–$19. **Wine** Bottles, $35 and up; $11–$24 by the glass. **Beer** $7–$12. **Dress** Mostly suits in evenings; looser later. **Specials** None. **Food available** Light fare and desserts (from the kitchen of adjacent Brasserie 44). **Hours** Sunday–Tuesday, noon–1 a.m.; Wednesday–Saturday, noon–2 a.m.

WHO GOES THERE 30s to 60s; tourists, businessmen, pre-dinner drinkers.

WHAT GOES ON This is an ideal break-the-ice meeting place for a before-dinner

NAME	DESCRIPTION
GRAMERCY PARK AND MADISON SQUARE (CONTINUED)	
Rodeo Bar	Cowboy bar with high-quality eclectic live music
MIDTOWN WEST, TIMES SQUARE, AND THE THEATER DISTRICT	
Bar 44 at Royalton Hotel	Swanky but strangely cozy hotel lobby bar
Carolines	Comedy club
Hudson Bar	Chic hotel bar
O'Flaherty's Ale House	Irish pub after-show hideaway
Rudy's Bar and Grill	Quintessential dive bar
Swing 46	Swing dance club
MIDTOWN EAST	
Campbell Apartment	Sophisticated bar/lounge
P. J. Clarke's	Old-time New York bar
Sakagura	Hidden suave sake bar
Top of the Tower	Romantic bar/restaurant with superb views
UPPER WEST SIDE	
Smoke	Jazz club and lounge
UPPER EAST SIDE	
Café Carlyle at The Carlyle	Sophisticated New York nightspot
Club Macanudo	Upscale cigar and whiskey bar
BROOKLYN	
Barbès	Welcoming, innovative bar/performance space
Excelsior Bar	Neighborhood gay bar
Galapagos	Bar and performance space
Ginger's	Friendly gay bar with pool table
Union Hall	Neighborhood bar, music venue, and bocce court

drink, be your companions business associates, in-laws, or a hot date. It's just stylish enough to set an elegant tone, but comfy enough (lots of well-cushioned couches and chairs positioned for maximum intimacy) not to intimidate. Urbane conversation flows easily; as you look around the room, you notice that everyone seems very, very engaged, very, very glib. It's not just the clientele; it's the room. Good lighting combined with the atmospheric coziness also make this a choice spot for a late-night tête-à-tête.

At-a-glance Club Guide

ARTY

Barbès
Cornelia Street Café
Galapagos
KGB
Kush
Mercury Lounge
Union Hall

BEER/NEW YORK LANDMARKS

The Ginger Man
O'Flaherty's Ale House
P. J. Clarke's
Rudy's Bar and Grill

BOWLING

Bowlmor Lanes

CHIC/TRENDY

Bongo
Campbell Apartment
Excelsior Bar
Flatiron Lounge
Hudson Bar

COMEDY

Carolines

COZY

Angel's Share
Barbès
The Bubble Lounge
O'Flaherty's Ale House

DANCE/DISCO

Joe's Pub
Lava Gina
Rodeo Bar
S.O.B.'s
Swing 46
Webster Hall

GAY

Excelsior Bar
Ginger's

HOTEL

Bar 44 at Royalton Hotel
Café Carlyle at The Carlyle
Hudson Bar at Hudson Hotel
Top of the Tower Bar & Lounge at
    the Beekman Tower Hotel

JAZZ CLUBS

The Blue Note
Smalls
Smoke
The Village Vanguard

KARAOKE

Planet Rose

MUSIC VENUES—VARIOUS GENRES

Barbès
Cornelia Street Cafe
Galapagos
Joe's Pub
Lava Gina
Mercury Lounge
S.O.B.'s
Union Hall

POOL

Slate

SAKE BARS/JAPANESE

Angel's Share
Sakagura

THEME

Café Carlyle at The Carlyle

WHISKEY/COCKTAILS/CHAMPAGNE

Angel's Share
The Bubble Lounge
Campbell Apartment
Club Macanudo
d.b.a.
Flatiron Lounge
Little Branch

SETTING AND ATMOSPHERE The recently renovated cocktail area and restaurant share a similar wood-and-leather design but in different shades, from rich chocolate to honey-colored to pale beige. The comfortable seats invite guests for pre- and post-theater drinks or a meal at the attached brasserie.

IF YOU GO Try one of the signature cocktails from the seasonal menu.

Barbès

WELCOMING, INNOVATIVE BAR-PERFORMANCE SPACE

**376 Ninth Street (near Sixth Avenue), Park Slope, Brooklyn;
☎ 347-422-0248; www.barbesbrooklyn.com**

Cover Only for the event space; strongly suggested donation of $10. **Minimum** None. **Mixed drinks** $6–$10. **Wine** $6–$8 by the glass. **Beer** $4–$9. **Dress** Casual or cool. **Specials** Happy hour Monday–Friday, 5–7 p.m. ($2 off any drink). **Food available** Just peanuts. **Hours** Monday–Thursday, 5 p.m.–2 a.m.; Friday and Saturday, noon–4 a.m.; Sunday, noon–2 a.m.

WHO GOES THERE 20s and up; locals, musicians, artists.

WHAT GOES ON Socializing, hanging out, and an interesting array of live events.

SETTING AND ATMOSPHERE Entrance is right off the street in a residential neighborhood, so loud crowds and events are not encouraged. One enters the main area, which features a long bar along one wall with tables and stools narrowly opposite as well as a nook with stools and table on the side between the end of the bar and front window. The performance space is past the bar into a smaller enclosure, and this is where attractions such as poetry readings, art-house films, acoustic guitarists, and unplugged brass bands squeeze in.

IF YOU GO Know that space gets tight when a popular event takes place, but if you persevere, you'll find a nook or standing position where you can at least drink your beer. On the first Sunday of every month, it hosts a 7 p.m. reading series, which has featured Paul Auster, Chuck Klosterman, and other luminaries.

Blue Note

JAZZ CLUB

**131 West Third Street, Greenwich Village; ☎ 212-475-8592;
www.bluenote.net**

Cover $10–$65 at tables, $5–$45 at bar; brunch, $24.50. **Minimum** $5 at tables, 1 drink at bar. **Mixed drinks** $9–$20. **Wine** Bottles, $30–$200; $9–$15 by the glass. **Beer** $6–$8. **Dress** Fancy-schmancy. **Specials** Monday nights are usually bargains (rarely more than $20 for a table); Fridays and Saturdays after the last set, late-night groove series until 4 a.m. for $5–$10 cover. **Food available** Full menu, for the gastronomically reckless. **Hours** Shows at 8 and 10:30 every night, and 12:30 on most Fridays and Saturdays; Sunday, jazz brunch, noon–6 p.m.; shows at 12:30 and 2:30 p.m.

WHO GOES THERE 22 to 90; tourists.

WHAT GOES ON It's amazing how many tourists think the Blue Note is a historic jazz institution, even though the place didn't open until the late date of 1981. But hordes of visitors continue to pay stratospheric prices to sit in uncomfortable chairs packed *way* too close together in a small, dark, boxy room. It's worth it, however, when the Blue Note brings in acts who normally don't play clubs (Herbie Hancock, Dave Brubeck, etc.), many of whom shine in the more intimate setting. But the entertainment here can be more "jazzish" than jazz; performers such as Roberta Flack, Tito Puente, and Steve Allen have played here. The Village Vanguard (see page 454) and Iridium (see page 421) are far more pure-minded in their bookings.

SETTING AND ATMOSPHERE Claustrophobic and tacky, done in dark tones and mirrors. A cheesy neon Manhattan skyline is the only "classy" touch.

IF YOU GO As at all jazz clubs in New York, avoid crowds by arriving for the last set or during bad weather (budget option: the revamped bar area now has good sight lines). Late jam sessions can be quite good.

Bongo

TRENDY HANGOUT–OYSTER BAR

299 Tenth Avenue, Chelsea; ☎ 212-947-3654; www.bongonyc.com

Cover None. **Minimum** None. **Mixed drinks** $9–$14 (but they're huge). **Wine** $8–$10 by the glass. **Beer** $6–$8. **Dress** Cool; suits may feel out of place after 8 p.m. **Specials** Complimentary sangria on Sundays, 5–6 p.m. **Food available** Superb oysters on the half shell, perhaps the best in town. **Hours** Monday–Tuesday, 5 p.m.–midnight; Wednesday, 5 p.m.–1 a.m.; Thursday–Saturday, 5 p.m.–2 a.m.

WHO GOES THERE 21 to 40; stylish small groups, couples, singles.

WHAT GOES ON While there are times when one wants to be in the center of things (and there's no better place than Manhattan for feeling "plugged in"), there are times when one prefers to retreat to the sidelines. Bongo is a tiny storefront hardly worth a second look from the outside. Yet despite the gritty area, you'll certainly not be roughing it inside, where cool ambience, great shellfish, and oversized cocktails are in the offing. It's no bargain, but there is a compelling coolness factor of knowing to take your date or business associate to this hip little place on the West Side. For those who like to nurse their drinks (the pace is slooow here) and turn the intensity down a notch—and chat up companions away from bustling crowds and prying ears—this alluring scene is a five-minute cab ride from Midtown. The owners have also re-created the vibe with a bigger, brighter version of Bongo in the West Village (395 West Street; ☎ 212-675-6555), just a block from the Hudson River.

SETTING AND ATMOSPHERE A tiny but chic storefront with ironically retro couches and chairs, soft lighting, and sultry music. The comfortable bar faces a backlit stage of trendy vodka bottles and other intriguing containers. Staff is aloof and cooler-than-thou (chalk it up to mystique).

IF YOU GO Don't miss the extraordinarily good (and well-priced) oysters, especially the rich, sweet Kumamotos. Mixed drinks are good (bartenders spray your glass with atomized vermouth for a *really* dry martini).

The place can get crowded later, though there's usually space at the bar. Skip the expensive lobster rolls (lots of fresh lobster, but overwhelmed by olive oil and basil).

Bowlmor Lanes

BOWLING WITH ATTITUDE

110 University Place (between 12th and 13th streets), Greenwich Village; ☎ 212-255-8188; www.bowlmor.com

Cover Changes frequently and depends on time, but expect to pay $10–$15 per person per game and $5–$8 for shoe rental. Ages 18 and over after 7 p.m. on weeknights; 21 and over after 7 p.m. on weekends. **Minimum** None. **Mixed drinks** $8–$16. **Wine** $7 and up by the glass. **Beer** $5–$8. **Dress** Jeans and T-shirts (though some do dress up). **Specials** Monday night, unlimited bowling, $24 per person; kids' birthday parties available weekend afternoons. **Food available** Surprisingly good (eat at the bar or take delivery directly to your lane!), including some of Manhattan's better burgers; beware the $25 credit-card minimum. **Hours** Monday and Thursday, 4 p.m.–2 a.m.; Tuesday and Wednesday, 4 p.m.–1 a.m.; Friday and Saturday, 11 a.m.–3:30 a.m.; Sunday, 11 a.m.–midnight.

WHO GOES THERE Stylishly pierced and ironic 20- to 30-somethings.

WHAT GOES ON Very, very hip, very, very ironic bowling, with a chic young crowd sprinkled with some oblivious oldsters. As the place is fond of saying, "This is not your father's bowling alley."

SETTING AND ATMOSPHERE A real old-time bowling alley (built in 1938) partially morphed into a way-cool hangout. Just because the ball-return lanes are painted baby blue and balls and pins are fluorescent pink and yellow doesn't mean Uncle Ernie and Aunt Ethel (who've come here for 30 years) don't feel at home bowling a few frames among the packs of 22-year-olds. There's a handsome old semicircular bar and old-fashioned tile floors. The place hasn't been totally revised—this is not so much a complete MTV makeover of a 1950s bowling alley as a slightly trippy touch-up. Enough of the old remains that the effect is more eerie than contrived. If you want your kitsch shiny and brand new, go upstairs to **Carnival** (☎ 212-255-8188; **www.carnivalnyc.com**), the bowling alley's new circus-themed club.

IF YOU GO Call ahead to check lane availability—this is not Paramus, New Jersey, so there's space for only a limited number of lanes. Try glow-in-the-dark bowling night (call for schedule).

The Bubble Lounge

CHAMPAGNE BAR

228 West Broadway, SoHo; ☎ 212-431-3433; www.bubblelounge.com

Cover None. **Minimum** $25 at tables. **Mixed drinks** $15–$16. **Wine** Champagnes $16–$22 per glass, less for half glasses. **Beer** Why bother? **Dress** Casual chic, dark colors. Dress code is strictly enforced. No sneakers, gym or workout garments, sandals, baseball caps, military or combat fatigues, or swimwear. **Specials** Happy hour, Monday–Friday, 5–7 p.m.; check Web site calendar for live music and cultural events. **Food available** Typical Champagne accompaniments, such as artisanal cheeses, salads, salmon, grilled sandwiches, crepes; all quite pricey. **Hours** Monday–Wednesday, 5 p.m.–1 a.m.; Thursday, 5 p.m.–2 a.m.; Friday and Saturday, 5 p.m.–4 a.m.; closed Sunday but available for private parties.

WHO GOES THERE 21 to 60; slinky, well-heeled lounge chicsters and locals.

WHAT GOES ON A Champagne bar where chic poseurs peacefully coexist with more down-to-earth locals, all feeling very, very grown-up. The bubbly itself is quaffed more as a style thing than as serious wine pursuit (sniff and swirl your glass like an oenophile here, and you'll get some strange looks), but there's no denying that sipping Dom Pérignon without shelling out big bucks for a whole bottle is a good thing. Twenty-four Champagnes are available by the glass, more than 250 Champagnes and sparkling wines by the bottle. A competing Champagne bar, **Flûte,** has two locations (205 West 54th Street; ☎ 212-265-5169; 40 East 20th Street; ☎ 212-529-7870; **www.flutebar.com**).

SETTING AND ATMOSPHERE An L-shaped space lush with red velvet draperies, exposed brick, couches, flickering candles, highly lacquered wood, and highly preened waitresses. Dracula would feel at home.

IF YOU GO Check out the downstairs Krug room, a Champagne-wine cellar with waitress service. Reservations are strongly recommended for parties of six or more.

Café Carlyle at The Carlyle

SOPHISTICATED NEW YORK NIGHTSPOT

35 East 76th Street, Upper East Side; ☎ 212-744-1600; www.thecarlyle.com

Cover $75–$150/table, $40–$100/bar. **Minimum** None. **Mixed drinks** $12 and up. **Wine** $10–$13.50 by the glass. **Beer** $10–$12. **Dress** Jackets required, of course, but you'd do well to pull out all the stops and wear your very best duds. **Specials** Save on the cover charge by watching from the cafe (reservations aren't accepted, though, and you'll pay full price even if there's only standing room). **Food available** Old-fashioned New York food served by old-fashioned professional New York waiters—expensive and available 6:30 p.m.–midnight. **Hours** Monday–Thursday, 7 p.m.–1:30 a.m., show at 8:45 p.m.; Friday and Saturday, 7 p.m.–1:30 a.m., shows at 8:45 p.m. and 10:45 p.m.; closed Sunday.

WHO GOES THERE 25 to 90; grown-ups.

WHAT GOES ON Pianist-singer Bobby Short was synonymous with Café Carlyle, and his death has left a void that aims to be filled by other talented musicians, including Judy Collins and the Eddy Davis New Orleans jazz band (often featuring Woody Allen on clarinet).

SETTING AND ATMOSPHERE One of the most famous cabarets in the world, Café Carlyle sets a nearly unreachable standard of elegant and intimate supper-club ambience. A splendid assortment of restored Marcel Vertes murals adds greatly to the magic. Only recently, the room was renovated by raising the ceilings and restoring the bar, but everything still remains classic New York.

IF YOU GO Have a low-key drink before or after the show (or instead of the show entirely if you're on a budget) in the hotel's Bemelmans Bar, an urbane time capsule of an older New York with fine—if less famous—piano entertainment.

The Campbell Apartment

SOPHISTICATED BAR-LOUNGE

15 Vanderbilt Avenue entrance at Grand Central Terminal, Midtown East; ☎ 212-953-0409; www.hospitalityholdings.com

Cover None. **Minimum** None. **Mixed drinks** $14–$18. **Wine** $9–$20 by the glass (Champagne also available). **Beer** Bottled only, $7–$10. **Dress** Business, chic (sneakers, T-shirts, shorts, etc., are not allowed, but smoking jacket and ivory-handled umbrellas are not required). **Specials** None. **Food available** No, just peanuts. **Hours** Monday–Thursday, noon–1 a.m.; Friday, noon–2 a.m.; Saturday, 3 p.m.–2 a.m.; Sunday, 3–11 p.m.

WHO GOES THERE 20s to 60s; commuters, after-work suits, the style-conscious.

WHAT GOES ON Drinking, socializing, and refined cruising.

SETTING AND ATMOSPHERE Apart from when the bar is buzzing with after-work socializing, the vibe is well suited for indulging in a vintage cocktail and admiring the scenery. Formerly an office–social area bought by a successful businessman in Grand Central Terminal, the space features a beamed ceiling with intricate painted detail, a stone fireplace, and a huge, multipaned leaded-glass window behind the bar. It's worth visiting just to see the grand interior, even if you don't want a drink.

IF YOU GO Unless you're commuting, try to arrive outside rush hour, which would be either pre–5 p.m. or post–9 p.m. The timing will give you a better chance to find a seat and enjoy the decor as opposed to rubbing elbows or backs with dozens of standing patrons eager for a drink. Specialty cocktails include the Vanderbilt Punch and the Oxford Swizzle.

Carolines

COMEDY CLUB

1626 Broadway, Times Square; ☎ 212-757-4100; www.carolines.com

Cover $15–$45, depending on the act. Must be 18 or older. **Minimum** 2 drinks. **Mixed drinks** $8–$10. **Wine** $7–$9 by the glass. **Beer** $5–$8. **Dress** Casual. **Specials** None. **Food available** T.G.I. Fridays–type menu in the monstrously commercial upstairs Comedy Nation restaurant. Snack menu in the club. **Hours** Sunday–Thursday, 5:30–11:30 p.m.; Friday and Saturday, 5:30 p.m.– 2 a.m.; shows at about 7 and 9:30 p.m. Monday–Wednesday, 8 and 10:30 p.m. Thursday and Sunday, and 8 p.m., 10:30 p.m., and 12:30 a.m. Friday and Saturday. Show times vary by performance (call for info). Box-office hours are Saturday–Wednesday, 10 a.m.–11 p.m.; Thursday and Friday, 9 a.m.–11 p.m.

WHO GOES THERE 21 to 60s; suburbanites on weekends, tourists and fans during the week.

WHAT GOES ON With Carolines's location smack-dab in the middle of Times Square, its 10:30 p.m. late set is a magnet for theatergoers with insatiable appetites for more entertainment. Like Broadway these days, the club relies on a steady diet of Big Names to pull in crowds, and this well-run operation—the most upscale of the big New York comedy clubs—gives them their money's worth.

SETTING AND ATMOSPHERE Though the Comedy Nation restaurant at street level is an utterly soulless space (comedy insiders call it "Planet Ha-Ha-Hollywood"), the actual club area, downstairs, is a nice, loungey hangout, a decent place for drinks even if you're not attending the show. The space doesn't have the mic-and-a-room pure minimalism of Gotham, but on entering it, one feels that something exciting is about to occur—and with the top-flight talent booked here, it often does.

Club Macanudo

UPSCALE CIGAR AND WHISKEY BAR

**26 East 63rd Street, Upper East Side; ☎ 212-752-8200;
www.clubmacanudonyc.com**

Cover None. **Minimum** None. **Scotch** $10–$300. **Wine** Vintage, tawny ports $12–$40 by the glass. **Beer** $7–$12. **Dress** Collared shirts for men, no sneakers, T-shirts, shorts, or flip-flops. **Specials** None. **Food available** Overpriced; stick with appetizers, tapas. **Hours** Monday and Tuesday, noon–1 a.m.; Wednesday–Saturday, noon–1:30 a.m.; Sunday, noon–8 p.m.

WHO GOES THERE 30s to 65; middle-aged suits, often stag but some towing either bored wives or trophy babes; some younger schmoozers.

WHAT GOES ON Some might expect that cigars and whiskey are fun things to be enjoyed lightheartedly. These people will not dig Club Macanudo. This place takes itself seriously. If it all wasn't very, very serious, people might not be inclined to fork over $700 a year to rent tiny personal humidors here (complete with shiny brass nameplates). They might wince at the over-the-top chummy, clubby, woody interior, or they might even break a smile. But the scotch selection *is* pretty serious stuff—it's America's only bar serving rare bottlings from the **Scotch Malt Whisky Society**—and the friendly bartenders are knowledgeable guides for neophytes. Go late enough that plenty of scotch has already been ingested, and you may strike up a stogie-based friendship with an exec who'd otherwise never take your calls. Varying genres of live music are featured.

SETTING AND ATMOSPHERE It's like being in an enormous cigar box (complete with wooden Indians) or spending time in an exclusive men's club.

IF YOU GO There are more than 150 cigars to choose from, at prices ranging from $7 to $180 (most are about $15). Don't worry too much about ordering the wrong thing; there are few dumb choices, drink- and cigar-wise. But do bone up on proper stogie cutting and lighting.

The Cornelia Street Café

INTIMATE PERFORMANCE CAFE

**29 Cornelia Street (between Bleecker and West Fourth streets),
Greenwich Village; ☎ 212-989-9319; www.corneliastreetcafe.com**

Cover Only downstairs; varies from $5 to $20. **Minimum** 1 drink per set. For food, there is a $25 minimum for credit-card use. **Mixed drinks** $7–$9. **Wine** $6–$10 by the glass. **Beer** $5–$8. **Dress** Casual. **Specials** None. **Food available** Yes, from snacks to full menu; $13–$22. **Hours** Daily, restaurant open from 10 a.m., but downstairs space usually open from 6 p.m. (unless there's an afternoon event); closes at midnight on weeknights and 1 a.m. on Friday and Saturday.

WHO GOES THERE 20s to 60s; regulars, the avant-garde.

WHAT GOES ON Listening, watching, and/or conversation.

SETTING AND ATMOSPHERE Although the cafe has several eating spaces, including the sidewalk in fair weather, this profile focuses on the snug downstairs performance space, which feels a bit like a blue-tinged wine cellar. The narrow quarters allow customers to sit at the long sides of the rectangular room. In spite of what seems like a minuscule stage, performers and five-plus-person bands use it and entertain happy audiences.

IF YOU GO Have an objective to see or hear an interesting, potentially experimental performance. The cafe has been in operation since 1977 and is very much a Greenwich Village institution, especially for artists and free thinkers. The restaurant offers breakfast through dinner and is especially popular for brunch. The downstairs space, which is often open only in the evenings, showcases events almost nightly. The cover is reasonable, and if the event isn't sold out and sounds appealing, give it a try.

d.b.a.

MECCA FOR ULTRA-HIGH-QUALITY DRINKS

41 First Avenue, East Village; ☎ 212-475-5097; www.drinkgoodstuff.com

Cover None. **Minimum** None. **Mixed drinks** $6 and up. **Wine** $8–$12 by the glass. **Beer** $6–$25. **Dress** Casual but hip. **Specials** Happy hour every day, 1–7:30 p.m. ($1 off everything). **Food available** None. **Hours** Daily, 1 p.m.–4 a.m.

WHO GOES THERE 21 to 50; drink freaks, ranging from nerdy home brewers to assured sybarites.

WHAT GOES ON No Schlitz here; rather, you'll find hand-pumped British (and British-style) ales, a whole bunch of taps (dated, so you can gauge freshness), and zillions of bottles. This is one of the few places in New York that serves properly poured ales and lagers at the proper temperature (never frigid, hand-pumps at cellar temperature) in the proper glasses, and there's a fine bourbon, scotch, and tequila collection as well. Servers have attitude, as do some of the customers.

SETTING AND ATMOSPHERE Low-lit, contemporary, and spare, this invariably crowded spot doesn't have much decor to distract from the reverent drinking, but it's certainly far more refined than your average beer hall. Nice garden out back, open in warm weather.

IF YOU GO Not sure what to order? Ask advice from any of the beer geeks at the bar, and you'll be guided by some of the city's most knowledgeable drinkers.

Excelsior Bar

NEIGHBORHOOD GAY BAR

**390 Fifth Avenue (between Sixth and Seventh streets), Brooklyn;
☎ 718-832-1599**

Cover None. **Minimum** None. **Mixed drinks** $6–$8. **Wine** $6–$7 by the glass. **Beer** On tap and bottled, $3–$6. **Dress** Casual or cool. **Specials** Happy hour, Monday–Friday, 6–8 p.m.; Saturday and Sunday, 2–8 p.m. **Food available** None, but you may call for deliveries. **Hours** Monday–Friday, 6 p.m.–4 a.m.; Saturday and Sunday, 2 p.m.–4 a.m.

WHO GOES THERE 20s to 50s; locals, gay, straight, and hip.

WHAT GOES ON There's usually a good rapport at the bar—whether you're here just to get a drink or to do some subtle cruising. From pretty boys to straight men and everything in between, all will enjoy themselves.

SETTING AND ATMOSPHERE Friendly, relaxed, and sophisticated-cool atmosphere. Sleek decor that mixes pseudo-Mondrian–esque designs with 1970s tackiness. There's a lot of red and angular lines; overall, the setting is crisp and clean. Old fans on the ceiling loom over clean wooden floors.

IF YOU GO Check out the jukebox, and after your selection has played, spend some time outside on the deck, or go downstairs into the garden and admire the two plastic pink flamingoes. You could also bar-hop to **Ginger's** (see page 442) across the street or get an order of tasty French fries at **The Park Slope Chip Shop** (383 Fifth Avenue; ☎ 718-832-7701; **www.chipshopnyc.com**).

Flatiron Lounge

CHIC SPECIALIST COCKTAILS

**37 West 19th Street, Gramercy Park; ☎ 212-727-7741;
www.flatironlounge.com**

Cover None. **Minimum** None. **Mixed drinks** $12–$16. **Wine** $8–$12 by the glass. **Beer** $8, but you don't come here for beer. **Dress** Chic or suited. **Specials** Downstairs room may be on offer for parties and special events. **Food available** Only free bar nibbles. **Hours** Sunday–Wednesday, 5 p.m.–2 a.m.; Thursday–Saturday, 5 p.m.–4 a.m.

WHO GOES THERE 20s to 40s; cocktail connoisseurs, stylish lounge types mixed with business suits and professionals.

WHAT GOES ON Cocktail consumption, socializing, looking fantastic.

SETTING AND ATMOSPHERE Great setting that comes at a price for the drinks. The space is Art Deco–inspired and –designed, with an arched ceiling at the entrance, dark wood, and plush, private group banquettes along the wall, beside open tables and a 30-foot bar. The 1920s-vintage bar was renovated to its "original splendor." There's a romantic quality to the place.

IF YOU GO Indulge in one or two of the bar's special cocktails using some of its own infused spirits; alternatively, you could order a flight of cocktails ($22) that provides a selection and avoids excessive alcohol consumption. The mixologist prepares drinks such as a "Metropolis," which includes Pearl vodka infused with green apples and finished with a touch of French apple brandy cider. A spiced pear drink is made with vodka infused with pear and cloves. Some drinks are prepared for certain seasons only.

Galapagos

BAR AND PERFORMANCE SPACE

16 Main Street, DUMBO, Brooklyn; ☎ 718-222-8500; www.galapagosartspace.com

Cover Free–$20, depending on the performance or film. **Minimum** None. **Mixed drinks** $6–$9. **Wine** $6–$10 by the glass. **Beer** $5–$8. **Dress** Grunge, casual, or simply cool. **Specials** Frequent special events; happy hour Monday–Saturday, 6–8 p.m. **Food available** None, but you may call for deliveries. **Hours** Sunday–Thursday, 6 p.m.–2 a.m.; Friday and Saturday, 6 p.m.–4 a.m.

WHO GOES THERE 20s to 50s; locals, art set, hipsters.

WHAT GOES ON Galapagos is a solid reason to get out of Manhattan for an evening. It has won several awards of distinction for its performance space, for its bar, and for being a top nightclub destination. These accolades are well deserved. There's almost always something going on—whether it be a DJ, an art installation, a film, music, theater, or a dance performance. You can go simply to get a drink or to soak up a bit of culture, no pressure—it's all very laid-back and comfortable.

SETTING AND ATMOSPHERE A multilevel space with curving couches and banisters, dim lighting, and winding walkways that lead to seating areas and a bare wooden stage. Be careful not to slip into the 1,600-square-foot lake, which forms a series of ponds below you and serves to heat and cool the building. It's part of the owners' effort to make this New York's first LEED-certified "green" cultural venue.

IF YOU GO Combine your visit to Galapagos with an exploration of DUMBO, where a thriving art scene, converted warehouse spaces, and sprawling waterfront parks have made it a favorite place for Brooklynites to live and play.

The Ginger Man

GIANT-SIZED BEER BAR

11 East 36th Street, Gramercy Park; ☎ 212-532-3740; www.gingerman-ny.com

Cover None. **Minimum** None. **Mixed drinks** $7 and up. **Wine** $5–$12 by the glass. **Beer** $5–$10. **Dress** Casual. **Specials** None. **Food available** Salads, soups, sandwiches, and Guinness Stout stew. **Hours** Monday–Thursday, 11:30–2 a.m.; Friday, 11:30–4 a.m.; Saturday, 12:30 p.m.–4 a.m.; Sunday, 3 p.m.–midnight.

WHO GOES THERE 21 to 60; throngs of businessmen and yuppies after work, varied at other times.

WHAT GOES ON On paper, this is New York's best beer hall. It boasts more than 60 mind-boggling taps, nearly all well chosen, plus decent Guinness stew to eat, friendly bartenders, and a comfy living room in the back. Prices are fair, and doors are open late, unheard of in this early-to-bed neighborhood. But there are problems: the beer's too cold (fine for light lagers, but some of the fancier British and Belgian ales turn flavorless at ballpark temperature), and peak hours—5:30 to 10 p.m. and all night on weekends—can be a crowded hell of noise.

SETTING AND ATMOSPHERE The huge, high-ceilinged space is classic New York, dominated by a mile-long bar and copper-plated Wall o' Taps. There are tables up front by the floor-to-ceiling windows and a relaxing parlor in back with sofas and armchairs.

IF YOU GO Midafternoons and late weeknights, you'll have the place largely to yourself; bring 20 or 30 friends, no problem!

Ginger's

FRIENDLY GAY BAR

363 Fifth Avenue (between Fifth and Sixth streets), Brooklyn; ☎ 718-788-0924

Cover None. **Minimum** None. **Mixed drinks** $6–$9. **Wine** $6 by the glass. **Beer** $4–$7. **Dress** Anything goes. **Specials** Happy hour Monday–Friday, 5–8 p.m. **Food available** None. **Hours** Monday–Friday, 5 p.m.–4 a.m.; Saturday and Sunday, noon–4 a.m.

WHO GOES THERE 20s to 70s; locals, gay, straight; truly diverse crowd.

WHAT GOES ON This is a great neighborhood bar, embracing all kinds. Lesbians are especially welcome. Amenities include a pool table, an outdoor garden, and the jukebox. Many have hailed the jukebox as being quite varied, but it sometimes plays a little too much Melissa Etheridge. Camaraderie is rampant, and you needn't sip your drink alone for long.

SETTING AND ATMOSPHERE The front part of the space is narrow, with the bar spanning one side. This is a very lively area and tends to get noisy and crowded quickly. The regulars know each other, and it's a good place to people-watch. The back room is more spacious and conducive to a quieter conversation—unless there's a dispute at the pool table. Ginger's is packed with knickknacks on the walls and loads of black-and-white photos. It's an incredibly cozy and homey space.

IF YOU GO Consider playing pool in the back room—but be aware that some of the ladies take their game very seriously. When it's warm, you can enjoy the outdoor garden.

Hudson Bar

ELEGANT HOTEL BAR

356 West 58th Street, Midtown West; ☎ 212-554-6217; www.hudsonhotel.com

Cover None. **Minimum** None. **Mixed drinks** $12–$20. **Wine** Bottles, $50 and up; $9–$17 by the glass; Cognac, $9–$35 by the glass. **Beer** $7–$9. **Dress** Casual dressy to ultra-chic or interestingly different; black always works. **Specials** None. **Food available** None, but hotel has restaurant and other food options. **Hours** Sunday–Wednesday, 5 p.m.–2 a.m.; Thursday–Saturday, 5 p.m.–3 a.m.

WHO GOES THERE 22 to 50; the beautiful, the trendy (and wannabes), and those interested in modern architecture.

WHAT GOES ON This is a great place to go when you're on an expense account, on an expensive date, or out for some extravagant fun. The Hudson Bar oozes cool and style, and it still manages to offer a genuinely friendly staff. The DJ nights aren't particularly stunning—many prefer the CDs pumped through the speakers on other evenings.

SETTING AND ATMOSPHERE Expectations are high when you enter an Ian Schrager hotel, and you won't be disappointed with the Hudson. Subtlety is key from the sidewalk until you enter through the glass doors and proceed up the chartreuse-hued, illuminated escalators. Once off the escalators, turn around and walk up a few stairs to the Hudson Bar. Before the stairs, there are a few tables in hidden corners with low light. Up the stairs, you're met with a long bar and a vast floor composed of large, illuminated, square tiles. There's plenty of space—one wall has pillowed banquettes with clear tables and a mixture of faux-period and ultra-modern, clear-plastic, high-backed chairs. The ceiling isn't too high, but you won't mind as you sip a strawbellini (strawberry puree and Champagne) and gaze at the dozens of candles throughout the room; your eyes may even happen upon a famous face.

IF YOU GO Don't go if you're having a bad hair day. Also visit Hudson's **Private Park**—a beautifully decorated outdoor bar that can be viewed through the lobby. In fair weather, this bar is usually open all day until 1 a.m.; it's closed during colder months. It has incredibly comfy chairs and love seats; you could easily become addicted to the atmosphere. Coffee and food are available here. During the winter, you could also try Hudson's **Library** bar, which is wood-paneled and cozy but not particularly chic.

Joe's Pub

NIGHTCLUB

425 Lafayette Street, East Village; ☎ 212-539-8778 for dinner reservations and show tickets (11 a.m.–5 p.m.), ☎ 212-967-7555 for show tickets (10 a.m.–9 p.m.); www.joespub.com

Cover $10–$35. **Minimum** Usually 2 drinks or $12 food minimum. **Mixed drinks** $10–$14. **Wine** $12 and up by the glass. **Beer** $6–$9. **Dress** Elegant on cabaret nights, elegantly sexy on other nights. **Specials** $25 prix-fixe dinner, 6–7:30 p.m. **Food available** Full menu until 12:30 a.m. **Hours** Daily, 6 p.m.–2 a.m.; shows usually start around 7, 9:30, and/or 11:30 p.m.

WHO GOES THERE 30s to 60s; a smart, chic set (younger later).

WHAT GOES ON Lots of cabaret (the more theatrical style, à la Ute Lemper—this is no piano bar). Also some rock, pop, and R&B—Amy Winehouse, Macy Gray, Norah Jones, Leonard Cohen, David Byrne, and countless others have played here. That's not to mention the jazz, world music, and well-chosen alternative bands (with music kept at a reasonable volume). The name is a joke—"Joe" is Joseph Papp, the highly respected director of the Public Theater, and this certainly is no mere pub . . . though it makes a good pun.

SETTING AND ATMOSPHERE Carpeted, with high ceilings, French windows, and softly glowing lamps. Highly atmospheric (where are the fog machines?) and very dramatic (not surprising, given the locale inside the Public Theater), Joe's Pub feels like a 1930s musical set—Marlene Dietrich would fit in well here. Yet it's not at all kitschy or contrived; it's just a great, dark, sexy, transportive place to dance, drink, or listen to music.

IF YOU GO Reserve tickets ahead of time. And don't forget to mix your music with some drama by enjoying a film or theater performance in the Public Theater.

KGB

SOCIALIST-THEMED LITERARY BAR

85 East Fourth Street, East Village; ☎ 212-505-3360; www.kgbbar.com

Cover None. **Minimum** None. **Mixed drinks** $6–$9. **Wine** $6–$8 by the glass. **Beer** $5–$7. **Dress** Understated. **Specials** None. **Food available** None. **Hours** Daily, 7 p.m.–4 a.m.; readings, 7–9 p.m.

WHO GOES THERE 21 to 40s; the literati, bookworms, activists, vodka-lovers.

WHAT GOES ON The age of the Beats in New York is long gone, but literary talents have been assembling to drink, discuss, and read at KGB since the early 1990s. The socialist slant of the venue isn't just posturing—in the 1940s, the building housed a socialist gathering place called the Ukrainian Labor Home. Don't expect to have political ideology forced down your throat, though. The focus here is on literature. You can catch fiction readings every Sunday, poetry on Mondays, nonfiction on Tuesdays, and a changing schedule of styles and genres during the rest of the week. All readings start at 7 p.m. Notable past readers include Philip Gourevitch, Jonathan Lethem, Francine Prose, and Joyce Carol Oates.

SETTING AND ATMOSPHERE Not surprisingly, red is the dominant color here, covering the walls, drapes, and seat cushions. Almost everything else is black. Nice selections of vodka and whiskey are served from the dark wood bar while framed portraits of socialist icons and Soviet flags loom overhead.

IF YOU GO Check the schedule of readings online. It's comprehensive and up-to-date, and will often give detailed background on upcoming readers. Also, leave the credit cards at home. These commies take only American greenbacks.

Kush

FUNKY MOROCCAN-THEMED BAR WITH VARIED ENTERTAINMENT

191 Chrystie Street (between Stanton and Rivington streets), Lower East Side; ☎ 212-677-7328; www.thekushnyc.com

Cover None. **Minimum** None. **Mixed drinks** $8–$14. **Wine** Not big selection, but has Lebanese wine, $8 by the glass. **Beer** Bottles, $5–$10. **Dress** Casual hip. **Specials** None. **Food available** Middle Eastern snacks, including fresh mint tea. **Hours** Wednesday–Saturday, 7 p.m.–4 a.m.; closed Sunday–Tuesday.

WHO GOES THERE 20s to 40s; locals, hipsters, smokers, and those interested in world music, international DJs, and belly dancing.

WHAT GOES ON Live, DJ, or "organic electronic" music played each night. Kush offers interesting entertainment, including belly dancing, world-class DJs, percussion, and Bulgarian harmonics. This is one of the few places where smoking (albeit hookahs) is permitted.

SETTING AND ATMOSPHERE Kush has a funky vibe, but it has gone a bit upscale recently and has (shock, horror) a velvet rope outside. Luckily, the rope isn't very hard to pass, so it may be in place to keep an eye on capacity. The Moroccan feel pervades, with dark lighting and Moorish touches. The space is bigger than you might expect, with a front and back bar and a central space that gets roped off for special events. All sections are connected by narrow passages.

IF YOU GO Make sure you catch some of the entertainment, and if you are inclined to smoke, rent a hookah with a choice of specially flavored tobaccos for $18 (inhaling not required).

Lava Gina

OFFBEAT MUSIC AND DRINK BAR

116 Avenue C (between Seventh and Eighth streets), East Village;
☎ **212-477-9319; www.lavagina.com**

Cover Not usually. **Minimum** None. **Mixed drinks** $10–$16. **Wine** $7–$10; bottles from $28. **Beer** Bottled only, $6–$10. **Dress** Casual, cool, or funky. **Specials** Happy hour Monday–Thursday, all night; Friday, until 10 p.m. **Food available** Tapas selection, $6–$8. **Hours** Tuesday–Saturday, 7 p.m.–4 a.m.; closed Sunday and Monday except for private parties.

WHO GOES THERE 20s to 40s; locals, world-music-DJ junkies.

WHAT GOES ON Sipping, socializing, and music appreciation.

SETTING AND ATMOSPHERE Unless one is averse to genitalia nuance, the distinctive V-shaped bar and overwhelming red hues in the room create a welcoming and positive vibe. Wooden African sculptures adorn the walls, as do velvet curtains by the windows. Although there's no grit, there's no cookie-cutter look for the clientele either. DJs spin nightly in the far corner, beyond the V. A medium-sized space, which makes the V-bar a definitive centerpiece.

IF YOU GO Don't be put off by the name. The eclectic music choices (modern world sounds, including material from Asia, the Middle East, Eastern Europe, South America, and Africa) are deftly spun, and Lava Gina sometimes features live music. Bartenders aren't warm, but they are certainly efficient. Specialty cocktails include the spicy Lavapolitan and the Giant Gina, which is a nod toward a communal drinkfest for close company, as it's 48 ounces of martini and costs $70.

Mercury Lounge

ROCK SHOWCASE

217 East Houston Street, East Village; ☎ 212-260-4700; www.mercuryloungenyc.com

Cover $10–$20. **Minimum** None. **Mixed drinks** $6–$7. **Wine** $6 by the glass. **Beer** $6. **Dress** Casual and hip. **Specials** None. **Food available** None. **Hours** Sunday–Wednesday, 7 p.m.–2 a.m.; Thursday–Saturday, 7 p.m.–4 a.m. Box office open Monday–Saturday, noon–7 p.m.

WHO GOES THERE 21 to 40; serious music fans, bohemian Lower East Side clubbers, some grunge.

WHAT GOES ON A showcase for newly signed (and hot about-to-be-signed) rock bands, with an excellent sound system. The performance space is perfect for listening to an eclectic mix of groups, from surprisingly big names (playing here to maintain their hip credentials) to up-and-comers and cult favorites. If you've never heard the name of a band playing here, you probably will soon.

SETTING AND ATMOSPHERE You enter through a mysterious-looking black bar with black curtains, and the music's through a door in the back. It's basically a box of a room, but exposed brick and great sound (blessedly, never head-bangingly loud) and lighting create an ambience that feels right.

IF YOU GO Walk down nearby Ludlow Street after the show to explore some cafes, music clubs, and late-night shops.

O'Flaherty's Ale House

IRISH PUB, AFTER-SHOW HIDEAWAY

334 West 46th Street, Midtown West; ☎ 212-581-9366; www.oflahertysnyc.com

Cover None. **Minimum** 1 drink. **Mixed drinks** $5–$7. **Wine** $5–$6 by the glass. **Beer** $4–$6. **Dress** Anything from suit and tie to jeans and T-shirt. **Specials** Happy hour daily, 4–7 p.m., with $3 pints, $3 Champagne, and $3 warm cocktails. **Food available** Surprisingly extensive Irish menu (shepherd's pie in several incarnations, stews, fried stuff). **Hours** Daily, noon–4 a.m.

WHO GOES THERE 25 to 55; locals and tourists until the 11 p.m. influx of the after-theater crowd (many actors and musicians).

WHAT GOES ON The beer's not super, but one of the selections is an interesting house-brewed honey lager. This is a great spot because among the winding passageways and copious alcoves there's an ambience to please almost anyone. The energy level picks up as theater people stop by for an after-work drink, and much of the crowd stays late. Part of the draw is the old-fashioned Irish bartenders, probably hired as much for their brogues as for their gregariousness. Live music daily from 10:30 p.m. to 2 a.m.

SETTING AND ATMOSPHERE Choose your surroundings: a book-filled study in the back with comfortable chairs and a pool table; a front corner of couches (great for groups); a handsome wraparound bar with adjoining dartboard; an outdoor garden with antique-style park benches. There's a nook or cranny for any occasion. It's all alcoves; there's no "main section" to speak of.

IF YOU GO If you're looking for a livelier time on this same block, see the profile for Swing 46, a jive-talking, swing-dancing nightspot.

P. J. Clarke's

915 Third Avenue, Midtown East; ☎ 212-317-1616; www.pjclarkes.com

Cover None. **Minimum** None. **Mixed drinks** $7 and up. **Wine** $6–$8 by the glass. **Beer** $5–$8. **Dress** Anything. **Specials** None. **Food available** Raw bar plus full menu until 3 a.m., including burgers, fries, salads, chicken, steak, desserts. **Hours** Daily, 11:30 a.m.–4 a.m. (dining room closes at 3 a.m.).

WHO GOES THERE 20s to 50s; businessmen after work, extremely varied later.

WHAT GOES ON A real New York legend, and one of the few old-time bars that hasn't turned cloyingly self-conscious. P. J.'s has long been known as a magnet for advertising people after work (it was featured prominently in an episode of *Mad Men),* but later the crowd turns amazingly diverse, from tourists to hard-boiled old guys to corporate moguls to Ratso Rizzo, with lots of interaction. A great jukebox plays well-chosen show tunes, swing, and rock.

SETTING AND ATMOSPHERE "Renovation" was a dirty word for the regulars a few years back, but after a year's closure, the place looks surprisingly the same as it ever did, except with stronger floorboards and an upstairs bar–dining room. Luckily, this single skinny little brick building has stubbornly remained as its onetime neighbors have fallen victim to progress. The atmosphere inside is so authentically old New York it's practically gas-lit. There's an oversized wooden bar; big, foggy mirrors plastered with photos of presidents, Irishmen, and deceased bartenders; and retro dining rooms where meals are served on tables with red-checkered tablecloths.

IF YOU GO Check out the antique men's urinals—tourist attractions in their own right. On the subject, other notable restrooms are the unisex see-through (until you close the latch) stalls at **Bar 89** (89 Mercer Street, ☎ 212-274-0989; **www.bar89.com**) and the podlike stalls at **SEA** (114 North Sixth Street, Brooklyn; ☎ 718-384-8850).

Planet Rose

219 Avenue A (at 13th Street), East Village; ☎ 212-353-9500; www.planetrosenyc.com

Cover None. **Minimum** $2 a song. **Mixed drinks** $6–$10. **Wine** $6–$8 by the glass. **Beer** $4–$6. **Dress** Anything goes. **Specials** Happy hour daily, 4–8 p.m. **Food available** None. **Hours** Sunday–Wednesday, 4 p.m.–2 a.m.; Thursday–Saturday, 4 p.m.–4 a.m.

WHO GOES THERE Hipsters, stage-frightened singers, small parties, the off-key.

WHAT GOES ON There's no stage in this unique karaoke bar, but the microphones are cordless, and the monitors are visible throughout the room, meaning you can warble while waltzing through the crowd, sitting at the bar, or lounging on a sofa. As the night wears on, it takes on a community sing-along atmosphere, with the microphone being passed from person to person and everyone trying to jump in on the chorus. The bartenders, good singers in their own rights, often join in the fun, but still manage to keep the service brisk and lively.

SETTING AND ATMOSPHERE The nondescript, metal-framed entrance doesn't hint at the garishness inside. Sure, it's tacky, but we're talking about a karaoke lounge. The rich red walls only help to make the zebra-print sofas and floors stand out. It's dark and not much bigger than a studio apartment inside, so be prepared to bump a few shoulders.

IF YOU GO Show up either very early or very late. No one likes to wait long to have a chance to sing, let alone to enter a bar. Coming in a group always assures more opportunities for sing-alongs, but private parties sometimes rent out the room, so be sure to call in advance. As odd as it might sound, don't be surprised if you see someone arrive in costume. It's just that type of place.

Rodeo Bar

COWBOY BAR WITH ECLECTIC LIVE MUSIC

✓ **375 Third Avenue, Gramercy Park; ☎ 212-683-6500; www.rodeobar.com**

Cover None. **Minimum** 2 drinks if watching a show, though it's not strictly enforced. **Mixed drinks** $5–$11. **Wine** $5–$8 by the glass. **Beer** $4–$7. **Dress** Jeans and whatever. **Specials** Happy hour daily, 4–9 p.m. **Food available** Tex-Mex (full meals or bar munchies). **Hours** Monday–Saturday, 11:30–4 a.m.; Sunday, 11:30–2 a.m. Shows start at 9 or 10 p.m. nightly.

WHO GOES THERE 20s to 60s; aging hippies, urban cowboys, music fans.

WHAT GOES ON Rodeo Bar isn't taken terribly seriously by New York music-scene cognoscenti, but it offers something extremely rare: good bar bands in regular rotation. Styles range from bluegrass to rockabilly to country rock, but the musical sensibility is always more New York hip than the saddles 'n' barrels decor would suggest; even the most country acts are *funky* country. The same bands play regularly, building audience and repertoire and honing skills. As a result, performances here are more polished than at nearly any other club in town, and there are loyal fans who come here first when they want to drink a beer and hear some dependably solid tunes without dropping dozens of dollars.

SETTING AND ATMOSPHERE So Wild West that you half expect Calamity Jane to come whooping past the bar; this place is tricked out with barrels, stirrups, rope-handle doorknobs, peanut shells, the works. Someone was decorating for a square dance, but thank goodness the music's much hipper than Cowboy Bob. A huge bull stares inquisitively at the performers from the side of the stage. Yee-haw.

IF YOU GO If the cow-punching vibe is too much for you, cross over to the restaurant next door for a quick city fix.

Rudy's Bar and Grill

QUINTESSENTIAL DIVE

627 Ninth Avenue, Midtown West; ☎ **212-974-9169;**
www.rudysbarnyc.com

Cover None. **Minimum** None. **Mixed drinks** $4–$6. **Wine** Avoid. **Beer** $3–$4 for a pint, $7–$9 for a pitcher. **Dress** Anything goes. **Specials** The regular prices are cheaper than most places' specials. **Food available** Free hot dogs and popcorn. **Hours** Daily, 8 a.m.–4 a.m.

WHO GOES THERE 20s to 60s; locals, hipsters, barflies, and other assorted characters.

WHAT GOES ON If you're looking for a quiet place to sip a well-mixed cocktail or a glass of wine, stay about as far away from Rudy's as possible. This is one of the city's most famous dives, and while word has been out for years about the dirt-cheap prices and the cheap and dirty atmosphere, it hasn't lost much of its authenticity. It's the type of place that harkens back to the rough-and-tumble New York of the 1970s and '80s, the type of place where a pitcher of beer costs less than $10 and you find yourself bellied up at the bar between a biker and a businessman. You can say you're slumming, but it will be hard to resist the infectious rowdiness of the crowd (thick on weekend nights), and you're sure to meet a breed of memorable folks not found at local wine bars or cocktail lounges.

SETTING AND ATMOSPHERE The giant pink pig outside serves as a beacon among the myriad bars and restaurants of Ninth Avenue. The interior is a monument to years of heavy use. The bathrooms are not as dirty as one might expect, but the writing on the walls certainly is. There have been better days for the plywood floors and red booths, which might have once been covered in leather but are now held together almost entirely by duct tape.

IF YOU GO Be brave and complement your cheap beer and whiskey with one or two free hot dogs, which are cooked nightly behind the bar on Rudy's "grill." Why not? Everyone else is eating them.

Sakagura

HIDDEN, SUAVE SAKE BAR

211 East 43rd Street, Midtown East; ☎ **212-953-SAKE;**
www.sakagura.com

Cover None. **Minimum** $10. **Mixed drinks** $7–$15. **Wine** $6–$25 for sake; 200 kinds imported from Japan. **Beer** $5–$8 (Japanese only). **Dress** Most men in jackets, but nice casual will do. **Specials** None. **Food available** Excellent, simple Japanese dishes such as *udon* (noodle soup) and *kinpira* (marinated burdock root). **Hours** Monday–Thursday, noon–midnight; Friday, noon–2 a.m.; Saturday, 6 p.m.–1 a.m.; Sunday, 6–11 p.m.

WHO GOES THERE 30 to 55; Japanese businessmen, sake aficionados.

WHAT GOES ON A treasure trove of sakes, plain, pricey, and odd. The drier sakes are usually the most interesting, and those who find sake an overly subtle drink should try *nama zake,* which has a much wider flavor of considerable complexity. If you can afford them, the aged *koshu* sakes (a particularly good one is *kamo izumi koshu*) have the length and complexity of great wine. Don't commit the faux pas of ordering your rice wine hot; the good stuff is drunk cold or at room temperature (very dry ones can be warmed a little). A couple of options: you can choose to sip from a *masu* (wooden box) rather than a cup, and a *hire* (nontoxic blowfish fin) can be added to impart a mellow, smoky flavor.

SETTING AND ATMOSPHERE Enter through a glarey office-building lobby, walk back toward the elevators, and descend a dank staircase to get to this supremely inviting inner sanctum that's all sleek lines and open space. There are some secluded tables, but there's lots more action at the big, handsome bar. It's sexy and peaceful, rarely crowded. Restrooms are hidden inside huge round wooden fermenting barrels.

IF YOU GO Try to talk your way into the odd private karaoke club; the door is just to your left as you enter the building's lobby.

Slate

SOPHISTICATED POOL HALL AND LOUNGE

54 West 21st Street, Chelsea; ☎ 212-989-0096; www.slate-ny.com

Cover None. **Minimum** None. **Mixed drinks** $8–$12. **Wine** $8–$10 by the glass. **Beer** $5–$8. **Dress** Preppy, casual chic. **Specials** Happy hour Monday–Friday, 5–8 p.m. **Food available** Full menu. **Hours** Daily, 11 a.m.–4 a.m.

WHO GOES THERE 20s to 30s; yuppies, couples, the occasional pool prodigy.

WHAT GOES ON Plenty of bars have pool tables. Plenty of pool halls have bars. At Slate, you get the best of both worlds. Sharks will appreciate the 30 impeccably maintained tables, while the less competitive will simply enjoy sipping cocktails, listening to the DJs, and mingling with the well-heeled crowd. A good-quality restaurant, a popular lounge known as **PLUS,** and six Ping-Pong tables round out the offerings, so when you hang up your cue, there's still plenty to keep you occupied.

SETTING AND ATMOSPHERE Designed by architect Jeanne Giordano, who renovated Grand Central Terminal, the sophisticated two-story venue is highlighted by a giant glass stairway. People tend to arrive in groups, then scatter to the tables, the sunken lounge, and the luminescent glass bar.

IF YOU GO Expect to pay more than you typically would at your neighborhood pool hall—an hour at the tables can set you back $20 to $30. Slate is a nightclub more than it is a place for hustlers to practice their wares. The pool is complimentary on Monday nights.

Smalls

183 West Tenth Street, Greenwich Village; ☎ 212-252-5091; www.smallsjazzclub.com

Cover $20 (good for the entire night); half price for after-hours shows. **Minimum** 1 drink. **Mixed drinks** $6–$10. **Wine** $5–$8 by the glass. **Beer** $4–$6. **Dress** Casual. **Specials** 1 cover charge allows you to go to Smalls and sister club Fat Cat (75 Christopher Street). **Food available** Snacks. **Hours** Daily, 6:30 p.m.– 4 a.m.; first band starts anytime between 7 and 9 p.m.; second band starts anytime between 9 p.m. and midnight; jam sessions on most nights after midnight.

WHO GOES THERE 21 and up, though kids are allowed with supervision; jazz aficionados, insomniacs, music students.

WHAT GOES ON Jamming, jazz, and listening. Each night highlights a different set of musicians.

SETTING AND ATMOSPHERE Smalls returned a few years ago after having been closed for more than a year, and the vibe is very much the same as it used to be, although the renovations have made space for a full bar service. Walk down a set of stairs and enter an intimate mecca of avantgarde and free jazz. In spite of the new bar, the focus is on the small stage, and stools and chairs are provided.

IF YOU GO Don't expect mainstream jazz. Old regulars are delighted at the resurrection, and newcomers are likely to get hooked on the caliber of musicians.

Smoke

2751 Broadway (between 105th and 106th streets), Upper West Side; ☎ 212-864-6662; www.smokejazz.com

Cover Varies; anywhere from free to $30. **Minimum** Varies; sometimes none, sometimes as high as $20. **Mixed drinks** $7–$10. **Wine** $6–$10 by the glass. **Beer** Bottled and draft, $6–$8. **Dress** Casual; lounge and/or accessorize with instrument, sheet music, or drumsticks. **Specials** None. **Food available** Full menu with sandwiches, steaks, and seafood. **Hours** Daily, 11:30 a.m.–2 a.m.

WHO GOES THERE All ages; jazz lovers, musicians, and any other affiliates.

WHAT GOES ON There's music every night of the week, most of it incredibly good. Smoke takes over from where the former Augie's Jazz Bar left off, so a great music tradition continues in this renovated space. You'll never know who'll be in the crowd listening or who'll come to the stage for a jam set, so no two visits are ever the same.

SETTING AND ATMOSPHERE An intimate, warm, relaxed setting for some great music; space can get tight because there's seating for only 50, but the overflow crowds the bar, and everyone gets a decent view. There's a real jazz-club ambience, with bar and lounge area complete with small octagonal tables, plush sofa and chairs, dark wood, red velvet curtains, candle sconces, and a few low-hanging, unobtrusive chandeliers; the only missing accoutrement is the club's namesake (eliminated by the smoking ban). Musicians and listeners alike praise the sound system; performances, including jam sessions, are given due respect and attention.

IF YOU GO Be prepared to listen, relax, and perhaps even be inspired.

S.O.B.'s

LATIN AND WORLD MUSIC; DANCE CLUB

204 Varick Street, SoHo; ☎ 212-243-4940; www.sobs.com

Cover Varies ($10–$25, more or less). **Minimum** $25–$50 per person at tables on weekend nights. **Mixed drinks** $10–$12. **Wine** Bottle, $30–$400; $8–$10 by the glass. **Beer** $6–$8. **Dress** Colorful and flashy. **Specials** Happy hour, Monday and Friday, discounted admission and free dance lessons (stay for the show). **Food available** Pretty good, overpriced pan-Latino and Brazilian dishes. **Hours** Monday, 5 p.m.–2 a.m.; Tuesday–Thursday, 6:30 p.m.–2 a.m.; Friday, 5 p.m.– 4 a.m.; Saturday, 6:30 p.m.–4 a.m.; Sunday, noon–2 a.m. (Bossa Nova brunch until 4 p.m.); music usually starts after 8 p.m.

WHO GOES THERE 21 to 40; music fans, salsa dancers, ethnic-music trollers.

WHAT GOES ON This is a fun enough club just for hanging out and listening, but for those who like to dance, it's one of the best parties in town. Friday nights smoke with famous salsa groups (the dance class will get your hips up to speed); other nights feature music from Brazilian to reggae—anything funky and tropical. The bands are tops in their genres; this is a great place for world-music neophytes to familiarize themselves with different styles. It's more nightclub than disco; bands are listened to as much as danced to, and even unaccompanied women feel "safe" on the dance floor.

SETTING AND ATMOSPHERE Large stage with sunken dance floor; the bar faces the stage, but visibility is bad in crowds. There are tables to the side of the stage. Bright and colorful with lots of tropical touches.

IF YOU GO Bear in mind that things can get crowded. FYI, S.O.B.'s stands for "Sounds of Brazil."

Swing 46

SWING-DANCE CLUB

349 West 46th Street, Midtown West; ☎ 212-262-9554; www.swing46.com

Cover $12–$15. **Minimum** 2 drinks at tables. **Mixed drinks** $7–$10. **Wine** $7–$9 by the glass. **Beer** $6–$8. **Dress** Smart casual; dancers dress up. **Specials** Happy hour daily at bar, 5–8 p.m.; free dance lessons on most nights; call for details. **Food available** Reasonably priced prix-fixe dinner before 7 p.m.; more expensive later in the evening; Sunday brunch. **Hours** Monday–Saturday, 5 p.m.– 2 a.m.; Sunday, noon–2 a.m.

WHO GOES THERE 25 to 90; swing-dance aficionados old and young, cool barflies.

WHAT GOES ON Live music seven nights a week; big bands and combos playing swing. Lindy Hoppers and jitterbugs are as hot as the music, and the place bristles with energy even on weeknights. The bar is as cool as the dance floor is hot, populated by older swing fans who prefer to sit and take it all in without getting personally involved. If you can overlook all the silly hepcat daddy-o spiel, it's all a pretty wild good time (neophyte dancers will not feel uncomfortable).

SETTING AND ATMOSPHERE The bar's up front, cut off from the frenzied action farther inside, but the bands can be clearly heard. The dance-nightclub room, framed with beige paneling, has a low ceiling and is close but not overly so. Tables have flickering candle lamps, and the dance floor is right up next to the band. An outdoor sunken terrace in front of the club is filled with tables in summer.

IF YOU GO Restaurant Row is actually a better block for bars than for eateries. Check out O'Flaherty's Ale House (page 446) on this same street.

Top of the Tower Bar & Lounge

ROMANTIC BAR-RESTAURANT WITH SUPERB VIEWS

3 Mitchell Place, at 49th Street and First Avenue (Beekman Tower Hotel), Midtown East; ☎ 212-980-4796; www.thetopofthetower.com

Cover None. **Minimum** None. **Mixed drinks** $10–$15. **Wine** $12–$15 by the glass. **Beer** Bottled only, $8–$13. **Dress** Upscale casual to business. **Specials** None. **Food available** Full menu, $23–$32. **Hours** Sunday–Thursday, 5 p.m.–1 a.m.; Friday and Saturday, 5 p.m.–2 a.m.

WHO GOES THERE 30s to 70s; tourists, lovers, vista seekers.

WHAT GOES ON Gazing, light canoodling, sipping, relaxing.

SETTING AND ATMOSPHERE The Top of the Tower is a perfect setting for either a date or a friendly tête-à-tête. Right off the elevator, you're in the middle of an open area complete with bar, baby grand piano (played from 9 p.m. on, except Mondays), small tables, and spacious high windows with Art Deco designs. There's no pretension in the air, but sneakers are not encouraged.

IF YOU GO Aim to get a table by a window during a sunset or later in the evening to see Midtown and the East River twinkle. The restaurant serves decent food, but the views are the main draw while you sip a drink or glass of Champagne. You're sufficiently high enough up to be away from the fray.

Union Hall

NEIGHBORHOOD BAR, MUSIC VENUE, AND BOCCE COURT

702 Union Street, Park Slope, Brooklyn; ☎ 718-638-4400; www.unionhallny.com

Cover None, but shows are usually $10–$25. **Minimum** None. **Mixed drinks** $6–$10. **Wine** $6–$8 by the glass. **Beer** $5–$7. **Dress** Casual and trendy. **Specials** Happy hour Monday–Friday, 4–7 p.m. **Food available** A menu of appetizers. **Hours** Monday–Friday, 4 p.m.–4 a.m.; Saturday and Sunday, noon–4 a.m.

WHO GOES THERE 21–35; hipsters, locals, musicians, young mothers earlier in the day.

WHAT GOES ON Plenty, from bocce and beers upstairs to rock, comedy, and karaoke downstairs. This Park Slope favorite advertises itself as a neighborhood bar, but it's really a jack-of-all-trades. During the day, it's a relaxed place to get a beer, read a book, and relax, as evidenced by the many moms with strollers that stop by. At night, local hipsters mob the two bocce courts as hip rock and comedy acts take the stage downstairs.

SETTING AND ATMOSPHERE The main level is designed as a study with fireplaces, weathered books, and comfy chairs. There's plenty of room to hold your own private powwow here, but mingling is encouraged. The bocce courts in the back are almost always occupied, as is the garden in fair weather. Downstairs is the dark and low-ceilinged performance space that hosts well-known acts in special performances, up-and-comers, and the occasional karaoke party. The whole place is 5,000 square feet total, bigger than many dance clubs.

IF YOU GO If you want to play bocce, show up early, and check the Web site to see when league nights are scheduled. Yes, there are league nights. Another bocce court can be found at Union Hall's sister bar, **Floyd** (131 Atlantic Avenue; ☎ 718-858-5810; **www.floydny.com**), a much smaller and humbler place. For more music in Brooklyn, try **The Bell House** (149 Seventh Street, Brooklyn; ☎ 718-643-6510; **www.thebellhouseny.com**), from the same owners.

The Village Vanguard

JAZZ CLUB

178 Seventh Avenue South, Greenwich Village; ☎ 212-255-4037; www.villagevanguard.com

Cover $30 or $35, which includes a $10 drink minimum. (*Note:* Credit cards can be used to reserve online but aren't accepted in the club.) **Minimum** Included in admission. **Mixed drinks** $7–$12. **Wine** $6–$11 by the glass. **Beer** $5–$7. **Dress** Dressy or nice casual. **Specials** None. **Food available** None. **Hours** Open 8 p.m. every night; closing time varies. Sets start at 9 and 11 p.m.; call to see if a third set is scheduled on Saturdays.

WHO GOES THERE 25 to 90, though "quiet" children are allowed; jazz pilgrims and Japanese tourists.

WHAT GOES ON This is it—the most famous jazz club in the world. Over the last 75 years, almost every major jazz musician has gigged in this room (many recorded landmark live albums here as well), and the ghosts are palpable. The service is crabby and the seating is cramped, but you become a tiny part of jazz history simply by walking through the door. The music is *finally* straying from strictly straight-ahead jazz and bebop: fusion, Latin, and even fresh blood are being heard here.

SETTING AND ATMOSPHERE Dank basement with a small bar in back . . . but the acoustics are wonderful, and it feels like jazz. Table service.

IF YOU GO Check out the Monday night Vanguard Jazz Orchestra (Thad Jones–Mel Lewis's band, sans leaders). Reservations are a good idea; the club fills up fast. No talking is allowed during performances, nor photography, videotaping, audio recording, or cell phones.

Webster Hall

DISCO THEME PARK

125 East 11th Street, East Village; ☎ 212-353-1600; www.websterhall.com

Cover None–$30. **Minimum** None. **Mixed drinks** $7–$9. **Wine** $7 by the glass. **Beer** $6–$7. **Dress** No sneakers, baseball hats, ripped jeans, or boots; dress to impress. **Specials** $1 pre-midnight admission and drink discounts are available through the Web site. **Food available** Probably somewhere; look around. **Hours** Thursday–Saturday, 10 p.m.–5 a.m.; Sunday–Wednesday, open only for concerts and special events.

WHO GOES THERE 21 to 35; equal parts New York University freshmen, beautiful party people, and paunchy 30-somethings clutching beers and looking wistful.

WHAT GOES ON An enormous disco theme park with dance floors, lounges, a (temporary) tattoo parlor, and a coffee bar. There are spending opportunities everywhere you look; even the bathroom attendants reign over little concession stands, selling candy, mouthwash, and hair products. Fridays and Saturdays are monstrously crowded mainstream disco free-for-alls, and Thursdays are known as "Girls Night Out" and feature a male revue. The staff seems to be instructed to act as peevish as possible. Lots of DJs; ladies get in free all Thursday night, while men get in for $10 before 11:30 p.m.

SETTING AND ATMOSPHERE Ground level is mostly a classic disco, complete with a go-go girl behind the bar. Upstairs, you enter a cavernous ballroom, like a junior high school auditorium taken over by aliens with superior technology—featuring amazing lighting tricks and a Sensurround-style bass response that makes your chest feel as if it's going to explode. More go-go girls and androgynous characters on stilts. Still farther upstairs is a balcony with tarot readings, temporary tattoos, body painting, and a tranquil lounge (wicker chairs, ferns) that hosts live bands Thursday and Friday nights (also check the bar here for drink specials). In the basement, yet another dance floor, this one with burning incense. The club is also a premier concert venue for established bands and ones that have just broken big. You can check **www .bowerypresents.com** for upcoming shows.

IF YOU GO Conceal no weapons (or beer bottles)—no happening disco would be complete without a security pat-down at the front door, and this is no exception.

INDEX

Unofficial Guide Reader Survey

If you would like to express your opinion in writing about New York City or this guidebook, complete the following survey and mail it to:

Unofficial Guide Reader Survey
P.O. Box 43673
Birmingham, AL 35243

Inclusive dates of your visit:_____

*Members of
your party:*   Person 1   Person 2   Person 3   Person 4   Person 5
Gender: M F   M F   M F   M F   M F
Age: _____

How many times have you been to New York City?_____
On your most recent trip, where did you stay?_____

Concerning your accommodations, on a scale of 100 as best and 0 as worst, how would you rate:

The quality of your room?   The value of your room?
The quietness of your room?   Check-in/checkout efficiency?
Shuttle service to the airport?   Swimming-pool facilities?

Did you rent a car?   From whom?

Concerning your rental car, on a scale of 100 as best and 0 as worst, how would you rate:

Pickup-processing efficiency?   Return-processing efficiency?
Condition of the car?   Cleanliness of the car?
Airport-shuttle efficiency?

Concerning your dining experiences:

Estimate your meals in restaurants per day? _____
Approximately how much did your party spend on meals per day? ____

_____

Favorite restaurants in New York City: _____

_____

Did you buy this guide before leaving?   while on your trip?

How did you hear about this guide? (check all that apply)

Loaned or recommended by a friend ☐   Radio or TV ☐
Newspaper or magazine ☐   Bookstore salesperson ☐
Just picked it out on my own ☐   Library ☐
Internet ☐

What other guidebooks did you use on this trip?_____

_____

_____

On a scale of 100 as best and 0 as worst, how would you rate them?

_____

_____

Using the same scale, how would you rate the *Unofficial Guide*(s)?

_____

Are Unofficial Guides readily available at bookstores in your area?_____

Have you used other *Unofficial Guides*? _____

Which one(s)? _____

_____

_____

Comments about your New York City trip or the *Unofficial Guide*(s):

_____

_____

_____

_____

_____

_____

_____

_____

_____

_____

_____

_____

_____

R.C.L.

SEP. 2010

G